EDITION

SOCIAL MARKETING

50 YEARS

SAGE was founded in 1965 by Sara Miller McCune to support the dissemination of usable knowledge by publishing innovative and high-quality research and teaching content. Today, we publish more than 750 journals, including those of more than 300 learned societies, more than 800 new books per year, and a growing range of library products including archives, data, case studies, reports, conference highlights, and video. SAGE remains majority-owned by our founder, and after Sara's lifetime will become owned by a charitable trust that secures our continued independence.

Los Angeles | London | Washington DC | New Delhi | Singapore | Boston

EDITION 5

SOCIAL MARKETING

Changing Behaviors for Good

NANCY R. LEE
*University of Washington and
Social Marketing Services, Inc.*

PHILIP KOTLER
Kellogg School of Management

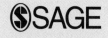

Los Angeles | London | New Delhi
Singapore | Washington DC | Boston

Los Angeles | London | New Delhi
Singapore | Washington DC | Boston

FOR INFORMATION:

SAGE Publications, Inc.
2455 Teller Road
Thousand Oaks, California 91320
E-mail: order@sagepub.com

SAGE Publications Ltd.
1 Oliver's Yard
55 City Road
London EC1Y 1SP
United Kingdom

SAGE Publications India Pvt. Ltd.
B 1/I 1 Mohan Cooperative Industrial Area
Mathura Road, New Delhi 110 044
India

SAGE Publications Asia-Pacific Pte. Ltd.
3 Church Street
#10-04 Samsung Hub
Singapore 049483

Acquisitions Editor: Maggie Stanley
Digital Content Editor: Katie Bierach
Editorial Assistant: Nicole Mangona
Production Editor: Libby Larson
Copy Editor: Rachel Keith
Typesetter: C&M Digitals (P) Ltd.
Proofreader: Dennis W. Webb
Indexer: Karen Wiley
Cover Designer: Candice Harman
Marketing Manager: Liz Thornton

Cover images courtesy of AT&T, Rotary International, and Colehour + Cohen.

Printed in the United States of America

A catalog record of this book is available from the Library of Congress.

ISBN 9781452292144

This book is printed on acid-free paper.

Certified Chain of Custody
SUSTAINABLE FORESTRY INITIATIVE Promoting Sustainable Forestry
www.sfiprogram.org
SFI-01268
SFI label applies to text stock

15 16 17 18 19 10 9 8 7 6 5 4 3 2 1

BRIEF CONTENTS

DETAILED CONTENTS

This book is dedicated to all current and future social marketers working to change behaviors to improve health, decrease injuries, protect the environment, build communities, and enhance financial well-being.

We hope that you'll find that this 10-step strategic planning approach enhances your success.

And to all instructors using the text, Nancy Lee offers you an opportunity for her to be "Skyped" in to your classroom for a 45-minute session to share her story about discovering social marketing. She can be reached at nancyrlee@msn.com.

FOREWORD

This fifth edition of *Social Marketing: Changing Behaviors for Good* makes a number of important changes in content and application that continue its tradition as the leading textbook for those seeking to be knowledgeable about, and adept in the use of, social marketing concepts and tools. Like earlier editions, it provides a wide range of examples that give students and practitioners opportunities to see and use social marketing concepts and tools that address major (and sometimes more minor) social challenges. Twenty-five new cases guide readers to effective use of the concepts and tools provided.

This book continues to be one of the most readable volumes in a growing array of texts and readers. To provide an especially rewarding experience for its readers, models and frameworks have been explained in more depth and breadth and set aside in a separate chapter. This very much reflects the historical development of the field of social marketing in terms of the expansion of the scientific basis of its planning, execution, and evaluation of real-world social challenges. In addition, the book continues to emphasize the field's scientific underpinnings by drawing from the social sciences, and to highlight its practical challenges by drawing concepts and tools from for-profit marketing textbooks, theories, and practices.

Like all cutting-edge textbooks and practitioner's guides, this volume is replete with new approaches to research and implementation, including crowdsourcing, participatory action research, and Gerald Zaltman's metaphor elicitation technique. It makes use of current thinking on habit formation and behavioral economics (e.g., nudging). It offers practical (and especially needed) advice on midcourse corrections and essential evaluations that can ensure that applications have the intended effect—and that unexpected outcomes are recognized and responded to.

As before, readers will find a fluidity of discourse and argumentation that marks the prolific output of the two authors. They will continue to be enticed deeper into the material by both the real-world flavor and content and the clever and absorbing exposition that this volume offers.

Alan R. Andreasen
Georgetown University

Part I

Understanding Social Marketing

Chapter 1

DEFINING AND DISTINGUISHING SOCIAL MARKETING

Think of social marketing as the social change version of "Let's Make a Deal." We believe that all men and women have a right to determine what is valuable to them. Our job is not to change their values. That may be the mission of education or religion, but not of marketing. Our job is to offer people something they already value in exchange for a behavior which we believe will benefit not only them as individuals, but society as whole. Our most fundamental principle, the principle of exchange, is radically democratic and populist.

—Dr. Bill Smith
Emeritus editor, *Social Marketing Quarterly*[1]

Social marketing, as a discipline, has made enormous strides since its distinction in the early 1970s, and has had a profound positive impact on social issues in the areas of public health, injury prevention, the environment, community involvement, and more recently, financial well-being. Fundamental principles at the core of this practice have been used to help reduce tobacco use, decrease infant mortality, stop the spread of HIV/AIDS, prevent malaria, help eradicate polio, make wearing a bike helmet a social norm, decrease littering, stop bullying, increase recycling, encourage the homeless to participate in job-training programs, and persuade pet owners to license their pets and "scoop their poop."

Social marketing as a term, however, is still a mystery to most, misunderstood by many, and increasingly confused with other terms such as *behavioral economics* (a framework we consider in this book) and *social media* (one of many potential promotional tactics to choose from). A few even worry about using the term with their administrators, colleagues, and elected officials, fearing they will associate it with socialism, manipulation, and sales. This chapter is intended to create clear distinctions and to answer common questions:

- What is social marketing?
- When did it originate?
- How does social marketing differ from commercial marketing, nonprofit marketing, public sector marketing, and education?

- What is its relation to behavioral economics, nudge, social change, community-based social marketing, community-based prevention marketing, social media, and cause promotion?
- Do people who do social marketing actually call themselves social marketers? Where do they work?
- What social issues can benefit from social marketing?

We support the voices of many who advocate an expanded role for social marketing and social marketers, challenging professionals to take this technology "upstream" to influence other factors that effect positive social change, including laws, enforcement, public policy, built environments, school curricula, community organizations, business practices, celebrities, and the media. We also encourage distinguishing and considering "midstream" audiences, those influential others closer to our target audiences, such as family, friends, neighbors, health care providers, teachers, and community leaders.

We begin this chapter, like the rest of the chapters in the book, with an inspiring case story; this one is from India. We conclude with one of several Marketing Dialogues that feature discourses among practitioners seeking to shape, evolve, and transform this discipline.

MARKETING HIGHLIGHT

Ending Polio in India

From 200,000 to Zero

(1988–2012)

Background

In 1979, Rotary International began a partnership with the government of the Philippines to immunize close to six million children in the country against polio. Based on the success of this initiative, this humanitarian organization launched PolioPlus in 1985, when more than 125 countries were polio endemic and there were over 350,000 cases worldwide.[2] Rotary has since supported the immunization of over 2 billion children

worldwide and helped establish the Global Polio Eradication Initiative in 1988 in partnership with the United Nations Children's Fund (UNICEF), the World Health Organization (WHO), and the U.S. Centers for Disease Control and Prevention, with support from the Bill and Melinda Gates Foundation.

Since the launch of PolioPlus in 1985, more than 10 billion doses of the oral polio vaccine have been administered worldwide, and cases diagnosed annually have declined by over 99.9%, with just

223 cases recorded in 2012, 217 of those in just three countries: Afghanistan, Pakistan, and Nigeria.[3]

India was long regarded as the most difficult place to end polio, and in 2009 accounted for nearly half the world's polio cases. This case highlights social marketing strategies contributing to this country's 27-year journey to the finish line, with not a single case recorded since 2011.

Target Audiences and Desired Behaviors

This polio eradication initiative focused on administering two drops of the oral polio vaccine to all children under the age of five. Priority target audiences included newborns, especially those in remote areas of northern India; the at-risk migrant, mobile, and nomadic populations; and groups with the greatest resistance to vaccinations, primarily those with religious objections.

To facilitate identification of missed children, finger marking of every vaccinated child was launched in 1999. The little finger on the left hand of the child was marked with indelible ink. To ensure completeness of coverage, the vaccinators used chalk to mark houses as "P" (all children in the house immunized) or "X" (children missed).[4]

Audience Insights

There were geographic and logistic challenges to reaching widely dispersed populations across treacherous terrains, especially migrant and nomadic groups. There was lack of availability of the vaccine for some and, for many, a persistent mistrust of medicine, suspicion of health care workers, and community skepticism. One of the most resistant groups was Muslims, some of whom believed the vaccine was against Islam and many of whom were concerned about a rumor that it would make their children impotent and was actually a ploy to reduce the population of this community.[5] Many in low-literacy populations believed that polio was "a curse from God and that nothing could be done to keep it from spreading or occurring."[6]

Marketing Mix Strategies

What did it take to overcome these barriers and fully immunize the children of India? It took, as Esha Chhabra stated in a 2013 article in the *Stanford Social Innovation Review*, "a web of coordination and collaboration . . . to penetrate dense neighborhoods, remote villages, and makeshift colonies." And it is this infrastructure that can "now serve as a blueprint for future public health campaigns."[7] These advancements took billions of dollars in investment, with Rotary contributions in India alone totaling $178 million.

A sampling of the marketing mix strategies that were used follows, intended to illustrate the need for and power of utilizing all four tools in the marketing intervention toolbox:

Product

The vaccination procedure involved giving each child two drops of vaccine. Individual vaccines were carried in bags and kept cool with ice packs. Since 2005, the development and utilization of more efficacious vaccines has helped curtail outbreaks of different strains of the virus.[8]

Figure 1.1 Popular Bollywood star Amitabh Bachchan promoting vaccinations.

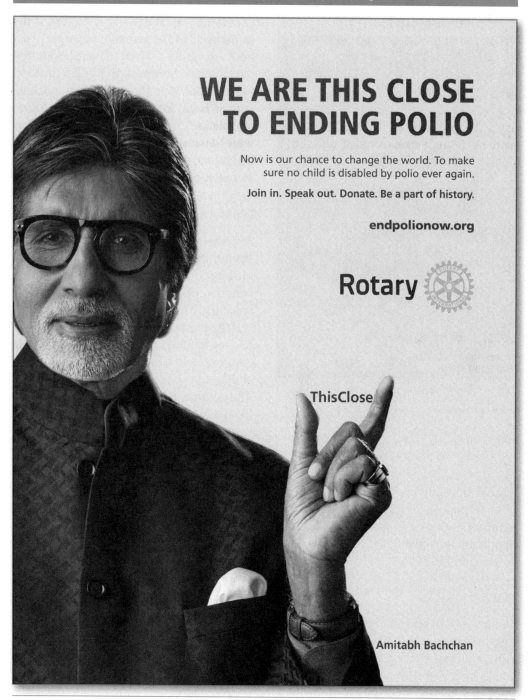

Source: Rotary International.

Figure 1.2 Poster promoting "For my child, two drops every time."

Source: UNICEF.

Price

Vaccinations are provided free of charge. The Global Polio Eradication Initiative estimates that on average, it takes approximately $0.60 to protect a child from polio for life.[9]

Place

Volunteer workers, including Rotarians, community mobilizers, and health officials, made vaccination convenient for some families by administering vaccines at the children's homes; a database was utilized to locate eligible children. Vaccination booths were pervasive; as stated by Chhabra, "the immensity of the Indian campaign [was] hard to grasp. There [were] 700,000 vaccination booths led by 2.5 million vaccinators, who [had] 2 million vaccine carrier bags, kept cool with 6.3 million ice packs."[10] Transit vaccination teams were also deployed at train stations, highways, and prominent road crossings to reach children in transit.

Promotion

Messages: Messages focused on promoting strong community ownership. Specific messages emphasized the disease, the benefits of polio vaccination, and the inaccuracy of misconceptions.

Messengers: To combat false rumors, Rotary in India formed a Muslim ulema committee to educate the Muslim clerics about the benefits of immunization. They wrote notes of affirmation in the local languages, which were then used by health workers to convince hesitant families that the vaccine was safe.[11] UNICEF India enlisted celebrities to appear annually in mass-media campaigns, including Amitabh Bachchan, one of the most popular Bollywood stars, who has been an ambassador for polio for a decade now (see Figure 1.1). India's cricketers have also been instrumental, with popular players publicly calling on parents to immunize their children.

Creative elements: To distinguish the polio campaign from other health-related programs, a brand using bright colors, including yellow and magenta,

Figure 1.3 Branded campaign targeting transit users.

Source: UNICEF.

was supported with catchy taglines that evolved from "Two drops of life" to "Every child, every time" to "For my child, two drops every time," emphasizing the responsibility of parents to ensure the well-being of their children (see Figure 1.2).

Communication channels: Traditional channels have included messages on billboards, posters, bus panels, and rickshaws as well as a presence at national immunization day events, community festivals, and large public gatherings (see Figure 1.3). Over the last several years, the polio program has adopted innovative ways to reach people, including text messages on cellular phones.

Outcomes

In 1988, there were an estimated 200,000 polio cases in India; by 2002, there were 1600; by 2011, just one person had polio. No cases have been reported as of September 2014.[12] One activity contributing to this success was a rigorous monitoring effort. Data were collected to find out where and among whom polio cases were being reported so that implementation strategies could be directed to reach population segments most at risk. Tim Peterson, a polio expert with the Gates Foundation, commented, "We understood exactly why certain children were being missed. We kept going back to them until we figured it out."[13]

WHAT IS SOCIAL MARKETING?

Social marketing is a distinct marketing discipline, one that has been labeled as such since the early 1970s and refers primarily to efforts focused on influencing behaviors that will improve health, prevent injuries, protect the environment, contribute to communities, and, more recently, enhance financial well-being. Several definitions from social marketing "veterans" are listed in Box 1.1 of this chapter, beginning with one we have adopted for use in this text and one from the International Social Marketing Association (iSMA).

We believe that after you have reviewed all these definitions, it will seem clear there are several common themes. Social marketing is about (a) influencing behaviors, (b) utilizing a systematic planning process that applies marketing principles and techniques, (c) focusing on priority target audience segments, and (d) delivering a positive benefit for individuals and society. Each of these themes is elaborated upon in the next four sections.

We Focus on Behaviors

Similar to commercial sector marketers' objective, which is to sell goods and services, social marketers' objective is to successfully influence desired behaviors. We typically want to influence target audiences to do one of four things: (1) *accept* a new behavior (e.g., composting food waste); (2) *reject* a potentially undesirable behavior (e.g., starting smoking), which is why we refer more to behavior influence than behavior change; (3) *modify* a current behavior (e.g., increase physical activity from three to five days of the week or decrease the number of fat grams consumed); or (4) *abandon* an old undesirable behavior (e.g., texting while driving). We may be encouraging a one-time behavior (e.g., installing a low-flow showerhead) or hoping to establish a habit and prompt a repeated behavior (e.g., taking a five-minute shower). More recently, Alan Andreasen suggested a fifth arena, in which we want to influence people to *continue* a desired behavior (e.g., giving blood on an annual basis), and a sixth, in which we want people to *switch* a behavior (e.g., take the stairs instead of the elevator).[14]

Although benchmarks may be established for increasing knowledge and skills through education, and although efforts may need to be made to alter existing beliefs, attitudes, or feelings, the bottom line for the social marketer is whether the target audience adopts the behavior. For example, a specific behavior that substance abuse coalitions want to influence is women's consumption of alcohol during pregnancy. They recognize the need to inform women that alcohol may cause birth defects and convince them that this could happen to their baby. In the end, however, their measure of success is whether the expectant mother abstains from drinking.

Perhaps the most challenging aspect of social marketing (and also its greatest contribution) is that it relies heavily on "rewarding good behaviors" rather than "punishing bad ones" through legal, economic, or coercive forms of influence. And in many cases, social marketers cannot promise a direct benefit or immediate payback in return for adopting the proposed behavior. Consider, for example, the task of influencing gardeners

Box 1.1
Definitions From a Few Social Marketing Veterans (Obtained via Personal Correspondence) and the International Social Marketing Association (iSMA)

Social Marketing is a process that uses marketing principles and techniques to change target audience behaviors to benefit society as well as the individual. This strategically oriented discipline relies on creating, communicating, delivering, and exchanging offerings that have positive value for individuals, clients, partners, and society at large.

—Nancy R. Lee, Michael L. Rothschild,
and Bill Smith, personal communication

Social Marketing seeks to develop and integrate marketing concepts with other approaches to influence behaviours that benefit individuals and communities for the greater social good.

—iSMA, 2013[a]

Social Marketing is the application of commercial marketing concepts and tools to influence the voluntary behavior of target audiences to improve their lives or the society of which they are a part.

—Alan Andreasen, 2014

Social Marketing 2.0, not to be confused with social media marketing (which is often mislabelled as social marketing), is the systematic application of interactive marketing principles and techniques that harness audience participation to deliver value and achieve specific behavioral goals for a social good.

—Jay Bernhardt, 2014

Social Marketing is the application of commercial marketing principles and tools in social change interventions where the primary goal is the public good.

—Rob Donovan, 2014

Social Marketing is a set of evidence- and experience-based concepts and principles that provide a systematic approach to understanding behaviour and influencing it for social good. It is not a science but rather a form of "technik"; a fusion of science, practical know-how, and reflective practice focusing on continuously improving the performance of programmes aimed at producing net social good.

—Jeff French, 2014

Social Marketing critically examines commercial marketing so as to learn from its successes and curb its excesses.

—Gerard Hastings, 2011

(Continued)

(Continued)

Social Marketing is a planned approach to social innovation.

—Craig Lefebvre, 2014

Social Marketing is a process that involves (a) carefully selecting which behaviors and segments to target, (b) identifying the barriers and benefits to these behaviors, (c) developing and pilot testing strategies to address these barriers and benefits, and, finally, (d) broad scale implementation of successful programs.

—Doug McKenzie-Mohr, 2014

Social Marketing is a way to reduce the barriers and increase the facilitators to behaviors that improve the quality of life for individuals and society. It uses concepts and planning processes from commercial marketing to make behaviors "fun, easy, and popular." It goes beyond communication, public service announcements, and education to give you a 360-degree view of potential causes and solutions for health and human service problems.

—Mike Newton-Ward, 2014

Social Marketing is the activity and processes for understanding, creating, communicating, and delivering a unique and innovative solution to contribute to societal well-being.

—Sharyn Rundle-Thiele, 2014

Social Marketing is the commercial marketing activity and processes which engage and empower individuals and society to facilitate and support societal well-being.

—SocialMarketing@Griffith 2013

Social Marketing is the use of commercial marketing strategies, terms and techniques to achieve societal wellbeing. It is used by government and nonprofit organisations as a way of delivering goods and services that provide sufficient customer value for people to improve their lives. It can be a primary strategy or can be used in combination with education and law/policy.

—Rebekah Russell-Bennett, 2014

Social Marketing is the use of marketing principles and techniques to promote the adoption of behaviors that improve the health or well-being of the target audience or of society as a whole.

—Nedra Weinreich, 2014

a. International Social Marketing Association, "Social Marketing Definition" (n.d.), accessed September 9, 2014, http://www.i-socialmarketing.org/.

to pull their dandelions instead of using harmful chemicals. It's tough to show the healthier fish their actions helped to support. And it's tough to convince youth who want to look good to use sunscreen so that they will (maybe) avoid skin cancer later in life. As you will read in subsequent chapters, this is why a systematic, rigorous, and strategic planning process is required—one that is inspired by the wants, needs, and preferences of target audiences and focuses on real, deliverable, and near-term benefits. It should be noted, however, that many believe that this heavy reliance on individual voluntary behavior change is outdated and have moved on to applying social marketing technologies to influencing other change factors in the environment (e.g., laws, public policies, media, and corporations). This is elaborated upon later in this chapter.

We Use a Systematic Planning Process That Applies Traditional Marketing Principles and Techniques

The American Marketing Association defines marketing as "the activity, set of institutions, and processes for creating, communicating, delivering, and exchanging offerings that have value for customers, clients, partners, and society at large."[15] The most fundamental principle underlying this approach is application of a *customer orientation* to understanding barriers target audiences perceive to adopting the desired behavior and benefits they want and believe they can realize. The process begins with alignment on the *social issue* to be addressed and an *environmental scan* to establish a purpose and focus for a specific plan. A *situation analysis* (SWOT) helps identify organizational strengths to maximize and weaknesses to minimize, as well as external opportunities to take advantage of and threats to prepare for. Marketers then select *target audiences* they can best influence and satisfy. We establish clear *behavior objectives* and *target goals* the plan will be developed to achieve. *Formative research* is conducted to identify audience barriers, benefits, and motivators; the competition; and influential others. This inspires the *positioning* of the offer, one that will appeal to the desires of the target audience, and the game requires that we do this more effectively than the competition. We then consider the need for each of the major intervention tools in the marketer's toolbox, the "4Ps," to influence target audiences: product, price, place, and promotion, also referred to as the *marketing mix*. An *evaluation* methodology is established, leading to a *budget* and *implementation* plan. Once a plan is implemented, ideally first with a pilot, results are *monitored* and *evaluated*, and strategies are altered as needed. Table 1.1 summarizes this strategic planning process using the 10-step model this text follows. Examples of marketing techniques are included.

We Select and Influence a Target Audience

Marketers know that the marketplace is a rich collage of diverse populations, each having a distinct set of wants and needs. We know that what appeals to one individual may not appeal to another and therefore divide the market into similar groups (market segments), measure the relative potential of each segment to meet organizational and marketing objectives, and then choose one or more segments (target audiences) on which to concentrate our efforts and resources. For each target, a distinct mix of the 4Ps is developed, one designed to uniquely appeal to that segment's barriers, benefits, motivators, competition, and influential others.

Considering, again, a more expanded view of social marketing, Robert Donovan and Nadine Henley (among others) advocate also targeting individuals in communities who have the power to make institutional policy and legislative changes in social structures (e.g., school superintendents). In this case, efforts move from influencing (just) an individual with a problem or potentially problematic behavior to influencing those who can facilitate behavior change in individuals.[16] Techniques, however, remain the same.

The Primary Beneficiary Is Society

Unlike commercial marketing, in which the primary intended beneficiary is the corporate shareholder, the primary beneficiary of the social marketing program is society. The question many pose and banter about is, who determines whether the social change created by the program is beneficial? Although most causes supported by social marketing efforts tend to draw high consensus that the cause is good, this model can also be used by organizations who have the opposite view of what is good. Abortion is an example of an issue where both sides argue that they are on the "good" side, and both use social marketing techniques to influence public behavior. Who, then, gets to define "good"? Some propose the United Nations' Universal Declaration of Human Rights (http://www.un.org/en/documents/udhr/) as a baseline with respect to the common good. Some share the opinion of social marketing consultant Craig Lefebvre, who posted the following on the Georgetown Social Marketing Listserve:

> "Good" is in the eye of the beholder. What I consider to be an absolute right and therefore worthy of extensive publicly funded social marketing campaigns, you may consider to be an absolute wrong. Organ donation is an absolute wrong for those whose religious beliefs preclude the desecration of bodies yet it is considered an important cause worthy of social marketing dollars by those not constrained by the same belief structure.[17]

Alan Andreasen's comments on the listserv focused on the role of the social marketing consultant versus the client or funder:

> We need to be clear that social marketers are "hired guns" (excuse the metaphor). That is, give us a behavior you want influenced and we have some very good ways of making it happen. Each of us is free to work on behavior-influence challenges with which we feel comfortable and "comfort" is both a matter of personal ethics and a matter of expertise. The decision about which behaviors ought to be influenced is not ours to make. Clients, or even societies or governments, make those judgments.[18]

Table 1.1 Social Marketing Planning Process: Phases, Steps, Techniques, and Feedback Loops

Phase	Scoping		Selecting		Understanding	Designing		Managing		
Step	1. Purpose and focus	2. Situation analysis	3. Target audience	4. Behavior objectives and target goals	5. Barriers, benefits, motivators, competition, and influential others	6. Positioning	7. Marketing mix: the intervention tools	8. Evaluation plan	9. Budget	10. Plan to implement
Technique examples	Literature reviews, epidemiological and scientific data	SWOT analysis, peer interviews	Andreasen's nine criteria (see Chapter 5)	McKenzie-Mohr's three criteria (see Chapter 6)	Knowledge, attitudes, and practice studies	Perceptual maps	The 4Ps	Logic model	Objective and task method	Include a pilot prior to rollout
Feedback loops					Findings at this step may suggest adjustments to the target audience and/or behavior objectives and target goals		A pretest of draft strategies may suggest changes in the 4Ps design			A pilot may suggest changes, especially in the marketing mix

WHERE DID THE CONCEPT ORIGINATE?

When we think of social marketing as "influencing public behaviors," it is clear that this is not a new phenomenon. Consider efforts to free slaves, abolish child labor, influence women's right to vote, and recruit women into the workforce (see Figure 1.4).

Launching the discipline formally more than 40 years ago, the term *social marketing* was first introduced by Philip Kotler and Gerald Zaltman, in a pioneering article in the *Journal of Marketing*, to describe "the use of marketing principles and techniques to advance a social cause, idea or behavior."[19] In intervening decades, interest in and use of social marketing concepts, tools, and practices has spread from the arena of public health and safety and into the work of environmentalists, community advocates, and poverty workers, as is evident in the partial list of seminal events, texts, and journal articles in Box 1.2.

Figure 1.4 "Rosie the Riveter," Created by the War Ad Council to Help Recruit Women

Source: Provided by the National Archives and Records Administration, Washington, DC.

HOW DOES SOCIAL MARKETING DIFFER FROM COMMERCIAL MARKETING?

There are a few important differences between social marketing and commercial marketing.

In the commercial sector, the primary aim is selling goods and services that will produce a *financial gain* for the corporation. In social marketing, the primary aim is influencing behaviors that will contribute to *societal and individual gain.* Given their focus on financial gain, commercial marketers often favor choosing primary target audience segments that will provide the greatest volume of profitable sales. In social marketing, segments are selected based on a different set of criteria, including prevalence of the social problem, ability to reach the audience, readiness for change, and other factors that will be explored in depth in Chapter 5 of this text. In both cases, however, marketers seek to gain the greatest returns on their investment of resources.

Although both social and commercial marketers recognize the need to identify and position their offering relative to the competition, their competitors are very

Box 1.2
Social Marketing: Seminal Events and Publications

1970s

1971:   A pioneering article by Philip Kotler and Gerald Zaltman, "Social Marketing: An Approach to Planned Social Change" in the *Journal of Marketing*, coins the term social marketing.

Other distinguished researchers and practitioners join the voice for the potential of social marketing, including Alan Andreasen (Georgetown University), James Mintz (Federal Department of Health, Canada), Bill Novelli (cofounder of Porter Novelli Associates), and Dr. Bill Smith.

1980s

The World Bank, World Health Organization, and Centers for Disease Control start to use the term and promote interest in social marketing.

1981:   An article in the *Journal of Marketing* by Paul Bloom and William Novelli reviews the first 10 years of social marketing and highlights the lack of rigor in the application of marketing principles and techniques in critical areas of the field, including research, segmentation, and distribution channels.

1981:   The Social Marketing Unit is created as part of the Health Promotion Directorate of Health Canada.

1988:   An article in the *Health Education Quarterly*, "Social Marketing and Public Health Intervention" by R. Craig Lefebvre and June Flora, gives social marketing widespread exposure in the field of public health.

1989:   A text by Philip Kotler and Eduardo Roberto, *Social Marketing: Strategies for Changing Public Behavior*, lays out the application of marketing principles and techniques for influencing social change management.

1990s

Academic programs are established, including the Center for Social Marketing at the University of Strathclyde in Glasgow and the Department of Community and Family Health at the University of South Florida.

1992:   An article in the *American Psychologist* by James Prochaska, Carlo DiClemente, and John Norcross presents an organizing framework for achieving behavior change, considered by many the most useful model developed to date.

(Continued)

(Continued)

1994:	A publication, *Social Marketing Quarterly* by Best Start Inc. and the Department of Public Health, University of South Florida, is launched.
1995:	A text by Alan Andreasen, *Marketing Social Change. Changing Behavior to Promote Health, Social Development, and the Environment*, makes a significant contribution to both the theory and practice of social marketing.
1995:	The first edition of the *Tools of Change* workbook by Jay Kassirer and Doug McKenzie-Mohr is published.
1998:	The Tools of Change website is created, offering specific community-based social marketing tools and case studies.
1999:	The Social Marketing Institute is formed in Washington, D.C., with Alan Andreasen from Georgetown University as interim executive director.
1999:	A text by Doug McKenzie-Mohr and William Smith, *Fostering Sustainable Behavior*, provides an introduction to community-based social marketing.
2000s	
2001:	The University of South Florida offers a social marketing certificate program.
2003:	A text by Rob Donovan, *Social Marketing: Principles & Practice*, is published in Melbourne, Australia.
2004:	Tools of Change introduces webinars.
2004:	The first National Social Marketing Strategy in the UK is developed.
2005:	The National Social Marketing Centre, headed by Jeff French and Clive Blair-Stevens, is formed in London, England.
2005:	The 10th annual conference for Innovations in Social Marketing is held.
2005:	The 16th annual Social Marketing in Public Health conference is held.
2006:	A text by Alan Andreasen, *Social Marketing in the 21st Century*, describes an expanded role for social marketing, including influencing target audiences upstream (e.g., policymakers).
2007:	Gerard Hastings's book *Social Marketing: Why Should the Devil Have All the Best Tunes?* is published.

2008: The first World Social Marketing Conference is held in Brighton, England.

2009: Social marketing approaches are included in Australia's National Preventative Health Strategy, and in the UK, National Operating Standards for social marketing are published.

2010s

2010–2011: The International Social Marketing Association is launched, providing member benefits including online access to information on conferences and meetings, tools and resources, jobs, and listserv/discussion forums; free webinars; discounts on conferences, trainings, and subscriptions; and networking online and in person with social marketing experts. The Australian Social Marketing Association and European Social Marketing Association are also launched.

2010–2013: The 20th, 21st, and 22nd Social Marketing in Public Health conferences are held in Florida. The second and third World Social Marketing conferences are held in Dublin and Toronto (the fourth will be held in Sydney, Australia, in 2015).

2010–2013: More books are published, including the third and fourth editions of *Social Marketing: Influencing Behaviors for Good* by Nancy Lee and Philip Kotler; the second edition of *Hands-On Social Marketing* by Nedra Weinreich; *Social Marketing for Public Health: Global Trends and Success Stories* by Hong Cheng, Philip Kotler, and Nancy Lee; *Social Marketing to Protect the Environment: What Works* by Doug McKenzie-Mohr, Nancy Lee, Wesley Schultz, and Philip Kotler; *Social Marketing and Public Health: Theory and Practice* by Jeff French; *Social Marketing and Social Change* by Craig Lefebvre; the second edition of *Social Marketing, From Tunes to Symphonies* by Gerard Hastings and Christine Domegan; *Social Marketing Six-Volume Series* (published by SAGE); and the third edition of *Fostering Sustainable Behavior* by Doug McKenzie-Mohr. The *Journal of Social Marketing* is launched in Australia.

2010–2014: In the United States, social marketing objectives are included in the Healthy People objectives for schools of public health and practice objectives for departments of health. In Australia, the minister for health and aging releases *Taking Preventative Action*, the government's response to the report of the National Preventative Health

(Continued)

(Continued)

	Taskforce. In the UK, the new coalition government endorses the previous government's strategic support of social marketing. A second, updated National Social Marketing strategy, called "Changing Behaviour. Improving Outcomes," is released in 2011.
2011:	The University of South Florida offers an online social marketing certificate program; George Washington University School of Public Health offers an MPH with a social marketing concentration.
2011–2012:	A TEDx event, "Changing Behaviors for Good," is launched by the Pacific Northwest Social Marketing Association, and Bill Smith presents the TED Talk *Reinventing Social Marketing*.
2012:	The first-in-the-world MBA in social marketing and behavior change program is launched from the University of Stirling.
2012:	The first European Social Marketing Conference is held in Lisbon, Portugal.
2013:	The first social marketing career center is launched by the International Social Marketing Association.

different in nature. Because, as stated earlier, the commercial marketer most often focuses on selling goods and services, the *competition is often identified as other organizations offering similar goods and services.* In social marketing, *the competition is most often the current or preferred behavior of the target audience* and the desired benefits associated with that behavior, including the status quo. This also includes any organizations selling or promoting competing behaviors (e.g., the tobacco industry).

For a variety of reasons, we believe social marketing is more difficult than commercial marketing. Consider the financial resources the competition has to make drinking alcohol look cool, yard cleanup using a gas blower easy, fried food look tasty, and bright green lawns the norm. And consider the challenges faced in trying to influence people to do any of the following:

- Give up an addictive behavior (e.g., stop smoking)
- Change a comfortable lifestyle (e.g., reduce thermostat settings)
- Resist peer pressure (e.g., be sexually abstinent)
- Go out of their way (e.g., take unused paint to a hazardous waste site)
- Be uncomfortable (e.g., give blood)
- Establish new habits (e.g., exercise five days a week)

- Spend more money (e.g., buy recycled paper)
- Be embarrassed (e.g., let lawns go brown in the summer)
- Hear bad news (e.g., get an HIV test)
- Risk relationships (e.g., take the keys from a drunk driver)
- Worry about unintended consequences (e.g., get an HPV vaccine for your 12-year-old to help prevent sexually transmitted diseases)
- Give up leisure time (e.g., volunteer)
- Reduce pleasure (e.g., take shorter showers)
- Give up looking good (e.g., wear sunscreen)
- Spend more time (e.g., flatten cardboard boxes before putting them in recycling bins)
- Learn a new skill (e.g., create and follow a budget)
- Remember something (e.g., take reusable bags to the grocery store)
- Risk retaliation (e.g., drive the speed limit)

Despite these differences, we also see many similarities between the social and commercial marketing models:

- *A customer orientation is critical.* The marketer knows that the offer (product, price, place) will need to appeal to the target audience by promising to solve a problem they have or satisfy a want or need.
- *Exchange theory is fundamental.* The target audience must perceive benefits that equal or exceed the perceived costs they associate with performing the behavior.[20] As Bill Smith says in this chapter's opening quote, we should think of the social marketing paradigm as "Let's make a deal!"[21]
- *Marketing research is used throughout the process.* Only by researching and understanding the specific needs, desires, beliefs, and attitudes of target adopters can the marketer build effective strategies.
- *Audiences are segmented.* Strategies must be tailored to the unique wants, needs, resources, and current behaviors of differing market segments.
- *All 4Ps (product, price, place, promotion) are considered.* A winning strategy requires an integrated approach, one utilizing all relevant intervention tools in the toolbox, not just relying on advertising and other persuasive communications.
- *Results are measured and used for improvement.* Feedback is valued and seen as "free advice" on how to do better next time.

HOW DOES SOCIAL MARKETING DIFFER FROM OTHER RELATED DISCIPLINES, BEHAVIOR CHANGE THEORIES AND MODELS, AND PROMOTIONAL TACTICS?

Social marketing is often confused or equated with several other related *disciplines* (nonprofit marketing, public sector marketing, and education), emerging behavior change *theories and frameworks* (behavioral economics, nudge, social change, community-based social marketing, community-based prevention marketing), and popular *promotional tactics* (social media, advertising, cause promotion). This section briefly helps distinguish 10 of these from the social marketing discipline, and the following section elaborates on the application of social marketing by corporations, nonprofit/nongovernmental organizations, and public sector agencies. Note as well that each of the behavior change theories and frameworks is elaborated on in Chapter 8 and that promotional tactics are described further in Chapter 14.

- *Nonprofit/NGO marketing.* Those responsible for marketing in the nonprofit/NGO sector most often focus on supporting utilization of the organization's programs and services (e.g., ticket sales for a new museum exhibit), purchases of ancillary products and services (e.g., at museum stores), volunteer recruitment (e.g., for museum docents), advocacy efforts (e.g., inviting elected officials to visit a museum), and fundraising (e.g., for expansion efforts).
- *Public sector marketing.* In this domain, marketing efforts are most often counted on to support utilization of governmental agency products and services (e.g., the post office, community clinics), engender citizen support (e.g., for road improvements), and increase compliance (e.g., with policies regarding public health practices at farmers' markets).
- *Education.* Educational efforts designed to address social issues focus primarily on increasing awareness and understanding. Although social marketers may use education as a tactic (e.g., sharing information about why pet waste is dangerous for fish), it is rarely sufficient to actually influence behaviors, as it does not often address major barriers, benefits, and motivators a target audience has in regard to adopting the behavior (e.g., access to plastic bags to pick up pet waste).
- *Behavioral economics.* This psychological framework proposes theories on why and when people make irrational choices, and then focuses on how changes in the external environment can prompt and promote positive, voluntary, individual-level behavior change. Social marketers can (and do) explore these insights when developing social marketing strategies.
- *Nudge.* This framework, introduced by Richard Thaler and Cass Sunstein in 2009, proposes that behaviors that improve health, wealth, and happiness can be influenced by presenting choices (e.g., children in a school cafeteria can be influenced to choose healthier options by placing them at eye level and/or at the beginning of the food display). This is an innovative strategy that can inspire social marketers.[22]
- *Social change.* We see social marketing as only one approach to creating positive social change. Others include advocacy (e.g., for gay marriage), innovation (e.g., electric cars), technology (e.g., the iPhone), infrastructure (e.g., bike lanes), science (e.g., a cure for HIV/AIDS), corporate business practices (e.g., calories posted on menu boards), funding (e.g., for malaria nets), and laws (e.g., prohibiting texting while driving). Although the focus of social marketing is on influencing individual

behaviors, you will read in the final sections of this chapter the role we see for social marketers to play in influencing these alternate social change strategies.

- *Community-based social marketing (CBSM).* This behavior change approach, developed by Doug McKenzie-Mohr in 1999, focuses on behaviors to protect the environment. It emphasizes several of the steps in the 10-step social marketing planning model presented in this text: selecting behaviors, identifying barriers and benefits, developing strategies, piloting, and then broad-scale implementation and evaluation.[23]

- *Community-based prevention marketing.* This practice engages influential and relevant community members in the process of identifying problems, mobilizing resources, planning and implementing strategies, and tracking and evaluating progress toward objectives and goals. It is not focused just on achieving behavior change but also on building community.[24] Social marketers can (and do) benefit from this practice by engaging community members and organizations in the planning, implementing, and evaluation process.

- *Social media.* This is a communication channel that social marketers use and includes Facebook, Twitter, blogs, YouTube, and other social networking sites. It is only one of numerous promotional tactics that social marketers use.

- *Cause promotion.* These promotional efforts are designed to increase awareness and concern for a social cause (e.g., global warming). Social marketers leverage these efforts by focusing on behaviors to alleviate these concerns.

WHAT IS SOCIAL MARKETING'S UNIQUE VALUE PROPOSITION?

In March 2011, Nancy Lee, Mike Rothschild, and Bill Smith wrote a document to address two very narrow questions: (a) What does social marketing add to the already considerable understanding of social change developed by many other disciplines? and (b) What is social marketing's unique value proposition? See Box 1.3 on pages 22, 23, 24, and 25 for their response.

WHO DOES SOCIAL MARKETING?

In most cases, social marketing principles and techniques are used by those on the front lines who are responsible for influencing public behaviors to improve public health, prevent injuries, protect the environment, engender community involvement, and, more recently, enhance financial well-being. It is rare that these individuals have a social marketing title. More often, they are program managers or those working in community relations or communication positions. Efforts usually involve multiple change agents who, as Robert Hornik points out, may or may not be acting in a consciously coordinated way.[25] Most often, organizations sponsoring these efforts are *public sector agencies*: international agencies such as WHO; national agencies such as the Centers for Disease Control and

Box 1.3
A Declaration of Social Marketing's Unique Principles and Distinctions

Nancy R. Lee, Michael L. Rothschild, and Bill Smith

March 2011

Principles Shared With Other Disciplines

Many of Social Marketing's key characteristics have been widely adopted by other fields, and in turn Social Marketing has integrated practices developed elsewhere. Among the important characteristics it shares with others are:

- AUDIENCE ORIENTATION: Social marketers view their audience as decision-makers with choices, rather than students to be educated, or incorrigibles to be regulated. Social Marketing begins with a bottom-up versus a top-down perspective, and therefore rejects the paternalist notion that "experts know what is best and will tell people how to behave for their own good" in favor of an audience-centered approach which seeks to understand what people want and provide them support in acquiring it.
- SEGMENTATION: In order to enhance efficiency and effectiveness, subsets of populations are selected, evaluated, and then prioritized as targets based on useful aggregation variables. The segments selected are those most likely to adopt the intended behavior or most important to the organization's goals, and most likely to provide value in yielding societal benefit. Even among difficult to reach populations, strategies are developed that appeal to those within the chosen population that are the "most ready for action."
- BEHAVIOR FOCUS: Behavior is defined as an individual's observable action or lack of action. Social Marketing is interested in behavior that results in societal benefit. Many marketing strategies also have intermediate responses, but Social Marketing success is ultimately measured on whether the desired behavior was adopted. It is not sufficient to merely change awareness, knowledge, attitudes, or behavioral intentions.
- EVALUATION: Efforts are evaluated, focusing on ongoing measurement of outcomes (levels of target audience behavior change) and the intended impact this has had on societal benefits. Social Marketing is a continuous process in which evaluation and monitoring provide data on the audience's preferences and the environmental changes necessary to maintain and expand the impact of programs.
- CONSIDERATION OF UPSTREAM & MIDSTREAM TARGET AUDIENCES: Efforts to influence individuals downstream are often enhanced by also targeting those who are upstream (policymakers, corporations) and/or those who are midstream (e.g. friends, family and influential others).

Unique Principles

While social marketing integrates many characteristics common to other forms of behavior change, four core principles remain truly unique to Social Marketing.

- VALUE EXCHANGE: Social Marketing is unique with respect to other behavior change tools in that the offer that is made is based on an understanding of the target audience's perceived self-interest, which will be rewarded for performing the desired behavior. The concept of value exchange states that consumers will choose a behavior in exchange for receiving benefits they consider valuable and/or reducing barriers that they consider to be important. An exchange may result when the marketer has created a program that is perceived by each side to provide value.
- RECOGNITION OF COMPETITION: In a free-choice society there are always alternative options available. Competition can be described in terms of choice offerings available in the environment that lead to alternative behaviors. Social Marketing strategies lead to a unique exchange offering that is perceived by the audience to have greater value than that of any other available option.
- THE 4Ps OF MARKETING: Product, Place, Price, and Promotion represent the fundamental building blocks of Social Marketing interventions. These tools are used to reduce the barriers that make it difficult for people to behave as desired, and to increase the benefits that induce people to be more likely to behave. The tools are used in concert to develop a favorably perceived relationship that is more appealing than all alternate choices. Social marketers assess and then balance the need for, and use of, these four elements to influence optimal change.
- SUSTAINABILITY: Sustainability results from continuous program monitoring and subsequent adjustment to changes occurring in the audience and environmental condition. This is necessary to achieve long run behavior.

Distinctions

It also is important to be clear about how Social Marketing differs from other important approaches to behavior change. Being different does not make any approach superior to any other, but these distinctions signal opportunities for Social Marketing to make a unique contribution.

- COMMERCIAL MARKETING: Social Marketing is built upon many of the traditional processes and principles of commercial marketing, especially Customer Orientation, Exchange Theory, Competition, Segmentation, the 4Ps, Relationships, and a Service Orientation. Social Marketing differs in that the primary responsibility of commercial marketers is to increase the company's wealth by

(Continued)

(Continued)

increasing individuals' well-being, whereas the primary responsibility of social marketers is to increase individual and societal well-being.

- COMMUNICATIONS: Communications is a process involved with every human activity and is widely used by many approaches to behavior change. In Social Marketing, communications refers to the activity that describes the benefits of the offering, its price and accessibility to the target audience. Communicating the integrated value of the marketing mix is unique to social marketing, and is not offered by any other communication discipline. Communications alone generally is not sufficient to influence behaviors.

- REGULATION: Regulation also seeks to influence behaviors for the benefit of society, but often does so by increasing the cost of undesired competing behaviors (e.g., penalties for breaking laws) rather than increasing the benefits of desired behaviors. Those regulations that offer a benefit for an appropriate behavior (e.g., various tax incentives) more closely fit within the rubric of Social Marketing. Social marketers also have a role to play in influencing policymakers to adopt regulations (upstream changes) that complement and accelerate behavior changes among large-scale audiences, and to increase compliance with existing regulations.

- SOCIAL MEDIA: Social media leverage the social networks of target audiences, and are more personal and interactive forms of message delivery than are the traditional mass media. From a conceptual perspective, though, these electronic systems are similar to print, broadcast, and outdoor, in that each are ways of delivering messages and are, therefore, a subset of communications.

- NONPROFIT MARKETING: The marketing function for nonprofit organizations often focuses on fund-raising, advocacy, and program development, as well as supporting utilization of the organization's products and services.

- BEHAVIORAL ECONOMICS: Behavioral economics merges economics, psychology, sociology, and anthropology theory and research that focus on how changes in the external environment prompt and promote voluntary individual level behavior change. Social Marketing is a process that should apply these insights along with others to maximize the efficiency and effectiveness of large-scale behavior change.

Unique Value Proposition

Social Marketing's unique position in the marketplace of behavior change ideas is to integrate the shared and unique characteristics described above into a program of behavior change. Social Marketing is a process rooted in the belief that more than words and/or regulations are needed in order to succeed at influencing people's behavior. Social marketers understand and build upon the consumer's perception of

- self-interest
- barriers to behavior, and
- competitive forces that create attractive choices.

These lead to interventions that

- reduce barriers, and
- increase benefits that matter to the audience and, in the end, move people to action.

Acknowledgments

We wish to thank the following colleagues whose feedback and insights were invaluable to this document: Alan Andreasen, John Bromley, Carol Bryant, Stephen Dann, Rob Donovan, Jeff French, Phil Harvey, Gerard Hastings, Phil Kotler, Francois Lagarde, Craig Lefebvre, Rowena Merritt, Mike Newton-Ward, Sharyn Rundle Thiele. Ultimately any flaws are ours, not theirs.

Prevention, the Ministries of Health, the Environmental Protection Agency, and the National Highway Traffic Safety Administration; state agencies such as departments of health, social and human services, and fish and wildlife; and local jurisdictions, including public utilities, fire departments, schools, parks, and community health clinics.

Nonprofit organizations and foundations also get involved, most often supporting behaviors aligned with their agency's mission. For example, the American Heart Association urges women to monitor their blood pressure, the Kaiser Family Foundation uses their Know HIV/AIDS campaign to promote testing, and the Nature Conservancy encourages actions that protect wildlife habitats.

Professionals working in for-profit organizations in positions responsible for corporate philanthropy, corporate social responsibility, marketing, or community relations might support social marketing efforts, often in partnership with nonprofit organizations and public agencies that benefit their communities and customers. Although the primary beneficiary is society, they may find that their efforts contribute to organizational goals as well, such as a desired brand image or even increased sales. Safeco Insurance, for example, provides households with tips on how to protect rural homes from wildfire; Crest supports the development of videos, audiotapes, and interactive lesson plans to promote good oral health behaviors; and thousands of customers at Home Depot's stores have attended weekend workshops focusing on water conservation basics, including drought-resistant gardening (see Figure 1.5).

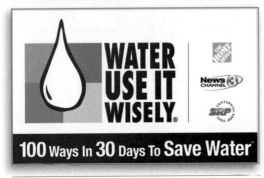

Figure 1.5 Home Depot's Arizona stores offered weekend workshops on water conservation basics, including drought-resistant gardening. More than 3,100 consumers attended.

Source: Courtesy of Park and Company.

Finally, there are marketing professionals who provide services to *organizations engaged in social marketing campaigns*, firms such as advertising agencies, public relations firms, marketing research firms, and marketing consulting firms—some that specialize in social marketing.

WHAT SOCIAL ISSUES CAN BENEFIT FROM SOCIAL MARKETING?

Table 1.2 presents 50 major social issues that could benefit from the application of social marketing principles and techniques. This is only a partial list, with data only for the United States, but representative of the aforementioned five major arenas social marketing efforts usually focus on: health promotion, injury prevention, environmental protection, community involvement, and financial well-being. For each of the social issues listed, the status could improve if and when we are successful in increasing the adoption of desired related behaviors.

WHAT ARE OTHER WAYS TO IMPACT SOCIAL ISSUES?

Social marketing is clearly not the only approach to impacting a social issue, and social marketers are not the only ones who can be influential. Other forces and organizations, which some describe as upstream factors and midstream influential others, can affect individual behaviors downstream. Included upstream are technological innovations, scientific discoveries, economic pressures, laws, improved infrastructures, changes in corporate business practices, new school policies and curricula, public education, and the media. Midstream influences are family members, friends, neighbors, church leaders, health care providers, entertainers, Facebook friends, and others our target audiences listen to, observe, or look up to.

Technology: Many new gas pumps inhibit the ability to top off the tank, thus avoiding ozone-threatening spillage. Some cars have automatic seatbelts that wrap around the passenger when the door is closed. In some states, ignition locks require Breathalyzers for serious offenders, and Mothers Against Drunk Driving (MADD) is advocating that automobile manufacturers be required to include high-tech alcohol sensors in all new cars. Imagine the impact on trip reduction if cars were designed to give feedback on how much that trip to the grocery store just cost, given the current price of a gallon of gas.

Table 1.2   50 Major Issues Social Marketing Can Impact in the U.S. Alone

Health-Related Behaviors to Impact	
Tobacco Use	Almost one in five (19%) adults 18 and older smokes cigarettes.[a]
Heavy/Binge Drinking	More than a fourth (28.2%) of 18- to 24-year-olds binge drink (have five or more drinks on one occasion).[b]
Fetal Alcohol Syndrome	4% of pregnant women use illicit drugs, including cocaine, Ecstasy, and heroin.[c]
Obesity	Almost half (48.4%) of adults do not exercise at recommended levels.[d]
Teen Pregnancy	38% of sexually active 9th- through 12th-graders did not use a condom during their last sexual intercourse.[e]
HIV/AIDS	Almost a fifth (18.1%) of Americans living with HIV are unaware of their infection.[f]
Fruit and Vegetable Intake	More than three out of four adults (76.5%) do not consume the recommended five or more servings a day.[g]
High Cholesterol	21% of adults have never had their cholesterol checked.[h]
Breastfeeding	59% of mothers do not meet recommendations to breastfeed infants until they reach at least six months.[i]
Breast Cancer	25% of women 40 and older have not had a mammogram within the past two years.[j]
Prostate Cancer	47% of men 40 and older have not had a PSA test within the past two years.[k]
Colon Cancer	35% of adults 50 and older have never had a sigmoidoscopy or colonoscopy.[l]
Birth Defects	60% of women of childbearing age are not taking a multivitamin containing folic acid.[m]
Immunizations	25% of 19- to 35-month-old children are not receiving all recommended vaccinations.[n]
Skin Cancer	Only 9% of youth wear sunscreen most of the time.[o]
Oral Health	30% of adults have not visited a dentist or dental clinic in the past year.[p]
Diabetes	One fourth of the 23 million Americans with diabetes are not aware that they have the disease.[q]
Blood Pressure	19% of the estimated 78 million Americans with high blood pressure don't know they have it.[r]
Eating Disorders	57% of college students cite cultural pressures to be thin as a cause of eating disorders.[s]
Injury Prevention–Related Behaviors to Impact	
Drinking and Driving	24% of high school students report having ridden one or more times in the past year in a car driven by someone who had been drinking.[t]
Texting or Emailing While Driving	32.8% of high school youth reported texting or emailing while driving.[u]

(Continued)

Table 1.2 (Continued)

Head Injuries	Among the 70% of high school youth who had ridden a bicycle in the past year, 87.5% had rarely or never worn a bicycle helmet.[v]
Proper Safety Restraints for Children in Cars	83% of children ages four to eight ride improperly restrained in adult safety belts.[w]
Suicide	7.8% of 9th- through 12th-graders have attempted suicide one or more times during the past 12 months.[x]
Domestic Violence	One in four women (25%) has experienced domestic violence in her lifetime.[y]
Gun Storage	One third of all households with children younger than 18 have a gun, and more than 40% of gun-owning households with children store their guns unlocked.[z]
School Violence	5% of students in high schools reported carrying a gun onto school property during a given month.[aa]
Fires	60% of reported home fire deaths resulted from fires in homes with no operational smoke alarm.[bb]
Falls	More than one third of adults 65 and older fall each year. In 2009, more than 20,400 people 65+ died from injuries related to falls.[cc]
Household Poisons	Medications are the leading cause of child poisoning. Every year, around 67,000 children go to an emergency room for medicine poisoning. That's one child every eight minutes.[dd]
Environmental Behaviors to Impact	
Waste Reduction	Only 55% of aluminum beer and soda cans, 34% of glass containers, and 29% of plastic bottles and jars are recycled.[ee]
Wildlife Habitat Protection	Roughly 70% of the major marine fish stocks depleted from overfishing are being fished at their biological limit.[ff]
Forest Destruction	About 15 million trees are cut down annually to produce the estimated 10 billion paper bags we go through each year in the United States.[gg]
Toxic Fertilizers and Pesticides	An estimated 76% of households use harmful insecticides, and an estimated 85% have at least one pesticide in storage.[hh]
Water Conservation	A leaky toilet can waste as much as 200 gallons a day.[ii]
Air Pollution From Automobiles	An estimated 76% of commuters in the United States drive alone to work.[jj]
Air Pollution From Other Sources	If every household in the United States replaced their five most frequently used light fixtures with bulbs that have the ENERGY STAR label, more than 1 trillion pounds of greenhouse gas emissions would be prevented.[kk]
Composting Garbage and Yard Waste	An estimated 28% to 56% of all trash that ends up in a landfill in the United States could have been composted.[ll]
Unintentional Fires	An average of 106,400 wildfires are estimated to break out each year in the United States; about 9 out of 10 are started by carelessness.[mm]
Litter	65% of cigarette butts are discarded as litter each year, with most (85%) ending up on the ground.[nn]

Watershed Protection	At least 38% of Americans don't pick up their dogs' waste.[oo]
Community Involvement Behaviors to Impact	
Organ Donation	As of July 30, 2013, 119,013 patients were on a waiting list for an organ transplant.[pp]
Blood Donation	38% of the U.S. population is eligible to give blood, but less than 10% do in a given year.[qq]
Voting	Only 62% of the eligible voting-age population voted in the 2012 U.S. presidential election.[rr]
Literacy	Only 33% of children are read a bedtime story every night, and 50% of parents say their children spend more time with TV or video games than with books.[ss]
Animal Adoption	3 to 4 million dogs and cats in shelters are not adopted and are euthanized each year.[tt]
Financial Behaviors to Impact	
Identity Theft	About 15 million U.S. residents have their identities used fraudulently each year, with financial losses totaling upwards of $50 billion.[uu]
Establishing Bank Accounts	Nearly a quarter of the workforce in the United States has no bank account.[vv]
Bankruptcy	Job loss is a big cause of bankruptcy because people who don't have emergency funds often live off credit cards while they are unemployed.[ww]
Fraud	More than a quarter (26%) of adults have been victimized by fraudulent telemarketing techniques at some point in their lives.[xx]

Note: Statistics are estimated and approximate. Data are for the United States, and dates for these statistics are given in the table notes.

Science: Medical discoveries may eventually provide inoculations for certain cancers, such as the HPV vaccine released in 2009 for 11- to 26-year-olds to help prevent cervical cancer. And, in 2006, researchers at the Mayo Clinic announced that they felt they were close to discovering a shot that could be given that would help a smoker quit (if not ensure smoking cessation).[26]

Legal/political/policymaking/law enforcement: Sometimes when all else fails, the laws have to get tougher, especially when the vast majority of the market has adopted the behavior and only the most resistant are still holding out (late adopters and laggards, as they are labeled in marketing). As of September 2014, 44 states, the District of Columbia, Puerto Rico, Guam, and the U.S. Virgin Islands have banned text messaging for all drivers.[27] All U.S. states now have a 0.08% blood alcohol level limit for drinking and driving, more strict than the prior 0.10%. Some states have considered laws requiring deposits on cigarettes similar to those requiring deposits on beverage containers (and rewarding their return). And in a policy statement published in December 2006 in the journal *Pediatrics*, the American Academy of Pediatrics asked Congress and the Federal Communications Commission to

Figure 1.6 Making the calories per container more obvious.

impose severe limits on children-targeted advertising, including the banning of junk food ads during shows viewed predominantly by those under age eight.[28] And, in 2013, a law enforcement crackdown on sex trafficking rescued dozens of victims.[29]

Improved infrastructures and built environments: If we really want more people to ride bikes to work, we'll need more bike lanes, not just bike paths. If we really want to reduce cigarette butt littering on roadways, perhaps automobile manufacturers could help out by building in smoke-free cigarette butt containers so that disposing a cigarette inside the car is just as convenient as tossing it out the window. If we want to reduce electricity consumption, perhaps more hotels could ensure that lights in rooms can be turned on only when the room key is inserted in a master switch and therefore are automatically turned off when guests leave the room with their key. And if we want more people at work to take the stairs instead of the elevators, we may want to have elevators skip the first three floors except in cases of emergency or to accommodate those with a physical disability, and we certainly want to take a look at the cleanliness and lighting of the stairway. How about a little music? Social marketers can play a huge role in influencing policymakers and corporations to make these changes.

Changes in corporate policies and business practices: In 2010, the American Beverage Association announced their Clear on Calories initiative in support of First Lady Michelle Obama's antiobesity campaign. Instead of printing the number of calories per serving on the back of the can in small print, members will print the number in large print on the front of the can—and the number will represent the total calories per container, versus per serving, since most consumers drink the entire can (see Figure 1.6).

Schools: School district policies and offerings can provide channels of distribution for social marketing efforts and contribute significantly in all social arenas: health (e.g., offering healthier options in school cafeterias and regularly scheduled physical activity classes), safety (e.g., requiring students to wear ID badges), environmental protection (e.g., providing recycling containers in each classroom), and community involvement (e.g., offering school gymnasiums for blood donation drives).

Education: As mentioned earlier, the line between social marketing and education is actually a clear one, with education serving a useful tool for the social marketer but one rarely working alone. Most often, education is used to communicate information and/or build skills but does not give the same attention and rigor to creating and sustaining behavior adoption. It primarily applies only one of the four marketing tools, that of promotion. Many in the field agree that when the information is motivating and "new" (e.g., the finding that secondhand tobacco smoke increases the risk of sudden infant death syndrome), it can move a market from inaction—even resistance—to action very quickly. This, however, is unfortunately not typical. Consider the fact that death threats for tobacco use have been posted right on cigarette packs for decades, and yet WHO estimates that 29% of youth and adults (ages 15 and older) worldwide still smoke cigarettes.[30] Marketing (reducing barriers and offering benefits in exchange for behaviors) has often been missing in action.

Media: News and entertainment media exert a powerful influence on individual behaviors, as they shape values, are relied on for current events and trends, and create social norms. Many argue, for example, that the casual and sensational attitude of movies and television toward sex has been a major contributor to the problems we see among young people today.[31] On the flip side, the media were a powerful factor influencing people to donate time and resources to victims of the earthquake in Haiti, the tsunami in Japan, the shootings at Sandyhook Elementary school in Connecticut, and the severe and destructive hurricane in New Jersey.

WHAT IS THE SOCIAL MARKETER'S ROLE IN INFLUENCING UPSTREAM FACTORS AND MIDSTREAM AUDIENCES?

As noted earlier, many believe that to date we have been placing too much of the burden for improving the status of social issues on individual behavior change and that social marketers should direct some of their efforts to influencing upstream factors and midstream influentials. We agree. (See Box 1.4 for examples of audiences midstream and upstream.)

Alan Andreasen describes this expanded role of social marketing well:

Social marketing is about making the world a better place for everyone—not just for investors or foundation executives. And, as I argue throughout this book, the same basic principles that can induce a 12-year-old in Bangkok or Leningrad to get a Big Mac and a caregiver in Indonesia to start using oral dehydration solutions for diarrhea can also be used to influence politicians, media figures, community activists, law officers and judges, foundation officials, and other individuals whose actions are needed to bring about widespread, long-lasting positive social change.[32]

Consider the issue of the spread of HIV/AIDS. Downstream, social marketers focus on decreasing risky behaviors (e.g., unprotected sex) and increasing timely testing (e.g., during pregnancy). If they moved their attention upstream, they would notice groups and organizations and corporations and community leaders and policymakers that could make this change a little easier or a little more likely, ones that could be a target

Box 1.4
Examples of Potential Midstream and Upstream Audiences to Influence

Potential Influential Midstream Audiences

Family Members
Friends
Neighbors
Colleagues
Health care providers
Pharmacists
Teachers
Librarians
Community leaders
Church members
Checkout clerks at retail stores

Potential Upstream Audiences

Policymakers
Corporations
Media
Law enforcement
Celebrities
School districts
Nonprofit organizations

audience for a social marketing effort. Social marketers could, with others, influence pharmaceutical companies to make testing for HIV/AIDS quicker and more accessible. They could work with physician groups to create protocols to ask patients whether they have had unprotected sex and, if so, encourage them to get an HIV/AIDS test. They could encourage offices of public instruction to include curricula on HIV/AIDS in middle schools. They could support needle exchange programs. They could provide the media with trends and personal stories, maybe even pitching a story to producers of soap operas or situation comedies popular with the target audience. They might look for a corporate partner that would be interested in setting up testing at their retail location. They could organize meetings with community leaders such as ministers and directors of nonprofit organizations, even providing grants for them to allocate staff resources to community interventions. They could visit hair salons and barbershops, engaging owners and staff in spreading the word with their clients. They could testify before a senate committee to advocate increased funding for research, condom availability, or free testing facilities. And midstream, they might appeal to parents to talk with their teens about how HIV/AIDS is spread and to midwives to speak to pregnant women about the importance of testing.

The marketing process and principles are the same as those used for influencing individuals: utilizing a customer orientation, establishing clear behavior objectives and target goals, conducting audience research, crafting a position statement, developing a marketing mix, and conducting monitoring and evaluation efforts. Only the target audience has changed.[33]

CHAPTER SUMMARY

Social marketing is a process that uses marketing principles and techniques to change target-audience behaviors that will benefit society as well as the individual. This strategically oriented discipline relies on creating, communicating, delivering, and exchanging offerings that have positive value for individuals, clients, partners, and society at large.[34]

There are a few important differences between social marketing and commercial marketing. Social marketers focus on influencing behavior for societal gain, whereas commercial marketers focus on selling goods and services at a financial gain for the organization. Commercial marketers position their products against those of other companies, while the social marketer competes with the audience's current behavior and its associated benefits.

Social marketing is often confused or equated with several other related *disciplines* (nonprofit marketing, public sector marketing, and education), emerging behavior change *theories and frameworks* (behavioral economics, nudge, social change, community-based social marketing, community-based prevention marketing), and popular *promotional tactics* (social media, cause promotion).

Social marketing principles and techniques are most often used to improve public health, prevent injuries, protect the environment, increase involvement in the community, and enhance financial well-being. Those engaged in social marketing activities include professionals in public sector agencies, nonprofit organizations, corporate marketing departments and advertising, public relations, and market research firms. A social marketing title is rare, and social marketing is most likely to fall within the responsibility of a program manager or community relations or communications professional.

Other approaches to changing behavior and impacting social issues include technological innovations, scientific discoveries, economic pressures, laws, improved infrastructures, changes in corporate business practices, new school policies and curricula, public education, and the media. Many agree that influencing these factors and audiences is well within the purview of social marketers—and even their responsibility.

When Is Social Marketing "Social Marketing"?
When Is It Something Else?

In February 2010, a member of the Georgetown Social Marketing Listserve of 2,000-plus members sent a message with the subject line "To Stir the Pot." The message included a link to an announcement of a new type of speed bump unveiled in West Vancouver, Canada, one intended to persuade motorists to slow down in the vicinity of an elementary school. A pavement painting appears to rise up as the driver gets closer to it, reaching a full 3D image of a child playing, creating the illusion that the approaching driver will soon hit the child (link: http://beta.news.yahoo.com/blogs/upshot/canada-unveils-speed-bump-optical-illusions-children.html). As anticipated, several members were adamant that this effort was not social marketing: "This is not marketing. Where's the exchange? What does the driver get [benefit] in exchange for slowing down?" Counterarguments stressed that "by slowing down [the cost], the driver gets a great benefit—a reduced probability of hitting a child!" Some were troubled by unintended secondary effects ("cultivating resentful drivers not liking to be tricked"), and others weren't impressed with the potential efficacy, convinced that "it might work once but then wouldn't be sustainable." A few felt it met the basic criteria for social marketing: "Since social marketing's basic purpose is to change behavior for the good or betterment of society as a whole, I think this initiative seems to fit well into that criteria. However, I question whether or not it will work."

The authors of this text offer the following opinions on common questions and reactions, such as whether an effort is—or is not—social marketing. As will be apparent, we make a distinction between what defines social marketing and what are its best practices:

- *Does the effort have to use all 4Ps in order to be called social marketing?* No, but this is a best practice. Your efforts will be more successful when you do, because most of the time all four intervention tools are needed to overcome audience barriers, increase benefits, and upstage the competition.
- *Does there have to be a narrowly defined and targeted audience segment?* No, but this is also a best practice, based on there being very few homogeneous populations, and the fact that different segments within these populations have different barriers and benefits and therefore require different interventions.
- *Is a communications-only campaign a social marketing campaign?* It might be. A campaign that is intended to influence a behavior (e.g., putting infants on their back to sleep) to benefit individuals and society (e.g., prevent sudden infant death

syndrome) but uses only words (e.g., "Back to Sleep" printed on the strip of a newborn diaper) meets the basic criteria for a social marketing effort. However, it is more likely to be successful if other influence tools are used as well (e.g., demonstrations as part of a free class for new moms at a local hospital).

- *What needs to be present for an effort to be called social marketing?* An effort can be considered a social marketing effort when it is intended to influence a target audience behavior to benefit society as well as the target audience. And we should keep in mind that the target audience may be a school district or corporation upstream.

DISCUSSION QUESTIONS AND EXERCISES

1. How does social marketing, as described in this chapter, differ from what you thought it was in the past?

2. Share an example of a social marketing effort that you are aware of.

3. What is the biggest distinction between social marketing and commercial marketing?

4. Reflect back on Table 1.2. What other social issues could social marketing impact?

5. Reflect back on the Marketing Highlight. What was the key to success in ending polio in India?

CHAPTER 1 NOTES

1. W. Smith, "Social Marketing and Its Potential Contribution to a Modern Synthesis of Social Change," *Social Marketing Quarterly* 8, no. 2 (Summer 2002): 46.

2. Rotary Down Under (Australia), "Can Rotary End Polio?" (n.d.), accessed July 12, 2013, http://www.rotarydownunder.com.au/latest-news?id=6f4820c6-31a9-1633-e037-51a587753a42.

3. Global Polio Eradication Initiative, "Fact File: Polio Eradication and Endgame Strategic Plan 2013–2018" (n.d.), accessed July 12, 2013, http://www.polioeradication.org/portals/0/docu ment/resources/strategywork/gpei_plan_factfile_en.pdf.

4. Polio Summit 2012 organized by the Government of India, Ministry of Health and Family Welfare, and Rotary International, *From 200,000 to Zero: The Journey to a Polio-Free India*, accessed July 12, 2013, from http://www.unicef.org/india/Polio_Booklet-final_(22-02-2012)V3.pdf.

5. E. Chhabra, "The End of Polio in India: An Immense Cross-Sector Partnership Is Responsible for the Immunization Success Story," *Stanford Social Innovation Review* (2012), accessed July 12, 2013, http://www.ssireview.org/articles/entry/the_end_of_polio_in_india.

6. S. Deshpande and N. R. Lee, *Social Marketing in India* (New Delhi, India: SAGE, 2013), chap. 15.

7. Chhabra, "End of Polio."

8 Polio Summit 2012, *From 200,000 to Zero.*

9. Rotary International, "Rotary's PolioPlus Program Fact Sheet as of February 2012" (n.d.), accessed July 2013, http://www.rotary.org/RIdocuments/en_pdf/polioplus_fact_sheet_en.pdf.

10. Chhabra, "End of Polio."

11. Ibid.

12. UNICEF India, "Polio Eradication" (n.d.), accessed July 12, 2013, http://www.unicef.org/india/health_3729.htm.

13. Chhabra, "End of Polio."

14. Personal communication from Alan Andreasen to Philip Kotler, April 28, 2011.

15. American Marketing Association, "AMA Definition of Marketing" (December 17, 2007), accessed July 24, 2013, http://www.marketingpower.com/aboutama/pages/definitionofmarketing.aspx.

16. R. Donovan and N. Henley, *Social Marketing: Principles and Practices* (Melbourne, Australia: IP Communications, 2003).

17. Message posted to the Georgetown Social Marketing Listserve, March 16, 2006.

18. Ibid.

19. P. Kotler and G. Zaltman, "Social Marketing: An Approach to Planned Social Change, *Journal of Marketing* 35 (1971, July): 3–12.

20. R. P. Bagozzi, "Marketing as Exchange: A Theory of Transactions in the Marketplace," *American Behavioral Science* (March/April 1978): pp. 535–556.

21. Smith, "Social Marketing and Its Potential Contribution."

22. R. Thaler and C. Sustein, *Nudge: Improving Decisions About Health, Wealth, and Happiness* (New York: Penguin Books, 2009).

23. D. McKenzie-Mohr, *Fostering Sustainable Behavior: An Introduction to Community-Based Social Marketing* (Gabriola Island, BC, Canada: New Society, 2011).

24. C. Lefebvre, *Social Marketing and Social Change: Strategies and Tools for Improving Health, Well-Being, and the Environment* (San Francisco: Jossey-Bass, 2013).

25. R. Hornik, "Some Complementary Ideas About Social Change," *Social Marketing Quarterly* 8, no. 2 (Summer 2002): 11.

26. M. Marchione, "Doctors Test Anti-smoking Vaccine" (2006), accessed July 31, 2007, http://www.foxnews.com/printer_friendly_wires/2006Ju127/0,4675,TobaccoVaccine,00.html.

27. Distraction.gov: Official US Government Website for Distracted Driving, "State Laws" (n.d.), accessed September 2014, http://www.distraction.gov/content/get-the-facts/state-laws.html.

28. I. Teinowitz, "Pediatricians Demand Cuts in Children-Targeted Advertising: Doctors' Group Asks Federal Government to Impose Severe Limits," *Advertising Age* (December 4, 2006), accessed June 29, 2011, http://adage.com/print?article_id=113558.

29. NBC Connecticut, "Dozens of Girls Rescued in Cross-Country Sex-Trafficking Sweep" (July 2013), accessed July 29, 2013, http://www.nbcbayarea.com/news/national-international/Dozens-of-girls-rescued-in-cross-country-child-sex-trafficking-sweep-21742 1071.html.

30. G. E. Guindon and D. Boisclair, *Past, Current and Future Trends in Tobacco Use* (February 2003), accessed September 9, 2014, http://siteresources.worldbank.org/HEALTHNUTRITIONANDPOPULATION/Resources/281627-1095698140167/Guindon-PastCurrent-whole.pdf.

31. A. R. Andreasen and P. Kotler, *Strategic Marketing for Non-profit Organizations*, 6th ed. (Upper Saddle River, NJ: Prentice Hall, 2003), 490.

32. A. R. Andreasen, *Social Marketing in the 21st Century* (Thousand Oaks, CA: SAGE, 2006), 11.

33. P. Kotler and N. Lee, *Marketing in the Public Sector: A Roadmap for Improved Performance* (Upper Saddle River, NJ: Wharton School, 2006).

34. N. R. Lee, M. L. Rothschild, and W. Smith, *A Declaration of Social Marketing's Unique Principles and Distinctions* (unpublished manuscript, March 2011).

CHAPTER 1 TABLE NOTES

a. Centers for Disease Control and Prevention, "Adult Cigarette Smoking in the United States: Current Estimates" (n.d.), accessed July 30, 2013, http://www.cdc.gov/tobacco/data_statistics/fact_sheets/adult_data/cig_smoking/.

b. Centers for Disease Control and Prevention, "Vital Signs: Binge Drinking, Prevalence, Frequency, and Intensity Among Adults—United States, 2010," *Morbidity and Mortality Weekly Report* (January 13, 2012), accessed July 30, 2013, http://www.cdc.gov/mmwr/preview/mmwrhtml/mm6101a4.htm.

c. March of Dimes, "Illicit Drug Use During Pregnancy" (n.d.), accessed July 30, 2013, http://www.marchofdimes.com/pregnancy/illicit-drug-use-during-pregnancy.aspx.

d. Centers for Disease Control and Prevention, "Exercise or Physical Activity" (n.d.), accessed July 30, 2013, http://www.cdc.gov/nchs/fastats/exercise.htm.

e. Centers for Disease Control and Prevention, "Youth Risk Behavior Surveillance—United States, 2011," *Morbidity and Mortality Weekly Report* (June 8, 2012), accessed July 30, 2013, http://www.cdc.gov/mmwr/preview/mmwrhtml/ss6104a1.htm.

f. Centers for Disease Control and Prevention, "HIV in the United States: At a Glance" (n.d.), accessed July 30, 2013, http://www.cdc.gov/hiv/statistics/basics/ataglance.html.

g. Centers for Disease Control and Prevention, "Behavioral Risk Factor Surveillance System Prevalence and Trends Data" (n.d.), accessed April 27, 2011, http://www.cdc.gov/brfss/index.htm.

h. Centers for Disease Control and Prevention, "Behavioral Risk Factor Surveillance System Prevalence and Trends Data: Cholesterol Awareness—2011" (n.d.), accessed July 30, 2013, http://apps.nccd.cdc.gov/brfss/list.asp?cat=CA&yr=2011&qkey=8061&state=All.

i. Centers for Disease Control and Prevention, "Breastfeeding Report Card, United States: Outcome Indicators" (n.d.), accessed July 30, 2013, http://www.cdc.gov/breastfeeding/data/reportcard.htm.

j. Centers for Disease Control and Prevention, "Behavioral Risk Factor Surveillance System Prevalence and Trends Data: Women's Health—2010" (n.d.), accessed July 30, 2013, http://apps.nccd.cdc.gov/brfss/list.asp?cat=WH&yr=2010&qkey=4421&state=All.

k. Ibid.

l. Ibid.

m. WebMD.com, "CDC to Young Women: Take Folic Acid" (2008), accessed July 30, 2013, http://women.webmd.com/news/20080110/cdc-to-young-women-take-folic-acid.

n. Henry J. Kaiser Family Foundation, "Percent of Children 19–35 Months Who Are Immunized" (2010), accessed July 30, 2013, http://kff.org/other/state-indicator/percent-who-are-immunized/.

o. Centers for Disease Control and Prevention, "Adolescent and School Health: Youth Risk Behavior Surveillance System (YRBSS)" (n.d.), accessed September 2014, http://www.cdc.gov/HealthyYouth/yrbs/index.htm.

p. Centers for Disease Control and Prevention, "Behavioral Risk Factor Surveillance System Prevalence and Trends Data: Oral Health 2010" (n.d.), accessed July 30, 2013, http://apps.nccd.cdc.gov/brfss/list.asp?cat=OH&yr=2010&qkey=6610&state=All.

q. "Hidden Risk: Millions of People Don't Know They Are Diabetic, *The Wall Street Journal* (2009), accessed July 30, 2013, http://online.wsj.com/article/SB124269507804132831.html.

r. American Heart Association, "High Blood Pressure Statistics" (2013), accessed July 3, 2013, http://www.heart.org/idc/groups/heart-public/@wcm/@sop/@smd/documents/downloadable/ucm_319587.pdf.

s. National Eating Disorders Association, "National Eating Disorders Association Announces Results of Eating Disorders Poll on College Campuses Across the Nation" [Press release] (September 26, 2006), accessed October 20, 2006, http://www.edap.org/ nedaDir/files/documents/PressRoom/CollegePoll_9–28–06.doc.

t. Centers for Disease Control and Prevention, "Youth Risk Behavior Surveillance—United States, 2011," *Morbidity and Mortality Weekly Report* (June 8, 2012), accessed July 30, 2013, http://www.cdc.gov/mmwr/pdf/ss/ss6104.pdf.

u. Ibid.

v. Ibid.

w. Safe Kids USA, "Preventing Accidental Injury. Injury Facts: Motor Vehicle Occupant Injury" (n.d.), accessed November 20, 2006, http://www.usa.safekids.org/tier3_cd.cfm?content_item_id=1133&folder_id=540.

x. Centers for Disease Control and Prevention, "Exercise or Physical Activity."

y. Domestic Violence Resource Center, "Domestic Violence Statistics" (2000), accessed July 30, 2013, http://dvrc-or.org/domestic/violence/resources/C61/.

z. M. A. Schuster, T. M. Frank, A. M. Bastian, S. Sor, and N. Halfon, "Firearm Storage Patterns in U.S. Homes With Children," *American Journal of Public Health* 90, no. 4 (2000): 588–594 (see p. 590).

aa. Centers for Disease Control and Prevention, "Exercise or Physical Activity."

bb. National Fire Protection Association, "Home Fires" (2011), accessed July 30, 2013, http://www.nfpa.org/research/fire-statistics/the-us-fire-problem/home-fires.

cc. Centers for Disease Control and Prevention, "Falls Among Older Adults: An Overview" (n.d.), accessed July 30, 2013, http://www.cdc.gov/homeandrecreationalsafety/falls/adultfalls.html.

dd. SAFE KIDS Worldwide, *An In-Depth Look at Keeping Young Children Safe Around Medicine* (March 2013), accessed July 30, 2013, http://www.safekids.org/research-report/depth-look-keeping-young-children-safe-around-medicine-march-2013.

ee. U.S. Environmental Protection Agency, *Municipal Solid Waste—Recycling and Disposal in the United States* (2011), accessed July 30, 2013, http://www.epa.gov/osw/nonhaz/municipal/pubs/MSWcharacterization_508_053113_fs.pdf.

ff. Bill Moyers reports: Earth on edge, "Discussion Guide" (June 2001), 4, accessed October 10, 2001, http://www.pbs.org/earthonedge/.

gg. A. Gore, *An Inconvenient Truth* (New York: Rodale, 2006), 316.

hh. Northwest Coalition for Alternatives to Pesticides, "Pesticide Use Reporting Program" (n.d.), accessed January 31, 2007, http://www.pesticide.org/PUR.html.

ii. U.S. Environmental Protective Agency, "WaterSense" (n.d.), accessed July 30, 2013, http://www.epa.gov/WaterSense/pubs/fixleak.html.

jj. U.S. Census Bureau, "United States—Selected Economic Characteristics: 2007–2009" (n.d.), accessed July 1, 2011, http://factfinder.census.gov/servlet/ADPTable?_bm=y&-qr_name=ACS_2009_3YR_G00_DP3YR3&-geo_id=01000US&-gc_url=null&-ds_name=ACS_2009_3YR_G00_&-_lang=en&-redoLog=false.

kk. U.S. Environmental Protective Agency, "At Home" (n.d.), accessed January 29, 2007, http://epa.gov/climatechange/wycd/home.html.

ll. U.S. Environmental Protection Agency, "Municipal Solid Waste" (2011), accessed July 30, 2013, http://www.epa.gov/epawaste/nonhaz/municipal/index.htm.

mm. "Only You Can Prevent Wildfires" (n.d.), accessed January 31, 2007, http://www.smokeybear.com/couldbe.asp.

nn. Keep America Beautiful, *Litter in America* (2009), accessed July 30, 2013, http://www.preventcigarettelitter.org/files/downloads/researchfindings.pdf.

oo. P. Wish, "Dog Waste Is More Than a Pet Peeve" (October 2011), accessed July 30, 2013, http://www.heraldtribune.com/article/20111029/columnist/111029516.

pp. United Network for Organ Sharing, accessed July 30, 2013, http://www.unos.org/.

qq. Advancing Transfusion and Cellular Therapies Worldwide, "Blood FAQ" (n.d.), accessed July 30, 2013, http://www.aabb.org/resources/bct/pages/bloodfaq.aspx

rr. U.S. Census Bureau, *The Diversifying Electorate—Voting Rates by Race and Hispanic Origin in 2012* (May 2013), accessed July 30, 2013, http://www.census.gov/prod/2013pubs/p20-568.pdf.

ss. Reading Is Fundamental, "New Survey: Only One in Three Parents Read Bedtime Stories With Their Children Every Night; Children More Likely to Spend Time With TV or Video Games Than Books" (June 20, 2013), accessed July 30, 2013, http://www.rif.org/us/about/press/only-one-in-three-parents-read-bedtime-stories-with-their-children-every-night.htm.

uu. Identity Theft Info, "Identity Theft Victim Statistics" (n.d.), accessed July 30, 2013, http://www.identitytheft.info/victims.aspx.

tt. Humane Society of the United States, "Common Questions About Animal Shelters" (May 3, 2013), accessed July 30, 2013, http://www.humanesociety.org/animal_community/resources/qa/common_questions_on_shelters.html#How_many_animals_enter_animal_shelters_e.

vv. Get a New Bank Account: Banks That Do Not Use ChexSystems, "The Plight of the Unbanked Population" (n.d.), accessed April 28, 2011, http://www.getanewbankaccount.com/the-plight-of-the-unbanked-population.html.

ww. TFGI.com, "The Top Five Causes for Bankruptcy" (n.d.), accessed April 28, 2011, http://www.tfgi.com/201003/the-top-five-causes-for-bankruptcy/.

xx. Retirement Industry Trust Association, "Senior Fraud Initiative" (n.d.), accessed April 28, 2011, http://www.ritaus.org/mc/page.do?sitePageId=77992&orgId=rita.

Chapter 2

10 Steps in the Strategic Marketing Planning Process

I find the social marketing 10-step model has a galvanizing effect on groups and coalitions that come together around a common goal. It is a logical, step-by-step process that makes sense. It provides a clear roadmap for how the project will be conducted, and the idea that their work will involve continuous monitoring reassures the team that their efforts will be measured and refined along the way as needed.

—Heidi Keller
Keller Consulting

Although most agree that having a formal, detailed plan for a social marketing effort "would be nice," that practice doesn't appear to be the norm. Those in positions of responsibility who could make this happen frequently voice perceptions and concerns such as these:

- "We just don't have the time to get this all down on paper. By the time we get the go-ahead, we just need to spend the money before the funding runs out."
- "The train already left the station. I believe the team and my administrators already know what they want to do. The target audience and communication channels were chosen long ago. It seems disingenuous, and quite frankly a waste of resources, to prepare a document to justify these decisions."

We begin this chapter with an inspiring case story that demonstrates the positive potential return on your investment in the planning process. In the end, you will be able to answer:

- What are the 10 steps to developing a compelling social marketing plan?
- Why is a sequential planning process critical to success?
- Where does marketing research fit in the process?

We hope you see what we have seen, that those who have taken the time to develop a formal plan realize numerous benefits. Readers of your plan will see evidence that recommended activities are based on strategic thinking. They will understand why specific target audiences have been recommended. They will see what anticipated costs are intended to produce in specific, quantifiable terms that can be translated into an associated return on investment. They will certainly learn that marketing is more than advertising and will be delighted (even surprised) to see that you have a system, method, timing, and budget for evaluating your efforts. The Marketing Dialogue at the end of the chapter gives a glimpse at another passionate debate among social marketing professionals: "Is it all about the 'social' or is it all about the 'marketing'?"

MARKETING HIGHLIGHT

Water Sense, an EPA Partnership Program[1]

Saving Consumers 487 Billion Gallons of Water and Over $8.9 billion in Water and Energy Bills

(2006–2012)

Source: Colehour + Cohen.

Background

WaterSense is a partnership program developed by the U.S. Environmental Protection Agency (EPA) with a *purpose* of making water saving easy and a *focus* on a label indicating certification as a water-efficient, high-performing product. Water conservation, the *social issue* the plan is addressing, is a growing concern in the United States, with water managers in many states expecting local, statewide, or regional water shortages.[2] WaterSense partners with manufacturers, distributors, and utilities to bring WaterSense-labeled products to the marketplace, and also works with irrigation professionals to promote water-efficient irrigation practices. The program strategy is similar to EPA's successful ENERGY STAR program that influences consumers to choose appliances, lightbulbs, computers, and more with the ENERGY STAR label, and includes independent certification by a licensed certifying body for water efficiency and performance.

Case information was provided by Colehour+Cohen and EPA's WaterSense program staff.

Target Audiences and Desired Behaviors

The priority consumer *target audience* is homeowners, especially those interested in saving money on their utility bills as well as contributing to the environment. The desired *behavior* is to choose water-consuming products for the home that bear the WaterSense label. Although the focus of this highlight is on consumers, the program also targets manufacturers, retailers, businesses, builders, and irrigation professionals.

Audience Insights

Prior to launch, EPA conducted focus groups to help develop the WaterSense brand and further understand water-efficient product issues. Group discussions explored purchasing behaviors regarding water-using appliances and fixtures as well as preferences for water efficiency promotional messages and taglines.[3] Findings confirmed the value of having a label to look for when purchasing products, as well as the need to assure potential buyers through independent certification sponsored by a trusted government agency that the products would also perform well (e.g., showerheads and faucets would still have adequate water pressure).

A 2009 project in Atlanta, Georgia, helped verify consumer benefits when American Standard Brands provided WaterSense-labeled toilets and faucets and more efficient showerheads to 21 volunteer households. Using detailed water usage reports, it was determined that participating households experienced an average reduction of 18% to 27% in total water use, all without any noticeable difference in water pressure or performance. Families reported strong satisfaction with the fixtures, most commenting that they didn't notice a difference in water pressure, and many families commenting that they appreciated the attractive styling, greater comfort, and increased functionality of the WaterSense-labeled products (*benefits*).[4]

Marketing Mix Strategies

Product

Major consumer product categories for certification and labeling include toilets, faucets, faucet accessories, showerheads, flushing urinals, and irrigation controllers that act like a thermostat for a sprinkler system, turning it on and off using local weather and landscape conditions to tailor watering schedules to actual conditions. In order for a product to receive certification and display the WaterSense label, it is certified by a third party to ensure that the product conforms to WaterSense specifications for efficiency, performance, and label use. Licensed certifying bodies also conduct periodic market surveillance.

Price

Price strategies emphasize savings on water bills. For example:

- "Toilets are the main source of water use in most homes, accounting for nearly 30 percent of residential indoor water consumption."[5]
- "Consumers can reduce their water bills by as much as 30 percent by using WaterSense labeled products."[6]
- "By replacing old, inefficient toilets with WaterSense labeled models, the average family can reduce water used for toilets by 20 to 60 percent— that's nearly 13,000 gallons of water savings for your home every year! They could also save more than $120 per year in water costs, and $2,400 over the lifetime of the toilets."[7]
- "The average family spends $1,100 per year in water costs, but can save $350 from retrofitting with Water-Sense labeled fixtures and ENERGY STAR qualified appliances."

Contributions to the environment are made concrete: "Nationally, if all old, inefficient toilets in the United States were replaced with WaterSense labeled models, we could save 520 billion gallons of water per year, or the amount of water that flows over Niagara Falls in about 12 days."[8]

A "Rebate Finder" on the WaterSense website provides information on rebate programs for purchases of WaterSense–labeled products, helping consumers find programs in their local communities, such as one offered by Colorado Springs Utilities that offers rebates of up to $75 on a WaterSense–labeled toilet.

Place

WaterSense–labeled products can be found on the shelves of most home-improvement and plumbing supply stores, including The Home Depot, Lowe's, and Ferguson. In some cases, retailers indicate that WaterSense–labeled fixtures constitute all, or the vast majority of, specific fixture types displayed in stores. The WaterSense brand and labeled products are also prominently featured on retail websites (see http://www.ecooptions.homedepot.com/water-conservation/ and http://www.lowes.com/cd_WaterSense_95987783).

Promotion

Key messages, as mentioned in the prior "Price" section, emphasize water and cost savings. There are also key messages assuring that products perform as well or better than standard models, and that this is determined by testing and independent certification.

To build awareness of the WaterSense label and the need to use water efficiently, the program annually promotes Fix a Leak Week in March. The focus of the week is to encourage consumers to take easy steps to find and fix leaks, which are estimated to waste 1 trillion gallons of water a year. WaterSense partners have embraced Fix a Leak Week and have developed their own campaigns and events to promote water efficiency in their communities. In 2012, for example, Delta Faucet worked with a variety of partners to sponsor events in nine cities to fix leaks and retrofit low-income households and community facilities with WaterSense–labeled products (see http://www.deltafaucet.com/landing/fix-a-leak-week.html).

WaterSense has benefited from earned media, including public service announcements; features on programs such as *CNN*, *The Today Show*, and *Good Morning America*; and articles in newspapers, including *USA Today*, and magazines, including *Consumer Reports*, *Newsweek*, and *National Geographic*. The program

Figure 2.1   A graphic in the WaterSense toolkit that can be used by partners—for instance, as a utility bill statement stuffer.

Source: Colehour + Cohen.

owes much of its promotional success to the more than 2,100 utilities, government entities, nonprofit organizations, manufacturers, builders, and retailers who have helped promote the WaterSense label and spread the word about the importance of water efficiency (see Figure 2.1).

Social media tactics were ramped up in 2010 and include utilizing Facebook and Twitter, engaging nearly 10,000 fans (see Figure 2.2). In 2012, WaterSense hosted its first annual Fix a Leak Week Twitter party, which was tweeted by its partners more than 1,000 times. During summer's hottest months in 2012, six national blogs, from *The Huffington Post to Big Green Purse*, reached more than 32,000 followers.[9]

Results

In terms of *outcomes*, as indicated in Table 2.1, the number of WaterSense–labeled product models has grown steadily over the life of the program.

A significant challenge is that consumers still do not give water efficiency the same level of importance that they give energy efficiency, and only about 12% consider it one of the top three environmental home improvements (Shelton Pulse Focus Groups, June 2012; Shelton EcoPulse Survey, July 2012). Although awareness of the WaterSense label is much lower than that of the ENERGY STAR label, when consumers unfamiliar with the label are exposed to it, they react positively (Shelton Pulse Focus Groups, June 2012). A 2012 survey of consumers indicated that 30% had replaced a plumbing product with a water-efficient model (Shelton Green Living Pulse Survey, March 2012).[10]

What about *impact*? A 2012 Accomplishments Report estimates that since the program's launch in 2006, WaterSense has helped consumers save 487 billion gallons of water and over $8.9 billion in water and energy bills.

Figure 2.2 Facebook postings offering water-saving tips.

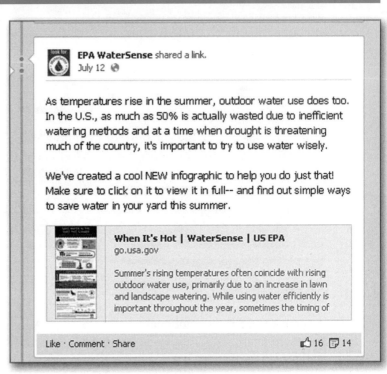

Source: Colehour + Cohen.

Table 2.1 Certification of WaterSense-Labeled Products

Product Labeled	2008	2009	2010	2011	2012
Toilets	252	451	613	905	1,647
Faucets	703	1,620	2,304	3,053	5,516
Showerheads	0	0	245	528	1,118
Total	955	2,071	3,162	4,486	8,281

And use of these products since 2006 has contributed to reductions of 64.7 billion kilowatt-hours of electricity and 24 million metric tons of carbon dioxide.[11]

What's next? WaterSense will continue to label additional residential indoor and outdoor products, support its program to label water-efficient new homes, and ramp up its activity in the commercial sector.

MARKETING PLANNING: PROCESS AND INFLUENCES

To set the stage for developing a tactical social marketing plan, we begin with a description of the traditional marketing planning process, the evolution of the marketing concept, and a few of the most recent shifts in marketing management philosophy and practice.

The Marketing Planning Process

In theory, there is a logical process to follow when developing a marketing plan—whether for a commercial enterprise, NGO/nonprofit organization, or public sector agency. You begin by noting background information leading to the development of the plan and clarifying the purpose and focus of your new effort; you move on to analyzing the current situation and environment relative to that purpose and focus, identifying target audiences, establishing marketing objectives and goals, conducting research to deepen your understanding of your target audiences and competitors, determining a desired positioning for the offer, and designing a strategic marketing mix (4Ps); and then you develop evaluation, budget, and implementation plans. Some conceptualize the process more easily with these broader headings: Why are you doing this? Where are you today? Where do you want to go? How are you going to get there? How will you keep on track?

Evolution of the Marketing Concept

The cornerstone of the marketing concept is a customer-centered mindset that sends marketers on a relentless pursuit to sense and satisfy target audiences' wants and needs and to solve their problems—better than the competition does. Marketers haven't always thought this way. Some still don't. This customer-centered focus didn't emerge as a strong marketing management philosophy until the 1980s and is contrasted with alternative philosophies in the following list provided by Kotler and Keller.[12] We have added a few examples relevant to social marketing.

- The Production Concept is perhaps the oldest philosophy and holds that consumers will prefer products that are widely available and inexpensive, and therefore that the organization's focus should be to keep costs down and access convenient. Early efforts to encourage condom use to prevent the spread of HIV/AIDS may have had this philosophical orientation, unfortunately falling on deaf ears for those who did not see this behavior as a social norm and feared their partner's rejection.
- The Product Concept holds that consumers will favor products that offer the most quality, performance, or innovative features. The problem with this focus

is that program and service managers often become caught up in a love affair with their product, neglecting to design and enhance their efforts based on customers' wants and needs. Otherwise known as the "Build it and they will come" or "Make it and it will sell" philosophy, this orientation may explain the challenges community transit agencies face as they attempt to increase ridership on buses.

- The Selling Concept holds that consumers and businesses, if left alone, will probably not buy enough of the organization's products to meet its goals, and that as a result, the organization must undertake an aggressive selling and promotion effort. Communications encouraging adults to exercise and eat five or more servings of fruits and vegetables a day do not begin to address the barriers perceived by many in the target audience—such as how to make time when holding down a full-time job or raising a family, or simply not liking vegetables.

- The Marketing Concept stands in sharp contrast to the Product and Selling concepts. Instead of a "make and sell" philosophy, it is a "sense and respond" orientation. Peter Drucker went so far as to proclaim, "The aim of marketing is to make selling superfluous. The aim of marketing is to know and understand the customer so well that the product or service fits him and sells itself."[13] If a city utility's natural yard care workshop is exciting, and better yet those who attend are able to keep their lawn weed free without the use of harmful chemicals, they are bound to share their enthusiasm and this newfound resource with their neighbors—and go back for more!

- The Holistic Marketing Concept is a 21st-century approach, recognizing the need to have a more complete, cohesive philosophy that goes beyond traditional applications of the marketing concept. Three relevant components for social marketers include relationship marketing, integrated marketing, and internal marketing. The Farmers' Marketing Nutrition Program of the U.S. Department of Agriculture encourages clients in the Women, Infants, and Children (WIC) program to shop at farmers' markets for fresh, unprepared, locally grown fruits and vegetables. Keys to success include relationship building (e.g., counselors in WIC offices work with clients to overcome barriers to shopping at the markets, such as transportation), integrated marketing (e.g., farmers' stands at the markets carry signage and messages regarding the program similar to those that clients see in WIC offices), and internal marketing (e.g., counselors in WIC offices are encouraged to visit the markets themselves so they are more able to describe places to park and what clients are likely to find fresh that week).

Shifts in Marketing Management

Kotler and Keller also describe philosophical shifts in marketing management that they believe smart companies have been making in the 21st century.[14] A few of theirs and others that are relevant to social marketers in the planning process include the following:

- From "marketing does the marketing" to "everyone does the marketing." Programs encouraging young partygoers to pick a designated driver are certainly supported (even funded) by more than public information officers within departments of transportation. Schools, parents, police officers, law enforcement, judges, healthcare providers, advertising agencies, bars, and alcohol beverage companies help spread the word and reinforce the program.
- From organizing by product units to organizing by customer segments. Clearly, an effective drowning-prevention program plan would need to have separate strategies—even separate marketing plans—based on the differing ages of children. Focuses might be toddlers wearing life vests on beaches, young children taking swimming lessons, and teens knowing where they can buy cool life vests that won't "ruin their tan."
- From building brands through advertising to building brands through performance and integrated communications. The "Makeover Mile," launched in the United States in 2011, is well on its way to building a brand that is a catalyst for positive change, one supported by communications that are both consistent and pervasive. Seeking to turn back the tide of obesity-related diseases that threaten nearly two thirds of Americans, on February 23, 2011, Dr. Ian Smith announced the launch of this grassroots initiative that stages a one-mile walk ending at a health fair in communities most adversely affected by weight-related illnesses and lack of access to health care.[15] The walks are constructed with the intention of influencing participants to "seize the moment today in order to steer their lives towards a healthier tomorrow."[16] At the end of the mile walk, participants participate in a sponsored health fair that provides free health screenings for adults, including eye exams, blood pressure checks, cholesterol screening, and bone density tests; healthy cooking and fitness demonstrations; and giveaways and activities for children. As of April 1, 2011, a total of 3,947 people had pledged, "I'm going to the Makeover Mile," in one of seven cities: Houston, Dallas, Los Angeles, Atlanta, Philadelphia, Chicago, and Washington, D.C.[17]
- From focusing on profitable transactions to focusing on customers' lifetime value. We would consider the approach many city utilities take to increasing recycling among residential households to be one focused on building customer relationships and loyalty (to a cause). Many begin with offering a container for recycling paper and then eventually offer those same households a separate container for glass and plastic. Some then take the next relationship-building step as they add containers for yard waste and food waste to the mix. A few are now providing pickup of used cooking oils, which can then be used to produce biodiesel fuel, and some cities (San Francisco for one) are considering collecting pet waste and turning it into methane to use for heating homes and generating electricity. At least one state (Minnesota)

also suggests to customers that they put unwanted clean clothing and rags in a plastic trash bag and set it out for pickup on regular curbside recycling days.

- From being local to being "glocal"—both global and local. Efforts by the U.S. Environmental Protection Agency (EPA) to encourage households to use energy-saving appliances seems a great example, where communications regarding ENERGY STAR appliances and fixtures stress the link between home energy use and air pollution and at the same time provide detailed information on how these options can both save taxpayer dollars and lower household utility bills.
- From a goods-dominant to service-dominant focus. Referred to as Service Dominant Logic (S-D Logic), this mindset, first described by Vargo and Lusch in 2004, proposes that marketers focus on the service, or value, that a product offers the customer, versus the features of the tangible or intangible good itself. It proclaims that the tangible (product) or intangible offering (service) has value only when the customer "uses" it.[18] As you will read in Chapter 10, the concept of a product platform is presented, with the "core product" representing the benefit the target audience wants in exchange for performing the behavior—addressing the S-D Logic recommendation. It answers the question, "What's in it for me?" Households with children and pets, for example, are more likely to be inspired to reduce their use of chemical fertilizers and pesticides when they find out how toxic these chemicals are for their children and pets than they are to respond to a general concern for water quality.
- From traditional consumer formative research techniques to crowdsourcing. This practice refers to tapping a large group of people, ideally your target audience, to inform and inspire real-time marketing strategies versus conducting a small number of focus groups and highly structured interviews. It is gaining in popularity, primarily as a result of the growing presence of active online communities, including social media. An example of one effort in Brazil is described as a "new wave of law enforcement." A Brazilian professor created a website where victims of crime can post the details of the crimes they experienced, including time, place, and profile of the attacker. Some citizens evidently believe that the site can provide a way for citizens to be more aware of high-crime areas.[19]

10 STEPS TO DEVELOPING A SOCIAL MARKETING PLAN

Our first of several primers in this book is presented in Table 2.2, outlining the 10 distinct and important steps to developing a strategic social marketing plan. They are described briefly in this chapter, with Chapters 4 through 17 providing more detailed information on each step. Worksheets are presented in Appendix A (a downloadable version is available at socialmarketingservice.com), and sample plans using this model are presented in Appendix B.

Table 2.2   Social Marketing Planning Primer

Executive Summary

Brief summary highlighting the social issue the plan is intended to impact, and its purpose, focus, target audience(s), major marketing objectives and goals, desired positioning, marketing mix strategies (4Ps), and evaluation, budget, and implementation plans.

1.0   Social Issue, Background, Purpose, and Focus

What social issue is this plan intended to impact (e.g., water quality)? What brief background information led to this decision? What is the intended purpose of this effort relative to the social issue (e.g., reducing chemicals from runoff)? What population (e.g., single-family homes) and/or solution (e.g., natural yard care) will be your focus? Who is the sponsor (e.g., public utility)?

2.0   Situation Analysis

2.1   SWOT: organizational Strengths and Weaknesses and external Opportunities and Threats

2.2   Key learnings from a review of similar prior efforts and additional exploratory market research

3.0   Target Audiences

3.1   Descriptions of priority target audiences, including demographics, geographics, readiness to change, relevant behaviors, values and lifestyle, social networks, and community assets relative to the plan's purpose and focus

3.2   Market research findings providing a rationale for targeted audiences, including factors such as size, problem incidence, problem severity, defensiveness, reachability, potential responsiveness to marketing mix elements, incremental costs, and organizational match, relative to the plan's purpose and area of focus

4.0   Behavior Objectives and Target Goals

4.1   Behaviors that target audience(s) will be influenced to adopt (e.g., planting native plants), ones that are single and simple with lowest current penetration, highest willingness, and most potential impact

4.2   SMART (specific, measurable, achievable, relevant, time-bound) goals quantifying desired behavior outcomes as well as changes in knowledge, beliefs, and behavior intent

5.0   Target Audience Barriers, Benefits, and Motivators; the Competition; and Influential Others

5.1   Perceived barriers and costs associated with adopting the desired behavior

5.2   Desired benefits the target audience wants in exchange for performing the desired behavior

5.3   Potential strategies the target audience identifies that might motivate them to perform the behavior

5.3   Competing behaviors/forces/choices

5.4   Others who have influence with the target audience

6.0   Positioning Statement

How you want the target audience to see the targeted behavior, highlighting unique benefits and the value proposition

7.0   Marketing Mix Strategies (4Ps)

7.1   Product: *Benefits from performing behaviors and features of goods or services offered to assist adoption*
Core product: Audience-desired benefits promised in exchange for performing the behavior (e.g., greater safety for children and pets)
Actual product: Features of any goods or services offered/promoted (e.g., 100 native plants to choose from)
Augmented product: Additional goods and services to help in performing the behavior or increase appeal (e.g., workshops on how to design a native plant garden)

7.2   Price: *Costs that will be associated with adopting the behavior and price-related tactics to reduce costs*
Costs: money, time, physical effort, psychological, lack of pleasure
Price-related tactics to decrease costs and increase benefits:
Monetary incentives (e.g., discounts, rebates)

(Continued)

Table 2.2 (Continued)

Nonmonetary incentives (e.g., pledges, recognition, appreciation)
Monetary disincentives (e.g., fines)
Nonmonetary disincentives (e.g., negative public visibility)

7.3   Place: *Convenient access*
Creating convenient opportunities for audience(s) to engage in the targeted behaviors and/or access goods and services, including developing partnerships for distribution channels and reinforcing desired behaviors

7.4   Promotion: *Persuasive communications highlighting benefits, features, fair price, and ease of access*
Decisions regarding messages, messengers, creative strategies, and communication channels
Consideration of incorporating prompts for sustainability

8.0   Plan for Monitoring and Evaluation
8.1   Purpose and audience for monitoring progress and evaluating final results
8.2   What will be measured: inputs, outputs, outcomes (from Step 4), and (potentially) impact and return on investment (ROI)
8.3   How and when measures will be taken

9.0   Budget
9.1   Costs of implementing the marketing plan, including additional research and monitoring/evaluation plan
9.2   Any anticipated incremental revenues, cost savings, or partner contributions

10.0   Plan for Implementation and Sustaining Behaviors
Who will do what, when—including partners and their roles (pilot projects are strongly encouraged prior to full implementation)

Note: This is an iterative, nonlinear process, with numerous feedback loops (e.g., barriers to a behavior may be determined to be so significant that a new behavior is chosen). Marketing research will be needed to develop most steps, especially exploratory research for Steps 1 and 2, formative research for Steps 3 through 6, and pretesting for finalizing Step 7.

Developed by Philip Kotler and Nancy Lee with input from Alan Andreasen, Carol Bryant, Craig Lefebvre, Bob Marshall, Mike Newton-Ward, Michael Rothschild, and Bill Smith in 2008.

Although this outline for the most part mirrors marketing plans developed by product managers in for-profit organizations, three aspects of the model stand out:

1. Target audiences are selected before objectives and goals are established. In social marketing, our objective is to influence the behavior of a target audience, making it important to identify the target (e.g., seniors) before determining the specific behavior the plan will promote (e.g., joining a walking group).

2. The competition isn't identified in the situation analysis. Because we haven't yet decided the specific behavior that will be encouraged, we wait until Step 4, when we conduct audience research related to the desired behavior.

3. Goals are the quantifiable measures of the plan (e.g., number of seniors you want to join a walking group) versus the broader purpose of the plan. In this model, the plan's purpose statement (e.g., increase physical activity among seniors) is included in Step 1. Certainly, labels for any part of the plan can and probably should be changed to fit the

organization's culture and existing planning models. The important thing is that each step be taken and developed sequentially.

Steps in the plan are described briefly in the following sections and illustrated using excerpts from a marketing plan to reduce litter in Washington state.

Step 1: Describe the Social Issue, Background, Purpose, and Focus

Begin by noting the social issue the project will be addressing (e.g., carbon emissions) and then summarize factors that have led to the development of the plan. What's the problem? What happened? The problem statement may include epidemiological, scientific, or other research data related to a public health crisis (e.g., increases in obesity), a safety concern (e.g., increases in cell phone use while driving), an environmental threat (e.g., inadequate water supply), or need for community involvement (e.g., need for more blood donations). The problem may have been precipitated by an unusual event such as a tsunami or may simply be fulfilling an organization's mandate or mission (e.g., to promote sustainable seafood).

Next, develop a purpose statement that clarifies the benefit of a successful campaign (e.g., improved water quality). Then, from the vast number of factors that might contribute to this purpose, select one focus (e.g., reducing the use of pesticides).

Litter Plan Excerpt: In the early 2000s, it was estimated that every year in Washington state, over 16 million pounds of "stuff" was tossed and blown onto interstate, state, and county roads. Another 6 million pounds was tossed into parks and recreation areas. Programs funded through the Department of Ecology (Ecology) spent over $4 million each year, but staff estimated that only 25% to 35% was picked up. Litter creates an eyesore, harms wildlife and their habitats, and is a potential hazard for motorists, who may be struck by anything from a lit cigarette to an empty bottle of beer, or even a bottle of "trucker's pee." In 2001, Ecology developed a three-year social marketing plan with the *purpose* of decreasing littering and a *focus* on intentional littering on roadways.

Step 2: Conduct a Situation Analysis

Now, relative to the purpose and focus of the plan, conduct a quick audit of factors and forces in the internal and external environments that are anticipated to have some impact on or relevance in subsequent planning decisions. Often referred to as a SWOT (strengths, weaknesses, opportunities, and threats) analysis, this audit recognizes organizational *strengths* to maximize and *weaknesses* to minimize, including factors such as available resources, expertise, management support, current alliances and partners, delivery system capabilities, the agency's reputation, and priority of issues. Then make a similar list of external forces in the marketplace that represent either *opportunities* your plan should take advantage of or *threats* it should prepare for. These forces are typically not within the marketer's control but must be taken into account. Major categories include cultural, technological, natural, demographic, economic, political, and legal forces.[20]

Time taken at this point to contact colleagues, query listservs, and conduct a literature—even Google—search for similar campaigns will be well spent. Lessons learned from others regarding what worked and what didn't should help guide plan development, as should reflection on prior similar campaigns conducted by the organization sponsoring this new effort.

Litter Plan Excerpt: The greatest organizational strengths going into the campaign included the state's existing significant fines for littering, social marketing expertise on the team, management support, and other state agency support, including critical involvement and buy-in from the state patrol and Department of Licensing. Weaknesses to minimize included limited financial resources, competing priorities faced by law enforcement (traffic safety issues such as drinking and driving and use of seatbelts), and lack of adequate litter containers in public areas.

External opportunities to take advantage of included the fact that litterers were not always aware of the significant fines for littering (as indicated by formative research), the strong environmental ethic of many citizens, and many businesses that were "part of the problem" but also potential campaign sponsors (e.g., fast-food establishments, beverage companies, minimarts). Threats to prepare for included the argument that litter was not a priority issue and that litterers were not motivated by environmental concerns.

Step 3: Select Target Audiences

In this critical step, select the bull's-eye for your marketing efforts. Provide a rich description of your target audience using characteristics such as stage of change (readiness to buy), demographics, geographics, related behaviors, psychographics, social networks, community assets, and size of the market. A marketing plan ideally focuses on a primary target audience, although additional secondary markets (e.g., strategic partners, target audience opinion leaders) are often identified and strategies included to influence them as well. As you will read further in Chapter 5, arriving at this decision is a three-step process that involves first segmenting the market (population) into similar groups, then evaluating segments based on a set of criteria, and finally choosing one or more as the focal point for determining a specific desired behavior, positioning, and marketing mix strategies.

Litter Plan Excerpt: Surveys indicate that some of us (about 25%) would never consider littering. Some of us (about 25%) litter most of the time. Almost half of us litter occasionally but can be persuaded not to.[21] There were two major audiences for the campaign: litterers and nonlitterers. Target audiences for littering include the five behavior-related segments creating the majority of intentional litter on roadways: (a) motorists or passengers who toss (1) cigarette butts, (2) alcoholic beverage containers, and (3) food wrappers and other beverage containers out the window, and (b) those who drive pickup trucks and are (1) not properly covering or securing their loads and (2) not cleaning out the backs of their pickup trucks before driving on roadways. Campaign strategies were also developed and aimed at nonlitterers traveling on Washington state roadways.

Step 4: Set Behavior Objectives and Target Goals

Social marketing plans always include a *behavior* objective—something we want to influence the target audience to do. It may be something we want our target audience to accept (e.g., start composting food waste), reject (e.g., purchasing a gas blower), modify (e.g., water deeply and less frequently), abandon (e.g., using fertilizers with harmful herbicides), switch (e.g., to cooking oils lower in saturated fat), or continue (e.g., donating blood on an annual basis). Often our research indicates that there may also be something the audience needs to know or believe in order to be motivated to act. *Knowledge objectives* include information or facts we want the market to be aware of (e.g., motor oil poured down the street drain goes directly to the lake)—including information that might make them more willing to perform the desired behavior (e.g., where they can properly dispose of motor oil). *Belief objectives* relate more to feelings and attitudes. Home gardeners may know the pesticide they are using is harmful, and even that it works its way into rivers and streams, but they may believe that using it once or twice a year won't make "that much difference."

This is also the point in the marketing plan where we establish quantifiable measures (goals) relative to our objectives. Ideally, goals are established for behavior objectives, as well as any knowledge and belief objectives—ones that are specific, measurable, attainable, relevant, and time-bound (SMART). You should recognize that what you determine here will guide your subsequent decisions regarding marketing mix strategies. It will also have significant implications for your budgets and will provide clear direction for evaluation measures later in the planning process.

Litter Plan Excerpt: Campaign strategies were developed to support three separate objectives: (a) a short-term objective to create *awareness* that there were significant fines associated with littering and that there was a (new) toll-free number to report littering, (b) a midterm objective to convince litterers to *believe* that their littering would be noticed and that they could be caught, and (c) a long-term objective to influence litterers to *change their behaviors*: to dispose of litter properly, cover and secure pickup truck loads and clean out the backs of their trucks before driving on roadways. Telephone surveys were conducted to establish a baseline of public awareness and beliefs about the littering, and field research was done to measure current quantities and types of litter.[22]

Step 5: Identify Target Audience Barriers, Benefits, and Motivators; the Competition; and Influential Others

At this point, you know who you want to influence and what you want them to do. You (theoretically) even know how many, or what percentage, of your target audience you are hoping to persuade. Before rushing to develop a positioning and marketing mix for this audience, however, take the time, effort, and resources to understand what your target audience is currently doing or prefers to do (the competition) and what real and/or perceived barriers they have to this proposed behavior, what benefits they want in exchange, and what would motivate them to "buy" it. In other words, what do *they* think of your idea? What are some of the reasons they are not currently doing this or don't want to (barriers)? What do they come up with when asked "What can you imagine would be in it for you to do this behavior?" (benefits)? Do they think any of your potential strategies would work for them, or do they have better ideas (motivators)? Their answers should be treated like gold and considered a gift.

Litter Plan Excerpt: Focus groups with motorists who admitted to littering (yes, they came) indicated several perceived barriers to the desired behaviors of disposing of litter properly, covering pickup loads, and cleaning out backs of trucks: "I don't want to keep the cigarette butt in the car. It stinks." "If I get caught with an open container of beer in my car, I'll get a hefty fine. I'd rather take the chance and toss it." "I didn't even know there was stuff in the back of my truck. Someone in the parking lot keeps using it as a garbage can!" "The cords I have found to secure my load are just not that effective." "What's the problem, anyway? Doesn't this give prisoners a way to do community service?"

And what strategies can they imagine and would motivate them? "You'd have to convince me that anyone notices my littering and that I could get caught." "I had no idea the fine for littering a lit cigarette butt could be close to a thousand dollars! And if I thought I could get fined, I wouldn't do it." (Notice their concerns were not about helping keep Washington green!)

Step 6: Develop a Positioning Statement

In brief, a positioning statement describes how you want your target audience to see the behavior you want them to buy relative to competing behaviors. Branding is one strategy to help secure this desired position. Both the positioning statement and brand identity are inspired by your description of your target audience and its list of competitors, barriers, benefits, and motivators to action. The positioning statement will also guide the development of a strategic marketing mix. This theory was first popularized in the 1980s by advertising executives Al Ries and Jack Trout, who contended that positioning starts with a product, but not what you do to a product: "Positioning is what you do to the mind of the prospect. That is, you position the product in the mind of the prospect."[23] We would add, "where you want it to be."[24]

Litter Plan Excerpt: "We want motorists to believe that they will be noticed and caught when littering and that fines are steeper than they thought. In the end, we want them to believe disposing of litter properly is a better, especially cheaper, option."

Step 7: Develop a Strategic Marketing Mix (4Ps)

This section of the plan describes your product, price, place, and promotional strategies. As noted in Chapter 1, the 4Ps are the intervention tools, those you use to influence your target audience to adopt the desired behaviors. Some suggest adding to this list other important components of a social marketing plan that start with a *p* (where each of these components fit in this strategic model is noted in parentheses): pilot (an implementation strategy); partners (potential messengers, funding sources, distribution channels, and/or implementation strategies); and policymakers (a target audience or influential others).

It is the blend of these elements that constitutes your marketing mix, also thought of as the determinants (independent variables) used to influence behaviors (the dependent variable). Be sure to develop the marketing mix in the sequence that follows, beginning with the product and ending with a promotional strategy. After all, the promotional tool is the one you count on to ensure that target audiences know about your product, its price, and how to access it. These decisions obviously need to be made before promotional planning.

Product

Describe core, actual, and augmented product levels. The *core product* consists of benefits the target audience values that they believe they will experience as a result of acting and that you will highlight. Your list of desired benefits and potential motivators and positioning statement are a great resource for developing this component of the product platform. The *actual product* describes actual features of the desired behavior (e.g., how a pickup load should be secured) and any tangible goods and services that will support the desired behavior. The *augmented product* refers to any additional tangible objects and/or services that you will include in your offer or that will be promoted to the target audience (e.g., guaranteed anonymity when reporting litterers).

Litter Plan Excerpt: It was determined that a new service, a toll-free number, would be launched for motorists who witnessed people throwing trash from vehicles or losing materials from unsecured loads. When they called the hotline, they would be asked to report the license number, a description of the vehicle, time of day, type of litter, whether it was thrown from the passenger's or driver's side of the car, and approximate location. Within a couple of days, the registered owner of the car would receive a letter from the state patrol, alerting the owner, for example, that "a citizen noticed a lit cigarette butt being tossed out the driver's side of your car at 3 P.M. on Interstate 5, near the University District. This is to inform you that if we had seen you, we would have pulled you over and issued a ticket for $1,025." All "Litter and it will hurt" campaign materials, from road signs (see Figure 2.3) to litterbags, stickers, and posters, would feature the campaign slogan and the litter hotline telephone number.

Price

Mention here any program-related *monetary costs* (fees) the target audience will pay (e.g., cost of a gun lockbox) and, if offered, any *monetary incentives* such as discount coupons or rebates that you will make available. Also note any *monetary disincentives* that will be emphasized (e.g., fines for not buckling up), *nonmonetary incentives* such as

Figure 2.3 Road sign for reporting littering

Litter and it will hurt.

REPORT VIOLATORS
866-LITTER-1

Source: Courtesy of Washington State Department of Ecology.

Figure 2.4 Washington state's litter campaign focused on a hotline and stiff fines.

$1,025

Want to litter? Fine.

Litter and it will hurt.

Source: Courtesy of Washington State Department of Ecology.

public recognition (e.g., plaques for backyard sanctuaries), and *nonmonetary disincentives* such as negative public visibility (e.g., publication of names of elected officials owing back taxes). As you will read in Chapter 11 on pricing, arriving at these strategies begins with identifying major costs the target audience associates with adopting the behavior—both monetary (e.g., paying for a commercial car wash versus doing it at home) and nonmonetary (e.g., the time it takes to drive to the car wash).

Litter Plan Excerpt: Fines for littering would be highlighted in a variety of communication channels, with an emphasis on targeted behaviors (lit cigarette butts $1,025, food or beverage container $103, unsecured load $194, illegal dumping $1,000 to $5,000 plus jail time), with notes that fines would be subject to change and might vary locally. The image in Figure 2.4 was used on billboards, posters, and litterbags.

Place

In social marketing, place is primarily where and when the target audience will perform the desired behavior and/or acquire any campaign-related tangible goods (e.g., rain barrels offered by a city utility) or receive any services (e.g., tobacco quitline hours and days of the week) associated with the campaign. Place is also referred to as a delivery system or distribution channel, and you will include here any strategies related to managing these channels. Distribution channels are distinct from communication channels, through which promotional messages are delivered (e.g., billboards, outreach workers, websites).

Litter Plan Excerpt: The hotline would be available 24 hours a day, seven days a week, as would a website where littering could be reported (www.litter.wa.gov/c_hotline.html). Litterbags (printed with fines for littering) were to be distributed at a variety of locations, including fast-food restaurant windows, car rental agencies, and vehicle licensing offices.

A litterbag was also enclosed with each letter sent in response to a litter hotline report.

Promotion

In this section, describe persuasive communication strategies, covering decisions related to *key messages* (what you want to communicate), *messengers* (any spokespersons, sponsors, partners, actors, or influential others you will use to deliver messages), *communication channels* (where promotional messages will appear), and creative elements (any logos, taglines, graphics). Include decisions regarding slogans and taglines as well. Information and decisions to this point will guide your development of the promotional plan—one that will ensure that your target audiences know about the offer (product, price, place), believe they will experience the benefits you promise, and are inspired to act.

Litter Plan Excerpt: Communication channels selected to spread the "Litter and it will hurt" message included roadway signs, television, radio, publicity, videos, special events, websites, and messages on state collateral pieces, including litterbags, posters, stickers, and decals. There were even special signs to be placed at truck weigh stations targeting one of the state's "most disgusting" forms of litter—an estimated 25,000 jugs of urine found on the roadsides each year (see Figure 2.5).

Figure 2.5   Washington state's litter poster at truck weigh stations.

Source: Courtesy of Washington State Department of Ecology.

Step 8: Develop a Plan for Monitoring and Evaluation

Your evaluation plan outlines what measures will be used to evaluate the success of your effort and how and when these measurements will be taken. It is derived after first clarifying the purpose and audience for the evaluation and referring back to goals that have been established for the campaign—the desired levels of changes in behavior, knowledge, and beliefs established in Step 4. This plan is developed before devising a budget plan, ensuring that funds for this activity are included. Measures typically fall into one of four categories: *input* measures (resources contributed to the campaign), *output* measures (campaign activities), *outcome* measures (target audience responses and changes in knowledge, beliefs, and behavior), and *impact* measures (contributions to the effort's purpose, e.g., improved water quality).

Litter Plan Excerpt: A baseline survey of Washington state residents was planned to measure and then track (a) awareness of the stiff fines associated with littering and

(b) awareness of the toll-free number for reporting littering. Internal records would be used to assess the number of calls to the hotline, and periodic litter composition surveys would be used to measure changes in the targeted categories of roadway litter.

Step 9: Establish Budgets and Find Funding Sources

On the basis of draft product benefits and features, price incentives, distribution channels, proposed promotions, and the evaluation plan, summarize funding requirements and compare them with available and potential funding sources. Outcomes at this step may necessitate revisions of strategies, the audience targeted, and goals, or the need to secure additional funding sources. Only a final budget is presented in this section, delineating secured funding sources and reflecting any contributions from partners.

Litter Plan Excerpt: Major costs would be associated with campaign advertising (television, radio, and billboards). Additional major costs would include road signs, signage at governmental facilities, and operation of the toll-free litter hotline number. Funding for litterbag printing and distribution and retail signage was anticipated to be provided by media partners and corporate sponsors who would augment advertising media buys.

Step 10: Complete an Implementation Plan

The plan is wrapped up with a document that specifies *who* will do *what*, *when*, and for *how much*. It transforms the marketing strategies into specific actions. Some consider this section "the real marketing plan," as it provides a clear picture of marketing activities (outputs), responsibilities, time frames, and budgets. Some even use this as a stand-alone piece that they can then share with important internal groups. Typically, detailed activities are provided for the first year of a campaign along with broader references for subsequent years.

Litter Plan Excerpt: Three phases were identified for this three-year campaign. In summary, first-year efforts concentrated on awareness building. Years 2 and 3 would sustain this effort as well as add elements key to belief and behavior change.

A news release from the Department of Ecology in May 2005 regarding the results of Washington state's litter prevention campaign touted the headline "Ounce of Prevention Is Worth 4 Million Pounds of Litter." The results from a litter survey three years into the campaign found a decline from 8,322 tons to 6,315 tons (24%) compared to a baseline survey. This reduction of more than 2,000 tons represented 4 million pounds less litter on Washington's roadways. And calls to the hotline were averaging 15,000 a year.

WHY IS A SYSTEMATIC, SEQUENTIAL PLANNING PROCESS IMPORTANT?

Only through the systematic process of clarifying your plan's *purpose and focus* and *analyzing the marketplace* are you able to select an appropriate target audience for your efforts.

Only through taking the time to *understand your target audience* are you able to establish realistic behavior *objectives and goals*. Only through developing an *integrated strategy* will you create real behavior change—an approach that recognizes that such change usually takes more than communications (promotion) and that you need to establish what product benefits you will be promising, what tangible goods and services are needed to support desired behaviors, what pricing incentives and disincentives it will take, and how to make access easy. Only by taking time up front to establish how you will measure your performance will you ensure that this critical step is budgeted for and implemented.

The temptation, and often the practice, is to go straight to advertising or promotional ideas and strategies. This brings up questions such as these:

- How can you know whether ads on the sides of buses (a communication channel) are a good idea if you don't know how long the message needs to be?
- How can you know your slogan (message) if you don't know what you are selling (product)?
- How can you know how to position your product if you don't know what your audience perceives as the benefits and costs of their current behavior compared to the behavior you are promoting?

Although planning is sequential, it might be more accurately described as spiral rather than linear in nature. Each step should be considered a draft, and the planner needs to be flexible, recognizing that there may be a good reason to go back and adjust a prior step before completing the plan. For example:

- Research with target audiences may reveal that goals are too ambitious, or that one of the target audiences should be dropped because you may not be able to meet its unique needs or overcome its specific barriers to change with the resources you have.
- What looked like ideal communication channels might turn out to be cost prohibitive or not cost effective during preparation of the budget.

WHERE DOES MARKETING RESEARCH FIT IN THE PLANNING PROCESS?

You may have questions at this point regarding where marketing research fits into this process, other than at the step noted for conducting research to determine barriers, benefits, motivators, and competitors. As you will read further in Chapter 3, and as is evident in Figure 2.6, research has a role to play in the development of each step. And properly focused marketing research can make the difference between a brilliant plan and a mediocre one. It is at the core of success at every phase of this planning process, providing critical insights into the target audience, the marketplace, and organizational realities. For those concerned (already) about the resources available for research, we will discuss in Chapter 3 Alan Andreasen's book *Marketing Research That Won't Break the Bank*.[25]

Figure 2.6   Summary of marketing planning steps and research input.

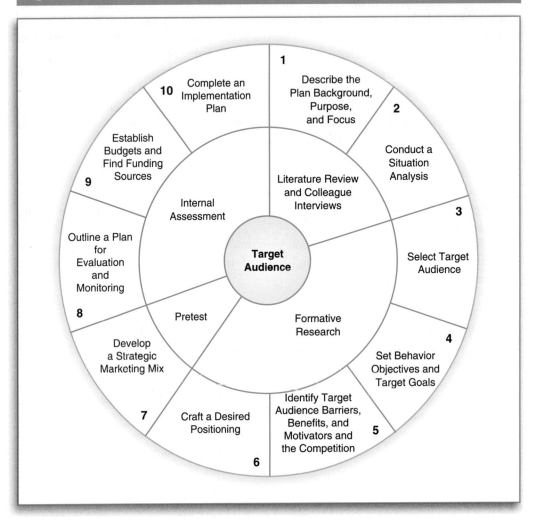

CHAPTER SUMMARY

Marketing planning is a systematic process, and a 10-step model is recommended for developing social marketing plans. You begin by identifying the social issue your plan will address and clarifying the purpose and focus of your plan, then move on to analyzing the current situation and environment; identifying target audiences; establishing marketing objectives and goals; understanding your target audience's barriers, benefits, and motivators as well as competing alternatives and influential others; determining a desired positioning for the offer; designing a strategic marketing mix (4Ps); and then developing evaluation, budget, and implementation plans.

Although planning is sequential, the process is more accurately described as spiral rather than linear—a draft the first time around—as you may need to go back and adjust a prior step before completing the plan. Given the customer-centered nature of all great marketing programs, planning efforts will revolve around the target audience, and research—both external and internal—will be essential to your success.

MARKETING DIALOGUE

Social Marketing

"It's About 'Marketing'; No, It's About 'Social'!"

In April 2013, the third World Social Marketing Conference was held in Toronto, Canada, bringing together nearly 900 leading practitioners and academics in social marketing from around the globe. In addition to numerous plenary and breakout presentations, the forum each year showcases one additional tradition: "The Big Debate."

For this debate, the conference chair, Jeff French of the UK, recruits four debaters, two for each side of an issue. The debate topic is different at each conference. This year, two of the debaters were asked to argue "It's about 'marketing'." The other two were asked to argue "It's about 'social'." Ground rules emphasize that even though the debates are on a serious issue, they are supposed to be fun and good spirited.

Prior to speaking, the chair asked the audience for a predebate vote by show of hands, and a rapid count was taken: those who agreed "It's about marketing" (29% raised their hands), those who agreed "It's about social" (44% raised their hands), and those who wished to abstain (27% raised their hands). The chair then invited the participants forward, one at a time, and

each was given 10 minutes to defend his or her position. Major points made by each debater are summarized below, followed by results of the postdebate vote:

Speaking for "the social":

Craig Lefebvre, Chief Maven, socialShift

- Social and public health challenges are what drive people to look for new solutions, including ones that apply marketing principles and techniques.
- It isn't social marketing if social issues, social problems, and, ultimately, social improvements are not at the core of the approach.
- Marketing offers a framework for developing approaches to social puzzles.
- Social theories take marketing to where it belongs, providing a way to facilitate change among large numbers of people and improve the social and physical conditions in which they live.
- Marketing, per se, has no such aspirations. It is the theories that are applied within a marketing framework that

determine what puzzles are addressed, how, under what circumstances, to what ends (e.g., sales, repeat visits, behavior change, social transformation), and with whom.

Christine Domegan, National University of Ireland, Galway

- This debate has me recall March 6—a day of two meetings.
- The first was with Coca Cola and a small group of public health researchers and practitioners invited to hear about the corporation's response to the obesity epidemic. They demonstrated the potential power of marketing, including paid advertising, to engage and mobilize.
- Public health representatives were skeptical that that this effort would contribute more to decreasing obesity than market share for Coke.
- The second meeting was with a group concerned with fair trade, including two Malawian farmers presenting how fair trade was benefiting them, their families, their community, and ultimately, their society. The impact it was having was moving for all.
- The "social" problems humanity and mankind faces are massive and multifaceted. They require not just ad hoc interventions but individual and community empowerment—not just one but many social movements to bring about change.

Speaking for "the marketing":

Jim Mintz, Centre of Excellence for Public Sector Marketing, Canada

- From time to time, the term *social marketing* is misunderstood and increasingly confused with concepts like socialism and most recently social media.
- Social marketing should be seen as one branch of marketing where the branch reflects the area of application (e.g., sports marketing, business-to-business marketing, and public sector marketing).
- Marketing makes the discipline of social marketing different from other approaches to behavior change. Without a clear commitment to both the social and the marketing, the social marketing field will remain focused on education and communications.
- One expert in the field, Bill Smith, laments that "the problem with the social marketing practice is clear; there is often little or no marketing."
- So let's agree today that social marketing has "two parents": a "social parent" and a "marketing parent."

Nancy Lee, Social Marketing Services, Inc., USA, and University of Washington

- It's not about social OR marketing. It's about social AND marketing.
- One is not more important than the other. They are equally important. They simply have different roles to play.
- Social is the beneficiary. Marketing is the strategy. They go together like a "horse and carriage."
- Social is a sector, marketing is a function, just as in nonprofit sector marketing, public sector marketing, and private sector marketing.
- Without marketing, the carriage is going nowhere, and without a

carriage, the horse has no mission, and the social marketer (riding the horse) is without a purpose.

• We should not be fighting. This one calls for some uniting.

The chair repeated the vote, adding a fourth option at the request of Nancy Lee: "It's about social *and* marketing." In the end, 7% voted for marketing, 7% voted for social, and 86% voted for social

and marketing. (Note: A video of the debate is available at http://www.youtube.com/watch?v=m6DT4FOW0YY. The fourth World Social Marketing Conference will be held in Sydney, Australia, on April 19 through 21, 2015, and the fifth will be held in 2017 at a location yet to be determined. Find out more at http://wsmconference.com/sydney-2015 so you don't miss the next "Big Debates.")

DISCUSSION QUESTIONS AND EXERCISES

1. Reflect back on Table 2.2 (Social Marketing Planning Primer). Review the order of the 10 steps and discuss any that are not in a sequence you are familiar with using, or that you question.

2. Similarly, reflect back on the sequence of determining the 4Ps: product, price, place, promotion. Why is it recommended they be determined in this order?

3. Reflect back on the litter campaign example. Why did they develop the toll-free number for reporting litterers? If the letter violators get isn't a ticket, why does it appear that it worked to deter littering?

4. Reflect back on the Marketing Dialogue. In the end, how would you have voted: (a) It's about social, (b) It's about marketing, or (c) It's about social and marketing?

CHAPTER 2 NOTES

1. U.S. Environmental Protection Agency (EPA), *WaterSense Accomplishments 2012* (n.d.), accessed August 1, 2013, http://www.epa.gov/watersense/docs/ws_accomplishments2012_508.pdf.

2. EPA, "WaterSense / Every Drop Counts!" (n.d.), accessed July 16, 2013, http://www.epa.gov/WaterSense/pubs/every.html.

3. EPA, *Every Drop Counts: WaterSense 2006 Accomplishments* (n.d.), accessed August 1, 2013, http://www.epa.gov/watersense/docs/2006_accomplishment508.pdf.

4. Responsible Bathroom, *The Results Are In: Serenbe Watersense Conversion Reduces Household Water Usage 27%* (n.d.), accessed August 1, 2013, http://responsiblebathroom.com/education/stream/blue-success-stories/serenbe-watersense-conversion-reduces-household-water-usage/.

5. Colorado Springs Utilities, "WaterSense Toilets" (n.d.), accessed July 16, 2013, https://www.csu.org/pages/watersense-toilets.aspx.

6. EPA, "WaterSense / Every drop counts."

7. EPA, "WaterSense / Toilets" (n.d.), accessed August 1, 2013, http://www.epa.gov/WaterSense/products/toilets.html.

8. Ibid.

9. EPA, *WaterSense Accomplishments 2012.*

10. Communication August 23, 2013, from Colehour+Cohen on behalf of EPA WaterSense.

11. EPA, *WaterSense Accomplishments 2012.*

12. P. Kotler and K. L. Keller, *Marketing Management*, 12th ed. (Upper Saddle River, NJ: Prentice Hall, 2005), 15–23.

13. P. F. Drucker, *Management: Tasks, Responsibilities, Practices* (New York, NY: Harper & Row, 1973), 64–65.

14. Kotler and Keller, *Marketing Management*, 27–29.

15. PR Newswire, "Dr. Ian Smith, Celebrity Physician and Diet Expert, Launches the Makeover Mile to Raise Health and Wellness Awareness in Underserved Communities" [Press release] (February 28, 2011), accessed April 4, 2011, http://thestreet.com/print/story/11025223.html.

16. Accessed April 1, 2011, from Makeover Mile website: http://www.makeovemiles.com.

17. Ibid.

18. C. Lefebvre, *Social Marketing and Social Change* (New York: Wiley, 2013), 28.

19. "Wikicrimes: The New Wave of Law Enforcement" (n.d.), accessed August 2, 2013, http://www.fastcase.com/wikicrimes-the-new-wave-of-law-enforcement/.

20. P. Kotler and N. Lee, *Marketing in the Public Sector* (Upper Saddle River, NJ: Wharton School, 2006), 283–284.

21. Washington State Department of Ecology, "Litter Campaign" (2006), accessed October 10, 2006, http://www.ecy.wa.gov/programs/swfa/litter/campaign.html.

22. Washington State Department of Ecology, *Washington 2004 State Litter Study: Litter Generation and Composition Report* (Olympia, WA: Author, March 2005).

23. A. Ries and J. Trout, *Positioning: The Battle for Your Mind* (New York: Warner Books, 1986), 2.

24. Kotler and Lee, *Marketing in the Public Sector*, 113.

25. A. R. Andreasen, *Marketing Research That Won't Break the Bank* (San Francisco: Jossey-Bass, 2002).

Part II

Analyzing the Social Marketing Environment

Chapter 3

DETERMINING RESEARCH NEEDS AND OPTIONS

Social marketing demands a passionate commitment to understanding consumers. Although existing data are used whenever possible, original research is usually needed to fully understand how people view the benefits, costs, and other factors that influence their ability to adopt new behaviors. This research does not always need to be expensive or complex, but it must be done. Without these unique insights, it is impossible to develop an effective, integrated marketing plan.

—Dr. Carol Bryant
University of South Florida

Alan Andreasen, a renowned marketing professor and social marketer at Georgetown University, captures the mood of many regarding research with his list of common myths below—coupled with his counterpoints for each:[1]

Myth 1: *"I'm already doing enough research."* Almost always, they aren't, but there are simple decision frameworks that will help you find out.

Myth 2: *"Research is only for big decisions."* Research is not only for big decisions, and sometimes big decisions don't even need it.

Myth 3: *"Market research is simply conducting surveys, and surveys are expensive."* All research is not surveys, and even surveys can be done inexpensively.

Myth 4: *"Most research is a waste."* Research can be a waste, but it need not be, especially if you use a systematic approach to developing a plan, beginning with determining key decisions to be made using the research results.

This chapter on research will only begin to debunk these myths and only scratch the surface of this important discipline and its contribution to successful campaigns. Its focus is on ensuring that you are familiar with

- Commonly used research terms and their distinctions
- The steps involved in developing a research plan
- Some ways that research can be conducted that "won't break the bank"

More-detailed research case stories appear at the end of this and all remaining chapters, intended to cover the range of research methodologies as well as applications for social marketing campaigns. We open with a case that highlights the numerous contributions research can make in the development of a social marketing plan.

MARKETING HIGHLIGHT

Decreasing Use of Mobile Phones While Driving

What Global Research Efforts Are Contributing

The Problem

In a 2011 World Health Organization (WHO) report, concern for the growing problem of distracted driving is made concrete with the statistic that "trends suggest that between now and 2030, road traffic injuries will rise from being the ninth leading cause of death globally to become the fifth."[2] In fact, they are the leading cause of death worldwide among those 15 to 29 years of age.[3] The report focuses on driver distraction as a major factor, largely because of drivers' increasing use of mobile phones . . . around the world. It also references numerous research efforts to understand and describe the issue, as well as strategies to reduce the problematic behavior.

Research to Understand the Problem With the Current Behavior

Technical research studies have identified four major types of driver distraction:

(a) visual (e.g., looking away from the road), (b) cognitive (e.g., participating in a conversation), (c) physical (e.g., taking one's hands off the steering wheel), and (d) auditory (e.g., responding to a noise such as a text notification). The problem with talking, and especially texting, on a mobile phone while driving is that it often involves all four of these distractions, explaining in part why talking with a passenger in the car, which typically involves only one of these distractions, is less concerning.

Research to Determine the Incidence of Problem Behaviors

A number of research efforts from around the world attempt to estimate the incidence of talking on a phone or texting while driving, helping to locate and determine the size of the problem. One from Johannesburg, South Africa, used *observation research* to estimate the incidence. Among a total of 2,497 drivers who were observed during a one-hour study at a busy intersection during peak time, 7.8% were seen holding a mobile phone and either talking or texting.[4] Other studies use *self-reported* data from quantitative surveys, including one in the United Kingdom finding that 45% of drivers reported text messaging while driving; one in Australia showing that 58% of drivers ages 17 to 29 years regularly read text messages while driving and that 37% send text messages; and one in Sweden in which 30% of all drivers with mobile phones reported using them daily while driving.[5] *Internal police crash reports* can be used to track problem incidence, with one state in the U.S., for example, estimating that based on internal reports, mobile phone use while driving more than doubled between 2001 and 2005.[6]

Research to Prioritize Target Audiences

The WHO report describes several studies conducted to determine how the incidence and degree of distraction vary by demographics and related behaviors, with implications for selecting priority target audiences. Relative to age and gender, a study in the UK, for example, examined *simulated laboratory studies* that concluded that younger drivers found it more difficult than others to divide their attention effectively between driving and talking on the phone. Others, which involved subjects *observing a video* of driving situations, suggested that because older drivers (50+) often have decreased visual and cognitive capacities, it is more difficult for them to conduct two tasks

concurrently, resulting in increased reaction time and therefore risk.[7] And in terms of gender, another study found that while male drivers were more likely to text while driving, females were more impaired in the process.[8]

Research to Assess Audience Attitudes

In 2010, and again in 2012, the U.S. National Highway Transportation Safety Commission conducted a survey to assess attitudes and self-reported behaviors related to distracted driving, mobile phones, and texting.[9] Findings are being used to contribute to the development of countermeasures and interventions to reduce distracted driving. A 20-minute *telephone survey* was conducted with drivers 16 and older and included households with landline telephones as well as ones relying solely on mobile phones. In 2012, more than 6,000 respondents completed the anonymous survey. Highlights of findings related to audience attitudes include the following:

- *Driver types.* Based on a pattern of responses across 10 questions concerned with distracted driving, respondents were classified into two distinct groups of drivers: distraction-prone drivers (33%) and distraction-averse drivers (67%). Those classified as distraction prone were more likely to be younger and more affluent and to have more formal education than distraction-averse drivers.
- *Perceptions of safety.* Ninety-five percent of distraction-averse drivers reported that they felt very unsafe as

a passenger if their driver were reading or sending text messages, compared to 67% of distraction-prone drivers.

- *Support for laws.* While the majority (74%) support state laws banning talking on a handheld cell phone while driving, an overwhelming majority (94%) support state laws that ban texting or emailing while driving.
- *Perceived risk of getting caught.* Forty-four percent of respondents in states with laws banning some form of cell phone use believed a driver who regularly talks on a mobile phone is unlikely to be ticketed. Fewer (37%) thought it was unlikely that drivers who frequently sent text messages or emails while driving would get a ticket.

Research to Test Potential Strategies

In a special section of the WHO report on potential interventions, it is highlighted that despite a rapidly expanding body of research on the use of mobile phones, the lack of evidence regarding intervention effectiveness to date has made it difficult to make scientifically based policy decisions. Perhaps this reality is what drove the U.S. transportation secretary in 2012 to fund two *pilot* projects to test the efficacy of a scaled-up campaign.

The secretary announced that the states of California and Delaware will be provided $2.4 million of federal support to examine whether increased police enforcement coupled with a high-profile public campaign using paid media and news media coverage can significantly reduce distracted driving. A press release commented, "We know from the success of national efforts like 'Click It or Ticket' that combining good laws with effective enforcement and a strong public education campaign can and does change unsafe driving behavior."[10] The release also referenced data from the 2012 Distracted Driving Attitudes and Behaviors Survey (mentioned in the prior section of this highlight), stating that this helped inform this decision.

The multimarket efforts in California and Delaware will mirror a smaller-scale demonstration project in 2011 in Connecticut and New York that led to a 72% decrease in texting in Hartford and a 32% decrease in Syracuse. The question the pilot will help answer is whether this effort can have an impact on a larger, multimarket area.

Summary

As the highlighted terms in the case indicate, a variety of methodologies are contributing to developing programs to reduce talking and texting on mobile phones while driving, including technical and observation research, internal records (e.g., crash reports), telephone surveys, personal interviews, simulated laboratory studies, and pilots.

MAJOR RESEARCH TERMINOLOGY

The first primer in this chapter presents some of the most commonly used research terms (see Table 3.1). They have been grouped according to whether they refer to the objective of the research, when the research is conducted in the planning process, the source of data and information, the technique used, or approaches to collecting primary data. More-detailed descriptions and an illustrative example are presented in the next several sections.

Research Characterized by Research Objective

Exploratory research has as its objective gathering preliminary information that helps define the problem.[11] It would be most characteristic of research conducted at the beginning of the marketing planning process, when you are seeking to determine the purpose and focus for your plan. A city wanting to persuade restaurants to recycle their cooking oil, for example, might begin by reviewing data on the estimated amount of cooking oil that is currently being dumped down drains or put in garbage cans and the impact it is having on infrastructures and the environment.

Descriptive research has as its objective describing factors such as the market potential for a product or the demographics and attitudes of potential target audiences.[12] It would be expected, for example, that the city developing the cooking-oil-recycling campaign would want to know the numbers, types, and locations of restaurants in the city that were generating the most cooking oil and where and how they were currently disposing of the oil.

Causal research is done to test hypotheses about cause-and-effect relationships.[13] We can now imagine the city managers "running the numbers" to determine how much in oil disposal costs they might be able to defray if they concentrate on Chinese restaurants in Phase 1 of their efforts and how this potential outcome stacks up against the suggested funding at various cooperation (market penetration) levels.

Research Characterized by Stage in Planning Process

Formative research, just as it sounds, refers to research used to help form strategies, especially to select and understand target audiences and draft marketing strategies. It may be qualitative or quantitative. It may be new research that you conduct (primary data), or it may be research conducted by someone else that you are able to review (secondary data). In June 2002 in Washington State, for example, formal observation studies indicated that 82% of drivers wore seatbelts. Although some might think this market share adequate, others, such as the Washington Traffic Safety Commission, were on a mission to save more lives and wanted to increase this rate. And formative research helped select target markets and form strategies. Existing data from the National Highway Traffic Safety Administration helped identify populations with the lowest seatbelt usage rates (e.g., teens and men 18 to 24, among others). Focus groups conducted around the

Table 3.1 A Marketing Research Primer

Marketing research is the systematic design, collection, analysis, and reporting of data and findings relevant to a specific marketing situation facing the organization.[a]
Characterized by Research Objective
Exploratory research helps define problems and suggest hypotheses.
Descriptive research is used to describe existing characteristics of a population, situation, or market, but does not offer causes or predictions.
Causal research tests hypotheses about cause-and-effect relationships.
Characterized by Stage in Planning Process
Formative research is used to help select and understand target markets and develop the draft marketing mix strategy.
Pretest research is used to evaluate draft marketing mix strategies and then make changes prior to finalizing the marketing plan and communication elements.
Monitoring research provides ongoing measurement of program outcomes through periodic surveys.
Evaluation research most often refers to research conducted at the conclusion of a campaign pilot or effort.
Characterized by Source of Information
Secondary data were collected for another purpose and already exist somewhere.
Primary data are freshly gathered for a specific purpose or for a specific research project.
Characterized by Approach to Collecting Primary Data
Key informant interviews are conducted with colleagues, decision makers, opinion leaders, technical experts, and others who may provide valuable insight regarding target markets, competitors, and strategies.
Focus groups usually involve 8 to 10 people gathered for a couple of hours with a trained moderator who uses a discussion guide to focus the discussion.
Surveys use a variety of contact methods, including face-to-face, mail, telephone, online/Internet, intercept, and self-administered surveys, asking people questions about their knowledge, attitudes, preferences, and behaviors.
Crowdsourcing is, in part, a technique that taps online communities for formative, pretest, and evaluative research efforts (crowd research). It also refers to efforts for fundraising (crowd funding), to recruit workers (crowd labor), and to generate creative elements, typically for a communications strategy (creative crowdsourcing).[b]
Participatory action research is a collaborative approach to research that involves community members and organizations in the research process, the objective being to determine the most effective actions in the community for positive social change.
Experimental research efforts, such as Randomized Controlled Trials (RCTs), are used to capture cause and effect relationships; primary data are gathered by selecting matched groups of subjects, giving them different treatments, controlling related factors, and checking for differences in group responses.[c]
Observation is the gathering of primary data by observing target audiences in action, in relevant situations.

(Continued)

Table 3.1 (Continued)

Ethnographic research is considered a holistic research method, founded in the idea that to truly understand target markets, the researcher will need an extensive immersion in their natural environment.
Mystery shoppers pose as customers and report on strong or weak points experienced in the buying process.
Mobile technology research efforts use mobile phones for conducting surveys; this is of particular interest in developing nations where utilization of mobile phones is pervasive and Internet infrastructures and landlines in homes are lacking.
The Zaltman metaphor elicitation technique (ZMET) is an in-depth interviewing technique developed by Professor Gerald Zaltman that seeks to tap the right brain and unconscious and explore what deep metaphors reveal about the minds of consumers.[d]
Neuromarketing is a relatively new field of marketing research that studies the brain's response to alternate marketing stimuli, the objective being to inform development of product features and promotions that have the most positive appeal.
Characterized by Rigor of the Technique
Qualitative research is exploratory in nature, seeking to identify and clarify issues. Sample sizes are usually small, and findings are not usually appropriate for projections to larger populations.
Quantitative research refers to research that is conducted in order to reliably profile markets, predict cause and effect, and project findings. Sample sizes are usually large, and surveys are conducted in a controlled and organized environment.

a. P. Kotler and G. Armstrong, *Principles of Marketing*, 9th ed. (Upper Saddle River, NJ: Prentice Hall, 2001), 140.

b. C. Parvanta, Y. Roth, and H. Keller, "Crowdsourcing 1010: A Few Basics to Make You the Leader of the Pack," *Health Promotion Practice* 14, no. 2 (January 8, 2013): 163–167, doi: 10.1177/1524839912470654

c. Kotler and Armstrong, *Principles of Marketing*, 146.

d. P. Kotler, *Marketing Insights From A to Z* (New York: Wiley, 2003), 117–118.

state with citizens who didn't wear seatbelts on a regular basis presented clear findings that current positive coaching messages, such as, "We love you. Buckle up," were not motivating. A primary seatbelt law, tougher fines, and increased enforcement were what they said it would take (although they wouldn't like it).

Pretest research is conducted to evaluate a short list of alternative strategies and tactics, ensure that potential executions have no major deficiencies, and fine-tune possible approaches so that they speak to your target audiences in the most effective way.[14] It is typically qualitative in nature (e.g., focus groups, intercept interviews), as you are seeking to identify and understand potential responses your target audiences may have to various campaign elements. It is most powerful when you can participate in, or at least observe, the interviews. Referring back to the Washington state seatbelt story, potential slogans, highway signs, and television and radio ad concepts were developed based on findings from the formative research and then shared once more with focus groups. Among the concepts tested was a successful campaign from North Carolina called "Click It or Ticket." Although focus group respondents certainly "didn't like it" (i.e., that they would be fined $86 for not wearing a seatbelt and that a part of the effort included increased law enforcement), their strong negative reaction indicated that it would certainly get their attention and likely motivate a behavior change. Findings indicated that elements of the North Carolina television and radio spots, however, left people with the impression that the enforcement effort was happening somewhere else in the country, and thus they could psychologically dismiss the message. Advertisements were developed locally to counteract this.

Monitoring research provides ongoing measurement of program outputs and outcomes and is often used to establish baselines and subsequent benchmarks relative to goals. Most important, it can provide input that will indicate whether you need to make course corrections (midstream), alter any campaign elements, or increase resources in order to achieve these goals. Once launched, the state's Click It or Ticket campaign was monitored using several techniques, including reviewing data from the state patrol on the number of tickets issued, analyzing news media coverage, and, most important, conducting periodic formal observation studies the first year. Findings indicated that in the first three months after the campaign was launched, seatbelt usage rates increased from 82% to 94%. Even though strategies appeared to be working, the decision was made to increase the fine from $86 to $101, and more grants were provided to support increased enforcement in hopes of reaching a goal of zero traffic deaths and serious injuries by 2030 (Target Zero). In 2007, data from research and monitoring efforts turned the state's attention to nighttime drivers, whose seatbelt usage was lower; motorists driving at night had a death rate about four times higher than that of those driving during the day. Twice-yearly law enforcement and publicity mobilizations stressed the importance of buckling up at night and that special patrols "were watching" (see Figure 3.1).

Evaluation research, distinct from monitoring research, according to Andreasen "typically refers to a single final assessment of a project or program, and may or may not involve comparisons to an earlier baseline study."[15] Important attempts are made in this effort to measure and report in the near term on campaign outcomes and in the longer term on campaign impacts on the social issue being addressed—both relative to campaign outputs. (Both monitoring and evaluation techniques

Figure 3.1 A new road sign emphasizing night seatbelt usage.

Source: Reprinted with permission from the Washington Transportation Safety Commission.

will be discussed in depth in Chapter 15.) Each year, a nationwide observational seatbelt survey is conducted. In Washington state, over 90,000 vehicle drivers and passengers are observed. Summarizing the results of the seatbelt campaign in Washington State, a press release in August 2006 from the Washington Traffic Safety Commission reported that results from the latest observational research survey of seatbelt use had shown that the use rate had climbed to 96.3%. It was the highest seatbelt use rate in the nation and the world, and research indicated that buckling up was attributable to seatbelt road signs, aggressive local law enforcement, and educational activities at all levels of government. And, by 2012, the numbers were getting even better, reaching 96.9%. Most important, in terms of impact on the social issue, vehicle occupant deaths dropped from 501 in 2002, to 292 in 2013, and serious injuries dropped from 2336 in 2002 to 1184 in 2013 (see Table 3.2).

Research Characterized by Source of Information

Secondary research, or secondary data, refers to information that already exists somewhere, having been collected for another purpose at an earlier time.[16] It is always worth a first look. The agency's internal records and databases will be a good starting point. Searching through files for information on prior campaigns and asking around about what has been done before and what the results were is time well spent. It is likely, however, that you will need to tap a wide variety of external information sources, ranging from journal articles to scientific and technical data to prior research studies conducted for other, similar purposes. Some of the best resources are peers and colleagues in similar organizations and agencies around the world, who often have information on prior similar efforts that they are willing to share. Unlike commercial marketers competing fiercely for market shares and profits, social marketers are known to rally around social issues and to treat each other as partners and team players. Typical questions to ask peers responsible for similar issues and efforts include the following:

- What target audiences did you choose? Why? Do you have data and research findings that profile these audiences?
- What behaviors did you promote? Do you have information on what benefits, costs, and barriers your target audience perceived? Did you explore their perceptions regarding competing alternative behaviors?
- What strategies (4Ps) did you use?
- What were the results of your campaign?
- What strategies do you think worked well? What would you do differently?
- Are there elements of your campaign that we could consider using for our program? Are there any restrictions and limitations?

There may also be relevant electronic mailing lists to query (e.g., the Georgetown Social Marketing Listserve at http://www.socialmarketingpanorama.com/social_marketing_panorama/georgetown-social-marketi.html, the International Social Marketing

Table 3.2 Vehicle Occupant Deaths and Serious Injuries in Washington State

Year	Passenger Vehicle Occupant Deaths			Passenger Vehicle Occupant Serious Injuries		
	All Hours	Daytime	Nighttime	All Hours	Daytime	Nighttime
2002	501	266	231	2,336	1,535	798
2007	401	212	188	1,817	1,136	628
2009	338	164	174	1,705	1,604	641
2010	312	179	133	1,614	1,083	531
2011	286	158	125	1,302	780	522
2012	258	149	107	1,275	762	513
2013	292	151	136	1,184	725	459

Association at http://www.i-socialmarketing.org/, and the Fostering Sustainable Behavior Listserv at http://www.cbsm.com/forums/index.lasso?p=6203), online database services (e.g., LexisNexis for a wide range of business magazines, journals, research reports), and Internet data sources (e.g., the Centers for Disease Control and Prevention's Behavior Risk Factor Survey Surveillance, which will be described further in Chapter 6). (See Appendix C for additional resources.)

Primary research, or primary data, consists of information collected for the specific purpose at hand, for the first time. This journey should be undertaken only after you have exhausted potential secondary resources. A variety of approaches to gathering this data will be described in the following section. A hypothetical example of a water utility interested in a sustainable water supply will be used throughout.

Research Characterized by Approaches to Collecting Primary Data

Key informant interviews are conducted with decision makers, community leaders, technical experts, and others who can provide valuable insights regarding target markets, competitors, and potential strategies. They can be useful in helping to interpret secondary data, explain unique characteristics of the target audience (e.g., in a country other than where you live), shed light on barriers to desired audience behaviors, and provide suggestions for reaching and influencing targeted populations. Though typically informal in nature, a standard survey instrument (questionnaire) is often used to compile and summarize findings. For example, a water utility interested in persuading households to fix leaky toilets to conserve water might interview engineers on staff to understand more about what causes toilets to leak and what options customers have to fix them. They might then want to interview a few retail managers of home supply and hardware stores to learn more about what types of questions customers come to them with regarding leaky toilets and what advice they give them.

Focus groups are a very popular methodology for gaining useful insights into target audiences' thoughts, feelings, and even recommendations on potential strategies and ideas for future efforts. Perceived as a group interview, a focus group usually involves 8 to 10 people "sitting around a table" for a couple of hours participating in a guided discussion—hence the term *focus group.* In terms of numbers of groups to conduct, Craig Lefebvre offers,

> My rule of thumb is to plan to do as many as you can afford *only* for segments that you will truly develop a specific marketing mix for. The advice I have gotten is to do at least three for any segment, but stop once you start hearing the same thing.[17]

This chapter's second primer highlights focus group terminology and key components (see Table 3.3). For the leaky toilet project, focus groups with homeowners could help identify reasons they did not test their toilets (*barriers*), what they would want in exchange for doing the behavior (*benefits*), and what it would take to persuade them (*motivators*). Households in targeted areas of the city might be contacted by a market research firm that would screen potential participants and then invite to the upcoming group those with the following profile: homeowner, person in the home most responsible for household maintenance and repairs, having a toilet older than 1994 that has not been checked for leaks in the past five years, and having some concern about whether or not his or her toilet has a leak and what should be done.

Surveys use a variety of contact methods and include mail, telephone, online/Internet, intercept, and self-administered surveys, asking people questions about their knowledge, attitudes, preferences, and behaviors. Findings are typically quantitative in nature, as the intent of the process is to project findings from a representative segment of the population to a larger population and to then have large enough sample sizes to enable the researcher to conduct a variety of statistical tests. These samples are designed by determining first *who* is to be surveyed (sampling unit), then *how many* people should be surveyed (sample size), and finally how the people will be *chosen* (sampling procedure).[18] Back to our leaky toilet example. A telephone survey might be conducted following the focus groups to help prioritize and quantify barriers and benefits identified by participants in the groups. Findings might also be used to identify the demographic and attitudinal profile of target audiences (those most likely/ready to test their toilets) and to test potential marketing strategies. How would interest increase (or not) if the utility were to host demonstrations on how to fix leaky toilets (*product*), provide monetary incentives for replacing old high-water-use toilets with new water-efficient ones (*price*), and offer to pick up old toilets (*place*)?

Crowdsourcing is, in part, a technique that taps online communities for formative, pretest, and evaluative research efforts (crowd research). A vivid example in the private sector of crowdsourcing as a formative research technique is one conducted by Starbucks, where a special website (MyStarbucksIdea.com) is dedicated to sharing, voting on, and discussing ideas. Examples of ideas posted for new products include a raspberry and

Table 3.3 Focus Group Primer

Focus Groups: A research methodology where small groups of people are recruited from a broader population and interviewed for an hour to an hour and a half utilizing a focused discussion led by a trained moderator. Results are usually considered qualitative in nature and therefore not projectable to the broader population.

Planning: The first step in the focus group planning process is to establish the purpose of the group. What decisions will this research support? From there, informational objectives are delineated, providing guidance for discussion topics.

Participants: The ideal number of participants is between 8 and 12. With fewer than 8 participants, discussions may not be as lively nor input as rich. With more than 12 participants, there is not typically enough time to hear from each person in depth.

Recruitment: Ten to 14 participants are usually recruited in order to be assured that 8 to 12 will show up. A marketing research firm is often involved in recruiting participants, using a screener developed to find participants with the desired demographic, attitudinal, and/or behavioral profile.

Discussion Guide: This detailed outline of discussion topics and related questions distributes the 60 to 90 minutes to ensure informational objectives are achieved. It usually begins with a welcome, statement of purpose, and ground rules and concludes with opportunities for the moderator and participants to summarize highlights of the discussion. It is likely to include time for numerous probes (e.g., "Please say more about that") to achieve the intended in-depth understanding and insights.

Moderator: The group facilitator is usually (but doesn't have to be) a trained professional. Important characteristics include strong listening and group dynamics skills, knowledge of the topic, genuine curiosity about the findings, and ability to synthesize and report on findings relative to research objectives.

Facility: Many groups are held in designated focus group rooms at market research firms, which include two-way mirrors so that observers (e.g., the client for the research) can witness participants' expressions and body language as well as slip notes to the moderator regarding additional questions or probes. Groups are often audiotaped and sometimes videotaped in order to prepare reports and share findings with others. Some focus groups are now conducted online, via the telephone, and/or via video conferencing.

Incentives: Participants are usually provided monetary incentives for their time (e.g., $50 to $60) and offered light refreshments when they arrive. The opportunity to share opinions and even contribute to an important social issue is a strong motivator as well.

caramel frappe; for enhanced experiences, more comfy leather chairs; and for corporate social responsibility, a tree-planting campaign. For social marketers working to increase timely immunizations, a pretesting idea using crowdsourcing would be to post alternative campaign endorsements on a popular "mommy's blog" to solicit ratings on messenger credibility. And for evaluation, social marketers could consider engaging clients at Supplemental Nutrition Program for Women, Infants, and Children (WIC) clinics to provide feedback online as to how they were treated at the farmers' market when using their coupons. In a 2013 *Health Promotion Practice* article on Crowdsourcing 101, authors Parvanta, Roth, and Keller described the appeal of market research online communities (MROCs), where an organization may establish an MROC website and recruit a specific group of people to participate in a shared topic of interest.

Like focus groups, MROCs allow hosts to have a conversation with the participants and explore topics in depth. Like consumer panels, hosts are able to go back to the same people repeatedly over a specific period of time. An MROC project can have 50 to 500 participants and be accomplished in a week, if desired. The average cost for running an online research community through a vendor for a month is $5,000.[19]

Experimental research efforts, sometimes referred to as controlled experiments, involves the gathering of primary data to capture cause-and-effect relationships by selecting matched groups of respondents (similar on a variety of characteristics), giving them different treatments (exposing them to alternative marketing strategies), controlling related factors, and checking for differences in group responses.[20] Some might even call it a pilot, where you measure and compare the outcomes of one or more potential strategies among similar market segments. For example, let's assume the utility was trying to decide whether they needed to provide homeowners with dye tablets to use to test for a leak or whether it worked just as well to provide instructions on how to use ordinary food coloring from the household pantry. If the incidence of testing for leaks is not higher among households who have been mailed a tablet than those who have simply been mailed instructions, the utility will likely decide to roll out the campaign without the added costs of the tablet.

Observational research, not surprisingly, involves gathering primary data by observing relevant people, actions, and situations. In the commercial sector, consumer packaged-goods marketers visit supermarkets and observe shoppers as they browse the store, pick up products, examine the labels (or not), and make purchase decisions.[21] In social marketing, observational research is more often used to provide insight into difficulties people have performing desired behaviors (e.g., recycling properly), to measure actual versus reported behaviors (e.g., seatbelt usage), or to simply understand how consumers navigate their environments in order to develop recommended changes in infrastructures (e.g., removing their computers from their bags as they approach airport security screeners). It would be useful for the managers working on the leaky toilet project to watch people at local home supply stores as they check out repair kits for their toilets.

Ethnographic research is considered a holistic research method, founded in the idea that to truly understand target audiences, the researcher will need an extensive immersion in their natural environment. It often includes observation as well as face-to-face interviews with study participants. For example, the utility might want to actually observe and interview people in their homes as they test their toilets for leaks and (if warranted) make decisions regarding repair or replacement. Findings can then be used to develop instructional materials that will be most helpful to others as they then engage in these behaviors.

Mystery shoppers pose as customers and report on strong or weak points experienced in the buying process. This technique may include interfacing with an agency's personnel with an interest in observing and reporting what the target audience sees, hears, and feels during the exchange and how personnel respond to their questions. For example, utility managers may want to call their own customer service center and ask questions regarding the mailer on testing for leaky toilets "they" received as well as questions regarding options for repairing and replacing the toilets. They may also want to visit the website for the project, post a comment or question, and note how quickly their question is acknowledged.

Mobile technology research efforts use mobile phones for conducting surveys. This method is increasingly popular in developing nations where utilization of mobile phones is pervasive and Internet infrastructures and landlines in homes are lacking. Some survey methods use talking on the phone, some use SMS, and others include a mixed mode, using a combination of telephone, SMS, and web during interviews. An example of one study using mobile technology in Africa was described in a paper by authors working for the World Bank and the Gates Foundation.[22] There is high interest in and a huge demand for timely, high-frequency, and high-quality information about socioeconomic indicators in developing countries. A pilot project in 2010 in Tanzania and South Sudan was intended to inform a larger-scale adoption of the use of mobile phones for data collection. For the South Sudan pilot, 1,000 panel respondents were provided mobile phones and were called on a monthly basis from a call center. Questions included this one regarding hunger: "In the last month, how often, if ever, have you or a member of your household gone without enough food to eat?" and another regarding education: "In the last week, did your child receive any homework?" Concluding comments in the report suggest that mobile surveys such as this can collect, in a very timely manner, quality data that are of use to a wide range of data users.

The *Zaltman metaphor elicitation technique (ZMET)* is an in-depth interviewing technique developed by Professor Gerald Zaltman that seeks to tap the right brain and unconscious and explore what deep metaphors reveal about the minds of consumers.[23] Research study participants are usually asked to collect a set of pictures that represent their thoughts and feelings about the topic of interest and then discuss these in an interview. A study that OlsonZaltman Associates conducted for the Robert Wood Johnson Foundation (RWJF), for example, helped create a new framework for discussing health care issues that would resonate across the political spectrum. As a result, RWJF discontinued using language of inequality in its communications and developed a framing that appealed to both Republicans and Democrats. The tagline "Health starts where you live, work and play" has helped RWJF gain bipartisan support for initiatives in areas including childhood obesity, access to health care, and healthy family eating.[24] The research highlight at the end of this chapter provides a more in-depth example of this technique.

Research Characterized by Rigor of the Technique

Sometimes a research project is characterized as either a qualitative or a quantitative study. The differences between these two techniques are described in the following section and illustrated by a research effort conducted to inform the development of a social marketing campaign to combat the spread of HIV/AIDS in Ethiopia, where the infection rate is one of the world's highest.

Qualitative research generally refers to studies where samples are relatively small and the findings are not reliably projected to the greater population. That isn't their purpose. The focus instead is on identifying and seeking clarity on issues and understanding current knowledge, attitudes, beliefs, and behaviors of target audiences. Focus groups, personal interviews, observations, and ethnographic studies are commonly used, as they are often qualitative in nature.[25]

In October 2005, an article titled "Managing Fear in Public Health Campaigns" by Cho and Witte appeared in *Health Promotion Practice*, a journal of the Society for Public Health Education (SOPHE).[26] It described, in depth, the role that formative research played in the development of strategies to influence HIV/AIDS-preventive behaviors among teens and young adults (ages 15 to 30) living in Ethiopia. This research was grounded in a fear appeal theory called the Extended Parallel Process Model.[27] Thus, the variables studied were not selected at random but were purposely chosen. Once the researchers discovered what people believed regarding these variables, they would have specific guidance from the theory about how to influence their beliefs in the direction providing the most behavior change.

Focus groups were conducted first to better understand urban youths' perceptions about HIV/AIDS-prevention issues by exploring, among other factors, their current knowledge, attitudes, beliefs, and behaviors regarding HIV/AIDS and condom use. Four focus groups were conducted in the two most populous towns in each of five regions in Ethiopia. Of specific interest were perceptions of consequences associated with HIV/AIDS. Participants in groups identified a variety: dysentery, weight loss, family breakdown, increase in orphans, social stigma, long-term disability, and death. The groups also revealed negative perceptions of condoms, including embarrassment, reduction of sexual pleasure, breakage during sexual intercourse, reduction of faithfulness between partners, and a perception among some that condoms actually spread HIV/AIDS. Also interesting was who participants considered to be most at risk for HIV infections: commercial sex workers, drivers, soldiers, youth in and out of school, government employees, and sexually active young adults. Most important, "participants expressed that condom promotion campaigns were either absent or ineffective in most of their localities" and that some totally ignored the HIV/AIDS-prevention messages.[28]

Quantitative research refers to studies conducted to reliably profile markets, predict cause and effect, and project findings. This reliability is created as a result of large sample sizes, rigorous sampling procedures, and surveys conducted in a controlled and organized environment.

For the HIV/AIDS-prevention study in Ethiopia, a quantitative effort followed the qualitative focus group phase. The study plan included a sample of 160 households per region, for a total of 800 households, drawn from a representative sample. A total of 792 household participants ages 15 to 30 years were interviewed from the 10 towns of priority regions. Of interest was the measurement and analysis of levels of agreement on a five-point scale (*strongly agree*, *agree*, *neutral*, *disagree*, and *strongly disagree*), with statements related to four beliefs often considered to be predictive of behavior change:

- Perceived susceptibility: "I am at risk of getting infected with HIV/AIDS."
- Perceived severity: "Getting infected with HIV/AIDS would be the worst thing that could happen to me."
- Perceived response efficacy: "Condoms work in preventing HIV/AIDS infection."
- Perceived self-efficacy: "I am able to use condoms to prevent HIV/AIDS infection."

Next, the data were analyzed within the theoretical framework. Based on previous research, the researchers knew they needed high levels of each of the four variables listed above to promote behavior change. If just one of the variables was at a low level, then they knew they had to focus on that variable in a subsequent campaign. The authors of the article embarked on five steps to analyze the data:

1. Examine the frequency distribution of each variable (agreement levels for each of the four variables).

2. Compare the mean score for each variable (average level of agreement) to assess whether average beliefs are all at high levels (i.e., 4 or 5).

3. Categorize the four variables into weak, moderate, and strong belief categories. Perceived severity was strong, and thus there was no need to address it in a campaign. However, perceived susceptibility was weak and response and self-efficacy moderate, thus needing to be strengthened in a subsequent campaign.

4. Strengthen targeted beliefs by examining the psychological, social, cultural, and structural bases of these beliefs to determine what caused low perceived susceptibility and only moderate levels of self-efficacy and response efficacy. For example, the researchers found that simply talking with partners about condom use was one key to increased perceived self-efficacy.

5. Then the research was entered into a chart of key beliefs to introduce, change, and reinforce. This chart guided writers and program planners in the development and production of a 26-week radio soap opera.[29] (See Table 3.4.)

STEPS IN DEVELOPING A RESEARCH PLAN

Andreasen recommends that we begin our research journey with the end in mind. He calls this "backward research" and states, "The secret here is to start with the decisions to be made and to make certain that the research helps management reach those decisions."[30]

Nine traditional steps to take when planning a research project are described in the following section, beginning with this critical purpose statement. We'll use a case

Table 3.4 Chart of Beliefs to Change, Introduce, and Reinforce for HIV/AIDS Prevention

Theoretical Variables	Beliefs to Introduce	Beliefs to Change	Beliefs to Reinforce
Susceptibility	Talk with partner(s) about HIV/AIDS and prevention methods.	HIV/AIDS prevention services are easy to get.	Talk with partner(s) about HIV/AIDS and prevention methods.
Severity	Partner(s) believes HIV/AIDS is serious problem.		Partner(s) believes HIV/AIDS is serious problem
Response Efficacy	Using condoms is good, positive, safe, accepted idea.	Quality of HIV/AIDS prevention services is good.	Using condoms is good, positive, safe, accepted idea.
Self-Efficacy	Talk with partner(s) about HIV/AIDS and prevention methods. Generate positive, nonjudgmental talk in community about HIV/AIDS and prevention methods. Best friends are supportive of HIV/AIDS prevention methods.	Generate positive, nonjudgmental talk in community about HIV/AIDS and prevention methods. Generate approval of condoms as a prevention method. Quality of HIV/AIDS prevention services is good.	Using condoms is good, positive, safe, accepted idea.

Source: H. Cho and K. Witte, "Managing Fear in Public Health Campaigns: A Theory-Based Formative Evaluation Process," *Health Promotion Practice* 6, no. 4 (2005): 483–490.

example to illustrate this process from an article by Simons-Morton, Haynie, Crump, Eitel, and Saylor that appeared in *Health Education and Behavior*.[31] Here the authors present a comprehensive research study they conducted for the National Institutes of Health to assess "peer and parent influences on smoking and drinking among early adolescents."

1. *Purpose:* What decisions will this research help inform? What questions do you need this research to help answer?

Existing research indicated to the study team that less than 10% of sixth-graders reported smoking or drinking in the past 30 days, and yet 19.1% of eighth-graders and 33.5% of 12th-graders reported smoking and 24.6% of eighth-graders and 51.3% of 12th-graders reported drinking in the past 30 days.[32] The purpose of the new research effort was to help determine what interventions would be most effective in reducing this prevalence, and with what audiences. Key to this decision were data answering the question, "To what extent do peers and parents influence smoking and drinking among middle school students?"

2. *Audience:* For whom is the research being conducted? To whom will it be presented?

Research findings would be presented to and utilized by health professionals working with youth populations.

3. *Informational objectives:* What specific information do you need to make this decision and/or answer these questions?

Major topics to be explored included those related to dependent variables (e.g., incidence of smoking and drinking among middle school students) and independent variables (e.g., peer- and parent-related factors). Relative to dependent variables, factors to be queried included demographics (gender, race, school attended, mother's education, family structure) and whether any adults living at the student's home smoked cigarettes. Relative to the students' peers, topics of interest included levels of direct peer influence (e.g., peer pressure) and indirect influence (e.g., how many of the respondent's five closest friends smoked and how many drank alcohol). Relative to their parents, insights were needed regarding perceived parent awareness, expectations, monitoring, support, involvement, and conflict—primarily related to drinking and smoking behaviors.

4. *Respondents:* From whom do you need information? Whose opinion matters?

Sixth-, seventh-, and eighth-grade students in all seven middle schools in a Maryland school district located in a suburb of Washington, D.C., would be recruited for the study. The county was predominantly white but included a relatively large minority of African Americans. Student and parent consent would be needed, as would review and approval of the study protocol by the Institutional Review Board of the National Institute of Child Health and Human Development. Authorization would be needed from the school district.

5. *Technique:* What is the most efficient and effective way to gather this information?

An anonymous self-administered questionnaire would be used for data collection. Once the technique is determined, draft the survey instrument.

6. *Sample size, source, and selection:* How many respondents should you survey, given your desired statistical confidence levels? Where will you get names of potential respondents? How do you select (draw) your sample from this population to ensure that your data are representative of your target audience?

A total of 4,668 students were selected after 417 special education students with reading difficulties were excluded. (In the end, the parents of 302 students refused to allow their children to participate, and 103 students were absent on both the initial and makeup dates for taking the survey. In total, 4,268, or 91.3%, of the students completed the survey, having the following demographic profile: 49.1% boys, 50.9% girls, 67.1% White, 23.5% African American, and 7.2% another race.)

7. *Pretest and fielding:* With whom will the survey instrument (e.g., questionnaire, focus group discussion guide) be pretested? Who will conduct the research, and when?

Extensive pretesting of the measures and the questionnaire was done with repeated samples of volunteer students in the same schools the year prior to initiation of the study. These assessments included small-group sessions where students were asked about the meanings of certain words, phrases, and statements being considered for use in the survey. For the final survey, students were to complete the questionnaire in class or during a makeup session, and two trained proctors were to oversee data collection in each class of 20 to 30 students. Classroom teachers were to remain in the classroom and be responsible for student discipline but were instructed not to circulate around the room or otherwise be involved while students completed surveys.

8. *Analysis:* How and by whom will data be analyzed to meet the planners' needs? A variety of statistical procedures will be considered and applied. This chapter's third primer, on basic statistical terminology, is presented in Table 3.5.

The prevalence of drinking and smoking behaviors within the past 30 days was to serve as the dependent variable for all analyses. Advanced statistical techniques would be used to determine the impact of each of the independent variables on these behaviors.

9. *Report:* What information should be included in the report, and what format should be used for reporting?

Final reports and discussions of findings were to include tables displaying results for each of the dependent variables (e.g., friends' problem behavior), cross-referenced by each of the independent variables (e.g., smoking in the past 30 days), and the "odds" that these variables would influence the youths' behavior. Discussions would include a description of the prevalence of drinking and smoking relative to national data as well as the degree to which the findings supported (or not) a positive association between direct and indirect peer pressure and smoking and drinking.

RESEARCH "THAT WON'T BREAK THE BANK"

Alan Andreasen's book *Marketing Research That Won't Break the Bank* has more than 250 pages of suggestions for reducing research costs, a few of which are described in the following section.

Table 3.5 A Statistical Primer

Statistics are numbers that help make sense of data. Statistical procedures are tools that are used to organize and analyze the data in order to determine this meaning. The following terms are described very briefly and are only a few among those used in the field.[a]

Terms Describing the Distribution of the Data

Mode: The response or score that occurs with the greatest frequency among findings.

Median: The value (score) halfway through the ordered data set, below and above which lies an equal number of values.

Mean: The simple average of a group of numbers, often thought of as the one number that best describes the distribution of all other numbers/scores.

Range: Determined by subtracting the lowest score from the highest score.

Terms Describing Measures of Variability

Margin of Error: A measure indicating how closely you can expect your sample results to represent the entire population (e.g., plus or minus 3.5%).

Confidence Interval: A statistic plus or minus a margin of error (e.g., 40% plus or minus 3.5%).

Confidence Level: The probability associated with a confidence interval. Expressed as a percentage, usually 95%, it represents how often the true percentage of the population lies within the confidence interval.

Standard Deviation: A measure of the spread of dispersion of a set of data. It gives you an indication of whether all the data (scores) are close to the average or whether the data are spread out over a wide range. The smaller the standard deviation, the more "alike" the scores are.

Terms Describing Analytical Techniques

Cross-Tabs: Used to understand and compare subsets of survey respondents, providing two-way tables of data with rows and columns allowing you to see two variables at once (e.g., the percentage of men who exercise five times a week compared to the percentage of women who exercise five times a week).

Factor Analysis: Used to help determine what variables (factors) contribute (the most) to results (scores). This analysis, for example, might be used to help determine the characteristics of people who vote (or don't) in every election.

Cluster Analysis: Used to help identify and describe homogeneous groups within a heterogeneous population, relative to attitudes and behaviors used to identify market segments.

Conjoint Analysis: Used to explore how various combinations of options (alternatives features, prices, distribution channels, etc.) affect preferences and behavior intent.

Discriminant Analysis: Used to find the variables that help differentiate between two or more groups.

Terms Describing Samples

Population: A set that includes all units (people) being studied, usually from which a sample is drawn.

Sample: A subset of the population being studied.

Probability Sample: Based on some form of random selection. Each population member has a known chance of being included in the sample. This chance measure helps determine the confidence level to be used when interpreting data.

Nonprobability Sample: A sample that was not selected in a random fashion. As a result, results are not representative of the population, and a confidence level cannot then be determined and used when interpreting data.

a. *Webster's New World Dictionary* (Cleveland, OH: William Collins, 1980); R. J. Senter, *Analysis of Data: Introductory Statistics for the Behavioral Sciences* (Glenview, IL: Scott, Foresman, 1969); A. R. Andreasen, *Marketing Research That Won't Break the Bank* (San Francisco: Jossey-Bass, 2002); D. Rumsey, *Statistics for Dummies* (Indianapolis: Wiley, 2003); P. Kotler and G. Armstrong, *Principles of Marketing*, 9th ed. (Upper Saddle River, NJ: Prentice Hall, 2001); Ellen Cunningham of Cunningham Environmental Consulting.

- Use available data, because they are almost always cheaper to gather than new data and are often "simply lying about as archives waiting to be milked for their marketing and management insights."[33] One place to look is at prior primary research projects conducted for your organization but not analyzed thoroughly or with your new research questions in mind. There may also be existing internal records or documents, such as attendance levels at events, tallies of zip codes and ages of clients, and anecdotal comments captured by telephone customer service staff. Externally, there are commercial enterprises that sell major marketing research data (e.g., *Advertising Age* magazine), and there are also free options, often easily found on the web (e.g., Centers for Disease Control and Prevention's Behavior Risk Factor Surveillance System).

- Conduct systematic observations, as they represent "the ultimate in cheap but good research."[34] And just because they're "free" doesn't dismiss the need for using a systematic and objective process to collect and interpret the data. For example, a state drowning coalition may decide they want to measure increases in life vest usage among children as a result of their campaign by observing toddlers on beaches in public parks. A standardized form for volunteers to use and a designated time and day of the week to conduct the research will be important to ensure reliability of the data when comparing pre- and post-campaign measures.

- Try low-cost experimentation, a technique often used in the private sector and referred to as "test marketing." In the social sector, it may be more familiar as a "pilot." In either case, the objective is to try things out before rolling them out. There are several advantages, including the ability to control the intervention so that it closely matches the strategic options under consideration. If your experiment is carefully designed, you can control extraneous variables and findings can be used to confirm (or not) cause and effect. And this approach is also "often speedier and more efficient than many other approaches."[35]

- Use quota sampling instead of the more costly probability sampling method by developing a profile of the population to be studied and then setting quotas for interviewers so that the final sample matches the major profile of the broader population. For example, a researcher who wanted a projectable sample of opinions of mental health care providers regarding various recovery models might control interviews to match the types of health care organizations in the state (e.g., clinical settings vs. hospital settings vs. school-based programs). Some maintain that these results can still be projectable to the larger similar population "if the quotas are complex enough and interviewers are directed not to interview just easy or convenient cases."[36]

Additional options to consider include *participating in shared cost studies*, sometimes called omnibus surveys. With these studies, you can pay to add a few additional questions to a survey being conducted by a research firm for a variety of other organizations, targeting an audience you are interested in. A county department of natural resources, for example, may want to estimate the percentage of households who might be willing to drop off unused prescription drugs at local pharmacies (market demand). They might then take advantage of a marketing research firm's offer to add that question to their monthly countywide survey that queries households on a variety of questions for similar clients. Another option is to *ask professors and students* at universities and colleges to volunteer their assistance. They may find your research proposal to be of interest and benefit to their current projects and publication goals.

CHAPTER SUMMARY

It may be easiest for you to remember (even understand) familiar research terms by recognizing the criteria used to categorize them:

- By research objective: exploratory, descriptive, causal
- By stage in planning process: formative, pretest, monitoring, evaluation
- By source of information: secondary, primary
- By approaches to collecting primary data: key informant, focus groups, surveys, experimental research, observational research, ethnographic research, mystery shoppers
- By rigor of the technique: qualitative, quantitative

There are nine steps for you to take when developing a research plan, beginning "with the end in mind":

1. Get clear on the purpose of the research.

2. Determine the audience for the research findings.

3. Identify informational objectives.

4. Determine respondents for the research.

5. Find the best technique, given the above.

6. Establish sample size and source, and how it will be drawn.

7. Draft survey instrument, pretest, and field.

8. Create an analytical approach.

9. Outline contents and format for reporting, helping to ensure that the methodologies will provide the desired management information.

Enhancing QUITPLAN® Services of ClearWay Minnesota℠

(2013)

Earlier in this chapter, the ZMET interviewing technique developed by Professor Gerald Zaltman was highlighted as a unique interviewing method that explores what deep metaphors reveal about the minds of consumers. This research highlight describes how this methodology not only inspired strategies to increase usage of smoking cessation services, but also informed development of subsequent formative research efforts.

Background

ClearWay Minnesota is an independent, nonprofit organization that improves the health of Minnesotans by reducing tobacco use and exposure to secondhand smoke through research, action, and collaboration. The organization is funded by 3% of the settlement Minnesota received from the tobacco companies in 1998. The funds are used to help Minnesotans quit smoking and tobacco use, and to fund research, public policy, and community development projects about the state.

Launched by ClearWay Minnesota in 2001, QUITPLAN Services has helped over 100,000 Minnesotans in their efforts to quit tobacco use. QUITPLAN Services offers all Minnesotans free access to quit-smoking counseling via telephone and can provide individuals with nicotine patches, gum, or lozenges. Importantly, the program offers options for smokers who may not want to use telephone counseling, providing an online, interactive quit-smoking program including personalized quit plans, counselors to "chat" with, access to a community forum of current and former smokers who share the ups and downs of the quitting process, and tools to track quit progress and calculate next steps. Timely emails help celebrate progress and milestones.

While these services have been effective, over the past few years service volumes have been declining. With an estimated 70% of Minnesotans who smoked saying they wanted to quit, it was unclear why these services were not more used. ClearWay Minnesota wanted meaningful consumer insights to help answer this question; these would guide the organization in designing and promoting a service that would be more appealing than the desire to "go it alone" or continue to smoke.

Methodology

CultrDig Minneapolis, a research firm specializing in cultural insights and behavioral intelligence, proposed the idea of an online bulletin board group methodology. This method offers several advantages, including speed, convenience, richness, and candor—features critical to engaging smokers and understanding their interior and exterior worlds.

Researchers designed a weeklong online bulletin board study using Dub's IdeaStream™ research platform with smokers and former smokers from across Minnesota. Online participants were recruited by a research facility through phone calls. They identified smokers and former smokers willing to participate online and ensured statewide representation. Thirty-one participants were recruited for the online discussions. Respondents were asked to share their lifestyles, surroundings, triggers, motivators, and obstacles, providing an "immersive look into the role smoking played in their lives and psyche."[37] Through this methodology, researchers hoped to learn what was truly relevant to a smoker who was contemplating a quit attempt.

Each day, new questions were posted on the online bulletin board for participants to respond to with comments as well as images. Three sample questions and responses are illustrated in Box 3.1, all from one participant.

Box 3.1
Questions to the Online Community Group Board

Questions Regarding Triggers

Triggers: "Today is Sunday and you get to use your camera or cellphone to take some photos and share them! Please take and upload 5–10 images of things that make you want to smoke such as sights, sounds, smells or certain activities. You can also upload images from the internet. Explain in text what it is about this image that stimulates your urge to smoke."

One participant's response:

"Stress in general makes me want to smoke! Specifically right now it is the stress of graduate school. Any time I am in the car I want to smoke. I especially want to smoke when in a social atmosphere like a concert or a social event that involves alcohol. Also, I enjoy smoking while on vacation. Finally, after eating I crave a smoke!" (See Figure 3.2.)

Questions Regarding Motivators

Motivators: "Please take and upload 5–10 images of things that make you want to quit smoking. Explain in text what it is about this image that gets you thinking about quitting:"

One participant's response:

"I do not want my children to think it's okay to smoke . . . because it's NOT! It is a bad unhealthy addictive habit. I love to be active and I enjoy being healthy. I do not want to have health issues that would inhibit my ability to watch my kids grow up or be involved in their or my husband's life. The financial requirement to support the smoking habit." (See Figure 3.3.)

Source: ClearWay Minnesota.

Figure 3.2 Images depicting triggers for smoking.

Source: ClearWay Minnesota.

Figure 3.3 Images depicting motivators for quitting.

Source: ClearWay Minnesota.

Questions Regarding Signs of Attempting to Quit

Quitting signs: "What clues would you point out to me that would be tell-tale signs of an attempt at quitting? Please take screenshots or pictures to share as much detail about this evidence as possible. Are there objects that serve as replacements such as gum, candy or a nicotine patch? Might there be an app on your phone? What about websites you visited or posts you shared on Twitter or Facebook?"

One participant's response:

"Choose a quit day, pregnancy, identified a reward of monthly massage/facial for quitting. Identified subs of running on treadmill or 1 square of a Caramello." (See Figure 3.4.)

Figure 3.4   Images depicting signs of attempting to quit..

Source: ClearWay Minnesota.

Findings from the online bulletin board groups were then used to inform focus group discussion guides, where key insights and potential solutions were then explored further. For example, one in-depth discussion with focus group respondents concentrated on what gets people "over the hump" from thinking about quitting to actually making a quit attempt. Participants shared that it was very important to them that it be easy to get the help they wanted, elaborating that they didn't want to have to fill out extensive forms and provide lots of information about themselves to be able to see posts in an online support community.

Implications

Findings from this research were used to redesign ClearWay Minnesota's QUITPLAN Services. Beginning in March 2014, QUITPLAN Services launched a new array of services with a focus on meeting smokers where they are in the quitting process and engaging as many Minnesota tobacco users as possible to access quit services available. Key changes to the services include

- Lowering barriers to quitting by reducing the amount of personal information required to receive a service. For example, a user will no longer be required to log in to use web-based services.

- Offering a wider variety of tools to help smokers make a quit attempt. These include stand-alone text and email programs, quit coach support through the QUITPLAN Services' Facebook page, or simply a quit guide sent to the user.

- Encouraging more smokers to make a quit attempt. This will include offering a two-week free starter kit of nicotine replacement therapy (patches, gum, lozenges) to any Minnesotan.

- More motivation for smokers to quit. The services will help smokers overcome their ambivalence to quitting by showing them how the cost of smoking outweighs the benefits of smoking.

Information for this highlight was provided by Marietta Dreher, director of marketing and communications for ClearWay Minnesota; Molly Hull, brand development supervisor at Clarity Coverdale Fury; and Valeria Esqueda at CultrDig Minneapolis.

DISCUSSION QUESTIONS AND EXERCISES

1. What, in your experience, are the biggest barriers to conducting research for a social marketing effort?

2. What type of research is most often conducted: formative, pretest, or monitoring/ evaluation? Which is least often conducted? Why?

3. Why do the authors strongly recommend that a research project begin with asking the question, "What decisions will you be making that this research is intended to inform?"

4. Crowdsourcing is a relatively new research technique. Are you familiar with any application of this?

5. In the Research Highlight, what do you think program planners learned from this ZMET technique that they might not have discovered using more traditional techniques, such as face-to-face interviews or focus groups?

CHAPTER 3 NOTES

1. A. R. Andreasen, *Marketing Research That Won't Break the Bank* (San Francisco: Jossey-Bass, 2002), 6–11.

2. World Health Organization, *Mobile Phone Use: A Growing Problem of Driver Distraction* (2011), 5, accessed August 7, 2013, http://www.who.int/violence_injury_prevention/publications/road_traffic/distracted_driving/en/index.html.

3. Ibid., 5.

4. Ibid., 16.

5. Ibid., 16–17.

6. Ibid., 15.

7. Royal Society for the Prevention of Accidents, *The Risk of Using a Mobile Phone While Driving* (2002), accessed August 8, 2013, http://www.rospa.com/roadsafety/info/mobile_phone_report.pdf.

8. U.S. Department of Transportation, "NHTSA Survey Finds 660,000 Drivers Using Cell Phones or Manipulating Electronic Devices While Driving at any Given Daylight Moment" (2013), accessed August 8, 2013, http://www.dot.gov/briefing-room/nhtsa-survey-finds-660000-drivers-using-cell-phones-or-manipulating-electronic-devices.

9. Ibid.

10. U.S. Department of Transportation, "U.S. Transportation Secretary Lahood Issues Blueprint for Ending Distracted Driving" (June 7, 2012), accessed August 8, 2013, http://www.distraction.gov/content/press-release/2012/06-7.html.

11. P. Kotler and G. Armstrong, *Principles of Marketing*, 9th ed. (Upper Saddle River, NJ: Prentice Hall, 2001), 140.

12. Ibid.

13. Ibid.

14. A. R. Andreasen, *Marketing Social Change: Changing Behavior to Promote Health, Social Development, and the Environment* (San Francisco: Jossey-Bass, 1995), 120.

15. Andreasen, *Marketing Social Change*, 127.

16. Kotler and Armstrong, *Principles of Marketing*, 141.

17. C. Lefebvre, message posted to the Georgetown Social Marketing Listserve, January 21, 2007.

18. Kotler and Armstrong, *Principles of Marketing*, 152.

19. C. Parvanta, Y. Roth, and H. Keller, "Crowdsourcing 101: A Few Basics to Make You the Leader of the Pack," *Health Promotion Practice* 14, no. 2 (January 8, 2013): 163–167, doi: 10.1177/1524839912470654.

20. Ibid., 146.

21. Ibid., 144.

22. K. Croke, A. Dabalen, G. Demombybes, M. Giugale, and J. Hoogeveen, "Collecting High Frequency Panel Data Using Mobile Phones" (2012), accessed October 6, 2014, https://editorialexpress.com/cgi-bin/conference/download.cgi?db_name=CSAE2012&paper_id=299.

23. P. Kotler, *Marketing Insights From A to Z* (New York: Wiley, 2003), 117–118.

24. OlsonZaltman Associates, "Success Stories" (n.d.), accessed August 9, 2013, http://www.olsonzaltman.com/process.htm.

25. P. Kotler and N. Lee, *Marketing in the Public Sector: A Roadmap for Improved Performance* (Upper Saddle River, NJ: Wharton School, 2007), 259.

26. II. Cho and K Witte, "Managing Fear in Public Health Campaigns: A Theory-Based Formative Evaluation Process," *Health Promotion Practice* 6, no. 4 (2005): 483–490.

27. K. Witte, "Putting the Fear Back Into Fear Appeals: The Extended Parallel Process Model," *Communication Monographs* 59 (1992): 329–349.

28. Cho and Witte, "Managing Fear," 484.

29. Ibid., 484–489.

30. Andreasen, *Marketing Social Change*, 101.

31. B. Simons-Morton, D. Haynie, A. Crump, P. Eitel, and K. Saylor, "Peer and Parent Influences on Smoking and Drinking Among Early Adolescents," *Health Education and Behavior* 23, no. 1 (2001): 95–107.

32. L. D. Johnston, P. M. O'Malley, and J. G. Bachman, J. G., *National Survey Results on Drug Use From the Monitoring the Future Study, 1975–1994: Vol. 1. Secondary School Students*, NIH Pub. No. 95–4206 (Rockville, MD: United States Department of Health and Human Services, National Institute on Drug Abuse, 1995).

33. Andreasen, *Marketing Research That Won't Break the Bank*, 75.

34. Ibid., 108.

35. Ibid., 120.

36. Ibid., 167.

37. Dub, "Evolution of an Insight: A Tale of Mixed Methodologies" (June 24, 2013), accessed September 6, 2013, http://www.greenbook.org/marketing-research.cfm/mixed-methodologies-cultrdig-39086.

Chapter 4

CHOOSING A SOCIAL ISSUE, PURPOSE, AND FOCUS FOR YOUR PLAN AND CONDUCTING A SITUATION ANALYSIS

Bring as many people, from all relevant disciplines you can think of, to the table, as early as possible . . . and find out how they would define success in the initiative.

—Dr. Katherine Lyon Daniel[1]
Associate Director for Communication, CDC

With this chapter, the strategic marketing planning process begins, following the 10-step model presented in Chapter 2. Whether you are a student developing a plan for a course assignment or a practitioner working on a project for your organization, this practical approach is intended to guide you in creating a final product destined to "do good." (In Appendix A, you will also find worksheets that follow this planning outline; you can also download an electronic version of this document from www.socialmarketingservice.com.) For those among you who are reading this "just for fun," the process is illustrated with a variety of examples to make it come to life.

This chapter outlines

- Step 1: Describe the social issue, background, purpose, and focus of your plan
- Step 2: Conduct a situation analysis (SWOT)

Since both are relatively brief, they will be covered together in this chapter. As mentioned earlier, this model begins "with the end in mind," inspiring your decision-making audiences with the problem your plan will address and the possibility it intends to realize. With this background, you will then paint a vivid picture of the marketplace where you will be operating and will be honest about the challenges you face and what you will need to address and prepare for to be successful.

In our opening Marketing Highlight, a compelling purpose with a single focus inspired a lifesaving marketing strategy.

Increasing Timely Childhood Immunizations: Every Child By Two

The Program's History and Current Situation Analysis

(2013)

Background

Every Child By Two: Carter/Bumpers Champions for Immunization (ECBT) was founded in 1991 by former first lady Rosalynn Carter and former first lady of Arkansas Betty Bumpers following a measles epidemic that killed more than 120 people, many of them children. The organization's stated mission is "to protect all children from vaccine-preventable diseases by raising parental awareness of the critical need for timely infant immunizations, fostering the establishment of a systematic method to locate and immunize children, and providing convenient access to immunization services into the future."[2] Read on about the work they have done . . . and the work ahead of them.

Target Audiences and Desired Behaviors

ECBT's informative and educational websites (www.ecbt.org and www.vaccinateyourbaby.org) have special sections for each of their three major target audiences—parents (downstream), health care providers (midstream), and advocates (upstream)—with information, outreach activities, resources, and "words of encouragement" for action.

Parents, who are the target audience for ECBT's Vaccinate Your Baby website, are encouraged to talk to their child's health care provider regarding any questions they have about vaccines during their baby's office visits and to follow the immunization schedule recommended by the Centers for Disease Control and Prevention (CDC). The Vaccinate Your Baby website also focuses on the concerns people may have and provides evidence-based information and personal appeals to encourage timely vaccinations. Families are encouraged to get an annual flu vaccine and a booster of pertussis vaccine (Tdap) to help bring the outbreak of whooping cough under control throughout the nation and to prevent future outbreaks.

Healthcare providers are considered essential for success and are encouraged to take advantage of each contact with a child (well and sick visits) to review the child's immunization status, and, when appropriate, to vaccinate. They are also encouraged to talk with the child's parents, listening and then addressing their concerns using evidence-based tactics that have been proven successful in allaying unfounded fears about vaccine safety. Furthermore, health care providers are encouraged to join their local Immunization

Information System (i.e., confidential, population-based, computerized database that records all immunization doses administered by participating providers) to better assess their patients' immunization status at each visit and avoid missed opportunities to vaccinate.

Advocates are seen as critical to influencing policymakers, especially to supporting annual funding for state immunization programs and pro-vaccine legislation. Advocates are encouraged to work with the media to encourage science-based reporting on vaccines and to conduct activities in local communities to ensure access to vaccines.

Audience Insights

Parents may have one or more barriers to the timely vaccination of their children. Some are concerned about the safety of the vaccines, with one of the most recent misconceptions being the fear that vaccines are associated with autism. Some parents mistakenly believe that their children are fully vaccinated. In addition, language barriers and socioeconomic factors may lead to children's missing vaccinations. With the availability of the Vaccines for Children Program (VFC) and the upcoming implementation of the Affordable Care Act, financial barriers to immunization should no longer be as significant an issue.

Healthcare providers report that one of the major obstacles to immunizing children is excess time spent counseling parents about the necessity of vaccines and alleviating concerns about the safety of vaccines. OB-GYNs are newer to the vaccine program and require guidance on

how to properly store vaccines and avoid missed opportunities to vaccinate their adolescent and adult patients, particularly pregnant women. Pregnant women are advised to receive vaccines to protect themselves and their infants from pertussis and influenza.

Advocates are not always aware of the most effective strategies for increasing immunization rates and influencing policymakers.

Examples of Strategies

Strategies to address *parental* barriers include the writing and distribution of articles on the safety of vaccines; the distribution of information on how to evaluate vaccine-related materials and studies to determine their credibility; the development, distribution, and promotion of science-based vaccination resources, such as the CDC-recommended immunization schedules and disease fact sheets; the promotion of videos and written stories that provide testimonials from parents who have lost a child or who have a child that suffered from a vaccine-preventable disease; the creation and promotion of short videos featuring experts responding to frequently asked questions about vaccines and their safety; and the distribution of information regarding government programs available for those who cannot afford vaccines (e.g., the Vaccines for Children Program). ECBT also uses social media to reach people with immunization messages. The organization's Vaccinate Your Baby Facebook page has more than 75,000 "likes" and reaches nearly 500,000 individuals with immunization messages weekly. The Shot of Prevention blog

Figure 4.1 The range of social media channels used by ECBT.

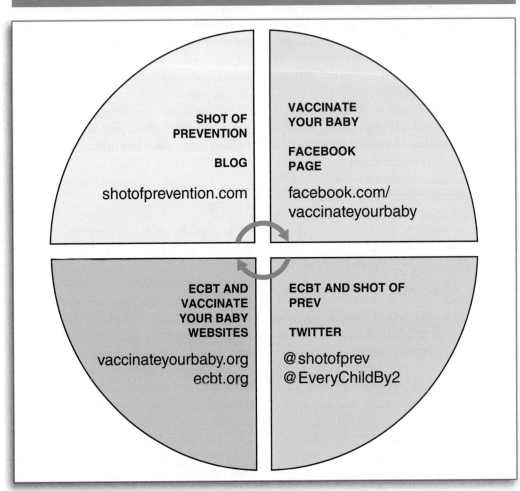

Source: Every Child By Two.

includes approximately three posts per week on issues related to vaccines for all age groups. Two Twitter accounts, @EveryChildBy2 and @ShotofPrev, are utilized to disseminate links to blog posts and vaccine-related news stories. (See Figure 4.1.)

Provider strategies include providing easy access to educational materials for their patients and promoting training resources that help teach providers how to better communicate with hesitant parents about immunizations. Information on the ECBT's website also highlights the benefits that providers receive by participating in an immunization information system, including increased assurance of proper reimbursement, reduction in overvaccination of new patients, automatic calculation of immunizations needed, ability to generate reminder and recall postcards, and staff time savings in seeking immunization histories from previous providers. Additionally, ECBT encourages providers to sign up for its *Daily News Clips* in order to prepare for parents' questions, which often arise from local and national news stories.

ECBT's *advocate* strategies includes teaming up with other immunization partners to create the 317 Coalition, promoting this Coalition to potential advocates, and urging them to get involved. The 317 Coalition advocates increased federal funding for immunizations. Commonly known as "Section 317" of the Public Health Service Act, this funding provides a "safety net" to states so that they are able to immunize children, adolescents, and adults who have no other means to pay for vaccinations.[3]

Situation Analysis

The U.S. *Healthy People 2020* objectives set childhood vaccination targets as indicated in Table 4.1. CDC's annual National Immunization Survey (NIS) tracks progress toward these objectives using a random-digit-dialed sample of telephone numbers to reach households with children aged 19 to 35 months in the 50 states and selected local areas and territories. A follow-up mail survey is then sent to the child's provider to collect vaccination information.

Findings from the 2012 survey indicate that childhood vaccination coverage remains near or above national target levels for doses of four vaccines (MMR, HepB, poliovirus vaccine, varicella) and below 2020 target objectives for five vaccines (DTaP, Hib, PCV, HepA, Rotavirus). As the study points out, however, coverage

varied significantly by state and tended to be lower among children in families with incomes below the federal poverty level. The CDC's report on these findings offered implications for public health practices: "Sustaining current coverage levels and increasing coverage for those vaccines below national target levels is needed to maintain the low levels of vaccine-preventable diseases and prevent a resurgence of these diseases in the United States."[4]

SWOT Analysis

A SWOT (strengths, weaknesses, opportunities, and threats) analysis recognizes organizational *strengths* to maximize and *weaknesses* to minimize, including factors such as available resources, expertise, management support, current alliances and partners, delivery system capabilities, the agency's reputation, and priority of issues. A similar list is made of external forces in the marketplace that represent either *opportunities* your plan should take advantage of or *threats* it should prepare for. These forces are typically not within the marketer's control but must be taken into account. Major categories include cultural, technological, natural, demographic, economic, political, and legal forces.

Potential Organizational Strengths for ECBT to Maximize

- Continued collaboration with ECBT's celebrity spokesperson Amanda Peet, which has raised visibility of the Vaccinate Your Baby program and resulted in more than 500 million print and television impressions.

Table 4.1 Estimated Vaccination Coverage Among Children Aged 19 to 35 Months—National Immunization Survey, United States, 2012. (Highlighted vaccines are near or above 2020 objectives.)

Vaccine	# Doses	2012	2020 Healthy People Objective
Diphtheria, tetanus, and pertussis (DTaP)	≥ 4	82.5%	90%
Measles, mumps, and rubella vaccine (MMR)	≥ 1	90.8%	90%
Hepatitis B vaccine (HepB)	≥ 3	89.7%	90%
Poliovirus Vaccine	≥ 3	92.8%	90%
Varicella vaccine	≥ 1	90.2%	90%
Haemophilus influenza Type B vaccine (Hib)	Full Series	80.9%	90%
Pneumococcal conjugate vaccine (PCV)	≥ 3	81.9%	90%
Hepatitis A vaccine	≥ 2	53.0%	85%
Rotavirus	1	68.6%	80%

Source: Centers for Disease Control and Prevention, "National, State, and Local Area Vaccination Coverage Among Children Aged 19–35 Months—United States, 2012," *Morbidity and Mortality Weekly Report*, accessed September 13, 2013, http://www.cdc.gov/mmwr/preview/mmwrhtml/mm6236a1.htm?s_cid=mm6236a1_w.

- The continued dedication of the ECBT cofounders, former first lady Rosalynn Carter and former first lady of Arkansas Betty Bumpers.
- The organization's strong reputation for mobilizing grassroots campaigns.
- The organization's ability to affect state and federal public policy decisions regarding immunizations, including funding for state immunization programs responsible for the delivery of vaccines to uninsured and underinsured children.
- Partnership with the Centers for Disease Control and Prevention in conducting educational programs for health care providers and promoting the implementation and use of immunization information systems (IIS) throughout the country.
- Obtaining a presidential directive to ensure that children who receive benefits from the Supplemental Nutrition Program for Women, Infants, and Children (WIC) are screened at each visit to ensure timely immunizations.
- A strong board of directors, including the executive director of the American Academy of Pediatrics, numerous professors of medicine, and well-known, highly regarded pediatricians and other vaccine experts.
- Partnerships with numerous immunization advocacy groups that form the 317 Coalition.

Potential Organizational Weaknesses for ECBT to Minimize

- Fluctuations in organizational funding may result in inability to conduct large-scale programs, particularly those targeting nationwide audiences.
- Congressional budget instability and ongoing budget deficits serve as a barrier to the 317 Coalition, who strive to obtain increased/necessary funding for immunization programs throughout the nation.
- Outbreaks of diseases such as pertussis and measles require ECBT to refocus efforts, often to the detriment of ongoing program goals.

Potential External Opportunities to Take Advantage Of

- Numerous cost–benefit analyses show that vaccination against the most common childhood diseases delivers large returns on investment—saving $16.50 in medical costs and indirect costs, such as disability, for every $1 spent on immunization.[5]
- The federal Affordable Care Act may increase affordability of and access to timely immunizations, especially for the poor.
- Immunization information systems (IIS) can locate communities with low immunization rates. This can assist in providing targeted interventions to these communities, thereby protecting more children from disease. Many IIS also provide appointment reminder notes, integrate immunization services with other public health functions such as lead screening and vision screening, and effectively utilize precious financial resources.
- Outbreaks, particularly in communities with low coverage, are an opportunity to increase motivations for timely immunizations.

Potential External Threats to Prepare For

- Budget cuts at the national, state, and local levels. Federal appropriation for immunizations not keeping pace with the real costs of immunization.
- Outbreaks.
- Renewed or continued skepticism about vaccines.
- Increase in number of new vaccines recommended, which increases the cost of fully vaccinating each child and requires ongoing provider and public education.
- Potential for repeal of the Affordable Care Act.
- Continued decrease in the number of pharmaceutical companies making vaccines.
- Vaccine shortages, delays, and distribution problems occur.
- Although vaccines are important disease prevention tools and have significant societal value, they often generate lower revenues than other pharmaceuticals.

Case information was provided by Jennifer Zavolinsky and Amy Pisani of ECBT.

To illustrate the first two steps in planning, we have chosen, for the most part, scenarios from China that represent social marketing opportunities to address a variety of social issues. Our intention is for you to capture the worldwide applicability of this very portable model.

STEP 1: DESCRIBE THE SOCIAL ISSUE, BACKGROUND, PURPOSE, AND FOCUS OF YOUR PLAN

Social Issue and Background

Begin the first section of your social marketing plan by briefly identifying the social issue, sometimes referred to as the wicked problem, your plan will be addressing—most likely a public health problem, safety concern, environmental threat, or community need. Then identify the organization(s) involved in developing and implementing the plan, and move on to present information and facts that led your organization to take on the development of this plan. What's the problem? How bad is it? What happened? What is contributing to the problem? How do you know? This description may include epidemiological, scientific, or other research data from credible sources—data that substantiate and quantify the problem for the reader. The development of the plan may have been precipitated by an unusual event, such as a school shooting, or it may simply be a means of fulfilling one of your organization's mandates. In either case, this section should leave the reader understanding why you have developed the plan and wanting to read on to find out what you are proposing to do to address the social issue.

It wouldn't be surprising, for example, to find the first paragraph of the following illustration in the social issue and background section of a social marketing plan developed to reduce air pollution in China. It also gives a glimpse of the subsequent intended purpose and chosen focus.

In September 2013, an article in the *New York Times*[6] described the Chinese government's new plan to curb air pollution (*social issue*). *Background* information described how Chinese cities suffer from some of the worst air pollution in the world, and residents in China's largest cities "grapple with choking smog that can persist for days and even weeks." Some estimate that air pollution accounts for 1.2 million premature deaths a year, that it is changing everyday lives, and that face masks are becoming ubiquitous.[7] For years, evidently, China had a variety of strict environmental standards, and leaders seemed concerned about the need to improve the environment, but enforcement was lax. Interestingly, the article mentions that one impetus for this new plan was a Twitter feed from the United States Embassy that was publishing the hourly fine-particulate matter level, known as PM 2.5, and that Chinese citizens increased the pressure on the government to have cities start to release their PM 2.5 levels, considering how deeply it penetrates the lungs and enters the bloodstream.

The article goes on to describe the government's intention to reduce this pollution (*purpose*). One of two plans would seek to reduce this pollution by curbing coal burning (*focus*). Evidently, China burns half of all the coal consumed in the world.[8] A second plan has a *focus* on removing all high-polluting "yellow-label" vehicles (those registered before the end of 2005).

Purpose

Given this background, you now craft a broad purpose statement for the campaign. It answers the questions, "What is the potential impact of a successful campaign?" and "What difference will it make?" This statement is sometimes confused with objective or goal statements. In this planning model, it is different from each of these. An *objective* in a social marketing campaign is what we want our target audience to do (behavior objective) and what they may need to know (knowledge objective) or believe (belief objective) to be persuaded. Our *goals* establish a desired level of behavior change as a result of program and campaign efforts. They are quantifiable and measurable. The campaign *purpose*, by contrast, is the ultimate impact (benefit) that will be realized if your target audience performs the desired behaviors at the intended levels. Typical purpose statements, like the background information, should inspire support for the plan. They don't need to be long or elaborate at this point. The following are a few examples:

- Decrease the spread of HIV/AIDS among African Americans
- Reduce the amount of time it takes to get through airport security
- Improve water quality in Lake Sammamish
- Increase the percentage of spayed and neutered pets in the county
- Eliminate the stigma surrounding mental illness

A plausible social marketing plan addressing pedestrian injuries in China illustrates this sequential thought process. The background section of this plan would likely include statistics describing pedestrian-related injury rates, locations where injuries occurred, and populations most affected—such as the estimate in 2004 that traffic injuries claimed the lives of more than 18,500 children ages 14 and under in China each year. And that further analysis of motor vehicle collisions typically shows two main reasons for child traffic injuries: children (a) suddenly running into driveways or (b) crossing a street behind or just in front of a car. Surveys also indicate that 65% of children ages 8 to 10 walk to school, but only 15% are accompanied by adults. And among the 40% of children surveyed who had problems crossing roads, lack of traffic signs and crosswalks were the major problems.[9]

Several related *purpose* statements might then be considered, including *increasing proper use of crosswalks by students* and *decreasing accidents among children in driveways*. As you can probably tell, each of these purpose statements will lead to a different focus, with the crosswalk problem being more likely solved by a focus on infrastructures such as flashing lights and the driveway problem being more likely addressed by a focus on parents walking with children to school and teaching them about navigating driveways. In the end, one would be chosen as the purpose for the plan (as a start).

Focus

Now, to narrow the scope of the plan, a *focus* is selected from the vast number of potential options contributing to the plan's *purpose* (e.g., decreasing accidents among children in driveways). This decision-making process can begin with brainstorming several major potential approaches (*foci*) that might contribute to the plan's *purpose*. These may be approaches that the agency has discussed or undertaken in the past; they may be new for the organization, recently identified as areas of greatest opportunity or emerging need; or they may be approaches other organizations have used that should be considered for your organization. Table 4.2 lists different social issues and possible foci of each. The areas of potential focus may be behavior-related, population-based (although a target market segment has not yet been chosen), or product-related strategies, but they are broad at this point. They will be narrowed further in the subsequent planning process.

Several criteria can be used to choose the most appropriate focus from your initial list of options:

- *Behavior change potential:* Is there a clear behavior within this area of focus that can be promoted to address the issue?
- *Market supply:* Is this area of focus already being addressed adequately in this way by other organizations and campaigns?
- *Organizational match:* Is this a good match for the sponsoring organization? Is it consistent with its mission and culture? Can the organization's infrastructure support promoting and accommodating the behavior change? Does it have staff expertise to develop and manage the effort?
- *Funding sources and appeal:* Which focus area has the greatest funding potential?
- *Impact:* Which area has the greatest potential to contribute to the social issue?

The best focus for a social marketing campaign would then have high potential for behavior change, fill a significant need and void in the marketplace, match the organization's capabilities, have high funding potential, and contribute most to alleviating the social issue. (See Table 4.3.)

STEP 2: CONDUCT A SITUATION ANALYSIS

Now that you have a purpose and focus for your plan, your next step is to conduct a quick audit of organizational strengths and weaknesses and external opportunities and threats that are anticipated to have some impact on or relevance for subsequent planning decisions. As may be apparent, it is critical that you selected a *purpose* and *focus* for your plan first, as they provide the context for this exercise. Without it, you would be scanning

Table 4.2• Identifying Potential Focuses for Your Campaign

Social Issue (and Hypothetical Sponsoring Organization)	Campaign Purpose	Options for Campaign Focus
Family planning (nonprofit organization)	Decrease teen pregnancies	• Condoms • Birth control pills • Abstinence • Sexual assault prevention • Talking to your child about sex
Traffic injuries (state traffic safety commission)	Decrease drinking and driving	• Designated drivers • Underage drinking and driving • Advocating tougher new laws with policymakers • Military personnel • Repeat offenders
Air pollution (regional air quality council)	Reduce fuel emissions	• Carpooling • Mass transit • Walking to work • Telecommuting • Not topping off gas tanks • Gas blowers
Senior wellness (city department of neighborhoods)	Increase opportunities for community senior gatherings	• Tai chi classes in parks • Walking groups in pedestrian malls • Disco dancing under overpasses • Neighborhood watch programs

Table 4.3 Potential Rationale for Choosing a Campaign Focus

Campaign Purpose	Campaign Focus	Rationale for Focus
Decrease teen pregnancies (nonprofit organization)	Abstinence	• Recent governmental funding for campaigns promoting abstinence in middle schools and high schools • Controversial nature of "safe-sex" campaigns in school environments
Decrease drinking and driving (state traffic safety commission)	Designated drivers	• Opportunities to work with restaurants and bars • Familiarity with brand, yet little recent promotion in past several years
Reduce fuel emissions (regional air quality council)	Not topping off gas tanks	• Consumer research in other regions revealing a high level of willingness to stop topping off gas tanks after hearing the (low) costs and potential benefits • Ease of getting the message out in partnership with gas stations
Increase opportunities for community senior gatherings (city department of neighborhoods)	Tai chi classes in parks for seniors	• Availability of space at parks and existing roster of tai chi instructors • Increasing popularity of this form of exercise and camaraderie for seniors

all aspects of the environment versus just the strengths, weaknesses, opportunities, and threats (SWOT) relevant to your specific plan. It would be overwhelming indeed.

Figure 4.2 presents a graphic overview of the factors and forces that are anticipated to have some impact on your target audience and therefore your efforts. As indicated, picture your target audience at the center of your planning process. (A specific segment of the population you will be targeting will be selected in Step 3, in part based on this analysis.) In the first concentric circle are the 4Ps, the variables that you as a marketer have the most control over. Next, a little farther away from the target, are factors associated with the sponsoring organization for the campaign, thought of as the *microenvironment.* The outer concentric circle depicts the *macroenvironment,* forces the marketer has little or no control over but that have influence on your target audience and therefore your effort.

The Microenvironment: Organizational Strengths and Weaknesses

The microenvironment consists of factors related to the organization(s) sponsoring or managing the social marketing effort—oncs therefore considered internal:

- *Resources:* How are your levels of funding for the project? Is there adequate staff time available? Do you have access to expertise related to the social issue or target populations that you can easily tap?
- *Service delivery capabilities:* Does the organization have distribution channels available for current products and services or ones you might develop? Are there any concerns with the current or potential quality of this service delivery?
- *Management support:* Does management support this project? Have they been briefed on it?
- *Issue priority:* Within the organization, is the social issue your plan will be addressing a priority for the organization? Are there other issues you will be competing with for resources and support, or is this one high on the list?
- *Internal publics:* Within the organization, who is likely to support this effort? Who might not? Are there groups or individuals whose buy-in will be needed for the campaign to be successful?
- *Current alliances and partners:* What alliances and partners does the sponsoring organization have that could potentially provide additional resources such as funding, expertise, access to target populations, endorsements, message delivery, and/or material dissemination?
- *Past performance:* What is the organization's reputation in regard to projects such as this? What successes and failures are relevant?

Strengths

Make a (bulleted) list of major organizational strengths relative to this plan, based at least in part on an audit of these seven internal factors. These points will be ones your

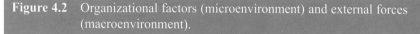

Figure 4.2 Organizational factors (microenvironment) and external forces (macroenvironment).

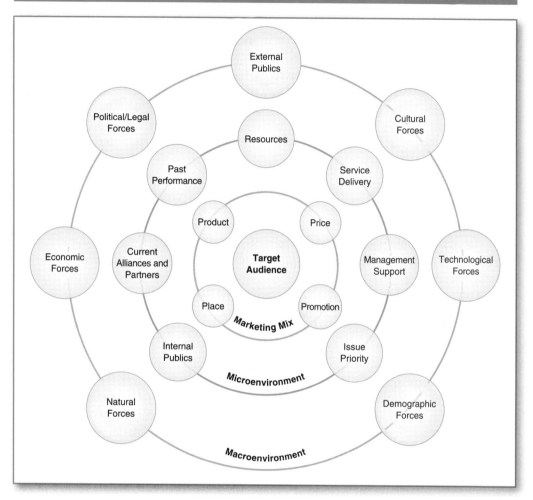

plan will want to *maximize.* You may not have something to note for each of the factors. You should be aware that this list will guide you in many subsequent decisions, such as which target audiences you can best reach and serve, what products (programs and services) you have the resources and support to develop, prices you will (need to) charge, incentives you will be able to afford to offer, and existing alliances you might be able to tap for delivery of products, services, promotional materials, and messages.

For another brief illustration from China, consider a plan with the purpose of reducing energy consumption and a focus on reducing commercial electrical use, a plan spurred by statistics indicating that, in 2004, the energy efficiency rate of

China stood at 33%, 10 percentage points lower than the average advanced world level.[10] We can imagine that a national group charged with the responsibility of developing this plan would begin fully aware of one of their major strengths to maximize—that as a result of blackouts experienced in dozens of provincial-level power grids, energy saving had topped the government agenda earlier in the decade. (In the end, this may have led to changes in infrastructure, such as self-activated escalators in hotel lobbies and hotel rooms that require room keys to be inserted for lights to go on. And of course, lights then go off as guests leave the room with the key that they will need when they return.) The team's pitch to leadership would remind the government of earlier responses and successes.

Weaknesses

On the flip side, a similar list is made of factors that don't look as positive for your effort—ones you may need a few action items, even strategies, to *minimize*. This bulleted list is constructed by reviewing each of the same seven internal factors, noting ones that stand out as potential concerns in developing and implementing a successful plan. Most frequently for governmental agencies and nonprofit organizations (the likely sponsors of a social marketing effort), concerns involve resource availability and issue priority, as in the following example.

Consider organizational factors challenging those charged with developing a plan to reduce teen smoking in China, where there are more than 100 million smokers under the age of 18.[11] According to an article in the *China Daily* in May 2006, a nongovernmental organization, the China Tobacco Control Association, wants to educate the public about the dangers of teen smoking, "but without money, what can we do?"[12] The article cites a lack of government funds (resources) for antismoking education and a historical lack of priority for this issue. In Beijing, for example, a regulation was issued 10 years ago banning smoking in public areas, but enforcement is apparently weak (an issue priority for a key partner organization in this case) and "smoking is still rampant in these places."[13]

The Macroenvironment: External Opportunities and Threats

The macroenvironment is the set of forces typically outside the influence of the social marketer that must be taken into account, as they either currently have an impact on your target audience or are likely to in the near future. In each of the following seven categories, you will be noting any major trends or events you may want to take advantage of (*opportunities*) or prepare for (*threats*). Remember, you are interested in those related to the purpose and focus of your plan.

- *Cultural forces:* Trends and happenings related to values, lifestyles, preferences, and behaviors, often influenced by factors such as advertising, entertainment, media, consumer goods, corporate policies, fashion, religious movements, health concerns, environmental concerns, and racial issues.

- *Technological forces:* Introduction or potential introduction of new technologies and products that may support or hinder your effort.
- *Demographic forces:* Trends and changes in population characteristics, including age, ethnicity, household composition, employment status, occupation, income, and education.
- *Natural forces:* Forces of "nature," including famine, fires, drought, hurricanes, energy supply, water supply, endangered species, tsunamis, and floods.
- *Economic forces:* Trends affecting buying power, spending, and perceptions of economic well-being.
- *Political/legal forces:* Potential or new laws and actions of governmental agencies that could affect campaign efforts or your target audience.
- *External publics:* Groups outside the organization other than current partners and alliances, including potential new partners, that could have some impact on your efforts (good or bad) and/or your target audience.

As discussed in Chapter 1, it is important to note that social marketing experts are now recommending that you also consider the role you can play in influencing decision makers who can impact these upstream forces (e.g., focusing on school district administrators to increase formal physical activity programs in elementary schools).

Opportunities

A major purpose for scanning the external environment is to discover opportunities that you can take advantage of and build into your plan. Your activities can be leveraged by benefiting from the visibility and resources that other groups may be bringing to your issue or the increased awareness and concern that you find is already out there in the general public, as it was in the following example.

According to yet another article in the *China Daily* in May 2006, the number of pet owners in China had been soaring, as were the associated social problems—pet waste left on sidewalks, increases in rabies, and abandonment of pets when owners turned out to be ill prepared for the responsibility. Several organizations were picking up the challenge, including the country's Ministry of Health and the International Fund for Animal Welfare. An environmental scan on their part would likely identify several external forces impacting their target populations, ones they would consider potential opportunities as they prepared their approach to influencing public behaviors. Most cities in China removed the ban on dog rearing in the urban area in the 1980s after food rationing was scrapped (political/legal forces); 2006 was the Year of the Dog on the Chinese calendar (cultural); having a pet is now a symbol of prosperity, whereas it was once looked upon as a bourgeois way of life (economic); and some have attributed the popularity of pets to a growing sense of loneliness among city dwellers, particularly the elderly living alone and single white-collar workers (demographic).[14]

Threats

On the other hand, some of these forces will represent potential threats to your project, and you will want your plan to address or prepare for them. Understanding the influences on your target population can provide insight, as shown in the following example.

Referring again to the problem with tobacco use in China and the interest in reducing teen smoking, numerous external factors threaten success of the campaign along with the organizational weaknesses noted earlier. Imagine the following powerful and entrenched cultural, economic, and legal forces operating in the marketplace—also mentioned in the May 2006 *China Daily* article:[15]

- People begin smoking at an early age, especially in tobacco-planting areas.
- Parents and teachers smoke in front of children.
- China is the world's largest tobacco producer and consumer, so smoking is accepted, even supported, given the close relationship between the production and consumption of tobacco and the national economy.
- Cigarette companies are still allowed to advertise their brands.
- There are no national laws or regulations in China to forbid selling cigarettes to youngsters.

REVIEW OF PAST OR SIMILAR EFFORTS

One social marketing principle for success is to begin your marketing planning with a search and review of prior efforts undertaken by your organization and similar campaigns planned and launched by others. When reviewing past efforts, you are looking for lessons learned. What worked well? What didn't? What did evaluators think should have been done differently? What was missing? One of the benefits of working in the public and nonprofit sectors is that your peers and colleagues around the world often can and will help you. They can share research, plans, campaign materials, outcomes, and war stories. Finding these resources (and people) can be as simple as joining social marketing listservs, such as those mentioned in Appendix C of this book, that have thousands of members around the world. It can also be as simple as watching what others have done, as illustrated in this next example from China.

Nations and communities around the world interested in increasing bicycling (especially as a mode of commuting) could benefit from observing what China has done over the decades to make bicycling a social norm. They provide bike lanes, not just paths, that are protected from cars that might be opening a door (see Figure 4.3). At many intersections, there's a traffic signal—just for cyclists—that gives them their own time and space (see Figure 4.4). In Beijing, there are sports coliseums for biking events, adding to the excitement (and status) of bikers. For those concerned about "overexertion," electric bicycles costing about the same as a cell phone and getting the equivalent of 1,362 miles per gallon of gas are common and certainly not a "sign of weakness." For those concerned about costs, the government makes the competition (cars) very unattractive through escalating gas prices and high fees for vehicle licensing, such as the $5,000 licensing fee in Shanghai that at the time the article was written doubled the cost of the cheapest cars.[16] And for those concerned about rain, they've thought of everything, including form-fitting heavy-duty ponchos that protect legs, heads, packages—even two riders (see Figure 4.5).

Figure 4.3   Bicycle lanes.

THE ROLE OF EXPLORATORY RESEARCH IN STEPS 1 AND 2

As mentioned in Chapter 3, exploratory research is conducted to describe the marketplace relative to the *social issue* you are addressing, a process that assists in making decisions regarding the *purpose* and *focus* of your plan (Step 1). Consider, for example, a program manager developing a plan to address a country's continued increase in new cases of HIV/AIDS. Exploratory research can help determine a purpose and focus for the plan by answering several important questions: (a) What are the number of new cases each year? (b) What populations represent the greatest increases? (c) What are the major ways this disease was transmitted in the past year?

Figure 4.4   Traffic signals.

Figure 4.5   Ponchos.

(d) What percentage of those infected are aware of their status? Findings may point, as they did for the Centers for Disease Control and Prevention (CDC) in 2006, to developing a social marketing plan with the purpose of increasing testing and a focus on African Americans, the population segment representing the greatest number of new cases at the time.[17] (Note: A specific target audience within this heterogeneous population would be selected in Step 3.)

Exploratory research also assists in identifying *organizational strengths and weaknesses* (Step 2) by assessing such factors as levels of support from management and key internal publics, resources available for the effort, the organization's past performance on similar efforts, and the capacity for incremental service delivery. For example, this research would be insightful for a large metropolitan hotel interested in increasing water conservation (*purpose*) with a *focus* on water utilized for laundering guest towels and sheets. Before selection of target audiences and desired behaviors, a work team would be interested in knowing the levels of behaviors influenced by existing cards in bathrooms that encourage guests to leave towels on the rack if they don't need a clean one and a card on a pillow if sheets don't need to be changed. They would also be curious about any feedback from guests and anecdotal comments from staff regarding the program.

Finally, exploratory research will enrich the identification of external forces that represent *opportunities* as well as *threats*. A citizen advocacy group interested in having the state legislature pass a law making texting while driving a primary, versus secondary, offense will find it useful to conduct informal interviews before speaking at a senate subcommittee hearing. What if they heard, for example, that four of the eight members of the committee were planning to recommend against the bill? This potential threat would certainly guide their selection of a target audience (Step 3) and underscore the urgent need to conduct subsequent formative research with these four to identify perceived barriers, desired benefits, and potential motivators (Step 5) relative to a "yes" recommendation.

ETHICAL CONSIDERATIONS WHEN CHOOSING A FOCUS FOR YOUR PLAN

Conscientious social marketers will no doubt face ethical dilemmas and challenges throughout the planning and implementation process. Although ethical considerations are varied, several themes are common: social equity, unintended consequences, competing priorities, full disclosure, responsible stewardship, conflicts of interest, and whether the end justifies (any) means.

For each of the planning steps covered in this text, major potential ethical questions and concerns will be highlighted at the completion of most chapters, beginning with this one. We present more questions than answers, with the intention of increasing awareness of "ethical moments" and the chances that your decisions will be based on a social conscience that leads all of us to "higher ground."

When you brainstormed potential focuses and then picked one for your current plan, your first ethical question and challenge probably popped up: "What will happen to the ones we didn't pick?" For decreasing drunk driving, potential foci include choosing designated drivers, promoting a tougher new law, and focusing on specific populations, such as military personnel or repeat offenders. Since each of these choices would lead to a different marketing strategy, you can only (effectively) deal with one at a time. One potential way to address this challenge is to present a comprehensive organizational plan for the social issue, indicating when important areas of focus will be handled and why they have been prioritized as such.

An additional common question and challenge regarding your focus may also come up, often from a colleague or peer: "If you are successful in accomplishing this, won't you make it tougher for me to accomplish mine?" Some argue, for example, that if you choose the focus of increasing the number of teens who choose a designated driver, won't you increase the number of teens who drink? Won't it look like "the government" approves of teen drinking? Good questions. And to answer, you will want to be prepared with your background and SWOT data as well as outcomes from prior similar efforts conducted by other agencies in other markets that support your decision making.

CHAPTER SUMMARY

This chapter has introduced the first two of the 10 steps in the social marketing planning model.

Step 1 is intended to help you (and others) clarify why you are embarking on this project and, in broad and brief terms, what you want to accomplish and where you will focus your efforts. This will include

- Identifying the social issue your plan will address
- Noting the organization(s) that will be sponsoring the effort
- Gathering and presenting background information relative to the social issue
- Choosing a campaign purpose
- Brainstorming and then selecting a focus for this plan

Step 2 provides rich descriptions of the marketplace where you will be vying for your customers and entails creating a common understanding of the organizational and external challenges you will face by conducting an analysis of

- *Organizational strengths* to maximize and *weaknesses* to minimize related to organizational resources, service delivery, management support, issue priority, internal publics, current alliances and partners, and past performance
- *External opportunities* to take advantage of and *threats* to prepare for related to cultural, technological, demographic, natural, economic, and political/legal forces,

as well as external publics other than current partners and alliances

- *Prior similar campaigns*, with an interest in lessons learned as well as opportunities for using existing research, plans, and materials developed by others

Exploratory research informs the process of identifying a purpose and focus and conducting a situation analysis and also provides a rationale for your decisions.

RESEARCH HIGHLIGHT

Pigs for Peace

Improving Health and Well-Being for Conflict-Affected Populations in the Democratic Republic of the Congo

(2008–Present)

This research case highlights the power of *participatory action research* to inspire a clear focus for a program intervention. As noted in Chapter 3, participatory action research is a systematic inquiry into a topic of importance to a community (*social issue*), with the objective of informing action for social change. In this case, a community-based approach to the research was used, involving strong partnerships with indigenous experts and local organizations. You'll read how this made all the difference.

Background

In the last decade, the population in the eastern provinces of the Democratic Republic of Congo (DRC) in Central Africa has "suffered brutal attacks, including rape, torture, and mutilation—weapons of war, imposed by rebels and soldiers alike. Survivors are further traumatized by infectious disease, poverty, stigma, and social isolation. Men can leave their wives, women are traumatized, families are

traumatized, and entire communities are destabilized by conflict-related violence," says Dr. Nancy Glass, a professor at the Johns Hopkins School of Nursing.[18]

In 2008, a research partnership was formed to obtain evidence for developing and implementing a sustainable intervention to address the social determinants of health, including poverty and traumatic stress for survivors and their families in eastern DRC. Partners included two U.S.-based organizations (Johns Hopkins University School of Nursing and Great Lakes Restoration) and two Congolese-based organizations (Programme d'Appui aux Initiatives Economiques du Kivu [PAIEDEK] and Rama Levina Foundation).

Method

These community and academic partners met multiple times over one year to develop a research plan including informational objectives, respondent profiles and sampling techniques, methodologies for information gathering, interview and focus group questions, and approaches for analysis and dissemination of findings. Once the team agreed on research questions and procedures, partners trained research assistants living in the DRC who would conduct 50 face-to-face interviews with survivors of conflict-related violence, including sexual assualt. Interviews were conducted as well with their husbands, health care providers, and village leaders—all to begin to "understand the complex, inter-related factors that influence exile or reintegration of survivors of violence."[19]

Interviews with survivors lasted 60 to 90 minutes and were conducted in safe and convenient locations, examining several key factors:

- *Individual factors*, including survivors' experiences of conflict-related violence, with a focus on sexual and gender-based violence, mental health, stigma, exile, and reintegration into the family and the village
- *Household factors*, including food security, employment, income, children in school, and access to health care
- *Village-level factors*, including availability of health care services, schooling, and employment associated with the exile or reintegration of survivors

Face-to-face interviews with health care providers, religious leaders, and village leaders provided further information on the health, economic, and social disparities of survivors and their families. All interviews were digitally recorded, and respondents were provided small tokens of appreciation for their time. At the end of each day, the research team met with interviewers for a debriefing and to make any needed changes prior to the next day's research activities.

Findings

A rigorous thematic analysis involving multiple reads of transcripts and subsequent discussions identified two themes. The first related to the significant health consequences of sexual violence for survivors as well as family members, including consequences related to reproductive health, infection diseases such as HIV/AIDS, and trauma. The second theme was one of women's worth, suggesting that a survivor needs a way to regain her "worth" in the family and the village through productive contributions. Based on follow-up discussions with a variety of stakeholders, it was decided to prioritize economic empowerment by assisting women and their families in rebuilding their economic resources, leading to increased health and well-being for them and their families. The challenge ahead was to develop a program that would address a consistent finding that participants did not have access to affordable financial services, and that traditional microcredit (loans) were not an appealing option given this group's economic shock and stress. A new microfinance program, one custom designed especially for this group, was needed. A village-led, animal husbandry approach was chosen.

Program Response

The *purpose* of the village-led animal husbandry microfinance project is to improve the economic, health, and social well-being of women and their families. The *focus* is on providing a "loan" of a pig as a means to generate income. Why pigs? Pigs

Figure 4.6 Ms. Cebeya of the village Bulenga declares, "I will take care of her like a baby."

Source: Great Lakes Restoration.

provide a sustainable supplemental income by giving birth a couple of times a year to 6 to 12 piglets. In addition, there are no cultural taboos, the women can manage the pigs, the pigs don't need a lot of space, and they eat local resources including bananas and sweet potatoes. The program was named Pigs for Peace (PFP) and was a simple one, with village members inviting a PFP coordinator through PAIDEK microfinance to explain the program to village households (*promotion*). If a village makes the decision to join, it creates a village-based association to support the activities of both male and female partners. A female pig is then delivered to families living in the village (*product and place*), with the female head of household being the primary target audience. Families agree to repay their "loan" by giving two piglets (one to repay the loan and one to pay interest on the loan) to the project from the first litter of piglets (*price*). After the repayment, the original pig and remaining piglets are the family's to provide a financial resource for the families, with some being

sold at the market or, in the case of male pigs, being used for stud services in the community. The project also provides adult male pigs to the village to start the project. The village association supports the women and their families in managing the pigs, from building enclosures to vet services to education on the food and health of pigs and how to bring others into the association (*products*).

Postscript

PFP was implemented in December 2008 with just four families in one rural village receiving "loan" piglets from the project. By August 2013, these totals had expanded to 492 families in 23 villages in South Kivu (see Figure 4.6).

On July 12, 2011, a blog from Dr. Nancy Glass Professor, Johns Hopkins School of Nursing, regarding the project comments on continued success:

> We still have many families to visit, but the first 65 visits have me convinced of the power of low-cost, village-led development and health projects. We have 186 families involved in the program, and the average village household is eight members (parents and six children). So we have provided a household income resource that has the potential to influence $186 \times 8 = 1,488$ villagers for the cost of $14,000. That is an average of $9.40 per individual. I think our Pigs for Peace project has the early evidence of cost and economic impact in Eastern DRC, and I think we have a model to build on and that is sustainable. Exciting![20]

DISCUSSION QUESTIONS AND EXERCISES

1. What is the distinction between a social issue and a campaign purpose?

2. Identify four potential areas of focus for an effort to decrease youth gun violence.

3. How are strengths and weaknesses distinguished from opportunities and threats?

4. Give an example of a campaign that is "already out there" that an organization planning a similar effort could take advantage of.

CHAPTER 4 NOTES

1. National Social Marketing Centre, *Effectively Engaging People: Views From the World Social Marketing Conference 2008* (2008), 10, accessed July 15, 2011, http://www .tcp-events. co.uk/wsmc/downloads/NSMC_Effectively_engaging_people_conference_version.pdf.

2. Every Child by Two [website], accessed September 13, 2013, http://www.ecbt.org/index. php/about/index.php.

3. 317 Coalition, "Removing Financial Barriers to Immunization," accessed September 13, 2013, http://www.317coalition.org/.

4. Centers for Disease Control and Prevention, "National, State, and Local Area Vaccination Coverage Among Children Aged 19–35 Months—United States, 2012," *Morbidity and Mortality Weekly Report*, accessed September 13, 2013, http://www.cdc.gov/mmwr/preview/mmwrhtml/ mm6236a1.htm?s_cid=mm6236a1_w.

5. F. Zhou, J. Santoli, M. L. Messonnier, H. R. Yusuf, A. Shefer, S. Y. Chu, L. Rodewald, and R. Harpaz, "Economic Evaluation of the 7-Vaccine Routine Childhood Immunization Schedule in the United States, 2001," *Archives of Pediatric and Adolescent Medicine* 159 (December 2005): 1136–1144.

6. E. Wong, "China's Plan to Curb Air Pollution Sets Limits on Coal Use and Vehicles," *The New York Times* (September 12, 2013), accessed September 19, 2013, http://www.nytimes. com/2013/09/13/world/asia/china-releases-plan-to-reduce-air-pollution.html?_r=0.

7. Ibid.

8. Ibid.

9. C. Qide, "Campaign to Teach Kids About Road Safety," *China Daily* (April 1, 2004), accessed November 20, 2006, http://www.chinadaily.com.cn/english/doc/2004–04/01/con tent_319588.htm.

10. U.S. Energy Information Administration, "International Energy Outlook 2013" (July 25, 2013), accessed September 19, 2013, http://www.eia.gov/forecasts/ieo/world.cfm.

11. Q. Quanlin, "Campaign Aims to Smoke Out Young Addicts," *China Daily* (May 30, 2006), 1, 5.

12. Z. Feng, "Current Anti-smoking Efforts Failing to Make an Impact," *China Daily* (May 30, 2006), 1.

13. Ibid.

14. L. Qi, "Pets Bring Host of Problems," *China Daily* (May 29, 2006), 5.

15. Feng, "Current Anti-smoking Efforts," 1, 5.

16. K. Holder, "China Road," *UCDAVIS Magazine Online* (2006), accessed November 28, 2006, http://www-ucdmag.ucdavis.edu/current/feature_2.html.

17. P. Kotler and N. Lee, *Social Marketing: Influencing Behaviors for Good*, 3rd ed. (Thousand Oaks, CA: Sage, 2007), 132–134.

18. Johns Hopkins Center for Global Health, "Healing the Heart of Africa, One Pig at a Time" (February 1, 2011), accessed September 11, 2013, http://www.hopkinsglobalhealth.org/news_center/headlines/2011/nancy-glass.html.

19. N. Glass, P. Ramazani, M. Tosha, and M. Mpanano, "A Congolese–US Participatory Action Research Partnership to Rebuild the Lives of Rape Survivors and Their Families in Eastern Democratic Republic of Congo," *Global Public Health: An International Journal for Research, Policy and Practice* 7, no. 2: 184–195.

20. Johns Hopkins School of Nursing, "Pigs for Peace Success Stories in Congo" (July 12, 2010), accessed September 12, 2013, http://blogs.nursing.jhu.edu/pigs-for-peace-success-stories-in-congo/.

PART III

SELECTING TARGET AUDIENCES, OBJECTIVES, AND GOALS

Chapter 5

SEGMENTING, EVALUATING, AND SELECTING TARGET AUDIENCES

We need to value segmentation beyond the "casting call" for images and voices and think about it as it can impact behavior offerings, product and service design, benefits offered and distribution strategies.

—Dr. Craig Lefebvre[1]
University of South Florida

Selecting target audiences probably makes sense to you by now and sounds good in theory. It's the practice that creates the greatest angst for many, reflected in these common musings addressed in this chapter:

- "We're a governmental agency and expected to treat everyone the same. How can we justify allocating a disproportionate share of our resources to a few population segments? Even worse, how can we justify eliminating some segments altogether?"
- "I keep hearing about 'the low-hanging fruit' and that we should go after them first. In my community clinic, I interpret that to mean that we focus our resources on clients who are ready to lose weight, ready to exercise. I don't get it. Don't the ones who aren't ready need us the most to convince them they should?"
- "If a marketing plan is built around and for a particular segment of the population, does that mean we'll need separate and multiple marketing plans for every audience we try to influence? That seems over the top."
- "Sometimes this just sounds like fancy language for something that never really happens. When we do a billboard for organ donation, everyone in town sees it. How is that target marketing?"

In this chapter, you'll read in depth about the benefits of segmentation and learn a three-step process for selecting a target audience for a specific program effort:

1. Segment a population into homogeneous groups

2. Evaluate segments based on a variety of factors

3. Choose one or more segments to target

We believe this inspiring opening case breaks the traditional segmentation mold, choosing to target audiences most open to change as a result of a life-stage event.

MARKETING HIGHLIGHT

Increasing Alternative Transportation by Targeting a Group Open to Change

Portland, Oregon

(2011–Present)

Source: Portland SmartTrips

Background

Portland, Oregon, is a city well known for building strong infrastructures that support active and alternative transportation modes, including bicycling, walking, and transit. They even brought back the street-car. And they see these investments as wise ones. Given that the region is dependent on trade and freight, the economy benefits from less road congestion. This choice also builds health, safety, and communities.

Program managers recognize, however, that it's not enough to just "build it and

they will come." They have therefore focused their efforts on identifying unique target audiences and then leveraging their insights in the decision-making process and in the identification of barriers, wants, and needs to create innovative strategies. In 2002, the Portland Office of Transportation brought an individualized marketing program called TravelSmart to the United States from Australia and Europe. After a pilot in 2004, the program was modified and branded SmartTrips, and over the next eight years it reached 80% of households in the city and reduced millions of vehicle miles traveled.[2] Planners recognized, however, that even successful programs must continually transform and respond to new market opportunities. The opportunity they responded to in 2011—which is highlighted in this case—was an opportunity to develop an innovative strategy for a distinct, attractive audience: new residents to the Portland area.

Case information was provided by Andrew Pelsma, program specialist, and Linda Ginenthal, program manager, for the Portland Bureau of Transportation, Active Transportation Division, and Jay Kassirer of Tools of Change and Cullbridge Marketing and Communications.

Target Audiences and Desired Behaviors

Why new residents? First, with an average of 15% of the U.S. population moving each year, new residents represent a significant, identifiable audience segment, one defined using a life-stage variable.[3] A second reason was their "readiness for action." When a person changes residence, new decisions need to be made, including how to get to work, to school, and to the store. In other words, new residents are open to change, and at this time of change, opportunities to create new habits (*behaviors*) are greatest. For those new to a neighborhood, for example, knowledge gaps need to be bridged, such as knowing where a bus goes, how to catch it, and how much it will cost. The opportunity for SmartTrips was to fill these gaps (*needs*). A third reason was an opportunity for long-term program savings based on the prediction that incremental costs of long-term program operations will decrease when targeting a population that continually "refreshes itself."

For this program, new movers were defined as residents who had moved to or within Portland during the sixth-month period prior to program implementation. Names and addresses were purchased from data services companies who used the U.S. Postal Service's National Change of Address Database. New movers were further segmented into one of three very disparate geographic regions. *North Portland* is about 7 miles from downtown and is a diverse mixture of residential, commercial, and industrial areas. Significantly for program planning, the terrain is characterized as primarily flat, with sidewalks and bike-friendly streets. The area also includes frequent and standard service bus lines as well as light rail. By contrast, *Southwest Portland* is composed primarily of residential homes, business districts, and larger institutions such as a university. Its steep hills and challenging terrain are noteworthy, presenting connectivity barriers for bicyclists and walkers. On the other hand, the area is serviced well by buses. Finally, *East Portland* is a mixture of residential and commercial areas. Although bike-friendly routes exist, unpaved roads and a lack of sidewalk connectivity present barriers. The area is serviced well, however, by buses and light rail. These three regions were targeted, as there was less access to healthy and active modes of transportation here than in the downtown core and inner part of Portland, and program planners wanted to reach areas that hadn't been targeted with a residential program in the past.

With a *purpose* of reducing vehicle miles traveled, the program promotes several behavior alternatives to driving alone: walking, biking, ride sharing, carpooling, buses, and light rail. Although many transportation-demand-management programs focus on the work trip, this program also focused on neighborhood and home-based trips, such as shopping. As you will read, a highly personalized and interactive strategy was developed to assist individual residents in choosing the most attractive option, given their unique situations and preferences.

Audience Insights

The list of potential perceived barriers to alternative modes of transportation is typically long, ranging from increased time spent to weather disruptions, risks to personal safety, equipment breakdowns (e.g., bicycle failure), and concerns about socioeconomic stigma. This list is lengthened for new residents, adding system intimidation, as new movers are easily overwhelmed by the complexity of a system as large as Portland's. Knowledge is also a barrier, given the lack of familiarity with what travel options are available and where to find more information concerning bike paths, safe walking routes, and transit pickup locations, destinations, and costs. Add to that the often chaotic mindset associated with changes in location and living arrangements, making it difficult to capture people's attention. Program planners clearly knew what they were up against, and this knowledge informed and inspired their strategies.

Planners also recognized benefits their audience would find worth their while, including wanting to be healthy, save money, contribute to the environment, and enjoy their local community. Given that

perceived benefits must exceed perceived costs in order for an exchange to take place, strategic planners were challenged—a challenge they were able to meet, as you will read.

Marketing Mix Strategies

Portland's new-mover program, branded "SmartTrip Welcome," was launched in 2011 and is uniquely focused on delivering program options through customized and personal communications and intent on creating a dialogue with new residents. Program options are organized by alternative transportation mode and packaged with a variety of products (*goods and services*), incentives (*price*), and promotional materials (see Figure 5.1), described below. You will read later about the program's unique delivery system (*place*).

- *Walking.* A "Ten Toe Walking" kit includes an area walking map; an "Oregon Crosswalk Laws" brochure; a schedule of neighborhood walking tours, including one for Senior Strollers; a "Walk to Wellness" brochure highlighting area programs focused on walking and health; walking logs to keep count of daily steps; and a free pedometer donated by Kaiser Permanente.
- *Bicycling.* The "Portland by Cycle" kit includes citywide and neighborhood bicycle maps; tips and rules of the road for cyclists; schedules of cycle rides and workshops; a "Bicycle Helmet" brochure; and a "Women on Bikes" resource guide.
- *Transit.* Informational materials include bus and light rail schedules,

Figure 5.1 Promotional materials for program options.

Source: Portland SmartTrips.

Figure 5.2 Front of postcard mailed to new residents.

Source: Portland SmartTrips.

an "Honored Citizen's Guide" especially for seniors, and a personalized tracker card that gives the bus stop ID numbers and schedules for the four stops closest to the resident's home.

- *Driving.* Information on car sharing and carpooling is made available, as well as road safety tips for seniors.

Program planners believe one of the reasons the SmartTrips effort has been successful over the years is because participants receive information and services "they want." The planners break their communication approach into three steps: (1) connecting with new movers, (2) processing and filling the orders, and (3) personal delivery of relevant materials. They begin with a postcard, designed to be humorous and eye-catching and to stand out from typical junk mail and inspire the resident to go online to take the next steps to express interest and request more information (see Figure 5.2). Residents then receive an online order form, or one can be mailed, where they can indicate their specific interests and requests for further information. Information from these order forms is then entered into a database, allowing for ease of tracking and targeting future communications. Once an order form is processed, each person receives a thank-you letter, pledge form, and local area coupon sheet. Based on the participant's interest, an individualized package is prepared, and in keeping with a personalized approach, these materials are placed in a reusable tote bag and the fun part begins—bike delivery! Having staff deliver orders by bike is seen as a cost-effective and efficient method. Program managers believe it brings credibility to the commitment of the Portland Bureau of Transportation to active transportation and provides program participants an opportunity to speak with the transportation expert face to face (see Figure 5.3).

Follow-up *prompts* increase responsiveness and include a phone call made two weeks after delivery of materials, giving residents an opportunity to ask additional questions and providing continued support and encouragement. Then a series of targeted emails are sent, tailored to unique resident profiles including their knowledge levels, attitudes, needs, vocations, and demographic information. The first customized and personal email blast addresses the residents' primary commute mode choice, and the second addresses their primary neighborhood mode choice, as indicated by the online trip diary attached to their order form.

Figure 5.3 Staff delivering program materials requested and answering any questions.

Source: Portland SmartTrips.

Outcomes

Three approaches were used to measure outcomes from the fall 2011 program launch: a new-mover analysis, a regional analysis, and a longer-term panel analysis.

- *New-resident analysis.* A sample population of new residents was separated into two groups: a control group and a survey group. This division helped control factors that might apply to the target new-resident community, such as weather, unemployment rates, and gas prices. Three weeks prior to program launch, a paper survey was mailed to the targeted survey group ($n = 5,400$) and to those in the control group ($n = 1,352$), with 953 (18%) of the survey group and 230 (17%) of the control group responding. The survey queried work and neighborhood modes of transportation and awareness of transportation information resources. After completion of the pilot SmartTrips Welcome program, a follow-up survey was issued through the mail to both target

and control groups using the same format. A raffle of a $50 grocery store coupon was offered as an incentive.

- *Regional analysis.* This analysis focused on comparing the three geographic regions that were targeted, with an interest in understanding the influence of regional variances including differing topography, transit service, and active transportation infrastructures.

- *Long-term panel analysis.* A longitudinal panel measured and recorded participants' progress over a longer term: a one-year period. A select group ($n = 356$) of respondents who ordered materials online were asked to fill out a trip diary and survey questionnaire, establishing baseline data for evaluation. After implementation of the individualized marketing component and provision of continued encouragement and reinforcement throughout the year, participants were issued the same survey one year later.

Findings from the 953 new-resident surveys, compared with the 230 control group surveys, indicated that vehicles miles traveled were reduced by 1,076,118— equivalent to 200 miles per new resident per year and a 10.4% reduction in drive-alone trips. All three regions (North, Southwest, and East Portland) showed improvements over control groups in those regions. And the panel participants showed a 7% decrease in drive-alone trips and a 9% increase in environmentally friendly trips one year later.

STEP 3: SELECT TARGET AUDIENCES

At this point in the planning process, you have established the following components of your plan (illustrated using a utility as a hypothetical example):

- *Purpose* (e.g., decrease landfill and hauling costs)
- *Focus* (e.g., backyard composting of food waste)
- *Strengths* to maximize (e.g., as a utility, access to the customer base)
- *Weaknesses* to minimize (e.g., the utility's curbside yard waste collection service just started accepting food waste, an internal competitor for the food waste)
- *Opportunities* to capture (e.g., continued community interest in natural gardening)
- *Threats* to prepare for (e.g., potential to increase rodent populations)
- Possible discovery of *existing campaigns* that will be useful for your efforts (e.g., one from a list of success stories on a state department of ecology's website)

You are now ready to select one or more target audiences for your campaign, defined as *a set of buyers sharing common needs or characteristics that the company decides to serve.* They are subsets of the larger group (population) that may also be exposed to your efforts. In the utility example, residential households are the implied population of focus for the backyard composting campaign, but not the target audience. Your marketing strategy will be crafted to be particularly effective with one or more subsets of these diverse residents.

STEPS INVOLVED IN SELECTING TARGET AUDIENCES

Determining these targets for your campaign is a three-step process involving *segmentation*, *evaluation*, and then *selection*. Each of these steps is described briefly in the following section and elaborated upon in the remaining sections of the chapter.

1. Segment the Market

First, the most relevant (larger) population for the campaign is divided into smaller groups who will likely require unique strategies in order to be persuaded to change their behavior. The groups you end up with should have something in common (needs, wants, barriers, motivations, values, behavior, lifestyles, etc.)—something that makes them likely to respond similarly to your offer. Based on background information about attitudes toward composting indicating that avid gardeners are the most interested in composting, this city utility might identify four market segments to consider. As you will see, their segmentation is based initially on a combination of values, lifestyle, and behavior variables:

- Avid gardeners putting most of their food waste in their *yard waste container*
- Avid gardeners putting most of their food waste in the *garbage* or *down the drain*
- Avid gardeners putting most of their food waste in a *backyard composter*
- Remaining households who aren't avid gardeners

2. Evaluate Segments

Each segment is then evaluated based on a variety of factors described later in the chapter, ones that will assist you in prioritizing (perhaps even eliminating some) segments. For the food-waste-composting scenario, planners should be very eager to know more about each of these segments, beginning with *size* (number of households in the group), as a way to understand the impact that the segment is having on the solid waste stream. They should also consider their *ability to reach* each identified segment and *how receptive* they might be to the idea of composting food waste in their backyard. Avid gardeners, for example, are likely to be the most interested in taking on this new practice, as they will likely see the value in the compost for their gardens.

3. Choose One or More Segments to Target

Ideally, you are able to select only one or a few segments as target audiences for the campaign and then develop a rich profile of their distinguishing characteristics that will inspire strategies to uniquely and effectively appeal to them. Keep in mind that if you select more than one audience, it is likely that you will need a different marketing mix strategy for each. A campaign to influence avid gardeners who are currently putting their food waste with their yard waste to instead put it in a composter would have different incentives and messages, and perhaps even communication channels, than one intending to persuade those who aren't avid gardeners to start composting their food waste. In fact, it is likely that the utility would make the latter segment its last priority, given the challenges they would face in creating and delivering value to this segment in exchange for their effort.

This segmentation and targeting process, though sometimes tedious and complex, provides numerous benefits—ones long familiar to corporate sector marketers who "know that they cannot appeal to all buyers in their markets, or at least not all buyers in the same way":[4]

- *Increased effectiveness.* Outcomes (numbers of behaviors successfully influenced) will be greater, as you have designed strategies that address your target audience's unique wants and preferences and therefore "work." (It's like fishing. If you use the bait that the fish you want like, you're more likely to catch the ones you want . . . and more of them!)
- *Increased efficiency.* Outcomes relative to outputs (resources expended) are also likely to be greater, again as a result of targeting your efforts and resources to market segments with a higher likelihood of responding to your offer. (And back to the fish analogy. You are also likely to catch all these fish in a shorter time and with less bait.)
- *Input for resource allocation.* As a result of evaluating each of the segments, you have objective information that will assist you in distributing your resources and providing this rationale to others.
- *Input for developing strategies.* This process will leave you with detailed profiles of a segment that will then provide critical insights into what will influence an audience to buy your behavior.

Even if, for a variety of purposes, programs are developed for all markets, segmentation at least organizes and provides a framework for developing strategies that are more likely to be successful with each of the markets.

VARIABLES USED TO SEGMENT MARKETS

Potential variables and models for segmenting a market are vast, and still expanding. Traditional approaches used by commercial marketers for decades are described in this section, as are unique models successfully applied by social marketing theorists and practitioners.

Keep in mind that in this initial segmentation process, before you have actually chosen a target audience, your objective is to create several attractive potential segments for consideration. You will select variables to characterize each group that are the most meaningful predictors of market behavior, ending up with groups that are likely to respond similarly to your offer (*products*, *price*, *place*) and your promotional elements (*messages*, *messengers*, *creative elements*, and *communication channels*).

Traditional Variables

Segmentation variables typically used to categorize and describe consumer markets are outlined in Table 5.1 on page 133. Each is applicable to a social marketing environment (marketplace) as well.[5]

Demographic segmentation divides the market into groups on the basis of variables common to census forms: age, gender, marital status, family size, income, occupation (including the media, legislators, physicians, etc.), education, religion, race, and nationality. Sometimes referred to as sociodemographic or socioeconomic factors, these are the most popular bases for grouping markets, for several reasons. First, they are some of the *best predictors* of needs, wants, barriers, benefits, and behaviors. Second, this type of information about a market is *more readily available* than it is for other variables, such as personality characteristics or attitudes. Finally, these are often the easiest ways to *describe and find a targeted segment* and to share with others working to develop and implement program strategies.

Example: A demographic basis for segmentation could be quite appropriate in planning an immunization campaign, because immunization schedules vary considerably according to age. Planners might understandably create unique strategies for each of the following population segments in their local community:

- Birth to 2 years (3%)
- 3 to 6 years (5%)
- 7 to 17 years (20%)
- Adults, 18 to 64 years (52%)
- Seniors, 65 years and over (20%)

Geographic segmentation divides a market according to geographic areas, such as continents, countries, states, provinces, regions, counties, cities, schools, and neighborhoods, as well as related elements, such as commute patterns, places of work, and proximity to relevant landmarks.

Example: An organization focused on reducing the number of employees driving to work in single-occupant vehicles might find it most useful to develop strategies based on *where employees live* relative to the worksite, current van pools, current car pools, and each other. The planner might then decide that the first four groups represent the greatest opportunity for "hooking up" employees with attractive alternative and/or existing forms of transportation:

- Employees living on current van pool routes (10%)
- Employees living within 5 miles of current car pools (5%)
- Employees living within 5 miles of each other (15%)
- Employees living within walking or biking distance of the workplace (2%)
- All other employees (68%)

Psychographic segmentation divides the market into different groups on the basis of social class, lifestyle, values, or personality characteristics. You may find that your market varies more by a personal value, such as concern for the environment, than by some demographic characteristic, such as age.

Example: A campaign to reduce domestic violence might find it most important to develop campaign programs based on levels of self-esteem among potential victims:

- High self-esteem (20%)
- Moderate self-esteem (50%)
- Low self-esteem (30%)

Behavior segmentation divides the market on the basis of knowledge, attitudes, and behaviors relative to the product being sold. Several variables can be considered within this approach: segmenting according to *occasion* (when the product is used or decided on), *benefit sought* (what the segment wants from using the product), *usage levels* (frequency of use), *readiness stage* (relative to buying), and *attitude* (toward the product/offering).

Example: A blood donation center may increase efficiency by prioritizing resource allocation according to donation history, allocating the most resources to loyal donors (those who have given in the past):

- Gave more than 10 times in the past five years (10%)
- Gave 2 to 10 times in the past five years (10%)
- Gave only once, less than five years ago (5%)
- Gave only once, more than five years ago (5%)
- Never gave at this blood center (70%)

In reality, marketers rarely limit their segmentation to the use of only one variable as we did to illustrate each of these variables. More often, they use a combination of variables that provide a rich profile of a segment or help to create smaller, better-defined target groups.[6] Even if, for example, the blood center decided to target the 20% of the market who had given more than once in the past five years, they might further refine the segment by blood type if a particular type was in short supply and high demand.

Stages of Change

The *stages of change model*, also referred to as the *transtheoretical model*, was originally developed by Prochaska and DiClemente in the early 1980s[7] and has been tested and refined over the past decades. In a 1994 publication, *Changing for Good*, Prochaska, Norcross, and DiClemente describe six stages that people go through to change their behavior.[8] As you read about each one, imagine the implications for a specific population you are working with or, if you are a student, one you have chosen for the focus of a class project.

Precontemplation: "People at this stage usually have no intention of changing their behavior, and typically deny having a problem."[9] Relative to the behavior you are "selling," you could think of this market as "sound asleep." They may have woken up and thought about it at some point in the past, but they have gone back to sleep. In the case of an effort to convince people to quit smoking, this segment is not thinking about quitting, doesn't consider their tobacco use a problem, or tried once in the past but decided not to try again.

Contemplation: "People acknowledge that they have a problem and begin to think seriously about solving it."[10] Or they may have a want or desire and have been thinking about fulfilling it. They are "awake but haven't moved." This segment of smokers is considering quitting for any number of reasons but hasn't definitely decided and hasn't taken any steps.

Table 5.1 Major Segmentation Variables for Consumer Markets

Variable	Sample Classifications
Geographic	
World, region, or country	North America, Canada, Western Europe, Middle East, Pacific Rim, China, India, Brazil
Country or region	Pacific, Mountain, West North Central, West South Central, East North Central, East South Central, South Atlantic, Middle Atlantic, New England
City or metro size	Under 5,000; 5,000–20,000; 20,000–50,000; 50,000–100,000; 100,000–250,000; 250,000–500,000; 500,000–1,000,000; 1,000,000–4,000,000; over 4,000,000
Density	Urban, suburban, exurban, rural
Climate	Northern, southern
Demographic	
Age	Under 6, 6–11, 12–19, 20–34, 35–49, 50–64, 65 and over
Gender	Male, female
Family size	1–2, 3–4, 5 or more
Family life cycle	Young, single; married, no children; married with children; single parents; unmarried couples; older, married, no children under 18; older, single; other
Income	Under $10,000; $10,000–$20,000; $20,000–$30,000; $30,000–$50,000; $50,000–$100,000; $100,000–$250,000; over $250,000
Occupation	Professional and technical; managers, officials, proprietors; clerical, sales; craftspeople; supervisors; operatives; farmers; retired; students; homemakers; unemployed
Education	Grade school or less, some high school, high school graduate, some college, college graduate
Religion	Catholic, Protestant, Jewish, Muslim, Hindu, other
Race	Asian, Hispanic, Black, White
Generation	Baby boomer, Generation X, Millennials
Nationality	North American, South American, British, French, German, Russian, Japanese, other
Psychographic	
Social class	Lower lower, upper lower, working class, middle class, upper middle, lower upper, upper upper
Lifestyle	Achievers, strivers, strugglers
Personality	Compulsive, outgoing, authoritarian, ambitious
Behavioral	
Occasions	Regular occasion, special occasion, holiday, seasonal
Benefits	Quality, service, economy, convenience, speed
User status	Nonuser, cx-user, potential user, first-time user, regular user
Usage rate	Light user, medium user, heavy user
Loyalty status	None, medium, strong, absolute
Readiness stage	Unaware, aware, informed, interested, desirous, intending to buy
Attitude toward product	Enthusiastic, positive, indifferent, negative, hostile

Source: From *Principles of Marketing*, 9th ed. (p. 252), by P. Kotler and G. Armstrong. Copyright © 2001. Reprinted by permission of Pearson Education, Inc., Upper Saddle River, NJ.

Preparation: "Most people in the Preparation Stage are (now) planning to take action . . . and are making the final adjustments before they begin to change their behavior."[11] Back to our analogy, they are "sitting up"—maybe they even have their feet on the floor. In this segment, smokers have decided to quit and may have told others about their intentions. They probably have decided how they will quit and by when.

Action: "The Action Stage is one in which people most overtly modify their behavior and their surroundings. They stop smoking cigarettes, remove all desserts from the house, pour the last beer down the drain, or confront their fears. In short, they make the move for which they have been preparing."[12] They have "left the bed." This segment has recently stopped smoking cigarettes. However, it may not be a new habit yet.

Maintenance: "During Maintenance individuals work to consolidate the gains attained during the action and other stages and struggle to prevent lapses and relapse."[13] Individuals in this segment have not had a cigarette for perhaps six months or a year and remain committed to not smoking. However, at times they have to work to remind themselves of the benefits they are experiencing and distract themselves when they are tempted to relapse.

Termination: "The Termination stage is the ultimate goal for all changers. Here, a former addiction or problem will no longer present any temptation or threat."[14] This segment is not tempted to return to smoking. They are now "nonsmokers" for life.

One of the attractive features of this model is that the authors have identified a relatively simple way to assess a market's stage. They suggest four questions to ask, and, on the basis of responses, respondents are categorized in one of the four stages.[15] Table 5.2 summarizes the groupings by stage of change on the basis of the four responses.

In the model shown in Box 5.1, the "name of the marketer's game" is to move segments to the next stage. The authors (Prochaska, Norcross, and DiClemente) offer cautions:

Linear progression is a possible but relatively rare phenomenon. In fact, people who initiate change begin by proceeding from contemplation to preparation to action to

Table 5.2 Determining Stage of Change

Decision/Response Taken	Decision/Response Taken By:				
	Precontemplation Segment	Contemplation Segment	Preparation Segment	Action Segment	Maintenance Segment
I solved this problem more than 6 months ago	No	No	No	No	Yes
I have taken action within the past 6 months	No	No	No	Yes	Yes
I intend to take action in the next month	No	No	Yes	Yes	Yes
I intend to take action in the next 6 months	No	Yes	Yes	Yes	Yes

---

Box 5.1
Stages of Change Progression

Precontemplation ⇒ Contemplation ⇒ Preparation ⇒
Action ⇒ Maintenance ⇒ Termination

---

maintenance. Most, however, slip up at some point, returning to the contemplation or sometimes even the precontemplation stage before renewing their efforts.[16]

Figure 5.4 is Prochaska et al.'s graphic representation of the more likely patterns of change, a spiral one.

Diffusion of Innovation

Commercial marketers have long referred to Everett Rogers's diffusion of innovation theory, which states that when a product is introduced into the marketplace, the first to buy are the *Innovators* and *Early Adopters*. Next are the *Early* and *Late Majorities*. And finally, there are the *Laggards*, sometimes never buying. Some consider this model one of the more important ones for attempting to segment the market and influence the behavior of large groups of people. Kotler and Roberto describe this concept of diffusion (or spread) of the adoption of new behaviors through a population-referencing original work by Rogers and Shoemaker:

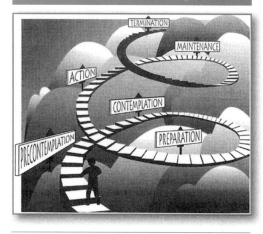

Figure 5.4 The spiral of change.

Source: J. Prochaska, J. Norcross, and C. DiClemente, *Changing for Good* (New York: Avon Books, 1994), 40–56.

> The ability of social marketers to plan and manage the diffusion or spread of adoptions to the largest possible target-adopter population requires an understanding of both individual behavior and the mechanisms by which new ideas and practices spread to the larger group or population of target adopters. . . .

Innovation diffusion research suggests that different types of adopters accept an innovation at different points in time. Table 5.3 summarizes the size, timing of adoption, and motivations for adoption of each target-adopter segment. The diffusion process begins with a small (2.5 percent) segment of innovative-minded adopters. These adopters are drawn to novelty and have a need to be different. They are followed by an early segment of target adopters (13.5 percent), who are drawn by the social product's intrinsic value. A third early majority segment (34 percent) perceive the spread of a product and decide to go along with it, out of their need to match and imitate. The late majority (34 percent) jump on the bandwagon, and the remaining segment, the laggards (16 percent), follow suit as the product attains popularity and broad acceptance.[17]

Social marketers make use of this model as well. See Box 5.2 for a version reinterpreted for social marketers.

Table 5.3 Elements of the Diffusion of Innovation Model That Are Useful for Diffusion Planning

Target-Adopter Segments	Hypothetical Size (%)	Timing Sequence of Adoption	Motivation for Adoption
Innovator segment	2.5	First	Need for novelty and need to be different
Early Adopter segment	13.5	Second	Recognition of adoption object's intrinsic/convenience value from contact with innovators
Early Majority segment	34.0	Third	Need to imitate/match and deliberateness trait
Late Majority segment	34.0	Fourth	Need to join the bandwagon triggered by the majority opinion legitimating the adoption object
Laggard segment	16.0	Last	Need to respect tradition

Source: Adapted with permission of The Free Press, a division of Simon & Schuster, Inc., from *Communications of Innovations: A Cross-Cultural Approach* (2nd ed.), by Everett M. Rogers, with F. Floyd Shoemaker. Copyright @ 1962, 1971 by The Free Press.

Healthstyles Segmentation

Another segmentation model used for health-related program planning appears in Table 5.4. This system incorporates several segmentation variables, including demographics, psychographics, and knowledge, attitudes, and current behaviors related to personal health. Resulting segments provide planners with a rich and memorable picture of each potential target audience, aiding in the development of winning strategies for that market. For example, a physical activity campaign wanting to influence *Decent Dolittles*, who may not have confidence in their ability to exercise, might emphasize the benefits of moderate physical activity, how it can fit into everyday life and activities, and the opportunities to "hang out with friends" while doing it. By contrast, a strategy to influence the *Tense but Trying* segment would switch the emphasis to the health benefits of exercise, especially for stress-related illnesses.

Box 5.2
"Show Me"/"Help Me"/"Make Me": A Social Marketing Version of the Diffusion of Innovation Model

When a new behavior is introduced into the marketplace, the first two groups (innovators and early adopters) usually only need someone to show them what to do to be healthy, prevent injuries, protect the environment, and contribute to their communities. Information and education are typically all it takes with this group, so we call them the "just *Show Me* group."

The two middle, and typically largest, groups (early and late majority) have some interest in doing the behavior, or at best are not opposed to it. But they have barriers to action. They need goods and services to stop smoking, like tobacco quitlines. They need incentives to insulate their attic, like reduced electrical bills. And they need more convenient times and locations to recycle their unwanted prescription medications, like at their pharmacy. We call this group the "please *Help Me* group." This is the group that social marketers were "born for," the one that should receive most of our attention and resources.

And the final group (laggards) aren't at all interested in doing the behavior, and most likely won't unless we pass and enforce laws and fines. We call them the "you'll have to *Make Me* group."

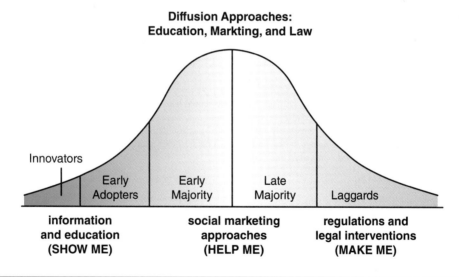

**Diffusion Approaches:
Education, Markting, and Law**

Innovators

Early Adopters | Early Majority | Late Majority | Laggards

information and education (SHOW ME) | **social marketing approaches (HELP ME)** | **regulations and legal interventions (MAKE ME)**

Graphic based on Everett Rogers's diffusion of innovations model, reinterpreted by Jay Kassirer, Mike Rothschild, Dave Ward, and Kristen Cooley.

Table 5.4 Healthstyles Segmentation System, American Healthstyles Audience Segmentation Project

Decent Dolittles (24%)

They are one of the less health-oriented groups. Although less likely to smoke or drink, they also are less likely to exercise, eat nutritiously, and work to stay at their ideal weights. Decent Dolittles know that they should be performing these behaviors to improve their health, but they do not feel that they have the ability. Their friends and family tend to avoid these behaviors as well. They describe themselves as "religious," "conservative," and "clean."

Active Attractives (13%)

They place a high emphasis on looking good and partying. Active Attractives are relatively youthful and moderately health oriented. They tend not to smoke and limit their fat intake more than do other groups. They are highly motivated, intending to exercise and keep their weight down, but they do not always succeed at this. Alcohol consumption is an important part of their lifestyle, and Active Attractives often are sensation seekers, constantly looking for adventure. They describe themselves as "romantic," "dynamic," "youthful," and "vain."

Hard-Living Hedonists (6%)

They are not very interested in health and tend to smoke and drink alcohol more heavily and frequently than do other groups. They also enjoy eating high-fat foods and do not care about limiting their fat intake. Despite this, they tend not to be overweight and are moderately physically active. Although they are the group least satisfied with their lives, they have no desire to make any health-related changes. Hard-Living Hedonists also are more likely to use stimulants and illicit drugs than are other segments. They describe themselves as "daring," "moody," "rugged," "independent," and "exciting."

Tense but Trying (10%)

They are similar to the more health-oriented segments except that they tend to smoke cigarettes. They are average in the amount of exercise they get and in their efforts to control their fat intake and weight. They have a moderate desire to exercise more, eat better, and control their weight more effectively as well. The Tense but Trying tend to be more anxious than other groups, with the highest rate of ulcers and use of sedatives and a higher number of visits to mental health counselors. They describe themselves as "tense," "high-strung," "sensitive," and "serious."

Noninterested Nihilists (7%)

They are the least health oriented and do not feel that people should take steps to improve their health. Accordingly, they smoke heavily, actively dislike exercise, eat high-fat diets, and make no efforts to control their weight. Despite this, they tend to drink alcohol only moderately. Of all the groups, Noninterested Nihilists have the highest level of physical impairment, the most sick days in bed, and the most medical care visits related to an illness. They describe themselves as being "depressed," "moody," and "homebodies."

Physical Fantastics (24%)

They are the most health-oriented group, leading a consistently health-promoting lifestyle. They are above average in not smoking or drinking, exercising routinely, eating nutritiously, and making efforts to control their weight. They tend to be in their middle or latter adult years and have a relatively large number of chronic health conditions. Physical Fantastics follow their physicians' advice to modify their diets and routinely discuss health-related topics with others.

Passive Healthy (15%)

They are in excellent health, although they are somewhat indifferent to living healthfully. They do not smoke or drink heavily and are one of the most active segments. Although they eat a high amount of dietary fat, they are the trimmest of all the groups. The Passive Healthy do not place much value on good health and physical fitness and are not motivated to make any changes in their behaviors.

Source: Reprinted by permission of Sage Publications Ltd. from Maibach, E. A., Ladin, E. A. K., and Slater, M., "Translating Health Psychology Into Effective Health Communication: The American Healthstyles Audience Segmentation Project," in *Journal of Health Psychology, I,* pp. 261–277. As appeared in Weinreich, N., *Hands-On Social Marketing: A Step-by-Step Guide* (p. 55).

Environmental Segmentation

Professor Ed Maibach at George Mason University is passionate about audience segmentation:

> Selecting the right audience may be the most important decision you make. For both upstream and downstream social marketing programs, it is critically important to identify the people who you can influence, and who, if you succeed in influencing them, will make the biggest difference in improving the situation you seek to improve.[18]

With the goal of improving climate-change public engagement initiatives, Maibach, Leiserowitz, and Roser-Renouf conducted a national study to identify distinct and motivationally coherent groups within the American public.[19] In the fall of 2008, they conducted a nationally representative web-based survey to measure Americans' climate-change beliefs, issue involvement, policy preferences, and behaviors. Using market segmentation techniques, they identified six distinct groups and described them as follows (see also Figure 5.5 on page 145):

- The *Alarmed* (18%) are the segment most engaged in the issue of global warming. They are completely convinced it is happening, caused by humans, and a serious and urgent threat. The Alarmed are already making changes in their own lives and support an aggressive national response.
- The *Concerned* (33%) are moderately convinced that global warming is a serious problem, but while they support a vigorous national response, they are distinctly less involved in the issue and less likely than the Alarmed to take personal action.
- The *Cautious* (19%) also believe that global warming is a problem, although they are less certain that it is happening than the Alarmed or the Concerned. They don't view it as a personal threat and don't feel a sense of urgency to deal with it through personal or societal actions.
- The *Disengaged* (12%) haven't thought much about the issue. They are the segment most likely to say that they could easily change their minds about global warming, and they are the most likely to select the "don't know" option in response to every survey question about global warming where "don't know" is presented as an option.
- The *Doubtful* (11%) are evenly split among those who think global warming is happening, those who think it isn't, and those who don't know. Many within this group believe that if global warming is happening, it is caused by natural changes in the environment, that it won't harm people for many decades into the future, if at all, and that America is already doing enough to respond to the threat.
- The *Dismissive* (7%), like the Alarmed, are actively engaged in the issue, but on the opposite end of the spectrum. The large majority of the people in this segment believe that global warming is not happening, is either not a threat to people or is not caused by humans, and is not a problem that warrants a personal or societal response.

Subsequently, Maibach and colleagues developed a brief (15-item) survey instrument—and accompanying SPSS and SAS macros—so that other researchers and campaign planners can identify the prevalence of the Six Americas within their target population.

Figure 5.5 Proportions of the U.S. adult population in the Six Americas.

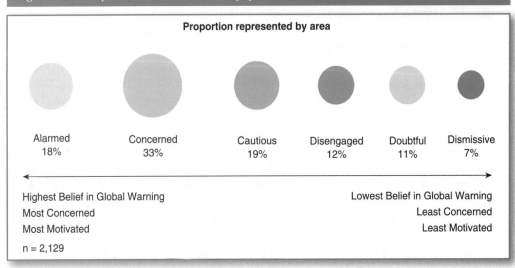

Source: A. Leiserowitz and E. Maibach, *Global Warming's "Six Americas": An Audience Segmentation* (Fairfax, VA: George Mason University, Center for Climate Change Communication, 2010).

Generational Segmentation

Some researchers and theorists point to the power of market segmentation on the basis of generation. Every generation is profoundly influenced by the times in which it grows up—the music, movies, politics, technological advances, economics, and defining events of the period (e.g., the Great Depression, 9/11, world wars). Demographers refer to generational groups as *cohorts*, members of which share similar major cultural, political, and economic experiences.[20] The five groups in Table 5.5 are a blend of several popular generational segmentation typologies.[21]

Of significance to social marketers is that these cohort segments and characteristics may provide unique insight into current beliefs, attitudes, and other behavioral influences. Kotler and Keller suggest, however, that we consider the impact that additional variables have on these cohorts. For example, two individuals from the same cohort (Baby Boomers) may differ in their *life stages* (e.g., one recently divorced and the other never married); *physiographics*, that is, conditions related to a person's age (e.g., one coping with hair loss and the other diabetic); and/or *socioeconomics* (e.g., one having recently lost a job and the other having received an inheritance).[22] This more multivariate analysis will lead to greater insights and therefore more efficient and effective targeting, a technique illustrated in the research highlight at the end of this chapter.

Cluster Systems: PRIZM and VALS

Two well-known commercial models used to group consumer markets into homogeneous segments, often referred to as clusters, are the PRIZM NE and VALS products.

PRIZM NE is a geodemographic classification system offered by the Claritas Corporation that describes every U.S. neighborhood in terms of 66 distinct social group

Table 5.5   Generational Segments

Born	Name	Age (2014)	Major characteristics
1927–1945	Traditionalists	69–87 yrs.	Loyal, hardworking, disciplined, patriotic, civic minded
1946–1964	Baby Boomers	49–68 yrs.	Optimistic, driven, competitive, career centered
1965–1977	Generation X	27–49 yrs.	Cynical, self-starters, independent, resourceful, media savvy
1978–1994	Generation Y	20–26 yrs.	Edgy, focused on urban style, more idealistic than Gen-X
1995–2002	Millennials	12–19 yrs.	Tech savvy, multicultural, grew up in affluent society

types, called "segments."[23] Each zip code is assigned one or several of these 66 clusters based on the shared socioeconomic characteristics of the area. This system is based on the fundamental premise that "birds of a feather flock together" and that when choosing a place to live, people tend to seek out neighborhoods compatible with their lifestyles, where they find others in similar circumstances who have similar consumer behavior patterns. Segments are given snappy, memorable names like "God's Country," "Red, White & Blues," "Kids & Cul-de-Sacs," and "Blue Blood Estates." Each segment is then described for the user, providing demographic as well as lifestyle-related behaviors. For example, a state department of ecology interested in reducing litter might be interested in having Claritas analyze the addresses and zip codes of citizens receiving tickets for littering, which will provide information that will help the department with messages and communication strategies, such as what bus routes in the city would be best for ads promoting the $1,025 fine for littering lit cigarette butts.

The well-known VALS segmentation system categorizes U.S. adult consumers into one of eight segments, indicative of personality traits considered to be determinants (drivers) of buying behaviors. The eight primary VALS consumer types are shown graphically in the VALS framework (see Figure 5.6.) The horizontal dimension in the figure represents the primary motivations and the vertical dimension represents resources. Using the primary motivation and resources dimensions, VALS defines eight primary types of adult consumers who have different attitudes and exhibit distinctive behavior and decision-making patterns. How would you use this? If you are a nonprofit organization with a mission of increasing voter turnout, this system might be very helpful in first identifying segments representing the greatest opportunities for increased voting, creating an offer this group would find particularly motivating, and then, by using the GeoVALS system, targeting a direct-mail campaign or get-out-to-vote effort in zip codes with high concentrations of these types.

Segmenting Target Audiences Midstream and Upstream

To this point, we have been focusing on market segmentation variables for those we are interested in targeting for adoption of a behavior, sometimes referred to as

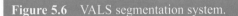

Figure 5.6 VALS segmentation system.

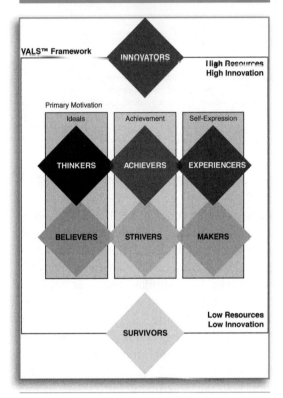

Source: SRI Consulting Business Intelligence (SRIC-BI).

downstream audiences. As you read in Chapter 1, however, real social change strategies benefit from influencing markets midstream and/or upstream from the individual:

- *Midstream audiences* include family members, friends, neighbors, church leaders, health care providers, teachers, law enforcement, entertainers, media, Facebook friends, and others closer to your target audience, especially ones they listen to, observe, or look up to.
- *Upstream audiences* include policymakers, school districts, corporations, foundations, and other groups with decision-making power and/or resources for creating infrastructures, business practices, and environments that support behavior change (e.g., bike lanes, labeling of serving sizes on packages, Breathalyzers in bars, placement of healthy foods in school cafeterias).

The segmentation process is the same for these populations, but the variables are likely to differ. Family members, for example, may be segmented by spouses versus children, and healthcare providers may be segmented by pharmacists versus pediatricians. Politicians might be segmented by what committees they serve on or by political party. The corporate market will more likely be segmented by industry type, schools by administrative level, and foundations by areas of focus. Once the market is segmented, you will still proceed to the next two steps of evaluation and selection.

Combination of Variables

As noted earlier, it is rare that a market will be segmented using only one variable. However, one base is often used as a primary way to group a market (e.g., age for immunization); then each segment is further profiled using descriptive variables (e.g., related behaviors) and perhaps narrowed by using additional important and relevant variables that predict response to strategies (e.g., education and income levels within each of the age segments for immunization).

"The most appropriate segmentation variables are those that best capture differences in the behavior of target adopters."[24] For social marketing planning, we encourage you to consider using behavior-related segmentation variables as the primary base for profiling the market, similar to the ones in the stages of change model described earlier. Segments are then profiled using other meaningful variables. Table 5.6 illustrates a hypothetical profile of market segments that a planner might compile at this stage in the planning process. References to how these relate to the diffusion model are noted. This profile uses Andreasen's version of the stages of change model, which collapses the six stages to four, a model more manageable for some programs. The issue is litter on roadways. The market is people who smoke in cars.[25]

CRITERIA FOR EVALUATING SEGMENTS

Once the marketplace has been grouped into meaningful population segments, the next task is to evaluate each segment in preparation for decisions regarding selection of target audiences.

For social marketers, Andreasen cites nine factors for evaluating segments relative to each other.[26] A list of these factors follows, with typical questions that might be asked to establish each measure. To further illustrate each factor, a situation is described in which a state health agency is deciding whether middle school students would be the most attractive segment for promoting safe sex. This segment would then be compared to a similar evaluation of high school students.

1. *Segment size:* How many people are in this segment? What percentage of the population do they represent? (How many middle school youth are sexually active?)

2. *Problem incidence:* How many people in this segment are either engaged in the "problem-related behavior" or not engaged in the "desired behavior"? (What percentage of middle school youth are having unprotected sex?)

3. *Problem severity:* What are the levels of consequences of the problem behavior in this segment? (What is the incidence of sexually transmitted diseases and pregnancy among middle school youth?)

4. *Defenselessness:* To what extent can this segment "take care of themselves" versus needing help from others? (What percentage of middle school youth have easy access to condoms?)

5. *Reachability:* Is this an audience that can be easily identified and reached? (Are there communication channels and other venues that we can use for safe-sex messages specifically targeting middle school youth?)

6. *General responsiveness:* How "ready, willing, and able" to respond are those in this segment? (How concerned are middle school youth about sexually transmitted diseases and pregnancy? How do they compare with high school students or college students in this regard? Which group has been most responsive to similar campaign messages in the past?)

Table 5.6 Hypothetical Segmentation Using Stages of Change as Primary Bases

Stage of Change	Precontemplation (The Make Me's)	Contemplation (The Help Me's)	Preparation for or in Action (The Help Me's)	Maintenance (The Show Me's)
Behavior and intent	Throw cigarette butts out the window and aren't concerned about it.	Throw cigarette butts out the window, feel bad about it, and have been thinking about not doing it.	Sometimes throw cigarette butts out the window and sometimes use ashtray. Trying to increase use of ashtray.	Never throw cigarette butts out the window; use ashtray instead.
Size	20%	30%	30%	20%
Geographics (residence)	Rural (10%) Suburban (40%) Urban (50%)	Rural (8%) Suburban (55%) Urban (37%)	Rural (6%) Suburban (65%) Urban (29%)	Rural (5%) Suburban (70%) Urban (25%)
Demographics (age)	16–20 (60%) 21–34 (25%) 35–50 (10%) 50+ (5%)	16–20 (53%) 21–34 (22%) 35–50 (15%) 50+ (10%)	16–20 (45%) 21–34 (20%) 35–50 (20%) 50+ (15%)	16–20 (30%) 21–34 (18%) 35–50 (27%) 50+ (25%)
Psychographics (environmental ethic)	Environmentally: Concerned (10%) Neutral (30%) Not concerned (60%)	Environmentally: Concerned (15%) Neutral (45%) Not concerned (40%)	Environmentally: Concerned (30%) Neutral (40%) Not concerned (30%)	Environmentally: Concerned (60%) Neutral (30%) Not concerned (10%)

7. *Incremental costs:* How do estimated costs to reach and influence this segment compare with those for other segments? (Are there free or inexpensive distribution channels for condoms for middle school youth? How does this compare with those for high school and college students? Are there campaigns from other states that have been proven to work well with middle school youth, or will we need to start from scratch?)

8. *Responsiveness to marketing mix:* How responsive is this market likely to be to social marketing strategies (product, price, place, and promotion)? (What are the greatest influences on middle school youths' decisions relative to their sexual activity? Will the parents of middle school youth, more so than those of high school or college students, be concerned about potential programs and messages?)

9. *Organizational capabilities:* How extensive is our staff expertise and the availability of outside resources in terms of assisting in the development and implementation of activities for this market? (Is our experience and expertise with middle school youth as strong as it is with high school and college students?)

One potential evaluation methodology would use these nine factors to quantitatively score each segment, creating a rational way to then rank them. Two major steps are involved, the first calculating a *potential for effectiveness* score and the second a *potential for efficiency* score.

1. *Effectiveness scores* are determined from statistics and incidence data on four of the factors: segment size, problem incidence, problem severity, and defenselessness. The segment's population size is multiplied by percentages for incidence, severity, and defenselessness (i.e., size × incidence × severity × defenselessness). The resulting number becomes the segment's "true" market size relative to potential effectiveness.

2. *Efficiency scores* are determined from assessments of segments on the next five factors: reachability, responsiveness, incremental costs, responsiveness to marketing mix elements, and organizational capabilities. This process requires assigning some quantitative value or score to each segment relative to each factor.

HOW TARGET AUDIENCES ARE SELECTED

Market segmentation has identified and described relevant market segments. *Evaluation activities* provide information on each segment that will help you take the next step: deciding which and how many segments will be *target audiences* for the campaign or program being planned.

Three approaches are typical for commercial sector marketers and are useful concepts for the social marketer to consider:[27]

- *Undifferentiated marketing:* The organization decides to use the same strategy for all segments, focusing on what is "common in the needs of consumers rather than on what is different."[28] This approach is sometimes referred to as *mass-marketing* and involves trying to reach and influence the most people possible at one time. Undifferentiated campaigns include those promoting issues of concern to a large cross-section of the population (e.g., drinking eight glasses of water a day, wearing seatbelts, not drinking and driving, flossing teeth, sun protection, water conservation, learning CPR, voting, organ donation).
- *Differentiated marketing:* The organization develops different strategies for different audiences. This approach often includes allocating more resources to priority segments. Campaigns that would benefit from a differentiated strategy are those in which segments have clear and distinguishable wants and needs as well as recommended behaviors. This approach might be used for campaigns promoting water safety, physical activity, breast cancer screening, and commute reduction.
- *Concentrated marketing:* In this approach, some segments are eliminated altogether, and resources and efforts often concentrate on developing the ideal strategy for one or only a few key segments. Campaigns with narrow and concentrated foci might include those promoting folic acid to women of childbearing age, encouraging horse

farmers to cover manure piles to avoid contamination of streams, offering AIDS prevention outreach programs to drug abusers, or recruiting young single men as volunteers for mentoring youth at risk.

As introduced in the prior section, segments can be prioritized and ranked at this point using effectiveness and efficiency scores. This would be especially useful for campaigns using a differentiated or concentrated approach in which the most efficient and effective segments will be targeted.

WHAT APPROACH SHOULD BE CHOSEN?

Most organizations involved in social marketing (public sector agencies and nonprofit organizations) are faced with limited budgets. Segments will need to be prioritized, with a disproportionate amount of resources being allocated to the most effective and efficient segments. Some segments will need to be eliminated from the plan.

Target audiences (markets of greatest opportunity) emerge as those with the greatest need and are the most ready for action, easiest to reach, and best match for the organization. Measures used to assess each of these are as follows:

- *Greatest need:* size, incidence, severity, and defenselessness
- *Greatest readiness for action:* readiness, willingness, and ability to respond
- *Easiest to reach:* identifiable venues available for distribution and communication
- *Best match:* organizational mission, expertise, and resources

Targeting audiences of *greatest market opportunity* may run counter to a social marketer's natural desire and inclination (or mandate) to either (a) ensure that all constituent groups are reached and served (markets are treated equally) or (b) focus resources on segments in which the incidence and severity of the problem is the gravest (markets of greatest need). Concerns can be addressed by emphasizing that this is the most effective and efficient use of scarce resources, reassuring others that segmentation allows plans to be developed that are likely to succeed with individual segments, and explaining that additional segments can be addressed over time. You are simply prioritizing resources and efforts in an objective, systematic, and cost-effective way.

ETHICAL CONSIDERATIONS WHEN
SELECTING TARGET AUDIENCES

The musings at the beginning of the chapter expressing concern regarding resource allocation represent well the ethical dilemma at this phase in the planning process. In campaigns in which a majority of resources have been allocated to one or a few market segments, how do you address concerns about social inequity? Or what about reverse situations in which resources are allocated equally, when in fact only one or a few market segments have the greatest need? For example, a state water conservation effort may send messages to all residents in the state to voluntarily reduce water usage by a goal of 10% over the next six months: Take shorter showers. Flush one less time. But what if water levels and resources are actually adequate in half the state? Should residents on one side of the mountain (where it rains "all the time") be asked to make these sacrifices as well? What is fair?

Our recommendation, as it was when selecting a focus for your campaign, is that you present (or at least mention) a long-range plan that will eventually address groups you are not addressing in this phase.

CHAPTER SUMMARY

Selecting target audiences is a three-step process: (1) Segment the market, (2) evaluate segments, and (3) choose one or more segments for targeting. Traditional variables used to describe consumer markets include demographics, geographics, psychographics, and behavior variables. Five additional models frequently used by social marketing practitioners include stages of change, diffusion of innovation, healthstyles segmentation, environmental segmentation, and generational segmentation.

Target audiences are evaluated based on efficiency and effectiveness measures, using nine variables outlined by Andreasen and presented in this text: segment size, problem incidence, problem severity, defenselessness, reachability, general responsiveness, incremental costs, responsiveness to marketing mix, and organizational capabilities.

Three common targeting approaches include undifferentiated marketing (same strategy for all segments), differentiated marketing (different strategies for different audiences), and concentrated marketing (only a few key segments are targeted and with unique strategies).

It is recommended that the markets of "greatest opportunity" be recognized as those that have the greatest need, are most ready for action, are easiest to reach, and are the best match for the organization. (See Appendix A for a worksheet on prioritizing target audiences.)

RESEARCH HIGHLIGHT

Using Psychographic Segmentation to Inform Targeted Strategies to Reduce Substance Use Among College Students

(2010)

Segmenting a population into groups based on psychographic characteristics is probably more common among commercial marketers than among social marketers. As described earlier in this chapter, this technique groups individuals into homogeneous segments based on common values, lifestyles, and personality characteristics. Commercial marketers have found that these variables more often predict the appeal of an offer than do traditional demographic and geographic characteristics. This research highlight describes a psychographic segmentation effort of relevance for public health strategies. It is a summary of a lengthier article that appeared in the *Social Marketing Quarterly* in September, 2013: "Psychographic Segments of College Females and Males in Relation to Substance Use Behaviors," authored by Tiffany Suragh, Carla Berg, and Eric Nehl.[29]

Background

Public health efforts aimed at preventing tobacco, alcohol, and marijuana use and abuse in young adults are often tailored to characteristics of a specific group using demographics (e.g., college students), stages of change (e.g., not interested in reducing binge drinking), and/or health beliefs (e.g., low perceptions of risk). The authors of the case were intrigued, however, by the apparently effective use of psychographic segmentation by the tobacco and alcohol industries, and wondered if there would be applications for public health efforts. They learned, for example, that in the 1990s many private tobacco industry documents were released to the public as a part of the Master Settlement, revealing the industry's use of personality characteristics to advantageously design advertisements that would entice young adults to use their products.

In 2010, the authors conducted a research effort to identify and characterize segments of female and male college students using psychographic segmentation factors, and to then examine these segments to identify differences in substance use behaviors, controlling for sociodemographics.

Methodology

Respondents were recruited from six colleges in the Southeast, selected as a convenience sample to represent state universities (two), technical/community colleges (three), and a historically Black university (one). Three of the colleges were in urban areas and three were in rural settings. Random samples of 5,000 students at each school were drawn from a directory list and were sent an email invitation with a link to a consent form and then directed to the online survey. To increase response rates, students received up to three email invitations and were entered into a drawing for cash prizes of $1,000 (one prize), $500 (two prizes), and $250 (four prizes) at each participating school. A total of 4,840 (20.1%) students returned the survey, with a final count of 3,469 responses being used for analysis following elimination of those that did not answer questions key to determining psychographic characteristics.

The *online survey* took approximately 20 to 25 minutes to complete and included 230 questions related to the following topic areas:

- Health behaviors, including cigarette, other tobacco, alcohol, and marijuana use
- Sociodemographic characteristics, including age, gender, ethnicity, and type of school attended

- Psychographic characteristics, including nine questions adapted from Philip Morris tobacco industry surveys designed to assess personality characteristics, including self-descriptors (e.g. rebelliousness), descriptors of friends (e.g., most friends drink alcohol), future goals (e.g., chance of a happy family life), and religious service attendance.

Two additional assessments were used for cluster analyses, including the Brief Sensation Scale,[30] which assessed the appeal of sensation-seeking behaviors, such as "I would like to explore strange places" and "I like new and exciting experiences, even if I have to break the rules." A second assessment was the Ten-Item Personality Inventory,[31] measuring levels of extraversion, agreeableness, conscientiousness, emotional stability, and openness to experience, with two items measuring each factor.

Findings

In the end, three psychographically distinct groups were identified and described, with significant differences between males and females being noted (see Table 5.7):

- *The Safe Responsibles* were characterized as having high levels of agreeableness, conscientiousness, and emotional stability; high academic achievement; and regular attendance at religious services. Within this segment, both females and males had the overall lowest rates of drug use.

- *The Stoic Individualists* were characterized by lower scores on extraversion, sensation seeking, and openness and higher scores on a pessimistic outlook for future occupational and family success. Within this group, females had lower rates of tobacco use, marijuana use, and binge drinking than female Thrill-Seeking Socializers, but males had higher rates of tobacco and marijuana use than male Thrill-Seeking Socializers.

- *The Thrill-Seeking Socializers* were characterized by high levels of sensation seeking and extraversion. Among females, this group had the highest rates of tobacco, alcohol, and marijuana use, and males in this group had the highest rates of binge drinking.

Implications

Authors conclude that this study demonstrates the utility of cluster analysis to segment populations based on personality traits and on the association between these personality traits and rates of substance use among female and male college students. They encourage tailoring strategies to appeal to the unique personality of targeted segments, and to differences between females and males within each of these psychographic segments. For example, emphasis might be placed on preventing Safe Responsibles from engaging in progressively higher levels of substance abuse by appealing to their desire for high academic performance. For Stoic Individualists, a different approach is implicated for males than for females. For males, efforts might be explored that

Table 5.7 Summary of Substance Abuse by Psychographic Segments Among Females and Males

	FEMALES			MALES		
	Safe Responsibles	Stoic Individualists	Thrill-Seeking Socializers	Safe Responsibles	Stoic Individualists	Thrill-Seeking Socializers
Use Cigarettes	15.1%	19.8%	26.4%	26.1%	32.1%	27.6%
Use Other Tobacco Products	11.5%	11.1%	6.6%	24.8%	68.5%	31.5%
Binge Drink	14.6%	17.4%	27.1%	27.5%	35.8%	36.2%
Use Marijuana	8.1%	9.6%	16.5%	14.6%	27.0%	22.0%
Overall Drug Use	30.6%	35.5%	48.6%	46.4%	56.1%	56.8%

would promote alternative ways of externalizing behaviors, such as through exercise or increased interpersonal communications. And for females, it might be worthwhile to promote alternative ways of coping with emotions and difficult situations, such as speaking openly with friends or family. For Thrill-Seeking Socializers, planners could explore alternative, healthier ways of inducing pleasure and euphoria, ones that might involve group activities, given the value these individuals place on social interaction.

DISCUSSION QUESTIONS AND EXERCISES

1. In your own words, what is the difference between a population and a target audience? Give an example of each.

2. What segmentation variables are you most familiar with and/or use the most? Which new variables did you read about that interest you for future audience segmentation?

3. Describe the difference between a segmentation variable and a descriptive variable.

4. Reflect back on the Marketing Highlight on increasing alternative transportation in Portland. How would you justify the personal delivery of program materials to residents by a staff member on a bike? Or could you/would you?

5. What are the major criteria you would use to select among major potential target audiences?

CHAPTER 5 NOTES

1. R. C. Lefebvre, "An Integrative Model for Social Marketing," *Journal of Social Marketing* 1, no. 1 (2011): 62.

2. Tools of Change [website], http://toolsofchange.com/en/case-studies/detail/658.

3. Ibid.

4. P. Kotler and G. Armstrong, *Principles of Marketing* (Upper Saddle River, NJ: Prentice Hall, 2001), 265.

5. Ibid., 244.

6. Ibid., 253–259.

7. J. Prochaska and C. DiClemente, "Stages and Processes of Self-Change of Smoking: Toward an Integrative Model of Change," *Journal of Consulting and Clinical Psychology* 51 (1983): 390–395.

8. J. Prochaska, J. Norcross, and C. DiClemente, *Changing for Good* (New York: Avon Books, 1994), 40–56.

9. Ibid., 40–41.

10. Ibid., 40–41.

11. Ibid., 41–43.

12. Ibid., 44.

13. Ibid., 45.

14. Ibid., 46.

15. Ibid., 47.

16. "The Spiral of Change" from *Changing for Good* by James O. Prochaska, John C. Norcross, and Carlo C. Copyright © 1994 by James O. Prochaska. Used by permission of the author.

17. P. Kotler and E. L. Roberto (1989), *Social Marketing: Strategies for Changing Public Behavior* (New York: Free Press, 1989), 119, 126–127.

18. Personal communication from Edward Maibach to Nancy Lee, October 30, 2013.

19. A. Leiserowitz and E. Maibach, *Global Warming's "Six Americas": An Audience Segmentation* (Fairfax, VA: George Mason University, Center for Climate Change Communication, 2010).

20. P. Kotler and K. Keller, *Marketing Management* (Upper Saddle River, NJ: Prentice Hall, 2006), 251–252.

21. B. Tsui, "Generation Next," *Advertising Age* 72, no. 3, (January 1, 2001): 14–16; Anna Liotta, Resultance Incorporated, www.resultance.com.

22. Kotler and Keller, *Marketing Management*, 251–252.

23. SRI Consulting Business Intelligence (SRIC-B1).

24. Kotler and Roberto, *Social Marketing*, 149.

25. A. R. Andreasen, *Marketing Social Change: Changing Behavior to Promote Health, Social Development, and the Environment* (San Francisco: Jossey-Bass, 1995), 148.

26. Ibid., 177–179.

27. Kotler and Armstrong, *Principles of Marketing*, 265–268.

28. Ibid, p.266.

29. T. Suragh, C. Berg, and E. Nehl, "Psychographic Segments of College Females and Males in Relation to Substance Use Behaviors," *Social Marketing Quarterly* 19, no. 3 (2013): 172–187.

30. M. T. Stephenson, R. H. Hoyle, P. Palmgreen, and M. D. Slater, "Brief Measures of Sensation Seeking for Screening and Large-Scale Surveys," *Drug and Alcohol Dependence* 72 (2003): 279–286.

31. S. D. Gosling, P. J. Rentfrow, and W. B. Swann, "A Very Brief Measure of the Big-Five Personality Domains," *Journal of Research in Personality* 37 (2003), 504–528.

Chapter 6

SETTING BEHAVIOR OBJECTIVES AND TARGET GOALS

Focus. Tackle one "non-reducible" behavior at a time. As the name suggests, and Doug McKenzie-Mohr describes, a non-reducible behavior is one that cannot be divided further into more specific behaviors. This is critical, as barriers and benefits differ dramatically for different behaviors.

—Dr. Ed Maibach[1]
Director, Center for Climate Change Communication
George Mason University

We recognize the challenges, even resistance, some of you may have when it comes to this section in the planning process—that of setting campaign objectives (desired behaviors) and target goals (levels of behavior change). Do any of the following sound familiar?

- "I always have trouble choosing among the numerous optional good behaviors we want to promote. Why do we need to (once more) narrow our focus, as we did with target audiences? It seems to me the more we can get them to do, the better."
- "When I look at this model and the use of the terms *objective* and *goal*, I get confused, even discouraged. We were taught in public health programs that goals were what we were trying to accomplish, like decrease obesity. This model says that goals are the quantifiable measure of your objective. Does it matter?"
- "This goal setting is nice in theory but near to impossible, in my experience. If we haven't done this particular behavior change campaign before, how could we possibly know what kind of a target goal or milestone to set?"

In this chapter, steps will be outlined for:

- Selecting a specific behavior your effort is intended to promote
- Identifying any knowledge and belief objectives your effort will need to address in order to influence the desired behavior
- Setting target goals for levels of behavior change as a result of your effort

We chose this opening case to highlight the importance of giving a high priority to the behavior your target audience is most willing to do. As you will read, the behavior that was focused on in the past was one the target audience was not "buying."

MARKETING HIGHLIGHT

Reducing Deaths at Railroad Crossings in India

A Neuroscience Approach

(2010)

Background

Mumbai is not only a city with a railway system that carries nearly 7 million commuters on a daily basis, but it is also a city where a large number of people live in slums right next to the railway's tracks. For millions of these residents, the shortest route to work and/or the railway station is to cross the tracks at one of over 1,000 illegal trespassing points throughout the city (see Figure 6.1). This trespassing results in daily fatalities; in 2009 alone there were 3,706 deaths, averaging more than 10 every day. The Indian Railways had implemented numerous prevention strategies, including boundary walls, imprisonment of trespassers, human chains to block trespassing, warning signs, fences, advertising campaigns, and over-bridges. These efforts had failed, however, to significantly change behaviors, with the largest number of trespassing deaths occurring in the Central Railway, for example, right under a foot-overbridge.

In June 2009, Indian Railways approached FinalMile Consultants, a Mumbai-based behavior change consulting firm, to recommend new approaches. As

you will read, the firm conducted extensive ethnographic research and pertinent literature reviews, then recommended three new interventions using principles of cognitive neurology and behavioral economics to inspire behavior change strategies.

Target Audience, Desired Behavior, and Audience Insights

The team was first interested in understanding more about where and when the fatal trespassing incidents were occurring and who the major trespassers were. Based on the Railways' internal records, the team found that the vast majority of trespassing deaths happened far from the station. In fact, accidents were most likely to happen in places where very few people were crossing the tracks. Almost all accidents were happening during the day, and the individuals most likely to be in these accidents were men ages 15 to 39.

More than 200 hours of ethnographic research involved direct observation, with team members even crossing the railway tracks along with other trespassers, visiting exact locations where accidents had happened, and identifying likely causes of accidents. Their research led to the discovery of three major influencers of the trespassing behavior: (a) It was a *social norm*, with so many having crossed the tracks for so long; (b) it had become a *nonconscious behavior*, with most trespassers being preoccupied when crossing the tracks, either speaking on their phones or engaged in conversations with their friends; and (c) there was an *overconfidence bias*, with most having successfully crossed the tracks without incident thousands of times, believing "it's not going to happen to me."

A detailed review of relevant cognitive neuroscience literature was also inspiring. The Leibowitz Hypothesis, for example, suggests that people perceive larger objects, such as trains, to be moving more slowly than smaller objects approaching at the same speed.[2] Additionally, research has indicated that humans do not accurately estimate the rate at which space is closing between them and an approaching object, such as a train. Of interest were studies regarding deep-rooted unconscious mechanisms, including the *fight/flight response*, making it more likely that a trespasser, once alarmed, will run more quickly across the tracks—in front of another oncoming train on a parallel track. There is also the *cocktail party effect*, which happens, in this instance, when a trespasser faces two oncoming trains honking simultaneously. Focusing on one train, his brain drowns out the honk from the other train on a parallel track.

Based on these solid insights, the team concluded that because trespassing was most likely inevitable, the project should not focus on decreasing trespassing, but instead promote a behavior that would

Figure 6.1 Railway crossings result in daily fatalities.

Source: Photo courtesy of FinalMile Consulting.

reduce accidents while trespassing: crossing when it's safest.

Strategies

To promote crossing more safely, program planners developed four interventions and conducted a 12-month pilot at the Wadala station in Central Mumbai:

1. *Break overconfidence of trespassers by a radically different approach to signage.* This was accomplished by creating photos of a real person (representing the target audience) exhibiting fear-based facial expressions, and then presenting them in a repetitive manner at trespassing entry points (see Figure 6.2).

2. *Redesign the horn of the trains to improve alertness in trespassers.* Motormen were encouraged to break the horn into two distinct, discontinuous parts, creating a staccato effect instead of one long horn, based on the

Figure 6.2 Warning signs at entry points to break overconfidence.

Source: Photo courtesy of FinalMile Consulting.

Figure 6.3 Whistle boards warn trespassers before entering the track.

Source: Photo courtesy of FinalMile Consulting.

studies indicating the brain is more alert when there is a break in sound.

3. *Install whistle boards 120 meters from the tracks to warn trespassers before they cross.* This was designed to counter the flight response,

Figure 6.4 Yellow lines placed across tracks help trespassers more accurately determine speed of oncoming trains.

Source: Photo courtesy of FinalMile Consulting.

increase alertness, obviate the cocktail party effect, and dissuade the individual from crossing the tracks (see Figure 6.3).

4. *Provide more powerful speed references so that people can judge the speed of the train correctly.* Fluorescent yellow lines were placed across the tracks to help trespassers determine the speed of oncoming trains. As illustrated in Figure 6.4, the lines are placed closer together as the train gets closer.

Outcomes

During the first 12-month period of the experiment at one of the high-incident areas near the Wadala station, fatalities were reduced by 75%. As suspected, the number of trespassing incidents did not decrease, as the strategies highlighted in this case were intended to change the timing of the crossings. As of 2014, the Central Railway Zone of the Indian

Railways has scaled up implementation to include 51 locations across Mumbai.

Information for this case was provided by Biju Dominic of FinalMile Consulting and by a case study from S. Deshpande and N. Lee, *Social Marketing in India: Influencing Behaviors for Good* (New Delhi, India: SAGE, 2013).

STEP 4: SET BEHAVIOR OBJECTIVES AND TARGET GOALS

Once target audiences for a campaign have been selected, your next step is to establish *campaign objectives*, with the primary objective always being the very specific *behavior* you want to influence your audience to accept, modify, abandon, reject, switch, or continue. Social marketers are also encouraged to consider what are called "coupling behaviors" (e.g., checking your smoke alarm batteries when you change your clocks). As you will read, the key to success is to select single, doable behaviors—and then explain them in simple, clear terms.

This chapter presents examples of the three types of objectives associated with a social marketing campaign:

1. *Behavior objectives* (what you want your audience to do)

2. *Knowledge objectives* (what you want your audience to know)

3. *Belief objectives* (what you want your audience to believe or feel)

A social marketing campaign always has a behavior objective. When and if you determine there is something your audience needs to know or believe in order to "act," that objective is identified and incorporated as well. As will become clear, campaign behavior objectives (e.g., waiting until it is safest to cross a railway track) are different from the campaign purpose (e.g., reducing deaths at railway crossings), defined earlier in this model as the ultimate impact of a successful campaign on the social issue being addressed.

After determining campaign objectives, campaign *target goals* are established that are specific, measurable, attainable, relevant, and time sensitive (SMART).[3] Ideally, they specify targeted rates of change in behaviors, such as the increase in numbers of those in the target audience who will be performing the desired behavior at some future date. They may also establish desired changes in knowledge and belief, especially in cases where behavior change may be a long-term effort. We recognize that in some models, such as those used in public health, goals are the nonquantifiable components of a campaign. These, however, are usually referred to as "overarching goals." Target goals at this step in the planning process refer to campaign goals. This social marketing model is based on commercial marketing models, where goals are expressed as "sales goals." We recommend, however, that you feel free to reverse these labels to match your organization's language and culture.

Remember from Chapter 2 that this planning model should be considered spiral in nature? Objectives and goals established at this point should be considered *draft behavior objectives* and *target goals*. You may learn in Step 5, for example, when you "talk" with your target audience about these desired behaviors, that your objectives and target goals are not realistic, clear, or appropriate for them and should be revised. Your audience may express a misconception that will require an additional knowledge objective, or an attitude that a new belief objective will need to address. Or you might find when developing preliminary budgets that you will need to reduce your goals because of funding realities.

As a final overview of this step, keep in mind that objectives and goals will affect your campaign evaluation strategy. Given that campaign goals represent the foundation for campaign evaluation, it is crucial that goals be relevant to campaign efforts and able to be measured.

Table 6.1 illustrates key concepts that will be presented in this chapter, using an example of an effort that might be undertaken by a state department of transportation to reduce traffic injuries and deaths caused by drivers distracted while texting.

BEHAVIOR OBJECTIVES

All social marketing campaigns should be designed and planned with a specific behavior objective in mind. Even if the planner discovers that the campaign needs to include additional knowledge and belief objectives, a behavior objective will need to be identified that these additional elements will support. As you develop and consider potential behavior objectives for your efforts, the following five criteria should help you choose one with the greatest potential for meaningful change, or at least assist you in prioritizing them:

1. *Impact:* If your audience adopts the behavior, will it make a difference relative to the purpose of your campaign (e.g., decreasing teen pregnancies)? How does this compare with other behaviors being considered?

2. *Willingness:* Has your target audience heard of doing this behavior before? How willing or interested are they in doing this behavior? Do they perceive it will solve some problem or concern they have, or will it satisfy some unfulfilled need?

3. *Measurability:* Can the behavior be measured, either through observation, record keeping, or self-reporting? You should be able to "picture" your target audience performing the behavior (e.g., removing the plastic insert from the cereal box before sorting for recycling). And your target audience should be able to determine that they have performed the behavior (e.g., placing infants in cribs on their backs to reduce the risk of infant death).

4. *Market opportunity:* How many in the target audience are not currently doing the behavior? What, in other terminology, is the current penetration of this behavior in

Table 6.1   Example of a Campaign's Purpose, Focus, Objectives, and Goal

Campaign Purpose	Reduce traffic injuries and deaths
Focus	Texting while driving
Campaign Objectives	
Behavior Objective	To wait until you arrive at your destination to text
Knowledge Objective	To know the percentage of traffic accidents involving someone texting while driving
Belief Objective	To believe that texting while driving is a significant distraction
Target Goal	Decrease the number of traffic accidents associated with texting while driving by 25% in one year

the target audience segment? A behavior that few have adopted would garner a high score in terms of market opportunity.

5. *Market supply:* Does the behavior need more support? If some other organization is already "doing all that can be done" to promote this behavior, perhaps a different behavior would be more beneficial to the social issue.

At the end of Al Gore's book *An Inconvenient Truth*, 30 specific desired behaviors to reduce carbon emissions were listed. Ten were then selected for a handout titled "Tenthingstodo" and make an interesting prioritization exercise that could be approached using a grid like the one in Table 6.2.[4] Assume that once launched, efforts would then focus on highlighting two behaviors each year based on scores for each of the five criteria just mentioned. To keep it simple, each behavior could be rated on each criterion as high (3), medium (2), or low (1), as illustrated in the first row. Ideally, these ratings would be determined using objective information (e.g., citizen surveys, scientific data). In reality, the ratings might be more subjective in nature—which is still better than prioritizing behaviors using less rigorous means, such as informal conversations or hunches.

To increase the rigor (and value) of the exercise, you could also weight the criteria. For example, you could understandably decide that "Impact" was more important than other criteria and decide to double the score ($2 \times 2 = 4$). That way, something that was low impact (1) but had the highest scores on other criteria would not automatically surface as the number-one priority. In the Research Highlight for this chapter, you'll read in more detail about the steps involved in the systematic application of this process.

A behavior objective should be distinguished from several other planning components. It is not the same as a campaign slogan or campaign message, although it is used to develop both (e.g., "Eat five or more fruits and vegetables a day" became "5 a Day the Color Way™"). It is not quantifiable as we are defining it. The target goal is the quantifiable, measurable component that has implications for strategies and budget decisions and provides a benchmark for monitoring and measuring program success (e.g., did the

Table 6.2 Process for Prioritizing Behavior Objectives: High (3), Medium (2), Low (1)

Behaviors	Impact	Willingness	Measurability	Market Opportunity	Supply	Average
Change a light	2	3	3	3	1	2.4
Drive less						
Recycle more						
Check your tires						
Use less hot water						
Avoid products with a lot of packaging						
Adjust your thermostat						
Plant a tree						
Turn off electronic devices						
Spread the word						

average consumption of the number of fruits and vegetables increase from 2.5 to 4 per day by 2010?).

If you are familiar with logic models, you may be curious where social marketing objectives fit in the model. They should be noted as "outcomes" in the traditional model, reflecting behaviors changed as the result of program "outputs."

For those not familiar with logic models, these are visual schematics that show links between program processes (inputs, activities, and outputs) and program outcomes and impact. This tool will be discussed in more depth in Chapter 15, which covers evaluation.

Although a campaign may promote more than one behavior, it should be recognized that different tactics or strategies may be necessary to promote each one (e.g., getting people to use a litterbag will take different strategies than getting people to cover their loads in pickup trucks). Table 6.3 presents examples of potential behavior objectives in our familiar arenas of health, injury prevention, the environment, and community and financial well-being.

KNOWLEDGE AND BELIEF OBJECTIVES

When gathering background data and conducting the strengths, weaknesses, opportunities, and threats (SWOT) analysis, you probably learned from existing secondary

Table 6.3   Examples of Potential Behavior Objectives for Specific Audiences

Improving Health	
Tobacco use	Don't start smoking.
Heavy/binge drinking	Drink less than five drinks at one sitting.
Alcohol and drug use during pregnancy	Don't drink alcoholic beverages if you are pregnant.
Diabetes prevention	Exercise moderately 30 minutes a day, 5 days a week, at least 10 minutes at a time.
Teen pregnancy	Choose abstinence.
Sexually transmitted diseases	Use a condom.
Fat gram intake	Make sure total fat grams consumed are below 30% of total daily calories.
Water intake	Drink eight glasses of water a day.
Fruit and vegetable intake	Eat five servings of fruits and vegetables a day.
Obesity	Have your body mass index measured by a health care professional.
Breast cancer	Learn the proper procedure for examining your breasts.
Prostate cancer	Talk with your health care provider about an annual prostate exam if you are 50 years of age or older.
Oral health	Use a cup to give an infant juice instead of a bottle.
Osteoporosis	Get 1,000 to 1,200 milligrams a day of calcium.
Preventing Injuries	
Drinking and driving	Keep your blood alcohol level below 0.08% if you are drinking and driving.
Seatbelts	Buckle your seatbelt before you put your vehicle in gear.
Domestic violence	Have a plan that includes a packed bag and a safe place to go.
Gun storage	Store handguns in a lockbox or safe or use a reliable trigger lock.
Fires	Check smoke alarm batteries every month.
Falls	Include some form of strength building in your exercise routine.
Household poisons	Place recognizable stickers on all poisonous products in the kitchen, bathroom, bedroom, basement, and garage.
Bullying	Report bullying incidents to your teacher or parent.

(Continued)

Table 6.3 (Continued)

Protecting the Environment	
Waste reduction	Buy bulk and unpackaged goods rather than packaged items.
Wildlife habitat protection	Stay on established paths when walking through forests.
Forest destruction	Use materials made from recycled tires and glass for garden steps and paths.
Toxic fertilizers and pesticides	Follow instructions on labels and measure precisely.
Water conservation	Replace old toilets with new low-flow models.
Air pollution from automobiles	Don't top off the gas tank when refueling your car.
Air pollution from other sources	Use an electric or push mower instead of a gas-powered model.
Forest fires	Chip wood debris that can be used for composting instead of burning it.
Conserving electricity	Turn off computer monitors when leaving work at the end of the day.
Litter	Clean out litter that might blow out of the open back of your pickup truck.
Involving the Community	
Volunteering	Give five hours a week to a volunteer effort.
Mentoring	Encourage and support caring relationships between your child and a nonparent adult.
Acts of Terrorism	If you see something, say something.
Enhancing Financial Well-Being	
Bank accounts	Open a checking account.
Savings	Build a savings account equivalent to six months of income.
Using credit	Establish a monthly budget and follow it.

research or from prior similar campaigns that typical audiences need a little help before they are willing, sometimes even able, to act. They may need to have some *knowledge* (information or facts) and/or *belief* (values, opinions, or attitudes) before they are convinced that the action is doable and/or worth the effort. Those in the precontemplation stage, for example, typically don't believe they have a problem. Those in the contemplation stage may not have made up their mind that the effort (cost) is worth the gain (benefit). Even those in the action stage may not be aware of their accomplishments and therefore be vulnerable to relapses.

Knowledge objectives are those related to statistics, facts, and other information and skills your target audience would find motivating or important. Typically, the information has simply been unavailable to the audience or gone unnoticed. Here are examples:

- Statistics on risks associated with current behavior (e.g., percentage of obese women who have heart attacks versus those not medically obese)
- Statistics on benefits of proposed behavior (e.g., the amount of money you will have saved in a year by making small monthly deposits)
- Facts on attractive alternatives (e.g., lists of flowering native plants that are drought and disease resistant)
- Facts that correct misconceptions (e.g., cigarette butts are not biodegradable and can take more than 10 years to disintegrate completely)
- Facts that might be motivating (e.g., moderate physical activity has been proven to have some of the same important medical benefits as vigorous physical activity)
- Information on how to perform the behavior (e.g., how to prepare a home for an earthquake)
- Resources available for assistance (e.g., phone numbers where battered women can call to find temporary shelter)
- Locations for purchase of goods or services (e.g., locations where handgun lock-boxes can be purchased)
- Current laws and fines that may not be known about or understood (e.g., a fine of $1,025 can be imposed for tossing a lit cigarette)

Belief objectives are those related to attitudes, opinions, feelings, or values held by the target audience. The target audience may have current beliefs that the marketer may need to alter in order for them to act, or you may find that an important belief is missing, such as one of the following:

- That they will personally experience the benefits from adopting the desired behavior (e.g., increased physical activity will help them sleep better)
- That they are at risk (e.g., they currently believe they are capable of driving safely with a blood alcohol level of over 0.08)
- That they will be able to successfully perform the desired behavior (e.g., talk to their teenager about thoughts of suicide)
- That their individual behavior can make a difference (e.g., taking mass transit to work)
- That they will not be viewed negatively by others if they adopt the behavior (e.g., not accepting another drink)
- That the costs of the behavior will be worth it (e.g., establishing a bank account versus cashing paychecks at check-cashing services and pawn shops)
- That there will be minimal negative consequences (e.g., that organ donation information won't be shared with third parties)

These knowledge and belief objectives provide direction for developing subsequent strategies (positioning and the marketing mix). They have important implications *especially for developing a brand identity and key messages* that provide the information and arguments that will be most motivating. Advertising copywriters, for example, will reference these objectives when developing communication slogans, script, and copy. There are also opportunities for other elements of the marketing mix to support these additional objectives: for instance, an immunization product strategy that incorporates a free downloadable app to ensure that parents know the recommended schedule; an incentive offered by a utility for trading in gas mowers for mulch mowers as a way to convince homeowners of their harm to the environment; or a special website dedicated to purchasing booster seats, sponsored by a children's hospital, as a testimonial to the safety concern. Table 6.4 provides examples of each of the objectives described. It should be noted that even though each campaign illustrated has a knowledge and belief objective, this is neither typical nor required. As stated earlier, the behavior objective is the primary focus.

TARGET GOALS

Ideally, target goals establish a desired level of behavior *change* as a result of program efforts (e.g., from 10% of homeowners who check for leaky toilets on an annual basis to 20% in one year). To establish this target for the amount or percentage of change, you will, of course, need to know current levels of behavior among your target audience. In this regard, you are similar to commercial marketers, who establish sales goals for their products when developing annual marketing plans and then develop strategies and resource allocations consistent with these goals. Consider how the specificity and time-bound nature of the following goals would inspire and guide your planning and eventually help justify your resource expenditures:

- Increase by 25% in a 24-month period the percentage of women over the age of 50 in the country who get annual mammograms
- Increase the percentage of people in the state wearing seatbelts at checkpoints from 85% in 2011 to 90% by 2014
- Decrease the amount of glass, paper, aluminum, and plastic litter on interstate roadways by 4 million pounds in two years
- Increase the average number of caring adults in the lives of middle school youth in the school district from 1.5 to 3.0 over a period of three years

Target goals may also be set for knowledge and belief objectives, as illustrated in Table 6.5. Although the goals are hypothetical for the purposes of this illustration, the effort to increase the intake of folic acid as a way to prevent birth defects is real. The U.S. Public Service and the March of Dimes recommend that all women of childbearing age consume 400 micrograms of folic acid per day in a multivitamin in addition to eating a healthy diet (see Figure 6.5).

In reality, this process is difficult or impractical for many social marketing programs. Baseline data on current levels of behavior for a target audience may not be known or

Table 6.4   Purpose, Audience, and Objectives

Campaign Purpose	Target Audience	Behavior Objective	Knowledge Objective	Belief Objective
Reduced senior falls	Seniors 75 and older	Exercise five times a week, including strength and balance exercises.	One in three adults age 65 and older falls each year.	Risk of falling can be reduced by strengthening muscles and improving balance.
Reduced child injuries from automobile accidents	Parents with children ages 4 to 8	Put children who are ages 4 to 8 and weigh less than 80 pounds in booster seats.	Traffic accidents are the leading cause of death for children ages 4 to 8.	Children ages 4 to 8 weighing less than 80 pounds are not adequately protected by adult seatbelts.
Improved water quality	Small horse farmers within 5 miles of streams, lakes, or rivers	Cover and protect manure piles from rain.	Storm water runoff from piles can pollute water resources.	Even though your manure pile is small, it does contribute to the problem.
Increased number of registered organ donors	People renewing driver's licenses	Register to be an organ donor when you renew your driver's license.	Your family may still be asked to sign a consent form for your donation to occur.	Information will be kept private and can be accessed only by authorized officials.
Decreased number of unbanked in San Francisco	Residents relying on check cashers, pawn shops, and other fringe financial services charging high fees and interest rates	Open a Bank on San Francisco account, one established by a public-private partnership.	These accounts offer a low- or no-cost product with no minimum balance; consular identification cards are accepted as primary identification.	Participating banks will be easy to find; you will feel welcomed.

Table 6.5   Hypothetical Objectives and Target Goals

Purpose	Behavior	Knowledge	Belief
Reduce birth defects	What we want them to do	What they may need to know before they will act	What they may need to believe before they will act
Objective	Get 400 micrograms of folic acid every day	For it to help, you need to take it before you become pregnant, during the early weeks of pregnancy (see Figure 6.3).	Without enough folic acid, the baby is at risk for serious birth defects.
Target goal	Increase the percentage of women ages 18 to 45 who take a daily vitamin containing folic acid from 39% in 2008 to 50% by 2014.	Increase the percentage of women ages 18 to 45 who know folic acid should be taken before pregnancy from 11% in 2008 to 15% by 2014.	Increase the percentage of women ages 18 to 45 who believe folic acid prevents birth defects from 20% in 2008 to 30% by 2014.

Figure 6.5 Promoting daily use of a vitamin before pregnancy.

Get the **"B" Attitude**

That's "B" for the B vitamin folic acid.
Get the attitude by taking it every day. Folic acid may help save your baby from birth defects of the brain and spinal cord. But you have to take it every day before you get pregnant and in the first few weeks of your pregnancy for it to help.

B vitamin folic acid — Why you need it A baby needs folic acid right after it's conceived, before you even know you're pregnant. Folic acid helps the baby's brain and spinal cord develop properly. Without enough, the baby could have serious birth defects called neural tube defects.

March of Dimes

Source: Copyright © March of Dimes Birth Defects Foundation, 1999. Reprinted with permission.

may not be available in a timely or economically feasible way. Projecting future desired levels (goal setting) often depends on data and experience from years of tracking and analyzing the impact of prior efforts. Many social marketing efforts are being conducted for the first time, and historical data may not have been recorded or retained.

There are several excellent resources in the public health arena you can explore, however, that may provide data that guide efforts to establish baselines as well as goals.

- The Behavioral Risk Factor Surveillance System (BRFSS) was developed by the Centers for Disease Control and Prevention (CDC), headquartered in Atlanta, Georgia. It is used throughout the United States to measure and track the prevalence of major risk-related behaviors among Americans, including tobacco use, sexual behavior, injury prevention, physical activity, nutrition, and prevention behaviors, such as breast, cervical, and colorectal cancer screening. Details on this system are highlighted in Box 6.1.
- *Healthy People 2020* is managed by the Office of Disease Prevention and Health Promotion within the U.S. Department of Health and Human Services. It is a set of objectives with 10-year target goals designed to guide national health promotion and disease prevention efforts to improve the health of all people in the United States (see Box 6.2). It is used as a strategic management tool by the federal government, states, communities, and other public and private sector partners. Its set of objectives and targets is used to measure progress for health issues in specific populations and serves as a foundation for prevention and wellness activities across various sectors and within the federal government, as well as a model for measurement at the state and local levels.[5] Of interest to social marketers is the inclusion, for the first time, of three objectives related to social marketing (see Box 6.3).
- Explore the availability of data from peers in other agencies who may have conducted similar campaigns.
- Often nonprofit organizations and foundations with a related mission (e.g., the American Cancer Society) may have excellent data helpful in establishing meaningful campaign goals.

Box 6.1
The CDC's Unique State-Based Surveillance

In the early 1980s, the CDC worked with the states to develop the Behavioral Risk Factor Surveillance System (BRFSS). This state-based system, the first of its kind, made available information on the prevalence of risk-related behaviors among Americans and their perceptions of a variety of health issues. (See Figure 6.4.)

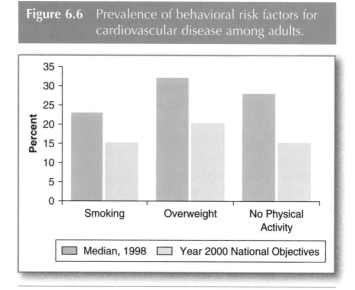

Figure 6.6   Prevalence of behavioral risk factors for cardiovascular disease among adults.

Source: Northeast Center for Agricultural and Occupational Health.

Now active in all 50 states, the BRFSS continues to be the primary source of information on major health risk behaviors among Americans. State and local health departments rely heavily on BRFSS data to:

- Determine priority health issues and identify populations at highest risk
- Develop strategic plans and target prevention programs
- Monitor the effectiveness of intervention strategies and progress toward achieving prevention goals
- Educate the public, the health community, and policymakers about disease prevention
- Support community policies that promote health and prevent disease

In addition, BRFSS data enable public health professionals to monitor progress toward achieving the nation's health objectives as outlined in *Healthy People 2020:*

(Continued)

(Continued)

National Health Promotion and Disease Prevention Objectives. BRFSS information is also used by researchers, volunteer and professional organizations, and managed care organizations to target prevention efforts.

The benefits of the BRFSS for states include the following:

- Data can be analyzed in a variety of ways. BRFSS data can be analyzed by a variety of demographic variables, including age, education, income, and racial and ethnic background. The ability to determine populations at highest risk is essential in effectively targeting scarce prevention resources.
- The BRFSS is designed to identify trends over time. For example, state-based data from the BRFSS have revealed a national epidemic of obesity.
- States can add questions of local interest. For example, following the bomb explosion at the Alfred P. Murrah Federal Building in Oklahoma City, the Oklahoma BRFSS included questions on such issues as stress, nightmares, and feelings of hopelessness so that health department personnel could better address the psychological impact of the disaster.
- States can readily address urgent and emerging health issues. Questions may be added for a wide range of important health issues, including diabetes, oral health, arthritis, tobacco use, folic acid consumption, use of preventive services, and health care coverage. In 1993, when flooding ravaged states along the Mississippi River, Missouri added questions to assess the impact of the flooding on people's health and to evaluate the capability of communities to respond to the disaster.

Although the BRFSS is flexible and allows for timely additions, standard core questions enable health professionals to make comparisons between states and derive national-level conclusions. BRFSS data have highlighted wide disparities between states on key health issues. In 2012, for example, the prevalence of current smoking among U.S. adults ranged from a low of 11% in Utah to a high of 28% in Kentucky. These data have also been useful for assessing tobacco control efforts. For instance, BRFSS data revealed that the annual prevalence of cigarette smoking among adults in Massachusetts declined after an excise tax increase and antismoking campaign were implemented.

Box 6.2
Healthy People 2020: **Topic Areas**

These topic areas of *Healthy People 2020* identify and highlight specific issues and populations. Each topic area is assigned to one or more lead agencies within the federal government that is responsible for developing, tracking, monitoring, and periodically reporting on objectives.

1. Access to health services
2. Adolescent health
3. Arthritis, osteoporosis, and chronic back conditions
4. Blood disorders and blood safety
5. Cancer
6. Chronic kidney disease
7. Dementias, including Alzheimer's disease
8. Diabetes
9. Disability and health
10. Early and middle childhood
11. Educational and community-based programs
12. Environmental health
13. Family planning
14. Food safety
15. Genomics
16. Global health
17. Healthcare-associated infections
18. Health communication and health information technology
19. Health-related quality of life and well-being
20. Hearing and other sensory or communication disorders
21. Heart disease and stroke
22. HIV
23. Immunization and infectious diseases
24. Injury and violence prevention
25. Lesbian, gay, bisexual, and transgender health
26. Maternal, infant, and child health
27. Medical product safety
28. Mental health and mental disorders
29. Nutrition and weight status
30. Occupational safety and health
31. Older adults
32. Oral health
33. Physical activity
34. Preparedness
35. Public health infrastructure
36. Respiratory diseases
37. Sexually transmitted diseases
38. Sleep health
39. Social determinants of health
40. Substance abuse
41. Tobacco use
42. Vision

Source: U.S. Department of Health and Human Services, Office of Disease Prevention and Health Promotion, http://www.healthypeople.gov/2020/topicsobjectives2020/default

---

Box 6.3
Healthy People 2020: **Health Communications and Health Information Technology Objectives Related to Social Marketing**

#13   To increase social marketing in health promotion and disease prevention:

13.1   Increase the proportion of State health departments that report using social marketing in health promotion and disease prevention programs

13.2   Increase the proportion of schools of public health and accredited master of public health (MPH) programs that offer one or more courses in social marketing

13.3   Increase the proportion of schools of public health and accredited MPH programs that offer workforce development activities in social marketing for public health practitioners

---

Source: HealthyPeople.gov, "Health Topics & Objectives," http://www.healthypeople.gov/2020/topicsobjectives2020/overview.aspx?topicid=18.

Pilots as a Way to Set Goals

Piloting is most often used to identify and address problems prior to campaign rollout and/or to test various potential strategies to determine which one(s) would be most effective. Pilots can also be used as a reference point for setting target goals. For example, a campaign to influence parents not to smoke around their children, with a focus on distribution of materials for children in elementary schools to take home to their parents, could be piloted at one school in a school district. A quantitative follow-up survey with parents regarding any changes in their behavior could help determine reasonable goals to set for campaign rollout in other schools. The advantages of this approach are not only the feedback you get from the target audience regarding the campaign, but also the increased credibility your effort will have with funders, providing an expected rate of return on their investments in terms of anticipated levels of behavior change. Methods for conducting pilots will be presented in Chapter 17.

Alternatives for Goal Setting

If baseline data are not available and setting target goals relative to behavior change is not practical or feasible at the time, the following alternatives might be considered for goal setting:

- Establish target goals for campaign awareness and recall. For example, a statewide tobacco prevention program establishes a goal for the first three months of an advertising campaign that 75% of the target audience (adults who smoke) will correctly recall the campaign slogan and two of the four television ads on an unaided basis. Results will then be presented to the state legislature to support continued funding of the campaign.

- Establish target goals for levels of knowledge. For example, a program for improved nutrition among low-income families sets a goal that 50% of women participating in a pilot project will correctly identify and describe the recommended daily servings of fruits and vegetables.
- Establish goals for acceptance of a belief. For example, a chain of gas stations is conducting a pilot project to influence customers not to top off their gas tanks and establishes a goal that 80% of customers, versus 25% prior to launch of the campaign, will report that they believe topping off a gas tank can be harmful to the environment.
- Establish target goals for a response to a campaign component. For example, a water utility will consider a campaign a success if 25% of residential customers call a well-publicized toll-free number or visit a website for a listing of drought-resistant plants.
- Establish target goals for intent to change behavior. For example, a state coalition promoting moderate physical activity is eager to know if a brief six-week pilot program increased interest in physical activity. They establish a goal that states their "reported intention to increase physical activity in the next six months from 20% to 30%, a 50% increase in behavior intent."
- Establish target goals for the campaign process. For example, a school-based program promoting sexual abstinence has a goal that 40 abstinence campaigns will be developed and implemented by youth in middle schools and high schools around the state during the upcoming school year.

In situations such as these, in which campaign goals are not specifically related to behavior change, it should be emphasized that campaign objectives should still include a behavior objective. Alternative goals relate to some activity that supports and promotes the desired behavior.

OBJECTIVES AND TARGET GOALS ARE ONLY A DRAFT AT THIS STEP

In Step 5 of this planning process, you will deepen your understanding of your target audience. You will learn more about their knowledge, beliefs, and current behaviors relative to objectives and goals established at this point, as well as their perceived barriers, desired benefits, and potential motivators. It is often necessary to then revise and finalize objectives and goals to make them more realistic, clear, and appropriate.

OBJECTIVES AND TARGET GOALS WILL BE USED FOR CAMPAIGN EVALUATION

One of the last steps (Step 8) in developing a social marketing plan will be to develop an evaluation plan, a process covered in Chapter 15. It is important to emphasize at this point, however, that the planner will need to return to Step 4 of the plan, setting campaign objectives and goals, and select methodologies and develop plans to measure these stated goals. Examples of items that would need to be measured include:

- Number of mammograms among women in the pilot community
- Number of people stopped at checkpoints wearing seatbelts
- Pounds of specific types of litter on roadways
- Number of caring adult relationships that middle school youth have
- Number of women in childbearing years taking folic acid
- Number of bank accounts opened by the unbanked in San Francisco

The message is simple. Establish a goal that is meaningful to campaign efforts and that will be feasible to measure.

ETHICAL CONSIDERATIONS WHEN SETTING OBJECTIVES AND TARGET GOALS

What if trends indicate that a behavior objective you are planning to support (e.g., putting food waste in curbside pickup containers) is in conflict with the desired behaviors of other agency programs (e.g., backyard composting)? Or what if your research reveals that the goals that your funders or sponsors would like to support are not realistic or attainable for your target audience? For example, a community clinic may know they are to encourage pregnant women to quit smoking—completely. But what if research has shown that cutting down to nine cigarettes a day would have significant benefits for those not able to quit? Can the clinic consider their efforts a success if they persuade pregnant women to decrease from 24 cigarettes a day to nine? Do they suggest a more attainable behavior (maybe using the foot-in-the-door technique) for this segment instead of just sending a "quit" message?

CHAPTER SUMMARY

The primary objective of a social marketing campaign is behavior change. All social marketing campaigns should be designed and planned with a specific behavior objective in mind—something we want our target audience to do. Behavior objectives should be clear, simple, doable acts—ones that can be measured and that the target audience will know they have completed.

Occasionally, the social marketer will also need to establish one or two additional objectives. *Knowledge objectives* (something you want your target audience to know) are those related to statistics, facts, and other information your target audience would find motivating or important. *Belief objectives* (something you want your target audience to believe) are those related to attitudes, opinions, or values held by the target audience. The target audience may have current beliefs that the marketer will need to alter in order for them to act, or an important belief may be found missing.

Target goals are quantifiable, measurable, and relate to the specific campaign focus, target audience, and time frame. Ideally, they establish a desired level of behavior change as a result of program and campaign efforts. When establishing and measuring behavior change is not practical or economically feasible, alternatives can be considered, including measuring campaign awareness, response, process, and/or increase in knowledge, beliefs, and intention.

Given that campaign target goals represent the foundation for campaign evaluation, it is critical that goals be relevant to program efforts and measurable.

RESEARCH HIGHLIGHT

Reducing Energy Use in Australia

A Community-Based Social Marketing Approach to Behavior Selection

(2011)

Background

For Doug McKenzie-Mohr, an environmental psychologist, founder of community-based social marketing, and author of *Fostering Sustainable Behavior*,[6] your first and most important decision, after selecting a target audience, is to determine what behavior your plan will be developed to promote. His process is a rigorous one, relying on scientific data and quantitative audience research to identify potential behaviors and to then select the one with the greatest possible return on investment

of resources. This highlight outlines his five steps to support this effort, illustrated using an example of reducing energy use in Australia.

Method

1. *Identify potential behaviors,* ones actually producing environmental benefits. Selection of potential behaviors for this list should be guided by two criteria. First, each behavior should be *nondivisible*, meaning that it does not include a subset of several optional behaviors. For example,

adding additional insulation to a home can be further divided into adding insulation to the attic, exterior walls, or the basement. And the reason it must be narrowed further to one of these more specific behaviors is that the barriers to these three behaviors differ, and therefore strategies to encourage them will necessarily differ. Second, each behavior should be *end state*; that is, it should actually contribute to the environmental issue being addressed. For example, purchasing a compact fluorescent lightbulb is not an end-state behavior, but installing one is. Doug suggests that to determine whether a behavior is end state, you must ask, "Will engaging in this behavior produce the desired environmental outcome?" If another behavior is needed, it is not an end-state behavior.

2. *Determine impact,* the potential environmental benefit of each behavior. Doug recommends two methods for assessing the impact of each of the behaviors being considered. The first, and preferred, method is to access existing information. If, for example, the purpose of your plan is to reduce CO_2 emissions, you would collect information on the emissions associated with each of the potential behaviors (e.g., installing and configuring a programmable thermostat versus turning down the water heater temperature). If reliable information does not exist (which is often the case), you should turn to technical experts and ask them to rate each of the potential behaviors. He suggests that you ask them to independently rate them using something like a five-point scale and then average the results.

3. *Determine probability,* the likelihood that the target audience will adopt the behavior. This step also has a preferred, as well as an alternative, method for scoring.

The ideal scenario would be that there are past programs for each of the behaviors being considered, ones with similar target audiences and measurable results. These would then provide an estimate of the percentage of a target audience likely to adopt the behavior. When this information doesn't exist, and especially when the potential list is long, a second method is used: surveying a representative and reliable sample of your target audience and asking them to rate the probability that they would engage in each of the behaviors. For ease of final scoring, a similar five-point scale could be used where 0 equals "no likelihood" and 4 equals "high likelihood."

4. *Determine penetration,* the current levels of adoption of the behavior. The most reliable, as well as realistic, method for determining penetration is to survey the target audience and combine this research objective with the survey to determine probability of adoption. As Doug elaborates, it is important to note that results from these audience surveys can provide fairly reliable *relative* measures for each of the behaviors, though not necessarily *actual* percentages of probability of adoption. This is because it is not uncommon for survey respondents to inflate their stated likelihood of adopting the behavior, as well as to accurately report how often they engage in a repetitive behavior (e.g., washing clothes in cold water).

5. *Calculate and select the behavior,* the one with the highest potential impact, highest probability, and lowest penetration. The highest-priority behavior, then, is the one that is expected to make the greatest relative impact, has the greatest relative chance of being adopted, and has the greatest potential market opportunity.

Table 6.6 illustrates an ideal format for summarizing the information gathered in the first four steps:

Column 1: A list of all potential behaviors being considered.

Column 2: A score for environmental impact. (Note that the score in Table 6.6 is actual impact on CO2. As noted earlier, when reliable estimates are not available, you would use an average of scores from scientific experts using a five-point scale, as illustrated in Table 6.7.)

Column 3: A score for probability of adoption, with an average score calculated from target audience surveys using a five-point scale for each behavior, with a 4 representing the highest probability.

Column 4: A score for current penetration levels, with the number indicating the percentage of the market that has not adopted the behavior. The actual score in column 4 is determined by subtracting the penetration percentage from 1.0 to obtain the number that have yet to participate in the behavior. For example, if 20% of households have installed water-efficient showerheads, the number in the penetration column would be 80%.

Column 5: A weighted score is determined by multiplying impact times probability times penetration. If environmental impacts are not known and estimates from technical experts on the five-point scale are used, similar calculations are used (see Table 6.7).

Table 6.6 Illustration of the Five Steps With a Hypothetical Example From Australia Where Actual Environmental Impacts Are Known

1 POTENTIAL BEHAVIOR	2 IMPACT (kg/ household/year)	3 PROBABILITY (0–4)	4 PENETRATION (% not engaged in behavior)	5 WEIGHT
Purchase Green Power	8,700	2.15	85	15,899
Install three high-efficiency showerheads	650	2.5	35	569
Wash clothes in cold water	450	3.09	63	876

Table 6.7 Illustration of the Five Steps With a Hypothetical Example From Australia Where Environmental Impacts Are Estimated by Averaging Scores From Technical Experts

1 POTENTIAL BEHAVIOR	2 IMPACT (0–4)	3 PROBABILTY (0–4)	4 PENETRATION (% not engaged in behavior)	5 WEIGHT
Purchase Green Power	4	2.15	85	7.31
Install three high-efficiency showerheads	2	2.5	35	8.75
Wash clothes in cold water	1	3.09	63	1.9467

Source: D. McKenzie-Mohr, *Fostering Sustainable Behavior: An Introduction to Community-Based Social Marketing*, 3rd ed. (Gabriola Island, BC, Canada: New Society, 2011), 11–20. This table is adapted from one on p.19, which includes the following note: "On behalf of Local Government Infrastructure Services of Queensland, Australia, the Institute for Sustainable Futures estimated the CO2 emission reductions associated with a variety of energy-efficiency behaviors. The probability values are from a state-wide survey conducted in Queensland, Australia by Local Government and Infrastructure Services. The penetration values are fabrications as these values were not available."

DISCUSSION QUESTIONS AND EXERCISES

1. Why do the authors stress that behaviors need to be specific, or as Doug McKenzie-Mohr says, "nondivisible"?

2. For a campaign addressing the social issue of suicide, share a potential purpose, focus, target audience, behavior objective, and target goal.

3. What is your experience with the use of the term *goal*?

4. In the opening highlight, why wasn't the behavior objective for the campaign to convince trespassers to stop using illegal crossings?

CHAPTER 6 NOTES

1. National Social Marketing Centre, *Effectively Engaging people: Views From the World Social Marketing Conference 2008* (2008), 8, accessed July 15, 2011, http://www.tcp -events .co.uk/wsmc/downloads/NSMC_Effectively_engaging_people_conference_version.pdf.

2. H. W. Leibowitz, "Grade Crossing Accidents and Human Factors Engineering," *American Scientist* 95 (1985), 558–562.

3. Project Smart, "Smart Goals" (n.d.), accessed August 11, 2007, http://www.projectsmart .co.uk/smart-goals.html.

4. Climate Crisis, "Ten Things to Do" (n.d.), accessed 2006, http://www.climatecrisis.net/ pdf/10things.pdf.

5. *Healthy People 2020.* SOURCE: U.S. Department of Health and Human Services, Office of Disease Prevention and Health Promotion, ODPHP Publication No. B0132 (November 2010), www.healthypeople.gov.

6. D. McKenzie-Mohr, *Fostering Sustainable Behavior: An Introduction to Community Based Social Marketing*, 3rd ed. (Gabriola Island, BC, Canada: New Society, 2011), 11–20.

Chapter 7

Identifying Barriers, Benefits, Motivators, the Competition, and Influential Others

You will have a much better chance of influencing people to adopt a behaviour if you: know more about them; understand that not all are likely to be at the same starting point; consider your competition; actually make it attractive and easy for people; partner with influential people; communicate effectively; and are in it for the long run.

Francois Lagarde[1]
Vice President, Communications
Lucie and Andre Chagnon Foundation

By the time you reach this stage in the planning process, you may (understandably) just want to "get going." You will probably be eager to design the product, brainstorm incentives, search for convenient locations, dream up clever slogans, and envision beautiful billboards. After all, you have analyzed the environment, have selected a target audience, and know what you want that audience to do. And you may think you know what they need to know or believe in order to act. The problem is, unless you are the target audience, you probably don't know how they really feel about what you have in mind for them, or what they may be thinking when approached to "behave" in ways such as these:

- Put all your liquids in a quart-sized resealable plastic bag before reaching security checkpoints.
- Reduce your lawn by half.
- Eat five or more fruits and vegetables a day, the color way.

You may not know what's really in the way of their taking you up on your offer. This is the time to find out. Five audience insights are important and will be described and illustrated in this chapter:

- *Perceived barriers.* Reasons your target audience doesn't want to do the behavior or don't think they can.

- *Desired benefits.* What your target audience says is "in it for them" if they do the behavior.
- *Potential motivators.* Your target audience's ideas on what someone could say to them, show them, do for them, or give to them that would increase the likelihood that they would adopt the behavior.
- *The competition.* Behaviors your target audience prefers to do instead, behaviors they have been doing "forever," and/or organizations and individuals who send messages that counter or oppose the desired behavior.
- *Influential others.* Those your target audience listens to, watches, and/or looks up to.

And by conducting this investigation well, the rest of your planning process will be grounded in reality and guided by the customer's hand, as it was in the following opening case.

MARKETING HIGHLIGHT

Reducing Litter in Texas

Don't mess with Texas®'s New "CANpaign"

(2013)

Figure 7.1 "I hate that feeling/Don't mess with Texas" trash can.

Source: Texas Department of Transportation.

Background

Back in 1986, the Texas Department of Transportation (TxDOT) decided to battle their big problem with litter on roadways. Based on extensive observation research and audience surveys, they identified the state's worst offenders, how best to reach them, and, most significantly in this case, how to "talk to them." Their tough-talking, award-winning "Don't mess with Texas" campaign slogan was developed by an Austin-based advertising agency, GSD&M, which was challenged by TxDOT to reduce litter by a minimum of 5% in the first year.[2] Its focus was on persuading Texans to keep their trash in the car and off the roads. Twelve months later, litter had decreased on roadways by an impressive 29%.[3] And between 1995 and 2001, it decreased by more than 50%, with cigarette butt litter decreasing by 70%.[4]

Fast forward to 2013, when a study commissioned by the transportation agency found 434 million pieces of trash along Texas roadways.[5] That same year, results of their biennial Attitudes and Behaviors Study on littering revealed that although awareness of the Don't mess with Texas campaign was very high (98%), and a majority (62%) recalled seeing advertising or public service announcements with the slogan in the past year, a third of residents admitted to littering in the past month.[6] Of additional interest for planners were findings that the most common forms of reported littering, by a wide margin, were food/organic materials, small pieces of paper (e.g., receipts, gum wrappers), and cigarette butts, with around 30% of smokers admitting to throwing cigarette butts out the window while driving. And there were notable differences by audience segments. With this news, TxDOT announced that the state's antilitter campaign was getting a makeover, with a new look and more. It needed to. It would have to appeal to a new target audience.

Target Audiences and Desired Behaviors

Who were the litterers? Findings from the online Attitudes and Behaviors Study of 1,206 Texas residents ages 16 and over revealed four groups with the highest incidence of reported littering: Millennials (born between 1980 and 2000, 13–33 years old in 2013), Hispanics, singles, and households with young children. The incidence of littering also skewed somewhat toward males. Millennials, most of whom had not been around or had been very young at the launch of the original campaign 27 years earlier, were selected as the "bulls-eye" target audience for the revived effort, with

48% admitting to having littered in the past month compared to 26% of adults ages 34 plus.[7] Although they were about the same age as those targeted in the 1986 campaign (18- to 34-year-old men), generations, like people, have unique personalities, and Millennials are no exception. According to the Pew Research Center,[8] they are:

- More ethnically and racially diverse than older adults
- Confident, connected, and open to change
- Self-expressive, with three fourths having created a profile on a social networking site
- On track to becoming one of the most educated generations in American history

The focused behavior for the original campaign beginning in 1986, as mentioned earlier, was to refrain from tossing litter out of cars. The revamped campaign focused on putting litter "where it belongs," and engaging this new generation in participating.

Audience Insights

Given the large sample size of the Attitudes and Behavior Study ($N = 1,206$), Millennials ($n = 285$) could be reliably compared to older adults ($n = 921$). The following summary findings related to perceived barriers, desired benefits, and potential motivators provided inspiration for strategies that would appeal (most) to this segment.

Perceived Barriers

For Millennials, major barriers to proper disposal included being more rushed from time, less certain than others that it is against the law, and less concerned overall with the seriousness of litter, especially small pieces of paper, food material, and cigarette butts, the major current litter components (see Table 7.1).

Desired Benefits

As indicated in Table 7.2, the majority of Millennials saw multiple benefits of not littering, especially protecting the environment, being a role model for children, wanting to keep Texas beautiful, and not wanting to participate in a socially unacceptable behavior.

Potential Motivators

The majority of Millennials were most motivated to dispose of litter properly by the prospect of being caught and fined (see Table 7.3). One section of the survey explored the idea of being able to report litterers, and although most indicated they would not report someone for littering, the likelihood to report increased if a letter would be sent to the offender, assuming anonymity for the person reporting. (As you will read in marketing mix strategies, this finding shaped renewed interest in making their "Report a Litterer" program more visible.)

Marketing Mix Strategies

Major strategies relied on all four intervention tools.

Product

To target the high volume of small pieces of litter, including fast-food packaging, cigarette butts, candy wrappers, and pieces of paper and plastic bags, special red-white-and-blue barrels became the centerpiece of the campaign (see Figure 7.2).

Table 7.1 Testing Potential Barriers

"How serious do you think each of these items is, in terms of litter?"		
Very Serious Litter Items	Millennials (16–33 yrs)	Older Adults (34+ yrs)
	$n = 285$	$n = 921$
Beer cans or bottles	79%	86%
Plastic bags/other plastics	79%	83%
Construction debris	80%	82%
Soda or other nonalcoholic beverage cans or bottles	75%	82%
Larger food wrappers (chip bags, candy wrappers, etc.)	70%	76%
Fast-food wrappers	68%	73%
Cigarette butts	65%	71%
Cardboard	56%	61%
Small pieces of paper (receipts, lottery tickets, gum wrappers, etc.)	34%	50%
Food/organic material, raw food	21%	32%

Source: Texas Department of Transportation, "2013 Litter Attitudes and Behaviors" (April 3, 2013), 31, accessed November 27, 2013, http://www.dontmesswithtexas.org/docs/DMWT_2013_Attitudes_Behaviors_Full_Report.pdf.

Table 7.2	Testing Potential Benefits

"Do you think keeping Texas clean and litter free is . . . ?"

	Past-Month Litterers	Nonlitterers	Millennials (16–33 yrs)	Older Adults (34+ yrs)
	$n = 353$	$n = 853$	$n = 285$	$n = 921$
More an environmental issue	21%	19%	31%	16%
More a Texas pride issue	18%	11%	14%	13%
Equally an environmental issue and a Texas pride issue	60%	70%	55%	71%

"Please rate how much you agree or disagree with each of the following statements."

	Past-Month Litterers	Nonlitterers	Millennials	Older Adults
	$n = 353$	$n = 853$	$n = 285$	$n = 921$
"It is important to instill antilittering values in children from a very young age."	81%	88%	74%	89%
"I take pride in not littering."	76%	86%	72%	87%
"I don't throw trash on the road because I want to 'Keep Texas Beautiful.'"	74%	87%	71%	87%
"Litter that accumulates on our roadways is a poor reflection on us as Texans."	73%	83%	68%	84%
"Littering is a socially unacceptable behavior."	68%	81%	69%	79%

Source: Texas Department of Transportation, "2013 Litter Attitudes and Behaviors" (April 3, 2013), 36, accessed November 27, 2013, http://www.dontmesswithtexas.org/docs/DMWT_2013_Attitudes_Behaviors_Full_Report.pdf.

Price

Litterers can be fined up to $500 for littering anything less than 5 pounds and face up to $2,000 fines and 180 days in jail for littering anything from 5 to 500 pounds. To capitalize on the fear of getting caught and fined, a program for reporting litterers (anonymously) was revitalized and described this way on a special section of the campaign's website:

So what can you do when you see trash blowing in the wind and eventually landing on the side of our highways? Instead of delivering your own method of justice, we suggest turning the litterer in through the Texas Department of Transportation's Report a Litterer Program. It's an anonymous way to gently remind litterbugs they Don't mess with Texas. When you see litter thrown from or flying out of a vehicle, intentionally or accidentally, take down the following information—license plate number, make and color of vehicle, date and time, location, who tossed the litter, and what was tossed.[9]

Table 7.3   Testing Potential Motivators[a]

"Here are a few facts about littering in Texas. What impact does each have on your likelihood of littering?"	Millennials (16–33 yrs)	Older Adults (34+ yrs)
	n = 285	n = 921
"If you're caught littering in Texas, you're likely to be fined up to $500, or possibly more in serious cases."	59%	67%
"The Texas government spends $46 million in litter pickup every year."	50%	58%
"It's against the law to litter in Texas."	44%	57%
"1.1 billion pieces of litter accumulate in Texas-maintained highways annually."	49%	55%
"47 million pieces of cigarette litter accumulate in Texas-maintained highways annually."	47%	54%
"In your own words, what would it take to reduce the frequency of littering in Texas?"		All Survey Respondents
Punishment/enforcement		33%
Fines		26%
Education/awareness (more/better forms of education regarding littering, more school involvement, more programs in schools regarding littering facts)		20%
Advertising (publication of littering episodes/news/enforcement of punishments)		11%

a. Percentages refer to the number of people who thought the statement would very likely have an impact on their likelihood of littering.

Source: Texas Department of Transportation, "2013 Litter Attitudes and Behaviors" (April 3, 2013), 29, 37, accessed November 27, 2013, http://www.dontmesswithtexas.org/docs/DMWT_2013_Attitudes_Behaviors_Full_Report.pdf.

Citizens are then directed to provide the information using an online form. TxDOT then compares the information through the Department of Motor Vehicles registration database, and when an exact match is located, sends the owner of the vehicle that was reported littering a Don't mess with Texas litterbag along with a letter reminding them to keep their trash off the roads. The letter includes information regarding litter fines and offers the recipient the option to order a (free) reusable pocket ashtray available through a grassroots partnership with Keep Texas Beautiful.

Place

The "CANpaign" is intended to be visible to Texans everywhere, with more than 300 barrels appearing across the state at a variety of locations, including travel information centers, popular tourist attractions, sports venues, and other high-traffic locations, to remind drivers to properly dispose of litter.

Promotion

TxDOT kicked off the campaign at a news conference featuring dancing iconic red-white-and blue "Don't mess with Texas" trash cans. Major promotional channels included televisions and radio spots in English and Spanish, billboards, news stories, and a major presence in social media. And as displayed in Figure 7.2, messages on cans were created to have special resonance with Millennials. To engage students, a Campus Cleanup Program

was designed and supported, and is described in Box 7.1.

Figure 7.2 A variety of slogans for the CANpaign appear on barrels placed around the state.

Source: Texas Department of Transportation.

Box 7.1
A Campus Cleanup Program to Appeal to Millennials in High Schools and Colleges

Campus Cleanup is a student-focused program intended to engage young Millennials at colleges and high schools in supporting the Don't mess with Texas effort. A variety of materials and suggestions are included in a toolbox to help students get organized and launch events. In its first two years, the program included a cleanup challenge between Texas colleges and universities, where students from across the state coordinated litter pickups on their campuses and picked up a significant amount of trash. TxDOT describes the program as a way to "help change the way your peers think about litter by getting out there and doing something about it. You'll be giving back to your community and participating in an event that will look great on your resume!"[10] Recommended locations include sporting events, neighborhoods, dorms, apartments, Greek houses, roadsides, and campus hot spots like

Figure 7.3 Poster for student groups to use to attract others to cleanup events.

Source: Texas Department of Transportation.

(Continued)

(Continued)

student unions, libraries, food service areas, parks, and other common areas. For the CANpaign, fun slogans were crafted for the cans that would especially appeal to these young Millennials:

- *Finally some* GOOD CLEAN FUN.
- *Enjoy lots of* EASY PICK UPS.
- *Let's get* DOWN *and* DIRTY.
- *Pick up* LITTER. *Pick up* DATES.

The toolkit includes posters for recruiting fellow students to an event (see Figure 7.3).

Source: Texas Department of Transportation.

Outcomes

Early signs of engagement in the new campaign are encouraging, with Facebook fans having increased from 15,000 in March 2013 to over 31,000 in January 2014. On YouTube, trash can video spots have been viewed more than 232,000 times since April 2013.

Information for this highlight was provided by Brenda Flores-Dollar, program administrator at TxDOT.

STEP 5: IDENTIFY TARGET AUDIENCE BARRIERS, BENEFITS, MOTIVATORS, THE COMPETITION, AND INFLUENTIAL OTHERS

In the marketing game, the winners almost always have one "maneuver" in common: a customer-centered focus. The best have a genuine curiosity, even hunger, to know what the potential customer thinks and feels about their offer. This fifth step in the planning process is designed to do just that—deepen your understanding of your target audience.

This chapter will first identify and discuss what current and specific knowledge, beliefs, attitudes, and practices will be helpful for you to know and understand. You then will read about how to gather this information and, finally, how you will use these insights in developing your strategies. First, a word about the exchange theory, another marketing cornerstone—one that will help you envision this "deal-making" process.

The Exchange Theory

The traditional economic exchange theory postulates that, for an exchange to take place, target audiences must perceive benefits equal to or greater than perceived costs.[11] In other words, they must believe they will get as much or more than they give. In 1972, Philip

Kotler published an article in the *Journal of Marketing* asserting that exchange is the core concept of marketing and that free exchange takes place when the target audience believes they will get as much or more than they give.[12] And earlier, in 1969, Kotler argued that exchange theory applies to more than the purchase of tangible goods and services, that it can in fact involve intangible or symbolic products (e.g., recycling), and that payments are not limited to financial ones (e.g., time and effort may be the only major perceived costs).[13] In 1974 and 1978, Richard Bagozzi broadened this framework by adding several ideas, including that more than two parties may be involved in the transaction and that the primary beneficiary of an exchange may in fact be a third party (e.g., the environment).[14] This is certainly consistent with the definition of social marketing used throughout this text, as it acknowledges that the intent is always to better society as well as the target audience.

Given this, five target audience perspectives, identified at the beginning of the chapter, are crucial and will be elaborated upon in the next section of this chapter.

WHAT MORE DO YOU NEED TO KNOW ABOUT THE TARGET AUDIENCE?

Perceived Barriers

Barriers are revealed in audience responses to a variety of questions. What concerns do they have regarding the behavior? What do they think they will have to give (up) in order to perform the behavior? Do they think they can do it? Why haven't they done it in the past, or on a regular basis? Why, perhaps, did they quit doing it? These could also be thought of as the "costs" the target audience perceives. Doug McKenzie-Mohr, the environmental psychologist highlighted in Chapter 6, notes that barriers may be *internal* to the individual, such as lack of knowledge or skill needed to carry out an activity, or *external*, as in structural changes that need to be made in order for the behavior to be more convenient. He also stresses that these barriers will differ by target audience and by behavior. In our planning process, that is why target audiences and the desired behavior (activity) are identified up front.[15]

Barriers may be related to a variety of factors, including knowledge, beliefs, skills, abilities, infrastructures, technology, economic status, or cultural influences. They may be *real* (e.g., taking the bus will take longer than driving alone to work) or *perceived* (e.g., people who take the bus can't really afford any other mode of transportation). In either case, they are always from the target audience's perspective and often something you can address.

Example: Safe Water Project. In 2006, in Malawi in southeast Africa, 90% of women in a pilot program developed by PATH, an international nonprofit organization, knew about an effective water treatment product called WaterGuard, but only 2% were currently using it. Nine months into the program, 61% were using it, as were 25% of their friends and relatives with young children.[16] How did this happen? The intervention succeeded because it addressed initial barriers and then focused on a single, simple solution.

Initial interviews with mothers identified primary barriers as affordability, availability, taste, and smell. A free trial offer included a sample of WaterGuard, a safe storage container, and up to three refills. This trial period let women experience firsthand how easy the product was to use and how much it could improve their family's health. It also gave them time to get used to the taste, which over time many came to associate with treated or safe water. Careful instruction about how to use WaterGuard also reduced the chances of overdosing, which had contributed to the strong smell and taste of chlorine. Health workers taught pregnant women about the health benefits of safe water, and outreach workers made follow-up home visits to reinforce the message.

Three years later, after the trial program had expired, 26% of participants (compared to 2% before the trial) and 18% of their friends and relatives were continuing to buy and use WaterGuard, and many others were treating their water with a free chlorine solution supplied by the government.[17]

Desired Benefits

Benefits are something your target audience wants or needs and therefore values and that the behavior you are promoting has the potential to provide.[18] What social marketers will need to address are any doubts their audience has that they will, in fact, experience these benefits. Again, these will be benefits in the eyes of the customer—not necessarily the same as yours. Bill Smith asserts that these benefits may not always be so obvious. For example,

> the whole world uses health as a benefit. [And yet] health, as we think of it in public health, isn't as important to consumers—even high-end consumers—as they claim that it is. What people care about is looking good (tight abdominals and buns). Health is often a synonym for sexy, young, and hot. That's why gym advertising increases before bathing suit time. There is not more disease when the weather heats up, just more personal exposure.[19]

In a 2014 webinar for the International Social Marketing Association, Hamilton Carvalho, a social marketer in Brazil, shared his checklist of fundamental human needs, ones we could consider to be desired benefit categories: (a) autonomy, (b) competence, (c) belonging, (d), meaning, (e) identity, (f) justice, (g), positive emotion, and (h) cognitive economy.[20]

Example: Saving the Crabs in Chesapeake Bay[21]. For centuries, Chesapeake Bay blue crabs were considered the best blue crabs in the world, but in 2003, the Chesapeake harvest hit a near historic low. With this knowledge at hand, a planned campaign theme of "saving the seafood" was born. While people in the DC area might have only limited concern for the bay, many are passionate about their seafood, as is evidenced by the many thriving seafood restaurants throughout DC and its Maryland and Virginia suburbs. Reframing the problem of a polluted bay as a culinary, not an environmental, problem was the cornerstone of the campaign developed by the nonprofit Academy for Educational Development (AED).

Branded "Save the Crabs. Then Eat 'em," promotional messages focused on skipping the spring fertilizing. Three television ads were developed, each encouraging viewers to wait until fall to fertilize their lawns and each using humor to lighten the message. One ad explained that "no crab should die like this," and, as a man bites into a lump of crab-meat, opines that "they should perish in some hot, tasty butter." Print ads ran in the *Washington Post* and in a free tabloid handed out at metro stops (see Figure 7.4). Drink coasters were printed and distributed without charge for local seafood restaurants to use and hand out to patrons (see Figure 7.5).

Figure 7.4 Out-of-home ad promoting fertilizing in the fall.	**Figure 7.5** Drink coasters distributed to local seafood restaurants.

Source: Academy of Educational Development for Chesapeake Bay Club.

Source: Academy of Educational Development for Chesapeake Bay Club.

To monitor campaign outcomes early on, random-digit-dial telephone surveys were administered to measure behavior intent before and after the campaign was launched. Interviews were completed with 600 area residents who reported they cared for their lawn or hired someone to do it. In 2004, prior to the campaign, 52% of those surveyed reported that they planned to fertilize that spring. In 2005, after the campaign had launched, that number had dropped to 39%, a 25% improvement.

Potential Motivators

Motivators are distinct from audience benefits. They are ideas your target audience shares with you, ones they think would make it more likely that they would adopt the desired behavior. Their answers to four questions will provide insight regarding strategies (the 4Ps): (1) "What could someone say to you that would make it more likely that you would consider adopting this behavior?"; (2) "What could someone show you that would make it more likely that you would adopt this behavior?"; (3) "Is there anything someone could give you that would help you adopt this behavior?"; and (4) "Is there anything someone could do for you that would help you adopt this behavior?" Responses are likely to fall into one of the 4P categories. We'll use an example of an effort to influence shoreline property owners to remove all or portions of seawalls and bulkheads on beaches to improve water quality and protect wildlife habitats. Audience members may mention that you could give them the native plants they would need to help decrease erosion as well as technical assistance with a design (*product strategies*). Further, having these plants delivered to their home, and having the technical assistance provided there, would be ideal (*place strategies*). They may mention that it would be motivating for them if they could get a decrease in property taxes in exchange for removing shoreline seawalls (*price strategy*). And they may mention that it would be persuasive to hear data on a potential increase in property values (*message*) as well as to hear from other homeowners in the area with success and satisfaction stories (*messengers*) at a special event (*communication channel*).

It should be noted that in this idea-generating interview process, you can also test ideas you have been thinking of that respondents don't mention. This is different from a formal pretest effort, which is recommended after strategies have been drafted based on these audience insights but prior to implementation.

Example: Breastfeeding. Studies show that babies who are breastfed for six months are less likely to develop ear infections, diarrhea, and respiratory illnesses. And some studies suggest that infants who are not breastfed have higher rates of obesity, diabetes, leukemia, and asthma. Yet, in 2004 in the United States, only about 33% of mothers were breastfeeding at the recommended six months postpartum, one of the lowest breastfeeding rates in the developed world.[22] The *Healthy People 2010* goal was to raise this to 50%. The U.S. Department of Health and Human Services, Office of Women's Health, took on this challenge.

Pre-campaign research findings provided a direction and focus for the campaign, revealing that there was no clear understanding of the duration goal for breastfeeding and that there were no known major perceived advantages of breastfeeding. Campaign messages were designed to address this confusion and to highlight advantages that would be most motivating. A media campaign was launched in June 2004 with the support of the Advertising Council, using ads driving home the message "Babies were born to be breastfed" and highlighting real health advantages— with a little humor (see Figure 7.6).[23]

In addition to mass media and the Internet, resources were directed to supporting community-based demonstration projects (CDPs) throughout the country. These projects involved funding local coalitions, hospitals, universities, and other organizations so that they could offer breastfeeding services, provide outreach to their communities, train health care providers, implement the media aspects of the campaign, and track breastfeeding rates in their communities.

Figure 7.6 Poster for a breastfeeding campaign in partnership with the Ad Council.[24]

Research after the first year of the campaign was encouraging. Awareness about breastfeeding had risen from 28% to 38%. More than half of respondents (63%) either correctly identified six months as the recommended length of time to exclusively breastfeed a baby or said the recommended duration was longer than six months. The number agreeing that babies should be exclusively breastfed in the first six months increased from pre-wave (53%) to post-wave (62%). And, most important, more of the women surveyed had breastfed a child (any duration) in the 2005 study (73%) than in the 2004 study (63%). An updated "report card" in 2012 indicates that breastfeeding rates are on the rise, with breastfeeding at six months having increased to 47.2% and the *Healthy People 2020* objective having now been set at 60.6%.[25]

The Competition

Identifying the Competition

The fourth area you'll want to explore with your target audience is the competition. Social marketers have tough competitors, because we define *the competition* as follows:

- Behaviors our target audience would prefer over the ones we are promoting (e.g., condoms may be preferred over abstinence as a way to prevent unwanted pregnancies)
- Behaviors they have been doing "forever," such as a habit that they would have to give up (e.g., driving alone to work or having a cigarette with a morning cup of coffee)
- Organizations and individuals who send messages that counter or oppose the desired behavior (e.g., the Marlboro Man)

Table 7.4 illustrates the challenges you (will) face. Consider the pleasures and benefits you are asking your target audience to give up. Consider the economic power of organizations and sponsors that are sending messages countering those you are sending. Consider the persuasiveness and influence of typical key messengers. And consider that the competition may even be your own organization! We call this "friendly" competition, where one program within the organization (e.g., a needle exchange program) may in fact potentially erode the success of another (e.g., a drug use reduction program).

Another potential framework (and way to identify the competition) is offered by Sue Peattie and Ken Peattie of Cardiff University in Wales.[26] They suggest that in social marketing, the competition is better thought of as a "battle of ideas" and that these competing ideas can come from four sources that can be considered potential competitors: (1) *commercial countermarketing* (e.g., cigarette companies), (2) *social discouragement* of your desired behavior (e.g., anti-gun-control activists), (3) *apathy* (e.g., when considering whether to vote), and (4) *involuntary disinclination* (e.g., physical addictions).

Identifying Perceived Barriers and Benefits of the Competition

Once competitors are identified, there is more you want to know while you're at it. McKenzie-Mohr and Smith provide a useful framework for capturing your research findings— one that will prepare you for developing your product's positioning and 4Ps marketing mix strategy in Steps 6 and 7. The name of this marketing game is to change the ratio of benefits to barriers so that the target behavior becomes more attractive. McKenzie-Mohr and Smith propose four ways (tactics), which are not mutually exclusive, to accomplish this:

1. Increase the benefits of the target behavior

2. Decrease the barriers (and/or costs) of the target behavior

3. Decrease the benefits of the competing behavior(s)

4. Increase the barriers (and/or costs) of the competing behaviors[27]

Table 7.5 is a simple illustration of what in reality (ideally) would include a more exhaustive list of benefits and barriers/costs created from audience research. Keep in mind that there is likely to be more than one preferred or alternative behavior identified as the competition.

Table 7.4 What and With Whom You May Be Competing

Behavior Objective	Competing Behaviors	Competing Messages and Messengers
Drink less than five drinks at one sitting	Getting really "buzzed"	Budweiser
Wear a life vest	Tanning	Fashion ads showing tan shoulders, midriffs, and arms
Give five hours a week to a volunteer effort	Spending time with family	The audience member's kids
Compost organic food waste	A habit of pushing scraps down the drain when cleaning dishes	Neighbors who say the backyard composter will attract rats

Table 7.5 Identifying Perceived Barriers and Benefits of the Competition

Audience Perceptions	Desired Behavior: Use a Litterbag in the Car	Competing Behavior: Tossing Fast-Food Bags Out the Window
Perceived benefits	• It's good role modeling for my kids. • I am doing my part for the environment. • I help save tax dollars. • I don't feel as guilty.	• It's easier. • I avoid the smell of old food in my car. • I avoid the trash all over my car. • It gives prisoners a job to do.
Perceived barriers/costs	• Having to find one and remember to put it in the car. • Having liquid spill out of it. • Looking like a nerd with a white plastic bag in my black leather interior car.	• I might have to do community service and pick up litter. • I could get caught and fined. • I'm contributing to the litter on the roadways that looks bad and will have to be picked up.

An important component of this research process will include attempting to prioritize these benefits and barriers/costs within each of the quadrants. You are most interested in the "higher values"—the key benefits to be gained or costs that will be avoided by adopting the desired behavior. In the example in Table 7.5, your research won't be complete until you determine how your target audience ranks benefits and barriers in each quadrant (e.g., what is the number-one benefit for using a litterbag?).

Example: Pet Adoption. On Saturday morning, October 14, 2006, an interview on a Seattle, Washington, radio station with a spokesperson for the Humane Society for Tacoma and Pierce County certainly highlighted the costs of doing nothing: "We have over a hundred cats and kittens that are likely to be euthanized tonight if they are not adopted today." Television news programs, newspaper articles, and blogs also helped spread the word to "*skadoodle over to Kittenkaboodle* and help us end the heartache of euthanasia by adopting a homeless cat or kitten." The event promised to be festive and was decked out with balloons and offered free face paintings for kids. An incentive topped off the offer—a $20 discount on the regular adoption fee, which ("today only") included spaying or neutering, a veterinary exam, a cat carrier, and even a cat toy.

On the following Monday, it was announced that a record-breaking 180 shelter pets had found homes in just eight hours! Evidently the shelter had made the cost of "doing nothing" (apathy) real and significant. Follow-up news stories and website postings assured those who missed out, "No problem. The shelter will be open all week, and there is sure to be a new and ample supply of adoptable animals."[28]

Influential Others

The fifth area to consider at this point is those your target audience listens to, watches, and/or looks up to, especially related to the desired behavior you have in mind. We think of them as midstream audiences, and they include social groups your target audience belongs to (e.g., a moms' support group or Facebook friends) as well as coworkers, classmates, neighbors, family members, physicians, counselors, pharmacists, the media, and entertainers. In some cases, it may be individuals the target audience finds trustworthy, likable, and as having expertise (e.g., a highly regarded scientist or entertainer). Knowing what these groups and individuals are saying and doing (or might say and do) regarding the desired behavior will have significant implications, especially for promotional strategies, perhaps warranting an additional target audience for your plan.

Example: Energy Conservation[29]. During an energy crisis on the U.S. West Coast in the winter of 2001, a popular, well-respected radio talk show host, Dave Ross of 97.3 FM KIRO in Seattle, Washington, was intrigued when he heard of a successful conservation effort in Israel more than 20 years before. He then tried a similar strategy with his listening audience of several hundred thousand.

The campaign in Israel had taken place immediately after a popular television show dramatized Israel's overuse of electricity. The show's host asked the audience to leave the room and go around the house and turn off all extra lights. The viewers then saw the impact of their actions on their television screens, from a camera focused on the Israeli Electric Company's electricity consumption gauges. Within a few seconds, the gauges dropped sharply. This experiment that helped alter the belief that "my lights don't make a difference" saved an estimated 6% in aggregate electricity consumption during the eight months of the campaign.[30]

Taking a similar approach, Dave announced on a preview for his show that he would try an experiment at 11:30 that morning and would be asking listeners to turn off and unplug anything electric that wasn't being used. He emphasized that he didn't want people to make any sacrifices; he just wanted them to turn off what they didn't need. At 11:28, the city's electric utility staff were standing by and read the current level of megawatts in use: "We're at 1,400 megawatts." At 11:30, the talk show host said, "Go!" and for the next five minutes he walked around the studios of the station with a handheld microphone and turned off conference room lights and computer monitors in empty offices. He then called his wife at home to make sure she was participating, all as an example for the listening audience.

At 11:35, the city utility public information officer came back on the air and reported impressive results. Usage had dropped by 40 megawatts to 1,360. The decrease was enough to power 40,000 homes and represented $300,000 worth of electricity. Excitement over the success generated an hour-long program the next day on ways to conserve electricity (e.g., doing laundry in nonpeak hours and purchasing energy-saving appliances). Dave was presented a conservation award on air (an energy-saving lightbulb) by a member of the city council. For several weeks thereafter, local home and garden supply stores featured energy-saving appliances and lightbulbs.

HOW DO YOU LEARN MORE FROM AND ABOUT THE TARGET AUDIENCE?

Formative research, as the name implies, will help you gain insights into audience barriers, benefits, and motivators; the competition; and influential others. It will assist you in developing draft strategies to then pretest. Existing behavior change theories and models that will be discussed in the next chapter will help deepen your understanding of your customer—and even develop empathy and compassion.

Formative Research

As usual, you should begin with a review of existing literature and research and discussions with peers and colleagues. If, after this review, informational gaps still exist, it may be important to conduct original research using qualitative methods, such as focus groups and personal interviews, to identify barriers, benefits, motivators, the competition, and important influential others. Quantitative instruments, such as telephone and web-based surveys, would be very helpful in prioritizing the benefits and barriers to, say, using a litterbag, such as those listed in Table 7.5.

One popular survey model to consider is the knowledge, attitudes, practices, and beliefs (KAPB) survey. As described by Andreasen,

> these are comprehensive surveys of a representative sample of the target population designed to secure information about the social behavior in question and on the current status of the target audience's Knowledge, Attitudes, Practices, Beliefs. KAPB studies are relatively common in social marketing environments, especially

in the area of health. They are very often carried out routinely by local govern-ments, the World Bank, or the United Nations. For this reason, they are sometimes available to social marketers as part of a secondary database.[31]

For example, a KAPB-type study has been conducted annually by the Gallup Organization for the March of Dimes, beginning in 1995, and is supported by the Centers for Disease Control and Prevention.[32] Telephone surveys conducted nationwide among women ages 18 to 45 are designed to track knowledge and behavior related to the impor-tance of taking folic acid before becoming pregnant to decrease the chances of birth defects. Consider how these summary findings in the year 2008 would shape campaign strategies and priorities:

- Nine out of 10 women (89%) did not know that folic acid should be taken prior to pregnancy.
- Eight out of 10 women (80%) did not know that folic acid could help prevent birth defects.
- Only about one in three women (39%) not pregnant at the time of the survey reported consuming a multivitamin containing folic acid daily.

An example of a more qualitative research approach to understanding a target audience was one conducted by Michael Jortner, an MBA candidate at the Institute for Social Marketing at the University of Stirling. Michael was interested in answering the question, "What desired benefits influence dog walkers in urban parks to keep their dogs on a leash [the preferred behavior] compared to those who don't?" He learned through personal interviews that dog walkers who leashed their dogs valued the "peace" in their walk, while those who didn't leash their dogs were looking for "joy" in their outing.[33] Perhaps those wanting to influence "nonleashers" to become "leashers" will want to challenge them-selves to answer the question, "How can we put more joy in walking a dog on a leash?"

HOW WILL THIS HELP DEVELOP YOUR STRATEGY?

If you understand (better yet, empathize with) your target audience's real and perceived barriers, benefits, motivators, competitors, and influential others relative to your desired behavior, it will be akin to having a guiding hand as you craft your positioning statement and 4Ps strategies. We'll illustrate this application and process with a brief case.[34]

In 2006, the Washington State Department of Health developed a social marketing plan with the purpose of decreasing falls among seniors and a focus on developing fitness classes that could be offered by a variety of community organizations. The target audi-ences for the pilot (first year) were seniors ages 70 to 79 living in one county of the state. Formative research with key informants and seniors in the target audience identified the following major perceived benefits, barriers, motivators, competition, and important others influencing seniors regarding joining and attending classes:

- Benefits desired: "It could improve my strength, balance, and fitness, and then perhaps I can live independent longer. I also want it to be fun and a chance to make new friends."
- Barriers to joining: "It depends on how much it will cost, where the class is located, the time of day it is offered, and who will be leading the class. I don't want some young instructor I can't relate to!"
- Barriers to attending regularly: "I'd probably drop out if it's too strenuous, I hurt myself, or I couldn't keep up. And I'd need to see improvements in my fitness for it to seem worthwhile."
- Motivators to attend regularly: "If the class is less than $50 a month, is located near my home, has free parking, includes others in the class like myself, and is taught by an instructor who understands seniors."
- Competition: "I can probably just do my own thing at home for free, at my own pace, by watching an exercise video or going out for a walk. I guess the advantage of the class, though, is that it's a way to make sure I do it!"
- Influential others: "My neighbor says that the gym instructor is younger than her grandkids and just as energetic. I wouldn't be able to keep up."

A *positioning* statement, as you will read in Chapter 9, describes how you want your target audience to see your desired behavior, especially relative to the competition. Planners wanted the fitness classes to be seen by their target audience of 70- to 79-year-olds as

a fitness class for seniors that *works*, as it will improve strength and balance; is *safe*, as it has experienced skilled instructors offering tested exercises; and is *fun*, as it offers an opportunity to meet others and get out of the house. It is an important and worthwhile activity for seniors wanting to stay *independent*, *be active*, and *prevent falls.*

The *product* platform includes a description of the core, actual, and augmented product, all inspired by your benefits, barriers, motivators, and competitive research. For the fitness classes, the *core* product (benefits of the classes) was subsequently refined to be "staying active, independent, and preventing falls." The *actual* product (features of the classes) would be one-hour fitness classes, with up to 20 participants, meeting three times a week. The classes would include strength exercises with wrist and ankle weights, balance exercises, and moderate aerobics. The exercises could be done standing or sitting, and the instructor would be a certified fitness instructor with special training in strength and balance exercises for seniors. The *augmented* product (extras to add value) would include a booklet giving information on fall prevention and describing how to conduct a self-assessment for fall risk and determine readiness to exercise (see Figure 7.7). External safety effectiveness assessments would be available as well.

Pricing strategies include *costs* for products, *fees* for services, and any *monetary* and *nonmonetary incentives* and *disincentives.* Based on target audience comments, it was determined that the recommended fee per class should be $2.00 to $2.50, enough to help cover the cost of the instructors, add to perceived value, and build commitment. It was also recommended that a coupon be offered for a free first class as well as a punch card giving 12 classes for the

Figure 7.7   Brochure cover for a fall-prevention class for seniors.

Source: Washington State Department for Health.

price of 11, and it was suggested that organizers build in a reward of a free class to participants who attended at least 10 classes in a month.

Place strategies refer to where and when behaviors are performed and tangible objects and services are accessed. For the exercise classes, nine sites were selected, eight of them at senior centers and one at a senior retirement facility. Suggested ideal start times were 9 or 10 a.m. or 1, 2, or 3 p.m. There was to be free, adjacent parking at each site.

Promotional elements include messages, messengers, and media channels. The recommended name of the program was S.A.I.L. (Stay Active and Independent for Life), with a tagline of "A strength and balance fitness class for seniors." Consistent with the desired positioning, key messages to incorporate in promotional materials included the following:

- "It works. You'll be stronger, have better balance, and feel better, and this will help you stay independent and active and prevent falls."
- "It's safe. Instructors are experienced and skilled, and exercises have been tested with seniors."
- "It's fun. You'll meet other seniors and make new friends, and this will get you out of the house three days a week."

Types of media channels to promote the class would include flyers, posters, articles in newsletters and local newspapers, packets for physicians, website information, sandwich board signs at senior centers, and a Q&A fact sheet for senior center staff.

POTENTIAL REVISION OF TARGET AUDIENCES, OBJECTIVES, AND GOALS

This new in-depth understanding of target audiences may signal a need to revise target audiences (Step 3) and/or objectives (Step 4), because it may reveal one or more of the following situations:

- One of the target audiences has beliefs that you would have a difficult time changing or may not want to: "Moderate physical activity like this is wimpy, and I'd rather increase vigorous activity from two to three days a week if I do anything more."
- The desired behavior has too many insurmountable barriers for one or more target audiences: "I can't get to the farmers' market to use my coupons because they close before I get off work."
- The audience tells us the behavior objective isn't clear: "I don't understand what reducing my BMI means."
- Perceived costs are too high: "Quitting smoking while I'm pregnant looks impossible, but I might be able to cut down to a half a pack a day."
- The behavior objective has already been met: "My child already has five caring adult relationships outside the home, so for you to suggest I go find one caring adult for my child says you're not talking to people like me."
- A major knowledge objective isn't needed but a belief objective is: "I already know that tobacco kills one out of three users. I just believe I'll be one of the two out of three who make it!"
- The original behavior objective isn't the solution to the problem: "I always cover the load in the back of my pickup truck with a tarp. The problem is, it still doesn't keep stuff from flying out. What we need is a net or cable that holds the tarp down."
- The goal is too high: "This latest survey says that 75% of high school seniors are sexually active, so a goal of 50% choosing abstinence looks impossible with this group!"

ETHICAL CONSIDERATIONS WHEN RESEARCHING YOUR TARGET AUDIENCE

Perhaps the greatest ethical concern when conducting activities to learn more about your target audience is the research process itself. Concerns range from whether questions will make respondents uncomfortable or embarrassed to deceiving respondents regarding the purposes of the research to assurance of anonymity and confidentiality.

Institutional review boards (IRBs) have been formed to help avoid these ethical problems. An IRB is a group formally designated to review and monitor behavioral and biomedical research involving human subjects. The purpose of IRB review is to ensure that appropriate steps are taken to protect the rights and welfare of humans participating as subjects in a research study. In the United States, IRBs are mandated by the Research Act of 1974, which defines IRBs and requires them for all research that receives funding, directly or indirectly, from the Department of Health and Human Services (HHS). These IRBs are themselves regulated by the Office for Human Research Protections within HHS and may be based at academic institutions or medical facilities or conducted by for-profit organizations.[35]

CHAPTER SUMMARY

In this important step in the marketing planning process, you take time out to deepen your understanding of your target audience. What you are most interested in knowing are perceived *barriers, benefits, motivators, competitors*, and *influential others*. What you are most interested in feeling are compassion and a desire to develop marketing strategies that decrease these barriers, increase benefits, are inspired by what the target audience says will motivate them, upstage your competition, and engage influential others.

These insights may be gathered through a literature review or other secondary research resources. They are more likely to involve at least some qualitative surveys, such as focus groups or personal interviews. Quantitative surveys, such as a KAPB (knowledge, attitudes, practices, and beliefs) survey, will help you prioritize your findings and provide sharp focus for your positioning and marketing mix strategies.

RESEARCH HIGHLIGHT

Protecting Water Quality in Backyard Ponds in Southern Florida

Focus Group Research to Identify Barriers, Benefits, and Potential Motivators

(2011–2013)

This research case highlights one of several formative research efforts to inform recommendations for a social marketing effort to protect backyard storm-water ponds in southwest Florida. The process began with focus groups to create an initial "list" of audience barriers, benefits, and potential motivators to desired behavior changes that would then be used to develop a quantitative survey to verify and prioritize findings.

Information for this case was provided by Paul Monaghan, assistant professor, University of Florida, Department of Agricultural Education and Communication. Funding for this research and extension

program has been provided by the Center for Landscape Conservation and Ecology at the University of Florida and the National Fish and Wildlife Fund.

Background

A majority of Florida's lakes, streams, rivers, and estuaries have been found to be impaired by harmful nutrients originating from municipal wastewater, septic tanks, and agricultural and urban storm water.[36] Homeowners, the focus for this social marketing effort, apply an estimated 35 million pounds of nitrogen fertilizer to their lawns every year, contributing to this runoff into watersheds and estuaries.[37] Better control of nutrients, such as fertilizer runoff and chemicals in the yards of homeowners living adjacent to ponds, will help protect water quality, as these ponds serve an environmental function by controlling flooding when it rains and treating polluted storm water before it can reach creeks and rivers downstream. The challenge for planners was that while the ponds are manmade, homeowners think of them as "lakes" that offer aesthetic benefits and increase property value.

The desired behavior explored in this research was for homeowners with property adjacent to or near these ponds to make several significant changes to their current landscape: (a) plant aquatic plants in the ponds; (b) plant recommended plants along the shore of the ponds; and (c) maintain a 10-foot "maintenance-free" zone around the pond that is not mowed or fertilized. Research to understand barriers, benefits, and potential motivators to then inform campaign strategies began with focus groups.

Method

Five focus groups were conducted with retirees in two planned communities in southwest Florida. Participants were recruited through snowball sampling, a technique where, as it sounds, a small pool of initial informants suggest others who might be willing or appropriate for the study, ones in their social networks who would likely meet eligibility criteria. In this case, many of the participants knew one another through their homeowner association, and several were members of the same local landscape committees. A total of 38 residents participated in the research, with 27 living directly on a storm-water pond,

usually located behind the home. A significant number lived in "maintenance-free" neighborhoods, where landscaping, maintenance, and fertilizing are taken care of by a single contractor hired by the homeowner association. Participants' identity was confidential, which was seen as key to gaining the trust of this audience and their continued participation through campaign implementation. Areas explored through questioning included:

- General knowledge about the function of storm-water ponds
- The perceived importance of the ponds' potential benefits, including filtering sediments and pollutants, controlling flooding, increasing property value, attracting birds and other wildlife, and creating open water views
- The likelihood that residents would implement or request that contractors modify pond landscaping approaches; reasons they might not; and what might motivate them to make these changes. Photographs illustrating the recommended practices were shared, as seen in Figure 7.8.

Findings

Transcriptions from the focus groups filled 400 pages of text, which were then analyzed using MaxQDA (http://www.maxqda.com/products/maxqda11) software, with quotes and comments then being categorized into themes of barriers, benefits, and potential motivators (4Ps), as summarized in Table 7.6.

These findings were then used to make preliminary recommendations for a Protect

Figure 7.8   Photographs used to illustrate current versus recommended landscaping practices for backyard ponds.

Current

1. Recommendation: Aquatic Plants

2. Recommendation: Shoreline Plants

3. Recommendation: No-Mow Zone

Source: Paul Monaghan and Shangchun Hu.

Our Ponds campaign that will be developed and implemented by the Cooperative Extension Service. A final report for planners emphasized that they should be forewarned of the barriers that many homeowners would initially have to change, having bought their homes with the appeal of manicured turf grass landscapes, the current norm. The good news is that when shown alternative stormwater pond landscaping practices, they will likely respond as focus group participants did, often preferring the aesthetics of shoreline plantings to the current turf. Homeowners apparently appreciate the beauty of a more diverse landscape and understand how it can benefit property owners, wildlife, and water quality.

Postnote

These findings informed the development of an online survey with more than 800 residents to gauge their knowledge and preferences for different landscapes and measure them against best practices.

Table 7.6 Highlights of Focus Groups Findings

Barriers	Benefits	Motivators
• Liking the current appearance of the lakes and having paid a premium for it • Concerned with neighbors' potential negative reaction, with most residents with lakefront property liking the current appearance • Costs of establishing plant beds and maintaining them versus turf lawn • Might attract undesirable wildlife, including snakes, rodents, alligators, and mosquitoes • Might create an erosion problem, as the sod has a dense root system and forms an effective barrier to bank erosion	• Cleaner ponds, free of algae problems • Helps to protect water quality in the region • Potential for increased property value if improves aesthetics and water quality • Might attract more wildlife • Improved aesthetics, with comments including: "The plantings in the water make it look like there's movement in it" and "The diversity of plants along the edges of the pond look interesting and make it look healthier"	• Encouragement, approval, and technical assistance from the homeowner association • Word of mouth and testimonials • Messengers including master gardeners and representatives of the Native Plant Society and garden clubs • Demonstration properties, with one or two at a time as a pilot study • Webpage that monitors progress of different landscape conversions and includes testimonials from property owners • Educational materials with packaged designs and options

DISCUSSION QUESTIONS AND EXERCISES

1. It is argued in this chapter that benefits to the target audience for performing a proposed behavior are likely to be different than those identified by the campaign sponsor. Referring back to the Research Highlight, what was primarily "in it" for the homeowners to change their landscape adjacent to ponds? What was in it for the environmental organizations supporting the effort?

2. What is the difference between perceived benefits and potential motivators? Why do you need to know both?

3. Discuss how you might influence dog walkers who value the benefit of "joy" in their outing to leash their dogs.

4. Why do you think the Texas Department of Transportation changed the behavior objective for their updated campaign from refraining from littering to putting it in the proper place?

CHAPTER 7 NOTES

1. F. Lagarde, "Views From the World Social Marketing Conference 2008" (2008), 15, accessed July 11, 2011, www.nsmcentre.org.uk.

2. "Don't mess with Texas" is a registered trademark owned by the Texas Department of Transportation.

3. Goodman Center, "Don't mess with Texas" (n.d.), accessed November 26, 2013, http://www.thegoodmancenter.com/resources/newsletters/dont-mess-with-texas/.

4. Tuerff-Davis EnviroMedia Inc., "'Don't mess with Texas' Litter Prevention Campaign" (n.d.), accessed August 25, 2003, http://www.enviromedia.com/study4/php.

5. S. Tressler, "Don't mess with Texas Re-launches Anti-litter Campaign," *San Antonio Express-News* (April 4, 2013), accessed November 26, 2013, http://www.mysanantonio.com/news/local_news/article/Don-t-Mess-With-Texas-re-launches-anti-litter-4409508.php.

6. Don't mess with Texas Research [website], accessed November 26, 2013, http://www.dontmesswithtexas.org/research.php.

7. Ibid.

8. PewResearch: Social & Demographic Trends, "Millennials: Confident. Connected. Open to Change" (February 24, 2010), accessed November 27, 2013, http://www.pewsocialtrends.org/2010/02/24/millennials-confident-connected-open-to-change/.

9. Texas Department of Transportation, "Report a Litterer" (n.d.), accessed November 27, 2013, http://www.dontmesswithtexas.org/programs/report-a-litterer.php.

10. Don't mess with Texas®, "Don't mess with Texas Campus Cleanup" (n.d.), accessed November 27, 2013, http://www.dontmesswithtexas.org/programs/campus-cleanup.php.

11. R. P. Bagozzi, "Marketing as Exchange: A Theory of Transactions in the Marketplace," *American Behavioral Scientist* 21 (March/April 1978): 535–556.

12. P. Kotler, "A Generic Concept of Marketing," *Journal of Marketing* 36 (April 1972): 46–54.

13. P. Kotler and S. J. Levy, "Broadening the Concept of Marketing," *Journal of Marketing* 33 (January 1969): 10–15.

14. R. P. Bagozzi, "Marketing as an Organized Behavioral System of Exchange," *Journal of Marketing* 38 (1974): 77–81; Bagozzi, "Marketing as Exchange."

15. D. McKenzie-Mohr, *Community Based Social Marketing: Quick Reference* (n.d.), accessed January 30, 2007, http://www.cbsm.com/Reports/CBSM.pdf.

16. PATH, "Promoting Water Treatment in Malawi" (n.d.), retrieved April 7, 2011, http://path.org/projects/safe-water-malawi.php.

17. Ibid.

18. P. Kotler and N. Lee, *Marketing in the Public Sector: A Roadmap for Improved Performance* (p. 199). (Upper Saddle River, NJ: Wharton School, 2006).

19. Smith, B. (2003). Beyond "health" as a benefit. *Social Marketing Quarterly* 9(4), 22–28.

20. See ww.procurandorespostas.com/checklist.xlsx or http://www.i-socialmarketing.org/index.php?option=com_community&view=profile&userid=24479552#.VBdYm3l3uUk.

21. Adapted from the Marketing Highlight "Save the Crabs. Then Eat 'em (2005–2006)," by Bill Smith, in the 3rd edition of this book (pp. 4–7).

22. U.S. Department of Health and Human Services, "Public Service Campaign to Promote Breastfeeding Awareness Launched" [Press release] (June 4, 2007), accessed April 6, 2007, http://www.hhs.gov/news/press/2004pres/20040604.html.

23. U.S. Department of Health and Human Services, "National Breastfeeding Awareness Campaign: Babies Are Born to Be Breastfed" (2005), accessed April 2007, http://www.4woman.gov/breastfeeding/index.cfm?page=campaign.

24. The National Women's Health Information Center (womenshealth.gov), a service of the Office on Women's Health in the U.S. Department of Health and Human Services.

25. Centers for Disease Control and Prevention, "Breastfeeding Report Card–United States, 2012," (n.d.), accessed November 22, 2013, http://www.cdc.gov/breastfeeding/data/reportcard/reportcard2012.htm.

26. S. Peattie and K. Peattie, "Ready to Fly Solo? Reducing Social Marketing's Dependence on Commercial Marketing Theory," *Marketing Theory Articles* 3, no. 3 (2003): 365–385.

27. D. McKenzie-Mohr and W. Smith, *Fostering Sustainable Behavior: An Introduction to Community-Based Social Marketing* (Gabriola Island, BC, Canada: New Society, 1999), 5.

28. The Humane Society, Tacoma and Pierce County, "Kittenkaboodle" (n.d.), accessed October 25, 2006, http://thehumanesociety.org/2006/09/kittenkaboodle/.

29. Case source: Nancy Lee, Social Marketing Services, Inc.

30. P. Kotler and E. L. Roberto, *Social Marketing: Strategies for Changing Public Behavior* (New York: Free Press, 1989), 102.

31. A. Andreasen. *Marketing social change: Changing behavior to promote health, social development, and the environment* (San Francisco, CA: Jossey-Bass, 1995, 108–109).

32. March of Dimes, "United States: Quick Facts: Folic Acid Overview" (2001), accessed December 23, 2010, http://www.marchofdimes.com/peristats/tlanding.aspx?reg=99&top=13&lev=0&slev=1%20.

33. Personal email communication from Michael Jortner, May 2013.

34. This case was taken from a draft of a social marketing plan for the Washington Department of Health, 2006. Ilene Silver, lead project manager.

35. "Institutional Review Board," *Wikipedia* (n.d.), accessed January 16, 2007, http://en.wikipedia.org/wiki/Institutional_Review_Board.

36. E. Stanton and M. Taylor, "Valuing Florida's Clean Waters" (Stockholm Environmental Institute—U.S. Center, 2012), citing Florida Department of Environmental Protection reports; the study found that 53% of river miles, 82% of lake and reservoir acres, and 32% of estuaries that had been assessed were considered impaired by nutrients.

37. Florida Department of Agriculture and Consumer Services, "Florida Consumer Fertilizer Task Force, Final Report" (2008), http://consensus.fsu.edu/Fertilizer-Task-Force/pdfs/Fertilizer_TF_EMail_Coms_12-13-07.pdf.

Chapter 8

Tapping Behavior Change Theories, Models, and Frameworks

Theories that explain what influences behaviour and models of behaviour that seek to describe the process of behaviour formation or change are vital to all social marketing practice. All practitioners, planners and strategists need to understand at the least the basics of behavioural theory if they are to develop effective social marketing interventions. Whilst there is usually not one theory or model that will fit exactly the issue and target group that you are working with, by reviewing a number of models and theories it should be possible to identify key triggers and possible points of intervention for a social marketing programme.

Professor Jeff French[1]

This chapter is intended to provide a convenient reference guide to 17 major theories, models, and frameworks that inform social marketing strategies and inspire social marketers:

Theories	Models
1. Diffusion of Innovation Theory	9. Health Belief Model
2. Self-Control Theory	10. Stages of Change Model
3. Goal-Setting Theory	11. Service Dominant Logic Model
4. Self-Perception Theory	12. Ecological Model
5. Social Cognitive Theory/Social Learning Theory	13. Community Readiness Model
6. Theory of Reasoned Action/Planned Behavior	14. Hierarchy of Effects Model
7. Social Norms Theory	**Frameworks**
8. Exchange Theory	15. Behavioral Economics & Nudge Tactics
	16. Science of Habit Framework
	17. Carrots, Sticks, and Promises

Although most of these theories, models, and frameworks can inform multiple steps in the strategic planning process, we have grouped them in this chapter by their strongest applicability, that is, by which of the following categories they inform:

1. Selecting target audiences

2. Setting behavior objectives and goals

3. Understanding audience barriers, benefits, and motivators; the competition; and influential others

4. Developing social marketing mix strategies

MARKETING HIGHLIGHT

Preventing Domestic Violence Among Women in West Africa

A Social Norms Approach

(2010–2012)

The social norms theory states that much of our behavior is influenced by our perceptions of what is "normal or "typical."[2] (Why else would high school youth in the United States wear basketball shorts to school during the frigid winter months?) These norms are most commonly thought of as the "rules" that a group uses to determine appropriate and inappropriate behaviors. This marketing highlight illustrates a strategic effort to change a long-held *injunctive norm*, a behavior a community perceives as being approved of by others in the group. The setting is the Cote d'Ivoire in West Africa, the issue is domestic violence, and the outcomes are inspiring.

Background

In 2010, the International Rescue Committee's Gender-Based Violence (GBV) team in Cote d'Ivoire conducted a community survey with 1,271 women that quantified and confirmed the widespread incidence of domestic violence in the country. Two out of three (66.8%) women reported having experienced emotional, physical, and/or sexual violence in their lifetime.[3] The survey also confirmed that intimate partner violence against women was perceived as a social norm and as "part of life," and that the women perceived it as "something to be tolerated." Further, the study found that

in the case of men, there is a strong dysfunctional norm that violence within a partnership, particularly marriage, is sometimes necessary to keep their women in line . . . and that current social norms also favor inaction and silence over reporting and communicating when violence does occur.[4]

Over the next two years, with the guidance of social marketing consultant Virginia Williams, the team developed and launched a social marketing campaign focusing on changing these dysfunctional norms.[5] Highlights of that plan, as well as results of an evaluation survey two years into the campaign, are the focus for this highlight.

Target Audience, Desired Behavior, and Audience Insights

Table 8.1 summarizes the two primary target audiences, the two desired behaviors the campaign was to influence, and key audience insights that informed the development of marketing mix strategies, ones identified through focus groups with target audiences.

Strategies

Consistent with campaign objectives, the campaign was branded "Break the Silence." A launch event was held at the Palais de la Culture in Abidjan on March 5, 2012, with over 1,200 people attending, facilitated by each of the 14 social centers in the metropolitan area. The event's activities included presentation of the International Rescue Committee's mission by the county director; presentation of the campaign by the GBV manager; speeches expressing support from the ministers of health and women's affairs; a performance of one of the campaign's radio sketches; a testimonial from a courageous survivor; and finally a performance of the campaign

song created by hip-hop/reggae artists Nash, DJ Mix, and Kajeem to an enthusiastic crowd. The event was covered by the national television station and by several of the local papers.

Marketing mix strategies to promote the reporting of incidents of domestic violence and to alter current perceived norms included the following.

Product

Both target audiences (women and men) were encouraged to use a hotline to reach their local social center for help. A list of preapproved social service facilities in each community where the International Rescue Committee (IRC) has offices was made available to target audiences. Procedures for reporting were also streamlined, making the "when, how, and why" of reporting gender-based violence acts simpler for target audiences.

Price

One incentive offered for going through the approved social service facilities was that this would help expedite referrals for those needing access to temporary housing or to a hospital for treatment. (This also provided a mechanism for monitoring and tracking the incidence of actions taken based on campaign interventions.) An additional incentive for going through the IRC was that if a medical certificate was needed to access the services, the IRC would cover the cost of the certificate (US $60), a cost too few women could afford to pay. This certificate is also valuable, if not essential, for going to court and pressing charges for sexual assault.

Table 8.1 Audience Profile, Desired Behaviors, and Insights

Primary Target Audiences	Women 18–25	Men 18–25
Description	- The most vulnerable: married or cohabiting with a partner, not working, living in rural areas, less educated, and less aware of their human rights - Value the well-being of their family, the future of their children, and being treated with respect	- Are concerned about domestic violence against women, including their wives, girlfriends, and/or others they know in their neighborhood and the community - Value the well-being of their wives and girlfriends, adequate finances, the respect of their parents, and providing a safe environment for their children
Behavior	- Report violence - Promote the (new) injunctive norm that violence should not be tolerated in the home and is a danger to the well-being of the children	- Support the reporting of violence within the community and support survivors - Discourage violence among male peers
Insights		
Barriers	- Reprisal from own family or community for reporting - Stigma - Personal embarrassment or fear to report	- Reprisal from family of victim or perpetrator of violence for reporting - Stigma - Personal embarrassment to be seen as supporting women
Benefits	- Bettering their own well-being/self esteem - Creating a more stable household for their children - Wanting children to grow up in a healthy environment - Receiving consideration/respect from their partners - By being healthy, they are better able to work and make money for the family	- Bettering one's status as one who takes initiative - Being viewed as a model citizen - Experiencing personal pride - Protecting one's own partner
Competition	- Remaining silent - Doing nothing after witnessing or experiencing violence	- Remaining silent - Doing nothing after witnessing or experiencing violence
Positioning	We want these women to know that gender-based violence is wrong and that they should report it for the well-being of themselves and their family.	We want this group of men to see that reporting violence and encouraging women victims to report violence will help protect women in the future and help to change community norms.

Place

Over half the population of Cote d'Ivoire own a mobile phone, and the campaign capitalized on this by making the hotline available 24 /7 and accessible throughout all regions in the Cote d'Ivoire, with referrals then being made to over 25 social centers in the nine regions where the IRC had offices.

Promotion

Messages: Two messages were designed for each audience, one to influence action and one to influence new social norms. The women's action message was "Stand up against violence!" and the norms message was "In our house, violence has no place" (see Figure 8.1). For the men, the action message, "Protect women. It's your business too," and the norms message was, "We are a team against violence!"

Messengers: Influential members of the target audience were featured as messengers for the campaign, appearing in TV ads as well as on billboards and posters. These messengers were chosen based on focus groups with women and men (from target audiences) who indicated that these individuals were highly regarded leaders or models in the community. They included actresses, a football star and his wife, three of the country's most respected religious leaders, and three musical artists.

Figure 8.1   A poster bearing a norms message: "In our house, violence has no place."

Source: New View Media LLC for International Rescue Committee.

Figure 8.2 Poster bearing a message from influential others: "We are a team against violence."

Source: New View Media LLC for International Rescue Committee.

Communication channels: Communication channels for sending messages regarding the new social norm included television and radio public service announcements (PSAs), a "Break the Silence" song played on local radio stations, panel discussions and radio call-in programs, radio news features and sketches, radio contests, promotion via text messaging, billboards, and articles in newspapers announcing the launch of the campaign and celebrity involvement. Specific channels to support both women and men and prompt action included pocket calendars, bracelets, T-shirts, and stickers for the interior and exterior of auto vehicles. The campaign was also promoted on Facebook, YouTube, and Twitter, which are increasingly being used by Ivorians via smartphones.

Results

A campaign evaluation included a nationwide survey of 1,500 people and was conducted by 65 trained volunteers who worked for two days in their respective regions. Within the target group, 60% of those interviewed were women and 40% were men.[6] The questionnaire utilized 12 questions measuring exposure to the campaign, comprehension of the questionnaire's messages, attitudes and beliefs about domestic violence, perceptions of social norms related to domestic violence, and actions related to reporting violence and assisting survivors. Input forms from both the hotline and social centers provided tracking information on how respondents learned about the hotline and social centers. Results were both informative and encouraging:

- *Campaign awareness.* A majority of the target audiences (78.5%) reported that they had seen the messages five times or more, with billboards and television being the most cited forms of media.
- *Alignment with the new social norm.* An overwhelming majority (88%) agreed with the statement that violence was unacceptable by the community.
- *Intent to action.* Almost all (90%) said they would take action when someone experienced violence.
- *Calls to the hotline.* Once launched, the hotline averaged 226 callers per

month and proved to be a crucial link in women's and men's ability to take the next behavioral step to visit a social center, given that it provided an opportunity to ask questions anonymously. It also proved to be an invaluable tool for measuring actual behavior change related to action messages of the campaign, with caller data indicating that posters, TV spots, auto stickers, and calendars were the most frequently mentioned sources for learning about the hotline. It is noteworthy that a significant number of callers were men (35%) calling to denounce violence against a woman or girl or even to state their interest to improve the couple's communications (see Box 8.1).

- *Visiting social centers.* Of those visiting the centers to report violence, almost 92% had been exposed to the campaign (see Box 8.2).

Box 8.1
August Case Study: The Role That Men Can Play in Combating Violence Against Girls

Mr. X calls in defense of Miss Z, who, when she was six months pregnant, was beaten by her boyfriend and died of her injuries. Mr. X, as a friend of the family, is calling the hotline to get information on what steps to follow to pursue the matter so that justice will be done, because for him it is unacceptable that someone who has committed such violence would be released. He is referred to the court for the proper procedure to follow.

Box 8.2
October Case Study: Resolution of Death Threat Against Ms. X

Ms. X is a teacher in Daloa. Legally married to her husband, she lives in Daloa with him. For some time, Ms. X had gone through difficult times with her husband. One day she received a text message from her husband threatening, "Like my two fiancées before you, you will die." Frightened by this death threat from her husband, Ms. X confided in a friend, who encouraged her to call the Break the Silence hotline to report the situation. After her report, she was assisted by the local social center through the judicial process. After the court hearing, her husband was detained in prison.

Reflections

Virginia Williams commented in her evaluation report that

the structure of the project included holding a week-long social marketing training workshop for the GBV staff. Looking back, this capacity building of the staff worked extremely well in developing a strategic social marketing plan intent on real behavior and social norms change, one the staff was then able to get behind.[7]

Information for this highlight was provided by Virginia Williams, communications consultant/owner, New View Media.

INFORMING AUDIENCE SEGMENTATION AND SELECTION: THE DIFFUSION OF INNOVATIONS THEORY AND THE STAGES OF CHANGE/TRANSTHEORETICAL MODEL

The Diffusion of Innovations Theory

Some believe, like Craig Lefebvre, that "the diffusion of innovations theory offers one of the most robust theories for taking innovations in ideas, behaviors, and practices to scale."[8] As noted in Chapter 5, Everett Rogers first conceptualized this theory in the early 1960s, and in the fifth edition of his book *Diffusion of Innovations* (2003), Rogers defines diffusion as a process by which (a) an innovation (b) is communicated through certain channels (c) over time (d) among the members of a social system. Innovation diffusion research suggests that different types of adopters accept an innovation at different points in time. Five groups have been identified:

1. *Innovators* are motivated by a need for novelty and a need to be different

2. *Early adopters* are drawn by the product's intrinsic value

3. The *early majority* perceive the spread of a product and decide to go along with it out of their need to match and imitate

4. The *late majority* jump on the bandwagon after realizing that "most" are doing it

5. *Laggards* finally follow suit as the product attains popularity and broad acceptance

The implication for social marketers is that, for a relatively new behavior, you start by targeting innovators and early adopters and then, once that adoption is successful, move to the early majority and then the late majority. After these groups are on board, the assignment gets easier, as the laggards will be "outnumbered." Beginning in January 2010 in Washington, D.C., for example, a 5-cent tax was charged for grocery bags. Later, in October of that year, the *Wall Street Journal* reported on outcomes. Retail outlets went from handing out 68 million bags per quarter to only 11 million. The article, however, attributed this success to something more than the 5-cent tax. "No one got bags automatically anymore. Instead, shoppers had to ask for them—right in front of their fellow customers."[9] The article concluded that the magic ingredient was not the financial incentive. It was "peer pressure."

The Stages of Change/Transtheoretical Model

The stages of change model was originally developed by Prochaska and DiClemente in the early 1980s[10] and has been tested and refined over the past decades. It describes six stages that people go through to change their behavior. These stages create unique market segments:

1. *Precontemplation.* "People at this stage usually have no intention of changing their behavior, and typically deny having a problem."[11]

2. *Contemplation.* "People acknowledge that they have a problem and begin to think seriously about solving it."[12]

3. *Preparation.* "Most people in the Preparation Stage are (now) planning to take action . . . and are making the final adjustments before they begin to change their behavior."[13]

4. *Action.* "The Action Stage is one in which people most overtly modify their behavior and their surrounds. They stop smoking cigarettes, remove all desserts from the house, pour the last beer down the drain, or confront their fears. In short, they make the move for which they have been preparing."[14]

5. *Maintenance.* "During Maintenance (individuals) work to consolidate the gains attained during the action and other stages and struggle to prevent lapses and relapse."[15]

6. *Termination.* "The Termination stage is the ultimate goal for all changes. Here, a former addition or problem will no longer present any temptation or threat."[16]

For social marketers selecting a target audience, the most attractive segments may be those in the action, preparation, and/or contemplation stages (in that order), assuming that the size of the segment is large enough to meet targeted behavior adoption goals. The rationale for this is that those in these stages at least know about the behavior and are open to it. You don't need to spend scarce resources waking up those in precontemplation or convincing them that your idea is a good one. The three priority groups "simply" have barriers we need to address and/or benefits we need to assure and help provide.

INFORMING BEHAVIOR SELECTION AND GOALS: SELF-CONTROL THEORY, GOAL-SETTING THEORY, AND SELF-PERCEPTION THEORY

Self-Control Theory

Self-control theory encourages planners to consider that individuals have a limited resource of self-control strength to use for various exertions such as resisting temptations or breaking "bad," but pleasurable, habits.[17] According to this theory, exerting self-control consumes or depletes this resource for a short time, and as a result, individuals are prone to performing more poorly on concurring or subsequent tasks that require self-control. Implications for selecting behaviors for a social marketing effort are that you may want to avoid efforts to influence a target audience to take on more than one "depleting" behavior at a time. Rather, intervention success is likely to be greater when behavior changes are initiated sequentially rather than simultaneously.[18]

For example, consider efforts by a physician to influence a 45-year-old male patient who had recently suffered from a heart attack to stop smoking cigarettes and resist consumption of fast foods. The self-control theory suggests that instead, we recommend that the patient focus first and solely on one behavior (smoking cessation) and ignore weight management until he is confident that he will not relapse.

The Goal-Setting Theory

The goal-setting theory offers insight into crafting a behavior objective that is both motivating and instructional. Dr. Edwin Locke's pioneering research in the late 1960s found that specific, clear goals that are realistically achievable are more effective than ambiguous and easy ones.[19]

Consider the difference between an effort to "eat more fruits and vegetables a day" and "5 a Day"; between "exercise regularly" and "exercise five days a week at least thirty minutes at a time"; between "take shorter showers" and "take a five-minute shower;" between "pick up pet waste in your yard" and "pick up pet waste in your yard on a daily basis and put it in the trash"; or between "don't idle except when in traffic" and "don't idle more than 10 seconds except when in traffic." Behaviors that are specific, measurable, achievable, realistic, and time-bound (SMART) work to first communicate what it is we want the target audience to do, and second to assist them (and you) in knowing if they have accomplished it.

Self-Perception Theory

Self-perception theory suggests that the more we engage people in a behavior category (e.g., healthy behaviors, environmentally friendly behaviors), the greater the chances they will sustain these behaviors and even take on more. This happens as they begin to perceive themselves as the type of person who participates in these types of actions, which, upon reflection, alters their beliefs about themselves.[20]

Doug McKenzie-Mohr suggests we leverage this tendency by providing convenient opportunities for people to initiate and engage in a behavior. He cites an example where

> prior to curbside recycling being introduced, most individuals had no strongly held beliefs regarding the importance of waste reduction. However, when these same individuals received their new curbside containers and began to recycle, their participation in recycling led them to come to view themselves as the type of person who believed that waste reduction was important. Furthermore, it is likely these beliefs will be most strongly held when the opportunity exists to engage in these actions frequently.[21]

When someone engages, for example, in repetitive actions such as recycling and turning off computer monitors when not in use, this is likely to increase his or her belief in the importance of waste reduction and energy conservation.

DEEPENING YOUR UNDERSTANDING OF AUDIENCE BARRIERS, BENEFITS, MOTIVATORS, THE COMPETITION, AND INFLUENTIAL OTHERS: THE HEALTH BELIEF MODEL, THE THEORY OF REASONED ACTION AND THE THEORY OF PLANNED BEHAVIOR, AND THE SERVICE-DOMINANT LOGIC MODEL

The Health Belief Model

Kelli McCormack Brown clearly describes the model originally developed by social psychologists Hochbaum, Kegels, and Rosenstock, who were greatly influenced by the theories of Kurt Lewin:

> The Health Belief Model states that the perception of a personal health behavior threat is itself influenced by at least three factors: general *health values,* which include interest and concern about health; specific health beliefs about *vulnerability* to a particular health threat; and beliefs about the *consequences* of the health problem. Once an individual perceives a threat to his/her health and is simultaneously cued to action, and his/her perceived benefits outweigh his/her perceived costs, then

that individual is most likely to undertake the recommended preventive health action. Key descriptors include:

- Perceived Susceptibility: Perception of the likelihood of experiencing a condition that would adversely affect one's health
- Perceived Seriousness: Beliefs a person holds concerning the effects a given disease or condition would have on one's state of affairs: physical, emotional, financial, and psychological
- Perceived Benefits of Taking Action: The extent to which a person believes there will be benefits to recommended actions
- Perceived Barriers to Taking Action: The extent to which the treatment or preventive measure may be perceived as inconvenient, expensive, unpleasant, painful, or upsetting
- Cues to Action: Types of internal and external strategies/events that might be needed for the desired behavior to occur.[22]

This model suggests that you would benefit from reviewing or conducting research to determine each of these forces (susceptibility, seriousness, benefits, barriers, and perceptions of effective "cues to action") *before* developing campaign strategies. The National High Blood Pressure Education Program (NHBPEP) understands this well, as illustrated in the following highlight of their social marketing efforts and successes.

More than 65 million American adults, one in three, had high blood pressure in 2006, and less than 30% were controlling their condition.[23] Key to influencing desired behaviors (increasing monitoring and lifestyle and medication plans) is an understanding of perceived susceptibility, seriousness, and barriers such as the following:

- "It is hard for me to change my diet and to find the time to exercise."
- "My blood pressure is difficult to control."
- "My blood pressure varies so much; it's probably not accurate."
- "Medications can have undesirable side effects."
- "It's too expensive to go to the doctor just to get my blood pressure checked."
- "It may be the result of living a full and active life. Not everybody dies from it."

As you read on, you can see how messages in NHBPEP materials and related strategies reflect an understanding of these perceptions:

- "You don't have to make all of the changes immediately. The key is to focus on one or two at a time. Once they become part of your normal routine, you can go on to the next change. Sometimes, one change leads naturally to another. For example, increasing physical activity will help you lose weight."[24]
- "You can keep track of your blood pressure outside of your doctor's office by taking it at home."[25]

- "You don't have to run marathons to benefit from physical activity. Any activity, if done at least 30 minutes a day over the course of most days, can help."[26]

The year the program began in 1972, less than one fourth of the American population knew of the relationship between hypertension, stroke, and heart disease. In 2001, more than three fourths of the population were aware of this connection. As a result, virtually all Americans have had their blood pressure measured at least once, and three fourths of the population have it measured every six months.

The Theory of Reasoned Action and the Theory of Planned Behavior

The theory of reasoned action (TRA), developed by Ajzen and Fishbein in 1975 and restated in 1980, suggests that the best predictor of a person's behavior is his or her intention to act. This intention is determined by two major factors: a person's beliefs about the outcomes associated with the behavior and his or her perceptions of how people he or she cares about will view the behavior in question. Using language from other theories presented throughout this text, one's likelihood of adopting the behavior will be greatly influenced by perceived benefits, costs, and social norms. In 1988, Ajzen extended the TRA to include the influence of beliefs and perceptions regarding control—beliefs about one's ability to actually perform the behavior (e.g., self-efficacy). This successor is called the theory of planned behavior (TPB).[27] Stated simply, a target audience is most likely to adopt a behavior when they have a positive attitude toward it, perceive that "important others" would approve, and believe they will be successful in performing it.

The Social Cognitive Theory/Social Learning

Fishbein has summarized Bandura's description of the social cognitive theory, also referred to as the social learning theory:

> The Social Cognitive Theory states that two major factors influence the likelihood that one will take preventive action. First, like the Health Belief Model, a person believes that the benefits of performing the behavior outweigh the costs (i.e., a person should have more positive than negative outcome expectancies). [This should remind you of the exchange theory mentioned frequently throughout this text.] Second, and perhaps most important, the person must have a sense of personal agency or self-efficacy with respect to performing the preventive behavior, . . . [and] must believe that he or she has the skills and abilities necessary for performing the behavior under a variety of circumstances.[28]

Andreasen adds that this self-efficacy comes about at least in part from learning specific skills and from observing social norms, hence the name "social learning." This learning of specific new behaviors, he explains, has three major components: sequential approximation, repetition, and reinforcement. Sequential approximation acknowledges that individuals do not often instantly leap from not doing a behavior to doing it. They may prefer to work their way up to it. For example, one way of teaching smokers how to adopt a nonsmoking lifestyle is to reduce their consumption step by step, perhaps one cigarette at a time, starting with the easiest behavior to give up and working up to the most difficult. Encouraging repetition (practice) and providing reinforcement strategies will then make it more likely that the behavior will become a "part of a permanent behavioral repertoire."[29]

The Service-Dominant Logic Model

In a seminal article in 2004, Steve Vargo and Robert Lusch proposed the concept of a service-dominant logic model, asserting that a product (whether a tangible good or a service) has value only when a customer "uses" it, and that when he or she does, it improves the condition or well-being of that person in some way. They also stress that this value is determined by the customer, not the marketer, and therefore that the customer should be involved in the design and delivery of the product.[30]

In the 10-step social marketing model outlined in this book, this value is equivalent to the *core product* and best determined when conducting barriers and benefits research with the target audience. As described in more depth in Chapter 10, determining a product strategy includes three decisions. We'll use family planning as an example. First, what is the primary benefit (value) the target audience wants in exchange for adopting the behavior (e.g., having children when they can best provide for them)? This becomes the *core product*. Second, what tangible good or service will you be promoting, the *actual product* (e.g., birth control pills)? And, third, what additional goods and services (*augmented product*) will you be offering that will make it more likely that the target audience will acquire the product (e.g., family planning counselors)? The core product (desired benefit/value) then inspires product branding (e.g., the family welfare vitamin),[31] as well as additional promotional messages.

INSPIRING DEVELOPMENT OF SOCIAL MARKETING MIX STRATEGIES: THE SOCIAL NORMS THEORY, THE ECOLOGICAL MODEL, THE BEHAVIORAL ECONOMICS FRAMEWORK AND NUDGE TACTICS, THE SCIENCE OF HABIT FRAMEWORK, THE HIERARCHY OF EFFECTS MODEL, EXCHANGE THEORY, THE COMMUNITY READINESS MODEL, AND THE CARROTS, STICKS, AND PROMISES FRAMEWORK

The Social Norms Theory

The social norms theory states that much of people's behavior is influenced by their perceptions of what is "normal" or "typical."[32] Social norms are most commonly thought of as the "rules" that a group uses to determine appropriate and inappropriate behaviors as well as values, beliefs, and attitudes.[33] Several related terms include the following:

- *Injunctive norms* are behaviors a group perceives as being approved or disapproved of by others in the group.
- *Descriptive norms* are perceptions of what behaviors others are actually, or normally, engaged in, regardless of whether or not these are approved of by others.
- *Explicit norms* are those that are written or openly expressed.
- *Implicit norms* are those that are not openly stated, but understood to be the norm for a group.
- *Subjective norms* are expectations that individuals think valued others will have about how they will behave.
- *Personal norms* are an individual's standards for his or her own behavior.

Linkenbach describes the social norms approach to prevention, which has clear potential implications for strategy development:

> The social norms approach to prevention emerged from college health settings in the mid-1980s in response to the seemingly intractable issue of high-risk drinking by college students. Wesley Perkins and Alan Berkowitz, social scientists at Hobart, Williams, and Smith Colleges, discovered that a significant disparity existed between actual alcohol use by college students and their perceptions of other students' drinking. Simply put, most college students reported that they believed drinking norms were higher and riskier than they really were.
>
> The major implication of these findings is that if a student believes that heavy alcohol use is the norm and expected by most students, then regardless of the accuracy of the perception, he or she is more likely to become involved in alcohol abuse—despite his or her own personal feelings. Perkins came to call this pattern of misperception the "reign of error" and suggested that it could have detrimental effects on actual student drinking. According to Berkowitz, if students think "everyone is doing it," then heavy drinking rates rise due to influence from "imaginary peers."[34]

This norming theory highlights the potential benefit of understanding perceived versus actual behaviors among target audiences. Results may signal an opportunity to correct the perception. The research highlight at the conclusion of this chapter presents a more in-depth case on this social norms marketing approach.

The Ecological Model

One criticism of many theories and models of behavior change is that they emphasize the individual behavior change process but pay little attention to sociocultural and physical environmental influences on behavior—the ecological perspective.[35] The ecological approach places significant importance on the role of supportive environments, and four are typically cited: *individual* factors (demographics, personality, genetics, skills, religious beliefs), *relationship* factors (friends, families, colleagues), *community* factors (schools, work sites, health care organizations, media), and *societal* factors (cultural norms, laws, governance). This model argues that the most powerful behavior change interventions are those that simultaneously influence these multiple levels and that this will lead to greater and longer-lasting behavioral changes. The key to success is to assess each of these levels of influence and determine what is needed that will provide the greatest influence on the desired behavior.[36]

The Behavioral Economics Framework and Nudge Tactics

Behavioral economics is a growing body of science that looks at how environmental and other factors prompt personal decisions. The core idea that humans don't behave like rational economic agents was introduced several decades ago by Daniel Kahneman, Amos Tversky, and others. The central thesis is that people move between states of emotional hot and cold. As it sounds, when in a hot state, we are emotionally aroused (irrational), and in a cold state we are calm or neutral (rational). And as might be expected, arousal more often than not overrides reason. A young woman watching her budget may think before going to the mall to shop that she will only buy the shoes she heard were 50% off. When she gets there and sees the newest fashions, however, she is likely to succumb to her desires and pay full price.

Bill Smith argues in an article in the Summer 2010 *Social Marketing Quarterly* that "we have a new ally in Behavioral Economics"—one he is particularly excited about, as it has the potential to encourage the government "to arrange the conditions of life . . . and build policy contingencies so that it is fun, easy, and popular for people to make the right decision."[37]

To distinguish behavioral economics from social marketing, Philip Kotler offered the following thoughts in an article titled "Behavioral Economics or Social Marketing? The Latter!":

> Behavioral economics does not come with a rich tool box for influencing individual and group behavior . . . Behavioral economics is mainly interested in demonstrating the irrationality of human decision making, not finding a more comprehensive system to influence individual and group behavior . . . . Behavioral economics is simply another word for "consumer behavior theory" as used by marketers . . . and the bottom line is that those who want to influence social behavior for the good of the individual and society need to apply social marketing thinking, a much larger system than behavioral economics.[38]

In their book *Nudge*, Professors Richard Thaler and Cass Sunstein go beyond the more psychology-oriented behavioral economics theory to suggest concrete tactics this can inspire and improve public policy. They call them "nudges." Consider, for example, organ donation in Europe. In Germany, they note, only an estimated 12% of citizens consent to organ donation when getting or renewing their driver's license. By contrast, in Austria, nearly everyone (99%) does.[39] Why the difference? In Germany, citizens must "opt in"—check a box indicating they agree to be an organ donor. By contrast, in Austria citizens need to "opt out"—check a box indicating they don't agree. The same "choice architecture," as the authors call it, could be used to bolster retirement-savings plans (companies automatically enroll employees unless told otherwise) or to increase the chances that students in school cafeterias will choose healthier foods (healthy options are at the beginning of the line).

To distinguish Nudge from Social Marketing, Jeff French offers the following thoughts in *Think Paper: Autumn 2010*, a publication of Strategic Social Marketing:

> Nudging people into better health or away from criminality will seldom be enough to result in population level improvements because in many situations, evidence and experience make it clear that there is a need for other forms of intervention. Therefore, Nudges should be seen as a helpful part of the solution but not a magic bullet . . . and do not represent a full toolbox of possible forms of intervention . . . The selection of which form of intervention or combination of intervention types should always be driven by evidence and target audience insight.[40]

Relative to the 10-step model presented in this text, nudge tactics can usually be categorized as one of the 4P intervention tools, and are therefore only one of numerous interventions available, with the ideal strategies being those that consumer insight research or pilots indicate would have the most success in removing barriers, increasing benefits, and providing motivators for your target audience. The following nudge tactics are among some of the most familiar:

- A *product* nudge: Streamlining applications for financial aid for a college education
- A *price* nudge: Offering lower minimum amounts for workplace savings plans
- A *place* nudge: Placing the "good food" at the beginning of the school lunch line
- A *promotion* nudge: Having potential organ donors opt "out" versus opt "in"

Our hope is that program managers involved in developing behavior change strategies will recognize that "nudges" are simply one of a bundle of potential behavior change marketing tactics, ones that Jeff French describes as being more automatic or unconscious in nature.[41]

The Science of Habit Framework

Charles Duhigg's 2008 article in the *New York Times*, "Warning: Habits May Be Good for You," encourages those interested in influencing "good behaviors" to take a lesson from the playbooks of the Proctor & Gambles and Unilevers of the world:

If you look hard enough, you'll find that many of the products we use every day—chewing gums, skin moisturizers, disinfecting wipes, air fresheners, water purifiers, antiperspirants, colognes, teeth whiteners, fabric softeners, vitamins—are results of manufactured habits. A century ago, few people regularly brushed their teeth multiple times a day. Today . . . many Americans habitually give their pearly whites a cavity-preventing scrub twice a day.[42]

How is this useful to social marketers? Consider opportunities to "manufacture" new habits (e.g., walking a new puppy 30 minutes a day), or try embedding a new behavior into an existing habit (e.g., flossing your teeth while watching your favorite late night show).

The Hierarchy of Effects Model

The hierarchy of effects, a communications model created in the early 1960s by Robert Lavidge and Gary Steiners, suggests that there are six steps that a potential customer experiences from first viewing a product promotion to the end state, product purchase (see Figure 8.3).[43]

Implications for the social marketer are that promotional strategies should be designed to target the "buyer readiness" stage the target audience is in relative to adopting the behavior, and moving them to the next step.

The Exchange Theory

As mentioned in Chapter 7, the traditional economic exchange theory postulates that, for an exchange to take place, target audiences must perceive benefits (value) in the offer equal to or greater than perceived costs. In other words, they must believe they will get as much or more than they give.

Implications for social marketers are significant and guide the development of social marketing mix strategies, for if the target audience does not perceive benefits of adopting a behavior (e.g., exercise five times a week, 30 minutes at a time) to be equal to or greater than the costs, the marketer has "work to do." We must decrease costs and/or increase benefits, and we have four major tools to accomplish this: product (e.g., fun exercise classes for seniors), price (e.g., free), place (e.g., at a local community center), and promotion (e.g., positioned as a way to feel better and live longer).

The Community Readiness Model

The community readiness model offers a process for assessing the level of readiness that a community has to develop and implement programs to address a variety of health (e.g., drug and alcohol use, HIV/AIDS), injury prevention (e.g., domestic violence, suicide), environmental (e.g., alternative transportation modes), and community (e.g., animal control) issues. Proponents suggest that communities have found this model helpful, as it

Figure 8.3   The hierarchy of effects model: Six steps from awareness to purchase. Adapted from www.learnmarketing.net

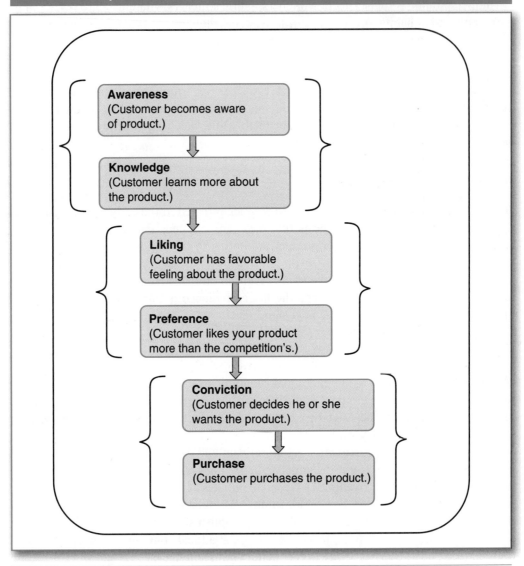

Source: Learn Marketing.net, "Hierarchy of Effects Model" (n.d.) accessed December 17, 2013, http://www.learnmarketing.net/ hierarchy_of_effects_model.html.

encourages use of local experts and resources and helps create community-specific and culturally specific interventions. It was developed at the Tri Ethnic Center at Colorado State University and can be used as "both a research tool to assess levels of readiness across a group of communities or as a tool to guide prevention efforts at the community level." [44] Assessment of readiness is determined for each of six key dimensions: (a) past efforts, (b) community knowledge of efforts, (c) leadership, (d) community climate, (e) community knowledge of the issues, and (e) resources. A level-of-readiness score, from 1 to 9, is assigned to each dimension. Scores are determined through in-depth interviews with key informants, who are chosen to represent important parts of the community (e.g., school, government, medical). Strategy development is based on these community readiness scores, with dimensions with the lowest levels of readiness typically being addressed first.

The Carrots, Sticks, and Promises Framework

Michael Rothschild, an emeritus professor for the School of Business at the University of Wisconsin, "shook" the social marketing world in a seminal article in the *Journal of Marketing* in October 1999 titled "Carrots, Sticks, and Promises: A Conceptual Framework for the Management of Public Health and Social Issue Behaviors."[45] The framework distinguishes three very distinct tools that governments can rely on to influence behaviors: marketing (the carrot), law (the stick), and education (the promise), and expresses concern that "current public health behavior management relies heavily on education and law while neglecting the underlying philosophy of marketing and exchange."[46]

Education, Rothschild writes, refers to messages that attempt to inform and/or encourage voluntary behaviors. They can create awareness about existing benefits of adopting the behavior, but cannot deliver them. *Law* involves coercion to achieve the behavior or threatens punishment for noncompliance or inappropriate behavior. *Marketing*, however, influences behaviors by offering incentives for voluntary exchange.

> The environment is made favorable for appropriate behavior through the development of choices with comparative advantage (products and services), favorable cost–benefit relationships (pricing), and time and place utility enhancement (channels of distribution). Positive reinforcement is provided when a transaction is completed.[47]

THEMES FROM ALL

Fishbein's summary of behavior change interventions melds themes from most of the theories, models, and frameworks presented in this chapter and provide a quick reference for gauging whether your target audience is "ready for action"—and, if not, what might be needed to help them out.[48]

Generally speaking, it appears that in order for a person to perform a given behavior, one or more of the following must be true:

1. The person must have formed a strong positive intention (or made a commitment) to perform the behavior.

2. There are no environmental constraints that make it impossible to perform the behavior (even better, there are "nudges" in the environmental infrastructure that make it more likely that the audience will choose the desired behavior).

3. The person has the skills necessary to perform the behavior.

4. The person believes that the advantages (benefits, anticipated positive outcomes) of performing the behavior outweigh the disadvantages (costs, anticipated negative outcomes).

5. The person perceives more social (normative) pressure to perform the behavior than to not perform the behavior.

6. The person perceives that performance of the behavior is more consistent than inconsistent with his or her self-image, or that its performance does not violate personal standards that activate negative self-actions.

7. The person's emotional reaction to performing the behavior is more positive than negative.

8. The person perceives that he or she has the capability to perform the behavior under a number of different circumstances.

Based on the science of habit framework, we would add a ninth point: The person is encouraged to form a *new habit* by connecting the new behavior with an existing one or new environmental cue.

CHAPTER SUMMARY

This chapter is intended to be used as a quick reference guide for identifying and understanding theories, models, and frameworks that can inform and inspire development of audience-driven social marketing strategies, including:

- Step 3: Selecting target audiences (diffusion of innovations theory, stages of change model/transtheoretical model)
- Step 4: Setting behavior objectives and goals (self-control theory, goal-setting theory, self-perception theory)
- Step 5: Understanding audience barriers, benefits, and motivators; the competition; and influential others (health belief model, theory of reasoned action and theory of planned behavior, service-dominant logic model)
- Step 7: Developing social marketing mix strategies (social norms theory; ecological model; behavioral economics framework and nudge tactics; science of habit framework; hierarchy of effects model; exchange theory; community readiness model; carrots, sticks, and promises framework)

As a practical tip, we recommend that you review these theories, models, and frameworks as you begin developing the relevant steps in the planning model. Not only will they be inspirational as you develop these steps, but your references to them will also help build confidence in your proposed strategies among funders, decision makers, and partners.

RESEARCH HIGHLIGHT

Reducing Drinking and Driving in Montana

Evaluating a Social Norms Approach

(2003)

Background

When a social marketing effort uses the social norms theory to inspire a campaign strategy, it is often referred to as *social norms marketing*. In 2001, the *New York Times Magazine* listed social norms marketing as one of the most significant ideas of the year, describing it as "the science of persuading people to go along with the crowd. The technique works because people are allelomimetic—that is, like cows and other herd animals, our behavior is influenced by the behavior of those around us."[49]

The theory was first introduced in a study by H. Wesley Perkins, a professor of sociology, who found that students consistently overestimated how much alcohol their fellow students drank. And then in an attempt to be more "normal," they drank more themselves. The theory states that

overestimations of problem behavior will increase these problem behaviors, while underestimations of healthy behaviors will discourage individuals from engaging in them. Thus, correcting misperceptions of group norms is likely to result in decreased problem behavior or increased prevalence of healthy behaviors.[50]

One of the first social norms campaigns took place at Northern Illinois University in 1990, where the message that "most students have fewer than five drinks when they party" was distributed using newspaper ads, posters, and handouts. By 1999, incidents of heavy drinking (five or more drinks at one sitting) was down 44%.[51]

While patterns of misperceptions were evident in college populations, they had never been identified in statewide populations of young adults.[52] If such misperceptions did exist, then a statewide campaign might have positive impacts.

The following case highlights a more recent effort and presents impressive evaluative results confirming the behavior change potential of this approach.

Campaign Overview

In 2002, Montana ranked first in the nation for alcohol-related fatalities per vehicle miles traveled, up from fourth in 1999.[53] Alcohol- and drug-related vehicle crashes accounted for approximately 10% of all crashes in Montana.[54] And young adults represented a disproportionate share of these crashes, with 21- to 30-year-olds accounting for nearly half of all alcohol- and drug-related crashes in Montana. In 2001, a statewide social norms media campaign was developed and then implemented from January 2002 to March 2003 (15 months) to test the potential for this model to reduce drinking and driving among youth ages 21 to 34. Campaign elements included television, radio, newspapers, theater slides, billboards, promotional items (e.g., T-shirts, key chains, pens, and windshield scrapers), and indoor advertisements in restaurants (see Figure 8.4). One TV ad depicted a ski lodge window with snow falling. A male voice reads the following script: "In Montana there are two things you need to know about snow: how to drive in it and how to ski on it. After a day on the slopes and some time in the lodge, my friends and I all take turns being designated drivers." The view widens to reveal the message written on the

Figure 8.4 Posters used in a 15-month campaign in western counties of Montana.

Source: J. W. Linkenbach and H. S. Perkins, "Most of Us Prevent Drinking and Driving: A Successful Social Norms Campaign to Reduce Driving Among Young Adults in Western Montana," DOT HS 809 869 (U.S. Department of Transportation, National Highway Traffic Safety Administration, 2005).

window, "Most of us (4 out of 5) don't drink and drive." The commercial closes with the voice asking, "How are you getting home?" Additional campaign messages pointed out that the majority of Montana young adults practice protective behaviors, such as taking cabs or using designated drivers.

Research Methodology

Researchers Perkins, Linkenbach, Lewis, and Neighbors used this opportunity to conduct a research study, for several reasons.[55] First, to date there had not been a peer-reviewed publication evaluating a social norms marketing campaign implemented on a statewide level. Second, rigorous evaluative results were needed, given the surge of social norms marketing campaigns being implemented widely in the United States, especially on college campuses. Third, the vast majority of interventions incorporating the social norms approach had been limited to school settings, so this would be one of the first studies to measure whether the approach worked in a broader marketplace. The research objectives were to evaluate whether the social norms media marketing campaign reached the target audience, whether it was effective in correcting misperceptions, and whether it resulted in adoption of key desired behaviors, including using a designated driver and not driving within an hour of having two or more drinks.

A quasi-experimental design was used, with regions of Montana being assigned to one of three groups. Fifteen counties in the western Montana region were assigned to receive a "high dosage" of the campaign. These counties were an optimal choice, as

a majority of Montanans ages 21 to 34 lived in those counties. Because radio and television messages could not be completely contained in intervention counties, counties in the buffer region (central Montana) were used to adjust for diffusion of social norms media messages outside the intervention counties. Counties in the control region were those on the eastern half of Montana and thus not in close geographical proximity to the counties in the campaign regions.

The target population was selected and surveyed a total of four times: once prior to the campaign ($n = 1,000$), once during the media interventions ($n = 1,000$), once immediately following the intervention ($n = 1,005$), and once three months after the conclusion ($n = 517$), with the final sample being reduced on account of cost considerations. Ten- to twelve-minute telephone interviews were conducted. Sampling frames were purchased that provided targeted lists of Montana households with residing adults ages 21 to 34, and numbers were then selected at random.

Results

As presented in Table 8.2, findings were encouraging. Overall, results revealed that the target audience noticed and recalled one or more of the campaign messages (70.5% in intervention counties versus 42.6% in control counties). (It should be noted that there had been MOST of Us® campaigns in several locations around the state in previous years. Thus, some recognition or recall at baseline was not unexpected. Therefore, analysis of the findings focused on difference of change.) Misperceptions of peer norms were reduced, with those in the intervention

Table 8.2 Differences Between Intervention and Control Counties for Perceived and Reported Behavior in November 2001 (Prior to Campaign) and June 2003 (Three Months After Completion of Campaign)

	Western Intervention Counties			Eastern Control Counties			Difference of Change
	Nov.	June	Change	Nov.	June	Change	
Percentage recalling social norms media as main message (unprompted recall)	53.8	70.5	16.7	50.7	42.6	−8.1	24.8
Percentage thinking average Montanan drove within one hour of consuming two drinks in past month	91.8	86.7	−5.1	91.9	94.3	2.4	−7.5
Percentage perceiving that majority of peers almost always have a designated driver when using a car after drinking	29.9	39.2	9.3	24.9	23.2	−1.7	11.0
Percentage driving within one hour of consuming two drinks in past month	22.9	20.9	−2.0	16.9	28.6	11.7	−13.7
Percentage reporting they always make sure they have a designated driver when using a car after drinking	41.7	46.4	4.7	42.3	32.0	−10.3	15.0

counties being less likely to believe that the average Montanan their age had, in the past month, driven within one hour of consuming one or more drinks (86.7% versus 94.3%) and more likely to believe that the majority of their peers almost always had a designated driver when using a car after drinking (39.2% versus 23.2%). Behaviors changed as well. The percentage of those in the intervention counties having driven, in the past month, within an hour after having two or more drinks decreased by 10%, and the percentage reporting they used a designated driver increased by 11%. And, most important, in 2003, alcohol-related crashes declined by 5% over 2001 in the intervention counties, while in the control counties, the rate actually increased by 2%.[56]

Details related to implementing this approach can be found in Linkenbach's toolkit titled *How to Use Social Norms Marketing to Prevent Driving After Drinking: A MOST of Us® Toolkit* (a publication of the

MOST of Us® Institute, Montana State University–Bozeman, 2006, available at www.mostofus.org).

Case information was provided by Dr. Jeffrey Linkenbach, director of the Center for Health and Safety Culture and a senior research scientist at Montana State University in Bozeman, Montana, where he directs the nationally acclaimed MOST of Us® Campaign (www.mostofus.org).

DISCUSSION QUESTIONS AND EXERCISES

1. Which of the 17 theories, models, and frameworks do you find most inspiring? Why?

2. Why do you think behavioral economics has gained more visibility to date than social marketing? In your own words, how does it differ from social marketing? What do the authors argue are the distinctions between social marketing and behavioral economics?

3. How does diffusion of innovations theory relate to the carrots, sticks, and promises and "Show me"/"Help me"/"Make me" frameworks presented in this text?

CHAPTER 8 NOTES

1. Personal communication from Jeff French, December 2013.

2. MOST of Us, "What Is Social Norms Marketing?" (n.d.), accessed December 18, 2013, http://www.mostofus.org/about-us/what-is-social-norms-marketing/.

3. M. Hossain, C. Zimmerman, L. Kiss, and C. Watts, "Violence Against Women and Men in Côte d'Ivoire: A Cluster Randomized Controlled Trial to Assess the Impact of the 'Men & Women In Partnership' Intervention on the Reduction of Violence Against Women and Girls in Rural Côte d'Ivoire—Results From a Community Survey" (London: London School of Hygiene &Tropical Medicine, 2010).

4. V. Williams (communications consultant, New View Media), "Break the Silence: Social Norms Marketing Campaign for the Prevention of Violence Against Women in Cote d'Ivoire" (December 2012), 7.

5. Virginia Williams, communications consultant, New View Media.

6. V. Williams, "Break the Silence."

7. Ibid.

8. C. Lefebvre, *Social Marketing and Social Change* (San Francisco: Jossey-Bass, 2012), 98.

9. S. Simon, "The Secret to Turning Consumers Green," *The Wall Street Journal* (October 18, 2010), accessed July 16, 2011, http://online.wsj.com/article/SB10001424052748704575304575296243891721972.html.

10. J. Prochaska and C. DiClemente, "Stages and Processes of Self-Change of Smoking: Toward an Integrative Model of Change," *Journal of Consulting and Clinical Psychology* 51 (1983): 390–395.

11. J. Prochaska, J. Norcross, and C. DiClemente, *Changing for Good* (New York: Avon Books, 1994), 40–41.

12. Ibid., 40–41.

13. Ibid., 40–41.

14. Ibid., 41–43.

15. Ibid., 43.

16. Ibid., 44.

17. D. Shmueli and J. Prochaska, "Resisting Tempting Foods and Smoking Behavior: Implications From a Self-Control Theory Perspective," *Health Psychology* 28, no. 3 (2009): 300–306.

18. B. Spring, S. Pagota, R. Pingitore, N. Doran, K. Schneider, and D. Hedeker, "Randomized Controlled Trial for Behavioral Smoking and Weight Control Treatment: Effect of Concurrent Versus Sequential Intervention," *Journal of Consulting and Clinical Psychology* 72 (2004), 785–796.

19. E. A. Locke, "Toward a Theory of Task Motivation and Incentives," *Organizational Behavior and Human Performance* 2, no. 3 (1968): 157–189.

20. D. McKenzie-Mohr, *Fostering Sustainable Behaviors: An Introduction to Community-Based Social Marketing* (Gabriola Island, BC, Canada: New Society, 2011), 45.

21. McKenzie-Mohr, *Fostering Sustainable Behaviors*, 45.

22. K. R. M. Brown, *Health Belief Model* (1999), accessed April 2, 2001, http://www.hsc.usf .edu/-kmbrown/Health_Belief_Model_Overview.htm.

23. United States Department of Health and Human Services, National Institutes of Health, National Heart Lung and Blood Institute, *National High Blood Pressure Education Program (NIIBPEP)* (n.d.), accessed September 18, 2001, http://hin.nhlbi.nih.gov/nhbpep_kit_about_m .htm.

24. Ibid.

25. Ibid.

26. Ibid.

27. I. Ajzen, "The Theory of Planned Behavior," *Organizational Behavior and Human Decision Processes* 50 (1991): 179–211.

28. A. R. Andreasen, *Marketing Social Change: Changing Behavior to Promote Health, Social Development, and the Environment* (San Francisco: Jossey-Bass, 1995), 266–268.

29. Ibid., 266–268.

30. Service-Dominant Logic [website], http://www.sdlogic.net/.

31. "Interview with Mechai Viravaidya" (July 23, 2007), *CNN.com/Asia*, accessed December 17, 2013, http://edition.cnn.com/2007/WORLD/asiapcf/07/22/talkasia.viravaidya/index .html?iref=allsearch.

32. MOST of Us, "What is Social Norms Marketing?"

33. Changing Minds.org, "Social Norms," (n.d.), accessed December 18, 2013, http://chang ingminds.org/explanations/theories/social_norms.htm.

34. Personal communication, 2001.

35. J. Grizzell, "Behavior Change Theories and Models" (n.d.), accessed June 9, 2008, http://www.csupomona.edu/~jvgrizzell/best_practices/betheory.html#Ecological%20Approaches.

36. P. Kotler and N. Lee, *Up and Out of Poverty: The Social Marketing Approach* (Upper Saddle River, NJ: Wharton School, 2009), 151.

37. B. Smith, "Behavioral Economics and Social Marketing: New Allies in the War on Absent Behavior," *Social Marketing Quarterly* XVI, no. 2 (Summer 2010), 137–141.

38. P. Kotler, "Behavioural Economics or Social Marketing? The Latter!," *The Sunday Times* (May 22, 2011), accessed December 28, 2013, http://www.sundaytimes.lk/110522/BusinessTimes/bt36.html.

39. R. Thaler and C. Sunstein, *Nudge: Improving Decisions About Health, Wealth, and Happiness* (New York: Penguin Group, 2009), 180–181.

40. J. French, "Why 'Nudges' Are Seldom Enough" (Strategic Social Marketing, 2010).

41. Ibid.

42. C. Duhigg, "Warning: Habits May Be Good for You," *The New York Times* (July 13, 2008), accessed July 16, 2011, http://www.nytimes.com/2008/07/13/business/13habit.html.

43. Learn Marketing.net, "Hierarchy of Effects Model" (n.d.) accessed December 17, 2013, http://www.learnmarketing.net/hierarchy_of_effects_model.html.

44. College of Natural Sciences, Tri-ethnic Center, "Community Readiness Model" (n.d.), accessed December 17, 2013, http://triethniccenter.colostate.edu/communityReadiness.htm.

45. M. Rothschild, "Carrots, Sticks, and Promises: A Conceptual Framework for the Management of Public Health and Social Issue Behaviors," *Journal of Marketing* 63 (October 1999): 24–37, accessed December 31, 2013, http://www.social-marketing.org/papers/carrot article.pdf.

46. Ibid, 24.

47. Ibid., 25–26.

48. M. Fishbein, in *Developing Effective Behavior Change Interventions* (pp. 5–6), as quoted in The Communication Initiative, *Summary of Change Theories and Models* (Slide 6), accessed April 2, 2001, http://www.comminit.com/power_point/change_theories/sld005.htm.

49. M. Frauenfelder, "The Year in Ideas: A to Z: Social-Norms Marketing," *The New York Times* (December 9, 2001), accessed July 16, 2011, http://www.nytimes.com/2001/12/09/maga zine/the-year-in-ideas-a-to-z-social-norms-marketing.html.

50. A. Berkowitz, *The Social Norms Approach: Theory, Research, and Annotated Bibliography* (August 2004), accessed July 16, 2011, http://www.alanberkowitz.com/articles/social_norms.pdf.

51. Frauenfelder, "The Year in Ideas."

52. J. Linkenbach and H. W. Perkins, "Misperceptions of Peer Alcohol Norms in a Statewide Survey of Young Adults," in *The Social Norms Approach to Preventing School and College Age Substance Abuse: A Handbook for Educators, Counselors, and Clinicians*, ed. H. W. Perkins (San Francisco: Jossey-Bass, 2003).

53. U.S. Department of Transportation, National Highway Traffic Safety Administration, *State Alcohol-Related Fatality Rates 2002* (Washington, DC: Author, 2003).

54. Montana Department of Transportation, *Traffic Safety Problem Identification (FY 2004)* (Helena, MT: Author, 2003), State and Local Traffic Safety Program section.

55. H. W. Perkins, J. W. Linkenbach, M. A. Lewis, and C. Neighbors, "Effectiveness of Social Norms Media Marketing in Reducing Drinking and Driving: A State Wide Campaign," *Addictive Behaviors* 35 (2010), 866–874, doi: 10.1016/j.addbeh.2010.05.004.

56. J. W. Linkenbach and H. S. Perkins, "Most of Us Prevent Drinking and Driving: A Successful Social Norms Campaign to Reduce Driving Among Young Adults in Western Montana," DOT HS 809 869 (U.S. Department of Transportation, National Highway Traffic Safety Administration, 2005).

PART IV

DEVELOPING SOCIAL MARKETING STRATEGIES

Chapter 9

CRAFTING A DESIRED POSITIONING

It's about more than education! If communication and information based on rational process were enough, no one in the entire world would ever smoke a cigarette! Human behavior often occurs in an emotional context; the tobacco and fast-food industries depend on it! That's why changing behavior means addressing all the 4Ps: Product, Price, Place, and Promotion.

—Bob Marshall
Rhode Island Department of Health

Back in the early 1970s, a couple of advertising executives, Al Ries and Jack Trout, started a small revolution—a marketing revolution, that is. They introduced the concept and art of positioning. It was more than a new approach. It was, as they described it, a creative exercise.

Positioning starts with a product—a piece of merchandise, a service, a company, an institution, or even a person. But positioning is not what you do to a product. Positioning is what you do to the mind of the prospect. That is, you position the product in the mind of the prospect.[1]

Ries and Trout's premise was that our mind, as a defense against the volume of today's communications, screens and rejects much of the information offered it and accepts only that which matches prior knowledge or experience. They advocated the oversimplified message as the best approach to take in our overcommunicated society:

The average mind is already a dripping sponge that can only soak up more information at the expense of what's already there. Yet we continue to pour more information into that supersaturated sponge and are disappointed when our messages fail to get through. . . . In communication, as in architecture, less is more. You have to sharpen your message to cut into the mind. You have to jettison the ambiguities, simplify the message, and then simplify it some more if you want to make a long-lasting impression.[2]

And as you no doubt have discovered, or at least have read so far in this text, different markets have different needs, and your challenge is to position your offer "perfectly" in the mind of your desired prospect. The positioning exercise you will explore in this chapter will help provide that clarity and will illustrate the following positioning strategies:

- Behavior-focused positioning
- Barriers-focused positioning
- Benefits-focused positioning
- Competition-focused positioning
- Repositioning
- Positioning-inspired brands

And in the following opening case story, you'll experience the power this can have.

MARKETING HIGHLIGHT

truth® Youth Smoking Prevention Campaign

Helping Youth Reject Tobacco for More Than a Decade
American Legacy Foundation (Legacy®)

(2000–2014)

Figure 9.1   The truth® van reaching out.

Source: Photo courtesy of Patricia McLaughlin.

This case highlight is one we have featured in the 2nd, 3rd, and 4th editions of this text as a powerful example of a clear desired positioning and superior branding effort. From the beginning, the truth® youth smoking prevention campaign was developed based on extensive formative research and fueled by the gravity of one of the greatest public health issues in the United States: youth tobacco use. Our focus for this edition is on how the campaign has stuck with its original positioning and protected its brand for more than a decade—no doubt because it has worked. You'll also read how Legacy, the campaign's founder, has adjusted promotional strategies (messages, messengers, creative elements, and especially communication channels) to appeal to significant changes in the past 14 years as youth lifestyles, values, and preferences continue to evolve.

Background, Target Audiences, Desired Behavior, and Audience Insights

Nearly 80% of all smokers begin smoking before age 18, and nearly 90% begin before age 20.[3] Consider, then, that in the year 2000, 440,000 persons died of a cigarette-smoking-attributable illness.[4] With tobacco use taking a grim toll on our families, communities, and the American economy, it was timely that Legacy® launched truth® that year, intending to influence youth to reject tobacco, saving young people from lives of potential addiction and disease or death.

Strategies

At the core of the truth® campaign's promotional strategies are messages about the marketing tactics of the tobacco industry, as well as the health effects, social costs, addictiveness, and ingredients/additives found in tobacco. The campaign doesn't preach or talk down to teenagers. Instead, it presents potentially life-saving information in a creative, attention-getting fashion. By working through media that teens watch, read, and hear on a daily basis, as well as through the communications tactics teens use every day in their personal relationships, truth® is able to best reach its audience. To ensure that the campaign stays relevant to teens and young people, teens are involved in testing advertising concepts and are encouraged to provide suggestions and feedback through the truth® website at http://www.thetruth.com.

The style and tone of truth® ads are "in your face" and hard-hitting, responding to teens' desire for powerful messages (see Figure 9.2). As the media landscape has changed, the campaign has expanded the

| Figure 9.2 | Appealing to teens' desire for "in-your-face" messages. |

Source: Photo courtesy of thetruth.com.

| Figure 9.3 | truth® ON THE ROAD. This annual grassroots tour is one of the best ways to bring the campaign to life, allowing teens and young people to really see, hear, and interact with the campaign firsthand. |

Source: Photo courtesy of Joshua Cogan Photography.

reach of truth® by adding advanced online and social media components. And, as might be expected, teens and young people are also front and center when truth® embarks on extensive grassroots efforts. Every summer, iconic orange truth® trucks and a crew of truth® youth ambassadors crisscross the country, making stops at popular summer musical and sporting events where teens naturally gather. In a typical summer, the tour makes stops in more than 50 cities and 25 states (see Figure 9.3).

Table 9.1 provides highlights of promotional executions over the past 14 years. Campaign elements have included television, radio, print, online, and cinema advertising; a website; social networking sites; video-sharing sites; interactive elements; special events; branded entertainment integrations; branded truth® apparel; and grassroots outreach through summer and fall tours.

Table 9.1   Highlights of Promotional Executions Over the Past 14 Years (2000–2013)

Year	Campaign Launch Highlights
2000	*truth* was launched at a youth summit attended by 1,000 teens from across the country.
2001	*Infect truth* educated teens on the facts about cigarette design and engineering.
2002	*A Look Behind the Orange Curtain* shed light on the tobacco industry's marketing tactics and included such topics as addiction and the health consequences of smoking.
2003	*Crazyworld* showed teens how tobacco companies play by a different set of rules than other companies. While many companies recall products at the first sign of danger to a consumer, the tobacco industry makes a product that kills 1,200 of its customers every day in the United States.
2004	*Connect truth* used an orange dot icon to link together pieces of information to reveal the larger picture about the effects of smoking and the chain of events from the marketing of tobacco products to consumer illnesses to death.
	Shards o' Glass featured a fictitious company that manufactures freeze pops with glass shards in them, a dangerous product analogous to cigarettes. The satirical ad is meant to raise consumer awareness about the harmful effects of smoking.
	Seek truth used a Q&A format to encourage teens to ask questions and seek answers about the tobacco industry and its marketing and manufacturing practices.
2005	*Fair Enough* took a new approach to advertising with a sitcom-styled television campaign that featured a cast and theme music. The commercials used tobacco industry documents to reveal marketing ideas.
	truth found pointed big orange arrows at some of the people and places targeted and affected by Big Tobacco.
2006	*truth documentary* used a documentary filmmaking style to capture real people's reactions to the marketing tactics of the tobacco industry. Named for the style in which the ads were shot, *truth documentary* featured one correspondent and a camera crew investigating the reasoning behind some ideas from Big Tobacco.
	Infect truth called attention to the marketing tactics of the tobacco industry and the health consequences of tobacco in such a way as to "infect" people with that knowledge and encourage active peer-to-peer participation.

(Continued)

Table 9.1 (Continued)

Year	Campaign Launch Highlights
2007	*truth documentary phase II* built on the approach of *truth documentary* to continue to highlight the absurdity of statements found in tobacco industry documents.
2008	*The Sunny Side of truth* used animation, Broadway-style choreography, and sarcasm to illustrate the "sunny side" of smoking tobacco. *ReMix* involved nine innovative and well-known DJs and bands putting new spins on the songs from the *Sunny Side of truth* campaign by remixing them in styles from hip-hop to house to electro. The music tracks were then packaged as a special compilation CD and made available for download online as part of a comprehensive effort to reach more of the teen audience through technology, alternative media, and entertainment outlets already popular with teens.
2009	*Do You Have What It Takes to Be a Tobacco Executive?* featured an actor posing as a corporate recruiter asking real-life job seekers whether they "had what it takes" to be an executive for Big Tobacco. Through references to tobacco-related facts and situations, the spots illuminated the types of decisions and situations that tobacco industry executives make or have encountered.
2010	Two new TV spots resurrected the theme of the 2004 campaign *Shards o' Glass*, highlighting the continued irony of tobacco companies producing a dangerous product. New web and interactive elements advanced the campaign's message.
2011	*Unsweetened truth* vividly illustrated the impact of smoking on health and highlighted how tobacco-related diseases are not just about dying—having such diseases is also about living with the effects of cancers of the mouth, throat, and neck; chronic obstructive pulmonary disease (COPD); emphysema; and loss of voice. In the spot, six real people suffering from tobacco-related disabilities were featured on a parade float traveling through the heart of Hollywood. Online components of the campaign featured video vignettes showcasing the daily lives and struggles of each of these real people.
2012	*Flavor Monsters*, a new mobile game, highlighted the many different flavorings—more than 45— found in tobacco products. Although most flavors are banned for use in cigarettes, tobacco companies still use them in many other tobacco products, some of which closely resemble cigarettes. *truth* had offered games via the campaign's website in the past, but with the release of *Flavor Monsters* and more of a presence in the gaming space, the campaign continues to evolve and connect with teens through their "passions," using entertainment channels like gaming, music, and sports to continue a conversation with teens around the issue of tobacco use. Also in 2012, truth launched its first-ever college music tour, called **truthlive**. This campus outreach effort traveled to five college campuses—Pennsylvania State University, the University of Maryland, the University of Virginia, the University of Tennessee, and Clemson University—offering an on-campus concert and grassroots outreach to connect with college students.
2013	*Ugly truth* revealed sets of thought-provoking facts, designed to illicit responses to how the tobacco industry characterizes potential customers and has developed its products. Through television spots and affiliated outreach online, viewers and visitors were encouraged to weigh the gravity of two different facts and decide "What's the ugliest truth?" through an online vote and voting in the field at *truth* tour stops.

Outcomes

According to research published online in February 2009 by the *American Journal of Preventive Medicine* (*AJPM*), truth® was directly responsible for keeping 450,000 teens from starting to smoke during its first four years. A second study released through *AJPM* in February 2009 found that the campaign had not only paid for itself in its first two years, but also saved between $1.9 and $5.4 billion in medical care costs to society.

Since its inception, the truth® campaign has been recognized for its creativity, its unique approach, and its results. The campaign has won more than 400 awards and has been lauded by leading federal and state officials and agencies including the Centers for Disease Control and Prevention and the U.S. Department of Health and Human Services.

What's Next?

In today's cluttered media landscape, an increased investment in paid advertising is vital to reaching a national audience. Over the next three years, Legacy will devote new and significant resources to truth® to help augment the important work being conducted by the federal government in both youth prevention and adult cessation. This national paid advertising will supplement truth's extensive grassroots and digital outreach—"connecting all dots" with the youth audience that the campaign strives to reach in strategic ways. The campaign continually strives to reach young people through their personal passions and interests and communication channels popular with them. Partnerships with like-minded campaigns, continued grassroots touring, and branded entertainment will continue to play a role in the campaign's reach moving forward.

Smoking prevalence among 8th-, 10th-, and 12th-graders has recently declined to just below 10%. With an increased paid media push behind the truth® campaign, Legacy hopes to work toward a "Generation Free" of tobacco use.

Case information and some editorial content was provided by Patricia McLaughlin, associate vice president of communications for Legacy®, a national public health foundation with the mission to keep young people from smoking and help all smokers quit. Legacy was created as a result of the 1998 Master Settlement Agreement between the tobacco industry, 46 states, and 5 U.S. territories.

POSITIONING DEFINED

Positioning is the act of designing the organization's actual and perceived offering in such a way that it lands on and occupies a distinctive place in the mind of the target audience—where you want it to be.[5] Keep in mind that your offering, which you will design in the next three chapters, includes your product, its price, and how it is accessed—place. The desired positioning for this offer is then supported by promotional components including messages, messengers, creative elements, and communication channels.

Think of your target audience as having a perceptual map that they will use to locate your offer. Consider further that they have a different map for each product category (one each for cars, airlines, fast food, beverages, etc., and, more relevant for social marketers perhaps, one each for exercise, workplace safety, recycling, organ donation, etc.). Figure 9.4 illustrates a simplified version of a perceptual map, showing which brands are perceived as being similar and which are competing against each other. Most perceptual maps for products and services use data from consumer surveys evaluating those products and services on specific attributes.

There is a good reason we present and recommend you take this step *after* you have selected and researched your target audience and *before* you develop your marketing mix strategy. Since offers are positioned differently for different markets (e.g., exercise for tweens versus seniors), choosing an audience comes first. And since your product, price, place, and promotion will determine (to a great extent) where you land, it makes sense to know your desired destination. This will help guide your marketing strategy by clarifying the brand's essence, what goals it helps the consumer achieve, and how it does so in a unique way.

Figure 9.4   A perceptual map.

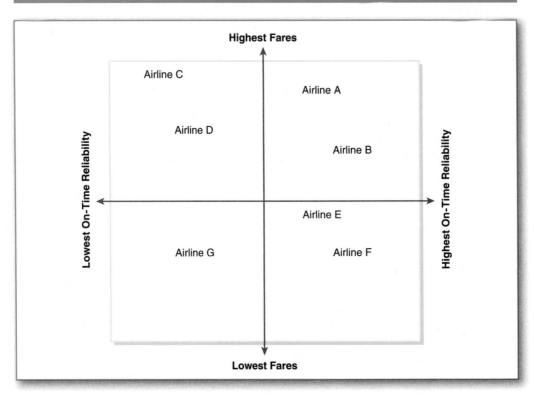

As you may recall, we have defined social marketing as a process that applies marketing principles and techniques to create, communicate, and deliver value in order to influence target audience behaviors. The result of positioning is the successful creation of a customer-focused value proposition, that is, a cogent reason why the target audience should buy the product—from you![6]

Positioning in the Commercial Sector

Perhaps because the commercial sector has embraced this positioning concept for decades, great examples of clear positioning and the value proposition are easy to find, as suggested in Table 9.2. In the Focus column, we have linked these value propositions to social marketing theories and models we have discussed in prior chapters: benefits, barriers, and competition. One new option, now that we have introduced the positioning concept, would be a focus on repositioning—where a brand manager is interested in moving a product from its current location in the mind of target audiences to a new, more desirable one (see Figure 9.5).

Figure 9.5   Repositioning milk as "cool."

Source: Photo courtesy of the National Dairy Council.

Commercial marketers also often consider and establish *points of difference* and *points of parity*, which are described by Kotler and Keller.[7] Points of difference are attributes or benefits consumers strongly associate with a brand and believe they could not find with a competing brand. Examples include FedEx (guaranteed overnight delivery), Costco (lower costs for similar products), and Lexus (quality). Points of parity, by contrast, are associations that are not necessarily unique to the brand but may be considered essential to a legitimate offering within a certain product or service category (e.g., a bank needs to at least offer access to ATM machines, online banking services, and checking accounts in order to be considered a bank). Competitive points-of-difference positioning might instead or also work to negate the competitors' points of difference. One good example Kotler and Keller highlight is a Miller Lite advertising strategy that ends with the tagline, "Everything you've always wanted in a beer and less."[8]

STEP 6: DEVELOP A POSITIONING STATEMENT

Positioning principles and processes for social marketing are similar to those of commercial marketing. With the profile of your target audience in mind, including any unique

Table 9.2   Commercial Sector Brand-Positioning Examples

Category	Brand	Focus	Value Proposition
Car	Volvo	Benefits	Safety
Fast food	Subway	Barriers	Fresh, healthy options
Airlines	Southwest	Competition	No frills, lower costs
Beverages	Milk	Repositioning	From boring to cool

demographic, geographic, psychographic, and behavior-related characteristics and the findings from your research on perceived barriers, benefits, competitors, and influential others, you will now "simply" craft a positioning statement.

One way to develop a positioning statement is to fill in the blanks to this phrase, or one similar to it:

> We want [TARGET AUDIENCE] to see [DESIRED BEHAVIOR] as [ADJECTIVES, DESCRIPTIVE PHRASES, SET OF BENEFITS, OR WHY THE DESIRED BEHAVIOR IS BETTER THAN COMPETING BEHAVIORS]

Keep in mind that this positioning statement is "for internal use only." It is not your ultimate message to your target audiences. It will, however, be shared with others working with you on your effort to develop your marketing mix strategy and help to unify and strengthen decision making. Consider how agreement on the following statements would guide these teams:

- "We want pregnant women to see breastfeeding exclusively for the first six months as a way to bond with their child and contribute to their health and as more important than concerns about nursing in public."
- "We want media reporters to see using nonstigmatizing mental health labels (e.g., 'this person has schizophrenia' versus 'this person is schizophrenic') as a way to help those with mental illnesses and as a way to be a respected and leading role model in the profession."
- "We want homeowners who love gardening to see composting food waste as an easy way to contribute to the environment and create great compost for their garden at the same time, and to see that this is better for the environment than putting it in the garbage, which then goes to the landfill, or down the kitchen disposal and into water that has to be treated."
- "We want people shopping for a puppy to visit the Humane Society's website first to see if the pet they have in mind is just waiting for someone to adopt it, and that this is likely to be a less expensive and more convenient option than going to the classified ads."

Inspiration for your descriptive phrase will come from the lists of barriers and benefits identified in your research. As you may recall, the ideal research will have included a prioritization of barriers and benefits, giving you a sense of what factors would be most important to highlight. You are searching for the "higher value," the key benefits to be gained or costs that will be avoided by adopting the desired behavior.

To leverage prior steps in the planning model, you may find it advantageous to consider a focus for your positioning statements, choosing from among those that drive home specific *behaviors*, highlight *benefits*, overcome *barriers*, upstage the *competition*, or *reposition* an "old brand." More detail on each of these options is presented in the next five sections, with a couple of brief examples and one longer illustration.

BEHAVIOR-FOCUSED POSITIONING

For some social marketing programs, especially those with a new and/or very specific desired behavior in mind, you may benefit from a behavior-focused positioning. In these cases, a description of your behavior will be highlighted, as shown in these examples:

Figure 9.6   A behavior-focused positioning from the TSA on a wallet card for travelers.

Source: Transportation Security Administration, *311 for carry-ons* (n.d.), accessed January 19, 2007, http://www.tsa.gov/assets/pdf/311-credit-card.pdf.

- 3 Days 3 Ways, a campaign sponsored by King County (Washington) Emergency Management, encourages citizens to be prepared for emergencies and disasters in three ways: (a) Make a plan, (b) build a kit, and (c) get involved[9]
- 311, the Transportation Security Administration's travel tip effort, was developed in 2006 to support travelers in knowing what liquids and gels they could carry on and how many (see Figure 9.6)

In these cases, making sure target audiences know the specifics of the desired behavior is key to successful outcomes, as illustrated in the following example.

Example: 5 a Day. In 1991, the National Cancer Institute (NCI), in cooperation with the Produce for Better Health Foundation, created "5 a Day for Better Health," a national program that approaches Americans with a simple, positive message: "Eat five or more servings of vegetables and fruit daily for better health" (see Figure 9.7).

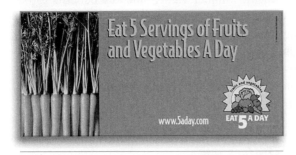

Figure 9.7 The Produce for Better Health Foundation's behavior-focused positioning.

Source: Photo courtesy of the Produce for Better Health Foundation.

This key message has been repeated using a well-integrated strategy and a multitude of venues over the years: plastic produce bags, grocery bags, in-store signage and displays, produce packaging labels, supermarket tours, recipe cards, brochures, grocery store flier ads, magazine articles, newspaper ads, news stories, the Internet, radio news inserts, television news inserts (cooking/recipe spots), radio public service announcements (PSAs), television PSAs, billboards, CD-ROMs in elementary schools, nutrition newsletters, patient nutrition education materials, pay stubs, school curricula, preschool programs, food assistance program materials, church bulletins and newsletters, posters, restaurant menus, Girl/Boy Scout badges, 4-H materials, food bank program materials, health fairs, county fairs, cookbooks, children's coloring books, and videotapes. In 2006, a new slogan, "The Color Way," was added to promote more variety in the 5 a Day mix we choose.

A press release from the Produce for Better Health Foundation in November 2005 reported good outcome news. According to the ACNielsen study of nearly 2,600 households, the number of Americans claiming to eat five or more daily servings was 18% in 2004, up 50% from 2003. The study also found a clear link between awareness and consumption, with a jump in consumption of five or more daily servings reported by those claiming awareness of the foundation's Color Way messages. More than 30% of those who were most aware of the Color Way message reported consuming five or more servings of fruits and vegetables a day, compared to less than 10% of those who were not aware of the campaign. This is further backed up by purchasing data, which show that those most aware of the Color Way message spent $111 more annually on fruits and vegetables than those not aware of the campaign.[10]

BARRIERS-FOCUSED POSITIONING

With this type of focus, you want your offer's positioning to help overcome or at least minimize perceived barriers, such as concern about self-efficacy, fear, or perceived high costs associated with performing the behavior:

- For tobacco users who want to quit, quitlines are often positioned as hopeful and encouraging, as in the following poem (perhaps more like a rap) that appeared on the Washington State Department of Health's website in 2007:

In the New Year, make smoking a thing of the past

Put yourself first and your habit last

Start the year right; start out on top

And make '07 the year that you stop

Tobacco products will harm your health

They'll deplete your energy as well as your wealth

Although smoking is a hard habit to break

With determination and support it's a change you can make

Call the Washington State Tobacco Quit Line to learn how

A quit coach will assist you at 1–800–QUIT–NOW

A customized plan and one-on-one counseling you'll get

To help make '07 smoke-free, and your best year yet

The call is confidential, the service is free

And can double your chance of quitting successfully

More than 80,000 Washingtonians have made the call

For free counseling and quit kits available for all

Don't hesitate; call the quit line today

And in the New Year, you'll be well on your way![11]

- Some women avoid or postpone having mammograms when they are afraid to get bad news. This explains why many organizations have positioned mammograms as "early detection," a way to get treatment before it spreads.

In the following illustration, the positioning reflects audience concerns about time, effort, cost, and "know-how."

Example: Recycling Your Cell Phone Is as Easy as 1, 2, 3. According to some estimates, there are over 800 million retired cell phones discarded in drawers and desks in the United States, and over 140 million more enter the waste stream each year.[12] Perceived barriers to recycling them range from not knowing how and where to considerations about the time involved in going to a special recycling station to understanding why it even matters. INFORM, a nonprofit organization in the United States, has a goal to "empower citizens, businesses and government to adopt practices and policies that will sustain our planet for future generations."[13] One of their initiatives is to support cell phone recycling, and their offer and its positioning appear to address consumer barriers head on. They say, "It's as easy as 1–2–3!" Just follow these steps posted on their website:

1. Print out the prepaid mailing label and cut it out along the dotted line.

2. Place your cell phone, charger, and accessories in the envelope and affix the mailing label.

3. Drop it off at the post office or in a mailbox. Postage is already paid, so shipping is free![14]

Additional messages on the website stress the problem with disposing of unwanted cell phones in the garbage, describing their toxic substances and how, when dumped in landfills, they pollute the environment and potentially harm human health.

BENEFITS-FOCUSED POSITIONING

When the best hook seems to be related to the WIFM ("what's in it for me") factor, perceived benefits become the focus of the positioning:

- Natural yard care practices, such as pulling weeds versus spraying them, are positioned as ways to ensure the health of your children and pets.
- Moderate physical activity, such as raking leaves and taking the stairs instead of the elevator, is positioned as something you can fit into your daily routine.
- Reading to your child 20 minutes each night is positioned as a way to help ensure he or she will do well in school.

In the following illustration of benefit-focused positioning, the focus is once more on benefits your target audience wants and believes they can get.

Example: Road Crew. Michael Rothschild, professor emeritus at the University of Wisconsin, believes that good positioning begins with a clear understanding of the target and their competitive choices. He also believes that when developing this positioning, a marketer needs to learn about the target, current usage patterns, and why existing competitive brands are succeeding. This is exactly what a team he led in Wisconsin in the spring of 2000 did for the Wisconsin Department of Transportation.

The "assignment" was to reduce alcohol-related crashes in rural Wisconsin. There was ample prior evidence that the group of people most likely to drink, drive, and crash were 21- to 34-year-old single men. The team conducted 17 focus groups, 11 with the target audience and 6 more with those who observed the target (e.g., bar owners, law enforcement ambulance drivers, judges). Meetings with the target were held in the back of local taverns so that respondents would feel comfortable discussing the issues. By asking the target why they drove after drinking, the team learned about reasons for driving drunk: to get home; to avoid the hassle of coming back in the morning to get the vehicle; everybody does it; at 1:00 a.m. the target is fearless; and there is a low risk of getting caught. When asked to help design a ride program that they would use, they asked for:

- Vehicles that were at least as nice as their own
- A ride from home to the bar, between bars, and then home again, as they wouldn't want to leave their cars behind and wanted to go between bars
- The right to smoke and drink in the vehicles

This is exactly what they were then offered. The resulting service uses limousines and other luxury vehicles to pick people up at their home, business, or hotel; take them to the bar of their choice; take them between bars; and then take them home at the end of the evening. As allowed by local ordinances, passengers may smoke and drink in the vehicles. The cost to the passenger is $15 to $20 for the evening.

Figure 9.8 shows the initial poster that was used to raise awareness. It doesn't tell people not to drive drunk; it focuses on Road Crew's position. That is, it tells people that they can have more fun if they

Figure 9.8 Repositioning Road Crew as a cool way to get around and have fun.

Source: Road Crew, University of Wisconsin.

use Road Crew than if they drive themselves. Research had shown that the target wanted to have fun and that drinking was a part of having fun. The target didn't feel that driving drunk was fun, but that it was necessary in order to have fun earlier in the evening.

By 2008, the program was operating in 32 small communities in rural Wisconsin and had provided over 97,000 rides and prevented an estimated 140 alcohol-related crashes and six alcohol-related fatalities. The costs incurred from an alcohol-related crash are approximately $231,000, but the cost to avoid a crash through the use of Road Crew is approximately $6,400. This means that it is about 37 times more expensive to incur a crash than it is to avoid one. Total net savings through the use of Road Crew has been more than $31 million. Of special note is that research shows that while driving behavior has changed dramatically, people are not drinking more as a result of getting rides. After receiving seed money to begin the program, communities are able to self-sustain from ride fares and tavern contributions.[15]

Road Crew has succeeded because it is well positioned relative to its competition. Rather than being told that drunk driving is bad, people are told that using Road Crew is more fun than the competitive choice. Road Crew offers more benefits than driving. In the past, driving was often the only choice available; anyone who admitted to not being able to drive home was seen as a "wimp." But now, choosing the Road Crew is a sign of being cool. (For more insights on Road Crew, go to www.roadcrewonline.org.)

COMPETITION-FOCUSED POSITIONING

A fourth option for focus is the competition, one quite appropriate when your target audience finds "their offer" quite appealing and your offer "a pain":

- Youth abstinence advocates have tough competitors, including the media, entertainment, peer pressure, and raging hormones. Positioning abstinence as postponing sex, versus "no sex," has become an easier sell for many.
- In 2003, New York City announced a convenient and cost-saving alternative to dialing 911—dialing 311 instead. With a vast majority of the more than 8 million annual calls to 911 representing nonemergency situations, the service was anticipated to delight citizens and decrease operating costs. All calls are answered by a live operator, 24 hours a day, seven days a week, and can be translated into 170 languages.[16]
- Consequences of tobacco use are often positioned as gross, realistic, and shocking (see Figure 9.9).

Because consumers typically choose products and services that give them the greatest value, marketers work to position their brands on the key benefits that they offer relative to competing brands. Kotler and Armstrong illustrate this with six possible value propositions, as shown in Table 9.3.[17]

An additional model for developing competitive advantage focuses on creating *competitive superiority*, a more rigorous objective. Four tactics are used in tandem, as illustrated in Table 9.4. A *benefit-to-benefit superiority* tactic appeals to values higher than those perceived for the competition (e.g., a child who wants and needs a parent is compared to the short-term pleasures of smoking). A *cost-to-benefit superiority* tactic focuses on decreasing costs of or barriers to adopting the desired behavior and, at the same time,

Figure 9.9   Positioning tobacco use.

Reprinted with permission of Pilgrim Plastics, Brockton, MA.

Table 9.3   Illustrating Value Propositions Based on Price and Product Quality

More for More	Starbucks
More for the Same	Lexus vs. Mercedes Benz
Same for Less	Amazon
Less for Much Less	Motel 6
More for Less	Costco
Less for Much Less	Southwest Airlines

decreasing perceived benefits of the competition (e.g., success stories from cessation classes include a testimonial from a spouse about how nice it is to have clean air in the house). A *benefit-to-cost superiority* tactic emphasizes the benefits of the desired behavior and the costs of the competing behavior(s) (e.g., abilities of teen athletes who don't smoke as compared to those of teen athletes who do). A *cost-to-cost superiority* tactic relies on a favorable comparison of costs of the desired behavior relative to those of the competition (e.g., short-term nicotine withdrawal symptoms are compared with living with emphysema).

Example: Broccoli's Makeover[18]. A six-page article in the November 3, 2013, *New York Times Magazine* announced that broccoli was about to get a serious makeover by ad agency Victors & Spoils, which had created campaigns for some of the biggest brands in the food industry, including Coca-Cola. Michael Moss, the author of the *Times* article, followed the team's vision quest for a campaign, and at the beginning challenged them with a couple of questions: "How would you get people to want to buy and eat broccoli? . . . What would you do that all the well-intentioned government-funded campaigns have failed to do for generations?"[19]

Table 9.4   Creating Competitive Superiority

Competing Behavior	Desired Behavior	
	Increase Benefits	Decrease Costs/Barriers
Decrease Benefits	Tactic A: Benefit-to-benefit superiority tactic	Tactic B: Cost-to-benefit superiority tactic
Increase Costs/Barriers:	Tactic C: Benefit-to-cost superiority tactic	Tactic D: Cost-to-cost superiority tactic

From there, the firm's team set out on a research journey to get a handle on what the public felt about broccoli—a crowdsourcing exercise. Impressions shared included "overcooked, soggy"; "hiding under cheese"; "told not to leave the table until I eat it"; and "brown, squishy, and smelly." When asked what an epitaph for broccoli might be, the team heard comments like, "Good-bye, poor friend" and "I hardly spent time with you, mainly because I didn't like you." They heard from a chef that broccoli wasn't thought of as much as a food as it was as a divider in the display case between meat and fish. And when looking through various food and cooking magazines, the team ran across a recent issue of *Bon Appétit* that featured the "vegetable revolution" and 10 different vegetables. Broccoli didn't even make the list.

Back in the firm's conference room for a brainstorming session, potential positioning and message strategies were considered, including that perhaps it should be seen as a flower and you could give someone broccoli bouquets. Or maybe they should change its name, or at least have Italians pronounce it!

Their "Aha!" moment finally came when, as they reviewed sales data, they discovered that broccoli ranked 20th among vegetables, doing far better than kale in 47th place, which had been rocketing to fame over the past several years. "Let's pick a fight with kale!"—just like the great soda war between Pepsi and Coca-Cola. From there, the team created multiple slogans, including "Broccoli: Now 43 Percent Less Pretentious Than Kale" and "Eat Fad Free: Broccoli v. Kale."

The agency estimated that the total cost of the campaign would be between $3 million and $7 million, including advertising fees, if they were to execute it for real. Moss shared that the month previously (October 2013), the Produce Marketing Association had intended to announce their new initiative soon.

REPOSITIONING

What happens when your program has a current positioning that you feel is in the way of your achieving your behavior change goals? Several factors may have contributed to this wake-up call and the sense that you need to "relocate." For instance, you might need to attract *new audiences* to sustain your growth, and these new markets may not find your current position appealing. For example, adults over 50 not engaged in regular physical activity may have tuned out messages regarding exercise long ago, as they could hear only the "vigorous aerobic" recommendation. Planners would be more successful emphasizing moderate physical activity with this group.

Or you may be suffering from an image problem. When bike helmets were first promoted to youth, they balked. Making the behavior "fun, easy, and popular" for the audience is Bill Smith's recommendation and could well describe the strategy in Figure 9.10. These three words focus program managers on how to change behavior by giving people what they want along with what we feel they need.

- *Fun* in this context means to provide your audience with perceived benefits they care about.
- *Easy* means to remove all possible barriers to action and make the behavior as simple and accessible as possible.
- *Popular* means to help the audience feel that this is something others are doing, particularly others the audience believes are important to them.[20]

Or you may have just received (as do lots of others) the results of an *evaluation* indicating disappointing outcomes as a result of your current positioning strategy, as was the case in the following example.

Example: Police as Guardians Versus Soldiers[21]

In 2013, the Seattle Police Department adopted federally mandated reforms to curb the use of excessive force. Breaking away from years of tradition, the academy shifted from fashioning "warriors" in a military mold to training "guardians" of the communities. Graduates of the Police Academy will still learn the basics of police work, such as handcuffing, writing reports, and handling firearms, but as described by the director of the academy in a *Seattle Times* article, the instruction will now include

> an increased emphasis on expressing empathy, following constitutional requirements, and treating citizens with respect and dignity. . . . More emphasis will be put on communication and behavioral psychology as a tool to gain control and compliance. Recruits need to learn how to make quick judgments, measure behaviors and consider options like social skills to de-escalate a conflict.

The first class embraced the idea, choosing "Guardians of the Gate" as one of their mottoes—even having T-shirts made with the inscription. One participant in the program, who had spent 12 years in the Army, was asked for his reaction to the new approach. His response was, "Thank goodness, I'm done being a warrior. I don't want to do that anymore."

Figure 9.10   Positioning of wearing protective gear as fun, easy, and popular.

Safety Tips

1: Wear protective gear, including a helmet, pads or guards on the arms, wrists and knees, and be sure to wear proper shoes, not flip-flops or bare feet

2: Never ride a scooter at night. Unlike bikes, scooters don't have reflectors.

3: Children under 8 should always be supervised by an adult when riding a scooter. Older kids should be supervised if crossing streets on a scooter.

Source: From *Newsweek* (October 2, 2000), © 2000 Newsweek, Inc. All rights reserved. Reprinted by permission. Photograph © Nicole Rosenthal.

HOW POSITIONING RELATES TO BRANDING

Although the concept of the brand and the branding process will be covered in the next chapter focusing on product, you may have immediate questions regarding positioning and how it relates to branding that we will address briefly at this point. It helps to distinguish the two by referring to a few basic definitions:

- Brand is a name, term, sign, symbol, and/or design that identifies the maker or seller of a product (e.g., ENERGY STAR® identifies products that are energy efficient, according to the Environmental Protection Agency [EPA]).[22]
- Brand identity is how you (the maker) want your target audience to think, feel, and act with respect to your brand (e.g., EPA wants citizens to see products with the ENERGY STAR label as a way to help the environment and save on electrical power bills).
- Brand image is how your target audience actually ends up thinking, feeling, and acting relative to your brand (e.g., what citizens know about the ENERGY STAR label and whether they associate it with energy and cost savings).
- Branding is the process of developing an intended brand identity (e.g., activities that EPA has undertaken to determine and ensure this desired brand identity).

Your positioning statement is something you and others can count on to provide parameters and inspiration for developing your desired brand identity—how you want the desired behavior to be seen by the target audience. It will provide strong and steady guidance for your decision making regarding your marketing mix, as it is the 4Ps that will determine where your offer lands in the minds of your target audience. And when your brand image doesn't align with your desired positioning (brand identity), you'll look to your 4Ps for "help" in repositioning the brand.

ETHICAL CONSIDERATIONS WHEN DEVELOPING A POSITIONING STATEMENT

When developing your positioning statement, several ethical questions may (and actually should) come to your mind. You will notice that many of these relate to the familiar "truth in advertising" code.

If your positioning statement is *behavior focused*, ensure that your recommendations are accurate. For 5 a Day the Color Way, detailed information on the website clarified why these specific behaviors are important: "Blue/purple fruits and vegetables contain varying amounts of health-promoting phytochemicals such as anthocyanins and pheno-lics, currently being studied for their antioxidant and anti-aging benefits."[23]

If your positioning statement focuses on *benefits* for the target audience, you will want to be certain that you can really deliver these benefits. A campaign promoting moderate physical activity should make it clear to potential "buyers" what levels and types of physical activity are needed to achieve any health gains promised, and at what levels.

If your positioning statement focuses on how the target audience will be able to over-come their *barriers*, you will want to be certain you paint a realistic picture. Communications promoting quitlines as a way to quit smoking should be certain to include rates of success and the fact that not all those who call will be able to quit. If you reread the poem from the Washington State Department of Health's website, note that the quitline delivers on its positioning as "hopeful and encouraging" but doesn't mention any guarantees.

If your positioning statement focuses on the *competition*, be certain that what you say about them is really true and not exaggerated. As you read, New York City promises bet-ter and "seamless" service when you call 311 rather than 911 for a missing car. It wouldn't take many citizens not getting quick help to spread the word that 911 will get you better service faster.

And if your positioning statement focuses on *repositioning* the brand, be sure your offer is really "new and improved." The Police as Guardian program will need to be obvi-ously distinct from the prior program.

CHAPTER SUMMARY

Positioning is the act of designing the organization's offering in such a way that it lands on and occupies a distinctive place in the mind of the target audience—where you want it to be. Step 6 in the marketing planning process recommends that you develop a positioning statement at this point. The research on your target audience's barriers, benefits, competitors, and influential others in Step 5 will provide the inspi-ration you need. It will also help build consensus among your colleagues and partners, ensuring fewer surprises and disappointments as you move forward to developing your strategies.

Positioning statements may be focused on behaviors, barriers, benefits, the competition, and/or on repositioning. Your decisions will reflect your value proposition, a reason why the target audience should buy the product—from you!

Take time and care to develop this statement, as you will refer to it frequently when developing each of the 4Ps. This will help ensure the "proper landing" you have in mind.

RESEARCH HIGHLIGHT

"Global Warming" or "Climate Change"?

Which Name Should We Use?

Imagine you could go back in time to 2005 and advise Al Gore on the development of his documentary film *An Inconvenient Truth*, the promotional materials that would accompany it, a website, and then his 2006 book *An Inconvenient Truth: The Planetary Emergency of Global Warming and What We Can Do About It*. Given the focus of this chapter on positioning and branding, here's the question: Would you advise him to go ahead and use the term *global warming*, or would you urge him to use the term *climate change* instead?

We would like to think that based on reading the first half of this text, you would first ask important questions to guide this recommendation. Number one, what problem is this effort intended to solve? Second, who is the target audience that could have the greatest impact on this problem? Third, what behavior or behaviors do you want to influence that target audience to do? And fourth, what term (brand) is most likely to motivate your priority audiences to take action?

The following research highlight provides a summary of a research study that examined differences in public preference for these terms and how they varied by target audience characteristics, including beliefs regarding causes of climate change, political affiliation, sociodemographics, and whether, relative to levels of concern with global warming, they were (a) alarmed/concerned, (b) cautious/engaged, or (c) doubtful/dismissive.[24]

The study was conducted in 2010 by Karen Akerlof and Edward W. Maibach, professors at George Mason University. Their specific objective was to identify whether three different terms (*global warming*, *climate change*, and *global climate change*) are favored uniformly by the public, or whether there are significant factors that influence preferences (and if so, what audience characteristics are most influential).

Background

As defined by EPA, the term *global warming* "refers to the recent and ongoing rise in global average temperature near earth's surface. It is caused mostly by increasing concentrations of greenhouse gases in the atmosphere. Global warming is causing climate patterns to change."[25] *Climate change* "refers to any significant change in the measures of climate lasting for an extended period of time."[26] A third term, *global climate change*, is also often used to describe the issue, and was therefore included in the study.

Method and Respondents

This research study was funded by Superior Watershed Partnership and Land Trust in an initiative in collaboration with Pictured Rocks National Lakeshore in Michigan. In June 2010, a mail survey was sent to 1,336 residents in Alger County, Michigan. Survey Sampling International provided a random sample from a frame of 4,613 addresses using address-based sampling. Each survey was addressed to "Alger County Resident" with instructions for the adult with the most recent birthday to complete the questionnaire. Geographically, the final sample closely resembled the zip code distribution for the initial mailing basis. To further verify the representativeness of respondent profiles, responses to the global warming questions were compared with a similar nationally representative survey fielded the same year. Responses of Alger County residents were only modestly different from those of the nationally representative sample.

Question areas included:

1. Preferred term for climate change (Global warming, Climate change, or Global climate change)

2. Global warming belief (Yes, No, or Don't know)

3. Global warming causation (Human activities, Natural changes, Both, or Global warming isn't happening)

4. Global warming's Six Americas (Alarmed/concerned, Cautious/disengaged, or Doubtful/dismissive).

5. Political affiliation (Republican, Democrat, or Independent/no party/ other)

6. *Sociodemographics* (Gender, Age, Education, or Income)

Analysis

Akerlof and Maibach explained,

> To evaluate the relationship between each independent variable and preferred name we performed a bivariate analysis using a Pearson chi-square test and Cramer's V values to measure the strength of association. Expected frequencies were greater than 5 in all cells, allowing for adequate approximation of the chi-square distribution. To evaluate the relative effect size of the independent variables we performed a hierarchical multinomial logistic regression analysis, using terminology preference as the dependent variable.[27]

Results

Overall, a bare majority of respondents (51.4%) preferred any of the three terms, and the percentages of those favoring *global warming* (18.0%) and *climate change* (20.5%) were statistically indistinct. When the percentages of those who prefer *climate change* and *global climate change* are added together, however, they represent a third of all respondents (33.4%; see Tables 9.5 through 9.7). This preference for *climate change* or *global climate change* was also true for each of the subgroups, with the exception of the "Doubtful/Dismissive" group that had a preference for a variety of other terms. It should be noted, however, that this group still preferred *climate change* or *global climate change* over *global warming* (see Table 9.6). (Note: For readers in a classroom setting, we suggest discussing your take on these findings as noted in the discussion section at the end of the chapter.)

Table 9.5 Term Preference by Belief in Whether Global Warming Is Happening

	Total (*n* = 715)	Is Global Warming Happening?		
		No (*n* = 172)	Yes (*n* = 400)	I Don't Know (*n* = 169)
Global Warming	18.0%	3.5%	30.3%	4.1%
Climate Change	20.5%	18.6%	19.8%	23.7%
Global Climate Change	12.9%	9.3%	16.5%	8.3%
Climate Change & Global Climate Change Combined	*33.4%*	*27.9%*	*37.3%*	*31.0%*
Other	8.3%	26.7%	2.8%	3.0%
No Preference	40.2%	41.9%	30.8%	60.9%

Note: Twenty-eight people did not respond to the question.

Table 9.6 Term Preference by Global Warming's Six Americas Collapsed Into Three Groups

	Sample Total (*n* = 715)	Alarmed/ Concerned (*n* = 333)	Cautious/ Disengaged (*n* = 222)	Doubtful/ Dismissive (*n* = 160)
Global Warming	18.0%	33.3%	7.2%	3.8%
Climate Change	20.5%	18.9%	25.2%	15.6%
Global Climate Change	12.9%	17.4%	11.3%	6.3%
Climate Change & Global Climate Change Combined	*33.4%*	*36.3%*	*36.5%*	*21.9%*
Other	8.3%	.9%	4.5%	28.8%
No Preference	40.2%	29.4%	51.8%	45.6%

Note: Twenty-eight people did not respond to more than 20% of the segmentation items.

Table 9.7   Term Preference by Political Party Affiliation

	Sample Total (*n* = 715)	Republican (*n* = 120)	Democrat (*n* = 225)	Independent/ Other (*n* = 262)	No Party/ No Interest in Politics (*n* = 102)
Global Warming	18.0%	15.8%	27.6%	14.5%	9.8%
Climate Change	20.5%	15.8%	20.0%	24.0%	20.6%
Global Climate Change	12.9%	8.3%	15.1%	13.4%	15.7%
Climate Change & Global Climate Change Combined	*33.4%*	*24.1%*	*35.1%*	*37.4%*	*36.3%*
Other	8.3%	14.2%	3.1%	11.5%	2.0%
No Preference	40.2%	45.8%	34.2%	36.6%	52.0%

Note: Thirty-four people did not respond to the question on party affiliation.

DISCUSSION QUESTIONS AND EXERCISES

1. One exercise that can inspire repositioning is to complete the following grid.

    If your agency/program were a dog, what dog would your key publics say you are? What dog do you want to be? Do the same for "car" and "a famous person."

	today	desired
a dog		
a car		
a famous person		

2. Referring back to the research highlight regarding using the term *climate change* versus *global warming*, what term would you advise using going forward? Or would you use both, depending on the target audience?

CHAPTER 9 NOTES

1. A. Ries and J. Trout, *Positioning: The Battle for Your Mind* (New York: Warner Books, 1982), 3.
2. Ibid., 7–8.
3. Legacy, "Keeping Young People From Using Tobacco" (n.d.), accessed January 13, 2014, http://www.legacyforhealth.org/what-we-do/national-education-campaigns/keeping-young-people-from-using-tobacco.

4. Centers for Disease Control and Prevention, "Cigarette Smoking–Attributable Mortality—United States, 2000," *Morbidity and Mortality Weekly Report* (September 5, 2003), accessed January 13, 2014, http://www.cdc.gov/mmwr/preview/mmwrhtml/mm5235a4.htm.

5. Adapted from P. Kotler and K. L. Keller, *Marketing Management*, 12th ed. (Upper Saddle River, NJ: Prentice Hall, 2005), 320.

6. Ibid.

7. Kotler and Keller, *Marketing Management*.

8. Ibid., 312–313.

9. King County Emergency Management, "3 Days, 3 Ways, Are You Ready?" (2006), accessed January 19, 2007, http://www.govlink.org/3days3ways/.

10. Produce for Better Health Foundation, "Fruit and Vegetable Consumption on the Rise for First Time in Nearly 15 Years" (November 30, 2005), accessed January 19, 2007, http://www.5aday.com/html/press/pressrelease.php?recordid=159.

11. Washington State Department of Health, "Tobacco Quitline" (2007), accessed January 22, 2007, http://www.quitline.com/.

12. Phones 4 Charity [website], http://www.phones4charity.org/.

13. Inform, Inc. [website], http://www.informinc.org/gs-recycle.php.

14. Ibid.

15. M. Rothschild, *The Impact of Road Crew on Crashes, Fatalities, and Costs* (June 2007), available upon request from roadcrew@mascomm.net; Show Case, "Road Crew" (n.d.), accessed July 29, 2011, http://www.thensmc.com/resources/showcase/road-crew?view=all.

16. Sun Microsystems, "Dial 311" (2007), accessed January 22, 2007, from http://www.sun.com/about-sun/media/features/311.html.

17. P. Kotler and G. Armstrong, *Principles of Marketing*, 9th ed. (Upper Saddle River, NJ: Prentice Hall, 2001), 273–275.

18. M. Moss, "Broccoli's Image Makeover," *The New York Times Magazine* (November 13, 2013), 30–35.

19. Ibid., 32.

20. B. Smith, "Social Marketing: Marketing With No Budget," *Social Marketing Quarterly* 5, no. 2 (June 1999), 7–8.

21. S. Miletich, "Police Academy 2.0: Less Military Training, More Empathy," *The Seattle Times* (July 13, 2013), accessed January 28, 2014, http://seattletimes.com/html/localnews/2021389398_policeacademyxml.html.

22. Kotler and Armstrong, *Principles of Marketing*.

23. Produce for Better Health Foundation, *5 a Day the Color Way* (n.d.), accessed January 29, 2007, http://www.5aday.com/html/colorway/colorway_home.php.

24. E. W. Maibach, A. Leiserowitz, C. Roser-Renouf, and C. K. Mertz, "Identifying Like-Minded Audiences for Global Warming Public Engagement Campaigns: An Audience Segmentation Analysis and Tool Development," *PLoS ONE* 6, no. 3 (2011): e17571.

25. U.S. Environmental Protection Agency, "Climate Change: Basic Information" (n.d.), accessed January 15, 2014, http://www.epa.gov/climatechange/basics/.

26. Ibid.

27. K. Akerlof and E. W. Maibach, "A Rose by any Other Name . . . ?: What Members of the General Public Prefer to Call "Climate Change," *Climate Change* 106 (April 2011): 699–710.

Chapter 10

PRODUCT

CREATING A PRODUCT PLATFORM

Product, not promotion, is the most important component of the marketing mix. Offer them benefits, not just fear. Offer them a tangible good or service to help them perform a behavior, not just a brochure. Adopt these principles and you shall win.

—Dr. Sameer Deshpande
University of Lethbridge

You are (finally) ready to develop your marketing strategy.

- You have identified a target audience and developed rich descriptions using relevant demographic, geographic, psychographic, and behavioral variables.
- You know what you want your audience to do and what they may need to know and/ or believe in order to act, and you've come to some agreement on levels of desired behavior change that you will develop a plan to achieve.
- You know what benefits and barriers your audience perceives relative to the desired behavior you have in mind, and what might motivate them to change.
- You know how this stacks up against the competition—most often your target audience's current or preferred behavior or the programs and organizations sponsoring it.
- You are aware of others your target audience considers influential.
- You have a positioning statement that will align and guide your team's decision making.

It is time to decide how you will influence your target audience to accept the desired behavior. You have four tools (product, price, place, and promotion) to help make this happen. And you'll probably need all of them to reduce barriers and create and deliver the value your target audience expects in exchange for this new behavior.

This chapter will focus on developing your product strategy, with an emphasis on exploring opportunities for goods and services that will support desired behaviors. You will read in this chapter about the three decisions you will make regarding the product offered:

1. *Core product:* The benefit the audience wants in exchange for performing the behavior

2. *Actual product:* Any tangible goods and services you will promote

3. *Augmented product:* Additional product elements to support behavior change

We begin with a case story where the product strategy is key to saving lives . . . of dogs and cats!

MARKETING HIGHLIGHT

Increasing Pet Adoption With Meet Your Match™

(2004–Present)

Source: American Society for the Prevention of Cruelty to Animals.

When we tally up the increases in adoptions, decreases in returns, decreases in euthanasia, and decreases in length of stay from shelters who have implemented the program, we are looking at literally tens of thousands of lives saved!

—Dr. Emily Weiss[1]

Background

The Humane Society of the United States reported in 2013 that 6 to 8 million cats and dogs entered shelters that year, and

because only 3 to 4 million were adopted, an estimated 2.7 million were euthanized.[2] It is also estimated that only about 30% of pets in homes come from shelters and rescues.[3] And although some pets in shelters are sick or have behavioral issues, this is not the case for the majority, as the American Society for Prevention of Cruelty to Animals (ASPCA) reports that "five out of ten dogs in shelters and seven out of ten cats in shelters are destroyed simply because there is no one to adopt them."[4]

Strategies to increase adoptions have ranged from rescue groups concentrating on saving and rehoming specific dog breeds (*product*) to waiving adoption fees (*price*) to off-site adoptions at stores like PetSmart (*place*) to branding strategies such as renaming animal shelters as pet adoption centers (*promotion*).

We think the strategy highlighted in this case is a great example of a new product designed to significantly decrease barriers to pet adoption and deliver on desired benefits.

Audience Insights

Maddie's Fund, a charitable foundation, identifies two obstacles to more shelter adoptions: fear and uncertainty.

> Many people believe shelter pets are "damaged goods." They're worried that they'll come with too much baggage, that they're sick or have serious behavior problems. They think of shelters as depressing, and can't handle selecting one pet while worrying that those they don't choose will die. What should be a happy family occasion starts to feel like a prison visit.[5]

A research study conducted by Ipsos Marketing for PetSmart Charities in 2011 showed that people who had recently acquired an animal from somewhere other than a shelter gave the reasons outlined in Table 10.1 as the top five reasons they chose not to adopt from an animal shelter.

Shelter personnel, the other target audience for the effort, were interested in improved strategies to increase adoptions, as these then would reduce euthanasia and potentially lead to shorter lengths of stay for animals. Increased adoptions and an enjoyable process for making this happen would also contribute to higher staff and volunteer moral. A strategy that would significantly increase adoption rates also had the potential to generate media interest, and therefore increased awareness and visits to the shelters.

Strategies

Dr. Emily Weiss, ASPCA's vice president of shelter research and development, had always been interested in animals. In college, she'd had a mentor who encouraged her to become a behaviorist, leading her to study everything from mice to elephants to Komodo dragons. Her work at ASPCA ranges from developing enrichment programs for animals in shelters to writing columns where she answers questions about horse behaviors.

In 2004, Dr. Weiss created an innovative way to address the concerns of potential pet parents and to increase adoptions. She developed models to predict how dogs and cats would behave in the home based on behaviors that could be measured in the shelter. Her innovation was branded Meet Your Match® and was designed to

Table 10.1   Top Five Reasons for Not Adopting from a Humane Organization

I wanted a purebred dog/cat	35%
The organization/shelter did not have the type dog/cat I was looking for	31%
You don't know what you'll get with a shelter animal	17%
The adoption process (application) is too difficult	12%
I do not know very much about pet adoption	9%

Note: Percentages add to more than 100 because multiple responses were allowed.

Source: PetSmart Charities, "Pet Adoption & Spay/Neuter: Understanding Public Perceptions by the Numbers" [webinar] (November 27, 2012).

scientifically match a shelter dog's personality, traits, and behavior characteristic with the traits and characteristics that adopters are seeking in a new animal companion. (We could perhaps think of this a pet version of eHarmony.com®!) There were two target audiences for program design: (a) shelter personnel who would be involved in assessing and characterizing the pets as well as working with potential adopters, and (b) potential adopters. Canine-ality™ was piloted with one shelter and launched nationally in 2004. Feline-ality™ followed in 2006 after a pilot with five shelters. Their marketing mix strategy is summarized in Table 10.2.

Table 10.2   The Meet Your Match™ Marketing Mix Strategy

Target Audience	Shelter Personnel	Potential Adopters
Desired Behavior	Help potential adopters find their best match.	Adopt a pet from a shelter, one that will be the best match.
The 4Ps:		
Product	*The Canine-ality and Feline-ality Assessments* These programs assess friendliness, playfulness, energy level, motivation and drive. Results place dogs into one of nine color-coded Canine-alities and cats into one of nine color-coded Feline-alities. (See Figure 10.1.) Staff are also provided a training, talking points, and more that help them work with adopters.	*Dog Adopter/Cat Adopter Surveys* Each survey consists of 18 questions to help determine which pet in the shelter best matches the adopter's expectations, experience, lifestyle, and home environment. Once it is completed, adopters receive a colored card that directs them to dogs or cats with cage cards that match the color of their guest passes. Shelter personnel provide individualized attention to the potential adopter and help her or him choose an animal more likely to be just the right companion, a service that pet stores and breeders don't always provide.
Price	ASPCA does not charge any fee for shelters to use the program. The guide and DVD cost $25, although the ASPCA often sends materials for free.	Shelters do not charge a fee for administering the adopter survey.
Place	Assessments are administered at the shelters.	Some shelters administer the adopter survey on paper in the facility. Others provide the survey online, so potential adopters can complete it in advance.
Promotion	Key messages include testimonials answering the question "What do you like about the program?" - "We were using a very long, two page application that made the adopter feel like the enemy. We required background checks, personal references, and we often made people go home empty handed while we did our research. After talking to Emily and going to a training, we learned to see the adopter as a friend."[a]	Key messages, as adapted by one shelter, include:[c] "You could be gazing at the animal of your dreams." "The Meet Your Match program wouldn't let you go home without knowing who's in that carrier or on that leash." "This is the only method in existence today that evaluates an animal's behavior and interests and matches them to an adopter's preferences."

"We get a lot of black Labrador retrievers and lab mixes that look alike . . . Now, rather than a black lab, one dog may be a 'teacher's pet', another may be a 'life of the party' each with different characteristics written out."[b]

The ASPCA works closely with shelters around the country. It introduced the Meet Your Match program primarily through one-on-one contact. Additional outreach is done via the ASPCApro website for shelters and at conferences.

Descriptions of specific personalities are appealing:

"Life of the Party. I think everything is fun, interesting and meant for play, especially you. Anything you do, I'll want to do too. With my own brand of surprises, life with me will keep you constantly on your toes, and the fun is guaranteed. (Socially motivated.)"[d]

The ASPCA provides a how-to publicity guide with tips and tools, such as sample media releases and pitch letters, to help shelters generate awareness. Individual shelters have also held launch events, inviting not only media but also board members, major donors, and leaders from other local humane groups.[e]

a. Maddie's Fund, "Meet Your Match: Does It Deliver?" (2006), accessed January 10, 2014, http://www.maddiesfund.org/Maddies_Institute/Articles/Meet_Your_Match.html. b. Ibid. c. Washington Animal Protection League, "Meet Your Match" (n.d.), accessed January 10, 2014, http://www.warl.org/adopt/meet-your-match/. d. ASPCA, "Meet the Canine-alities," accessed January 10, 2014, http://www.aspca.org/adopt/meet-your-match/meet-canine-alities. e. ASPCA, "MYM Mesmerizes Media at Jacksonville Humane," accessed January 10, 2014, http://www.aspcapro.org/node/72096.

Outcomes

The Meet Your Match program provides measurable results, with participating shelters achieving gains in adoption often reaching more than 15%—even 40% to 60% gains during heavy publicity.

Reflections

Upon reflection, Caryn Ginsberg notes,

> The Meet Your Match program is transformative in the way it redefines "product." People have traditionally chosen pets based on breed stereotype or an animal's appearance, often turning to breeders or pet shops as a result. Now shelters can help prospective pet parents rethink what it means to choose the very best animal to join their family. The adopter-friendly process takes service to a

Figure 10.1   The nine feline-alities.

Source: American Society for the Prevention of Cruelty to Animals.

new level, giving shelters competitive advantage over other outlets and reducing the number of animals killed for want of a home.[6]

Information for this case was provided by Caryn Ginsberg, author of *Animal Impact: Secrets Proven to Achieve Results and Move the World*.[7]

PRODUCT: THE FIRST "P"

A product is anything that can be offered to a market to satisfy a want or need.[8] It isn't, as many typically think, just a tangible offering like soap, tires, or hamburgers. It can be one of several types: physical goods, a service, an experience, an event, a person, a place, a property, an organization, information, or an idea.[9]

In social marketing, major product elements include: (a) the benefit the target audience wants in exchange for performing the behavior, (b) any goods and services you will be promoting to your target audience, and (c) any additional product elements you will include to assist your target audience in performing the behavior. As highlighted in the opening case about increasing pet adoption, the product benefit to pet adopters is in finding a pet from a shelter that will be their best match; the actual product is the adopter survey; and an additional product element to assist potential adopters is individualized attention from shelter staff. As you will read, all three elements are key to success. Certainly, what's in it for the audience in exchange for their performing the behavior needs to be highlighted. You will often find social marketing efforts that encourage audiences to increase consumption or utilization of existing products (e.g., childhood immunizations) or products that your program develops and makes available (e.g., a statewide immunization database for healthcare providers). We also encourage you to consider the critical role that additional product elements (augmented products) can play in reducing barriers to behaviors (e.g., providing a vaccine reminder application for the parent to download to keep track).

At this point, it is beneficial to distinguish between what we consider goods and what we consider services. We also distinguish between existing products and new products, as depicted in Table 10.3. While goods are usually "consumed" or "utilized" and are purchased or obtained for personal use (e.g., organic fertilizers), services are a product form that is essentially intangible and does not result in the ownership of anything (e.g., a workshop on natural yard care).[10] These distinctions are important primarily so that you are inspired to consider all four categories when developing a product strategy. Additional relevant terms often associated with product strategy in the commercial sector are presented in Table 10.4.

STEP 7: DEVELOP THE SOCIAL MARKETING PRODUCT PLATFORM

Traditional marketing theory propounds that from the customer's perspective, a product is more than its features, quality, name, and style and identifies three product levels you

Table 10.3   Examples of Existing and New Social Marketing Goods and Services

Potential Actual Products	Goods	Services
Existing Products	Condoms	Mammography
	Breast pumps	Gym membership
	Home blood pressure monitors	Taxis
	Immunizations	Blood donation
	Lockboxes for handguns at home	Pet neutering
	Low-flow showerheads	Home energy audits
	Organic fertilizers	Septic tank inspections
New Products Developed to Support Behaviors	Breathalyzers at bars	Road Crew for "bar hopping"
	Hot water temperature gauge cards	Tobacco quitline
	Drug test kits for parents of teens	Home visits for early learning
	Collapsible grocery carts suitable for walking to and from the store	Workshops on natural gardening
	Food waste containers for under the sink	Veggie Mobiles for inner-city residents
	Tablets to test for leaky toilets	Walking school bus programs
		Amber Alert for missing children

Table 10.4   A Product Primer

Product Type refers to whether the product is physical goods, services, experiences, an event, a person, a place, a property, an organization, information, or an idea

Product Line refers to a group of closely related products offered by an organization that perform similar functions but are different in terms of features, style, or some other variable[a]

Product Mix refers to the product items that an organization offers, often reflecting a variety of product types

Product Features describe product components (e.g., number of days or hours it takes to obtain results from an HIV/AIDS test)

Product Platform includes decisions regarding the core product (benefit), actual product (goods and services), and augmented product (additional product elements included to support the desired behavior)

Product Quality refers to the performance of the product and includes such valued attributes as durability, reliability, precision, and ease of operation[b]

Product Development is the systematic approach that guides the development and launch of a new product and is managed by a product manager, sometimes called a brand manager

[a] P. Kotler and G. Armstrong, *Principles of Marketing*, 9th ed. (Upper Saddle River, NJ: Prentice Hall, 2001), 300.

[b] Ibid., 299.

should consider when developing your product: *core product*, *actual product*, and *augmented product*.[11] This platform is illustrated in Figure 10.2, and each of these levels will be described in detail in the next three sections of this chapter. This will be helpful to you in conceptualizing and designing your product strategy.

Figure 10.2 Three levels of the social marketing product.

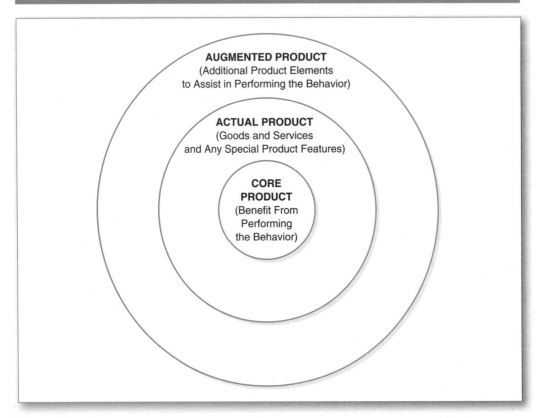

Briefly, your *core product* is the benefit the target audience wants and expects in exchange for performing the behavior. The *actual product* is any goods or services you will be influencing your target audience to "buy." And the *augmented product* includes any additional product elements that you may develop, distribute, sell, or just promote. Examples are presented in Table 10.4.

Core Product

The core product, the center of the product platform, answers the following questions: What's in it for the customer to adopt the behavior? What benefits will customers receive? What needs will the desired behavior satisfy? What problems will it solve? The core product is not the behaviors or accompanying goods and services you will be developing, providing, and/or promoting. It is the benefits your audience wants and expects to experience when they perform the behavior—benefits *they say* are the most valuable to them (e.g., "moderate physical activity will make me feel better, look better, and live longer"). As noted in Chapter 8, the service-dominant logic model asserts that a product has value only when a customer "uses" it, and that this value (core product) is determined by the customer, not the marketer. The great Harvard marketing professor Theodore Levitt was known to have told his students, "People don't want to buy a quarter-inch drill. They want a quarter-inch hole!" And Charles Revson, of Revlon, also provided a memorable quote illustrating the difference between product features (actual product) and product benefits (core product): "In the factory we make cosmetics; in the store, we sell hope."[12]

Decisions about the core product focus primarily on what potential benefits should be stressed. This process will include reviewing (from Step 5) audience perceptions of (a) benefits from the desired behavior and (b) perceived costs of the competing behaviors that the desired behavior can help the target audience avoid. You may have even identified this core product when constructing your positioning statement (in Step 6). Decisions are then made regarding which of these should be emphasized in a campaign. And keep in mind, the key benefit you should highlight is the benefit the target audience perceives for performing the behavior—not the benefit to your organization or agency.

Example. Interviews with teens often reveal several perceived benefits youth associate with not smoking: doing better in school, doing better in sports, being seen as smart, and looking and feeling good. They may also reveal the following perceived costs of smoking: You could get addicted and not be able to quit, you might die, you'll stink, and you won't be as good in sports. Further discussions may indicate that one of these (e.g., fear of addiction) is most concerning and should be highlighted in the campaign (see Figure 10.3). In this case, the core product for the campaign becomes "By not smoking, you don't risk addiction."

Figure 10.3 A testimonial used to persuade youth that tobacco is addictive.

Reprinted with permission of the Centers for Disease Control and Prevention's Media Campaign Resource Center.

Actual Product

Surrounding the core product are the *specific goods or services* you want your target audience to acquire, utilize, and/or consume—those related to the desired behavior. As noted earlier, it may be existing goods or services offered by a for-profit company (e.g., fruits and vegetables), a nonprofit organization (e.g., rapid HIV/AIDS test), or a governmental agency (e.g., community swimming pool). Or it may be goods or services your organization develops or advocates for development (e.g., Road Crew). In 1952, G. D. Wiebe raised the question, "Why can't you sell brotherhood like you sell soap?" and then embarked on a research journey to find the answer.[13] Dr. Wiebe, at the time a research psychologist for the CBS Radio Network and lecturer in psychology at the City College of New York, concluded after examining four social campaigns that "the more the conditions of a social campaign resemble those of a product campaign, the more successful the campaign will be."[14] One specific factor he felt was critical is a "mechanism" that enables the target audience to translate their motivation (wants, needs, awakened desires) into action. These physical goods and services may well provide this critical mechanism. The following example illustrates this principle well.

Example. At the 2013 World Social Marketing Conference, Shiraz Latiff, CEO of Hummingbird International, shared an inspiring "product development" story from Sri Lanka, an island nation in the Indian Ocean known to be one of the best and largest producers of black tea in the world. It is also known for its very high diabetes-related death rate, attributed in part to the 2 to 3 teaspoons of sugar added to several traditional cups of tea a day. In celebration of World Diabetes Day in 2011, the Diabetes Association of Sri Lanka piloted a new product, one designed to decrease sugar consumption. They called it a F'Poon, as in fact it was a "serrated" spoon that looked and functioned more like a fork than a spoon (see Figure 10.4). On this day, the F'Poon was distributed across a chain of leading restaurants and tea houses in the Colombo district, replacing the regular spoons in sugar bowls. Within six hours, over 1,500 tea drinkers used the F'Poon; 65% less sugar was consumed; and 100% of tea drinkers spoke with representatives of the Diabetes Association, most expressing that "it was a good idea" rather than a complaint. The success of the pilot with the major restaurants and tea houses was featured in the local electronic and print media and was commended by major governmental and nongovernmental institutions for its classic innovative concept and outcome. By 2013 , all major restaurants in three country districts had adopted the F'Poon at their own cost, with plans being discussed to roll this out among medium-scale and low-end tea boutiques across the island nation at no cost by 2015.

Figure 10.4 The F'Poon: A product designed to make it easier to have less sugar with a cup of tea.

Additional components at the actual-product level may include any *brand names* developed for the behavior (e.g., 5 a Day), the *campaign's sponsoring organization* (e.g., Produce for Better Health Foundation), and any *endorsements and sponsors* (e.g., National Cancer Institute or Centers for Disease Control and Prevention). The following

Source: Hummingbird International.

Table 10.5   Examples of Three Product Levels Products

Behavior objective	Core product (benefit from performing the behavior)	Actual product (goods and services and any special product features)	Augmented product (additional product elements to assist in performing the behavior)
For Improved Health			
Get tested for HIV/AIDS within six months of having unprotected sex	Early detection, treatment, and prevention of spreading the disease	Rapid HIV/AIDS test with results available in 30 minutes (versus two weeks as before)	Counseling for you and your partner
Conduct monthly breast self-exams and annual mammograms after age 50	Early detection and treatment	Mammogram	Laminated card for a shower to prompt and record exams
For Injury Prevention			
Do not text while driving	Preventing injuries and death	Thumb socks that make it difficult to text, given to teens when they get their driver's licenses	Special attachment for keeping the thumb socks on rearview mirror when not driving
Put a life vest on toddlers at the beach	Preventing drowning	Toddler life vests	Life vests for loan at beaches
To Protect the Environment			
Plant native plants	Protecting wildlife habitats	100 native plants to choose from	Workshops on designing a native plant garden
Reduce home energy consumption	Saving money and reducing carbon emissions	Home energy audits	Findings from the audit of potential anticipated savings
For Community Involvement			
Sign up to become an organ donor	Saving someone's life	Organ donor registry	Form that makes it clear that in the event of death, any family members will be asked to give final approval
To Enhance Financial Well-Being of the Poor			
Make regular deposits to a savings account	Children's education	Lockbox to keep at home for depositing money	Bank personnel make home visits to collect the money and deposit in a savings account

example highlights a product branding strategy, a topic covered in more detail at the end of this chapter.

   Example. Every year in the United States, an estimated 25,000 children die before their first birthday,[15] and one in every eight babies is born prematurely.[16] To address this public health crisis, the National Healthy Mothers, Healthy Babies Coalition (HMHB) has created text4baby, a free mobile information service providing pregnant women and moms whose babies are less than a year old with information to influence them to perform behaviors that will give their babies the best possible start in life. The program was launched in February 2010, and by December 2013, over 246,987 pregnant women and 409,938 mothers of new babies had registered.[17] Many consider this a success and have asked, "What are they doing right?" A strong brand is certainly one contributing factor, as is a strategic mix of all 4Ps to support the brand identity.

   First, the service (*product*) was developed with input from potential users. The HMHB tested the content and style of text messages in, for example, community clinics and Healthy Start programs. According to Judy Meehan, the chief executive officer of HMHB, "We worked on tone—so the messages sound like they're coming from a friend. Not 'you should do this' but 'have you thought about this?'"[18] Balanced, informative, 160-character messages are delivered directly to cell phone inboxes.

   Second, the service is free (*price*). One program partner, CTIA–The Wireless Association, a nonprofit advocacy group, persuaded wireless carriers to transmit messages free of charge, similar to what has been done to send Amber Alerts—messages about child abductions.

   Third, signup is simple (*place*): All you need to do is send a text message to the number 511411 with the message BABY or BEBE (for Spanish messages). You are then prompted for your due date or your child's birth date and your zip code, and immediately you begin receiving three messages a week offering actionable, evidence-based information relevant to your stage in pregnancy or your child's development.

   Finally, information (*promotion*) reaches mothers in all 50 states in a variety of ways, including through libraries, churches, billboard ads, health care providers, employers, health fairs, and networks such as the American Academy of Pediatrics. In some states, women learn about the program when applying for Medicaid, and in others, such as New York City, every birth certificate promotes the program.

Augmented Product

This level of the product platform includes any *additional product elements* you will be providing and/or promoting along with the actual product. Although they may be considered optional, they are sometimes exactly what is needed to provide encouragement (e.g., a walking buddy), remove barriers (e.g., a detailed resource guide and map of local walking trails and organized walking programs), or sustain behavior (e.g., a journal for tracking exercise levels). They may also provide opportunities to brand

and to "tangibilize" the campaign, creating more attention, appeal, and memorability for target audiences.[19]

Example. WalkBoston is a nonprofit organization with a mission to create and preserve safe walking environments that build vital communities. One behavior they promote is walking 30 minutes a day. One audience benefit they appeal to is the opportunity to see and experience things that would be missed using other modes of travel. One product they created certainly fits the augmented product profile: maps. One map features lines that indicate five-minute walking increments, helping to plan routes to work, a meeting, or lunch, and lets users estimate how long the walk will be. Other maps feature over 50 places that are

wonderful to walk, easy to navigate, and convenient to get around. Created by those who know the area best—either local people or experts in the walk's particular theme—each self-guided walk has a detailed route as well as distances and descriptions of sights and scenes.[20]

Decisions Regarding Physical Goods

You will face several decisions in regard to developing or enhancing physical goods that your campaign will encourage audiences to acquire, utilize, or consume.

Is there a need for new physical goods that would greatly support the behavior change? For example, many adults with diabetes conduct finger-prick blood tests to monitor their blood sugar levels. A painless, needle-free mechanism that would provide reliable readings would be a welcome innovation and might result in more regular monitoring of blood sugar levels. Not all new products will require retooling or significant research and development costs, as illustrated in the following example.

Example. In December 2012, news around the world featured the story of a 23-year old student in Delhi, India, who was gang-raped on a public bus. She died 13 days later. The attacks sparked not only mass anger and demonstrations, but also the imagination and determination of three engineering students from the SRM Institute of Science and Technology in Tamil Nadu, India, who then created electronic underwear they believed would help protect women from sexual assault. The female engineers of the team commented to news sources that current laws and lack of enforcement are not enough to keep women safe in India. The lingerie (actual product) will deliver electric shock waves of 3,800,000 volts to an attacker, is designed to track the wearer's location by GPS, and can send text message alerts to police and/or family in case of emergencies.[21] The protective underwear, named Society Harnessing Equipment (SHE), won the 2013 Gandhian Young Technology Innovation Award, and is expected to be mass produced and distributed.[22]

Do current goods need to be improved or enhanced? For example, typical compost bins require the gardener to use a pitchfork to regularly turn the yard waste to enhance compost development. New and improved models that a social marketing campaign might make known to target audiences are suspended on a bracket that requires only a regular "tumble."

Consider that until recent years, most users (and especially nonusers) have perceived life vests as bulky and uncomfortable. Teens have raised concerns about tan lines and the "ugly" orange color. New options are vastly improved, with a look similar to that of suspenders and a feature for automatic inflation using a pull tab. Consider also the clear need for an improved product within a product category in the next example.

Example. An environmental scan of bullying prevention apps available in 2013 conducted by the Substance Abuse and Mental Health Services Administration (SAMHSA) identified something critical missing. Most bullying prevention apps available focused on reporting bullying incidents, by either the person being bullied or an onlooker. Some also provided educational content (e.g., signs of bullying and what actions to take). And yet, formative research with technical experts indicated that children look (more) to their parents and caregivers for guidance on tough choices, peer pressure, and making decisions. And that parents and caregivers who spend at least 15 minutes a day talking with their child can build the foundation for a strong relationship and offer reassurance that he or she can come to them for any problem. A new bullying prevention app was designed by SAMHSA to fill this product gap. It aids parents and caregivers prevent bullying by helping them to:

- Understand bullying and how to recognize warning signs
- Learn pointers on talking with a child about bullying
- Set reminders to talk with a child
- Establish a profile for a child so they can easily navigate to age-appropriate content and manage reminders
- Share conversation tips, advice, and resources from the app with others via Facebook, Twitter, email, and text message[23]

Is there a need or opportunity for a substitute product?[24] A substitute product is one that offers the target audience a "healthier and safer" way to satisfy a want, fulfill a need, or solve a problem. The key is to understand the real benefit (core product) of the competing behavior and to then develop and/or promote products offering the same or at least some of the same benefits. These include, for example, food and beverages such as nonalcoholic beers, garden burgers, fat-free dairy products, nicotine-free cigarettes, and decaffeinated coffee; natural fertilizers, natural pesticides, and ground covers to replace lawns; an older sibling (versus a parent) taking a younger teen to a community clinic for STD screening; and a package containing a can of chicken soup, tissues, and aspirin "prescribed" to patients suffering from colds, in an effort to reduce the overuse of antibiotics.

Chakravorty defines a substitute product as "a product offered to a market that is thought of and used by those in the market as a replacement for some other product."[25] She further surmises,

> An acceptable and accessible substitute product may promote desirable behaviors by enhancing the user's perceived self-efficacy. Self-efficacy is expected to be strengthened to the extent that many of the behaviors required in using a substitute are similar to behaviors associated with reference product use.[26]

For example, a heavy coffee drinker may come to believe that eliminating coffee will lead to improved cardiac health. The prospective former coffee drinker may decide that she is very likely to quit coffee if she replaces it with decaffeinated coffee. A variety of factors may have contributed to this perception. First, she may feel that as a result of her coffee drinking behavior, she "knows how" to execute the behaviors required in drinking decaf. The beverage will be consumed in the same container, at the same temperature, and she will not have to make great adjustments to the flavor of the substitute. If she is able to consume decaf in all the same situations where she usually drinks coffee (i.e., at home, work, favorite restaurant), her efficacy for "decaf drinking" behavior may rise as she estimates that she will be able to perform the new behavior across a wide variety of settings.[27]

Decisions Regarding Services

Services are often distinguished as offerings that are intangible and do not result in the ownership of anything.[28] In the social marketing environment, examples of services that support the desired behavior change might include *education-related services* (e.g., parenting workshops on how to talk to your kids about sex), *personal services* (e.g., escorts for students back to their dorms at night), *counseling services* (e.g., a crisis line for people considering suicide), *clinical services* (e.g., community clinics for free immunizations), and *community services* (e.g., hazardous waste mobiles for disposal of toxic waste products). It should be noted that services that are more sales oriented in nature (e.g., demonstrations on the efficiency of low-flow toilets) fall into the promotional category and will be discussed in Chapter 14. You will also face several decisions regarding any services you offer.

Should a new service be developed and offered? For example, given the apparent success and popularity of toll-free tobacco quitlines to support smoking cessation in other states, a community without one might want to develop and launch a line to accompany mass-media campaigns encouraging adults to quit smoking. In the past few years, apps such as those highlighted in the following example have become a new popular service for social marketers to explore.

Example. As part of First Lady Michelle Obama's Let's Move! campaign to reduce childhood obesity, a competition was announced in March 2010. Apps for Healthy Kids challenged software developers, game designers, students, and other innovators to develop fun and engaging software tools and games that would influence (even excite) children, especially "tweens" (ages 9 to 12), to eat better and be more physically active. Entries were required to use USDA nutrition guidelines.[29] The tool winning first place, announced in September 2010, was Pick Chow!, an online tool allowing children to create meals by dragging and dropping foods onto their virtual plate (see Figure 10.5). The Add It Up! meter then shows the nutritional value of the meal, rating it with one to five stars, helping children learn quickly how their choices make a difference in creating a well-balanced meal. And perhaps the most sustainable feature is the one that allows the children to then "send their 'chow' to their parents, who then receive an email with what their child has chosen to be a healthy choice for breakfast, lunch or dinner, along with the menu, recipe, shopping list and coupons."[30]

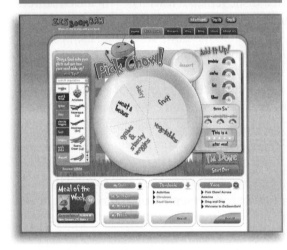

Figure 10.5   Pick Chow! An app developed by Karen Laszlo, Mike Carcaise, and Lisa Lanzano.[31]

Does an existing service need to be improved or enhanced? For example, what if customer surveys indicate that an estimated 50% of callers to the state's 800 number for questions about recycling hang up because they typically have to wait more than five minutes on hold? Relative to enhanced services, what if customer feedback also indicates that residents would be interested in (and would pay for) recycling of yard waste in addition to glass, paper, and aluminum?

Example. Doug McKenzie-Mohr is an environmental psychologist specializing in designing programs that support sustainable behaviors. One of the tools he encourages social marketers to use is making norms visible: "Norms guide how we should behave. If we observe others acting unsustainably . . . we are more likely to act similarly. In contrast, if we observe members of our community acting sustainably, we are more likely to do the same."[32]

Opower, an energy efficiency and smart grid software company, has developed a program whereby residents receive information about their own level of household energy consumption compared with the norm for their local community. They say their company was "founded on a simple premise: It's time to engage the 300 million Americans who are in the dark about their energy use."[33] One of their products is a home energy report that not only provides the utility's customers information and trends on their energy usage, but also includes comparisons to their neighbors, including the use of symbolic "smiley faces" (see Figure 10.6). According to Opower, leading utilities across the country provide home energy reports to nearly 1 million households nationwide, and these utility customers have cut their annual gas or electricity usage by 1.5% to 3.5% annually after receiving these reports.[34]

DESIGN THINKING

Tim Brown, CEO and president of IDEO, a leading design company, frequently writes and speaks about design thinking, and in a 2009 TED talk in Oxford, he described the difference between *design* and *design thinking*. Design, as he describes it, focuses on making a product attractive, easy to use, and ultimately more marketable. By contrast, design thinking focuses less on an object and more on an approach to designing products that fulfill human desires, solve problems, and create world-changing innovations. He calls for a shift to a more local, collaborative, and participatory process to fully understand what humans need, test preliminary idea with prototypes, and then design products that fulfill human needs and desires.[35]

Design thinking is very consistent with the product platform outlined in this chapter, where we begin with determining the core product, the value the target audience wants in exchange for adopting the behavior. What benefits do *they* say they want the behavior to provide? We then, and only then, move on to determining the features of tangible

Figure 10.6   Home Energy Report comparing "you" to your neighbors.

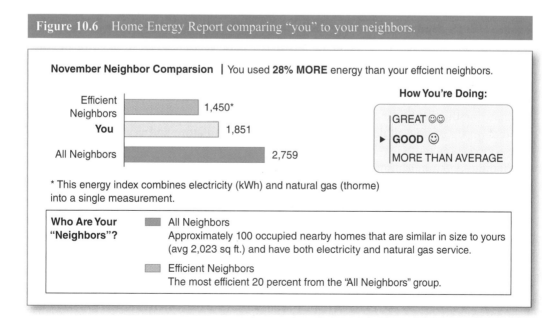

goods and services (actual and augmented products). Here is when and where we apply the elements of design—shape, size, color, sound, texture, process—to arrive at the actual features of the physical object or the experiencing process, as illustrated in the following example.

Example. To increase access to clean water among low-income households, PATH, an international nonprofit organization focusing on sustainable, culturally relevant public health solutions, launched the Safe Water Project in 2006. The five-year project is funded by the Bill and Melinda Gates Foundation.[36]

One of the primary challenges in developing a household water treatment and safe storage (HWTS) product for low-income households is a lack of understanding of how, when, why, and by whom such products might be used—or not. To address this challenge, PATH contracted with Quicksand Design to codesign and conduct a *longitudinal ethnographic study* on user experiences with HWTS products. The study revealed much about what works and does not work, and helped identify key product attributes that might influence the adoption and sustained, correct use of future iterations of HWTS products.

The sample for the study focused on families living on less than US$5 a day per capita. Twenty households were selected from four districts in Andhra Pradesh, one of 28 states in India. Five different durable HWTS products were placed in study households, chosen to represent as much diversity as possible in product features. These included a ceramic water pot, a stainless steel filter, two multistage filters, and one portable hollowfiber filter. Research teams made six visits to each household over a six-month period, each lasting four to six hours. During the first visit, baseline information on participants' attitudes, perceptions, behaviors, and motivations related to water, HWTS, and health was gathered. A water treatment device was randomly assigned and introduced to each household at the second visit. Some households received an unopened package without any detailed instructions. In other cases, members of the research team posed as shopkeepers who provided cursory instructions about how to set up and use the product, or as traveling salespeople who set up the product for the family and demonstrated cleaning and maintenance procedures. And another group of households was sent to an actual retail store and given money to purchase the product.

Findings and implications from the study indicated that design and development efforts need to focus on product features and attributes that improve the user's experience. For example, devices should be designed to let users know how much water is left by using transparent containers or water level indicators. Clear signals of a product's operational status and prompts for maintenance can reduce frustration and enable users to correct problems. Designers can make HWTS products more desirable by responding to consumers' preferences for certain materials and forms and also by appealing to their desire for modernity. Steel is respected for its durability and traditional place in the kitchen. And although plastic has a more modern appeal, consumers are extremely sensitive to the grade and quality of plastic. Cylindrical shapes that resemble existing vessels in homes may be considered old-fashioned when compared with asymmetrical or angular shapes.

In the research highlight at the end of this chapter, you'll read about "The Lucky Fish," another great example of using design thinking, this time to reduce anemia in Cambodia.

BRANDING

Branding in the commercial sector is pervasive and fairly easy to understand and recognize. A brand, as mentioned earlier, is a name, term, sign, symbol, or design (or a combination of these) that identifies the maker or seller of a product (see Table 10.6).[37] You have contact with brands when you start your day with a Starbucks, search for directions on your iphone, drive your Volvo, listen to music on your iPod, like a friend on Facebook, tweet a super-bowl score on Twitter, use Microsoft Word, run in your Nikes, and TiVo the CBS News.

Branding in social marketing is not as common, although we would like to encourage more of it, as it helps create visibility and ensure memorability. The following list includes a few of the stronger brands. In these cases, brand names that have been used to identify programs and products are used consistently in an integrated way. Most are accompanied by additional brand elements, including graphics and taglines:

- Wildfire prevention: **Smokey Bear**
- Poison prevention: **Mr. Yuk**
- Maternal and child health: **Text4Baby**
- Nutrition: **5 a Day**
- Traffic safety: **Click It or Ticket**
- Physical activity: **VERB**
- Crime protection: **McGruff the Crime Dog**
- Safe produce: **USDA Organic**
- Sustainable seafood: **Seafood Watch**
- Waste reduction: **Reduce. Reuse. Recycle.**
- Drinking and driving: **Road Crew**
- Tobacco prevention: **truth®**
- Litter prevention: **Don't mess with Texas**
- Pet waste: **Scoop the Poop**
- Youth drug prevention: **Parents. The Anti-Drug.**
- Voting: **Rock the Vote**
- SIDS: **Back to Sleep**
- Water conservation: **Water—Use It Wisely**
- Water quality: **Chesapeake Club**
- Energy conservation: **ENERGY STAR**
- Schoolchildren's safety: **Walking School Bus**
- Senior fall prevention: **S.A.I.L. (Stay Active and Independent for Life)**
- Protected sex: **Number One condoms**

Figure 10.7 Previous packaging and new packaging.

Source: Population Services International.

In 1994, PSI Cambodia (PSI/C) launched the Number One condom brand and aggressively grew it over time through well-funded promotion and distribution efforts. By 2006, however, PSI/C was becoming a victim of its own success. The Number One brand had a disproportionately large share of the condom market (88%), which led donors to question how much longer they would have to support the costs. To this end, PSI/C decided to reposition this flagship condom as a more upscale brand, one that would be designed to appeal to those engaged in unprotected "sweetheart sex" (e.g., between two people who share an affectionate bond) and priced to recover costs. They also wanted to leverage the tremendous brand equity of Number One that had built up over 15 years. Changes to the product's packaging appear in Figure 10.7. It kept the visual elements that were so closely associated with the brand (such as the color blue and the boxy logo) while updating them to better express the new positioning (impressing one's partner) and brand personality (being successful and classy).[38]

ETHICAL CONSIDERATIONS RELATED TO CREATING A PRODUCT PLATFORM

One way to highlight ethical considerations relative to product decisions is to revisit each component of the product platform.

The *core product* promises the target audience a benefit they will receive (or cost they will avoid) if they perform the behavior. Can you be sure? How much should you disclose about the probability of success? Tobacco prevention specialists emphasize the health costs of smoking cigarettes, and yet how many times have you seen or read the research that claims that much of the physiological damage done by smoking during the first 10 to 20 years will be repaired by the body if and when you quit? Should this information be prominently displayed?

For the *actual product*, decisions are made relative to a specific behavior you will be promoting (e.g., 5 A Day) and any name and sponsors that will be associated with the behavior (e.g., Produce for Better Health Foundation). Perhaps one major ethical consideration here is whether you make the actual sponsor/funder of the project very visible or not. For example, should the funder of the campaign be visible on a teen pregnancy prevention

Table 10.6 A Branding Primer

Brand is a name, term, sign, symbol, or design (or a combination of these) that identifies the maker or seller of a product or service.
Brand Identity is how you (the maker) want consumers to think, feel, and act with respect to your brand.
Brand Image is how your target audience actually does think, feel, or act with respect to your brand.
Branding is the process of developing an intended brand identity.
Brand Awareness is the extent to which consumers recognize a brand.
Brand Promise is the marketer's vision of what the brand must be and do for consumers.
Brand Loyalty refers to the degree to which a consumer consistently purchases the same brand within a product class.
Brand Equity is the value of a brand, based on the extent to which it has high brand loyalty, name awareness, perceived quality, strong brand associations, and other assets such as patents, trademarks, and channel relationships. It is an important, although intangible, asset that has psychological and financial value to a firm.
Brand Elements are those trademarkable devices that serve to identify and differentiate the brand.
Brand Mix or **Portfolio** is the set of all brands and brand lines a particular firm offers for sale to a buyer in a particular category.
Brand Contact can be defined as any information-bearing experience a customer of prospect has with the brand.
Brand Performance relates to how well the product or service meets customers' functional needs.
Brand Extension is using a successful brand name to launch a new or modified product in a new category.
Cobranding is the practice of using the established brand names of more than one company on the same product or marketing them together in the same fashion.

Source: P. Kotler and N. Lee, *Marketing in the Public Sector: A Roadmap to Improved Performance* (Upper Saddle River, NJ: Wharton School, 2006). Reprinted with permission.

campaign poster? And consider this product introduced in January 2011 in Placer, California. Law enforcement and schools there began offering parents a home alcohol and drug screening kit at a deeply discounted price. The kit included a 10-panel drug screening for $10, which would sell for about $40 in stores; alcohol test strips sell for $2. A deputy who launched the program said authorities were not asking parents to turn in kids who tested positive for illicit drugs and that it was meant to help keep kids safe. Are you as concerned as one representative of the New York–based Drug Policy Alliance, who noted that "asking kids to urinate in a cup could further erode a rocky relationship with parents"?[39] This may be where the rule of thumb "Do more good than harm" can help you decide.

For the *augmented product*, decisions regarding additional tangible goods and services are similar to those in the private sector, although in this case you are often dealing with taxpayer-funded programs, a different constituent group with agendas different from those of shareholders. Does your product "perform as promised"? If you distribute condoms in high school, do those concerned with sending a "sex is okay" message have a good point? In terms of services, can you deliver and provide good service if you are successful in generating demand?

CHAPTER SUMMARY

The *product* platform has three levels: the core product (the benefit of the behavior), the actual product (any goods and/or services your effort will be developing or promoting), and the augmented product (any additional product elements needed to support behavior change).

Decisions are faced at each level. At the core product level, decisions will need to be made regarding what potential benefits should be stressed. At the actual product level, you will consider whether existing goods (e.g., bike helmets) or services (e.g., home energy audits) should be promoted or whether new or improved products are needed to support behavior adoption (e.g., a tobacco quitline or a bullying app for parents). We encourage you to also consider whether there are additional product elements (augmented products) that would provide support for the target audience, ones not "required" but that might make the difference in whether the audience is moved to action (e.g., life vests available for loan at beaches).

RESEARCH HIGHLIGHT

Reducing Anemia in Cambodia

Canadian's Lucky Iron Fish Saves Lives in Cambodia[40]

By Louise Brown*

November 12, 2011

University of Guelph grad student Chris Charles helped in the development of this iron fish that poor village women in Cambodia put in their cooking pots, allowing iron to leach into the food and therefore raising the levels of iron in their bodies. They tried several designs but *finally chose a lucky fish. Charles holds one of the lucky fish on the Guelph University Campus.*

GUELPH — At the heart of this tale is a lucky little fish.

How it became the answer to a dire medical problem deep in the Cambodian

*Reprinted with permission-Torstar Syndication Services.

Figure 10.8 Charles and fish.

Source: Glenn Lowson/Record news services.

jungle is something University of Guelph researcher Christopher Charles swears is no fish tale.

It began three years ago when this science whiz from Milton, who had just graduated from Guelph with a bachelor in biomedical science, took on a gritty little summer research gig in Cambodia. The task was to help local scientists try to persuade village women to place chunks of iron in their cooking pots to get more iron in their diet and lower the risk of anemia. Great in theory, but the women weren't having it.

It was an enticing challenge in a country where iron deficiency is so rampant, 60 per cent of women face premature labour, hemorrhaging during childbirth and poor brain development among their babies.

A disease of poverty, iron deficiency affects 3.5 billion people in the world. This was frontier research. Chris Charles was hooked — but he was also due to start his master's back in Guelph.

Mere weeks before he was to leave, Charles called his academic adviser to pull the plug on his master's in hormone research. To his credit, his adviser refused to let him quit. Instead, he told Charles he had found his true master's project.

From his new base in a bamboo hut on stilts, Charles took on the task with two researchers from Research Development International in Cambodia, with funding from the University of Guelph, the International Development Research Centre in Ottawa and the Canadian Institutes of Health Research's doctoral research award.

"Some nights I wondered what I had got myself into; here I was in a village with no running water, no electricity and no way to use my computer—it was like a (research) baptism by fire," he recalled.

The people they worked with—"the poorest of the poor"—can't afford red meat or pricey iron pills, and the women won't switch to iron cooking pots because they find them heavy and costly. Yet a small chunk of iron could release life-saving iron into the water and food. But what shape would the women be willing to place in their cooking pots?

"We knew some random piece of ugly metal wouldn't work . . . so we had to come up with an attractive idea," he said. "It became a challenge in social marketing."

The research team tried a small circle of iron. The women wouldn't use it.

They crafted iron shaped like a lotus flower. The women didn't like that either.

But when Charles's team came up with a piece of iron shaped like a local river fish believed to be lucky? Bingo. Women were happy to place it in their cooking pots and in the months that followed, the iron levels in the village began to climb.

"We designed it about 3 or 4 inches long, small enough to be stirred easily but large enough to provide up to about 75 per cent of the daily iron requirement," said Charles. They found a local scrap metal worker who could make them for $1.50 each, and so far they have been reusing the fish roughly three years.

"We're getting fantastic results; there seems to be a huge decrease in anemia and the village women say they feel good, no dizziness, fewer headaches. The iron fish is incredibly powerful."

In three years, Charles has discovered an answer to the iron problem that is stunning in its simplicity, is likely to save lives, and has earned him a master's and very nearly his PhD. Along the way the 26-year-old learned the Khmer language, mastered the art of taking a blood sample from someone sitting in a dugout canoe while balancing in a second canoe, and caught dengue fever.

Today, Charles is back at Guelph, crunching numbers, preparing to submit the research for publication and putting final touches on his PhD.

Almost as excited is the adviser he called three years ago: endocrinology professor Alastair Summerlee, who also happens to be president of the university.

Summerlee knew he had taken a chance when he let Charles change academic gears.

"We were flying by the seat of our pants, Chris working in a field placement where he had to learn everything (including Khmer) by trial and error and me worrying about whether or not this was the right decision. Did he have the skills to pull it off?" recalled Summerlee.

"But his results are spectacular. He has presented his findings in Asia, Europe and North America to acclaim, and there is a serious possibility that this simple discovery will have a profound influence on the health status of women in Asia."

One more lesson Charles learned? That marketing is the flip side of science.

"You can have the best treatment in the world, but if people won't use it, it won't matter."

DISCUSSION QUESTIONS AND EXERCISES

1. In the opening highlight addressing pet adoption, there were two target audiences. Why did program planners develop a strategy for the animal shelters as well as potential adopters?

2. How do the authors define *core product*? What is its relation to *service-dominant logic*?

3. What examples could you add to the list of social marketing brands, even if they are not well known?

CHAPTER 10 NOTES

1. E. Weiss, "Meet Your Match Save Lives" (May 27, 2010), accessed January 16, 2014, http://aspcapro.org/meet-your-match-saves-lives.

2. Humane Society of the United States, "Pets by the Numbers" (September 27, 2013), accessed January 8, 2014, http://www.humanesociety.org/issues/pet_overpopulation/facts/pet_ownership_statistics.html.

3. Ibid.

4. American Society for the Prevention of Cruelty to Animals, "Pet Statistics" (n.d.), accessed January 8, 2014, http://www.aspca.org/about-us/faq/pet--statistics.aspx.

5. Maddie's Fund, "The Shelter Pet Project By the Numbers—And Something More" (2009), accessed January 10, 2014, http://www.maddiesfund.org/Maddies_Institute/Articles/The_Shelter_Pet_Project_By_the_Numbers.html.

6. Personal communication from Caryn Ginsberg, January 16, 2014.

7. "Animal Impact" (n.d.), accessed January 16, 2014, http://priorityventures.com.

8. P. Kotler and K. L. Keller, *Marketing Management*, 12th ed. (Upper Saddle River, NJ: Prentice Hall, 2005), 372.

9. Ibid.

10. P. Kotler and G. Armstrong, *Principles of* Marketing, 9th ed. (Upper Saddle River, NJ: Prentice Hall, 2001), 291.

11. Ibid., 294.

12. Ibid.

13. G. D. Wiebe, "Merchandising Commodities and Citizenship on Television," *Public Opinion Quarterly* 15 (1951–1952): 679–691.

14. P. Kotler and G. Zaltman, "Social Marketing: An Approach to Planned Social Change," *Journal of Marketing* 35 (1971): 3–12.

15. Centers for Disease Control and Prevention, "Infant Mortality" (n.d.), accessed January 6, 2014, http://www.cdc.gov/reproductivehealth/maternalinfanthealth/infantmortality.htm.

16. Centers for Disease Control and Prevention, "National Prematurity Awareness Month" (n.d.), accessed January 6, 2014, http://www.cdc.gov/features/prematurebirth/.

17. Text4baby, "Enrollment Data" (n.d.), accessed January 6, 2014, https://text4baby.org/index.php/get-involved-pg/partners/national-organization/7-partner-resources/105.

18. D. Bornstein, "Mothers-to-Be Are Getting the Message," *The New York Times* (February 7, 2011), accessed April 15, 2011, http://opinionator.blogs.nytimes.com/2011/02/07/pregnant-mothers-are-getting-the-message/?pagemode=print.

19. P. Kotler and E. L. Roberto, *Social Marketing: Strategies for Changing Public Behavior* (New York: Free Press, 1989), 156.

20. WalkBoston, "Maps" (n.d.), accessed January 24, 2011, http://www.walkboston.org/resources/maps.htm.

21. A. Edelman, "Engineers in India Create Electronic Rape-Preventing Underwear, GPS Included," *New York Daily News*, http://www.nydailynews.com/life-style/health/engineers-create-rape-preventing-underwear-article-1.1305842.

22. N. Garun, "Three Engineer Students Invent an Electronic Anti-rape Undergarment," *Digital Trends* (April 3, 2013), accessed January 6, 2014, http://www.digitaltrends.com/home/three-engineer-students-invent-an-electrifying-anti-rape-undergarment/.

23. Information for this example was provided by Ingrid Donato, chief of the Mental Health Promotion Branch of the Center for Mental Health Services (CMHS) at the Substance Abuse and

Mental Health Services Association (SAMHSA) under Task Order No. HHSS2832007000271/ HHSS28342001T, directed by contracting officer's representative Anne Mathews-Younes. Contributing authors include Ingrid Donato, SAMHSA, CMHS; James Wright, SAMHSA, CMHS; Erin Reiney, HRSA; Katie Gorscak, ASPA; Stephanie Rapp, Department of Justice; Sharon Burton, Department of Education; and Alana Vivolo, CDC; SAMHSA has been assisted in the development of the SAMHSA Bullying Prevention App by IQ Solutions, Inc.

24. B. Chakravorty, as quoted in B. Chakravorty, "Product Substitution for Social Marketing of Behaviour Change: A Conceptualization," *Social Marketing Quarterly* (1996), 5, accessed July 19, 2011, http://degraysystems.com/aedmichael/Vol%203/3-2/Full%20Text/III.2.Chakravorty .pdf.

25. Ibid., 5.

26. Ibid., 10.

27. Ibid., 9–10.

28. Kotler and Roberto, *Social Marketing*, 155–157.

29. Apps for Healthy Kids, "Application Gallery" (n.d.), accessed January 26, 2011, http:// www.appsforhealthykids.com/application-gallery.

30. ZisBoomBah, "Where It's OK to Play With Your Food!" (n.d.), accessed January 26, 2011, http://www.zisboombah.com/.

31. An application developed by Karen Laszlo, Mike Carcaise, and Lisa Lanzano.

32. D. McKenzie-Mohr and W. Smith, *Fostering Sustainable Behavior: An Introduction to Community-Based Social Marketing*, 2nd ed.(Gabriola Island, BC, Canada: New Society, 1999), 156.

33. Opower, "About Us" (n.d.), accessed January 26, 2011, http://www.opower.com/Company/ AboutUs.aspx.

34. Opower, "Special Delivery: Energy Savings" (n.d.), accessed January 26, 2011, http:// www.opower.com/Products/HomeEnergyReport.aspx.

35. M. Trost, "A Call for 'Design Thinking': Tim Brown on TED.com," *TED Blog* (July 2009), accessed January 7, 2014, http://blog.ted.com/2009/09/29/a_call_for_desi/.

36. Information from this case was taken from PATH's project brief, "Extended User Testing of Water Treatment Devices in Andhra Pradesh," published August 2010.

37. Kotler and Armstrong, *Principles of Marketing*, 301.

38. Population Services International, Global Social Marketing Department, "A Total Marketing Approach to Better Marketing in Cambodia" (March 2010).

39. "Drug Test Kits a Bargain for Parents," *Chicago Sun-Times* (January 22, 2011), accessed January 26, 2011, http://www.suntimes.com/lifestyles/3412644-423/parents-drug-kids -schools-test.html.

40. "Canadian's Lucky Iron Fish Saves Lives in Cambodia," *The Record.com*, accessed January 20, 2014, http://www.therecord.com/news-story/2591989-canadian-s-lucky-iron-fish-saves-lives-in-cambodia/.

Chapter 11

PRICE

DETERMINING MONETARY AND NONMONETARY INCENTIVES AND DISINCENTIVES

Social marketers need to use the whole of the marketing mix to win their target audience's business—there's no use tying one hand behind your back and only using promotion when the competition has price, distribution, and, more often than not, a better product.

—Dr. Stephen Dann
Australian National University

On March 19, 2007, a Canadian news network announced that the new federal budget would include several environmental protection–related strategies. These strategies, which are still in effect in 2014, appear to use, as Michael Rothschild would describe them, carrots as well as sticks: "Gas guzzlers will be dinged with a new tax of up to $4,000, fuel-efficient cars will get a rebate worth up to $2,000 and old wrecks will be offered a short-cut to the junkyard."[1]

This chapter introduces "price," the second tool in your marketing toolbox and one you may find especially helpful in overcoming financial barriers associated with adopting your behavior. You will find it useful in "sweetening the pot"—and not necessarily with just monetary incentives that could add significant costs to your program budget. You may also find it effective in reducing the appeal of the competition's offer. You'll read how others have used creative monetary and nonmonetary incentives to add value, sometimes just enough to tip the exchange in their favor:

- How gift cards increased blood donation by more than 50% in a research trial
- How coupons helped increase the use of bike helmets from 1% to 57% in one community
- How rewarding youth hockey teams for reducing foul plays decreased (actually eliminated) head injuries for teams in Minnesota

- How a social marketing approach succeeded in persuading legislators to toughen the laws and fines for texting while driving
- How a group of teens convinced their peers to postpone having sex by sharing the pain of pubic lice (crabs)

You'll read that the price tool has four "attachments":

1. Monetary incentives (e.g., discount coupons)

2. Nonmonetary incentives (e.g., positive public recognition)

3. Monetary disincentives (e.g., fines)

4. Nonmonetary disincentives (e.g., negative public recognition)

MARKETING HIGHLIGHT

Reducing Tobacco Use Through Commitment Contracts

"Put Your Money Where Your Butt Is"[2]

(2010)

This case highlights the exchange principle at its finest. You will read how the "loads" of benefits in a uniquely designed offer tipped the scales by outweighing the costs of giving up a highly addictive behavior. This is the story, in part, of the application of two strategic price tools, a monetary and a nonmonetary incentive, aimed at fulfilling three strong desires for the target audience: (a) to quit smoking, (b) to save money, and (c) to keep a promise. And a randomized controlled trial (RCT) proved it worked. Information for this case is based on a study conducted by Xavier Gine, Dean Karlan, and Jonathan Zinman, published in 2010 in the *American Economic Association Journal: Applied Economics.* The study was conducted in partnership with Innovations for Poverty Action and the Green Bank of Caraga and funded by the World Bank.

Background, Target Audiences, and Audience Insights

The setting for the field experiment was the island of Mindanao in the Philippines where, as in most regions of the country in 2009, over 28% of Filipinos age 15 years and older were current smokers.[3] In addition to incurring serious health effects, smokers were spending approximately US$2 per week on cigarettes, representing nearly 15% of their monthly income. The intriguing finding for the researchers, however, was that 72% of survey respondents reported they wanted to stop smoking at some point in their life, about 18% said they want to stop smoking now, and nearly 45% indicated they had tried within the last year.[4]

Researchers for the project were particularly interested in providing field evidence of the viability and effectiveness of voluntary commitment devices for smoking cessation. Could this mechanism disrupt consumers' impatience for near-term benefits (having a cigarette) in return for future, greater benefits (a healthier life and increased financial well-being)? And would a hard device (e.g., financial consequences for breaking a commitment) be more effective than a soft one (e.g., not keeping a promise)?

Strategies

The offer researchers tested was a voluntary commitment savings program, branded Committed Action to Reduce and End Smoking (CARES). The trial program being tested worked like this: A smoker wanting to quit would sign a commitment contract and open a savings account (*product*) with an initial deposit of about US$1, and would be encouraged to deposit the money he or she would normally spend on cigarettes into this account each week for six months (*price*). The savings account would not yield any interest. Clients could only make deposits to, and not withdrawals from, the CARES account during the six-month commitment period. If, at the six-month milestone, a nicotine test proved that the client was "tobacco free," the entire savings would be given back and the smoker would be encouraged to start a small enterprise (*monetary incentive*). If not, he or she would be required to give up the money and donate it to a charity (*monetary disincentive*). Every week, a Green Bank field staff would collect the money that the smoker had saved and deposit it in one of the bank's microfinance branches, saving him or her the weekly trip to the bank (*place*) as well as adding a component of social pressure

Figure 11.1   Weekly savings were deposited in a lockbox.

Source: Innovations for Poverty Action.

(see Figure 11.1). In cases where a client failed to show up for a scheduled nicotine test, he or she would be given three more weeks. Failure to appear again would mean forfeiture of his or her account balance. Green Bank promoted CARES by sending bank representatives into the street to target obvious smokers, providing them with an informational pamphlet on the dangers of smoking and a tip sheet on how to quit (*promotion*).

To provide evidence-based outcomes, this offer was tested against two alternatives. To recruit study participants, Green Bank of Caraga staff approached smokers on the street and asked them if they were interested in quitting smoking; if they said they were, they were asked to participate in a short survey on smoking (see Figure 11.2). A total of 2,000 smokers ages 18 or older completed the baseline survey. All respondents received an informational pamphlet on the dangers of smoking as well as a tip sheet on how to quit. Each respondent was then randomly assigned to receive one of the following three offers:

1. *CARES Contract group.* As described above, individuals were offered a savings account with an initial minimal deposit of about US$1, encouragement to deposit into this account the amount of money they would normally spend on cigarettes, weekly visits from deposit collectors, and the ability to deposit into, but not withdraw from, the account; no interest would be paid on the account.

2. *Cue Cards group.* Individuals were presented with four wallet-sized cards depicting the negative health consequences of smoking: (a) a premature baby (with copy stating, "Smoking harms unborn babies"), (b) bad teeth ("Smoking causes mouth and throat cancer"), (c) black lung ("Smoking causes lung cancer"), and (d) a child hooked up to a respirator ("Don't let children breathe your smoke"). They then chose the specific cards they wanted to keep and were encouraged by the marketers to place them in a prominent location.

| Figure 11.2 | People interested in quitting smoking were asked to complete a brief survey. |

Source: Innovations for Poverty Action.

3. *Comparison group.* These individuals received no additional information after the survey.

Six months after the baseline survey, all respondents were required to take a urine test to determine whether they were still smoking. As stipulated in the contract, those in Group 1, the CARES Contract group, who refused or failed the urine test were required to forfeit the entire balance in their bank accounts. Those in the Cue Cards and Comparison groups were paid US$.60 for taking the test. All respondents were paid US$.60 for taking another (surprise) test 12 months after the baseline.

Results

CARES Contract (Group 1)

- *Signing the contract.* Of the individuals who were offered CARES, 11% signed a contract; those most likely to sign were those indicating they wanted to quit and were optimistic about quitting or already trying to manage their cravings; those least likely to sign the contract were those reporting they wanted to quit more than a year into the future and showed signs of being heavy smokers.
- *Additional savings account contributions.* Of the individuals who were offered CARES, 80% made additional contributions to the account, on average every two weeks, and after six months had a final balance of US$11, equal to approximately six months' worth of cigarette spending and 20% of monthly income.
- *Smoking cessation.* Individuals in the CARES Contract group were 3.3

to 5.8 percentage points more likely to pass the six-month urine test than the control group and 3.4 to 5.7 percentage points more likely to pass the urine test after 12 months, representing a more than 35% increase in the likelihood of smoking cessation compared to baseline. The 12-month results lacked any incentives, as all commitment contract money had been returned or forfeited at six months and there was no financial consequence tied to the 12-month test result.

Cue Cards (Group 2)

- *Taking the cue cards.* Of the individuals who were offered the cue cards, 99% accepted them.
- *Using the cue cards.* Of the individuals taking the cue cards, 5% reported using the cards to manage their cravings, but one year later, fewer than half of that 5% remembered the cards or knew where they had put them.
- *Smoking cessation.* There was no effect of the cue cards on smoking cessation.

Implications

The authors of the study conclude that the results suggest that a commitment product such as CARES is an effective treatment for smoking cessation, comparing favorably to take-up rates and results from nicotine replacement therapy in randomized trials in other settings. They also believe that commitment contract take-up rates could potentially increase further as familiarity with, trust in, and information about a product such as this builds in a community. They further conclude that rough calculations suggest that CARES could pass a social costs/benefits test, taking into consideration a cost per quit in comparison to employer costs, health improvements, and increases in quality-adjusted years of life.

PRICE: THE SECOND "P"

Price is the cost that the target audience associates with adopting the desired behavior. Traditional marketing theory has a similar definition: "The amount of money charged for a product or service, or the sum of the values that consumers exchange for the benefits of having or using the product or service."[5]

Adoption costs may be *monetary* or *nonmonetary* in nature. Monetary costs in a social marketing environment are most often related to *goods and services* associated with adopting the behavior (e.g., buying a life vest or paying for a swim class for toddlers). Nonmonetary costs are more intangible but are just as real for your audience and often even more significant for social marketing products. They include costs associated with the *time, effort, and energy* required to perform the behavior, *psychological risks and losses* that might be perceived or experienced, and any *physical discomforts* that might be related to the behavior. You probably discovered most of these nonmonetary costs when you conducted barriers research, identifying concerns your target audience had about adopting the desired behavior. There may be more to add to the list, however, as you may have decided you want to include goods and services such as those listed in Table 11.1. This is the time to do that.

If your organization is actually the maker or provider of these tangible goods (e.g., rain barrels) or services (e.g., home energy audits), you will want to be involved in establishing the price your customer will be asked to pay. This is the time to do that as well, before developing the incentives that are the emphasis of this chapter. A section at the end of this chapter presents a few tips on price setting.

STEP 7: DETERMINE MONETARY AND NONMONETARY INCENTIVES AND DISINCENTIVES

Your objective and opportunity with this second marketing tool is to develop and provide *incentives* that will increase benefits or decrease costs. (It should be noted that *product* and *place* tools will also be used to increase benefits and decrease costs. The *price* tool is unique in its use of monetary incentives, as well as nonmonetary ones including recognition, appreciation, and reward.) The first four of the six price-related tactics focus on the desired behavior and the last two on the competing one(s).

1. Increase monetary benefits for *the desired behavior*
2. Increase nonmonetary benefits for *the desired behavior*
3. Decrease monetary costs for *the desired behavior*
4. Decrease nonmonetary costs for *the desired behavior*
5. Increase monetary costs for *the competing behavior*
6. Increase nonmonetary costs for *the competing behavior*

The next six sections of this chapter explain each of these in more detail and provide an illustration for each.

1. Increase Monetary Benefits for the Desired Behavior

Monetary rewards and incentives can take many forms familiar to you as a consumer and include *rebates, gift cards, allowances, cash incentives,* and *price adjustments* that reward customers for adopting the proposed behavior. Some are rather "tame" in nature (e.g., 3.5-cent credit for reusing grocery bags), others a little more aggressive (e.g., quit-and-win contests that offer a chance to win a $1,000 prize for successfully stopping smoking for at least one month;[6] a $20 annual license fee for a neutered dog versus $60 for an unaltered one), and a few quite bold (e.g., offering drug-addicted women a $200 incentive for voluntary sterilization; offering voters a chance at a $1 million lottery just for showing up at the polls).

Where would you place the following example on that continuum?

Table 11.1   Potential Costs for Performing the Desired Behavior

Type of Cost	Examples
Monetary: Goods	• Nicotine patches • Blood pressure monitoring equipment • Condoms • Bike helmets, life vests, and booster seats • Breathalyzers • Earthquake preparedness kits • Smoke alarm batteries • Food waste compost tumblers • Natural fertilizers (vs. regular fertilizers) • Recycled paper (vs. regular paper) • Energy-saving lightbulbs • Electric mulch mowers
Monetary: Services	• Fees for family-planning classes • Smoking cessation classes • Athletic club fees • Suicide prevention workshops • Taxi rides home from a bar
Nonmonetary: Time, Effort	• Cooking a balanced meal • Pulling over to use the cell phone • Driving to a car wash versus washing at home • Taking the food waste outside to a composter
Nonmonetary: Psychological	• Finding out whether a lump is cancerous • Wondering about whether to believe the warning about eating too much fish when pregnant • Having a cup of coffee without a cigarette • Feeling "dorky" carrying a flag across a crosswalk • Listening to the chatter of others in a car pool • Asking your son whether he is considering suicide • Telling your husband you think he drinks too much • Using sunscreen and coming back from Hawaii "pale" • Letting your lawn go brown in the summer
Nonmonetary: Physical Discomfort	• Exercising • Pricking a finger to monitor blood glucose • Having a mammogram • Lowering the thermostat • Taking shorter showers

Example: Incentives for Blood Donation. In July 2013, the American Red Cross issued an emergency request for blood donations. Donations in June were about 10% lower than expected, representing 50,000 fewer donations.[7] That same summer a group of researchers, including Mario Macis, an assistant professor at Johns Hopkins Carey Business School, encouraged the World Health Organization (WHO) and other blood collection agencies to reconsider long-standing opposition to gift or monetary incentives for blood donation. They pointed out that these guidelines had been developed 40 years previously over two major concerns. One was that offering incentives for blood donation would have a detrimental impact on the frequency of donations, as those motivated by altruistic activities would lose interest. The other concern was that monetary incentives would motivate people in poor health to donate, resulting in more contaminated blood. The researchers argued that those concerns had been based on old evidence from unreliable studies, and that more recent research proved that real-world incentive programs have increased blood donations, and with no significant effect on the percentage of tainted blood received.

Macis and his fellow researchers had examined data from nearly 100,000 donors at 72 American Red Cross drives in northern Ohio where gift cards were offered at half the donor sites and no incentives were offered at the other half. The gift cards were promoted as tokens of appreciation, recognizing people for their generosity. To help ensure that people would not conceal any health concerns during screenings in order to get the reward, gift cards were distributed upon arrival, before the screening or donation process began. Results were impressive, with $5 gift cards increasing the likelihood of donating among people with a history of donating by 26%, and a $10 gift card increasing that number by 52%. "The findings make us conclude that one-time rewards can be used to smooth donations over time—increasing the donations at times or in places where they are scarce," Macis said.[8]

2. Increase Nonmonetary Benefits for the Desired Behavior

There are also ways to encourage changes in behavior that don't involve cash or free/discounted goods and services with significant monetary value. Instead, they provide a different type of value. In the social marketing environment, they often take the form of a *pledge/commitment*, *recognition*, and/or *appreciation* acknowledging the adoption of a desired behavior. In most cases, the benefit is psychological and personal in nature. By signing and keeping a pledge or commitment, a participant receives (in return) increased self-respect. If the pledge is made public, the value increases, with public respect increasing perceived value even further. Recognition or appreciation can be as simple as an email from a supervisor thanking an employee for commuting to work by bicycling, or as formal and public as an annual awards program recognizing the dry cleaner who has adopted the most significant green behaviors in the past year. These nonmonetary benefits are distinct from goods and services (e.g., safe bike storage) that are offered to help the target audience actually adopt the behavior. They are also distinct from sales promotion tactics that are more similar to gifts or prizes (e.g., T-shirts and coffee mugs). In the following example, the reinforcement (incentive) for a desirable behavior is a surprising and unique one, and based on the positive results, perhaps should be considered more often.

Example: Rewarding Fair Play. In 2000, a parent in a Boston suburb was killed by another parent at a grade school hockey game. The incident touched off a national discussion about excess in youth sports, and in 2004, Minnesota Hockey officials decided to do something to change their game's increasingly violent atmosphere. One youth coach described their games then as out of control, with "three, four, five fights a game, easy. Any time there was any body contact, they dropped the gloves."[9]

One revolutionary feature they implemented was called the "fair-play point," where a team would get an extra point for each game in which they took fewer than a designated number of penalty minutes. For championship awards, a team earns two points for winning a game and, if it takes fewer than 12 minutes of penalties, a third point for fair play. The losing team for a game also earns a fair-play point if it is under the penalty threshold. Within a year of instituting the fair-play point, the number of penalties dropped sharply, particularly for fouls from hits to the head, high-sticking, and fighting. The Mayo Clinic, a research partner, reported that penalties for hits to the head dropped from 12.4 per 100 youth games in the 2004–2005 season to 2 per 100 games the next season. By 2008–2009, no calls were being made for hits to the head.[10]

3. Decrease Monetary Costs for the Desired Behavior

Methods to decrease monetary costs are also familiar to most consumers: discount coupons, gift cards, trial incentives (e.g., eight free rides on a network of bus routes), cash discounts, quantity discounts, seasonal discounts, promotional pricing (e.g., a temporary price reduction), and segment pricing (e.g., price based on geographic locations). Many of these tactics are also available to you as a social marketer to increase sales. In July 2013, for example, a pet adoption extravaganza in Seattle waived adoption fees for cats one year and older and reduced fees for kittens, resulting in 203 adoptions in one weekend and breaking a 116-year history.[11] You yourself may have used a discount coupon from a utility for compost, taken advantage of a weekend sales event for water-efficient toilets, or received a discount on parking at work because you are part of a car pool. The social marketing organization may be involved in subsidizing the incentive, distributing coupons, and/or getting the word out, as illustrated in the following example.

Example: Bike Helmet Coupons. The website of the Harborview Injury Prevention and Research Center (HIPRC) reported in February 2000 that "more bicyclists in Seattle wear helmets than bicyclists in any other major city in the country where laws do not require it." The Washington Children's Helmet Bicycle Campaign had been launched in 1986 by physicians at Harborview Medical Center in Seattle, who were alarmed at the nearly 200 children they were treating each year with bicycle-related head injuries.[12] "Although bicycle helmets were available in 1985, just one child in 100 wears one." HIPRC physicians conducted a study to understand why parents didn't buy bike helmets for their children and what factors influenced whether children actually wore them.

The results, from a survey of more than 2,500 fourth graders and their parents, shaped the eventual campaign. More than two thirds of the parents said that they had never thought of providing a helmet and *another third cited cost as a factor* [italics added].

A campaign was designed around "four key objectives: increasing public awareness of the importance of helmets, educating parents about helmet use, overcoming peer pressure among children against wearing helmets, and lowering helmet prices."

The HIPRC formed a coalition of health, bicycling, and helmet industry and community organizations to design and manage a variety of promotions. As a result, parents and children heard about helmets on television, on the radio, in the newspapers, in their doctors' offices, at school, and at youth groups. The advertised discount coupons cut helmet prices by half, to $20. Nearly 5,000 helmets were distributed at no or low cost to needy families.

By September 1993 (seven years later), helmet use had jumped from 1% to 57% among children in the greater Seattle area, and adult use had increased to 70%. Five years into the campaign, an HIPRC evaluation revealed its ultimate impact: Admissions at five Seattle-area hospitals for bicycle-related head injuries had dropped by approximately two thirds for children 5 to 14 years old.

4. Decrease Nonmonetary Costs for the Desired Behavior

Tactics are also available for decreasing *time*, *effort*, and *physical* or *psychological* costs. Fox suggests reducing usage time by "embedding" a new behavior into present activities.[13] Thus, people might be encouraged to floss their teeth while they watch television. People can also be encouraged to "anchor" a new behavior to an established habit.[14] To encourage physical activity, for example, you can recommend that people climb the stairs to their third-floor office instead of taking the elevator.

Gemunden proposed several potential tactics for reducing other nonmonetary costs in this model:

1. Against a perceived psychological risk, provide social products in ways that deliver *psychological rewards such as public recognition.*

2. Against a perceived social risk, gather *endorsements from credible sources* that reduce the potential stigma or embarrassment of adopting a product.

3. Against a perceived usage risk, provide target adopters with *reassuring information* on the product or with a free trial of the product so they can experience how the product does what it promises to do.

4. Against perceived physical risk, solicit *seals of approval* from authoritative institutions, such as the American Dental Association, the American Medical Association, or other highly respected organizations.[15]

Example: Redeeming Farmers' Market Checks

Offices of the Supplemental Nutrition Program for Women, Infants, and Children (WIC) often distribute checks to qualified families to purchase fresh fruits and vegetables at local farmers' markets. Yet clients often face significant nonmonetary costs that lead to lower redemption rates than many WIC offices would like to see. Many experience increased *effort* in finding the market and parking, *embarrassment* around other shoppers when using a WIC check, *difficulty* in identifying qualified produce when signs are inconsistently displayed or hard to see, *concern* about not getting change back from checks, *frustration* with misplacing checks that are often stored in drawers or forgotten in strollers, and *fear* of what the WIC counselor will think if they decline the checks, even though their chances of using them are minimal, given work schedules that conflict with market hours.

These costs could be overcome with a variety of tactics related to the price tool as well as to the other Ps:

* Detailed maps showing the way to the market and parking areas printed on the backs of checks
* Electronic debit cards in place of the checks
* Signs on poles above the stands that display some recognizable logo that doesn't "brand" the client, such as the 5 a Day logo
* Printing checks in lower amounts, such as $1 denominations
* Packaging checks in sturdy check folders
* Offering hesitant clients fewer checks, and more if they use them all

5. Increase Monetary Costs for the Competing Behavior

In the social marketing environment, this tactic is likely to involve influencing policy-makers, as the most effective monetary strategies against the competition often require *increasing taxes* (e.g., on gas-guzzling cars), *imposing fines* (e.g., for not recycling), and/ or *decreasing funding* (e.g., if a school doesn't offer an hour of physical education classes). Referring back to the bike helmet example, the Harborview Injury Prevention and Research Center is now taking a more legislative and regulatory emphasis, since recent evaluations show that helmet use rates have stabilized—a possible sign, they say, that those not wearing helmets may respond only to laws and fines. As Alan Andreasen lays out in his book *Social Marketing in the 21st Century*, these policy changes may be critical to significant social change, and the social marketer can play a role in making this happen. "Our models and frameworks are flexible enough to guide efforts aimed at this kind of upstream behavior, especially for the many smaller organizations, especially at the local level, that cannot afford lobbyists."[16]

Andreasen proposes that you use familiar components of the social marketing model. You can segment the potential audience using the stages of change model, and in the legislative environment this may be translated into those who are opponents, undecideds, or supporters. You will then benefit from identifying and understanding your target audience's BCOS factors: *benefits*, *costs*, and *others* in the target audience's environment and their influence and *self-assurance* (perceptions of opportunity and ability).[17] These should sound familiar as well.

In the following example, a social marketing approach upstream helped pass a law to influence behaviors downstream, one expected to save lives.

Example: Persuading Legislators to Pass a Primary Cell Phone and Texting Law

As of January 2010, only 15 states and the District of Columbia had made it a primary offense to text and drive, and only five states and the District of Columbia had made it a primary offense to talk on handheld cell phones while driving. Washington State was one of the states where this was only a secondary offense, meaning a driver must have done something else wrong (e.g., weaving across lane markers) to be ticketed.[18] Two state legislators and a volunteer citizen task force stepped up efforts to persuade the legislature and the governor to pass a new law (*desired behavior*), one that would allow the police to pull over drivers talking on their cell phones or texting while driving. They used a social marketing approach, and their first step was to understand concerns legislators had about voting yes. Several major barriers were identified. A few are presented in Table 11.2, along with responses presented at testimonies to legislative committees.

Washington's new law was passed and went into effect on June 10, 2010. Tickets are $124 for talking on handheld cell phones while driving or texting while driving. Teens with intermediate driver's licenses or learner permits may not use a wireless device at all while driving, including a hands-free device, unless they're reporting an emergency.

6. Increase Nonmonetary Costs for the Competing Behavior

Nonmonetary tactics can also be used to increase actual or perceived nonmonetary costs associated with choosing the competing behavior. In this case, you may be creating or emphasizing negative public recognition. In the spring of 2013, dog owners in a village near Madrid, for example, started receiving unpleasant home deliveries if they failed to pick up their pets' waste on the streets. It worked like this: Volunteers waited for someone to abandon their dog's poop on the streets. While some of the volunteers snatched up the poop without being seen, others approached the dog owner and found out the dog's name and breed. Volunteers would then search the town's pet registration database to find the owner's address. The pet's waste was then dropped off at the corresponding address in a box labeled "Lost Property." One report on results indicated that the amount of dog poop seen on the streets of Brunete decreased by 70%.[19]

In Tacoma, Washington, a website features properties not in full compliance with municipal codes. They call it "The Filthy 15," and although property owners' names do not appear on the website, it does include photos of each building, specific reasons the property is on the list, and what is next in the cleanup process, including something a neighbor or other concerned citizen could track.[20]

In a different scenario, you might be highlighting the downsides of the competition, as illustrated in the following example, in which research was key to understanding what costs should be highlighted.

Table 11.2   Addressing Barriers to Passing a Primary Cell Phone and Texting Law

Major Concerns Expressed by Legislators	Responses From Advocates
"My constituents will argue that talking on a cell phone is no more dangerous than putting on makeup or eating food. They'll claim laws against this will be next."	Human factors experts tell us that there are three kinds of driving distractions. The first is visual—eyes off the road. The second is mechanical—hands off the wheel. The third is cognitive—when our mind is not fully engaged on the task of driving. Talking on a handheld cell phone or texting involves all three. As a result, one study shows that drivers talking on cell phones are as impaired as drunk drivers who have a 0.08% blood alcohol level, and those texting while driving are equivalent to those with a 0.24% blood alcohol level.
"I don't understand how talking on a phone is any different than talking with a passenger in the vehicle."	There is one very important difference. A passenger in a vehicle is aware of the driving situation and can even serve as an additional lookout for hazards. He or she also understands when there is a needed pause in a conversation.
"A law like this would not be enforceable."	Although we won't see all offenders, this law would give us the important ability, though after the fact, to assess additional penalties on those who have chosen to act recklessly or irresponsibly.

Example: Encouraging Teen Abstinence

The Teen Aware Project is part of a statewide effort to reduce teen pregnancy and is sponsored by the Washington State Office of Superintendent of Public Instruction. Funds are allocated through a competitive grant process to public middle/junior and senior high schools for the development of media campaigns to promote sexual abstinence and the importance of delaying sexual activity, pregnancy, and childbearing. These campaigns are substantially designed and produced by students. Student media products include video and radio productions, posters, theater productions, print advertising, multimedia, T-shirts, buttons, and websites. Campaign messages are distributed in local project schools and communities.

This particular research effort was conducted by teens at Mercer Island High School, a grant recipient. A team of nine students from marketing, health, and communications classes volunteered to develop the campaign, from start to finish. Several teachers and outside consultants served as coaches on the project.[21] At the time this research effort was undertaken, the team had chosen their campaign focus (abstinence), purpose (reducing teen pregnancies), target audience (eighth-graders), and campaign objective (to persuade students to "pause and think in a heated moment"). Information from existing student surveys indicated that about 75% of eighth-graders—but only 25% of seniors—were abstinent. It was decided that the campaign bull's-eye would be eighth-graders, who were seen as being the most vulnerable in terms of making choices regarding sexual activity.

The team of juniors and seniors wanted to refresh their memories about middle school years. As one student expressed it, "It's been a long time since I was an eighth-grader, and I don't have a clue what they know and think about sex these days." The primary purposes of their research were to (a) help with decision making regarding which benefits of abstinence and costs related to sexual activity should be highlighted in the campaign and (b) provide input for selecting a slogan for the campaign. More specifically, the study was designed to determine major perceived benefits of abstinence, costs associated with being sexually active, and messages (and tone) that would be most effective in influencing an eighth-grader to consider abstinence.

Each of the nine students agreed to conduct casual interviews with at least five eighth-graders over a one-week period. They used an informal script that explained the project and assured respondents that their comments would be anonymous. They recorded and summarized responses to the following three open-ended questions:

1. What's the most important reason you can think of for delaying having intercourse until you are older?

2. What are the worst things you can think of that can happen to you if you have intercourse before you are ready?

3. What would you say to your best friend if she or he told you that they thought they were going to have sex for the first time tonight?

Interviews were conducted, with district permission, before and after classes at the middle schools as well as at informal settings such as sports events, after-school programs, and friends' homes. Students returned to class the following week, shared summaries of their findings, and were guided to identify the following themes for each of the informational areas:

- Major reasons for delaying sex:
  - You won't get sexually transmitted diseases (STDs)
  - You can save it for someone special
  - You won't get pregnant

- The worst things that can happen:
  - They could drop you later for someone else
  - You could get pregnant, and childbirth really hurts
  - You can get really bad STDs, like crabs

- Words for a friend:
  - "You should wait until you are older."
  - "Are you sure he really loves you?"
  - "Do you have protection?"
  - "Are you ready for all the things that could happen?"

The team used this input to develop a campaign centered around three "gross" consequences of having sex before you're ready. They developed the campaign slogan "Are you ready?" and followed the question with each of the three consequences. Graphic, in-your-face images were reflected on the posters and depicted in radio scripts (see Figures 11.3, 11.4, and 11.5).

Radio spots that were played on the high school radio station followed the three gross consequence themes. In one, a male voice says,

> I remember the day I learned what an STD really was. I had seen little things crawling around in my . . . hair. I woke up in the middle of the night, my . . . you know . . . was burning from an itch. My entire crotch was swarming with miniature crabs. Finally, I had to get help. If you think you're going to have sex, ask yourself, "Are you ready for that?" (See Figure 11.3.)

In another approach, a girl graphically recounts the pain of giving birth (see Figure 11.4). And in the third spot, a girl sadly yet frankly relates how the guy she slept with immediately told everyone at school and found a new girlfriend. It took her years to trust a guy again (see Figure 11.5).

MORE ON COMMITMENTS AND PLEDGES

As noted earlier, we consider commitments and pledges as nonmonetary incentives, adding value to adopting a desired behavior, most often in the form of increased self-respect and/or public reputation. In terms of distinctions between commitments and pledges, many use the term *pledge* when referring to actually signing a form or clicking a box on a website, expressing the *commitment*. Doug McKenzie-Mohr encourages commitments and pledges that are public (versus private) and durable

Figure 11.3   Abstinence campaign poster.

Source: Copyright © 2001 by Washington State Office of Superintendent of Public Instruction.

Figure 11.4   Abstinence campaign poster.

Source: Copyright © 2001 by Washington State Office of Superintendent of Public Instruction.

Figure 11.5 Abstinence campaign poster.

Source: Copyright © 2001 by Washington State Office of Superintendent of Public Instruction.

(versus only visible temporarily), as they are the most likely to motivate individuals to keep their commitment as well as foster social diffusion.

In January 2014, we asked members of the Georgetown and International Social Marketing Association listserves for examples of the use of commitments and pledges in social marketing efforts. (Note: For most of these examples, a website link appears in the reference, providing more details on the effort.)

- Improved health
  - Nick Goodwin in Australia shared about Australia's "Hello Sunday Morning" program, a way for an individual to take a break from drinking and re-create the drinking culture. Since 2010, over 20,000 people have signed up to go three months or more without alcohol and blog about their journey on "Hello Sunday Morning."[22]
  - Niamh Gately in Ireland wrote to us about an Irish reality television show, *Operation Transformation*, which involves five overweight or obese people, or "leaders" as they are called on the show, who pledge to transform their lives and ultimately their health. The leaders receive guidance from a fitness expert, a dietician, a general practitioner, and a psychologist throughout the eight weeks of the program via structured exercise plans and meal plans, which are available for viewers to adopt as well. The television show documents the leaders' progress on a weekly basis, and members of the general public are asked to commit themselves to follow one of the five leaders' plans online and try to achieve the same lifestyle behavior change. Niamh shared initial outcomes: After the eight-week program, 52% of respondents had lost up to 6 pounds, 25% had lost 7 to 13 pounds, 13% had lost 14 to 21 pounds, and 10% had lost close to 22 pounds.[23]

- *Injury prevention*
  - Martha Jamieson in Canada shared about a safe-driving initiative in Alberta that focuses on drivers on a notoriously dangerous set of highways. A dedicated website contains a series of prompt messages and asks people to commit to acting responsible when driving these roads. As of February 2014, more than 3,000 had signed the pledge using email, Facebook, or Twitter. [24]
  - Kristina MacKenzie in the United States mentioned a partnership effort between AT&T, Verizon, T-Mobile, and Sprint to stop texting while driving. On the

Texting & Driving: It Can Wait website, which includes powerful videos and persuasive statistics, people are asked to take a pledge not to text while driving. "No text is worth a life. It Can Wait."[25]

- *Environmental protection*
  - Sara Isaac in Florida pointed us to an online pledge for Be Floridian, a fertilizer reduction campaign for the Tampa Bay Estuary that used Facebook for those wanting to make their pledge public. There was also a paper version for grass-roots outreach events.[26]
  - Sheila Sarhangi in Hawaii mentioned a pledge program in West Maui to reduce polluted runoff and more, with options for pledging to carry out a variety of actions, including "Use fertilizer wisely" and "Pick up after my pooch by putting the unmentionables in the garbage bin."[27]
  - Mike Walker in Massachusetts cited working with ENERGY STAR to create the "Low Carbon IT Campaign," with a major component being a pledge taken by facilities' sustainability and IT managers to activate computer sleep features. As of February 2014, they had received pledges to power-manage nearly 6 million computers, saving roughly 1.5 billion kilowatt hours.[28]
  - Sara Wicks in Canada shared about the Waterloo Region's 1000 Blue Barrel challenge, in which Reduce the Juice is challenging households in the Waterloo Region to reduce their carbon footprint by pledging to use their Green Bin.

- *Community involvement*
  - Caryn Ginsberg in Virginia noted that the Farm Animal Rights Movement (FARM) asks people to commit to eating fewer animal products after they have watched a four-minute video depicting what happens to animals in food production as part of the organization's "10 Billion Lives Tour." Eighty percent of viewers, primarily young adults, take the pledge, and 60% report acting on their pledge in follow-up surveys.[29]
  - Eric Green in Ohio is using a social marketing strategy to encourage men to get involved in a new statewide organization called the Ohio Men's Action Network and to pledge to carry out several actions, including not committing any act of violence against anyone regardless of age, sex, or gender identity; speaking out against sexual violence; and teaching friends and others about nonviolent and respectful relationships.
  - Nedra Kline Weinreich in California is involved in a mental health movement, Each Mind Matters, that is collecting pledges from Californians on how they will personally take action to end stigma and discrimination around mental health issues.[30]

SETTING PRICES FOR TANGIBLE GOODS AND SERVICES

Prices for tangible goods and services involved in social marketing campaigns are typically set by manufacturers, retailers, and service providers. Social marketers are more often involved in helping to decide what tangible goods and services would be beneficial in facilitating behavior change, recommending discount coupons and related incentives, and then promoting their use.

When a social marketer gets involved in the price setting, however, several principles can guide decision making. The first task is to reach agreement on your pricing objectives. Kotler and Roberto[31] outline several potential objectives:

- *Maximizing retained earnings* where the primary consideration is money making (e.g., charging advertisers for space on billboards above the Play Pumps in Africa, ones that decrease the time it takes for families to pump water from wells)
- *Recovering costs* where revenue is expected to offset a portion of costs (e.g., charging customers $32 for a rain barrel that cost the utility $45)
- *Maximizing the number of target adopters* where the primary purpose is to influence as many people as possible to use the service and/or buy the product (e.g., providing free condoms to farm workers)
- *Social equity* where reaching underprivileged or high-risk segments is a priority and different prices might be charged according to ability to pay (e.g., a sliding scale fee for bike helmets)
- *Demarketing* where pricing strategies are used to discourage people from adopting a particular social product (e.g., taxes on cigarettes)

Once the pricing objective is agreed upon, setting specific prices gets easier. Three options to consider include the following:

1. *Cost-based pricing*, where prices are based on a desired or established profit margin or rate of return on investment (e.g., condoms are sold at community clinics at prices to cover purchase costs)

2. *Competitive-based pricing*, where prices are more driven by the prices for competing (similar) products and services (e.g., a life vest manufacturer partnering on a drowning prevention campaign offers discount coupons to make pricing similar to less expensive vests that are not Coast Guard approved)

3. *Value-based pricing*, where prices are based on an analysis of the target adopters' "price sensitivity," evaluating demand at varying price points (e.g., food waste composters that require simple spinning are priced higher than those requiring manual tossing)

ETHICAL CONSIDERATIONS RELATED TO PRICING STRATEGIES

Ethical considerations related to pricing strategies include issues of *social equity* (e.g., fixed versus sliding scale fees), *potential exploitation* (e.g., offering monetary incentives to drug-addicted women for voluntary sterilization or, like a program in North Carolina to reduce teen pregnancy, giving a dollar for each day not pregnant to teens who have never been pregnant, want to attend college, and have a sister who gave birth as a teen), impact and fairness of *public shame* tactics (e.g., what if owners of one of the Filthy 15 buildings have lost their job, and this explains why they haven't repaired their dilapidated building), and *full disclosure* of costs (e.g., requirements to toss food composters daily in order to receive stated benefits). In the case of promoting farmers' markets to WIC clients, each of these issues might apply. Should clients receive additional checks if they use all of their first set, making it necessary to give some clients only half a pack? What do we do about the fact that many items at the market are less than the $2 check denomination, and yet change cannot be given? Are we consistent about telling our clients that they will probably need to pay $3 for parking while at the markets?

CHAPTER SUMMARY

The price of a social marketing product is *the cost that the target audience associates with adopting the new behavior.* Costs may be monetary or nonmonetary in nature. Your task is to use this second tool to help ensure that what you offer the audience (*benefits*) is equal to or greater than what they will have to give up (*costs*). As noted, the *product* and *place* tools are also used to increase benefits and decrease costs (e.g., providing more convenient locations to recycle is a *place* strategy). Your objective (and opportunity) with the *price* tool is to develop and offer *incentives* that can be used to provide one or more of the following six impacts. The first four tactics focus on the desired behavior and the last two on the competing one(s):

1. Increase monetary benefits for *the desired behavior*
2. Increase nonmonetary benefits for *the desired behavior*
3. Decrease monetary costs for *the desired behavior*
4. Decrease nonmonetary costs for *the desired behavior*
5. Increase monetary costs for *the competing behavior*
6. Increase nonmonetary costs for *the competing behavior*

Although most prices for tangible goods and services are established by manufacturers, retailers, and service providers, several principles can guide a social marketer faced with price-setting decisions, beginning with establishing pricing objectives. What do you want the price to accomplish for you? Once that is defined, you will likely decide to establish your price based on cost, the competition, or the perceived value that the product holds for your target audience.

Increasing Planting of Native Plants

Does "Free" Matter?

(2012)

In his book *Predictably Irrational*,[32] Dan Ariely describes a series of simple experiments that offered subjects something desirable—chocolate—at a variety of prices.

> Two types of chocolate were used— a Hershey's kiss and a Lindt chocolate truffle. While the kiss is an inexpensive and common treat, a Lindt truffle is a far more tasty confection that costs an order of magnitude more than the kiss.[33]

In one of the experiments, the truffle was offered at 14 cents and the kiss was free. More than two thirds of the subjects chose the free chocolate kiss over the bargain-priced truffle.[34] Ariely explains that this preference for "free" seems to be hardwired into our brains: "FREE! gives us such an emotional charge that we perceive what is being offered as immensely more valuable than it really is."[35]

The following research highlight confirms this power of "free," although in this case the value of the alternative to free is identical in price. The highlight consists of a brief summary of an article appearing in the December 2012 issue of *Social Marketing Quarterly* and authored by Bret Randall Shaw, Barry Radler, and John Haack: "Comparing Two Direct Mail Strategies to Sell Native Plants in a Campaign to Promote Natural Lake Shorelines."[36]

Background

Residential development around lakeshores in the Upper Midwest have been associated with reduced wildlife habitat, lower biodiversity, and degraded water quality.[37] One way to improve degraded lakeshores is through the planting of trees and plants next to water sources, often referred to as riparian buffers. And one approach used by local governments and other stakeholder groups to increase these plantings is to subsidize or discount the costs for lakeshore property owners of reestablishing native vegetation along shorelines.

Of interest in this study was what discount strategy would be the most effective in influencing purchase of these native plants. Would uptake vary by seemingly simple changes in promotional messaging? More specifically, which of two promotional direct mail strategies would yield the most coupon redemptions? Would it be the "$5 OFF" headline or the "FREE" headline? Or would it matter?

Method

Two versions of a coupon were included in a newsletter that was part of a larger social marketing campaign called Share Your Shore, designed to encourage natural shorelines in Burnett County located in northwest Wisconsin (see Figures 11.6 and 11.7). The coupons were identical in copy with the exception of the two different visually dominant elements in the upper left corner. Of significance to the research objectives, they are functionally the same offer:

1. With the "FREE" coupon, redeemers have two options. They can use it to procure a free pack of six small native plants, or they can use it to get $5 off one of the top 10 native shoreline plants.

2. With the "$5 OFF" coupon, redeemers have the same two options, just presented in reverse order. They can use it to get $5 off one of the top 10 native shoreline plants, or they can use it to get a free pack of six smaller native plants.

The newsletter the coupons were inserted into was sent to a subscriber list of 3,672 households. Random distribution was achieved by enclosing coupons in newsletters that were numerically sorted by zip code and randomly inserted into bulk mailing trays. Also included in the mailing was a colorful booklet called the *Top 10 Native Plans for Burnett County*, which described the types of wildlife the different plants would attract and featured plants most likely to survive the area's sandy soil (see Figure 11.8). Coupons could be redeemed at one of five participating nurseries in the county that stocked the 10 native plants featured in the booklet. There was a "point of purchase" poster at the nurseries with similar visual branding to both coupon versions and an accompanying brochure directing recipients to the promoted products.

Figure 11.6   Coupon featuring the "FREE Pack" prominently.

Source: Share Your Shore.

Figure 11.7   Coupon featuring the "$5 OFF" prominently.

Source: Share Your Shore.

Findings

In total, of the 263 coupons redeemed, about two thirds (66.2%) were the "FREE Pack" coupons. Authors of the study were interested, however, in determining how the probability of the obtained results compared to chance, and they applied a

Figure 11.8 Front cover of colorful booklet featuring 10 native plants.

Source: Share Your Shore.

chi-square goodness-of-fit statistic to the data. This analytical technique compares the frequency distribution of a single categorical variable against a theoretical frequency distribution, testing the match, or fit, between an obtained sample frequency distribution and a theoretically expected frequency distribution. Because equal numbers of both coupons were randomly distributed—each to half the households in the study—and because both versions of the coupon had the same absolute dollar value, the expected redemption rate (or distribution) of the coupons would have been 50/50. Table 11.3 confirms that significantly more of the "FREE" coupons were redeemed.

Discussion

Results from this study suggest that seemingly small changes in marketing messages can substantially influence how people respond to them. It is important to remind the reader that there was no functional difference in the messages contained within both coupon versions. Both gave the recipient $5 worth of native plants. However, a simple inversion of the messaging—focusing on the FREE Pack versus the $5 off—significantly altered response to the promotion.[38]

The authors also noted that in order to have a significant impact on protecting water quality, more plants would likely be needed than those that could be purchased with the free or $5-off coupon. Future research should look at whether the free offer resulted in a greater overall purchase of plants as compared to the $5 discounted offer, and whether redeemers with coupons (either one) made more purchases than those with no coupon at all.

Table 11.3 Chi-Square Test of Goodness of Fit Between Observed and Obtained Frequencies

	FREE Headline	**$5 OFF Headline**
Observed frequency (# of coupons redeemed)	174	89
Expected frequency (assuming 50/50)	131.5	131.5
Observed/expected (difference)*	42.5	–42.5

*$p < .001$

Source: Adapted from p. 278 of B. Shaw, B. Radler, and J. Haack, "Comparing Two Direct Mail Strategies to Sell Native Plants in a Campaign to Promote Natural Lake Shorelines," *Social Marketing Quarterly* XVIII, no. 4 (December 2012): 274–280.

DISCUSSION QUESTIONS AND EXERCISES

1. One of the concerns that has been expressed regarding the use of monetary incentives is their "durability," meaning that behaviors that are influenced primarily through monetary incentives might revert back once the incentive is removed, perhaps even dropping below initial levels. What are your thoughts on the implications of this potential for the blood donation example presented earlier in the chapter? How could you protect against this?

2. Share about pledges or commitment programs you have used or are aware of.

3. Discuss the outcomes of the opening case. Do you think the roughly five people out of 100 who quit in the CARES group constitute success? Why or why not?

CHAPTER 11 NOTES

1. D. Bueckert, "Federal Budget Hammers Gas-Guzzlers, Leaves Kyoto in the Air" (2007), accessed March 20, 2007, http://cnews.canoe.ca/CNEWS/Canada/2007/03/19/3783431-cp.html.

2. X. Gine, D. Karlan, and J. Zinman, "Put Your Money Where Your Butt Is: A Commitment Contract for Smoking Cessation," *American Economic Journal: Applied Economics* 2, no. 4 (October 2010): 213–235.

3. X. Gine, D. Karlan, and J. Zinman, "Cares Commitment Savings for Smoking Cessation in the Philippines" (n.d.), accessed January 31, 2014, http://www.povertyactionlab.org/evaluation/cares-commitment-savings-smoking-cessation-philippines.

4. Ibid.

5. P. Kotler and G. Armstrong, *Principles of Marketing* (Upper Saddle River, NJ: Prentice Hall, 2001), 371.

6. R. O'Connor, B. Fix, P. Celestino, S. Carlin-Menter, A. Hyland, & K. M. Cummings, "Financial Incentives to Promote Smoking Cessation: Evidence From 11 Quit and Win Contests," *Journal of Public Health Management and Practice* 12, no. 1 (2006), 44–51, accessed March 10, 2007, http://www.ncbi.nlm.nih.gov/entrez/query.fcgi?cmd=Retrieve&db=pubmed&dopt=Abstract&list_uids=16340515&query_hl=6&itool=pubmed_docsum.

7. A. Luthern, "Blood Shortage Risk Prompts Red Cross Request for Donors," *Milwaukee Wisconsin Journal Sentinel*, accessed February 3, 2014, http://www.jsonline.com/news/wisconsin/blood-shortage-risk-prompts-red-cross-request-for-donors-b9951666z1-214901141.html.

8. A. Woerner, "Should Monetary Incentives Be Offered for Blood Donation? Study Says Yes," *Fox News* (May 24, 2013), accessed February 3, 2014, http://www.foxnews.com/health/2013/05/24/should-monetary-incentives-be-offered-for-blood-donation-study-says-yes/.

9. J. Z. Klein, "Fair Play Shows Up in the Standings," *The New York Times* (December 21, 2010), accessed January 28, 2011, http://www.nytimes.com/2010/12/22/sports/hockey/22youth.html.

10. Klein, "Fair Play."

11. D. Rich, "Humane Society Adoptions Hit Record," *Mercer Island Reporter* (September 17, 2013), 8, accessed October 7, 2014, http://www.mi-reporter.com/opinion/letters/224089501.html.

12. Information in this example is from Harborview Injury Prevention and Research Center, University of Washington, Seattle; accessed October 1, 2001, http://www.hiprc.org.

13. K. F. Fox, "Time as a Component of Price in Social Marketing," in *Marketing in the '80s*, ed. R. P. Bagozzi et al. (Chicago: American Marketing Association, 1980), 464–467; as cited in P. Kotler and E. L. Roberto, *Social Marketing: Strategies for Changing Public Behavior* (New York: Free Press, 1989).

14. Ibid.

15. H. G. Gemunden, "Perceived Risk and Information Search: A Systematic Meta-analysis of the Empirical Evidence," *International Journal of Research in Marketing* 2 (1985): 79–100; as cited in Kotler and Roberto, *Social Marketing*, 182–183.

16. A. R. Andreasen, *Social Marketing in the 21st Century* (Thousand Oaks, CA: SAGE, 2006), 153.

17. Ibid., 102.

18. Driven to Distraction Task Force, "Frequently Asked Questions / Cell Phone Legislation Proposed by Senator Tracey Eide and Representative Reuven Carlyle" (n.d.), accessed January 28, 2011, http://www.nodistractions.org/The_Evidence.html.

19. thinkSPAIN, "Dog-Mess Not Cleared Up Hand-Delivered Back to Owners as 'Lost Property'" (April 2013), accessed February 3, 2014, http://www.thinkspain.com/news-spain/22852/dog-mess-not-cleared-up-hand-delivered-back-to-owners-as-lost-property.

20. City of Tacoma, "The Filthy 15" (2007), accessed March 21, 2007, http://www .cityofta-coma.org/Page.aspx?nid=167.

21. Students received creative and production assistance from Cynthia Hartwig (creative director), Shelley Baker (art director at Cf2Gs Advertising), Marlene Liranzo (Mercer Island High School teacher), Gary Gorland (Teen Aware program manager), and Nancy Lee (consultant).

22. Hello Sunday Morning [website], accessed February 10, 2014, https://www.hellosunday morning.org/pages/about.

23. Personal communication from Niamh Gately, March 6, 2014.

24. Coalition for a Safer 63/881, "These Albertans Pledged to Be Safer Drivers. Join Them" (n.d.), accessed February 10, 2014, http://www.safer63and881.com/thepledge/.

25. Texting & Driving: It Can Wait [home page], accessed February 10, 2014, http://www .itcanwait.com/.

26. Be Floridian: A Service of the Tampa Bay Estuary Program [website], accessed February 10, 2014, www.BeFloridian.org.

27. West Maui Kumuwai, "Take the Pledge" (n.d.), accessed February 10, 2014, http://west mauikumuwai.org/take-the-pledge/personal-pledge/.

28. ENERGY STAR, "Put Your Computers to Sleep: Save up to $50 per Computer Annually" (n.d.), accessed February 10, 2010, http://www.energystar.gov/index.cfm?c=power_mgt.pr_power_mgt_low_carbon_join.

29. FARM: Farm Animal Rights Movement, "10 Billion Lives North American Tour Fact Sheet" (n.d.), accessed February 10, 2014, http://www.10billiontour.org/10%20Billion%20Tour%20Media%20Fact%20Sheet.pdf.

30. Each Mind Matters: California Mental Health Movement, "Join the Movement: Make a Pledge" (n.d.), accessed February 10, 2014, http://www.eachmindmatters.org/join-the-movement/.

31. Kotler and Roberto, *Social Marketing*, 176–177.

32. D. Ariely, *Predictably Irrational: The Hidden Forces That Shape Our Decisions* (New York: HarperCollins, 2009).

33. Neuromarketing: Where Brain Science and Marketing Meet, "The Power of FREE!" (July 10, 2008), accessed February 5, 2014, http://www.neurosciencemarketing.com/blog/articles/the-power-of-free.htm.

34. Ibid.

35. "Predictably Irrational," *Wikipedia* (n.d.), accessed February 5, 2014, http://en.wikipedia.org/wiki/Predictably_Irrational.

36. B. Shaw, B. Radler, and J. Haack, "Comparing Two Direct Mail Strategies to Sell Native Plants in a Campaign to Promote Natural Lake Shorelines," *Social Marketing Quarterly* XVIII, no. 4 (December 2012): 274–280.

37. B. M. Henning and A. J. Remsburg, "Lakeshore Vegetation Effects on Avian and Anuran Populations," *American Midland Naturalist* 161 (2009): 123–133.

38. Shaw et al., "Comparing Two Direct Mail Strategies," 278.

Chapter 12

PLACE

MAKING ACCESS CONVENIENT AND PLEASANT

Avoid victim blaming and acknowledge that deficiencies in the structural environment can fuel social inequities and block change.

—Dr. Christine Domegan
National University of Ireland

Store-based retailers say that the three most important things in the success of their businesses are "location, location, location!" You may find this true for many social marketing efforts as well. Consider how much lower the following scores would be without the convenient-access component of these programs:

- *Recycling.* In 2011, Americans recycled 66% of paper, 57% of yard trimmings, 28% of glass, and 21% of aluminum.[1] Although this is certainly not as much as we would like to see, imagine how grim the statistics would be without curbside recycling and recycle containers in office buildings and most public places.
- *Pet waste pickup.* Although an estimated 40% of dog owners in the United States do not pick up their dog's waste, at least 60% do, and without Mutt Mitts available in parks and public places around the country, we can imagine that number would be smaller.[2]
- *Tobacco quitlines.* The prevalence of smoking among adults in the United States declined from about 25% in 1990 to 18% in 2012.[3] Most tobacco users across the states have access to quitlines, which provide telephone counseling to help them quit, and in some cases these lines provide limited access to medication. Quitlines overcome many of the barriers to traditional smoking cessation classes, as they require no transportation and are available at the smoker's convenience.
- *Organ donations.* Many initiatives around the world aim to increase the number of organs obtained from deceased donors. Convenience of registering as an organ donor is one important strategy, with many countries now offering registration through driver's license bureaus or departments of motor vehicles, where individuals can designate their wish to be an organ donor on their license.[4]

In this chapter, you'll read about 10 strategies for increasing convenience of access and making the desired behavior easier and more pleasant to carry out, as program organizers did in the following case highlight.

MARKETING HIGHLIGHT

Books: The Ultimate Toy for Toddlers

(2012–2014)

Lucie and André Chagnon Foundation

Quebec, Canada

We refuse to accept the inevitability of poverty. In a society such as ours, it is unacceptable that many, many children are still living and growing up in disadvantaged conditions. The poverty that affects these children and their families concerns all of us: theirs is not the only development that is compromised. The development of our society as a whole is at stake.[5]

—Claude Chagnon, President
Lucie and André Chagnon Foundation

Background

The mission of the Lucie and André Chagnon Foundation, based in Quebec, Canada, is to prevent poverty by focusing on the educational success of young Quebecers, helping them to develop their full potential from conception to age 17. Its intent is to create environments that meet the needs of these children as well as those of their families. Its strategies focus on mobilizing local communities, raising societal awareness, and inspiring actions to achieve optimal childhood development. The foundation develops and promotes early, sustained interventions to help ensure that children get off to a good start at school, and supports their parents in their role as educators.

The *purpose* of one of the foundation's social marketing initiatives, initiated in 2009, has been to encourage and support parents in providing appropriate stimulation for children under 6 years of age. Most recently, a campaign developed and launched in 2012 and continuing into 2014 has *focused* on books as the ultimate toy for toddlers. Studies have consistently shown that involving children, even toddlers, in reading and playing with books has the power to create interactional contexts that nourish language development.[6] As you will read, a core strategy has involved engaging multiple partners to provide convenient locations for parents to pick up books for their young children.

Information for this case was provided by François Lagarde, Vice President, Communications, at the Lucie and André Chagnon Foundation.

Target Audience and Desired Behavior

The Books for Toddlers effort targeted parents with children under 2 years of age, especially those in low-socioeconomic-status households. A single, simple, specific, and doable behavior was developed for the campaign: *Use a book to play with your child five minutes a day.*

Audience Insights

Early research conducted for the foundation explored parents' perceived barriers to reading with their toddlers, with findings indicating that 50% of parents were not reading with their child due to perceived lack of time.[7] They were also concerned about the convenience of access to and cost of books. In addition, parents' perceptions of the benefits of reading with their toddlers were not clear, as books were associated with school and some believed that toddlers should be playing, not learning. "Let them be babies!" they proclaimed.

What would motivate these parents to read more with their toddlers? Parents indicated that they were looking for more opportunities for immediate gratification, signaled by a smile and a laugh from their child. And they wanted to feel empowered and in control, not preached to or told what to do.

Marketing Mix Strategies

Using a book to play with your child was positioned as the ultimate fun toy—one with multiple benefits, including that reading a book takes only five minutes a day. Strategies for achieving this positioning and overcoming audience barriers included the following elements of the marketing mix:

Product

A unique and informative book was published for the campaign in French and English: *Kittycat & Friends: My Very Own Book.* Bookmarks for the book provided parents with inspirational tips on using the book as a toy (see Figures 12.1 and 12.2).

Price

The book was free.

Place

Close to 300,000 copies of the book were distributed between February 2013 and January 2014 throughout Quebec in a variety of locations and at a variety of events, especially those that would reach lower-income households:

- 250,000 copies were inserted in the *Naitre et grandir magazine* that the Foundation distributes through its own network.
- 9,700 copies were distributed through *organizations* who ordered directly from the foundation (community organizations, local health centers, day care centers).
- 3,800 copies were distributed through popular children/family *events* by trained individuals who directly interacted with parents of children under the age of six years.
- 4,300 copies were distributed through a network of local public *libraries.*

Figure 12.1 A new book published for the campaign for parents to use to play with their child.

Source: Lucie and André Chagnon Foundation.

Figure 12.2 Bookmarks for the book with tips for parents on how to use the book like a toy.

Source: Lucie and André Chagnon Foundation.

- 1,600 copies were distributed through *Moisson Montréal*, a large *food bank*. The copies were specifically distributed to families with at least one child under the age of six.
- 10,400 copies were distributed in *commercial and professional outlets* (drugstores, supermarkets, dental clinics) in selected underprivileged neighborhoods that committed to distributing the book to targeted consumers. In-store promotional materials were posted to increase pickup by the target audience.
- 6,400 copies were distributed through a partnership with the OLO Foundation, a food security initiative that reaches 17,000 of the lowest-socio-economic-status pregnant mothers in the province through a *network of dedicated and personalized local health, social, and prenatal services.*
- 11,600 copies were distributed by *Avenir d'enfants*, which supports local early childhood coalitions throughout the province, concentrating on *distribution in underprivileged areas.*

Promotion

A key message of the campaign, featured in a variety of communication channels, is that "playing with your child and a book is a gift that lasts forever." Communication channels include:

- Television and outdoor advertising
- Print advertising in selected weeklies (underprivileged neighborhoods)

- Web advertising and content (naitreetgrandir.com)
- Facebook
- A kit for professionals and leaders containing best practices, tips, and materials
- YouTube videos featuring the television advertisements (http://www .youtube.com/watch?v=qInSw_s Ftcc&feature=youtu.be and http:// www.youtube.com/watch?v=JKmR Hwd6agE&feature=youtu.be)

An additional effort, in partnership with the Quebec Literacy Foundation, invited citizens to buy new books in participating bookstores and libraries for needy children. The Literacy Foundation collected 18,700 books aimed at children ages 0 to 4, an increase of 47% from the previous year.

Outcomes

To establish a baseline of awareness, attitudes, and behaviors, a web-based survey was conducted with parents of children ages 0 to 5 in July 2013, with a total of 333 respondents. A tracking survey was completed in January 2014, with 702 web respondents and an additional 335 adults interviewed by phone; 501 respondents for the January 2014 survey were parents of children 0 to 5. Findings were encouraging:[8]

- Sixty-six percent of respondents recalled the campaign (aided and unaided).
- Sixty-seven percent understood (unaided) that campaign messages had to do with early childhood development, the introduction of books and reading as early as possible in a child's life, and the parental role in child development and reading.
- Ninety-five percent indicated that they thought the campaign messages were clear and easy to understand.
- Seventy-nine percent indicated that they had read a book with their child and/or let their child play with a book during the previous seven days, a significant (58%) increase from the July 2013 survey, where 50% indicated they had done this.
- The January 2014 study indicated that the self-reported frequency of reading with their child during the previous seven days for parents with a household income under CAN$40,000 was 6.7 times (up from 5.9 in July 2013). The corresponding figure for parents with a household income over CAN$40,000 was 7.7 times (up from 7.1 in July 2013). The greatest increase was among mothers with a household income under CAN$40,000 (up from 6.3 to 7.5 times). Program managers commented that while the causality is difficult to establish, this particular increase could suggest that the marketing mix, especially with a distribution focus on underprivileged neighborhoods, may be part of the explanation.
- Two specific behaviors highlighted in campaign materials increased significantly between July 2013 and January 2014: "Point out words and pictures" increased from 66% to 75%, and "Cuddle with him/her" increased from 62% to 71%.

Reflections

François Lagarde shared that

achieving optimal development for all children is one of the most complex undertakings. It can only be achieved through a combination of interventions including public policies, community mobilization to create supportive environments, appropriate measures and practices as well as the adoption of positive parental behaviors. As one element of a comprehensive strategy and based on formative steps, this Books for Toddlers effort addresses access issues through multiple points of distribution of free books and appropriate partnerships to help with the outreach. Continued community-based efforts are necessary to ensure that positive attitudes and behaviors are sustained.[9]

PLACE: THE THIRD "P"

Place is where and when the target audience will perform the desired behavior, acquire any related goods, and receive any associated services.

We live in a convenience-oriented world in which many of us place an extremely high value on our time, trying to save some of it for our families, friends, and favorite leisure activities. As a social marketer, you'll want to be keenly aware that your target audience will evaluate the convenience of your offer relative to other exchanges in their lives. And the convenience bar has been raised over the past decades for all marketers by companies such as Starbucks, McDonald's, Federal Express, Amazon.com, 1–800–Flowers, Netflix for online movie rentals, and of course, the Internet.

In commercial sector marketing, place is often referred to as the distribution channel, and options and potential examples for social marketing are pervasive:

- *Physical locations:* Recycle stations at retail outlets
- *Phone:* Domestic violence help line
- *Mobile phone apps:* To find out when the next bus arrives
- *Mail:* Postage-paid plastic bags for recycling mobile phones
- *Fax:* An agreement to quit smoking signed by both patient and physician and faxed to a quitline
- *Internet:* Rideshare matching
- *Mobile units:* For hazardous waste
- *Where people shop:* Mammograms in a department store
- *Where people hang out:* HIV/AIDS tests at gay bars
- *Drive-throughs:* For flu shots at medical centers
- *Home delivery/house calls:* Home energy audits

- *Kiosks:* For determining body mass index (BMI)
- *Vending machines:* Condoms

It is important to clarify and stress that place is *not the same as communication channel*, which is where your communications will appear (e.g., brochures, radio ads, news stories, and personal presentations). Chapter 14 presents a detailed discussion of communication channels.

STEP 7: DEVELOP THE PLACE STRATEGY

Your objective with the place marketing tool is to develop strategies that will make it as convenient and pleasant as possible for your target audience to perform the behavior, acquire any goods, and receive any services. It is especially helpful in reducing access-related barriers (e.g., lack of transportation) and time-related barriers (e.g., being at work all day). It can also break down psychological barriers (e.g., providing needle exchange programs on street corners versus at a community health clinic). You will also want to do anything possible and within reason to make the competing behavior (seem) less convenient. The next sections of this chapter will elaborate on 10 successful strategies for you to consider.

1. Make the Location Closer

Example: A Dental Office on Wheels. Many children don't get the regular dental care they need. They may be struggling with language barriers, poverty, rural isolation, or homelessness. A mobile clinic called the SmileMobile travels to communities all across Washington State. This modern dental office on wheels brings dental services directly to children age 13 and younger who don't otherwise have access to care. Children enrolled in Medicaid have no out-of-pocket expenses, and other children are charged on a sliding fee schedule. Families may even enroll in Medicaid at the SmileMobile.

The brightly painted clinic features three state-of-the-art dental operatories and includes x-ray facilities. A full-time dentist and teams of local volunteer dentists and their staffs provide a range of dental services, including diagnostic services (e.g., exams and x-rays), prevention services (e.g., cleaning and sealants), acute and emergent relief of pain (e.g., extractions and minor surgical procedures), and routine restorative services (e.g., fillings and crowns).

The SmileMobile was developed by Washington Dental Service, the Washington State Dental Association, and the Washington Dental Service Foundation (see Figure 12.3). Staff work closely with local health departments and community, charitable, and business organizations to coordinate visits to cities and towns throughout the state. Every effort is made to reach the neediest children and provide translators for non-English-speaking

Figure 12.3 Making dental care for children more accessible.

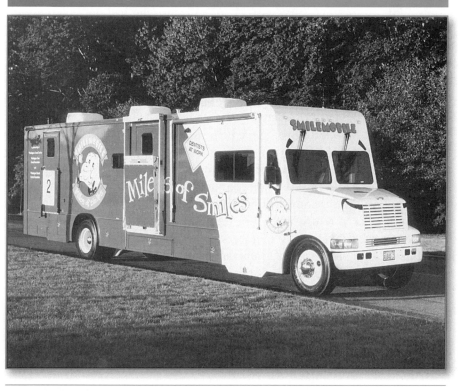

Source: Reprinted with permission from the Washington Dental Service Foundation, Making Dental Care for Children More Accessible. SmileMobile was developed by Washington Dental Service (WDS), the Washington State Dental Association (WSDA), and the Washington Dental Service Foundation (WDSF).

patients and their families. The mobile clinic first hit the road in 1995 and by 2013 had treated more than 25,000 children throughout the state.[10]

Additional examples illustrating ways to save your target audience a little time and travel include the following:

- Exercise facilities at work sites
- Flu shots at grocery stores
- Breastfeeding consultation provided during home visits
- Print cartridges recycled at office supply stores
- Litter receptacles that make it easy to drive by and deposit litterbags
- Dental floss kept in the TV room or, better yet, attached to the remote control
- Xmas tree recycling drop-off at the local high school
- Bins for unwanted clothing placed in residential buildings
- Mobile libraries reaching rural areas

2. Extend Hours

Example: Vote by Mail. A survey of 15,167 citizens who had not voted in the 2008 presidential election in the United States indicated that the number-one reason for this was that they were "too busy, or had a conflicting schedule."[11] Oregon, however, had one of the highest voter turnouts in the nation, with 86% of registered voters voting in the 2008 presidential election.[12] Perhaps this is because voting is so convenient, with Oregonians *voting only by mail.* There are no polling places, and election day is just a deadline to turn in your ballot and has been that way since 1998, when nearly 70% of Oregonians approved the Vote by Mail initiative. Some believe it is the most "effective, efficient and fraud-free way to conduct an election."[13]

Oregon's Vote by Mail system is simple, straightforward, and most of all, convenient. Ballots are mailed to registered voters 14 to 18 days before an election. Voters can complete the ballot "in the comfort of their own home" and on their own schedule. They have two weeks to return the ballot through the mail, or they can drop it off at one of many official conveniently located sites, including ones in a downtown park (see Figure 12.4). And there are additional advantages as well, including reduced election costs (since there are no polling places) and the fact that some feel voters give

Figure 12.4   One of Oregon's conveniently located ballot boxes in a park in downtown Portland.

more thought to how they mark their ballots, having access to campaign materials at their fingertips.

As one editorial opinion expressed it,

> while the idea of the polling place at your local elementary school is something that provokes nostalgia in many of us, the realities of modern life as well as the demands on election officials outstrip any nostalgia we may feel for voting at a polling place. . . . Isn't the true definition of "democracy in action" one where the mechanism for casting ballots advantages the voter, not the system set up to count the ballots?[14]

Additional examples of strategies that offer target audiences more options in terms of time and day of the week include the following:

- Licensed child care searches online (versus calling a telephone center during normal business hours)
- Twenty-four-hour help lines for counseling and information
- Recycling centers open on Sundays
- Natural yard care workshops offered weekday evenings

3. Be There at the Point of Decision Making

Many social marketers have found that an ideal moment to speak to the target audience is when they are about to choose between alternative, competing behaviors. They are at a fork in the road, with your desired behavior in one direction and their current behavior, or a potential undesirable one, in the other. Presenting the offer at a target audience's point of decision making can be powerful, giving you one last chance to influence their choice.

Example: Ecstasy Pill Testing at Nightclubs. DanceSafe is a nonprofit organization promoting health and safety within the rave and nightclub community, with local chapters throughout the United States and Canada. They report that they neither condone nor condemn the use of any drug. Rather, they engage in efforts to reduce drug-related harm by providing health and safety information and on-site pill testing to those who do use drugs.[15] Among other programs and services, volunteers in communities with chapters offer *on-site pill testing* to ecstasy users at raves, nightclubs, and other public events where ecstasy is being used socially. Users who are unsure of the authenticity of a pill they possess can bring it to a booth or table where trained harm-reduction volunteers will test it for use. DanceSafe reports on its website that volunteers staff booths at raves, nightclubs, and other dance events, where they also provide information on drugs, safe sex, and other health and safety issues concerning the dance community (such as driving home safely and protecting one's hearing).[16]

DanceSafe cites two fundamental operating principles: *harm reduction* and *popular education.* They believe that "combining these two philosophies enables them to create successful, peer-based educational programs to reduce drug abuse and empower young people to make healthy, informed lifestyle choices."[17] They believe that

> while abstinence is the only way to avoid all the harms associated with drug use, harm reduction programs provide non-abstentionist health and safety information under the recognition that many people are going to choose to experiment with drugs despite all the risks involved. Harm reduction information and services help people use as safely as possible as long as they continue to use.[18]

Other creative solutions that can influence decision making "just in time" include the following:

- Place a glass bowl of fruits and vegetables at eye level in the refrigerator versus in closed drawers on the bottom shelf.
- Negotiate with retailers to place natural fertilizers in a prominent display at the end of the aisle.
- Place a small, inexpensive plastic magnifier on fertilizer jugs so that gardeners can read the small print, including instructions for safe usage.

4. Make the Location More Appealing

Example: Bicycle Paths and Lanes in Los Angeles. One of the major barriers a potential bicyclist will cite for not commuting by bike to work is the lack of safe, pleasant, and interconnected bike paths and lanes. In 1994, the City of Los Angeles, led by its Department of City Planning, developed its first-ever comprehensive Bicycle Plan. It was adopted by the city council in 1996 and then provided the Department of Transportation a template for bicycle paths, lanes, and myriad bicycle amenities and policies to be implemented throughout the city.

And the plan has a goal, that of increasing bicycle travel in the city to *5% of all utilitarian trips taken* by 2025, the year the plan is expected to be fully implemented. Public input for the plan was provided primarily through the city's Bicycle Advisory Committee (no bicycle advocacy group existed in Los Angeles at the time). The public learned about potential bike routes by visiting the committee's "war room," which posted the city's arterial roadway system maps and provided an opportunity for citizen reactions and recommendations.

By 2014, the city had installed 56 miles of bicycle paths, 119 miles of bicycle routes, and 348 bike lanes (see Figure 12.5). In addition, the Los Angeles Department of Transportation had installed over 5,500 U bicycle racks and had developed and distributed over 500,000 comprehensive city bicycle maps.[20]

Additional examples of enhanced locations include the following:

- Conveniently located teen clinics that have reading materials and decor to which the market can relate
- Stairways in office buildings that employees would want to take—ones that are well lit, carpeted, and have art exhibits on the walls that get changed out once a month
- Organized walking groups for seniors in shopping malls

Figure 12.5   Making bicycling more appealing and safer in Los Angeles, with the orange line bike path built in conjunction with a metro bus rapid transit project.[19]

5. Overcome Psychological Barriers Associated With Place

Example: Pets on the Net. In 2014, it was estimated that close to 8 million dogs and cats end up in shelters across America every year and that only about 50% get adopted.[21] Potential pet owners have several considerations (*barriers*) associated with visiting animal shelters to see what pets are available. In addition to the time it takes to travel to a center, some describe the psychological risk—a concern that they might take home a pet that isn't what they were really looking for. They worry they won't be able to say no. Viewing pets available for adoption on the Internet can help reduce both of these costs.

Many humane societies across the country have created websites where all or some of the pets currently available for adoption are featured, 24 hours a day, seven days a week. As illustrated in the photo on Sacramento's Pets on the Net website (see Figure 12.6), detailed information on the pet includes a personality profile based on information provided by the previous owner. Website visitors are told that adoptions are offered on a first-come, first-served basis, and directions to the facility are provided.[22] Some websites include features such as daily updates, an opportunity to put a temporary hold on an animal, information on how to choose the right shelter pet, and reasons the pet was given up for adoption. A few national sites offer the ability to search nationwide for a pet by providing criteria such as desired breed, gender, age, size, and geographic locale.

Figure 12.6 Pets on the Net reduces concern about not being able to say no.

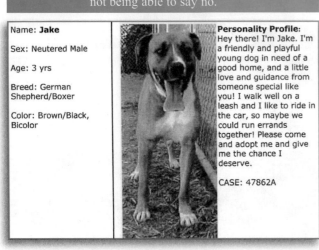

Name: **Jake**

Sex: Neutered Male

Age: 3 yrs

Breed: German Shepherd/Boxer

Color: Brown/Black, Bicolor

Personality Profile: Hey there! I'm Jake. I'm a friendly and playful young dog in need of a good home, and a little love and guidance from someone special like you! I walk well on a leash and I like to ride in the car, so maybe we could run errands together! Please come and adopt me and give me the chance I deserve.

CASE: 47862A

Source: http://www.sspca.org/ContactUs.html.

Additional examples of strategies that reduce psychological barriers regarding place include the following:

- Needle exchange services provided by a health clinic on a street corner or from a mobile van versus at the facility of a community clinic
- A website to help youth quit smoking, with an option to email a counselor instead of calling—an option some research with youth indicates just "isn't going to happen"

And finally, consider this example where well-intentioned program managers wanted to increase convenience of access. The question is whether they will end up creating place-associated psychological costs that will outweigh the attractive product and price components of the offer:

In October 2010, at a Department of Motor Vehicles branch in southwest Washington, D.C., a new program was launched, one that would provide residents an opportunity for a confidential HIV test as they waited for their driver's license. The DMV provided the space to a nonprofit organization, Family and Medical Counseling Service, that administered the tests. A spokesperson for the organization commented, "Many people have to wait for some of the DMV services, and the rapid HIV test takes only 20 minutes. It fits perfectly with the waiting times."[23] The oral test is free. In fact, test takers are given $15 to go toward the cost of their DMV services that day.

6. Be More Accessible Than the Competition

Example: School Lunch Line Redesign. Brian Wansink, a professor at Cornell University, argues that "the ideal lunchroom isn't one that eliminates cookies. The ideal lunchroom is the one that gets children to choose an apple instead of a cookie, but to think it's their own choice."[24] Wansink's Center for Behavioral Economics and Childhood Nutrition at Cornell aims to provide schools with research-based solutions that encourage healthier eating in the lunchroom. In an October 2010 article in the *New York Times*, Wansink and his colleague, David Just, shared a dozen strategies that they found nudge students toward making better choices on their own by changing the way their options are presented. Several are place-related strategies:

1. Place nutritious foods at the beginning of the lunch line

2. Use more appealing words to label healthy foods (e.g., "creamy corn" rather than "corn")

3. Give choices (e.g., carrots or celery versus just carrots)

4. Keep items like ice cream out of sight in the freezer with an opaque top

5. Pull the salad bar away from the wall

6. Have cafeteria workers ask children, "Do you want a salad?"

7. Provide food trays, as they appear to increase the likelihood of taking a salad

8. Decrease the size of cereal bowls

9. Place the chocolate milk behind the white milk

10. Place fruit in glass bowls rather than stainless-steel pans

11. Lunch tickets should cover fruit as a dessert, but not cookies

12. Provide a "healthy express" checkout line for those not buying chips or desserts

Other examples in which the desired behavior is made more accessible relative to the competition include the following:

- Family-friendly lanes in grocery stores where candy, gum, and adult magazines have been removed from the checkout stand
- High-occupant vehicle lanes that reward high-occupant vehicles with less traffic congestion (most of the time)

7. Make Access to the Competition More Difficult or Unpleasant

Example: Tobacco's "25-Foot Rule". On December 8, 2005, Washington became the fifth state to implement a comprehensive statewide law prohibiting smoking in all indoor public places and workplaces, including restaurants, bars, taverns, bowling alleys, skating rinks, and nontribal casinos. But this law went further than any state had up to that time. Unlike Washington's measure, most statewide bans exempt some businesses, such as bars, private clubs, card rooms, and cigar lounges. And no state at the time had a deeper no-smoking buffer than Washington's 25-foot rule that prohibits smoking within 25 feet of entrances, exits, windows that open, and ventilation intakes that serve indoor public places or places of employment.

This (upstream) measure, supported by the American Cancer Society and the American Lung Association, created a heated and emotional debate for months before the election on local talk shows and editorial pages. Opponents argued that bars would be put out of business, people would lose their jobs, all the patrons (and revenues) would just move to tribal casinos that would be exempt from the law, and outside dining would decline. And since people can simply choose to work at or frequent a nonsmoking restaurant or bar, why remove their choice? More than a year after the measure went into effect, some were still angry and lobbying with legislators to amend at least the "draconian" 25-foot rule: "It's overly harsh. It's turning my servers into cops. They are working for tips and to take care of customers—not to be authority figures."[25]

But research shows that state tobacco prevention programs must be broad based and comprehensive to be effective and that requiring smokers to "step out in the rain" would be a significant deterrent. With one of the lowest smoking rates in the country (16% of adults in 2013),[26] Washington's Tobacco Prevention and Control Program also provides services to help people, restricts the ability of kids to get tobacco, conducts public awareness and media campaigns, supports programs in communities and schools, and evaluates the effectiveness of its activities.[27]

Other examples of limiting access to competitive behaviors include the following:

- Offering coupons for lockboxes for safe gun storage and distributing brochures listing convenient retail locations for purchase
- Distributing padlocks for home liquor cabinets to reduce alcohol access for minors; better yet, advocating with home builders to make these standard in new homes
- Pruning bushes in city parks so that youth are not able to gather in private and share their cigarettes and beer

8. Be Where Your Target Audience Shops

Example: Mammograms in the Mall. The following excerpt from an article in the *Detroit Free Press* provides an example of reducing barriers through improving access and location appeal.[28]

Many women already pick up birthday gifts, grab dinner, and get their hair cut at the malls, so why not schedule their annual mammograms there, as well? With a concept that screams "no more excuses," the Barbara Ann Karmanos Cancer Institute will open a cancer prevention center at the Somerset Collection South in Troy in September. A first for Michigan and the Detroit Institute, the mall-located screening center will provide a comfortable, spalike atmosphere for patients in a less intimidating setting than a traditional doctor's office or hospital.

Targeting shoppers, mall workers—including about 3,000 women—and the 100,000 employees near the mall, Karmanos is renovating a 2,000-square-foot space in the lower level of the mall. The center initially will focus on breast cancer prevention, with clinical breast exams and mammography available. However, services could expand to prostate, lung, and gastrointestinal cancer screenings and bone density testing, said Yvette Monet, a Karmanos spokeswoman. Taking its cues from the spas, the Karmanos Prevention Center will pamper patients with privacy, peace and quiet, and warm terry cloth robes.

The center is expected to encourage regular mammograms and breast exams. Nearly 44,000 women in the United States died last year from breast cancer—including 1,500 in Michigan—even though American Cancer Society studies show early diagnosis can mean a 97% survival rate. The Karmanos Center is expected to reach women who think they are too busy to get mammograms or are afraid to do so. "This is intended to be a nonclinical-type setting that will feature soothing shades of blue and comfy couches," Monet said.

Other examples of similar opportunities to provide services and tangible objects where your target audience is already shopping include the following:

- Distributing sustainable seafood guides at the fish counter of fish markets
- Providing litterbags at gas pumps, similar to pet waste bags in parks
- Giving demonstrations on how to select a proper life vest at sporting goods stores
- Offering beauty salon clients laminated cards to hang on a shower nozzle with instructions and reminders to conduct a monthly breast self-exam

9. Be Where Your Target Audience Hangs Out

Example: HIV/AIDS Tests in Gay Bathhouses. A headline in the *Chicago Tribune* on January 2, 2004, exemplified this ninth place strategy: "Rapid HIV Tests Offered Where Those at Risk Gather: Seattle Health Officials Get Aggressive in AIDS Battle by Heading Into Gay Clubs, Taking a Drop Of Blood and Providing Answers in 20 Minutes." The article described a new and aggressive effort for Public Health–Seattle & King County, one that included administering rapid result HIV tests in bathhouses and gay sex clubs.[29]

Up to this point in time, it had been common for health counselors to visit bathhouses to administer standard HIV testing. Although this certainly made taking the test more convenient, it didn't address the place barrier associated with getting the results. Those who took advantage of these services would still need to make an appointment at a medical clinic and then wait at least a week to hear the results, a critical step in the prevention and early treatment process that was not always taken. With this new effort, counselors would be with clients to present their results within about 20 minutes of taking the test. To address concerns about whether people carousing in a nightclub could handle the sudden news if it turned out they were HIV positive, counselors would refuse to test people who were high, drunk, or appeared emotionally unstable.

Apparently, the bathhouse and sex club owners initially expressed concern with health officials about whether this effort might offend customers or even drive them away. Perhaps the fact that in 2014 (10 years later) one of the clubs still touts the availability of free and anonymous rapid HIV tests every Friday and Saturday nights from 10 P.M. to 2 A.M. on its website is an indication of how things actually turned out.[30] A tracking effort between July 2003 and February 2007 revealed that 1,559 rapid HIV tests were administered to gay male patrons of these bathhouses, identifying 33 new cases, a rate of 2.1%. In general, new-case-finding rates of greater than or equal to 1% are considered cost effective, and screening in the baths has substantially exceeded that threshold.[31]

By contrast, consider these dismal results when the place wasn't right. In Denmark in 2009, a government-sponsored pilot program was launched in Copenhagen to supply addicts with free heroin. You would think this offer would be welcomed. It included a doctor's prescription which guaranteed users a pure dose, and since addicts wouldn't have to steal money to buy their drugs, the crime rate was expected to go down. But the addicts weren't "biting." Out of Denmark's estimated 30,000 heroin addicts, only 80 took the government's offer. The problem was the "place." Users had to show up daily at a medical clinic to get their fix, which was then administered and supervised by a doctor. Evidently, this place took all the "fun and freedom" out of it.[32]

10. Work With Existing Distribution Channels

Example: Influencing the Return of Unwanted Drugs to Pharmacies. In the fall of 1999, in response to a request from British Columbia's minister of the environment, pharmaceutical industry associations voluntarily created an organization to administer a medications return program in British Columbia, Canada. The program provides the public with a convenient way to return (at no charge) unused or expired medications, including prescription drugs, nonprescription and herbal products, and vitamin and mineral supplements. Easy-to-find links for participating pharmacies are on the association's website, and information promoting the program is provided on annual recycling calendars, brochures, flyers, bookmarks, and posters. By 2012, 95% of pharmacies were participating, providing convenient access at over 1,098 locations. Many of the pharmacies are open extended hours, and most offer easy access to those with special needs. All containers returned from a pharmacy are tracked by pickup date, weight, and location and stored in a secure location until ready for safe destruction at a licensed destruction facility. The association's annual report indicated that in 2012, 87,429 kg of medication were collected.[33]

SOCIAL FRANCHISING

Social franchising can be described as the application of the principles of franchising originating in the commercial sector for companies like Starbucks and Subway to the nongovernmental organization (NGO) and public sectors . . . for social good. Fundamentally, it is a way to increase distribution channels for an existing program or product, which then increases utilization by offering convenience of access and quality assurance for users. It is a way of scaling up successful solutions and often builds on existing private sector infrastructures including private clinics, pharmacies, and community providers.

The first significant implementation of social franchising was conducted in the 1990s by Population Services, International, (PSI), when they created the Greenstar franchise in Pakistan, which provides family planning, sexual and reproductive health services, maternal and child health services, and tuberculosis diagnosis. Greenstar products and services are now distributed through a nationwide network of over 7,000 franchised clinics and 75,000 retail outlets and community-based distribution sites.[34] Franchising has grown rapidly around the world in the past 20 years, primarily in the health sector, addressing a widely recognized gap in accessibility and quality, especially in low-income countries. Franchise networks most frequently provide services and products related to family planning, sexual and reproductive health services, maternal and child health services, HIV/AIDS diagnosis and treatment, tuberculosis diagnosis and treatment, diarrhea treatment, malaria treatment, and respiratory infections.

Operationally, a *franchisor*, the owner and originator of the franchise brand and policies, offers a *franchisee*, the individual outlet owner, a variety of benefits, including access to new expertise and capital, the ability to replicate a successful model, opportunities for training, use of a highly visible brand, increased promotional activities that then increase clientele and revenue, and the opportunity to expand a range of services offered. In return, franchise members typically pay a franchise fee and maintain certain standards of quality determined by the franchise agency, and may receive funding through grants.

The International Centre for Social Franchising often refers to an inspirational quote from former President Bill Clinton: "Nearly every problem has been solved by someone, somewhere. The frustration is that we can't seem to replicate (those solutions) anywhere else."[35] The organization's mission is to take this challenge on by helping to replicate the most successful social impact projects.

MANAGING DISTRIBUTION CHANNELS

In situations in which tangible objects and services are included in your campaign or program, a network of intermediaries may be needed to reach target audiences through the distribution channel.

Kotler and Roberto describe four types of distribution levels to be considered, illustrated in Figure 12.7.[36] In a *zero-level channel*, there is direct distribution from the social marketer to the target audience. Tangible goods and services are distributed by mail, over the Internet, door to door, or through outlets managed by the social marketing organization (e.g., a health department providing immunizations at community clinics). In

Figure 12.7 Distribution channels of various levels.

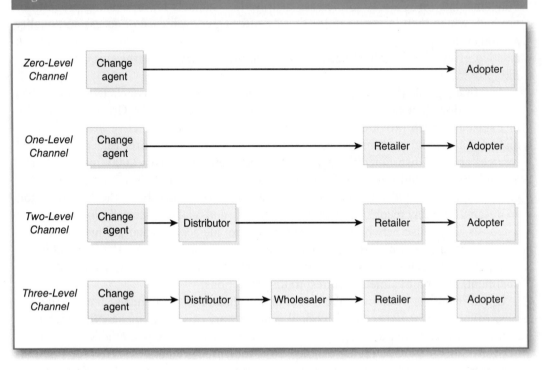

a *one-level channel*, there is one distribution intermediary, most commonly a retailer (e.g., grocery stores where health care officials set up tables for flu shots). In a *two-level channel*, you would be dealing with the local distributor as well as the retailer (e.g., working with distributors of life vests to include safety tips attached to the product). In a *three-level channel*, a national distributor finds local distributors.

Choices regarding distribution channels and levels are made on the basis of variables such as the number of potential target adopters, storage facilities, retail outlet opportunities, and transportation costs, with a focus on choosing the most efficient and cost-effective option for achieving program goals and reaching target audiences. This process can be guided by several principles offered by Coughlan and Stern:[37]

- The purpose of channel marketing is to satisfy end users, which makes it critical that all channel members focus on this and that channels are selected on the basis of the unique characteristic of each market segment.
- Marketing channels "play a role of strategic importance in the overall presence and success a company enjoys in the marketplace."[38] They contribute to the product's positioning and the organization's image, along with the product's features, pricing, and promotional strategies.

- Marketing channels are more than just a way to deliver the product to the customer. They can also be an effective means of adding value to the core product, evidenced, for example, by the fact that employees are often willing to pay a slightly higher price for the convenience of bottled water at a vending machine at a work site than they would in a retail location.
- Issues currently challenging channel managers include increasingly demanding consumers, management of multiple channels, and the globalization of markets.

In the following example from Malcom Gladwell's book *The Tipping Point*, program planners found they had the "perfect" distribution channel and the "perfect" distributors:[39]

In Baltimore, as in many communities with a lot of drug addicts, the city sends out a van stocked with thousands of clean syringes to certain street corners in its inner-city neighborhoods at certain times in the week. The idea is that for every dirty, used needle that addicts hand over, they can get a free clean needle in return. In principle, needle exchange sounds like a good way to fight AIDS, since the reuse of old HIV-infected needles is responsible for so much of the virus's spread. But, at least on first examination, it seems to have some obvious limitations. Addicts, for one, aren't the most organized and reliable of people. So what guarantee is there that they are going to be able to regularly meet up with the needle van? Second, most heroin addicts go through about one needle a day, shooting up at least five or six times—if not more—until the tip of the syringe becomes so blunt that it is useless. That's a lot of needles. How can a van, coming by once a week, serve the needs of addicts who are shooting up around the clock? What if the van comes by on Tuesday, and by Saturday night an addict has run out?

To analyze how well the needle program was working, researchers at Johns Hopkins University began, in the mid-1990s, to ride along with the vans in order to talk to the people handing in needles. What they found surprised them. They had assumed that addicts brought in their own dirty needles for exchange, that IV drug users got new needles the way that you or I buy milk: going to the store when it is open and picking up enough for the week. But what they found was that a handful of addicts were coming by each week with knapsacks bulging with 300 or 400 dirty needles at a time, which is obviously far more than they were using themselves. These men were then going back to the street and selling the clean needles for $1 each. The van, in other words, was a kind of syringe wholesaler. The real retailers were these handfuls of men—these *superexchangers*—who were prowling around the streets and shooting galleries, picking up dirty needles, and then making a modest living on the clean needles they received in exchange.

At first some of the program's coordinators had second thoughts. Did they really want taxpayer-funded needles financing the habits of addicts? But then they realized that they had stumbled inadvertently onto a solution to the limitations of needle exchange programs. "It's a much, much better system," says Tom Valente, who teaches in the Johns Hopkins School of Public Health. "A lot of people shoot on Friday and Saturday night, and they don't necessarily think in a rational way that they need to have clean tools before they go out. The needle exchange program isn't going to be available at that time—and certainly not in the shooting galleries. But these (superexchangers) can be there at times when people are doing drugs and when they need clean syringes. They provide twenty-four seven service, and it doesn't cost us anything."

One of the researchers who rode with the needle vans was an epidemiologist by the name of Tom Junge. He would flag down the superexchangers and interview them. His conclusion is that they represent a very distinct and special group. "They are all very well connected people," Junge says. "They know Baltimore inside and out. They know where to go to get any kind of drug and any kind of needles. They have street savvy. I would say that they are unusually socially connected. They have a lot of contacts. . . . I would have to say the underlying motive is financial or economic. But there is definitely an interest in helping people out." Does that sound familiar? The superexchangers are the Connectors of Baltimore's drug world. What people at Johns Hopkins would like to do is use the superexchangers to start a counter-drug epidemic. What if they took those same savvy, socially connected, altruistic people and gave them condoms to hand out, or educated them in the kinds of health information that drug addicts desperately need to know? Those superexchangers sound as though they have the skills to bridge the chasm between the medical community and the majority of drug users, who are hopelessly isolated from the information and institutions that could save their lives. They sound as if they have the ability to translate the language and ideas of health promotion into a form that other addicts could understand.

ETHICAL CONSIDERATIONS WHEN SELECTING DISTRIBUTION CHANNELS

Issues of equity and unintended consequences are common when planning access strategies. How do working mothers get their children to the free immunization clinic if it is only open on weekday mornings? How do drug addicts get clean needles if they don't have transportation to the exchange site? In these cases, "more" of this place tool may be just the answer, with mobile units, for example, traveling to villages and neighborhoods to reach more of the target population.

Do critics of the ecstasy-testing volunteers at dance clubs have legitimate and higher-priority concerns that this will increase use of the drug? What about those who argue that restricting access (e.g., of alcohol to teens in their homes) leads to more serious consequences (e.g., driving home drunk)? And does a safe gun storage campaign that distributes coupons for lockboxes send a message that having guns is a norm and thereby increase ownership? One strategy to consider when addressing the potential for unintended consequences is to conduct a pilot and measure actual behavior changes, both intended and unintended. These data can then be used to conduct a cost-benefit analysis and help guide decision making for future efforts and potentially a quantifiable rationale for a sustainable effort and expanded markets.

CHAPTER SUMMARY

Place, the third "P," is where and when the target audience will perform the desired behavior, acquire any related tangible goods, and receive any associated services.

Distribution channels, as they are often referred to in the commercial sector, include more than physical locations, with other alternatives that may be more convenient for your target audience, including phone, mail, fax, Internet, mobile units, drive-throughs, home delivery, kiosks, and vending machines.

Your objective with the *place marketing tool* is to develop strategies that will make it as convenient and pleasant as possible for your target audience to perform the behavior, acquire any goods, and receive any services. You are encouraged to consider the following winning strategies:

1. Make the location closer.

2. Extend hours.

3. Be there at the point of decision making.

4. Make the location more appealing.

5. Overcome psychological barriers related to "the place."

6. Be more accessible than the competition.

7. Make accessing the competition more difficult.

8. Be where your target audience shops or dines.

9. Be where your target audience hangs out.

10. Work with existing distribution channels.

And, finally, since this tool is often misunderstood, it is worth repeating that place is *not the same as the communication channel*, which is where your communications will appear (e.g., brochures, radio ads, news stories, personal presentations).

Addressing Opiate Overdose With Naloxone Distribution in Russia

Lessons Learned From Pilot Distribution Models

Foundation Center for Social Development and Information
An Affiliate of Population Services International (PSI)

Background

Opiate overdose is a major cause of mortality among drug users, and in Russia it is the cause of one in every five deaths related to injection drug use, or an estimated 70,000 deaths per year.[40] The focus for this research highlight is on one of the treatment choices, naloxone, a specific opioid receptor antagonist used to reverse an opiate overdose. Although it has been shown to be highly effective in counteracting overdoses and costs under US$1per dose, its availability in most countries, including Russia, has been limited to administration by medical professionals, and it is not commonly included in public

health programs designed for opiate users. Further, a baseline study conducted in 2009 by Population Services International (PSI) in Russia among people who inject drugs found that 67% of respondents had never heard of naloxone, 30.6% had heard of it but never used it, and only 2.4% had previously used it.[41]

Russia's naloxone program worked to increase both demand and supply. To increase demand, activities focused on increasing awareness, interest, and informed use among people who inject drugs and members of their families, while efforts to increase supply focused on influencing more medical specialists to prescribe the drug and more pharmacies to offer it at retail outlets. Three product distribution models were designed, piloted, and evaluated. The structure of these models and the lessons learned from each pilot are the focus of this research highlight, and demonstrate the power of utilizing existing distribution systems. Information for this case was provided by Robert Gray, IDU technical expert at PSI.

Method

Over a period of three years, two cities in Russia were targeted for the pilot project, St. Petersburg and Yekaterinburg. The three alternative distribution models are described below, including their structure and lessons learned from the pilot.

Model One: Free Distribution

Structure; In this implementation model, priority was given to saving lives and reaching high health impact within a short period of time. NGO staff obtained prescriptions from drug treatment specialists and then procured naloxone from pharmacies. Outreach workers provided peer counseling and mini-trainings in overdose symptoms, CPR, and administration of naloxone to people who used drugs. People who used drugs who received the counseling and training were given naloxone at no cost.

Lessons learned: On the plus side, the pilot demonstrated that it was possible to bring an intervention to scale within a short period of time and that it was not resource intensive. In terms of cons, it was a short-term fix, as it did not create linkages to sustainable supplies and might not be replicable in countries where naloxone is permitted to be distributed only by key personnel such as medical professionals.

Model Two: Sustainable Supply Through Private Pharmacies and Drug Treatment Clinics

Structure: This model focuses on involving the private sector pharmacies and drug treatment clinics in providing naloxone, and on building demand among drug users and willingness to pay for the product over the life of the program. NGOs provided trainings on overdose and administration of naloxone for drug treatment specialists and pharmacists, strengthened relationships with municipal medical institutions, influenced drug treatment clinics to provide prescriptions for obtaining naloxone from private pharmacies, and conducted outreach to drug users to build demand for drug treatment and for naloxone.

Lessons learned: On the plus side, this model revealed that drug treatment specialists are well positioned to provide consultation on naloxone use to drug users at risk of an overdose. The model also has greater potential for sustainability and to be more legally acceptable than the free distribution model. In terms of cons, it proved difficult to convince people who used drugs to go to drug treatment clinics to obtain the naloxone prescription, because the clinic would require them to register as a drug user. Further, when using this strategy, it takes more time to establish provider networks, change behavior, and generate demand and willingness to pay.

Model Three: Comprehensive OD Prevention Model

Structure: This model integrated an overdose component into the existing framework of a larger-donor HIV prevention program, introducing naloxone distribution into existing scopes of work for each of the parties involved. It engaged major stakeholders interacting with injection drug users and their families: NGOs, primary healthcare providers, drug treatment professionals, pharmacies, emergency care, and treatment centers for AIDS and tuberculosis (TB).

Lessons learned: On the plus side, this program offered a broader range of access points for naloxone, including by supporting private-sector supply of naloxone. The model successfully engaged health care professionals from other fields (e.g., HIV and TB). And it offered multiple incentives for drug users, including free initial distribution and longer-term subsidies to reduce the price of the product. In terms of cons, it is a resource-intensive model and dependent upon relationships and links between multiple stakeholders.

Conclusions

Program managers report that, through the various models outlined above, a total of 35,794 naloxone ampoules had been distributed by end of Year 3, with an estimated 1,238 lives having been saved. The programs helped to establish a positive dialogue between injection drug users and their family members, representatives of the official medical establishments, NGOs, and the private sector.[42] Program managers concluded that for the Russian context at that time, the third distribution model, the "Comprehensive OD Prevention Model," was the most appropriate and sustainable option, and endorsed inclusion of OD prevention and naloxone distribution into a package of services for people who inject drugs. The model was then introduced in three new sites, intending to be scaled up and replicated in other Russian regions. Program managers added that the experience of the project confirms that overdose prevention programs can be implemented at scale even in heavily regulated environments such as Russia, and are left confident that these models can be replicated in other countries as well. Each country, depending on its own context, should identify the model that is most appropriate.

DISCUSSION QUESTIONS AND EXERCISES

1. To further explore the strategy of being where your target audience hangs out, imagine places where these target audiences hang out that you might consider distribution channels for the services or tangible goods associated with your campaign:

    a. Where could you find groups of seniors so you can give them small, portable pedestrian flags to keep and wave when entering crosswalks?

    b. What would be a good place to distribute condoms to Hispanic farm workers who are having unprotected sex with prostitutes while away from home?

    c. In an effort to increase voting among college students, where could you distribute voter registration packets?

    d. Where could you efficiently provide dog owners a mail-in pet licensing form?

2. These questions were posed in the ethical considerations section of this chapter. Discuss responses to the following:

    a. Do critics of the ecstasy-testing volunteers at dance clubs have legitimate and higher-priority concerns that this will increase use of the drug?

b. What about those who argue that restricting access (e.g., of alcohol to teens in their homes) leads to more serious consequences (e.g., driving home drunk)?

c. Does a safe gun storage campaign that distributes coupons for lockboxes send a message that having guns is a norm and thereby increase ownership?

3. Regarding social franchising, what opportunities do you see that might be considered for existing programs or products?

CHAPTER 12 NOTES

1. U.S. Environmental Protection Agency, *Municipal Solid Waste in the United States: Facts and Figures for 2011* (2011), accessed March 13, 2014, http://www.epa.gov/osw/nonhaz/munici pal/pubs/MSWcharacterization_fnl_060713_2_rpt.pdf.

2. T. Watson, "Dog Waste Poses Threat to Water," *USA Today* (June 6, 2002), accessed February 11, 2007, http://www.usatoday.com/news/science/2002–06–07-dog-usat.htm.

3. Centers for Disease Control and Prevention, "Current Cigarette Smoking Among Adults—United States, 2005–2012," *Morbidity and Mortality Weekly Report* 63, no. 2 (2014): 29–34.

4. H. M. Nathan, S. L. Conrad, P. J. Held, K. P. McCullough, R. E. Pietroski, L. A. Siminoff, and A. O. Ojo, "Organ Donation in the United States," *American Journal of Transplantation* 3, no. 4 (2003): 29–40, accessed February 11, 2007, http://www.blackwell-synergy.com/links/doi/10.1034/j.16006143.3.s4.4.x/full/?cookieSet=1.

5. Fondation Lucie et André Chagnon [website], accessed March 14, 2014, http://www.fon dationchagnon.org/en/news/2014/message-from-the-president-working-tirelessly-to-prevent-poverty.aspx.

6. D. K. Dickinson, J. A. Griffith, R. Michnick Golinkoff, and K. Hirsh-Pasek, "How Reading Books Fosters Language Development Around the World," *Child Development Research* (2012), doi:10.1155/2012/602807.

7. Fondation Lucie et André Chagnon.

8. Personal communication from François Lagarde, March 14, 2014.

9. Personal communication from François Lagarde, March 17, 2014.

10. Delta Dental: Washington Dental Service, "SmileMobile" (n.d.), accessed March 13, 2014, http://www.deltadentalwa.com/Guest/Public/AboutUs/WDS%20Foundation/SmileMobile.aspx.

11. U.S. Census Bureau, "Voting and Registration in the Election of November 2008" (n.d.), accessed February 1, 2011, http://www.census.gov/prod/2010pubs/p20–562.pdf.

12. "Oregon Voter Turnout 85.76% in November," *The Oregonian* (December 4, 2008), accessed February 1, 2011, http://www.oregonlive.com/news/index.ssf/2008/12/oregon_voter_turnout_8567_in_n.html/.

13. J. Wright, "Mail-In Ballots Give Oregon Voters Control," *Seattle Post-Intelligencer* (November 23, 2004), http://seattlepi.nwsource.com/opinion/200682_ore gonvote23.html.

14. Ibid.

15. DanceSafe [website], accessed March 14, 2014, http://www.dancesafe.org/about-us/.

16. Ibid.

17. Ibid.

18. Ibid.

19. City of Los Angeles, California [website], http://www.lacity.org/index.htm.

20. Personal communication from Michelle.mowery@lacity.org, May 20, 2014.

21. Humane Society of the United States, "Pets by the Numbers" (January 30, 2014), accessed March 13, 2014, http://www.humanesociety.org/issues/pet_overpopulation/facts/pet_ownership_statistics.html.

22. Sacramento Society's Prevention of Cruelty to Animals, "Pets on the Net" (n.d.), accessed October 31, 2001, http://www.sspca.org/adopt.html.

23. F. Karimi, "Residents Can Get Tested for HIV as They Wait for Driver's License," *CNN Health* (October 6, 2010), accessed February 1, 2011, http://www.cnn.com/2010/HEALTH/10/06/washington.hiv.testing/index.html.

24. Smith, "How Smart Is Your School Cafeteria? 12 Small Lunchroom Changes That Make a Big Nutritional Difference" (November 16, 2010), accessed July 23, 2011, http://blog.syracuse.com/cny/2010/11/how_smart_is_your_school_cafeteria_12_small_lunchroom_changes_that_make_a_dig_nutritional_difference.html.

25. P. Dawdy, "Broke as a Smoke: Powerful State Legislators Explore Ditching the 25-Foot Rule as Barkeeps Struggle to Weather a Butt-Free Recession," *Seattle Weekly* (September 27, 2006), accessed February 19, 2007, http://www.seattleweekly.com/2006-09-27/news/broke-as-a-smoke.php.

26. Centers for Disease Control and Prevention, "Prevalence and Trends Data: Washington—2013 Tobacco Use," accessed October 8, 2014, http://apps.nccd.cdc.gov/brfss/display.asp?cat=TU&yr=2013&qkey=8161&state=WA.

27. Centers for Disease Control and Prevention, "Behavioral Risk Factor Surveillance System Prevalence and Trends Data: Washington—2012 Tobacco Use," (n.d.), accessed March 13, 2014, http://apps.nccd.cdc.gov/brfss/display.asp?cat=TU&yr=2012&qkey=8161&state=WA.

28. J. Bott, "Karmanos Site to Offer Mammograms at Mall," *Detroit Free Press* (April 28, 1999), accessed http://www.freep.com/news/health/qkamra28.htm. Reprinted with permission.

29. J. Kowal, "Rapid HIV Tests Offered Where Those at Risk Gather: Seattle Health Officials Get Aggressive in AIDS Battle by Heading to Gay Clubs, Taking a Drop of Blood and Providing Answers in 20 Minutes," *Chicago Tribune* (January 2, 2004), accessed July 23, 2011, http://www.aegis.com/news/ct/2004/CT040101.html.

30. P. Kotler and N. Lee, *Marketing in the Public Sector* (Upper Saddle River, NJ: Wharton School, 2006), 97.

31. Personal communication, March 2007. Data from the HIV/AIDS Program, Public Health–Seattle & King County.

32. N. Rytter, "Few Takers for Free Heroin," *The Week* (January 28, 2011), 19.

33. Health Products Stewardship Association, *Annual Report to the Director: 2012 Calendar Year* (June 30, 2013), accessed March 13, 2014, http://www.healthsteward.ca/sites/default/files/HPSA%20BC%20Annual%20Report%202012.pdf.

34. Greenstar Social Marketing [website], accessed March 12, 2014, http://www.greenstar.org.pk/.

35. International Centre for Social Franchising, "About" (n.d.), accessed March 12, 2014, http://www.the-icsf.org/.

36. P. Kotler and E. L. Roberto, *Social Marketing: Strategies for Changing Public Behavior* (New York: Free Press, 1989), 162.

37. T. Coughlan and L. W. Stern, "Market Channel Design and Management, in *Kellogg on Marketing*, ed. D. Iacobucci (New York, NY: Wiley, 2001), 247–267.

38. Ibid., 250.

39. M. Gladwell, *From the Tipping Point: How Little Things Can Make a Big Difference* (Boston: Little, Brown, 2000; copyright by Malcolm Gladwell), 203–206. Reprinted by permission of Little, Brown and Company, Inc.

40. N. N. Ivanets et al., "Mortality Among Drug Addicts in the Russian Federation," *Issues of Drug Treatment*, no. 3 (2008): 105–118; as cited in Foundation Center for Social Development and Information, "RUSSIA: Piloting Naloxone for OD Prevention" (November 2012).

41. PSI Research Division, "Russia (2009): Overdose Prevention Study of Injecting Drug Users (IDUs) in Ekaterinburg and St. Petersburg, Russian Federation. Round 1," *PSI TRaC Summary Report* (2009), http://www.psi.org/research/cat_socialresearch_smr.asp.

42. Foundation Center for Social Development and Information, "RUSSIA: Piloting Naloxone for OD Prevention" (November 2012).

Chapter 13

PROMOTION

DECIDING ON MESSAGES, MESSENGERS, AND CREATIVE STRATEGIES

Think for a moment about how our everyday lives are dominated by commercial enterprise. We wake in the morning to radio and television programmes interspersed with advertising messages, perform our ablutions courtesy of Procter & Gamble and the Body Shop, breakfast with Kellogg's and Quaker, then dress ourselves with the help of Nike, Topshop and Gap. Before we have even left the house, the commercial sector has not only succeeded in getting us to listen to their messages and use their products—they have turned us into walking adverts. . . . Over a century ago, General William Booth asked, "Why should the devil have all the best tunes?" I am not sure about his demonic metaphor, but the idea of learning from success is clearly a good one.

—Professor Gerard Hastings[1]

Consider for a moment the fact that this chapter on promotion is the 13th of 17 chapters in this book. Twelve chapters precede it. It is placed more than two thirds of the way into the journey to complete a social marketing plan. Those who started this book thinking, as many do, that marketing *is* promotion are probably the most surprised. However, we imagine and hope that, after reading the first 12 chapters, you understand that you wouldn't have been ready before now to explore or use this final tool in the marketing mix.

Many of you who are following the planning process are probably eager for the more creative, often fun-filled exercises associated with brainstorming slogans, sketching out logos, picking out colors, even screening potential actors. Others find this the most intimidating, even dreaded, process of all, having experienced in the past that it can be fraught with internal battles over words, colors, and shapes, and in the end, having experienced disappointment and frustration with their final materials or radio and television spots.

This time will be different. You have help. You know your target audience and a lot about them. You have clear behavior objectives in mind and understand what your potential customers really want out of performing the behavior and the barriers that could stop them in their tracks. You know now that this understanding is your inspiration, a gift—one that has already helped you craft a powerful positioning statement, build a product platform, find incentives, and select distribution channels.

In this chapter, you will read about the first three components of a promotional campaign: (1) deciding on intended messages, (2) choosing credible messengers, and (3) 12 tips to consider when developing creative elements of your campaign. Chapter 14 presents the fourth component, selecting communication channels. We think you'll be inspired by this opening story, one that focuses promotional efforts on supporting downstream audiences in becoming credible messengers to influence behaviors of critical midstream and upstream audiences.

MARKETING HIGHLIGHT

Seafood Watch®

Influencing Sustainable Seafood Choices

(2014)

Background

Seafood is one of the leading sources of the world's protein consumed by humans, with 200 billion pounds of fish and shellfish coming out of the ocean each year. But many of the world's major fisheries are in severe decline, and without intervention, global fish stocks will be depleted within a generation. Aquaculture can help relieve this pressure—and just in the past year (2013), more than half of all seafood was farmed—but this activity has its own environmental impact.

The good news is that it's not too late to restore global fisheries. The Monterey Bay Aquarium® seeks to inspire conservation of the oceans and its resources, and its Seafood Watch program creates market incentives for fishing and aquaculture

industries to reduce their environmental impact, actions that will increase the long-term availability of seafood and help protect ocean resources. It has also made it easier for consumers to make sustainable choices through products like consumer guides and mobile apps, the focus for this case highlight.

Target Audiences and Desired Behaviors

The following planned chain of events reflects the program's strategic intent to influence audiences *downstream* (consumers) to request and make purchases that then influence audiences *midstream* (e.g., restaurants, food service companies, grocery stores, and fish markets) to persuade those *upstream* (wholesalers and the fishing/aquaculture industry) to change their practices. Program managers began with the end in mind:

1. Consumers decide to buy more (or only) sustainable seafood.

2. Consumers start asking questions and making requests at restaurants, grocery stores, and fish markets, creating salience for the sustainable seafood issue.

3. These purveyors work with their suppliers to increase availability of sustainable seafood.

4. Suppliers shift purchasing.

5. In response to customer demand from major buyers, the fishing/aquaculture industry changes its harvesting practices or shifts to a different operation.

The priority initial consumer audience in 2004 was identified as "green consumers." New market research in 2010 identified a new, larger audience, those with a propensity to "try" the Seafood Watch program. ("Trying" is defined as being willing to refer to the recommendations at least once when purchasing seafood, and to talk with the person at the fish counter or restaurant about the choices being offered.) These "trialers" are 67.8 million strong and, importantly, may convince others in their circle of influence to try Seafood Watch. Through trialers, Seafood Watch intends to connect with a large, influential, and vocal audience. Thus, the feedback loop to businesses is maintained and their willingness to commit to change is strengthened.

Audience Insights

Perceived barriers to purchasing sustainable seafood were identified as:

- Difficulty adhering to sustainable seafood guidelines
- Disputing of recommendations at the point of sale
- Lack of availability of recommended choices

The primary benefit for this environmentally oriented target audience was to contribute to a sustainable supply of seafood.

Strategies

The tools and resources (*products*) Seafood Watch has created since 1999 tackle many of these barriers head on.

The initiative began with the Seafood Watch Consumer Guides—one for each of six regions in the United States, a national guide, and a sushi guide (see Figure 13.1). More than a promotion, these consumer guides are designed for point-of-purchase decision making and for prompting the question, "Do you sell sustainable seafood?" The most popular seafood options in each region are listed as either green (best choices), yellow (good alternatives), or red (avoid). And to address potential concerns about the credibility of the recommendations, assessment reports, fishery and aquaculture assessment criteria, and other information are posted on seafoodwatch.org. In producing the seafood reports, Seafood Watch uses research published in academic, peer-reviewed journals whenever possible. Other sources of information include government technical publications, fishery management plans

Figure 13.1   Seafood Watch consumer guide.

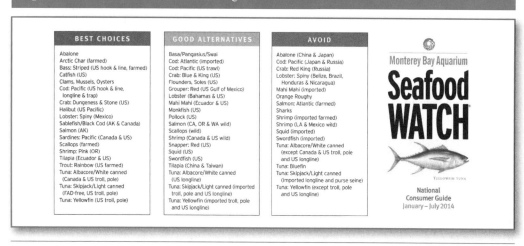

BEST CHOICES	GOOD ALTERNATIVES	AVOID
Abalone	Basa/Pangasius/Swai	Abalone (China & Japan)
Arctic Char (farmed)	Cod: Atlantic (imported)	Cod: Pacific (Japan & Russia)
Bass: Striped (US hook & line, farmed)	Cod: Pacific (US trawl)	Crab: Red King (Russia)
Catfish (US)	Crab: Blue & King (US)	Lobster: Spiny (Belize, Brazil,
Clams, Mussels, Oysters	Flounders, Soles (US)	Honduras & Nicaragua)
Cod: Pacific (US hook & line,	Grouper: Red (US Gulf of Mexico)	Mahi Mahi (imported)
longline & trap)	Lobster (Bahamas & US)	Orange Roughy
Crab: Dungeness & Stone (US)	Mahi Mahi (Ecuador & US)	Salmon: Atlantic (farmed)
Halibut (US Pacific)	Monkfish (US)	Sharks
Lobster: Spiny (Mexico)	Pollock (US)	Shrimp (imported farmed)
Sablefish/Black Cod (AK & Canada)	Salmon (CA, OR & WA wild)	Shrimp (LA & Mexico wild)
Salmon (AK)	Scallops (wild)	Squid (imported)
Sardines: Pacific (Canada & US)	Shrimp (Canada & US wild)	Swordfish (imported)
Scallops (farmed)	Snapper: Red (US)	Tuna: Albacore/White canned
Shrimp: Pink (OR)	Squid (US)	(except Canada & US troll, pole
Tilapia (Ecuador & US)	Swordfish (US)	and US longline)
Trout: Rainbow (US farmed)	Tilapia (China & Taiwan)	Tuna: Bluefin
Tuna: Albacore/White canned	Tuna: Albacore/White canned	Tuna: Skipjack/Light canned
(Canada & US troll, pole)	(US longline)	(imported longline and purse seine)
Tuna: Skipjack/Light canned	Tuna: Skipjack/Light canned (imported	Tuna: Yellowfin (except troll, pole
(FAD-free, US troll, pole)	troll, pole and US longline)	and US longline)
Tuna: Yellowfin (US troll, pole)	Tuna: Yellowfin (imported troll, pole	
	and US longline)	

Monterey Bay Aquarium

Seafood WATCH

YELLOWFIN TUNA

National Consumer Guide
January – July 2014

Source: Monterey Bay Aquarium.

and supporting documents, and other scientific reviews of ecological sustainability. New and updated recommendations are issued monthly on the website, and the consumer guide is updated twice a year. In 2009, a new app was launched, making it easier to get up-to-date recommendations for seafood and sushi, and the app is now available on Android phones and tablets as well. The app offers the ability to sort seafood by rating or to search for a specific seafood item (see Figure 13.2).

Pocket guides, including shipping, are free to the public, as is the mobile application (*price*). A link to download the app is provided on seafoodwatch.org. Seafood Watch also communicates and expands the reach of science-based recommendations through zoos, aquariums, educators, chefs, and others who are helping to build awareness about ocean-friendly seafood choices by distributing consumer guides and furthering messaging (*place*).

Seafood Watch raises consumer awareness primarily through its consumer guides, website, mobile app, presence on social

Figure 13.2   Seafood Watch app.

media, and special events (*promotion*). As the program has gained credibility, it has been featured in a broad array of popular media—from Oprah Winfrey's *O* magazine to Martha Stewart's television program, and from the *New York Times* and *Time* magazine to websites including NationalGeographic. com, TreeHugger.com, and Grist.org.

Results

Summary output and outcome highlights for consumers, partnership, and retailers were shared by Monterey Bay Aquarium program staff.[2]

Consumer Outputs and Outcomes

- *Consumer guides.* By 2014, more than 45 million guides had reached the pockets of consumers across the United States. Most had been distributed by partners in epicenters, including more than 7 million to visitors at the Monterey Bay Aquarium alone. Each year, more than 100,000 guides are inserted or reprinted in publications, with 140,000 having been distributed in 2013.
- *Website.* In 2013, there were 1,059,519 unique visitor sessions to seafoodwatch.org.
- *Special events.* Annual Cooking for Solutions events are attended by more than 15,000 people, and additional presentations at various conferences, trade shows, and special events reached an audience of more than 40,000 in 2013.
- *Outcomes.* Findings from a 2010 survey of 19,077 adults, representative of the U.S. population, indicated that 39.8% referred to the Seafood Watch program when making purchases.

Partnership Outcomes

By 2014, more than 150 restaurants and retailers had partnered with Seafood Watch and have pledged to not serve "avoid list" items, and to educate their customers and colleagues about the issues around seafood sustainability. Another 1,000 businesses at more than 100,000 locations use Seafood Watch recommendations. More than 100 zoos, aquariums, science museums, nature centers, and other nonprofits have partnered with the Seafood Watch program to promote sustainable seafood messaging. More than 50 culinary spokespeople share messaging at various events, conferences, and trainings and through social media.

Retail Outcomes

Monterey Bay Aquarium partners with the nation's two largest food service providers, Compass Group North America and ARAMARK, to help shift their purchase of millions of pounds of seafood per year toward more sustainable options. These companies have accounts at universities, sports venues, restaurant chains, and thousands of other locations across the United States.

In 2010, the Monterey Bay Aquarium and Blue Ocean Institute partnered with Whole Foods Markets, who on Earth Day 2012 removed all "avoid list" wild-caught seafood from their stores. Seafood Watch is also partnering with Mars Petcare US to meet its 2020 target of 100% sustainable seafood sourcing for its pet food ingredients. Its SHEBA® Entrées for Cats product line is the first to use only farmed or wild-caught fish from environmentally responsible sources. Additionally, Seafood Watch science is informing the purchasing decisions of companies including Target, Safeway, Wolfgang Puck Catering, and others across North America—more than 100,000 retail and food service outlets.

PROMOTION: THE FOURTH "P"

Promotions are persuasive communications designed and delivered to inspire your target audience to action.

You will be highlighting your product's benefits, features, and any associated tangible goods and services. You will be touting any monetary and nonmonetary incentives. And you will be letting target adopters know where and when they can access any tangible goods and services included in your program's effort and/or where you are encouraging them to perform the desired behavior (e.g., recycle motor oil). In this step, you create the voice of your brand and decide how you will establish a dialogue and build relationships with your customer.[3]

STEP 7: DEVELOP A PROMOTION STRATEGY

Developing this communication strategy is the last component of Step 7, developing a strategic marketing mix. Your planning process includes four major decisions:

1. *Messages:* What you want to communicate, inspired by what you want your target audience to do, know, and believe

2. *Messengers:* Who will deliver your messages or be perceived to be sponsoring or supporting your offer

3. *Creative strategy:* What you will actually say and show and how you will say it

4. *Communication channels:* Where and when your messages will appear (distinct, of course, from distribution channels)

This chapter discusses strategies for developing messages and choosing messengers and presents 12 tips for developing creative strategies ("how to say it"). As noted earlier, Chapter 14 covers communication channels.

A WORD ABOUT THE CREATIVE BRIEF

One of the most effective ways to establish clear messages, choose credible messengers, inspire winning creative strategies, and select effective communication channels is to develop a document called a creative brief, usually one to two pages in length.[4] It helps ensure that communications will be meaningful (pointing out benefits that make the product desirable), believable (the product will deliver on the promised benefits), and distinctive (how your offer is a better choice than competing behaviors).[5] Its greatest contribution is that it helps ensure that all team members, especially those in advertising and public relations firms working on the campaign, are in agreement with communication objectives and strategies prior to more costly development and production of communication materials. Typical elements of a creative brief are illustrated in the following section, and a sample creative brief is featured in Table 13.1.

Table 13.1 Creative Brief for a Youth Tobacco Prevention Campaign
Purpose and Focus:
Reduce tobacco use among youth with a focus on addictive components.
Target Audience Description and Insights:
Middle school and high school youth who don't currently smoke or chew tobacco, although they may have experimented with it in the past. They are vulnerable, however, to using tobacco because they have family members and friends who smoke or chew. They know many of the facts about the consequences of using tobacco. They've been exposed to them in health classes and may even have experienced the reality with family members who have smoking-related illnesses or who have died from smoking. The problem is, they don't believe it will happen to them. They don't really believe they will get addicted. There is much peer pressure to fit in by smoking. These youth have also heard that smoking is a great stress relief and is an appealing way to pass the time. Some think kids who smoke look older and cool.
Communication Objectives:
To Know: Addiction is real and probable.
To Believe: Smoking-related illnesses are shocking, "gross," and painful.
To Do: Refuse to try cigarettes or chew.
Benefits to Promise:
You will have a longer, healthier, and happier life, free of tobacco addiction.
Supports to Promise:
Real stories from real people who started smoking at a young age
Stories of personal loss involving a family member's dying or living with or dying from a smoking-related illness
Graphic visuals depicting real, shocking, and "gross" consequences to the body
Real facts from the American Cancer Society and surgeon general
Style or Tone:
Credible, realistic, and serious
Openings:
Engaging in social media including Facebook, Instagram, Twitter
Playing video games
Listening to the radio
Watching television
Surfing the Internet
Talking with friends
Positioning:
People who smoke are risking their health and hurting their future, families, and friends. It's not worth it.

Purpose of communications: This is a brief statement that summarizes the purpose and focus of the social marketing effort, taken from Step 1 in your plan.

Target audience: This section presents a brief description of the target audience in terms of key variables determined in Step 3. Most commonly, it will include a demographic and geographic profile of the target audience. It is helpful to include what you know about your audience's current knowledge, beliefs, perceived barriers, and behaviors relative to the desired behavior as well as to competing ones. Ideally, it describes the target's current stage of change and anything else that you think is special about them.

Communication objectives: This section specifies what you want your target audience to *know* (think), *believe* (feel), and/or *do* (behavior), based on exposure to your communications. This can be taken directly from decisions made in Step 4. (Social marketing campaigns will always have a behavior objective, and often have both a knowledge and belief objective.)

Positioning statement: The product positioning established earlier in Step 6 is presented here. This provides guidance to those selecting images and graphics and developing script and copy points.

Benefits to promise: Key benefits the audience hopes they will receive from adopting the behavior were identified as the *core product* when developing the product platform in Step 7. The primary benefit is sometimes expressed in terms of a cost that the audience can avoid by adopting the desired behavior (e.g., stiff penalties for drinking and driving).

Support for the promise: This section refers to a brief list of additional benefits and highlights from product, price, and place strategies established earlier in Step 7. The ones to be highlighted are those that would most help convince the target audience that they can perform the desired behavior, that the benefits are likely, and that they exceed perceived costs. This section also includes any available testimonials.

Style and tone: Come to some agreement on any recommended guidelines about the style and tone for creative executions. Also note whether there are any existing graphic standards or related efforts that should be taken into consideration (e.g., the logo and taglines used for any current similar or competing efforts).

Openings: This final important section will be helpful to those selecting and planning communication channels. Siegel and Doner describe openings as "the times, places, and situations when the audience will be most attentive to, and able to act on, the message."[6] Input for this section will come from profiles and audience behaviors explored in Step 5 (barriers benefits and motivators). Additional input may come from secondary and expert resources on the target audience's lifestyle and media habits.

MESSAGE STRATEGY

At this point, you are focused on the content of your communications, not the ultimate slogans, scripts, or headlines. That comes later. What those developing your creative strategies need to know first is what responses you want from your target audience. In our social marketing model, you've already done the hard work here and can simply fill in the blanks to the following by refining and elaborating on campaign objectives established earlier in Step 4 and referencing barriers, benefits, motivators, and your competition from Step 5. Bullet points are usually adequate.

What Do You Want Your Target Audience to Do?

What specific desired behavior is your campaign focused on (e.g., get an HIV/AIDS test three to six months after having had unprotected sex)? It will include any immediate calls to action (e.g., call this toll-free number for locations in your area for free, rapid HIV/AIDS tests). If your behavior objective was stated in fairly broad terms (e.g., practice natural yard care techniques), this is the time to break these down into more single, simple doable messages (e.g., leave grass clippings on the lawn).

What Do You Want Them to Know?

Select key facts and information regarding your offer that should be included in campaign messages. If you are offering tangible goods or services related to your campaign (e.g., free quart-sized resealable plastic bags at security checkpoints), you will want messages that inform target audiences *where and when they can be accessed.* There may be key points you want to make on *how to perform* the behavior (e.g., the limit for carry-on liquids is 3 ounces, and they must fit in a quart-sized resealable plastic bag). To highlight benefits of your offer, you may decide that a key point you want your audience to know relates to *statistics on risks* associated with competing behaviors (e.g., makeup and other liquids not in these bags will be taken and discarded) and *benefits you promise* (e.g., having liquids in the appropriate containers ahead of time can save you and fellow passengers up to 20 minutes in lines).

What Do You Want Them to Believe?

This question is different from what you want your target audience to know. This is about what you want your target audience to believe and/or feel as a result of your key messages. Your best inspiration for these points will be your barriers and benefits research. What did they say when asked why they weren't planning to vote (e.g., "My vote won't make a difference")? Why do they think they are safe to drive home after drinking (e.g., "I've done it before and was perfectly fine")? Why are they hesitant to talk with their teen about suicide (e.g., "I might make him more likely to do it")? These are points you will want your communications to counter. And what was their response when you asked what would motivate them to exercise five days a week (e.g., "believing I would sleep better"), fix a leaky toilet (e.g., saving 200 gallons of water a day), or take the bus to work (e.g., having Wi-Fi available for the duration)? These are points you'll want to put front and center.

Example: Reducing Binge Drinking on College Campuses

To further illustrate these communication objectives, we will use a campaign developed by students at Syracuse University, one that won first prize in the 2009 National Student Advertising Competition sponsored by the Century Council, in which over 140 schools competed. The assignment was to develop and present a campaign to curb the dangerous overconsumption of alcohol on college campuses. (A full description of contest entry materials can be found at http://www.centurycouncil.org/binge-drinking.)[7]

The student team's formative research included 1,556 in-depth surveys reaching all 50 states, 75 expert interviews, and 15 journals documenting sober and drunk weekends. The first revelation was "difference of opinions," with 92% of college students rejecting the definition of "binge drinking" as having five or more drinks (male) or four or more drinks (female) in about two hours. Students were quick to mention, however, that they were well aware of the negative consequences of drinking too much, and that there was definitely a line between "drinking" and "drinking too much." As one student put it, "There's always that one drink—that one shot that I wish I didn't have. It always makes things go downhill. Always." The problem, as students defined it, was knowing when they "crossed the line." That's when things went wrong.

The team found out what didn't work—statistics and authoritarian messages. And they learned that students got smarter about how they consumed alcohol by the time they were juniors and seniors. The team

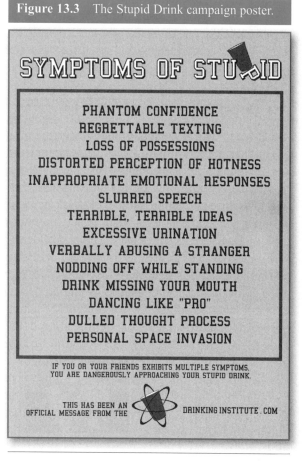

Figure 13.3   The Stupid Drink campaign poster.

Source: Courtesy of the Century Council.

saw their job as getting students to progress more quickly to that ability to moderate. Their message strategy was developed to do just that.

What Did They Want Students to Do? The Syracuse students wanted their campaign to influence students to refuse that "next drink," the one that would take them "over the line."

What Did They Need Them to Know? They wanted them to recognize that the point between drinking and drinking too much is actually . . . a drink.

What Did They Need Them to Believe? They wanted them to believe that by refusing that drink that would take them over the line, they would avoid negative consequences, ones their research indicated were "all too familiar" to their target audience and made them feel stupid: "sending drunk texts"; "blacking out"; "getting a DUI"; "ending up in an unwanted hookup"; "throwing up"; "arguing with my girlfriend"; "falling down stairs"; "acting like an idiot."

With this as their inspiration, the students developed a creative strategy, one that would identify and stigmatize the one drink that would separate enjoyable drinking from the negative consequences of "drinking too much." They called it "The Stupid Drink" (see Figure 13.3).

One-Sided Versus Two-Sided Messages

A one-sided message usually just praises the product, while a two-sided one also points out its shortcomings. In this spirit, Heinz ran the message, "Heinz Ketchup is slow good," and Listerine ran the message, "Listerine tastes bad twice a day."[8]

Intuitively, you might think that the one-sided presentations would be more effective (e.g., "Three out of four students drink fewer than four drinks at one sitting"). But research suggests that one-sided messages tend to work better with audiences who are initially favorably predisposed to your product. If your audience is currently "opposed" to your idea or has suspicions or negative associations, a two-sided argument might work better (e.g., "Although 25% of students drink more than four drinks at one sitting, most of us don't"). Furthermore, an organization launching a new brand whose other products are well accepted might think of favorably mentioning the existing products and then going on to praise the new one (e.g., "Click It or Ticket has saved lives, and now Drive Hammered, Get Nailed will too"). Research also indicates that two-sided messages tend to be more effective with better-educated audiences and/or those who are likely to be exposed to counterpropaganda. By mentioning a minor shortcoming in the product, you can take the edge off this communication from the competitor, much as a small discomforting inoculation now prevents a greater sickness later. But you must take care to inject only enough negative vaccine to make the buyer resistant to counterpropaganda, not to your own product.[9]

Example: Booster Seats as a Better Alternative

While great strides have been made to protect infants and toddlers in a motor vehicle crash, preschoolers and young children remain at high risk of injury. The U.S. Centers for Disease Control and Prevention report that many of the nation's children under age 12 still either ride in motor vehicles unprotected or use adult seatbelts that do not fit them properly.[10] Seatbelts alone can cause serious internal injuries and even death. Booster seats raise the child so that the lap and shoulder belts fit correctly. A booster seat provides a safe transition from child seats that have their own harness systems to adult lap and shoulder belts. And the ad in Figure 13.4 presents an example of a two-sided message encouraging proper restraints.

Figure 13.4   Wanting parents to see booster seats as less costly than the competition.

Source: Reprinted with permission of Harborview Injury Prevention and Research Center.

Messages Relative to Stages of Change

Messages will also be guided by your target audience's current stage of change. As mentioned in Chapter 5 on target audiences, the marketer's role is to move target adopters to the next stage, influencing precontemplators to become contemplators, contemplators to take action, and those in action to make it a habit (maintenance). Most important, there are different recommended message strategies for each stage.[11]

For *precontemplators*, your major emphasis is on making sure your target audience is aware of the costs of competing behaviors and the benefits of the new one. These are often stated using statistics and facts, especially those that your target audience was not aware of—ones that serve as a wake-up call. When these facts are big news, they can often move some target audience members very quickly through subsequent stages—all the way to maintenance in some cases (e.g., when it was discovered that aspirin given to children for flu is related to a potentially fatal disease called Reye's syndrome).

For *contemplators* (now that they are "awake"), your message options include encouraging them to at least try the new behavior and/or restructure their environment to make adoption easier (e.g., put a compost container under the kitchen sink). You'll want to dispel any myths (e.g., air bags are as good as seatbelts) and potentially address any barriers, such as a concern they have about their ability to successfully perform and maintain the behavior.

For those *in action*, you'll want them to start to see the benefits of having "gotten out of bed." Perhaps you will be acknowledging that they reached targeted milestones (e.g., 30 days without a cigarette) or persuading them to use prompts to ensure sustainability (e.g., put the laminated card to track monthly breast self-exams in the shower) or sign pledges or commitments to "keep up the good work." Your messages will target a tendency to return to old habits and at the same time prepare them to create a new one.

For those in *maintenance*, you still have a role to play, for as you learned earlier, behavior change is spiral in nature, and we can easily regress back to any of the stages—even go "back to sleep." This is the group whose behavior you want to recognize, congratulate, feature, and reward. You want to be sure they are realizing the promised benefits, and you may want to occasionally remind them of the long-term gains they are bound to receive or contribute to (e.g., a message on a utility bill that selectively thanks residents for helping to reduce peak hour electrical consumption by 6%).

MESSENGER STRATEGY

Who your target audience perceives to be delivering your message and what they think of this particular messenger can make or break the deal. And this is the right time to be choosing the messenger, as this decision will have important implications when you develop the creative strategy as well as select communication channels. You have six major messenger options (sole sponsor, partners, spokespersons, endorsements, midstream audiences, mascot), described next, followed by considerations for choosing.

The sponsoring organization can be the *sole sponsor*, with campaign communications highlighting the organization's name (somewhere). A quick audit of social marketing campaigns is likely to indicate a public sector agency sponsor (e.g., the EPA promoting energy-efficient appliances) or a nonprofit organization (e.g., the American Cancer Society urging colon cancer screenings). Although it is not as common, the sole sponsor might be a for-profit organization (e.g., Safeco Insurance promoting "10 Tips to Wildfire Defense").

For many efforts, there will be *partners* involved from the beginning in developing, implementing, and perhaps funding the campaign. In this scenario, target audiences may not be certain of the main or actual sponsors. These partners may form a coalition or just a project, one where the target audience may or may not be aware (or clear) what organizations are sponsoring the effort (e.g., a water quality consortium that includes utilities, departments of health, and an environmental advocacy group). In 2006, for example, a public, private, and nonprofit partnership was formed to influence 10,000 of the estimated 50,000 unbanked households in San Francisco to open a bank account. Estimates were that the average unbanked household was spending 5% of its income per year on check cashing alone, relying on check cashers, pawnshops, payday lenders, and other fringe financial services charging high fees and interest rates. City officials were able to persuade 75% of the banks and credit unions in the city to offer what were branded Bank on San Francisco accounts. Even those with a poor banking history were encouraged to open these "second-chance" accounts offering a low- or no-cost product with no minimum balance requirement, accepting consular identification, and waiving one set of overdraft fees per client. Two years after the program launched, more than 31,000 Bank on San Francisco accounts had been opened.[12]

Some organizations and campaigns make effective use of *spokespersons* to deliver the messages, often achieving higher attention and recall as well as increased credibility. In 2006, for example, Barack Obama traveled to Kenya and received a public HIV test. He then spoke about his trip on World AIDS Day:

> So we need to show people that just as there is no shame in going to the doctor for a blood test or a CAT scan or a mammogram, there is no shame in going for an HIV test. Because while there was once a time when a positive result gave little hope, today the earlier you know, the faster you can get help. My wife Michelle and I were able to take the test on our trip to Africa after the Centers for Disease Control informed us that by getting a simple 15-minute test, we may have encouraged as many as half-a-million Kenyans to get tested as well.[13]

Some programs have used entertainers to draw attention to their effort (e.g., Willie Nelson for the Don't Mess With Texas litter prevention campaign). The best choice would be someone highly recognized and appropriate for the effort. This strategy is not without risk, however, as there is a chance the celebrities you choose might lose popularity or, even worse, get caught in a scandal or embarrassing situation, as when Willie Nelson was arrested for drug possession.[14] You may want to include *endorsements* from outside organizations, which are often then seen as one of the messengers. These can range from simply including an organization's name or logo in your communications to displaying more formal testimonials in support of your campaign's facts and recommendations (e.g., the American Medical Association's verifying that a public health department's statistics on the dangers of secondhand tobacco smoke are scientifically based). In January 2009, Oprah Winfrey gave a big on-air boost for Starbucks' campaign to encourage volunteerism, called "I'm In," which encourages customers to pledge five hours of volunteer work to an organization of their choosing. Their goal, which seemed ambitious at the time, was to raise pledges for 1 million hours of service. By February 4, 2011, they had received pledges for more than 1.3 million hours.[15]

It may be very advantageous to engage *midstream audiences*, who typically have a closer relationship with your target, to be your messengers. Soul Sense of Beauty, for example, is an outreach program that trains hairstylists, considered confidants by many, to talk to their clients about health issues such as the threat and prevention of breast cancer. Hair salons evidently hold special meaning for African American women, the target audience for this effort. To many, the salons represent a place where women can go to be pampered and cared for consistently. Although the salon setting is important to the delivery of health messages, including videos and printed material, it is the relationship between the client and her stylist that creates the magic. After all, this confidant is likely to be someone she has had a personal history with for years, and since she "generally stands 6–8 inches from a woman's ear, who better to whisper some potentially lifesaving pearls of wisdom?"[16]

Finally, there is always the option of creating a *mascot* to represent the brand, like Smokey Bear or McGruff the Crime Dog. Others have used current popular characters such as Sesame Street's Elmo, who is featured in a *Ready, Set, Brush Pop-Up Book* intended to feature the fun side of good oral health habits (e.g., a wheel shows how much toothpaste you should use, and there is a pop-up whose teeth can be brushed with an attached toothbrush).[17]

How Do You Choose?

In the end, you want your target audience to see the messenger, or messengers, as a credible source for the message. Three major factors have been identified as key to source credibility: expertise, trustworthiness, and likability.[18]

Expertise is the perceived knowledge the messenger has to back the claim. For a campaign encouraging 12-year-olds to receive the new human papillomavirus (HPV) vaccine to help prevent cervical cancer, the American Academy of Pediatrics was an important messenger, in addition to local health care providers. *Trustworthiness* is related to how objective and honest the source is perceived to be. Friends, for example, are more trusted than strangers, and people who are not paid to endorse a product are viewed as more trustworthy than people who are paid.[19] This is why for-profit organizations often need the partnership or at least the endorsement of a public agency or nonprofit organization, with target audiences being innately skeptical about the commercial sector's motive (e.g., a pharmaceutical company encouraging childhood immunizations). *Likability* describes the source's attractiveness, with qualities such as candor, humor, and naturalness making a source more likable.

The most credible source, of course, would be the option scoring highest on all three dimensions. Perhaps that's what inspired the strategy in the following example.

Example: The Meth Project in Montana

The United Nations has identified methamphetamine abuse as a growing global pandemic. Law enforcement departments across the United States rank meth as the number-one crime problem in America. In response to this growing public health crisis, Montana rancher Thomas M. Siebel established the Meth Project to significantly reduce meth use through public service messaging, community action, and public policy initiatives.[20]

The state of Montana, where the Meth Project was first initiated, ranks among the top 10 states nationally in treatment admissions per capita for methamphetamine. The social costs reported on the project's website are staggering and the human costs incalculable: 52% of children in foster care are there because of meth, costing the state $12 million a year; 50% of adults in prison are there because of meth-related crime, costing the state $43 million a year; and 20% of adults in treatment are there for meth addiction, costing the state $10 million a year.

The Meth Project, launched in 2005, focuses on informing potential meth consumers about the product's attributes and risks. The integrated program consists of an ongoing, research-based marketing campaign—supported by community outreach and public policy initiatives—that realistically and graphically communicates the risks of methamphetamine use.

At the core of the Meth Project's effort is research-validated, high-impact advertising with the tagline "Not Even Once" and bold images that communicate the risks of meth use. Television, print, radio, and a documentary feature testimonials from youth meth users (see Figure 13.5). Approaching meth use as a consumer product marketing problem, the project aims to unsell meth. It organizes a broad range of com-

Figure 13.5   The primary messengers for this successful effort are youth meth users.

Source: Montana Meth Project [website], accessed March 26, 2007, http://www.montanameth.org/About_Us/index.php.

munity outreach programs to mobilize the people of Montana to assist in meth awareness and prevention activities. Through its Paint the State art contest, thousands of teens and their families were prompted to create highly visible public art with a strong anti-meth message. Today (2014), the project is a program of the national nonprofit organization The Partnership at Drugfree.org and has been adopted by other states including Colorado, Georgia, Hawaii, Idaho, and Wyoming.

CREATIVE STRATEGY

Your creative strategy will translate the content of your desired messages to specific communications. These will include everything from logos, typeface, taglines, headlines, copy, visuals, and colors in printed materials to script, actors, scenes, and sounds in broadcast media. You will be faced with choosing between informational appeals that elaborate on behaviors and their benefits and emotional appeals using fear, guilt, shame, love, or surprise. Your goal is to develop (or approve) communications that will capture the attention of your target audience and persuade them to adopt the desired behavior. We present 12 tips in these next sections for you to consider and to help you and others decide.

Creative Tip 1: Keep It Simple and Clear

Given a social marketing campaign's inherent focus on behaviors, try to make your instructions simple and clear.[21] Assume, for a moment, that your target audience is interested in adopting, even eager to adopt, the behavior. Perhaps it was something you said or something they were already inclined to do and they are just waiting for clear instructions. Messages like this are probably familiar to you. "Eat five or more fruits and vegetables a day." "Wash your hands long enough to sing the Happy Birthday song twice."

"Move right for sirens and lights." "Check your fire alarm batteries when you reset your clocks in the fall and spring." Consider how easy these messages make it for you to know whether you have performed the desired behavior and can therefore count on receiving the promised benefits. Often visual instructions can help make the behavior seem simple and clear. You have, no doubt, seen many versions of messages in hotel rooms asking us to let staff know if we are happy to sleep on our sheets another night and to reuse our towels. Notice how quickly you know what to do in a hotel with a sign such as the one in Figure 13.6.

Figure 13.6 Visual graphics make it easy and quick to know what to do.

Creative Tip 2: Focus on Audience Benefits

Since, as Roman and Maas suggest, people don't buy products but instead buy expectations of benefits,[22] creative strategies should highlight benefits your target audience wants (most) and expects in return for costs associated with performing the behavior. This will be especially effective when the perceived benefits already outweigh perceived costs. The target audience just needs to be prompted and reminded, as they were in the following example, shared by Mary Shannon Johnstone, a photographer and a tenured associate professor at Meredith College in Raleigh, North Carolina, with a passion for saving the lives of homeless dogs.

Example: Landfill Dogs

These are not just cute pictures of dogs. [See Figures 13.7 and 13.8.] These are dogs who have been homeless for at least two weeks, and now face euthanasia if they do not find a home. Each week for 18 months (late 2012–early 2014) I bring one dog from the county animal shelter and photograph him/her at the local landfill. The landfill site is used for two reasons. First, this is where the dogs will end up if they do not find a home. Their bodies will be buried deep in the landfill among our trash. These photographs offer the last opportunity for the dogs to find homes. The second reason for the landfill location is because the county animal shelter falls under the same management as the landfill. This government structure reflects a societal value; homeless cats and dogs are just another waste stream. However, this landscape offers a metaphor of hope. It is a place of trash that has been transformed into a place of beauty. I hope the viewer also sees the beauty in these homeless, unloved creatures. As part of this photographic process, each dog receives a car ride, a walk, treats, and about 2 hours of much needed individual attention. My goal is to offer an individual face to the souls that are lost because of animal overpopulation, and give these animals one last chance. This project will continue for one year, so that we can see the landscape change, but the constant stream of dogs remains the same.[23]

Creative Tip 3: When Using Fear, Follow Up With Solutions and Use Credible Sources

Social marketers frequently debate whether or not to use "fear appeals." Some researchers suggest that part of the reason is the lack of distinction between a fear appeal and what might better be called a "threat appeal."[24] They argue that threats simply illustrate undesirable consequences of certain behaviors (e.g., cancer from smoking) and that the emotion triggered may in fact not be fear, which some worry can immobilize the audience.

Rob Donovan, Professor of Behavioral Research at Curtin University in Australia, posted on the Georgetown Social Marketing Listserve in 2013 that "the issue is not so much whether fear, disgust, etc. work or not—but under what conditions and for whom are they appropriate, and when might they be counterproductive."[25] Kotler and Roberto point to research by Sternthal and Craig suggesting that decisions to execute fear-based messages should take several factors into account:[26]

- A strong fear-based appeal works best when it is accompanied by solutions that are both effective and easy to perform. Otherwise, you may be better off with a moderate appeal to fear (see Figure 13.9).

Figure 13.7 "This landfill is where I'll end up if I don't find a home."

Source: Shannon Johnstone, Associate Professor, Meredith College.

Figure 13.8 "I found a home!"

Source: Shannon Johnstone, Associate Professor, Meredith College.

Figure 13.9   A fear appeal followed by a solution.

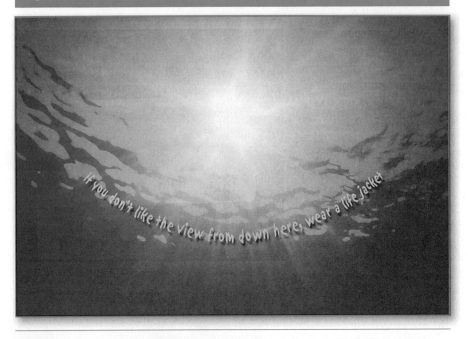

Source: Reprinted with permission of Children's Hospital and Regional Medical Center, Seattle, Washington.

Figure 13.10   A fear appeal from a credible source: "The surgeon general warns that smoking is a frequent cause of wasted potential and fatal regret."

Source: Image courtesy of www.adbusters.org.

- A strong fear-based appeal may be most persuasive to those who have previously been unconcerned about a particular problem. Those who already have some concern may perceive a message of fear as going too far, which will inhibit their change of attitudes or behaviors.
- An appeal to fear may work better when it is directed toward someone who is close to a potential target adopter than it is when directed to the target adopter. This may explain some research indicating that fear appeals are more effective when they are directed toward family members of the target audience.[27]

- The more credible the source, the more persuasive the fear-based appeal. A more credible source reduces the chances that the audience will discount or underestimate the fear-based appeal (see Figure 13.10).

Creative Tip 4: Try for Messages That Are Vivid, Concrete, and Personal

McKenzie-Mohr and Smith believe one of the most effective ways to ensure attention and memorability is to present information that is vivid, personal, and concrete.[28] They point to a variety of ways to make this happen.

Vivid information, they explain, increases the likelihood that a message will stand out against all the other information competing for our attention. Furthermore, because it is vivid, we are more likely to remember it at a later time. For example, one assessor conducting home energy audits was trained to present vivid analogies:

> You know, if you were to add up all the cracks around and under these doors here, you'd have the equivalent of a hole the size of a football in your living room wall. Think for a moment about all the heat that would escape from a hole that size.[29]

Information that is *personalized* uniquely addresses your target audience's preferences, wants, and needs, fully informed by their perceived barriers to and benefits of doing the behavior. For example, McKenzie-Mohr and Smith have a suggestion for utilities on how they might promote energy conservation: Show the percentage of home energy by use item. Rather than using bars for the graph, replace them with a picture of the item itself (furnace, water heater, major appliances, lighting, etc.) and the corresponding energy use in the home.[30]

McKenzie-Mohr and Smith also illustrate information that is *concrete* with an example of a more powerful way to depict waste. Instead of stating that Californians each produce 1,300 pounds of waste annually, Shawn Burn at California Polytechnic State University depicts Californians' annual waste as "enough to fill a two-lane highway, ten feet deep, from Oregon to the Mexican border."[31]

We think the postcard shown in Figure 13.11, used for a youth

Figure 13.11 A vivid, personal, and concrete creative strategy.

This is the size of the hole they'll cut in your throat if you continue to smoke.

Source: Washington Department of Health.

tobacco prevention campaign in Washington State, demonstrates that a creative strategy can be vivid, personal, and concrete.

Creative Tip 5: Make Messages Easy to Remember

The magic of persuasive communications is to bring your messages to life in the minds of the target audience. And as Kotler and Keller reveal, every detail matters. Consider, they suggest, how the legendary private sector ad taglines listed in Table 13.2 were able to bring to life the brand themes listed on the left. Consider, as well, how familiar many or most of them (still) are to you.

In their book *Made to Stick: Why Some Ideas Survive and Others Die*, the Heath brothers suggest six basic traits of sticky ideas—ones that are understood and remembered.[32] Note that they even make the six traits sticky by having them almost, but not quite, spell the word *success*:

1. **S**implicity: The Golden Rule

2. **U**nexpectedness: Southwest: the low-cost airline

3. **C**oncreteness: John Kennedy's "A man on the moon by the end of the decade"

4. **C**redibility: Ronald Reagan's "Before you vote, ask yourself if you are better off today than you were four years ago."[33]

5. **E**motions: "Don't Mess With Texas"

6. **S**tories: David and Goliath

Table 13.2 Sample Ad Taglines

Brand Theme	Ad Tagline
Our hamburgers are bigger.	Where's the Beef? (Wendy's restaurants)
Our tissue is softer.	Please, Don't Squeeze the Charmin (Charmin bathroom tissue)
No hard sell, just a good car.	Drivers Wanted (Volkswagen automobiles)
We don't rent as many cars, so we have to do more for our customers.	We Try Harder (Avis auto rental)
We provide long-distance phone service.	Reach Out and Touch Someone (AT&T telecommunications)

Source: P. Kotler and K. Keller, *Marketing Management*, 12th ed. (Upper Saddle River, NJ: Prentice Hall, 2005), 545.

A quick audit of familiar, perhaps even "famous," social marketing messages provides a few additional clues as to what seems to help target audiences remember what to do, especially when your communications aren't close at hand:

- Try rhyming techniques such as "Click It or Ticket" and "If it's yellow, let it mellow; if it's brown, flush it down."
- Those that surprise you may be more likely to stick with you, such as "Save the Crabs. Then Eat 'em."
- Create a simple and memorable mental picture, such as "Drop. Cover. Hold" in case of an earthquake.
- Connect the timing to some other familiar event, such as a birthday, as in "Get a colonoscopy when you turn 60."
- Leverage the familiarity of another brand or slogan, as "Just Say No" did with Nike's "Just Do It." Similarly, to help prevent kitchen fires, in 2013, the Kent Fire & Rescue Service in the UK created a song for targeted promotions titled "Stand By Your Pan" sung to the tune of "Stand by Your Man."

Creative Tip 6: Have a Little Fun Sometimes

Having fun with social marketing promotions is often as controversial as using fear-based appeals. We suggest that the key here is to know when it is an appropriate and potentially effective solution—and when it isn't. A host of variables will impact your success, including your target audience (e.g., demographics, psychographics, geographics), whether the social issue is one that your target audience can "laugh about," and how a humorous approach contrasts with what has been used in the past to impact this issue. The following successful example suggests the "fun" boundaries can be stretched further than we might think.

In 2007, the Bill & Melinda Gates Foundation announced that Thailand's Population and Community Development Association (PDA) had received the 2007 Gates Award for Global Health in recognition of its pioneering work in family planning and HIV/AIDS prevention. The prize honored Mechai Viravaidya, founder and chairman of the PDA and an ex-senator in Thailand with a passion for reducing unplanned pregnancies and the spread of HIV/AIDS in the country. He had decided to popularize condoms, thinking a "little fun" might make them more acceptable. His creative promotional strategies supported the "fun" theme:

- He spoke at a variety of events, proclaiming, "The condom is a great friend. You can do many things with it . . . You can use different colors on different days—yellow for Monday, pink for Tuesday, and black when you are mourning."[34]
- He organized condom "balloon-blowing" contests with prizes for kids and adults. He also made sure the media would take photos that he hoped would end up on the front page or on the evening news.

- He influenced tollbooths to hand out condoms with their tickets.
- He created a Cops and Rubbers program in which traffic police were given boxes of condoms to distribute on New Year's Eve.
- He demonstrated other uses for condoms, such as putting them over the barrel of a gun to prevent sand from getting into the barrel.
- He had monks bless condoms so that Thais would be assured there would be no ill effects after using them.
- He added condoms to fashion shows, with runs of condoms in different colors.
- He opened new restaurants branded "Cabbages and Condoms" with the slogan "Our food is guaranteed not to cause pregnancy"—and a condom, instead of a mint, comes with the bill.

Figure 13.12 A welcome approach in a subway in New York City.

Source: Author photo.

In general, humorous messages are most effective when they represent a *unique approach* to the social issue. For example, consider how surprised and perhaps delighted you would be to read a sign in a subway in New York like the one in Figure 13.12. There are probably opportunities for humor whenever your target audience would get a kick out of *laughing at themselves or with others.* The Ad Council's Small Steps campaign, launched in 2004 for the U.S. Department of Health and Human Services, is a great example. Campaign elements use humor to inspire overweight adults to incorporate some of the 100 suggested small steps into their hectic lives (see Figure 13.13).[35]

On the other hand, humorous messages are not as effective for *complex messages.* There would be no benefit, and perhaps even a detriment, to a campaign to influence parents to childproof their home, an effort involving multiple, specific instructions. Nor is it appropriate for issues with *strong cultural, moral, or ethical concerns* (e.g., child abuse or domestic violence).

Creative Tip 7: Try for a "Big Idea"

A "big idea" brings the message strategy to life in a distinct and memorable way.[36] In the advertising business, the big idea is thought of by some as the Holy Grail, a creative solution that in just a few words or one image sums up the compelling reason to buy.[37] It takes message strategy statements that tend to be plain, straightforward outlines of benefits and desired positioning and transforms them into a compelling campaign concept.[38] It might be inspired by asking yourself, if you had only "one thing" you could say about your product, how would you say it and how would you show it? Others suggest that getting the big idea is not a linear process, but rather a concept that might emerge while in the shower or in a dream. At Porter Novelli, a global public relations firm, the big idea is described as one that has a head, heart, hands, and legs.

Not only can The Big Idea straddle across a period of time through several campaigns, but at the same time it can stand astride any channel we choose. The Big Idea brings campaigns and channels together, rather than working as disconnected executional elements.[39]

Examples in the commercial sector to model include the well-known "Got milk?" campaign that has been adopted for a variety of celebrities and non-dairy products (e.g., "Got junk?"). A great social marketing example is one developed by the U.S. Department of Health and Human Services' Office on Women's Health's national breastfeeding campaign. The big idea for this

Figure 13.13 A graphic print ad with copy reading "Starts doing sit-ups during commercials. Gets 30 minutes a day of physical activity. No longer dependent on vertically striped shirts" and "Take a small step to get healthy. Get started at www. smallstep.gov."

Source: Ad Council.

campaign will seem more obvious when you see two of their ads, ones intended to increase knowledge about the benefits of breastfeeding exclusively for the first six months (see Figure 13.14).

Creative Tip 8: Consider a Question Instead of a Nag

Are you going to drink eight glasses of water today? Are you going to vote tomorrow? Some believe the very act of asking these questions can be a force for positive change, a technique referred to as the "self-prophecy effect," or the behavioral influence of a person making a self-prediction. Research conducted by Eric Spangenberg, professor of marketing, and Dave Sprott, assistant professor of marketing, both at Washington State University, has led them to believe that having people predict whether they will perform a socially normative behavior increases their probability of performing that target action. These researchers have even demonstrated successful application of self-prophecy

Figure 13.14   Part of a big campaign idea.

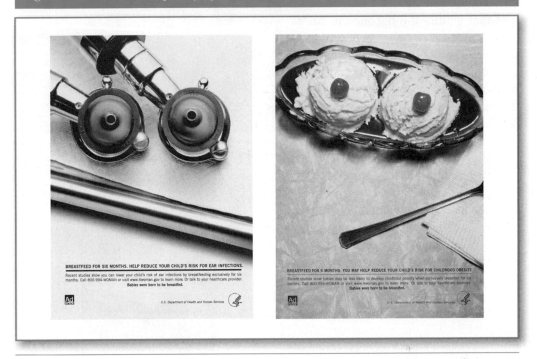

Source: Ad Council.

through mass-communicated prediction requests.[40] They have also found theoretical support for a dissonance-based explanation for self-prophecy.

Spangenberg and Sprott's studies show that when people predict they will do something, they are more likely to do it. These authors' analysis of the technique showed an average effectiveness rate of 20% immediately following the asking of the question, and sometimes behavior change would last up to six months after people predicted their behavior.[41] Specific studies have shown that self-prophecy has increased voter turnout in elections, improved attendance at health clubs, increased commitment to recycling aluminum cans, and increased the chances that a family will eat dinner together. The researchers believe this result can be explained by the phenomenon of cognitive dissonance, that uncomfortable feeling we humans sometimes get when we say we'll do something and then we don't. (Some of us would probably call it guilt.) This uncomfortable feeling then drives us to act consistently with our predictions. In other words, the prediction becomes a self-fulfilling prophecy.

Spangenberg stresses that for this to be successful, the target audience must see the behavior as a social norm and be predisposed to the behavior, or at least not have strong commitments to the other, undesirable one. For example, asking a group of drug users, "Are you going to stop using today?" is probably not going to work.[42]

Creative Tip 9: Make Norms (More) Visible

Social norms marketing, as mentioned in earlier chapters, is based on the central concept of social norms theory—that much of people's behavior is influenced by their perceptions of what is "normal" or "typical." When a behavior is not (yet) a social norm, however, one strategy is to increase perceptions that others are engaged in the behavior. In Figure 13.15, for example, note the sign on the curbside garbage container that states "We Scoop the Poop." The sticker is there not only to forewarn the garbage collectors as they dump the container, but also to "spread" the idea to other pet owners around the neighborhood.

Figure 13.15 A message intended to help make scooping the poop and placing it in the trash a norm.

Creative Tip 10: Tell Real Stories About Real People

Perhaps one of the reasons that real stories told by real people is such a great creative strategy is that they embody many of the message and messenger best practices mentioned in this chapter. The messenger, because he or she is a real person telling his or her own story, is viewed as *credible* and usually *likable*. And the messages, when they are true stories, have more possibility for providing *concrete* examples and creating *emotion*, two of the "sticky" principles. The following two examples illustrate these well.

Example: Heather Crowe's Story About Second-Hand Tobacco Smoke

My name is Heather Crowe. I'm 58 years old, and I'm dying from lung cancer caused by second-hand smoke in the work-place.

I was a waitress for over 40 years.

I worked in the hospitality industry because it let me earn a decent living for myself and my daughter. I worked long hours, sometimes more than 60 hours every week. The air was blue with smoke where I worked, but until recently nobody did or said anything about the smoke in our workplaces. Until last year, I had no idea that second-hand smoke was dangerous. People would say, "do you mind if I smoke?" and I said, "I really don't care." I didn't have any idea that the smoke in the restaurants could do me harm. I just wasn't protected. I just wasn't told.

My cancer was diagnosed last year. My health had usually been good, but last spring I noticed some lumps on my neck that didn't go away. Even though I wasn't feeling sick, my daughter encouraged me to visit the doctor. My doctor measured the lumps and sent me for some x-rays and tests. When she told me that results showed a cancerous tumour on my lung that was as big as my hand, I had trouble believing it. "Are you sure it's not tuberculosis?" I asked. "I've never smoked a day in my life."

When she was a university student, my doctor had worked in the same restaurant as me. She remembered how much smoke there was in that restaurant, and told me that she thought my lung cancer might be from second-hand smoke. It took many more weeks before they finished the tests and the specialists told me that my cancer was inoperable, and that they identified it as caused by second-hand cigarette smoke. When I learned this, I became exceptionally angry. I thought I had to put my anger and my stress into something positive. I looked for a way to prevent anyone else from getting sick this way. Because I didn't know I was at risk, I figured there were a lot of other people in the hospitality industry that were working in the smoke on a daily basis that also did not know that they might get sick as I had done.

I realized I wanted to increase awareness and I wanted workers in the industry to have some protection if they do happen to get sick. Waiters and waitresses do not have second-class lungs and there is no reason why we should continue to have second-class protection for our health. It's time legislation took over.

The first thing I did was to hire a lawyer to help me make a claim with the Workers Compensation Board. I figured by going forward with Workers Compensation claim it would help give other workers financial support as well as helping change the way workers in the hospitality sector are treated. Then I began to ask for letters to support my claim. I got some letters from my doctor, from the politicians, like the mayor and former mayor, and the medical officer of health for Ottawa, and from some Members of Parliament and councillors. To my surprise, the Board accepted my claim within 8 weeks. I learned that mine was the first claim accepted for illness caused by second-hand smoke in restaurants.

On the day after I had a biopsy of my lung, one of my regular clients asked me why I was favouring my left arm. I told him I had lung cancer from second-hand smoke. He worked at Health Canada and asked me if they could use me in an advertisement about second-hand smoke. This would help people learn about the need to protect workers, and I said yes. By coincidence, the advertisement started the same day that I learned that my claim for compensation had been accepted. My phone began ringing off the hook, there were so many newspapers and television stations interested in the claim.

Since then I have been across Canada talking to politicians, to schools and to communities about the need to protect workers from smoke. I think I help because I put a face to cancer. There are lots of statistics out there, but I am a person, and

I think that helps people understand that this is a real problem. I just want people to become a little more aware of what second-hand smoke can do.

I am hoping that the politicians will work at a solution and that we should get smoke-free workplaces right across Canada. I don't expect it all to be done in a very short time, I'm just hoping that they consider this is a very dangerous chemical, and that all workers should be equally protected. Some people say "well, if you don't like the smoke you don't have to work there," to which my reply is "if other people have protection in the workplace then why not us?" All I'm asking for is equal rights. We should not be disposable workers.

I'm not asking the smokers to give up smoking, I'm asking them to step outside when they smoke, to protect all workers.

There are four stages of cancer and that I am at the third stage. That means that there is no way I will be able to get well. I have had five big and five small rounds of chemo-therapy and thirty radiation treatments. The radiation was supposed to kill the actual cancer cells and the chemo-therapy was supposed to shrink the tumour. That may give me two or three years if I go into remission, but eventually the cancer will come back and it will be terminal.

It helps me to do this work. At least I'm out there trying to do something, trying to make a difference. It's too late for me, but it doesn't mean that I have to curl up in a ball and let it go, you know? It's not too late for future generations. My goal is to be the last person to die from second-hand smoke.[43]

Heather died at 8:00 P.M. on May 22, 2006.

When Heather started her campaign, very few workers were protected from second-hand smoke at work. Now, all provinces and territories and the federal government have banned smoking in public places and workplaces.

Example: Chloe Akahori's Choice Not to Drink and Drive

The following true story was presented in May 2013 by high school senior Chloe Akahori at a Communities That Care event to reduce underage drinking rates.

The roads were slick with fresh rain. The clouds were so black it was as though ink from a ballpoint pen had broken, permanently staining the sky. My friends and I pondered our night ahead when my phone lit up with a warm text message inviting us all to come over. Perfect, we had plans.

When we got to the house, it was not what we expected. Walking in, we were offered alcohol—everyone had a red cup in hand. Was it worth it? We chose not to drink and left after a few minutes.

Planning to drive off-island, I decided to head toward the freeway via East Mercer Way. I drove carefully as the sharpest turn on the road appeared. A figure flashed in the bottom field of my vision. I took greater control of the wheel and swerved to avoid it. Passing by, I saw someone lying in the middle of East Mercer Way. My mind worked quickly as I pulled over. After asking my friend to call the police, I ran to the woman and helped her out of the road. Seconds later, a red Porsche skidded around the corner on the wet pavement without a hint of hesitation. It was only later that I considered "what if."

I made a series of good choices that night that had a greater outcome than I could have ever anticipated. Often, since, I have thought about choices in general and how hard it is for students to make "good" choices with continual academic, parental and social pressures. I also realized that my decision not to drink that evening profoundly affected more lives than just my own.[44]

Creative Tip 11: Try Crowdsourcing

As noted in Chapter 3, crowdsourcing is often used to tap online communities for formative, pretest, and evaluative research efforts. It can also be used to generate creative elements, as Johnson & Johnson did for its Campaign for Nursing's Future, a multiyear corporate social marketing effort to underscore the value of the nursing profession and help increase the nursing workforce. One component the campaign undertook was the Art of Nursing: Portrait of Thanks Mosaic Project, designed to thank nurses for their hard work and dedication and to commemorate the campaign's 10th anniversary in 2012. Nurses from around the world were encouraged to upload a photo and brief information on the campaign's website, Discovernursing.com. The photo could be from on the job, a social event, or even a family outing. Photos were then compiled to create a single digital (mosaic) image, one intended to be a symbol of pride for nurses everywhere (see Figure 13.16). The mosaic includes nearly 10,000 photos submitted by nurses and nursing students. For every photo that was submitted to the project, the campaign pledged to donate $1 to fund student nursing scholarships.

Figure 13.16   The Johnson & Johnson's Campaign for Nursing's Future Portrait of Thanks. Once on the site, you can search through nearly 10,000 individual photos by keyword: name, hometown, specialty.

Source: Johnson & Johnson.

Creative Tip 12: Appeal to Psychographic Characteristics and Desires of the Target Audience

Psychographic traits such as personality, lifestyle, values, interests, and attitudes can often lead us deeper into persuasive factors than demographics alone. Curtis Carey, an adjunct professorial lecturer at American University, shared the following inspirational application:

If someone asks you about your best friend's defining characteristics, you are unlikely to start with where she lives or her age. Instead, you might explain that she's motivated, that she always reads something interesting in the book club, and that she is the first person to help out friends and family. You might even talk about the interesting activities and things she shares on Facebook or Twitter or the time she asked you to go water skiing. If she truly is your best friend, you'll tell us about her as a motivational and maybe inspirational person, not as a demographic.

Amid the devastation of the "Year of Tornadoes" in 2011, a creative team comprising communications experts and social scientists at the National Oceanic and Atmospheric Administration in Silver Spring, Maryland, coalesced around just such a compelling psychographic profile as they developed a tornado safety campaign. The team zeroed in on their target audience, describing these individuals as "Motivated Moms." With a dash of inspiration and an ample helping of gritty research grounded in the Actionable Risk Communication Model,[45] the team designed a message to elicit the strong need of Motivated Moms to feel empowered and be seen as actively leading others. Motivated Moms served as midstream influencers and were vital in inspiring both family members and friends in their close-knit social network to practice safe behavior during tornado warnings.

The creative message asked Motivated Moms to act on what came naturally to them— their instinctive desire to protect their family and friends.

The slogan—"Be a Force of Nature"—activated Motivated Moms, empowering them to first model the desired behavior and then to share it with friends and family. The kindergartner reading the script for the campaign's animated public service message targeting moms says,

> A tornado is a force of nature, but so are you! If you find yourself in the path of a tornado, immediately go to shelter, and then with a text, a status update, or a tweet you can alert your social network of the coming threat. In the face of severe weather send a message, save a life; be a force of nature.

The message, messenger, and creative materials all speak to the psychographic characteristics and desires of the Motivated Mom.[46]

PRETESTING

Appropriate Reasons for Testing

The primary purpose for pretesting potential messages and creative executions is to *assess their ability to deliver* on the strategies and objectives developed in Step 4 and highlighted in your creative brief. When faced with several potential executions, the process can also help you *choose the most effective options* or eliminate the least effective. It provides an opportunity to *refine materials* prior to production and distribution.

In addition, it helps identify any red flags—something about the potential ad that might interfere with communications or send the wrong message. This often happens when planners and campaign developers are too close to their work or don't have the same profile and characteristics as the target audience. For example, a potential tobacco prevention ad targeting teens with the fact that "all it takes is 100 cigarettes to become addicted" raised a couple of red flags when several youth commented, "Well, then I'll just have 99" and others expressed the idea that 100 cigarettes (to a nonsmoker) "sounds like a lot!"

Potential Pretesting Techniques

Techniques used for pretesting are typically qualitative in nature, and most include *focus groups* or *personal interviews* and *professional review* of materials for technical accuracy and readability (i.e., literacy levels). When a more quantitative, controlled approach is required, methodologies may include *theater* or *natural exposure testing* (e.g., ads are embedded between other spots or in the middle of programming) and/or a *larger number of focus groups*, *intercept interviews*, and *self-administered surveys*. This more extensive testing is often warranted when (a) interested parties are divided on their initial assessments of creative executions, (b) there will be significant economic and political implications to choices, and (c) the campaign needs to have a longer-term shelf life (e.g., years versus months).

Often these techniques vary according to stages in the pretest process. At early stages, when concepts and draft executions are being tested, qualitative instruments are usually most appropriate. After concepts have been refined, quantitative techniques may be important to help you choose from several potential executions.

Typical topics explored with respondents to assess the ability of potential executions to deliver on the strategy are listed as follows (responses are then compared with intentions developed in the creative brief).

1. "What is the main message you get from this ad?"

2. "What else are they trying to say?"

3. "What do you think they want you to know?"

4. "What do you think they want you to believe or think?"

5. "What action do you think they want you to do?"

6. If the respondent doesn't mention the desired behavior, say, "Actually, the main purpose of this ad is to persuade you and people like you to . . ."

7. "How likely do you think it is that this ad will influence you to take this action?"

8. "What about this ad works well for that purpose?"

9. "What doesn't work well for that purpose?"

10. "How does the message/ad make you feel about [doing this behavior]?"

11. "Where is the best place to reach you with this message/ad? Where would you most likely notice it and pay attention to it? Where are you when you make decisions about [this behavior]?"

A Word of Caution About Pretesting

The idea of pretesting potential messages, concepts, and executions is often dreaded among creative professionals. Many of their concerns are legitimate, grounded in experiences with respondents who typically don't like advertising, don't really want to adopt the desired behavior being promoted, want to be art directors, want to meet expectations to be an ad critic, can't imagine what the finished ad will really be like, or seize the opportunity to vent about the campaign's sponsor.

Principles and practices that can help to assuage these concerns and produce more effective results from testing efforts include the following:

1. *Inform respondents up front that this testing has nothing to do with whether they like or dislike the ads.* You are trying to find out whether they think the ad will work relative to stated objectives and why or why not. Respondents should be told (at some point) what the intended purpose of the ads is and then be asked to comment relative to that intention. One successful technique is to put the objective on a flip chart or whiteboard and continue to refer to the statement throughout discussions.

2. *Consider testing concept statements* that describe the theme and ad instead of using storyboards or illustrations, especially when dealing with executions that involve fantasy, humor, or other styles that are difficult to convey with two-dimensional descriptions.

3. *Test potential conceptual spots prior to showing finished ads* when evaluating several potential executions at the same time relative to each other.

4. *Ask respondents to write down their comments before discussing their reactions to ads.* They should be instructed that they can ask for clarification if needed, but to hold their comments until they have had a chance to capture them in writing.

5. *Thoroughly brief clients and colleagues not familiar with the creative testing process* on the limitations of this type of research and the potential pitfalls. Emphasize the importance of listening for what the ads are communicating and what components work and don't work relative to the intended objectives. Warn them not to be surprised or discouraged if participants don't like an ad and not to celebrate just because they do.

The CDC's Message Development and Testing Tool

CDC offers an online tool (CDCMessageWorks) to assist in picking the most effective message among several potential ones, revising and/or crafting new ones, and defending messages once they are developed. It is based on an empirical model developed by Keller and Lehmann in 2008 that provides 10 variables considered to be significant predictors for success. The intention of the tool is to assist program planners and their partners in developing and choosing health messages that will be the most *understood, relevant, compelling, worthwhile,* and *to the point* for promoting the desired behaviors of targeted audiences. The tool can be accessed at https://cdc.orau.gov/HealthCommWorks/ MessageWorks/MW/Features.

ETHICAL CONSIDERATIONS WHEN DECIDING ON MESSAGES, MESSENGERS, AND CREATIVE STRATEGIES

Many of the ethical issues regarding communications seem straightforward. Information should be accurate and not misleading. Language and graphics should be clear and appropriate for audiences exposed to the communications. Gray areas are hard to avoid, however, and what and whose criteria should be used to decide whether something is appropriate? Is this tagline in a teen sexual assault prevention campaign too risky—"If you force her to have sex, you're screwed"—even though it tested well with the target audience? Should someone blow the whistle on a local television station promoting the TV sitcom *Friends* on an outdoor billboard by featuring photos of the three slender stars and the headline "Cute Anorexic Chicks"? In most cases, the funders of the effort will likely be the ones to make the final call.

CHAPTER SUMMARY

Promotion is persuasive communication and the tool we count on to ensure that the target audience knows about the offer, believes they will experience the stated benefits, and is inspired to act. There are four major components of a communications strategy:

- *Messages:* What you want to communicate, inspired by what you want your target audience to do, know, and believe
- *Messengers:* Who will deliver your messages or be perceived to be sponsoring or supporting your offer
- *Creative strategy:* What you will actually say and show and how you want to say it
- *Communication channels:* Where and when your messages will appear (distinct, of course, from distribution channels)

Several tips are suggested to assist you in evaluating and choosing a creative strategy:

1. Keep it simple and clear.

2. Focus on audience benefits.

3. When using fear, follow up with solutions and use credible sources.

4. Try for messages that are vivid, personal, and concrete.

5. Make messages easy to remember.

6. Have a little fun sometimes.

7. Try for a "big idea".

8. Consider a question instead of a nag.

9. Make norms (more) visible.

10. Tell real stories about real people.

11. Try crowdsourcing.

12. Appeal to psychographics.

Before producing campaign materials, you are encouraged to pretest messages and creative concepts, even if informally. You will be testing their ability to deliver on the objectives for your campaign, especially those outlined in your creative brief. Potential pitfalls in testing are real and can be minimized by carefully constructing questioning and briefing respondents as well as colleagues and clients.

RESEARCH HIGHLIGHT

Bicycling in the Netherlands

What Went Right?

(2010)

At a minimum, this research highlight represents the application and value of *key informant interviews*. What makes it a rich example is that it also includes *observational*, *experiential*, and *ethnographic* research activities. It is the story of a trip to the Netherlands that a delegation of key decision makers from the San Francisco Bay Area took in search of the "twenty-seven percent" solution. They wanted to understand what the Netherlands had done to influence an impressive 27% of adults to ride a bike to work or to do errands. The trip was sponsored by the Bikes Belong Foundation, a nonprofit organization based in Boulder, Colorado, with a mission "to put more people on bicycles more often."[47] The organization regularly takes public officials on tours of cities where biking is popular.

Their story appeared on September 13, 2010, in an online article written by Jay Walljasper titled "A Week of Biking Joyously: An American Delegation Learns From the Dutch."[48]

Background and Research Purpose

Bikes have so shaped the image of the Netherlands that, for many people throughout the world, the country is almost synonymous with cycling. And evidently it is not, as some might believe, a function of their DNA. Rather, the Dutch made a conscious decision in the early 1970s to make biking safe, convenient, and appealing.[49] Importantly, their efforts have created cycling that appeals to women as well as men, to all age groups, and to all income classes, for a variety of trip purposes.[50]

The September 2010 delegation included elected officials, public sector managers, and other decision makers and influencers from the San Francisco Bay Area. Their research objective seemed simple: "What can we do back home, that they have done here, to increase cycling among adults as well as kids?"

Methodology

The delegation's "investigations" began in Utrecht, where their focus was on the staggering data indicating that 95% of older students (10 to 12 years) in the town bike to school at least some of the time. (This compares to 15% who either walk or bike to school in the United States, down from 50% in 1970 according to The National Center for Safe Routes to School Program.) Their next stop was The Hague, where bikes account for 27% (the national average) of all trips in the city, which has a population of 500,000. On the third day, they visited Rotterdam, where bike traffic share had been increasing by 3% annually for the last several years. And the fourth and final stop was Amsterdam, where their imaginations were further fueled by a bold new vision of urban life embodied in Java Island, where bikes and pedestrians (and boats) take priority over cars.

In each city, delegates attended presentations, interviewed local officials and decision makers, and experienced first-hand the support for cycling.

Findings

Strategies delegates discovered for making cycling safer, more convenient, and more appealing are summarized in Table 13.3, grouped by familiar components of the social marketing model, including the *promotion* "P" highlighted in this chapter. We have also included a few strategies not mentioned in the online article but listed in a separate article by John Pucher and Raphy Buehler at Rutgers University, "At the Frontiers of Cycling: Policy Innovations in the Netherlands, Denmark, and Germany."[51]

Delegates were evidently encouraged when they learned that it took the Dutch more than 25 years to construct their current complex bicycle system. And after they went home, delegates' comments reflecting their research findings were sure to make a difference in the San Francisco Bay area:

> The Dutch are not somehow exceptional people when it comes to biking. Everything we see here is the result of a deliberate decision to improve biking here. Even little things, like paint on the street, add up.
>
> They don't just think about bikes. Every presentation we heard tied

Table 13.3 Target Audience Barriers and Strategies to Overcome Them

Target Audience	Kids	Adults
Barriers	• Concern with personal safety • Lack of navigation skills	• Concern about personal safety • Concern about/experiences with theft • Lack of parking for bikes
Product	• A municipal program sends teachers into the schools to conduct bike safety classes • Students go to *Trafficgarden*, a miniature city complete with roads, sidewalks, and busy intersections, where they "learn safety by doing"	• Advance green lights for cyclists at most intersections • Well-maintained, fully integrated paths, lanes, and bicycle-dedicated streets • Increased numbers of bike racks and special bike shelters • Bright red asphalt clearly marking bike lanes for motorists to see • "Call a bike" programs where bikes can be rented by cell phone at transit stops • Intersection modifications and priority traffic signals • Traffic-calming mechanisms via speed limits and physical infrastructure deterrents • Regular surveys of cyclists to assess their satisfaction with cycling facilities and programs and to gather specific suggestions for improvement (*product quality research*)
Price	• At age 11, most kids in town are tested on their cycling skills and win a certificate of accomplishment that ends up framed on many bedroom walls	• In Gronigen, a guarded parking facility built in 1982 has a nominal fee, but the city now has 30 of these facilities, and 59% of urban trips made in this city are on bikes • Motorists are assumed by law to be responsible for almost all crashes with cyclists
Place		• Bike-only parking facilities available in the basements of new office developments and at strategic outdoor locations • Conversion of auto parking spaces to 10 bike spaces • Coordination with public transportation on routes and schedules • Bikes available for rent at train stations
Promotion		• Public awareness campaigns focusing on health benefits • Cycling ambassador programs • Annual cycling festivals and car-free days

things together—public transit, parking, cars, streets. The Dutch sense people are going to do what's easiest.

There is actually a road map of doable public policies we can adopt to get us where the Dutch are today.

DISCUSSION QUESTIONS AND EXERCISES

1. The authors suggested that you might be surprised that you are two thirds of the way through the planning process and just now getting to what some people think is marketing: promotion. Why is the promotional tool developed after selecting target audiences; a desired behavior; a positioning statement; and product, price, and place strategies?

2. What are the three major factors contributing to messenger credibility? Give an example of a credible messenger for a campaign you have seen. It can be for a commercial, nonprofit, or social marketing effort.

3. How might you use crowdsourcing to develop creative elements for a campaign to reduce texting and driving?

CHAPTER 13 NOTES

1. G. Hastings, *Social Marketing: Why Should the Devil Have All the Best Tunes?* (Burlington, MA: Butterworth-Heinemann, 2007).

2. Personal communication from Monterey Bay Aquarium communications staff, April 2014.

3. P. Kotler and K. L. Keller, *Marketing Management*, 12th ed. (Upper Saddle River, NJ: Prentice Hall, 2005), 536.

4. R. Reeves, *Reality in Advertising* (New York: Knopf, 1960).

5. M. Siegel and L. Doner, *Marketing Public Health: Strategies to Promote Social Change* (Gaithersburg, MD: Aspen, 1998), 332–333.

6. Ibid., 321.

7. Syracuse University, Newhouse School of Public Communications, "The Stupid Drink" (July 29, 2009), accessed February 5, 2011, http://www.slideshare.net/prceran/syracuse-universitys-the-stupid-drink-campaign-book?from=ss_embed.

8. A. E. Crowley and W. D. Hoyer, "An Integrative Framework for Understanding Two-Sided Persuasion," *Journal of Consumer Research* (March 1994): 561–574.

9. P. Kotler, *Marketing Management*, 3rd ed. (Upper Saddle River, NJ: Prentice Hall, 1976), 334–335.

10. U GRO, "Study: Many Children Are Still Not Properly Restrained in Cars" (n.d.), accessed March 31, 2014, http://www.u-gro.com/2014/03/study-many-children-are-still-not-properly-restrained-in-cars/.

11. Siegel and Doner, *Marketing Public Health*, 314–315.

12. "Pioneering S.F. Program Puts Bank Accounts in Reach of Poor," *Irvine Quarterly* (n.d.), accessed July 24, 2011, http://www.irvine.org/publications/irvine-quarterly/current-issue/947; City and County of San Francisco, Office of the Treasurer & Tax Collector, "Mayor Gavin Newsom and Treasurer José Cisneros Announce Over 24,000 Accounts Opened for Bank on San

Francisco Clients" [Press release], *Irvine Quarterly* (November 20, 2008), accessed July 24, 2011, http://www.sftreasurer.org/ftp/uploadedfiles/tax/news/PR%20Bank%20on%20SF.pdf.

13. B. Obama, "Race Against Time—World AIDS Day Speech" (December 1, 2006), accessed April 11, 2007, http://obama.senate.gov/speech/061201-race_against_time_world_aids_day_speech/index.html.

14. Kotler and Keller, *Marketing Management*, 12th ed., 547.

15. Starbucks Pledge 5 [website], accessed February 4, 2011, http://pledge5.starbucks.com/.

16. R. C. Browne, "Most Black Women Have a Regular Source of Hair Care—But Not Medical Care," *Journal of the National Medical Association* 98, no. 10 (October 2006), 1652–1653.

17. Sesame Street Store, Healthy Habits, "Ready, Set, Brush Pop-Up Book" [Product description] (n.d.), accessed February 4, 2011, http://store.sesamestreet.org/Product.aspx?cp=21415_214 77_21532&pc=6EAM0196.

18. H. C. Kelman and C. I. Hovland, "Reinstatement of the Communication in Delayed Measurement of Opinion Change," *Journal of Abnormal and Social Psychology* 48 (1953): 327–335; as cited in Kotler and Keller, *Marketing Management*, 12th ed., p. 546.

19. D. J. Moore, J. C. Mowen, and R. Reardon, "Multiple Sources in Advertising Appeals: When Product Endorsers Are Paid by the Advertising Sponsor," *Journal of the Academy of Marketing Science* (Summer 1994): 234–243; as cited in Kotler and Keller, *Marketing Management*, 12th ed., 546.

20. Montana Meth Project [website], accessed March 26, 2007, http://www.montanameth.org/About_Us/index.php.

21. D. McKenzie-Mohr and W. Smith, *Fostering Sustainable Behavior: An Introduction to Community-Based Social Marketing*, 2nd ed. (Gabriola Island, BC, Canada: New Society, 1999), 101.

22. K. Roman and J. M. Maas, *How to Advertise*, 2nd ed. (New York: St. Martin's, 1992).

23. Personal communication from Mary Shannon Johnstone, March 24, 2014.

24. Siegel and Doner, *Marketing Public Health*, 335–336.

25. Posting on Georgetown Social Marketing Listserve, March 3, 2012.

26. B. Sternthal and C. S. Craig, "Fear Appeals: Revisited and Revised," *Journal of Consumer Research* 3 (1974): 23–34; as summarized in P. Kotler and E. L. Roberto, *Social Marketing: Strategies for Changing Public Behavior* (New York: Free Press, 1989), 198.

27. J. L. Hale and J. P. Dillard, "Fear Appeals in Health Promotion Campaigns: Too Much, Too Little, or Just Right?," in *Designing Health Messages: Approaches From Communication Theory and Public Health Practice*, ed. E. Maibach & R. Parrott (Thousand Oaks, CA: SAGE, 1995), 65–80.

28. McKenzie-Mohr and Smith, *Fostering Sustainable Behavior*, 101.

29. Ibid., 85.

30. Ibid., 86.

31. S. M. Burn, "Social Psychology and the Stimulation of Recycling Behaviors: The Block Leader Approach," *Journal of Applied Social Psychology* 21 (1991): 611–629.

32. C. Heath and D. Heath, *Made to Stick: Why Some Ideas Survive and Others Die* (New York: Random House, 2007).

33. Ibid, 17.

34. Health Affairs, "Interview: From Family Planning to HIV/AIDS Prevention to Poverty Alleviation: A Conversation with Mechai Virabaidya," Web Exclusive (September 25, 2007), Glenn A. Melnick, gmelnick@usc.edu.

35. AdCouncil. (n.d.). *Obesity prevention*. Retrieved 2006 from http://www.adcouncil.org/default.aspx?id=54

36. P. Kotler and G. Armstrong, *Principles of Marketing*, 9th ed. (Upper Saddle River, NJ: Prentice Hall, 2001), 548.

37. V. Carducci, "The Big Idea" (n.d.), accessed March 28, 2007, http://www.popmatters.com/books/reviews/h/how-brands-become-icons.shtml.

38. Porter Novelli, "The Big Idea": Death by Execution" (2006), accessed March 28, 2007, http://www.porternovelli.com/site/pressrelease.aspx?pressrelease_id=140&pgName=news.

39. Ibid.

40. E. R. Spangenberg, D. E. Sprott, B. Grohmann, and R. J. Smith, "Mass-Communicated Prediction Requests: Practical Application and a Cognitive Dissonance Explanation for Self-Prophecy," *Journal of Marketing* 67 (July 2003): 47–62, http://www.atyponlink.com/AMA/doi/abs/10.1509/jmkg.67.3.47.18659.

41. M. Guido, "A More Effective Nag," *Washington State Magazine* (Spring 2004), accessed July 28, 2011, http://researchnews.wsu.edu/society/33.html.

42. Ibid.

43. Story provided by Physicians for a Smoke-Free Canada, 1226A Wellington Street Ottawa, Ontario, Canada, 613–233–4878, http://www.smoke-free.ca/heathercrowe/.

44. Personal communication from Chloe Akahori, March 24, 2014.

45. M. M. Wood, D. S. Mileti, M. Kano, M. M. Kelley, R. Regan, and L. B. Bourque, "Communicating Actionable Risk for Terrorism and Other Hazards," *Risk Analysis: An International Journal of the Society of Risk Analysis* 32, no. 4 (April 2012): 601–615.

46. Personal communication from Curtis Carey, March 31, 2014.

47. The Bikes Belong Foundation is a nonprofit arm of the Bikes Belong Coalition. Information accessed October 29, 2010, http://www.bikesbelong.org/what-we-do/.

48. J. Walljasper, "A Week of Biking Joyously: An American Delegation Learns From the Dutch" (September 13, 2010), accessed October 19, 2010, http://www.worldchanging.com/archives/0011581.html.

49. Ibid.

50. J. Pucher and R. Buehler, "At the Frontiers of Cycling: Policy Innovations in the Netherlands, Denmark, and Germany," *World Transport Policy and Practice* (December 2007), accessed July 29, 2011, http://policy.rugers.edu/faculty/pucher/Frontiers.pdf.

51. Ibid.

Chapter 14

PROMOTION

SELECTING COMMUNICATION CHANNELS

Social media platforms offer tremendous opportunities to engage our audiences deeply and widely. However, we can't approach social media with the "same old, same old" mindset and treat these channels like cyber brochures that we push to people. Social media is about meeting our audiences where they are both in cyberspace and in their daily lives, engaging them as part of the solution and listening. That being said, social media stills needs to be grounded in good strategic planning, as part of the marketing mix.

—Mike Newton Ward
Social Marketing Consultant
North Carolina Division of Public Health

In the third edition of this text (2008), there were only two pages describing the social media communication channel. In this fifth edition, there are more than 12, a reflection of the explosion of this channel in just the past six years. Smart marketers have moved from a reliance on traditional channels (e.g., television, radio, outdoor, print advertising, brochures), to an integrated media mix, one that now includes social media options (e.g., mobile phones, interactive websites, Facebook, YouTube, Instagram, blogs, Twitter, podcasts, online forums, wikis). Perhaps this shift has occurred in part because many marketers identify with a famous quote from John Wanamaker: "I know that half the money I spend on advertising is wasted, but I can never find out which half." In addition to providing lower costs per impression, social media options provide a more efficient method of collecting real-time data on whether target audiences have noticed and responded to the marketers' efforts (e.g., number of times a YouTube video was viewed and shared).

This chapter will guide you through the final step of developing your promotional strategy: deciding on the most efficient and effective mix of communication channels to reach and inspire your target audiences to action. It will

- Familiarize you with the major communication channel options you have
- Review eight factors that can guide your decisions

We begin with a case illustrating the power of social media to increase blood donations, and conclude with a story illustrating the persuasive power of a popular messenger to influence purchasing of healthier options.

MARKETING HIGHLIGHT

Increasing Blood Donations in Australia Using Social Media and More

The Australian Red Cross Blood Service

(2011–2013)

Background

The Australian Red Cross Blood Service is responsible for collecting, testing, processing, and distributing all blood in Australia, with the organization's success being dependent on the support and generosity of people donating their time and/or blood. The fact is that although one in three people in the country will need blood in their lifetime, only one in 30 currently donate.[1] Common barriers to participation include not knowing how and where to donate or whether potential donors are even eligible. Desired benefits have historically focused on internal desires to help others. Kathleen Chell, a PhD marketing student at Queensland University of Technology in Australia, writes about opportunities to provide potential donor benefits that are often overlooked:[2]

Blood donation is widely portrayed as an archetypal altruistic behaviour as it conforms to characteristics of a classic altruistic act, with the behaviour benefiting others at some cost to the donor, performed without external reward. This orientation is reflected in the ongoing rollout of education based promotions appealing to the audience's altruistic nature. As donation rates have failed to increase, however, the pivotal role of altruism as a motivator for blood donation is being questioned by scholars and practitioners. Recognizing this, many not-for-profit organizations have developed strategies that leverage self-interest rather than altruism by facilitating individuals to donate conspicuously. With the rise in web 2.0 technology and in particular social media, the opportunity to affordably leverage these tools to provide such recognition is increasing.

The following three blood donation campaigns using social media in Australia demonstrate that Chell's insights are probably right on.

Recharge Your Karma Campaign

This campaign targeting university students 18 to 25 years old was managed by a cross-functional team from the Blood

Service and Student Marketing Australia, an organization specializing in implementing on-campus campaigns. The campaign was designed to take students on a journey and engage them enough to want to take part, ultimately by giving blood (see Figure 14.1). The creative "Recharge Your Karma" approach was based on the rationale that

> everyone has done something they shouldn't have. At some point, everyone's regretted something they did, or didn't do. Most of the time you can't erase your mistakes but fortunately, there is a way to make up for them. You can "recharge your karma" by doing something good, something that helps other people and makes a positive difference. Like giving blood.[3]

All campaign collateral pieces encouraged visits to a *website* (donateblood.com.au/karma) which included a karma quiz, information about donating blood, a pledge-to-donate page, and a link to booking an appointment. Collateral also featured unique *QR codes*, allowing potential donors to take a photo of the QR code with their mobile device and then receive an *SMS message* with a karma message and a link to a specific landing page. In preparation for Donormobiles arriving on campus, teaser events were supported with a social media campaign encouraging students to talk about these blood donation opportunities on *Facebook* and take photos and forward them to their friends via their mobile device. Students then coming to the Donormobile for their appointment were encouraged to "hang out" in the Good Karma Zone, established next to the

Figure 14.1 Poster with a QR code for signing up.

Source: Australian Red Cross Blood Service.

Donormobiles to give donors a positive pre- and post-donation experience. The zone featured magazines, games, bean bags, music, and a Facebook "check-in" page, which meant that everyone who was a donor's friend on Facebook saw his or her check-in status. Word of the Donormobile on campus was also spread via *email* by the Student Marketing Association, which had compiled a database of students who had "opted in" to receive updates and deals, providing a unique opportunity to target thousands of students with key messages and encourage them to make an appointment online to give blood.

Campaign evaluators reported that all key objectives of the campaign were met, with there being an increase of more than 40% in blood donations compared to the same period the year before. A post-donation survey emailed to 852 respondents, with 300 (35%) completing the survey, indicated that positive results were also achieved in terms of brand awareness and intention to give again, with 78% indicating they were highly likely to give blood in the next six months.[4]

Soup's Influential Word of Mouth Campaign[5]

Soup, an agency in Australia specializing in harnessing the power of word of mouth, developed a campaign for the Australian Red Cross Blood Services targeting "highly influential" 30- to 54-year-olds, characterized as those who were well connected, both online and offline. Those selected had never donated blood or had not donated in the past five years. They were also family and community minded, worked or lived near a blood donation center, and were willing to go with a partner, friend, or colleague to donate blood. It was also important that they were regular users of Facebook and/or Twitter. Over a period of a month, influencers were encouraged to make a donation at their local blood center. They were asked to share their full experience online via Facebook and Twitter, explaining why they made the decision to donate, how the experience was, and how they felt afterward. Influencers also had the opportunity to create online reviews via the Social Soup review page.

Soup engaged 750 influencers, offered them packages of information and branded materials, and encouraged them to donate blood themselves and to then reach out to friends and family and encourage them to do the same. Results were impressive:

- There were 1,827 blood donations.
- Eighty-eight percent of the influencers who donated blood indicated they would do so again.
- Three hundred online reviews were created.
- Among the influencers who donated, almost all left a review, giving an average rating of 4.4 out of 5 for the experience.[6]

Battle of the Burbs' Public Engagement Effort

In Australia in 2012, the headline and opening paragraph of a press release from the Australian Red Cross Blood Service read:

> *"Battle of the Burbs" blood challenge is ON!* Is your suburb the best? Is it more generous than the others? Well the proof will be in the blood bag with the Australian Red Cross Blood Service's latest challenge . . . Local residents are being asked to show their community pride and spirit

Figure 14.2 Campaign graphic engaging the public to donate blood.

Source: Australian Red Cross Blood Service.

by donating blood and helping win the title of the most generous Brisbane suburb . . . All blood donations from 19 March until the end of April will help save lives and every drop will be counted towards your suburb's total for the 2012 challenge.[7]

The campaign targeted residents using traditional media, with cities using more social media to engage their citizens. And to put more "skin in the game," the challenge was extended to city councils, "pitting council against council to see which has the biggest heart." In the end, Southern Grampians won the challenge with 1.47% of residents donating in the nearly six-week-long campaign effort—the highest of all Victorian towns.[8]

PROMOTION: SELECTING COMMUNICATION CHANNELS

When selecting communication channels, you will be faced with making decisions regarding (a) types of communication channels, (b) specific media vehicles within these broader types, and (c) timing for communications. A brief explanation of each follows (see Box 14.1).

Box 14.1
Major Social Marketing Communication Channels

A. ADVERTISING (PAID MEDIA AND UNPAID PUBLIC SERVICE ANNOUNCEMENTS)	
Broadcast:	*Outdoor/Out of Home:*
Television	Billboards
Radio	Busboards
Internet: Banner ads	Bus shelter displays
Print:	Subways
Newspaper	Taxis
Magazine	Vinyl wrap on cars and buses
Direct Mail:	Sports events
Separate mailings	Banners
Paycheck and other stuffers	Postcard racks
Backs of Tickets and Receipts	Kiosks
Ads in Theaters	Restroom stalls
Ads on Internet/Web	Truckside advertising
	Airport billboards and signage

(Continued)

(Continued)

B. PUBLIC RELATIONS AND SPECIAL EVENTS	
Stories on television and radio	*Special Events:*
Articles in newspapers and magazines	Meetings
Op-eds	Speakers' bureaus
Public affairs/community relations	Conferences
Lobbying	Exhibits
Videos	Health screenings
Media advocacy	Demonstrations
C. PRINTED MATERIALS	
Brochures	Calendars
Newsletters	Envelope messages
Flyers	Booklets
Posters	Bumper stickers
Catalogs	Static stickers
D. SPECIAL PROMOTIONAL ITEMS	
Clothing:	*Functional Items:*
T-shirts	Key chains
Baseball hats	Flashlights
Diapers	Refrigerator magnets
Bibs	Water bottles
Temporary Items:	Litterbags
Coffee sleeves	Pens and pencils
Bar coasters	Bookmarks
Lapel buttons	Book covers
Temporary tattoos	Notepads
Balloons	Tote bags
Stickers	Mascots
Sports cards	Door hangers
	e-Games
	e-Cards
	Podcasts

E. SIGNAGE AND DISPLAYS	
Road signs	
Signs and posters on government property	
Retail displays and signage	
F. PERSONAL SELLING	
Face-to-face meetings, presentations, speakers' bureaus	
Telephone	
Workshops, seminars, and training sessions	
G. SOCIAL MEDIA CHANNELS AND TYPES	
Social networking sites such as Facebook, Twitter, and Instagram	RSS feeds (really simple syndications) on websites
Mobile technologies such as phones for text messaging	Buttons and badges
Email blasts and alerts	Image sharing
YouTube videos	Virtual worlds
Blogs and microblogs such as Twitter	Widgets
H. WEBSITES	
Banner ads	
Links	
I. POPULAR AND ENTERTAINMENT MEDIA	
Songs	Public art
Movie scripts, television, radio programs	Flash mobs
Comic books and comic strips	Product integration
Video games	

Communication Types

Communication channels, also referred to as media channels, can be categorized by whether they are *mass*, *selective*, or *personal*. Each approach may be appropriate, depending on communication objectives. Many campaigns and programs may warrant all three, as they are mutually reinforcing.

Mass media channels are called for when large groups of people need to be quickly informed and persuaded regarding an issue or desired behavior. There is a need, and perhaps a sense of urgency, for audiences to "know, believe, and/or do something." Typical mass media types for social marketers include *advertising, publicity, popular and entertainment media*, and *governmental signage*.

Selective media channels are used in cases where target audiences can be reached more cost effectively through targeted media channels and/or when they need to know more than is available in mass media formats. Typical selective media types include *direct mail, flyers, brochures, posters, special events, telemarketing,* and the *Internet.*

Personal media channels are sometimes important for achieving behavior change objectives and include *social networking sites such as Facebook, blogs, and microblogs such as Twitter, face-to-face meetings and presentations, telephone conversations, workshops, seminars, and training sessions.* This approach is most warranted when some form of personal intervention and interaction is required in order to deliver detailed information, address barriers and concerns, build trust, and gain commitment. It is also an effective and efficient way to create social norms and make them more visible.

Communication Vehicles

Within each of the major communication channels (media types) there are specific vehicles to select. Which TV stations, radio programs, magazines, websites, mobile technologies, and bus routes should you choose? At what events should you sign up for a booth? When are road signs warranted? Where should you put your fact sheets?

Communication Timing

Timing elements include decisions regarding months, weeks, days, and hours when campaign elements will be launched, distributed, implemented, and/or aired in the media. Your decisions will be guided by when your audience is most likely to be reached or when you have your greatest windows of opportunity for being heard (e.g., a drinking-and-driving campaign aimed at teens might be most effective immediately prior to and during prom and graduation nights).

Communication Funding Sources

Paid media has traditionally been referred to as communication channels that the brand (maker or seller of the product) pays for. *Earned media* refers to when the brand gets "free" visibility, either through public service announcements, articles in print media, or mentions in broadcast media. Relative to social media channels, earned media refers to visibility that others give to the brand (e.g., liking on Facebook a campaign or product). And with the dominance of the Internet, a third source has been proposed by some, one labeled *owned media*, defined by Corcoran and others as "a channel a brand controls, including a website, mobile site, blog, or Facebook or Twitter account."[9]

TRADITIONAL COMMUNICATION CHANNELS

Advertising and Public Service Announcements

Defined formally, advertising is "any paid form of nonpersonal presentation of ideas, goods, or services by an identified sponsor."[10] More commonly, you probably think of one or more of the popular, traditional mass media communication channels such as *television, radio, newspapers, magazines, direct mail, the Internet,* and a variety of *outdoor* (out-of-home) channels such as billboards, transit signage, and kiosks. In the commercial sector, these advertisements are most often placed (bought) by the organization's advertising or media-buying agency.

As a social marketer working for a public sector or nonprofit organization, you will also have opportunities for *unpaid advertising,* something you know of as public service announcements (PSAs). An obvious advantage of PSAs, of course, is the cost (often free, or at least deeply discounted); the disadvantage is that you do not have the same level of control over where the ad will actually appear in the newspaper or magazine or during what program or time of day it will air on television or radio. This perhaps is why some refer to a PSA as "people sound asleep."

There are several tactics you can use to increase your odds of obtaining public service placement of your advertisements and the likelihood they will appear when and where you would like. First, build a relationship with the public affairs or community relations personnel at your local television and radio networks. Know that what they will be most interested in (it's their job) are issues that their listeners and viewing audience care about and ones that their organization has chosen as a community priority. Ensure high quality of your productions, whether for television or radio, as they will consider them a reflection of their organization as well. Be prepared to negotiate. If they can't offer you free placement at times you are targeting, they may have interested corporate sponsors; and if they can't do it free of charge, they may be able to offer a discounted price (e.g., two for the price of one).

Example: Denver Water's Conservation Advertising Campaign. From 2002 to 2006, Denver Water's 1.2 million customers reduced their water usage by about 20% each year. The Denver mayor, however, wanted to continue this trend and announced a partnership in July 2006 to reduce use by 22% a year over the next decade, including a $500,000 advertising campaign intended to help make this happen. The campaign, with the tagline "Use Only What You Need," appeared in community newspapers, magazines, billboards, transit, and other out-of-home media (see Figure 14.3). The ads also appeared

Figure 14.3 A creative campaign and use of outdoor advertising for Denver Water.

in places you might not expect, such as on 20,000 drink coasters that went to local restaurants and bars, offering water conservation tips such as "Be a real man and dry shave, tough guy."[11] And in 2013 the campaign sent out a "Thank you for Using Even Less" message to customers, announcing they had exceeded their goal of reducing water use 10% throughout the summer: "Without your efforts, providing a secure water future is an exercise in futility."[12]

Public Relations and Special Events

Public relations is distinguishable by its most favorable outcome—free visibility for your campaign.[13] Successful activities generate free, positive *mentions of your programs in the media*, most commonly as news and special programming on radio and television and as stories, articles, and editorial comments in newspapers and magazines. Many refer to these accomplishments as *earned media*, contrasting it to paid media. Additional typical efforts in this channel include planning for *crisis communications* (e.g., responding to adverse or conflicting news), *lobbying* (e.g., for funding allocations), *media advocacy* (e.g., working with the media to take on and advance your social issue), and managing *public affairs* (e.g., issue management). Although some organizations hire public relations firms to handle major campaigns, it is more common for internal staff to handle day-to-day media relations.

Some believe this is one of the more underutilized channels, and yet a well-thought-out program coordinated with other communications-mix elements can be extremely effective. It provides more-in-depth coverage of your issue than is often possible with a brief commercial and is often seen as more objective than paid advertising. Tools used to generate news coverage include press releases, press kits, news conferences, editorial boards, letters to the editor, and strong personal relationships with key reporters and editors. Siegel and Doner recommend several keys to success:

> *Build relationships with the media* by first "finding out who covers what and then working to position yourself and your initiative as an important, reliable source of information so that the reporters will call you when they are running a story on your topic."[14]

> *Frame the issues* with the goals of the media in mind, "to appeal to the broadest number of audience members possible, and . . . tell a compelling story that is relevant to their audience and in the public's interest."[15]

> *Create news* by convening a press conference, special event, or demonstration. Consider a technique mastered by the Center for Science in the Public Interest (CSPI) in which their studies create "news that applies pressure to decision makers. For example, after [CSPI's] analysis of the nutrient content of movie popcorn was

reported in the media, many major movie chains began using oils lower in saturated fat or offering air-popped options."[16]

Special events can also generate visibility for your effort, offering the advantage of interaction with your target audience and allowing them to ask questions and express attitudes about your desired behaviors that you probably need to hear. The event may be a part of a larger public gathering such as a county fair, or it may be something you have organized just for your campaign. It might include a demonstration (e.g., car seat safety checks), or

Figure 14.4 Inside the Prevent Cancer Super Colon™

Source: Janet Hudson, Manager, Exhibit Services, Prevent Cancer Foundation, www.PreventCancer.org.

it might be a presentation at a location where your target audience shops, dines, or commutes, such as the one in the following example.

Example: An Unusual Tour for Colon Cancer Prevention. Times Square in New York City is a cultural hub featuring upscale hotels, Broadway theaters, music, nightlife, quality shops, and gargantuan promotional icons. In 2009 it added one more feature: a giant colon. Since 2003, the Prevent Cancer Foundation had been sponsoring the Prevent Cancer Super Colon™ exhibit, featuring a tour of an inflatable tube, 20 feet long and 8 feet tall—one that most could easily walk through. On February 27, it arrived in New York City to honor March as Colon Cancer Awareness Month, with the purpose of increasing timely colon cancer screening. As visitors take the tour, they get an up-close look at healthy colon tissue, tissue with nonmalignant colorectal disease, colorectal polyps, and various stages of colorectal cancer (see Figure 14.4). The Prevent Cancer Super Colon attracted over 1,500 visitors that week in Times Square, and then throughout 2009 traveled across the nation reaching out to people in small towns as well as big cities, stopping at health fairs, hospitals, and cancer centers.[17] As of 2014, the Super Colon has visited 49 states, the District of Columbia, and Puerto Rico.[18]

Printed Materials

This is probably the most familiar and utilized communication channel for social marketing campaigns. *Brochures, newsletters, booklets, flyers, calendars, bumper stickers, door hangers, and catalogs* provide opportunities to present more detailed information regarding the desired behavior and the social marketing program. Sometimes, but not as often as you might like, target audiences hold on to these materials, and ideally even share them with others. In some cases, special materials are developed and distributed to other key internal and external groups, such as program partners and the media. Included in this channel category are any collateral pieces associated with the program, such as *letterheads*, *envelopes*, and *business cards*.

Example: A Calendar to Increase Workplace Safety. "Keep Washington safe and working," the mission statement of the Washington State Department of Labor & Industries (L&I), also serves as the title of the annual calendar produced by L&I's Division of Occupational Safety and Health. First published in 2007, the calendar explains job hazards and provides safety tips. In 2009, the calendar began featuring real Washington State businesses and employees in a variety of industries. This educational tool brings important safety messages to employers and workers 365 days a year. L&I produces and distributes 12,000 copies a year (see Figure 14.5).

Figure 14.5 A weekly calendar intended to increase safety practices on construction job sites.

It's a death trap!

Eight times in five years, construction workers died when they fell through an unguarded skylight or roof opening.

October

14 | 15 | 16 | 17 | 18 | 19 | 20
SUN | MON | TUES | WED | THURS | FRI | SAT

Think About...

Know and follow the safety requirements for guarding or covering skylights, roof openings and floor openings.

Source: Washington State Department of Labor and Industries.

Special Promotional Items

You can reinforce and sometimes sustain campaign messages through the use of special promotional items, referred to by some in the industry as "trinkets and trash." Among the most familiar are messages on *clothing* (e.g., T-shirts, baseball hats, diapers, bibs), *functional items* (e.g., key chains, water bottles, litterbags, pens and pencils, notepads, bookmarks, book covers, refrigerator magnets), and more *temporary mechanisms* (e.g., bar coasters, stickers, temporary tattoos, coffee sleeves, sports cards, lapel buttons). Some campaigns, such as the one in the following example, create a treasure chest of these items.

Example: Temporary Tattoos and More for Pooper Scoopers. In Snohomish County, Washington, Dave Ward of the Snohomish County Public Works Department understands the difference between an awareness campaign and a social marketing campaign. He also understands how important it is to research target audiences' current attitudes and practices regarding picking up pet waste and to focus on creative strategies to promote very specific behaviors by solving the customer's problem.

His research among pet owners revealed that 42% picked up their dog's waste regularly and disposed of it properly in the trash; 42% were picking it up regularly but not disposing of it properly (e.g., they were

Figure 14.6 A promotional item, a flashlight, that also helps overcome barriers to "scooping the poop" in the dark.

Source: Washington State Department of Labor and Industries.

burying it on their property); and 16% were picking it up only sometimes or not at all. To promote "proper behaviors," the county created concrete and vivid communications: "More than 126,000 dogs live in Snohomish County, producing waste equivalent to a city of 40,000 people. More than 20 tons of dog waste are dropped in Snohomish County backyards every day." Observation research then helped define the problem even further. Although citizens appeared to be fairly reliable in picking up pet waste on public property such as sidewalks and parks (where they could be seen), they were less judicious in their own backyards.

Ask dog owners why they don't pick up their dog's waste in their yard, and you might hear what Dave did: "When I come home from work at night and let the dog out to go, it's too dark to see where they go." To address this barrier, a free functional promotional item was developed, a small flashlight that could be left by the door, serving not only as a way to follow the pet around the yard but also as a prompt for the desired behavior on a regular basis (see Figure 14.6). And to spread the word and recognize these pooper scoopers, another promotional item, a temporary tattoo for the hand with the words "I'm a pooper scooper," was especially popular among youth (see Figure 14.7).[19]

Figure 14.7 A temporary tattoo signaling "Good job, Aja!"

Signage and Displays

Many social marketing campaigns rely on signage and displays to launch and, especially, sustain campaign messages. Examples of those more permanent include *road signs* warning against drinking and driving, reminding people to use a litterbag, and asking motorists to "Move right for sirens and lights." *Signs on government property and establishments regulated by the government* can be used to target messages, such as signs in forests asking people to stay on the path, plaques in bars with messages warning about the dangers of alcohol when pregnant, and signs at airports urging us to remove computers from our bags before reaching the checkpoint. Displays and signage can also be used at point of purchase in *retail environments* (e.g., for life vests, tarps for covering pickup loads, energy-saving lightbulbs, natural pesticides). In this case, preparing signage and special displays will include selling the idea to distribution channel decision makers and coordinating distribution of any special signage and accompanying materials.

Personal Selling

Perhaps the oldest promotional channel is that of face-to-face selling. Kotler and Keller see this tool as being the most effective at later stages of the buying process and as one that helps build buyer preference, conviction, and action. They cite three distinctive qualities this tool provides: (a) personal interaction—involving an immediate and interactive relationship; (b) cultivation—permitting relationships to grow; and (c) response—making the buyer feel under some obligation for having listened to the "sales talk."[20] And, as illustrated in the following example, the experience doesn't have to be unpleasant.

Example: One Man Helping to Clear the Air Over China. Ma Jun, a well-known Chinese environmentalist who spoke at the 2013 World Social Marketing Conference in Toronto, was named by *Time* magazine in 2006 as one of the world's 100 most influential people. He has also been called an eco-warrior, an innovator, and a modern-day hero.[21] He must be what Margaret Mead had in mind with her famous quote: "Never doubt that a small group of thoughtful committed citizens can change the world. Indeed it's the only thing that ever has." Ma's strategy isn't typical, though, of an activist, who is more often drawn to communication channels such as sit-ins or demonstrations. Instead, he personally calls on corporate decision makers and shows them data that provide evidence of environmental pollution, and then persuasively talks about the benefits of change.

Although China had penalties for polluters, according to Ma, companies have found it "easier and cheaper to simply pay fines for polluting than to clean up their acts."[22] Concluding in 2006 that credible and "shocking" information was a primary motivator for change, Ma founded the Institute of Public and Environmental Affairs, an agency that gathers data from the government concerning water, air, and hazardous waste and then "exposes" this information. As of April 2013, Ma and his team had exposed more than 120,000 violations by multinational and local companies in China. At least 900 have made efforts to change their techniques,[23] including Apple, which made major efforts to clean up environmental violations in the company's supply chain.[24]

NONTRADITIONAL AND NEW COMMUNICATION CHANNELS

Social Media

In December 2009, Queen Rania of Jordan delivered a keynote speech at Europe's number-one technology event, attended by over 2,000 entrepreneurs, bloggers, and developers. She posed a challenging question, asking how to leverage the power of social media to alleviate social challenges in the real world—especially the state of global education. She sees social media as "a platform to collaborate and a mouthpiece to mobilize" and urged online activists to act on behalf of 75 million children in the world still being denied an education.[25] "You are the ones who can help link online activism to reality, to finally make life-streaming life-changing."[26] The Queen clearly recognizes what many social marketers are discovering—the power of social media. The Social Media Toolkit provided in 2009 by the Centers for Disease Control and Prevention (CDC) articulates these strengths well, seeing the potential of these technologies to[27]

- Increase the timeliness of communications
- Leverage the networks of target audiences
- Expand your reach
- Personalize and reinforce messages
- Facilitate interaction
- Influence desired behaviors

Example: Letting YouTube Bury the Argument for Brochures. As a sponsor of landmark menu-labeling legislation, the California Center for Public Advocacy in 2008 contracted with Brown-Miller Communications to increase support for the nation's first statewide menu labeling law, one that would require chain food facilities to disclose calories for each standard menu item directly on the menu next to the actual item. The fast-food industry was backing an alternative bill opting instead for nutrition brochures. Based on the old saying that a picture is worth a thousand words, the agency spent an afternoon filming people standing in line with fast-food outlets' complex brochures, trying, unsuccessfully, to quickly find simple information for the item they wanted. They then created a lighthearted man-on-the-street video showcasing their difficulties and posted it on YouTube (http://www.youtube.com/watch?v=zD4m6WN3Tlg) and sent it directly to fast-food industry representatives, legislators, and their staff, advocates, and the media. The secretary of health and human services and the governor were shown the video in one-on-one meetings. The YouTube video garnered over 5,000 views the first week, and over 80% of the comments directly attacked the fast-food industry's bill. Featured on the *New York Times* editorial blog, the video reached beyond the confines of

YouTube. The resulting public backlash prompted the fast-food industry to withdraw its legislation. State legislators who had previously been skittish about the bill and supportive of the fast-food industry's bill passed the first statewide menu-labeling law. The governor signed it into legislation, and California became the first state to pass statewide menu-labeling legislation.[28]

The CDC's toolkit also provides detailed definitions, descriptions, and tips for social media tools, which are summarized in Box 14.2. In the past several years, the CDC has developed a number of integrated social media campaigns, including the one described in the next example.

Example: 2009–2010 H1N1 and Seasonal Flu Outbreak Campaign. During the 2009–2010 H1N1 and seasonal flu outbreak, the CDC and the U.S. Department of Health and Human Services (HHS) created a media strategy that used a variety of social media tools: *buttons* to inform visitors of steps to take to stop the spread of the disease and direct them to additional information; *badges* that users could post to their individual social networking profiles or personal blogs; *widgets* for sharing guidance and health tips; *online videos*, the most popular being "Symptoms of H1N1 (Swine Flu)," viewed more than 2 million times; *podcasts*, including a special for children about flu prevention; *e-cards* allowing users to send flu-related health messages to friends, family, and coworkers (flu-related e-cards were sent more than 22,000 times and viewed a collective 103,000 times); *text messaging* providing three health messages a week to more than 16,000 subscribers; the *virtual world* Whyville for tweens featuring two different virtual flu viruses, the "Why Flu" and the "WhyMe Flu"; the CDC's *Twitter* accounts (which grew to a collective following of 1.28 million users); and the CDC's *Facebook* account, sharing flu updates and providing additional tools such as badges and widgets and a link to subject matter experts.

Box 14.2
A Social Media Primer

Badges are small graphic elements that include an image, a call to action, and a link for more information, often posted on personal profiles (e.g., "I got my flu shot").

Image sharing involves posting images such as photos and artwork to websites (e.g., a photo of what bacteria on hands looks like before washing).

RSS feeds (really simple syndications) provide the ability to aggregate and update information and provide links from many sites in one place (e.g., for emergency preparedness and response recommendations).

Podcasts are a convenient way to listen to or view digital media files by downloading on a portable media device or computer when and where convenient (e.g., for preventing type 2 diabetes).

Online video sharing is the posting of videos on online sites such as YouTube, Bing, and Yahoo (e.g., a YouTube video featuring simple things to do at home to conserve water).

Widgets provide interactive information and fresh content on a subject and can be accessed on an organization's website or downloaded to personal websites (e.g., a body mass index calculator).

e-Cards are electronic greeting cards sent to personal email accounts, often with a colorful greeting and some message that promotes or reinforces a desired behavior (e.g., congratulations for being tobacco free for six months).

e-Games are interactive electronic games played through applications such as the Internet, video game consoles, or mobile phones (e.g., actions youth can take to reduce, reuse, and recycle).

Mobile applications, such as texting, are the most portable and are quickly becoming a vital tool for timely and personalized communications (e.g., apps to help choose sustainable seafood while ordering a meal or shopping at a grocery store).

Blogs are regularly updated online journals with one or a team of regular authors (e.g., a physician at a children's hospital participating in a "mommy's" blog regarding childhood immunizations).

Microblogs, such as Twitter, are brief text updates 140 or fewer characters long (e.g., a specific Twitter encouraging sports injury prevention).

Social networking sites such as Facebook, Twitter, and Instagram are online communities where people can interact with friends, family, coworkers, and others with common interests. They provide social marketers with timely and personal ways to deliver products and promotional communications (e.g., UV alerts through a "Be Smart in the Sun" Facebook page).

Virtual worlds are online environments providing users an opportunity to create a virtual persona, or avatar, and then interact with other avatars in an online virtual environment (e.g., a virtual world on Second Life for preventing bullying).

Source: Adapted from the Centers for Disease Control and Prevention's "The Health Communicator's Social Media Toolkit" (August 2010), http://www.cdc.gov/healthcommunication/ToolsTemplates/SocialMediaToolkit_BM.pdf.

Twelve lessons learned that the CDC hopes will benefit others as they develop, implement, and evaluate social media efforts include the following:[29]

1. "Make strategic choices" based on the audience's profile and your communication objectives.

2. "Go where the people are" by reviewing user statistics and demographics.

3. "Adopt low-risk tools first," such as podcasts and videos.

4. "Make sure messages are science based," ensuring accuracy and consistency.

5. "Create portable content," such as widgets and online videos that can easily be shared.

6. "Facilitate viral information sharing" through sites such as Facebook and YouTube.

7. "Encourage participation," especially through two-way conversations

8. "Leverage networks" such as Facebook, where many in your target audience may have more than 100 "friends."

9. "Provide multiple formats" to increase accessibility, reinforce messages, and provide preferred ways to interact.

10. "Consider mobile phones," since 90% of adults in America subscribe to mobile services.

11. "Set realistic goals," as social media alone are unlikely to achieve aggressive communication or behavior change goals.

12. "Learn from metrics and evaluate efforts," an advantage afforded by digital communications.

Craig Lefebvre, a renowned social marketing expert experienced in social media applications, provides additional perspectives for success:[30]

The position a social marketer takes when using social media involves not just a new perspective, but another set of skills that focus on the network, not the individual. *To use these media successfully, we must become collaborators, conveners, facilitators, brokers and weavers.* By collaborators, we mean working inside what others have created—existing blogs, social network sites; creating platforms for group participation from the beginning—not just as static dissemination websites. As conveners we must think about using social media in new ways to bring people of common purpose together to get things done—not simply substitute computer-mediated meetings for in-person ones (aka the burgeoning scheduling of "webinars") to "talk." One of the major barriers to becoming a convener is that few people and organizations understand the effort that must go into changing the behaviors of their collaborators . . . . Being a broker means becoming a dynamic resource center—not a place where people go to check out job posts, and download toolkits and case studies, but where people can, among other things, exchange advice and information, solicit creative work, comment on works in progress, allow agencies to see who outside their usual networks might have the ways and means to reach priority groups. For example, why do so few health programs reach poor, underserved and rural populations through agricultural extension services or United Way agencies? And finally, agencies and organizations need to think about themselves as network weavers—pulling together what are usually (when you look for them) a number of diverse and isolated groups working on the same problem but do not have the connectors, or bridges, to bring them into contact with one another.

The creative use of social media and mobile technologies that moves past what they are as technologies, and focuses on how they fit into the lives of people we serve, will allow social marketing to become more effective and efficient at realizing behavior and social change at scale.[31]

Examples of the use of several major social media types for social marketing are featured in this next section.

Facebook

Facebook's free and robust advertising platform offers the exciting possibility for public health researchers and program developers to find their target audiences online. By targeting advertising to specific elements of users' Facebook profiles—things like location, gender, and age as well as "likes" or groups the user has joined—public health professionals can maximize what are often limited funds available for program promotion or study recruitment. Megan Jacobs, project manager at Legacy, shared the following example of using Facebook for a clinical trial recruitment effort.

Researchers at the Schroeder Institute for Tobacco Research and Policy Studies at Legacy used Facebook advertising to recruit study participants to install a quit-smoking app called UbiQUITous™ as part of a randomized controlled trial funded by the National Cancer Institute (http://apps.facebook.com/quitlab). They targeted paid advertising at specific Facebook users to try to find smokers who fit the eligibility criteria (e.g., United States resident; 18+ years old; likes "hookah"). Facebook's easily accessible and detailed advertising metrics made it easy to determine in real time which targeting variables most successfully and cheaply drove Facebook users to the app, enabling the research team to experiment frequently with images, ad copy, and targeting variables to maximize recruitment efficiency. Surprisingly, an image of a fluffy white dog wearing thick black glasses combined with text about a free quit-smoking app was the most effective at recruiting smokers (see Figure 14.8). The study recruited over 9,000 study participants within 10 months at a cost of only $15.56 each.[32]

Figure 14.8 The winning app and image for recruiting smokers.

UbiQUITous
Health & Fitness

Every day is a good day to quit smoking. Visit Dr. Youkwitz's lab for help quitting today!

Source: Legacy For Health.

Blogs

The National Institute of Drug Abuse (NIDA) believes that social media are an effective way to meet teens "on their turf by going where they are instead of pushing information in a top-down manner."[33] In July 2009, NIDA launched the "Sera

Bellum Blog" (featuring an older teen of unidentifiable race/ethnicity, with an air of mystery, peering through a spyglass or over the top of sunglasses) to speak to a range of teens about drug addiction as a brain disease (http://teens.drugabuse.gov/blog). Still active in 2014, this online community engages teens with NIDA scientists, teachers, and others to grow their curiosity about research-based science without fear or stigma. Here is one example of a conversation between a teen and NIDA:

TEEN MIKE: There are kids in my school who smoke pot and they seem okay, what's the big deal.

NIDA: Hi mike, there's no way to predict who will encounter the negative effects of marijuana and who will not. Actually, that's true for many drugs since there are so many differences between us all as individuals . . . we'll react differently depending on how the drug is made, what our genetic make-up is, and other factors. The point is why take the risk?"[34]

Twitter

In 2013, the world's second Global Police Tweet-a-Thon was joined by millions across several countries on Twitter using the same hashtag, #poltwt.[35] The effort, in part, was to increase understanding of the use of social media by the police and to increase awareness among citizens on how they can use Twitter to assist police on a variety of issues, including finding missing persons, notifying police of parking infractions, reporting car accidents, sending information on suspicious citizens carrying weapons, and more. The global event also used the opportunity to provide safety tips such as this one: "Cheshire Police @cheshirepolice: Lots of calls re snowballs. Throwing snowballs at traffic can be very dangerous. Don't do it!! #poltwt."[36]

Texting

South Africa has more HIV-positive citizens than any country in the world; in some provinces, more than 40% of the population is infected.[37] With many seeking care only after becoming symptomatic with end-stage AIDS, an ambitious initiative undertaken by Project Masiluleke is tackling this issue using text messaging to get the word out about testing for the virus. Cell phones are abundant in South Africa, with more than 90% of the population (including the young and the poor) using some kind of mobile technology.[38] The developers of Project Masiluleke struck a unique deal with a South African cellular company to send out messages accompanying 1 million "please call" messages each day for a year. Similar to a public service announcement, these messages are inserted in the unused space of a "please call me" (PCM) text message, which is a special free form of SMS text widely used in South Africa, substituting a call for a paid text message. One message reads "Frequently sick, tired, losing weight and scared that you might be HIV positive? Please call AIDS Helpline 0800012322." For each PCM message, an accompanying script and frequently asked questions have been provided to helpline operators to ensure consistent and accurate information. Project Masiluleke's PCM campaign is reported to have increased calls to the National AIDS Helpline in Johannesburg by 300%, and project managers believe the potential is to mobilize several hundred thousand South Africans to get tested.[39]

Instagrams

The Blairs, owned and managed by The Tower Companies, is an apartment community in Silver Spring, Maryland, and Molly King is program director for its Lifestyles Program, a community development and sustainability program for residents living at the 1,400-unit apartment community. Molly believes it's true that "a picture is worth a thousand words" and that, in the world of social media, an image and a short-and-sweet statement are going to grab the attention of an audience like nothing else. Audrey Glasebrook, Lifestyles Program coordinator at The Blairs, writes,

> Instagram is a perfect way to do this! The Blairs uses Instagram to create a visual of its green lifestyle, supporting the need to see it to believe it. We Instagram pictures of our bike fix-it stations, bike maps of the surrounding area, and coming soon—our bike lounge complete with washing station and cyclist-friendly vending machine. Residents can see every day that biking is not only a viable commuting option, but also a fun one with Instagram images of these free amenities! We encourage residents to correspond with us and with each other on Instagram. When you see photos of your neighbor setting up their free composting supplies or bringing old electronics, batteries, and CFLs to the recycling bins at the front desk, you are more likely to reduce the landfill waste coming from your own apartment. Instagram has become an important part of our interaction with residents, and even prospective residents, to encourage sustainable living in our community. We truly believe in engaging our community, and Instagram is one of many great tools to do this!

Online Videos

In 2013, a Warc Prize for Social Strategy was awarded to Lifebuoy, a corporation with a social mission (and corporate social marketing effort) to help more children reach their fifth birthday by supporting good hand-washing habits around the world. Every year, they report, 2 million children fail to reach their fifth birthday because of diseases like diarrhea and pneumonia, diseases that could (in part) be prevented by healthy hand-washing habits.[40] Program strategies include working directly with schoolchildren, new moms, and community groups to encourage hand washing with soap before eating, after using the toilet, and when bathing. The campaign was launched with an inspiring three-minute video (http://www.youtube.com/watch?v=GVhCQNSGF1w), one that offers a real, personal, and powerful perspective through the story of a father's journey to celebrate his son's fifth birthday. Those viewing the video are encouraged to share on

Facebook, with Lifebuoy making a contribution to the effort for every posting. With over 6 million views (as of 2013), the video has sparked strong emotions and is expected to increase hand-washing behaviors.

Websites

To increase visibility for your website, *search engine marketing* has evolved immensely in the past several years, and many of us are not fully exhausting recommended strategies to increase the visibility of our website when someone conducts a Google-type search (e.g., "natural gardening"). There are paid options to ensure a ranking, often with a "pay per click" fee structure, a strategy that probably makes more business sense in the for-profit sector. There are also numerous unpaid options to improve the chances that your site will make the first results page, if not the top of that page (i.e., your site's ranking). Ranking can be improved by enhancing a website's structure, content, and keyword submissions.

Websites are a critical "touch point" for your customer, one that not only impacts awareness and attitudes toward your organization but also makes a difference in whether your audience is inspired and supported to act (e.g., to pledge to keep a lawn pesticide free). Some even believe your website could be "the third place," a term referring to social surroundings different from the two usual social environments of home and the workplace (customers of Starbucks, for example, might classify their coffee spot as one of their third places).

To maximize the influence of your website, experts advise that you pay attention to your site's (a) ease of navigation, (b) ability to tailor itself to different users, (c) availability of related links, and (d) potential for two-way communications as illustrated in the following example.[41]

Example: A Website to Highlight Citizens Taking Action to Protect Ocean Health. West Maui Kumuwai is a movement to protect the ocean through inspiring personal action and community collaboration, a movement with many moving parts. Just Googling the name provides a glimpse of the multiple platforms that feature their work as well as their website, including Twitter, YouTube, Facebook, and Instagram. A core strategy is to feature individuals in the West Maui community taking personal action to reduce polluted runoff and to share their stories on the website along with photos of the individual and a personal quote. An example from Julie is typical:

> I was in Ace Hardware Hawaii in Lahaina, debating about what fertilizer to buy and I noticed a sticker that read "Ocean Preferred." It really helped, and was the deciding factor in my purchase. I appreciate Ace making it easy for customers to choose more environmentally responsible products. Mahalo!

Additional features on the website include opportunities to participate in volunteer activities (e.g., help clear invasive plants) and to post a pledge to take one of eight specific actions (e.g., use a drip water system), even showing individuals holding up a sign of what they have pledged (see Figure 14.9).

Popular Entertainment Media

A less well-known and underused media category employs popular forms of entertainment to carry behavior change messages, referred to as popular entertainment media by some and edutainment by others. These include movies, television series, radio programs, comic books, comic strips, songs, theater, video games, and traveling entertainers such as puppeteers, mimes, and poets. Social marketing messages integrated into programming, scripts, and performances have included topics such as drinking and driving, use of condoms, eating disorders, recycling, youth suicide, organ donation, HIV testing, avoiding loan fraud, and sudden infant death syndrome.

Alan Andreasen sees this approach as a very effective one in overcoming the problems of selective exposure and selective attention on the part of indifferent target audiences. "This has come to be called the Entertainment Education Approach.[42] It began in the 1960s with a soap opera in Peru called *Simplemente Maria*, which discussed family planning, among other topics."[43] And John Davies, an international social marketing consultant who refers to these initiatives as "edutainment," believes that although they can require substantial budgets, costs might be lowered by selling advertising time to multinational companies that market beneficial, affordable health products such as soap for hand washing, oral rehydration salts for babies, and vitamin/mineral tablets for women.[44]

On a local level, you might try persuading local celebrities popular with the target audience to develop special promotional products (e.g., songs on their CDs) to perform at special events or to be featured in advertisements. In a national award-winning television spot for Mississippi's antilitter campaign, for example, former first lady Pat Fordice magically appears in the cab of a pickup truck between two "Bubbas," one of whom has gleefully tossed trash out the window. Pinching the ears of the driver and his offending pal, Fordice admonishes the pair for littering Mississippi highways. The former first lady continued as a spokesperson and representative of the campaign with the tagline "I'm Not Your Mama! Pick It Up, Mississippi!"[45]

Efforts to make this happen on a large scale, however, are likely to be substantial and may include lobbying and partnership efforts with the entertainment industry. The CDC, for example, often partners with Hollywood executives and academic, public health, and advocacy organizations to share information with writers and producers about the

Figure 14.9 A posting on the website from Amanda pledging to use biodegradable detergents (http://westmauikumuwai.org/take-the-pledge/).

Source: West Maui Kumuwai.

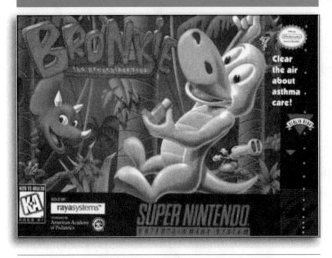

Figure 14.10 A video game helping to reduce asthma attacks.

Source: Social Impact Games, 2011.

nation's pressing health issues. Knowing that an estimated 88% of people in America learn about health issues from television, they believe prime time and daytime television programs are great outlets for health messages. To facilitate this, they provide tip sheets for TV writers and producers, conduct expert briefings for writers, and respond to inquiries for health information. They arrange expert briefings for the entire writing staff of a TV show, set up one-on-one conversations between a producer and a health expert to explore story line possibilities, and help find real people who deal with health issues firsthand. They also present awards and acknowledgments for exemplary portrayal of health issues, as they did in 2013 when they awarded a Sentinel for Health Award to HBO's *Enlightened* for its depiction of a character's struggle during drug rehab and why people relapse.[46]

Another impressive trend is also seen as an opportunity for popular media. By 2007, video games had surpassed movie rental, music, and box office films in terms of time and dollars spent. In fact, since 2005, an annual Games for Change Conference has been held in New York City to inspire organizations to use video games to further social change, and there is now a website (http://www.gamesforchange.org/) that provides a listing and description of over 125 games, including ones similar to the one described in the following example.

Example: Video Games for Asthma. *Bronkie the Bronchiasaurus*, created by Click Health in 1995, is a Super Nintendo video game designed to improve players' asthma self-management. Players take the role of either Bronkie or Trakie, two dinosaurs who have asthma (see Figure 14.10). To win the game, players must keep their dinosaur's asthma under control while also saving their planet from deadly dust clouds. To make sure Bronkie and Trakie stay in top form, the dinosaurs must be guided to measure and monitor their peak flow (breath strength), take medications as needed, follow a sick day plan, use an inhaler correctly, and avoid asthma triggers such as pollen, dust, smoke, and cold viruses shot through the air by Sneezers. The game has been used successfully in homes, hospitals, clinic waiting rooms, and asthma summer camps. Studies found that young people with asthma who had the Bronkie video game available to play at home reduced their asthma-related emergency and urgent care visits by 40% on average.[47]

Public Art

You have, no doubt, experienced public art intended to advocate a cause (e.g., white crosses in a park to protest a war), attract tourists (e.g., Cows on Parade in Chicago), or raise money for a nonprofit organization (e.g., quilts for AIDS victims). But what about public art intended to actually influence behaviors—behaviors to improve health, safety, the environment, or financial well-being? We think it is another emerging and untapped channel, with unique potential to sustain behaviors, create media attention, and be seen as a credible messenger. Channel types include *sculptures*, *exhibits*, *murals*, *paintings*, and more recently, "flash mobs," described in the next example.

Example: A Flash Mob to Protect Pedestrians in Crosswalks. Flash mobs are spontaneous public performances by a group (mob) designed to surprise shoppers, diners, commuters, and passers-by in a public place. The mob silently gathers in a public place, indistinguishable from normal passers-by. At a designated time, they break into action, sometimes a synchronized dance, sometimes just a song, maybe even a giant pillow fight. Sometimes participants are organized informally via social networks and consider it an opportunity for artistic expression. Others are more formal, sponsored by an organization with an agenda, as was the case in Seattle in November 2010.

In December 2009, the Seattle Department of Transportation chose the holiday shopping months to organize a flash mob to help reduce pedestrian injuries in the city, where on average there is more than one pedestrian/motor vehicle collision a day. The location was an indoor downtown shopping center near four intersections with the greatest number of collisions, ones that were already well lit, well marked, well signalized, and well engineered. They had run out of upstream engineering solutions and turned to influencing citizen behaviors. Deciding that a group of elected officials speaking at a busy mall might not draw a crowd, they chose a flash mob strategy instead, one that involved 60 people suddenly springing up on the ground floor of the center delivering their messages while doing "The Safety Dance." Then again in December 2010, another city-sponsored mob appeared downtown, this one at the popular Pioneer Square featuring dancers dancing to the tune "Singin' in the Rain" with umbrellas printed with the slogan "See You in the Crosswalk," a message to influence pedestrians to make sure they are seen before crossing the street. Comments on the YouTube blog posted the next day included, "Pretty cool. Fun to learn. Fun to do. Fun to watch. Good work all" (http://www.youtube.com/watch?v=S4CqTV9eEkI).

PRODUCT INTEGRATION

In the commercial sector, product placement is a specialty of its own, with marketers finding inventive ways to advertise during actual television programs and movies especially. You probably recognize this when you see a familiar logo on a cup of coffee in an actor's hand or the Swoosh on a star's baseball cap. In the James Bond film *Die Another*

Day, for example, 7UP, Aston Martin, Finlandia, Visa, and Omega all spent an estimated $100 million for product placement rights, with some critics nicknaming the film *Buy Another Day*.[48]

More relevant for social marketing is the integration of your desired behaviors into commercial products or their packaging. Sometimes corporations decide "all on their own" to take on an initiative. In the fall of 2006, for example, the toymaker Mattel unveiled Tanner, Barbie's new pet dog. Tanner comes with little brown plastic "biscuits" that he can be fed simply by lifting his tail. When he "releases them," Barbie can then scoop them up using her new, magnetic pooper-scooper and place them in the little garbage can included in the package.

More often, the social marketing organization approaches the corporation for support, as Seafood Watch did with Warner Home Video, who then agreed to include the 2007 Seafood Watch pocket guide in every copy of the Academy Award–winning animated film *Happy Feet* when millions of DVD copies became available in March 2007.

FACTORS GUIDING COMMUNICATION CHANNEL DECISIONS

Clearly, you have numerous channel options available for getting your messages to target audiences. Choices and decisions can be guided by a few important factors, eight of which are described in the following sections, in no particular order, since each is an important consideration. Some are even deal breakers.

Factor 1: Your Campaign Objectives and Goals

In Step 4 of your planning process, you ideally set a quantifiable goal for changes in behavior, behavior intent, awareness, and/or attitudes. Those measures/targets are now your guide for selecting communication channels.

For example, it makes sense that if you want 50 homes in a neighborhood of 500 homes on a river to be stream stewards, you will have a very different outreach (communication) strategy than if you want 5 million residents of a state to be aware of an E. coli outbreak. Confirming these numbers ahead of time with funders and team members will help you make the case for the strategies that you then propose.

Factor 2: Desired Reach and Frequency

Kotler and Armstrong describe *reach* as "a measure of the percentage of people in the target audience who are exposed to the ad campaign during a given period of time" and *frequency* as "a measure of how many times the average person in the target audience is exposed to the message."[49] This will be an important decision. For example, a state health department may want radio and television spots to reach 75% of youth ages 12 to 18 living in major metropolitan areas at least nine times during a two-month campaign. Media representatives will then use computer programs to produce media schedules and associated costs to achieve these objectives. The media planner often looks at the cost of the plan and calculates the cost per contact or exposure (often expressed as the *cost per thousand*—the cost of reaching 1,000 people using the medium).

Factor 3: Your Target Audience

Perhaps the most important consideration when planning media strategies will be the *target audience's profile* (demographics, psychographics, geographics, and behaviors) and their *media habits.* This will be especially important when selecting among social media platforms and using paid advertising and selecting specific media vehicles, such as radio stations, television programs, sections of the newspaper, magazines, and direct mail lists. Ideally, these were identified as "openings" when developing the creative brief. Again, media representatives will be able to provide audience profiles and recommendations. The goal will be to choose general media types, specific vehicles, and the timing most likely to reach, appeal to, and influence target audiences. *Compatibility* of the social marketing program and associated messages will also be key and will contribute to the ultimate impact of the given medium. For example, a message regarding safe gun storage is more strategically aligned with a parenting magazine than one on home decorating, even though both may have readerships with similar demographic profiles. And the timing of this ad would be best linked to special issues on youth violence or campus shootings.

Factor 4: Being There Just in Time

Many social marketers have found that an ideal moment to speak to the target audience is when they are about to choose between alternative, competing behaviors. They are at a fork in the road, and the social marketer wants a last chance to influence this decision. Tactics demonstrating this principle include the following:

- The use of the ♥ symbol on menus signifying a smart choice for those interested in options that are low in fat, cholesterol, and/or calories
- Calories posted on menu boards
- The familiar forest fire prevention signs that give updates on the current level of threat for forest fires in the park
- A message on the backs of diapers reminding parents to turn their infants over, onto their backs, to sleep
- The idea of encouraging smokers (in the contemplation stage) to insert their child's photo under the wrappers of cigarette packs
- A sign at a beach that makes the benefit of a life vest clear (see Figure 14.11)
- A key chain for teens with the message "You Don't Have to Be Buzzed to Be Busted"
- A handmade tent card next to a napkin holder suggesting that customers take only what they need

Figure 14.11 A sign at a beach shows the benefit of a life vest.

Factor 5: Being There "In the Event Of"

Communicators also want to prepare for events that are likely to motivate target audiences to listen, learn more, and alter their behaviors. Examples would include an earthquake, a teen suicide in a small community, the listing of an endangered species, threats of drought and power blackouts, a famous female entertainer diagnosed with AIDS, a governor injured in an automobile accident while not wearing a seatbelt, a college student sexually assaulted after a rave party, or a politician diagnosed with prostate cancer. Events such as these often affect levels of awareness and belief relative to costs and benefits associated with behavior change. The amount of time it will take to learn about and prepare a home for a potential earthquake will seem minor compared with suffering the costs and losses in a real earthquake. Though such events are often tragic, the silver lining is that target audiences in the precontemplation stage are often moved to contemplation, even action, and the social marketer can take advantage of the momentum created by heightened publicity and the need for practical information. Just as public relations professionals prepare for crisis communications, the social marketer wants to prepare for these *opportunity communications.*

Example: A Timely Message on Earthquake Preparedness. On Sunday, March 13, 2011, three days after the 8.9 earthquake off the coast of Japan, a front page headline in the *Seattle Times* read "GETTING READY FOR DISASTER. See Page A13 for a clip-and-save guide to make sure your family are ready if disaster strikes." Editors had likely been ready long before the quake with the full-page checklist, including tips on storing copies of important documents such as birth certificates, making a family emergency plan, having a list of important phone numbers, and knowing how and when to turn off the gas, as well as a list of supplies for the home as well as the car. Publishing this when readers "were awake" to the reality of disasters certainly ensured that more would look at the list—even clip it out and start checking off completed items.

Factor 6: Integrated Marketing Communications

Commercial marketers routinely invest millions of dollars in marketing communications, and this experience has led many companies to adopt the concept of *integrated marketing communications* (IMC), "where a company carefully integrates and coordinates its many communication channels to deliver a clear, consistent, and compelling message about the organization and its products."[50]

With integrated marketing communications, you achieve consistency in the use of slogans, images, colors, font types, key messages, and sponsor mentions in all media vehicles and customer touch points. It means that statistics and facts used in press releases are the same as those in printed materials. It means that television commercials have the same tone and style as radio spots and that print ads have the same look and feel as the program's social media.[51]

In addition, IMC points to the need for a graphic identity and perhaps even a statement or manual describing graphic standards. The integrated approach also addresses the need for coordination and cooperation among those developing and disseminating program materials and, finally, calls for regular audits of all customer touch points.

Benefits of an integrated approach are significant, including (a) increased efficiency in developing materials (e.g., eliminating the need for frequent debates over colors and typefaces and incremental costs of developing new executions) and (b) increased effectiveness of communications, given their consistent presentation in the marketplace.

Example: Friends Don't Let Friends Drive Drunk. In the early 1990s, the Ad Council and the U.S. Department of Transportation's National Highway Traffic Safety Administration introduced a new campaign encouraging friends to intervene in order to prevent a drunk person from getting behind the wheel. It was originally designed to reach 16- to 24-year-olds, who accounted for 42% of all fatal alcohol-related car crashes.[52] Eighty-four percent of Americans recall having seen or heard a PSA with the now famous "Friends Don't Let Friends Drive Drunk" tagline. More impressive, nearly 80% report they have taken action to prevent a friend or loved one from driving drunk, and 25% report they have stopped drinking and driving as a result of the campaign.[53] This hard-hitting campaign was instrumental, it is reported, in achieving a 10% decrease in alcohol-related fatalities between 1990 and 1991—the single largest one-year drop in alcohol-related fatalities ever recorded.[54] Communication channels have been consistent in their use of the tagline, emotional themes, and memorable

Figure 14.12 Magazine insert from a memorable campaign.

Source: Courtesy of the U.S. Department of Transportation and the Ad Council.

stories of "innocent victims" and have included PSAs produced for TV, radio, print, out-of-home, and online media outlets and, more recently, social media including Facebook (see Figure 14.12).

Factor 7: Knowing the Advantages and Disadvantages of Media Types

Media decisions should also be based on the advantages and limitations of each unique media type and should take into consideration the nature and format of key messages established in the creative brief. For example, a brief message such as "Choose a designated driver" can fit on a key chain or bar coaster, whereas a complex one such as "How to talk with your teen about suicide" would be more appropriate in a brochure or on a special radio program. Table 14.1 presents a summary of advantages and limitations for each of the major advertising categories.

Factor 8: Your Budget

Even when all other factors are considered, resources and funding may very well have the final say in determining communication channels. In the ideal scenario, as we have discussed, media strategies and associated budgets are based on desired and agreed-upon campaign goals (e.g., reach 75% of youth at least nine times). In reality, plans are more often influenced by budgets and available funding sources. For example, first estimates of a draft media plan to achieve the above goal may indicate that costs for the desired reach and frequency exceed actual and fixed budgets. In this (all-too-common) scenario, you will need to prioritize and allocate funding to media types and vehicles judged to be most efficient and effective. In some cases, it may then be necessary and appropriate to reduce campaign goals (e.g., reach 50% of youth at least nine times) and/or create a phased approach to campaign implementation (e.g., achieve the reach and frequency goals in half the state).

ETHICAL CONSIDERATIONS WHEN SELECTING COMMUNICATION CHANNELS

Options for communication channels are numerous, and several factors for consideration have been identified in this chapter, including audience profile and campaign resources. Ethical considerations will also be a factor. Does the end justify the means in a case where antiabortionists block the entrance to clinics and threaten the lives of doctors? Or what about a case in which activists threaten (but do not physically harm) a woman wearing a fur coat? Considerable mention has been made of channels involving access to computers, emails, and the Internet. What about the fact that many target audiences don't have this access, or even the skills, to fully utilize and benefit from these new media campaigns?

Organizations, understandably, have ethical and legal concerns about the use of social media, especially regarding security, staff productivity, and negative postings from readers. To address this, many organizations develop and distribute formal policy and best-practice statements.

Table 14.1   Profiles of Major Media Types

Medium	Advantages	Disadvantages
Newspapers	Flexibility, timeliness, good local market coverage, broad acceptability, high believability	Short life, poor reproduction quality, small pass-along audience
Television	Good mass-market coverage; low cost per exposure; combines sight, sound, and motion; appealing to the senses	High absolute costs, high clutter, fleeting exposure, less audience selectivity
Direct Mail	High audience selectivity, flexibility, allows personalization	Relative high cost per exposure, "junk mail" image
Radio	Good local acceptance, high geographic and demographic selectivity, low cost	Audio only, fleeting exposure, low attention ("the half-hear" medium); fragmented audiences
Magazines	High geographic and demographic selectivity, credibility, and prestige; high-quality reproduction; long life; good pass-along readership	Long ad purchase lead time, high cost, no guarantee of position
Outdoor	Flexibility, high repeat exposure, low cost, low message competition, good positional selectivity	Little audience selectivity, creative limitations
Social Media	Timeliness, ability to leverage target audience networks, provides for interactions and feedback, ability to personalize, ability to prompt and reinforce behaviors	Resource intensive, primarily audience controlled
Websites	High selectivity, low cost, immediacy, interactive capabilities	Small, demographically skewed audience; relatively low impact
Sales Promotions	Attention getting, stronger and quicker buyer response, incentives add value	Short life, potential image of "trinkets and trash"
Public Relations	High credibility, ability to catch prospects off guard, ability to reach prospects preferring to avoid salespeople and advertisements	Less audience reach and frequency
Events and Experiences	Relevance, high involvement and active engagement, "softer sell"	Less audience reach, high cost per exposure
Personal Selling	Effective for understanding consumer objections and for building buyer preference, conviction, action, and relationships	Audience resistance, high cost

Source: Adapted from P. Kotler and G. Armstrong, *Principles of Marketing* (Upper Saddle River, NJ: Prentice Hall, 2001), 553. Reprinted with permission.

And here's one to ponder: Is it wrong to advertise for a kidney donor? In 2010, in the United States, 19 people on average die each day waiting for an organ transplant, 10 of them waiting for a kidney.[55] MatchingDonors.com is a nonprofit organization trying to improve the odds of finding an organ donor for patients needing transplants. Reportedly, they have the world's largest database of available altruistic donors, ones who are not allowed to receive any financial benefit from organ donation. Some physicians wage campaigns against such websites, believing the practice is unethical and should be illegal, as it "bypasses" the national organ donor list. Proponents of the website argue that those on the organ donor list get organs harvested only from cadavers and that there are currently 70,000 people waiting for a kidney and that half of those on this list will die while waiting.[56]

CHAPTER SUMMARY

Communication channels, also referred to as media channels, can be categorized as one of three types: mass, selective, or personal. *Mass media* channels are called for when large groups of people need to be quickly informed and persuaded regarding an issue or desired behavior; *selective* channels are used when target audiences can be reached more cost effectively through targeted channels such as direct mail; *personal channels* include social networking sites as well as one-on-one meetings and conversations.

Traditional communication channels, as the label implies, are those you are probably most familiar with and exposed to:

- Advertising and PSAs
- Public relations and special events
- Printed materials
- Special promotional items
- Signage and displays
- Personal selling

You are encouraged to consider new media and other nontraditional options that may be more successful in "catching your audience by surprise." They may also allow your audience more time to consider your messages:

- Social media: Facebook, YouTube, Instagram blogs, online forums, texting, Twitter, texts on mobile phones
- Websites
- Popular entertainment media
- Public art
- Product integration

Eight factors are presented to guide your selection of communication types, vehicles, and timing:

Factor 1: Your campaign objectives and goals

Factor 2: Desired reach and frequency

Factor 3: Your target audience

Factor 4: Being there just in time

Factor 5: Being there "in the event of"

Factor 6: Integrated marketing communications

Factor 7: Knowing the advantages and disadvantages of media types

Factor 8: Your budget

RESEARCH HIGHLIGHT

Increasing Use of 1% Low-Fat Milk in Oklahoma

(2012)

This research highlight presents an example of using a comparison group to evaluate the impact of an intervention, in this case comparing two distinct, but similar, media markets. One of the markets received an intervention that included a campaign utilizing multiple media channels, with the comparison group receiving "nothing new." It is also noteworthy that outcomes are measured by using sales data from participating retail partners, providing more robust indicators of behavior change. Information for this case was provided by Robert John, professor of health promotion sciences at the University of Oklahoma Health Sciences Center, and was presented at the third World Social Marketing Conference in Toronto in April 2013.

Background

In 2012, the Oklahoma Nutrition Information and Education Project (ONIE) launched a campaign in the Oklahoma City media market to influence low-income individuals to switch from whole and 2% milk to 1% milk to decrease consumption of saturated fats. The primary target audience was the Supplemental Nutrition Assistance Program (SNAP) population, formerly known as the Food Stamp Program. The secondary audience was participants in the Supplemental Nutrition Program for Women and Infant Children (WIC; those under 185% of the Federal Poverty Level) with children over 2 years of age. Within both populations, the "bulls-eye" target audience was those using 2% milk, as formative research indicated they were most likely to switch. Additional formative research utilizing a telephone survey with 532 SNAP households indicated that 91.9% were not using low-fat or nonfat milk and that 73.9% considered 2% milk to be low-fat milk, even though the fat content in 2% is two thirds that of whole milk.

This misconception became the primary focal point of the campaign and guided the development of the campaign

slogan "1% Low-Fat Milk Has Perks" and several key messages, including the following factoids:

- 1% is not watered down whole milk
- 1% has the same nutrients as 2% and whole
- Only 1% is low-fat milk; it's a healthy protein drink
- 1% milk has the same amount of Vitamin D as 2% and whole

The campaign spokesperson was the popular Kendrick Perkins, center for the Oklahoma City Thunder NBA basketball franchise. Promotional materials featured messages focused on Perkins, including "When Kendrick Perkins found out about the fat content in 2% and whole milk, he decided to take the matter into his own enormous hands" (See Figure 14.13). The project also developed collaborative relationships with regional grocery stores, milk producers, and a trade association in the Oklahoma City media market.

The 12-week mass media campaign ran from June 11 to September 2, 2012, with nearly $250,000 being allocated to promotional elements. These included the following:

- Advertising: television, radio, magazine ads, bus wraps (see Figure 14.14)
- Social media: Facebook, twitter, blogs
- Website
- Point of sale: All participating retailers in the intervention area displayed some type of point-of-purchase material (a life-size cutout of Perkins, clings on dairy case doors, a nutrition education flyer, and, in some stores, discount coupons for 1% low-fat milk purchases)

| Figure 14.13 | The campaign's spokesperson was the popular Kendrick Perkins, center for the Oklahoma City Thunder NBA basketball franchise. |

Source: Oklahoma Nutrition Information and Education Project.

Figure 14.14 Bus wrap for the campaign.

Source: Oklahoma Nutrition Information and Education Project.

- Flyers distributed in elementary schools where more than 50% of the meals were free or reduced in price

Method and Findings

The intervention in the Oklahoma City media market was evaluated on several outcome measures: increases in awareness and understanding, levels of engagement with social media efforts, and, most importantly, increases in sales of 1% milk.

In terms of campaign recall, a random telephone survey of SNAP beneficiaries indicated that 18.0% recalled the campaign, with 58.6% of those recalling it accurately. To assess increases in understanding of important facts regarding 1% milk, a pre- and post-intervention telephone survey of SNAP beneficiaries indicated that several perceptions had been "corrected," primarily that 2% milk is not considered low-fat milk (see Table 14.2).

In terms of interaction with digital media, the webpage received 10,100 visits and 8,296 clicks; Pandora generated an estimated 3.35 million impressions, with 23,963 clicks; YouTube videos received

Table 14.2 Changes in Low-Fat Milk Knowledge

	Pre- and Post-Intervention Telephone Survey		
Fact Tested	**Pre: Correct Answers** $(n = 500)$	**Post: Correct Answers** $(n = 539)$	**% Increase**
1% milk is not watered-down whole milk	44.4%	50.5%	+13.7%
2% milk is not considered low-fat milk	26.1%	30.0%	+14.9%
1% has fewer calories and less fat but the same vitamins and minerals as whole milk	58.7%	65.5%	+11.6%

53,000 views; and a number of sports blogs posted the TV commercial on their site.

The most rigorous measure of impact was utilization of sales data to measure milk purchases at each participating grocery store in the Oklahoma City area compared with Tulsa, the comparison media market. Measurements of sales were obtained from retailers at four points in time: (a) at the same period in the prior year, (b) at a three-month period prior to intervention, (c) during the intervention period, and (d) at a three-month period after the intervention. As indicated in Table 14.3, there was a 15.0% increase in the purchase of 1% milk after the completion of the 12-week campaign and a 4.6% decrease in purchases of whole milk.

Table 14.3 Sales Data Based on Five Supermarket Chains (144 Retail Stores) in Oklahoma

	Monthly Milk Sales					
	Oklahoma City Media Market				Tulsa Media Market	
Type of Milk	**Pre**	**Post**	**% Difference**	**% Change**	**Pre**	**Post**
Whole	37.1%	35.4%	−1.7%	−4.6%	33.9%	34.2%
2% Reduced Fat	42.8%	43.3%	+0.5%	+1.2%	46.3%	46.0%
1% Low-Fat	10.0%	11.5%	+1.5%	+15.0%	8.5%	8.4%

DISCUSSION QUESTIONS AND EXERCISES

1. Why is the promotional tool the last of the 4P tools to be considered?

2. In the opening Marketing Highlight regarding blood donation, what was different about the desired benefit program managers were appealing to compared to the desired benefit in traditional blood donation campaigns?

3. How do you or would you answer this question: "What's the difference between social marketing and social media?"

4. Share examples of social marketing efforts using social media that you are aware of or have implemented.

CHAPTER 14 NOTES

1. Australian Red Cross Blood Service, "Battle of the Burbs' Blood Challenge Is ON!," accessed April 7, 2014, http://www.donateblood.com.au/media-centre/news/qld/%E2%80%98battle-of-the-burbs%E2%80%99-blood-challenge-is-on.

2. Personal communication from Kathleen Chell, December 2013.

3. C. Fratto, "2011 University Attack Test Campaign University of Queensland National Marketing Post Analysis Report November 2011" (Australian Red Cross Blood Service, November 2011), 5.

4. Ibid.

5. Campaign Brief, "Australian Red Cross Blood Service Case Study: How an Influential Word of Mouth Campaign Increased Blood Donations via Social Soup" (May 13, 2013), accessed April 7, 2014, http://www.campaignbrief.com/2013/05/australian-red-cross-blood-ser.html.

6. Ibid.

7. Australian Red Cross Blood Service, "Battle of the Burbs'."

8. Australian Red Cross Blood Service, "Battle of the Burbs" (n.d.), accessed April 7, 2014, http://www.donateblood.com.au/category/news-tags/battle-of-the-burbs.

9. Sean Corcoran's Blog, "Defining Earned, Owned and Paid Media," (December 16, 2009), accessed June 2, 2014, http://blogs.forrester.com/interactive_marketing/2009/12/defining-earned-owned-and-paid-media.html.

10. P. Kotler and K. Keller, *Marketing Management*, 12th ed. (Upper Saddle River, NJ: Prentice Hall, 2005), 546.

11. J. Dunn, "Denver Water's Ads Already Working Conservation Angle," *Denver Post* (July 13, 2006), accessed April 22, 2007, http://www.denverpost.com/portlet/article/html/fragments/print_article.jsp?articleId=4043. Ads developed by Sukle Advertising and Design.

12. Denver Water, "Thank You for Using Even Less" (n.d.), accessed April 21, 2014, http://www.denverwater.org/Conservation/UseOnlyWhatYouNeed/.

13. P. Kotler and N. Lee, *Marketing in the Public Sector* (Upper Saddle River, NJ: Wharton School, 2006), 152.

14. M. Siegel and L. A. Doner, *Marketing Public Health: Strategies to Promote Social Change* (Gaithersburg, MD: Aspen, 1998), 393.

15. Ibid., 394.

16. Ibid., 396.

17. Prevent Cancer Foundation, "Prevent Cancer Super Colon Exhibit" (n.d.), accessed March 7, 2011, http://www.preventcancer.org/education2c.aspx?id=156&ekmensel=15074e5e_34_38_btnlink.

18. Prevent Cancer Foundation, "Prevent Cancer Super Colon Exhibit" (n.d.), http://prevent-cancer.org/what-we-do/education/super-colon/.

19. For more information, go to http://www.petwaste.surfacewater.info.

20. Kotler and Keller, *Marketing Management*, 556.

21. "How One Man Has Fought to Clear the Air Over China's Polution," *Toronto Star* (April 23, 2013), accessed April 23, 2014, http://www.thestar.com/news/world/2013/04/23/environmentalist_ma_jun_fights_for_change_to_clean_up_chinas_pollution.html.

22. "Cleaning Up China," *Time* Magazine (June 24, 2013), accessed April 23, 2014, http://content.time.com/time/magazine/article/0,9171,2145500,00.html.

23. "How One Man Has Fought," *Toronto Star*.

24. "Cleaning Up China," *Time* Magazine.

25. Queen Rania Al Abdullah: The Hashemite Kingdom of Jordan, "Social Media for Social Good: Queen Rania Calls on Online World to Unite on Behalf of 75 Million Out of School Children" (December 11, 2009), accessed March 10, 2011, http://www.queenrania.jo/media/news/social-media-social-good-queen-rania-calls-online-world-unite-behalf-75-million-out-schoo.

26. Ibid.

27. Centers for Disease Control and Prevention, "The Health Communicator's Social Media Toolkit" (August 2010), accessed March 10, 2011, http://www.cdc.gov/healthcommunication/ToolsTemplates/SocialMediaToolkit_BM.pdf.

28. Information for this case was provided by Michael Miller of Brown-Miller Communications, March 8, 2011.

29. Adapted from the Centers for Disease Control and Prevention's "The Health Communicator's Social Media Toolkit."

30. For more on social media from a social marketing perspective, see R. C. Lefebvre, "Integrating Cellphones and Mobile Technologies Into Public Health Practice: A Social Marketing Perspective," *Health Promotion Practice* 10 (2009): 490–494; R. C. Lefebvre, "The New Technology: The Consumer as Participant Rather Than Target Audience," *Social Marketing Quarterly* 13 (2007): 31–42; R. C. Lefebvre, J. Preece, and B. Shneiderman, "The Reader-to-Leader Framework: Motivating Technology-Mediated Social Participation in AIS," *Transactions on Human-Computer Interaction* 1 (2009); 13–32; and the On Social Marketing and Social Change website, http://socialmarketing.blogs.com.

31. Personal communication from Craig Lefebvre, March 8, 2011.

32. Personal communication from Megan Jacobs, April 29, 2014.

33. E. Macario, C. Krause, J. C., Katt, S. Caplan, R. S. Payes, and A. Bornkessel, "NIDA Engages Teens Through Its Blog: Lessons Learned," *Journal of Social Marketing* 3, no. 1 (2013): 43.

34. Ibid., 48.

35. J. Cowhig, "2nd Global Police Tweet-a-Thon Friday, Nov 1st–Saturday, Nov 2nd," Chelsea Massachusetts Police Department (October 17, 2013), accessed April 21, 2014, http://chelseapolice.com/2nd-global-police-tweet-a-thon-beginning-at-8-a-m-friday-nov-1st.

36. C. Crawford, "World's 2nd Global Tweet-a-thon Is Here," *MercerIslandPatch* (October 31, 2013), accessed April 21, 2014, http://mercerisland.patch.com/groups/police-and-fire/p/friday-worlds-2nd-global-police-tweetathon-mercerisland?ncid=newsltuspatc00000001&evar4=picks-2-post&newsRef=true.

37. Pop!Tech,"Project Masiluleke: A Breakthrough Initiative to Combat HIV/AIDS Utilizing Mobile Technology & HIV Self-Testing in South Africa" (n.d.), accessed April 29, 2014, http://poptech.org/system/uploaded_files/27/original/Project_Masiluleke_Brief.pdf.

38. Ibid.

39. Ibid.

40. Lifebuoy, "Lifebuoy Helps More Children Reach Their 5th Birthday" (n.d.), accessed April 23, 2014, http://www.lifebuoy.com/socialmission/help-childreach5/helpchild.

41. Kotler and Keller, *Marketing Management*, 613.

42. E. M. Rogers et al., *Proceedings from the Conference on Entertainment Education for Social Change* (Los Angeles: Annenberg School of Communications, 1989).

43. A. R. Andreasen, *Marketing Social Change: Changing Behavior to Promote Health, Social Development, and the Environment* (San Francisco: Jossey-Bass, 1995), 215.

44. J. Davies, "Preventing HIV/AIDS With Condoms: Nine Tips You Can Use" (n.d.), accessed April 12, 2007, http://www.johndavies.com/johndavies/new2html/9tips_print.htm.

45. Keep America Beautiful, "I'm Not Your Mama: Mississippi's War Against Highway Litter" (n.d.), accessed April 13, 2007, http://www.kab.org/aboutus2.asp?id=642.

46. Centers for Disease Control and Prevention, "Entertainment Education: Overview" (n.d.), accessed October 10, 2006, http://www.cdc.gov/communication/entertainment_education.htm.

47. Social Impact Games, "Entertaining Games With Non-entertainment Goals" (n.d.), accessed April 12, 2007, http://www.socialimpactgames.com/modules.php?op=modload&name=News&file=article&sid=116&mode=thread&order=1&thold=0.

48. J. Weaver, "A License to Shill," *MSNBC News* (November 17, 2002), accessed July 25, 2011, http://www.msnbc.msn.com/id/3073513/.

49. P. Kotler and G. Armstrong, *Principles of Marketing* (Upper Saddle River, NJ: Prentice Hall, 2001), 552.

50. Kotler and Armstrong, *Principles of Marketing*, 513–517.

51. Ibid.

52. Ad Council, "Drunk Driving Prevention (1983–Present)" (n.d.), accessed April 18, 2007, http://www.adcouncil.org/default.aspx?id=137.

53. Ibid., "Campaign Description."

54. Ibid.

55. Matching Donors [website], accessed March 7, 2011, http://www.matchingdonors.com/life/index.cfm?page=main&cfid=12265246&cftoken=12950547.

56. S. Satel, "Is It Wrong to Advertise for Organs?," *National Review Online* (April 13, 2007), 16.

PART V

MANAGING SOCIAL MARKETING PROGRAMS

Chapter 15

DEVELOPING A PLAN FOR MONITORING AND EVALUATION

Marketing is a learning game. You make a decision. You watch the results. You learn from the results. Then you make better decisions.

—Dr. Philip Kotler[1]
Northwestern University

Now you've reached a step you may not be eager for—developing a plan for monitoring and evaluation. If this is true for you, your experiences and conversations may sound similar to the following common laments:

- "My administrators and additional funders think it's nice I can report on how many PSAs we ran and how many hits we got to our website, but I can see it in their eyes. It's not enough. They want to know how many more people got an HIV/AIDS test as a result of our efforts. And actually, that's not even enough. What they really want to know is how many positives did we find and how much did it cost us to find each one."
- "You think that's hard. In my line of work, they want to know if the fish are any healthier."
- "Most of the evaluation strategies I've looked at could cost as much as the small budget I have for this campaign. I honestly can't justify it. And yet, everyone seems to want it."
- "Quite frankly, my concern is with the results. What if it's bad news—that we didn't reach our goal? They like the plan, are going to fully fund it, and trust that we know what we're doing. Bad news could dampen any further work like this."

This chapter describes the five major components to be included in an evaluation plan, Step 8 in this model:

1. *Purpose*. Why are you conducting this evaluation and who is the audience?

2. *Results to be measured*. What will you measure in order to achieve the evaluation purpose?

3. *Methods*. How will you conduct these measurements?

4. *Timing*. When will these measurements be made and by whom?

5. *Budget*. How much will it cost?

MARKETING HIGHLIGHT

ParticipACTION

Increasing Physical Activity of Kids in Canada by Bringing Back Play

(2012–2013)

Source: Participaction.

This inspiring Marketing Highlight was chosen for this chapter on evaluation because it demonstrates the power of frequent monitoring of campaign outcomes, with findings informing new and improved directions. It is also impressive because rigorous assessments include the full array of outcome metrics described in this chapter. Information for this case

was provided by Tala Chulak-Bozzer (knowledge manager) and Rachel Shantz (marketing director) at ParticipACTION.

Background

ParticipACTION is a national nongovernmental (NGO) in Canada, originally launched as a government program in the 1970s to "get Canadians moving." For more than 30 years, the organization has worked in partnership with public, private, and other NGOs supporting solutions to turn Canada into a more active, healthier nation.[2] In 2008, they launched the Inactive Kids campaign, one hitting hard on the consequences of physical inactivity on children's lives. In 2010, the campaign focus changed, this time addressing subsequent research indicating that many moms thought their kids were already getting enough physical activity.[3] In response, Think Again was launched, a mass-media campaign informing moms of the recommended daily physical activity levels, and, as the campaign theme implies, helping them realize their kids weren't as active as they thought. Subsequent monitoring research on this campaign, however, showed that although awareness of recommended physical activity levels was increasing, moms saw the campaign as authoritarian. Once again, the team made a course correction, this time focusing on solutions rather than reinforcing the problem.

Target Audience and Desired Behavior

The team described their *target audience* as "moms with kids aged 5–11 who naturally want the best for their kids," those who wanted their kids to be happy, healthy, and self-confident but worried about their academic performance, circle of friends, problems at school, bullying, and more.[4] The *desired behavior* was for these moms to support their child in engaging in active play daily to help achieve the recommended 60 minutes of physical activity per day.

Audience Insights

The major focus on active play, versus physical activity per se, was in response to common perceptions among moms that physical activity required enrolling their kids in organized sports and/or regular classes. And although they believed organized physical activity was the best solution, they had financial considerations and time constraints, not seeing how they could easily squeeze another class or activity into their kids' schedules due to conflicting priorities in their households. They would also be competing with their kids' preference for "screen time."

Strategies

A strong *positioning* statement inspired the communication strategy, the primary intervention for this effort. Campaign planners wanted these moms to see active play as a simple and fun way to get their kids more physically active. They created a new tagline, "Bring Back Play," and wanted moms to think of the ParticipACTION brand as a friend who "speaks with" them, not a mentor who "speaks to" them. They wanted to highlight the benefits of physical activity as well as tap a nostalgic sentiment for the games the moms had played in their childhood.

Campaign *messages* stressed the importance of getting 60 minutes of physical activity a day and showcased simple ways to do so through play. *Creative elements* were developed to avoid pointing fingers at moms; rather, they took a more positive approach to make moms/parents feel as if they were all on the same team. The "Bring Back Play" concept was brought to life with visual images of kids of different ages engaging in classic active games (see Figure 15.1).

Communication channels reached out to these moms at major touch points: TV (paid and unpaid), print (posters, newspaper and magazine ads), radio, collateral materials, digital banners (available to provincial partners), mobile and social

Figure 15.1 Print media focusing on outdoor games "we used to play."

Source: Participaction.

Figure 15.2 One of several digital banners for the campaign.

media (Facebook, Twitter), and grassroots activities (see Figure 15.2). They

redesigned their Wall of Inspiration, an online application that integrates Google Maps and serves as a platform for people to share their stories and be inspired on how to be more physically active. Moms were invited to share stories, pictures, or videos on how they "bring back play" with their kids as well as read other moms' submissions for inspiration. A mobile "Bring Back Play" app was developed to provide moms with an at-hand tool to teach their kids the classic games they played as a kid. How to play, space required, and equipment needed were among the details provided for over 50 active games on the app. A Bring Back Play Funmobile, presented in partnership with Healthy Families BC, made 89 tour stops in 28 communities in British Columbia in Phase I of the tour (2012), making stops at schools, community centers, neighborhood parks, and festivals. Enthusiastic activators led kids through classic games and encouraged spontaneous free play with the skipping ropes, balls, chalk, and hula hoops provided. Parents present were engaged to inform them of the benefits of play (see Figure 15.3).

Results

An assessment of results for the campaign conducted by Vision Critical in March 2013 was encouraging, and is summarized in the outcomes section that follows. In addition, major campaign inputs and outputs are also noted.

Inputs

Core funding from the campaign was sourced from ParticipACTION's annual operational budget. For the first time, additional media funding came from provincial partners in British Columbia, Nova Scotia, and New Brunswick. In addition, campaign messages are disseminated and marketing resources are made available to 4,541 NGOs that are part of the ParticipACTION Network.

Outputs

In the first year, the campaign generated more than 353 million total media impressions, including more than 14 million earned media impressions.

Outcomes

As will be described in this chapter, outcome measures are those related to audience response to the intervention, including any changes in awareness, understanding, attitudes, and behaviors. This case highlight measured and reported on five major outcome metrics: awareness of the campaign, understanding of key messages, attitudes toward the desired behavior and communication strategies, engagement with campaign elements, and changes in

Figure 15.3   British Columbia's Funmobile.

Source: **Participaction.**

behavior as a result of the campaign. Statistics summarized in Box 15.1 represent findings from a 2013 Vision Critical online survey among moms with kids 5 to 11 years old ($n = 1,142$) and the general population ($n = 757$). In some cases, findings were compared with those from similar surveys for the prior ParticipACTION campaigns conducted in 2011 and 2012 with moms of children age 5 to 11.

Box 15.1
Outcome Measures for the 2012–2013 Bring Back Play campaign

Awareness among the target population was measured relative to awareness of the ParticipACTION brand:

- Thirty-six percent of moms were aware (unaided) of ParticipACTION, a 57% increase over 2011 results.
- Fifty-one percent of moms had prompted recall of the campaign and 89% correctly recalled the campaign messages (net).

Understanding among the moms was measured by their correctly identifying the physical activity guidelines for children:

(Continued)

(Continued)

- Twenty-two percent were aware of the 60-minutes-of-physical-activity guideline, a 57% increase over 2011 results.

Attitudes these moms had toward the brand, desired behavior, and campaign communications were assessed using the following metrics.

- Twenty-nine percent ranked daily physical activity as a top priority for their kids in terms of how they should spend their leisure time, a 14% increase over 2011 results.
- Ninety-four percent agreed that unstructured activities, like outdoor play with friends, are an effective way for kids to get the physical activity they need each day
- Eighty-four percent agreed that unstructured activities, such as outdoor play, are just as effective as structured physical activities in helping kids be healthy.
- Ninety-two percent agreed that the amount of physical activity recommended in the ads is achievable.
- Ninety-three percent agreed that the information presented in the ads was credible
- Eighty-seven percent agreed that "these ads were inspiring" versus 65% for the prior Think Again ads.
- Fifty-one percent indicated that the ads made them feel "happy," and 42% indicated that they made them feel "hopeful."

Engagement activities with the brand were measured with metrics from social media platforms:

- The campaign garnered 27,492 Facebook fans versus 1,000 prior to the campaign.
- Twitter followers reached 7,112.
- The Bring Back Play app had 11,479 visits between October 2012 and March 2013.

Behavior measures include intent to engage as well as actual engagement in the behavior:

- Moms reported that their kids were active (MVPA) for 60 minutes per day on 4.7 days of the week, a directional increase of 0.2 days over 2011.
- Seventy-two percent of moms who saw the ads took some sort of action as a result of the ads.
- Twenty-nine percent of moms started doing more physical activity by themselves or with their family, a 21% increase over 2011 results.

STEP 8: DEVELOP A PLAN FOR MONITORING AND EVALUATION

We recommend that you take time to develop a plan for monitoring and evaluating your social marketing effort before creating your budget in Step 9 and implementation plan in Step 10. You will want your final budget to include funding for this critical activity and your implementation plan to include action items to ensure that it happens.

This chapter will guide you in determining these funding needs and identifying related activities. It is intended to help by outlining components of a monitoring and evaluation plan mentioned earlier, posed in the form of questions you'll want to answer sequentially—starting with the toughest one, of course:

- Why are you conducting this measurement, and who is the audience for the results?
- What will you measure?
- How will you conduct these measurements?
- When will these measurements be taken?
- How much will it cost?

One distinction is important to clarify up front: the difference between the term *monitoring* and the term *evaluation.*

Monitoring refers to measurements conducted sometime after you launch your social marketing effort but before it is completed. Its purpose is to help you determine whether you need to make midcourse corrections that will ensure that you reach your ultimate marketing goals.

Evaluation, on the other hand, is a measurement and final report on what happened, answering the following bottom-line question: Did you reach your goals for changes in behaviors, knowledge, and attitudes? Additional questions are also likely to be addressed in the evaluation. Were activities implemented on time and on budget? Were there any unintended consequences that will need to be addressed now or in future projects? Which program elements worked well to support outcomes? Which ones didn't? Was there anything missing? What will you do differently next time, if there is a next time?[5]

WHY ARE YOU CONDUCTING THIS MEASUREMENT?

Your purpose for this measurement often shapes what you measure, how you measure, and when you measure. Consider the differing implications for your plan for each of the following potential reasons for your effort. Notice that audiences for the measurement results will also vary, depending on your purpose.

- To fulfill a grant requirement
- To do better the next time you conduct the same campaign
- To (hopefully) get continued or even increased funding
- To help you decide how to prioritize and allocate your resources going forward
- To alert you to midcourse corrections you need to make to achieve your goals

To fulfill a grant requirement. Sometimes the nature of the monitoring and/or evaluation will be predetermined by specifications in a grant. Consider a case where a city receives a grant from a state department of transportation (DOT) to increase the use of pedestrian flags in the city's eight crosswalks in a downtown corridor. Assume the DOT is hoping that this city's campaign strategies are successful and that these strategies can then be shared by the DOT with other cities in the state. The campaign's evaluation plan will certainly include measuring levels of flag usage before and after the campaign. And the funder (primary audience for the measurement) will need to be assured that the data were collected using a systematic, reliable, and verifiable methodology that can be replicated in other cities.

To do better next time. What if, instead, you are sincerely interested in measuring what happened so that you can improve results in your next similar effort? Perhaps it is a pilot and you want to evaluate the campaign elements to decide what worked well and should be repeated, what could be improved, and what elements should be "dropped" next time around. Imagine a countywide effort to reduce smoking around children in cars. A pilot is carried out the first year to help determine what elements of the campaign should be used when it is rolled out countywide in Year 2. The pilot includes a packet of materials sent home with children from the elementary schools and contains a secondhand tobacco smoke information card, a plug to replace the cigarette lighter, a smoke-free pledge card, and an air freshener with the campaign's slogan, "Please Smoke Outside." Follow-up surveys with parents will then measure changes in parents' levels of smoking around their child in the car as well as their ratings on which of the materials in the packet they noticed, used, and felt were influential. Imagine further that the results indicated that some of the parents thought the air freshener would reduce the harmful effects of the smoke, so they didn't change their habits. This finding, of course, would then lead the county (the primary audience for this measurement) to eliminate the $1.50 item when the campaign was rolled out countywide.

To get support for continued funding. Often the purpose of an evaluation is to persuade funders to reinvest in the project to sustain it into the future. As you can imagine, key to the success of this endeavor is identifying criteria the funders will use to make their decisions and then creating an evaluation plan that includes measures to provide this information. Consider the Road Crew case in Wisconsin, mentioned in Chapter 9, in which a service using limousines and other luxury vehicles picks up people at their home, business, or hotel; takes them to the bars of their choice; and returns them home at the end of the evening—all for about $15 to $20 an evening. A key statistic that funders of the program (the primary audience for this measurement) were interested in was a cost-benefit analysis, and the program's evaluation methodology provided just that. You may recall that it showed an estimated cost of $6,400 to avoid a crash through Road Crew, compared with $231,000, the estimated costs incurred from an alcohol-related crash.

To help determine resource allocation. Management may also, or instead, want to use an evaluation effort to help decide how resources should be allocated in the future. In King County, Washington, for example, the Department of Natural Resources and Parks wanted an evaluation survey to help decide which of some 30 community outreach efforts should receive more funding and which, perhaps, should be pulled back. This objective led to a plan to measure household behaviors that each of these 30 programs sought to influence (e.g., leave grass clippings on the lawn). The programs with the greatest potential market opportunity for growth were then considered first for increased support, with market opportunity being determined by the percentage of households doing the behavior sometimes but not on a regular basis (the action stage of change) or not doing the behavior at all but considering doing it (the contemplation stage of change).

To decide if course corrections are needed. This purpose will lead to a monitoring effort, measuring sometime after an effort launches but before completion, to determine whether goals are likely to be met based on how the market is responding.

Example: Pedestrian Flags. In 2007, the City of Kirkland in Washington state was interested in knowing the difference their 12-year PedFlag program was making. In 1995, in an effort to increase the visibility of pedestrians in crosswalks, they had installed pole holders with orange flags for pedestrians to carry when crossing streets in 37 locations around the city (see Figure 15.4). City officials estimated that about 5% of pedestrians used the flags, but no formal measure had confirmed this. They were interested in knowing what they could do to increase usage to a desired level of 40% by 2011. Observation research of more than 3,000 pedestrians over a 20-day period estimated usage at 11%, and barriers research with those not using the flags provided inspirational feedback. Many did not know what the orange flag was for, thinking it either was intended to alert drivers to a pedestrian crosswalk or signaled a construction zone—a *product* problem. Others noted that often there were no flags on their side of the street—a *place* problem. And the vast majority indicated they felt safe and were sure drivers could see them—a *promotion* problem. Enhancements to the program included redesigning the flags so that they had an immediate connection with pedestrian crosswalks and making them easy to grab by placing them in buckets instead of pole holders (see Figure 15.5). The number of flags at each crosswalk was increased from 6 to 18, and local businesses were engaged in notifying the city when they saw supplies running low. New promotional strategies included a slogan, "Take It to Make It," and messages intended to increase perception of risk (see Figure 15.6). Five

Figure 15.4 Original PedFlags were orange and had to be inserted carefully in the pole holder.

Figure 15.5 Enhanced PedFlags were yellow and were easy to grab and then replace in a bucket.

Figure 15.6 Campaign messages were intended to increase risk perception as well as the benefits of taking a flag.

months after the enhanced strategies had been implemented, the monitoring research methodology was replicated and indicated that usage had increased by 64% (from 11% to 18%).

WHAT WILL YOU MEASURE?

What you will measure to achieve your evaluation purpose is likely to fall into one or more of five categories: *inputs, outputs, outcomes, impacts,* and *return on investment* (ROI). As you will read, required efforts and rigor vary significantly by category.

Overview of a Modified Logic Model

A logic model is a visual schematic that organizes program evaluative measures into categories that can be measured and reported using a "logical" flow, beginning with program inputs and outputs, moving on to program effects in terms of outcomes and impact, and ending with (ideally) reporting on returns on investment (see Table 15.1). The difficulty of reporting increases the further one moves to the right on the model.

Table 15.1 A Modified Logic Model for Reporting on Social Marketing Efforts

Inputs	Outputs	Outcomes	Impact	Return on Investment
Resources allocated to the campaign or program effort	Program activities conducted to influence audiences to perform a desired behavior	Audience response to outputs	Indicators that show levels of impact on the social issue that was the focus for the effort	Value of changes in behavior and the calculated rate of return on the spending associated with the effort
• Money • Staff time • Volunteer hours • Existing materials used • Distribution channels utilized • Existing partner contributions	• Number of materials disseminated, calls made, events held, websites created, social media tactics employed • Reach and frequency of communications • Free media coverage • Number of special events held • Paid media impressions and cost per impression • Implementation of program elements (e.g., whether on time, on budget)	• Changes in behavior • Numbers of related products or services "sold" (e.g., safer pesticides) • Changes in behavior intent • Changes in knowledge • Changes in beliefs • Responses to campaign elements (e.g., YouTube videos shared, Facebook postings shared, Twitter followers, number of attendees at special events) • Campaign awareness • Customer satisfaction levels • New partnerships and contributions created • Policy changes	• Improvements in health • Lives saved • Injuries prevented • Water quality improved • Water supply increased • Air quality improved • Landfill reduced • Wildlife habitats protected • Animal cruelty reduced • Crimes prevented • Financial well-being improved	• Cost to change one behavior • For every dollar spent, dollars saved or generated • After subtracting expenses, the rate of return on investment

Input Measures

The easiest and most straightforward measures are those itemizing resources used to develop, implement, and evaluate the campaign. The most common elements include money spent and staff time allocated. In many cases there will also be additional contributions to the effort to report on, including any volunteer hours, existing materials, distribution channels utilized, and/or partner contributions. (Developing new partnerships for the effort would be noted in program outcomes.) The quantification of these resources will be especially important when determining return on investment, as they represent the amount invested.

Output/Process Measures

The next-easiest measures are those describing your campaign's outputs, sometimes referred to as process measures, which focus on quantifying your marketing activities as much as possible. They represent how you utilized program inputs and are distinct from outcome measures, those focusing on your target audience's response to these activities. Many are available in your records and databases.[6]

- *Number of materials distributed and media channels utilized.* This measure refers to the numbers of mailings, brochures, flyers, key chains, bookmarks, booklets, posters, or coupons put forth. This category also includes numbers and types of additional outreach activities, such as calls made, events held, websites created, and social media tactics deployed. Note that this does not indicate whether posters were noticed, brochures were read, or events were attended, YouTube videos were viewed—only the numbers "put out there."
- *Reach and frequency.* Reach refers to the number of different people or households exposed to a particular image or message during a specified period. Frequency is the number of times within this time frame, on average, that the target audience is exposed to the communication. It is a predictor of audience response but not an indicator of such.
- *Media coverage.* Measures of media and public relations efforts, also referred to as earned media, may include reporting on numbers of column inches in newspapers and magazines, minutes on television and radio news, and paid ads on websites and special programs, and people in the audience attending a planned speaker's events. Efforts are often made to determine and report what this coverage would have cost if it had been paid for.
- *Total impressions/cost per impression.* This measurement combines information from several categories, such as reach and frequency, media exposure, and material dissemination. Typically these numbers are combined to create an estimate of the total number of people in the target audience who were exposed to campaign elements. Taking this to the next level of rigor to achieve a cost per impression, total campaign costs associated with this exposure can be divided by the estimated number of people

exposed to the campaign. For example, consider a statewide campaign targeting mothers to increase children's fruit and vegetable consumption; the campaign may have collected exposure information from media buys (e.g., parenting magazines) and any additional efforts (e.g., messages on grocery bags). Let's assume they were able to estimate that 100,000 mothers were exposed to these campaign efforts and that the associated costs were $10,000. Their cost per impression would be $0.10. These statistics can then be used over time to compare the cost efficiency of varying strategies. Suppose, for example, that in a subsequent campaign, efforts reached 200,000 mothers after funds were redirected to sending messages from child care centers and preschools, thus reducing the cost per impression to $0.05.

- *Implementation of program elements.* An audit of major activities planned and implemented (or not) may shed light on campaign outputs and outcomes. Did you do everything you planned to do? Did you complete activities on time and on budget? This audit can help address the tendency many of us have to expect campaign goals to be achieved, even though we did not implement all planned activities or spend originally allocated funds in planned time frames.

Outcome Measures

Measuring outcomes is a little more rigorous, as you are now assessing customer response to your outputs, most likely involving some type of primary research surveys. Ideally, these measures were determined by the goals you established in Step 4, the specific measurable results you want your program to achieve—one or more of the following types:

- *Changes in behavior.* These may be measured and stated in terms of a change in percentage (e.g., adult binge drinking decreased from 17% to 6%), a percentage increase or decrease (e.g., seatbelt usage increased by 20%), and/or a change in numbers (e.g., 40,000 new households signed up for food waste recycling bins, increasing the total number of households participating from 60,000 to 100,000). In 2011, for example, results of a research study conducted by Michael Slater at Ohio State University regarding behavior outcomes for the U.S. federal antidrug campaign Above the Influence were encouraging:

  A study of more than 3,000 students in 20 communities nationwide found that by the end of 8th grade, 12 percent of those who had not reported having seen the campaign took up marijuana use compared to only 8 percent among students who had reported familiarity with the campaign.[7]

  Slater believed that the successful outcomes were due in part to the fact that the campaign appears to "tap into the desire by teenagers to be independent and self-sufficient." He cited, for example, one television ad in the campaign ending with the line "Getting messed up is just another way of leaving yourself behind."[8]

- *Changes in behavior intent.* This measure might be appropriate for campaigns with minimal exposure or when campaigns have been running for only short periods of time. It may be the most appropriate measure for campaigns targeting those in the precontemplation stage, when the social marketer's goal is to move them to contemplation and then (eventually) to the action stage.
- *Changes in knowledge.* This may include changes in awareness of important facts (e.g., five drinks at one sitting is considered binge drinking), information (e.g., an estimated 75,000 people are on waiting lists for organ transplants), or recommendations (e.g., eat five or more servings of vegetables and fruit daily for better health).
- *Changes in belief.* Typical indicators include attitudes (e.g., my vote doesn't count), opinions (e.g., native plants are not attractive), and values (e.g., tanning is worth the risk).
- *Responses to campaign elements.* Here you may be counting hits to your website, times a video was shared, comments on a blog, calls to an 800 number (e.g., for a booklet on natural gardening), attendees at an event, coupon redemptions (e.g., for a bike helmet), mail or Internet orders or requests for more information (e.g., for a free consultation on home earthquake preparedness), purchases of tangible objects that have been promoted (e.g., numbers of new low-flow toilets or energy-saving lightbulbs sold compared with the numbers the previous year), or services provided (e.g., number of blood pressure checks given at a mall event).
- *Campaign awareness.* Though not necessarily an indicator of impact or success, measures of awareness of campaign elements provide some feedback on the extent to which the campaign was noticed and recalled. Measurements might include levels of unaided awareness (e.g., what you have seen or heard lately in the news about legal limits for blood alcohol levels while driving); aided awareness (e.g., what have you seen or heard lately in the news about your state's new 0.08% legal limit); or proven awareness (e.g., where you read or hear about this change in the law).
- *Customer satisfaction levels.* Customer satisfaction levels associated with service components of the campaign provide important feedback for analyzing results and for planning future efforts (e.g., ratings on levels of satisfaction with counseling at Supplemental Nutrition Program for Women, Infants, and Children [WIC] clinics).
- *Partnerships and contributions created.* Levels of participation and contributions from outside sources are significant and represent positive responses to your campaign, even though they may not be a reflection of the impact on target audience behaviors. These may include numbers of hours spent by volunteers, partners, and coalition members participating in the campaign, as well as amounts of cash and in-kind contributions received from foundations, media, and businesses. It should be noted that these contributions would be included in determining returns on investment measures.
- *Policy changes.* A legitimate campaign goal may focus on causing an important change in policies or infrastructures that will encourage and/or support behavior change. In the interest of oral health for children, for example, efforts to persuade grocery stores to remove candy and gum from checkout lanes have paid off in some communities.

Impact Measures

This measure is the most rigorous, costly, and controversial of all measurement types. In this category, you are attempting to measure the impact that the changes in behavior you have achieved (e.g., more homeowners using natural fertilizers) have had on the social issue your plan is addressing (e.g., water quality). It would indeed be great to be able to report on the following types of impact measures in addition to outputs and outcomes:

- Lives saved (e.g., from reducing drinking and driving)
- Diseases prevented (e.g., from increased physical activity)
- Injuries avoided (e.g., from safer workplace practices)
- Water quality improved (e.g., from taking prescription drugs back to pharmacies)
- Water supply increased (e.g., from increased purchases of low-flow toilets)
- Air quality improved (e.g., from use of fewer leaf blowers in a community)
- Landfill reduced (e.g., from composting food waste)
- Wildlife and habitats protected (e.g., from decreases in littering)
- Animal cruelty reduced (e.g., from increases in spaying and neutering)
- Crimes prevented (e.g., from increases in the use of motion sensors for outdoor lighting)
- Financial well-being improved (e.g., from microcredit loans for farm animals)

The reality is that not only are these measures rigorous and costly to determine, but it may in fact be inappropriate and inaccurate to try to connect your campaign activities with these impacts, even though they were designed with them in mind.

Several key points can assuage you and others: First, you need to trust, or assume, that the behavior that was chosen for your campaign is one that can have an impact on the issue (e.g., that folic acid can help prevent some birth defects). Second, you may need to wait longer to measure, as there may be a lag between adopting the behavior and seeing the impact (e.g., increased physical activity to lower blood pressure levels). Finally, your methodology for measurement may need to be quite rigorous, controlling for variables that may also be contributing to the social issue (e.g., there may not be an improvement in water quality in a lake if during your campaign a new manufacturer in the area started polluting the same waters). You will need to be diligent and forthright about whether you believe you can even determine and claim this victory.

Return on Investment

Determining and reporting on return on investment (ROI) has several benefits. It can provide a solid rationale for *continued funding* for successful programs, funding that might be cut if it is perceived that the program is too costly or is a large-budget item. This will help agency directors address tough budget questions from policymakers, peers, constituents, and the media. Second, findings can help administrators *allocate resources*, providing a "disproportionate" share to programs with the highest ROI based on a rational, "apples-to-apples" comparison. And finally, if more and more programs calculate this, we can build and share a *database of ROIs* that will assist in evaluating programs' efficacy as well as replicating the most cost-effective ones.

Most ROIs can be determined with five simple (but not necessarily easy) steps:[9]

1. *Money spent.* Determine total costs of the campaign/program, including the value of staff time spent as well as direct expenses associated with research, development, implementation, and evaluation of the program. In other words, calculate total inputs.

2. *Behaviors influenced.* Estimate how many people were influenced to adopt the targeted behavior as a result of the campaign/intervention. Hopefully this was determined when conducting outcome research.

3. *Cost per behavior influenced.* This is the simpler step, completed by dividing the dollars spent by the numbers of behaviors influenced (Step 1 divided by Step 2).

4. *Benefit per behavior.* This step answers the question, "What is the economic value of this changed behavior?" This is the most challenging step for many, as it is most often stated in terms of costs avoided as a result of the behavior adoption (e.g., healthcare costs, response to injuries, landfills developed, environmental cleanup efforts). It some cases, it may be revenue generated by behavior adoption (e.g., from home energy audits conducted by a utility). The problem is that reliable data on the economic benefit of one changed behavior are not often readily available, and many are reluctant to use even reasonable estimates. This concern might be assuaged by being up front with audiences and presenting information as a "best estimate," explaining the rigor that was taken to create the estimates.

5. *ROI.* This takes three calculations:

   a. Number of behaviors influenced (from Step 2) *times* economic benefit per behavior (from Step 4) *equals* the gross economic benefit (#2 × #4 = gross economic benefit).

   b. The gross economic benefit *minus* the amount spent (Step 1) *equals* the net benefit.

   c. The net benefit divided by the investment costs (Step 1) times 100 *equals* rate of return on the investment.

Example: A Positive ROI for Public Health. The American Public Health Association's National Public Health Week in 2013 had a bold new theme—that "Public Health is ROI: Save Lives, Save Money"—supporting "the notion that spending a small amount of money on preventive efforts can avert a much larger expenditure years later."[10] Examples were featured in a two-minute animated YouTube video that included the calculated economic values of fluoridated drinking water, seatbelt use, workplace safety programs, vaccinations, food and nutrition education, and tobacco cessation programs. It notes, for example, that every $1 invested in a child safety seat has a $42 return in avoided medical costs, and that every $1 dollar invested in effective workplace safety programs may save $4 to $6 in avoided illnesses, injuries, and fatalities.[11]

Example: Reducing Deaths and Injuries on Roads in the UK and Saving Society Money. In 2010, the UK Department for Transport launched a comprehensive program to reduce the number of deaths and injuries on the road, with an in-depth case summary provided in the 2011 *Social Marketing Casebook,* coauthored by Jeff French, Rowena Merritt, and Lucy Reynolds.[12] The campaign, branded "THINK!," utilized a 3Es approach: enforcement, education, and engineering, an intervention mix focused on enhancing the physical environment to promote safe road use (e.g., speed cameras and traffic-calming measures); strategies to increase awareness and understanding; and an emphasis on enforcement and punishment for inappropriate and unsafe behaviors. Of interest relative to ROI, the authors provided an inspiring recap:

Based on the difference between the number of road deaths in 2008 and the 1994–8 baseline average, 1,040 lives have been saved and there have been 18,044 fewer serious injuries and 69,939 slight injuries, saving society £5.1 billion, or £4.2 billion if only killed or seriously injured (KSIs) are taken into account. This means that a reduction of only 418 KSIs is needed to cover all of "THINK!" costs.[13]

HOW WILL YOU MEASURE?

Our third step in developing an evaluation and monitoring plan is to identify methodologies and techniques that will be used to actually measure indicators established in the first step. Chapter 3 outlined typical research methodologies available to you, a few of which are most typical for evaluation and monitoring measures. In general, audience surveys will be the primary technique used in measuring outcomes, given your focus on the actual influence you have had on your target audience in terms of behavior, knowledge, and beliefs. Records will provide information for determining inputs; outputs will rely on records as well but will also tap information from contact reports, anecdotal comments, and project progress reports. Outcome measures usually require quantitative surveys, whereas impact measures may require more scientific or technical surveys.

Quantitative surveys are needed when reliable data are key to evaluation (e.g., percentage increase in levels of physical activity) and are most commonly conducted using telephone surveys, online surveys, self-administered questionnaires, and/or in-person interviews. These may be proprietary or shared-cost studies in which several organizations have questions for similar populations. They may even rely on established surveys, such as the Behavioral Risk Factor Surveillance System (BRFSS) presented in Chapter 6.

Randomized controlled trials (RCTs) are rigorously designed and implemented experiments to determine the effectiveness of one or more interventions by comparing results with a similar control group that didn't receive the intervention. (See Figure 15.7 for a schematic that illustrates this systematic process.) Sometimes a new intervention (e.g., providing one-on-one assistance in completing a college application) is compared against the status quo (e.g. not providing this one-on-one assistance). Other times the objective is to compare different levels of "dosage" (e.g., pregnant mothers receiving a text message encouraging healthy behaviors once a week compared with those receiving them daily). We are most familiar hearing about this approach in the context of testing one or more medical treatments, such as a new drug, two different forms of cancer surgery, or lifestyle modifications for reducing high blood pressure. RCTs are increasingly being used in international development to compare the cost effectiveness of different interventions for reducing poverty. Though not as commonly used for testing and evaluating social marketing interventions, it is a model worth considering, especially where the stakes are high, such as in the arena of policy development.

The Behavioural Insights Team in the UK, sometimes called the "Nudge Unit," uses RCTs to develop proposals and then test them empirically across the full spectrum of government policy.[14] Findings have been used to increase organ donation, payment of fines, employment, and recycling, to name a few. In 2012, the team published an in-depth paper on the use of RCTs and outlined nine recommended steps to set up such a scientific experiment, ones at the core of the team's "Test. Learn. Adapt." methodology:[15]

Figure 15.7 Hypothetical illustration of a randomized controlled trial to test a strategy to increase the number of high school graduates who go to college.

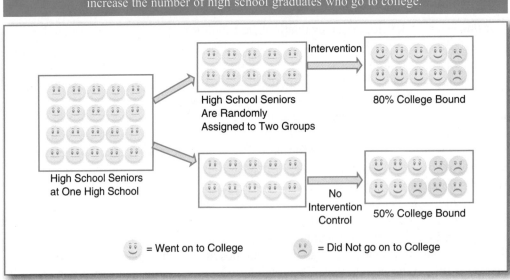

Source: Schematic adapted from L. Haynes, O. Service, B. Goldacre, and D. Torgerson, "Test, Learn, Adapt: Developing Public Policy With Randomised Controlled Trials" (Cabinet Office Behavioural Insights Team, June 2012).

- **Test**

  1. Identify two or more interventions to compare.

  2. Determine the outcome the intervention is intended to influence, as well as how it will be measured in the trial.

  3. Decide on the randomization unit (e.g., seniors in a high school, gas stations, worksites).

  4. Determine how many units are required to provide robust results.

  5. Assign each unit to one of the interventions, using a rigorous randomization method.

  6. Introduce the interventions to assigned groups.

- **Learn**

  7. Measure results and determine the impact of the intervention.

- **Adapt**

  8. Adapt the intervention based on findings.

  9. Return to Step 1 to continually improve your understanding of what works.

Nonrandomized control groups used in combination with quantitative and scientific or technical surveys will further ensure that results can be closely tied to your campaign and program efforts. A drug and alcohol prevention campaign might be implemented in high schools in one community but not in another similar community. Extra precautions can even be taken to ensure the similarity of the control groups by conducting surveys prior to the selection of the groups and then factoring in any important differences. Results on reported drug use in the control group of high schools are then compared with those in the other (similar) communities.

Qualitative surveys should be considered when evaluation requirements are less stringent or more subjective in nature and include methodologies such as focus groups, informal interviews, and capturing anecdotal comments. Focus groups might be appropriate for exploring with child care providers which components of the immunization tracking kits were most and least useful and why. This information might then refocus efforts for the next kit reprint. Informal interviews might be used to understand why potential consumers walked away from the low-flow toilet display, even after reading accompanying materials and hearing testimonials from volunteers. Anecdotal comments regarding a television campaign might be captured on phone calls to a sexual assault resource line.

Observation research is often more reliable than self-reported data and, when possible, the most appropriate technique for highly visible behaviors. It can be used for evaluating behaviors such as wearing a life vest, washing hands before returning to work, or topping off gas tanks. It may also provide more insight for assessing skill levels and barriers than self-reported data (e.g., observing people sorting garbage and placing it in proper containers or observing a WIC client finding her way around a farmers' market for the first time). An example of this method was carried out in Vancouver, British Columbia, in 2014 where there was a problem at one of the TransLink bus stops that most cities would envy: It was too popular. Commuters leaving the adjacent train station to catch a bus experienced long waiting lines, which curled around the block, creating safety hazards as well as blocking the sidewalks for pedestrians. Past efforts to manage the long lines had not always turned out well, with riders ignoring interventions or cutting through them. This time they tried a "real-time" observation approach where one morning they tested several interventions, video-recorded crowd response, and then reviewed results to determine the most effective strategy. This observation approach enabled the consulting firm Nelson/Nygaard to make recommendations to TransLink without undergoing a lengthy and more costly data gathering and analysis. They discovered, in part, that sidewalk tape was as effective as fences for keeping the sidewalk clear; stanchions (sturdy upright fixtures) were needed for switchbacks; and arrows on the ground worked better than posted signs. A senior associate at the consulting firm confirmed the benefits that observation research can have:

> Sometimes it's easy for us to be armchair planners and look at maps and this other stuff and attack a problem. But this is one of those cases that just by being there and observing over the course of a couple hours how people react to something it became clear what was going to work and what wasn't.[16]

Scientific or technical surveys may be the only sure methodology to assess the impact of your efforts. If you are charged with reporting back on the difference your efforts have made in reducing diseases, saving lives, improving water quality, and the like, you will need help designing and conducting reliable scientific surveys that not only are able to measure changes in these indicators but can also link these changes to your social marketing campaign.[17]

Records and databases will be very useful for several indicators, particularly those measuring responses to campaign elements and dissemination of campaign materials. This may involve keeping accurate track of number of visits to a website and length of time spent, numbers of calls (e.g., to a tobacco quitline), comments on Facebook (e.g., regarding tips to avoid the flu), views of a YouTube video (e.g., of a PSA persuading viewers to wear seatbelts), numbers of requests (e.g., for child care references), numbers of visits (e.g., to a teen clinic), numbers of people served (e.g., at car seat inspections), or numbers of items collected (e.g., at a needle exchange). This effort may also involve working with suppliers and partners to provide similar information from their records and databases, such as numbers of coupons redeemed (e.g., for trigger locks), tangible objects sold (e.g., compost tumblers featured in the campaign), or requests received (e.g., organ donation applications processed).

Comparative effectiveness research is a relatively new approach and is utilized primarily to inform health care decision making by providing evidence on the effectiveness, benefits, and potential harms of various treatment options. According to the U.S. Department of Health and Human Services, there are two ways this evidence is found. Researchers can look at all available evidence on the benefits and harms of each choice for different groups of people from existing clinical trials, clinical studies, and other research. They might also, or instead, conduct studies that generate new evidence of effectiveness or comparative effectiveness of a test, treatment, procedure, or health care service.[18] For social marketers, implications are similar to those of controlled experiments, where one or more interventions are evaluated based on a comparison of results.

Pilots, as Doug McKenzie-Mohr suggests, could be thought of as a "test run," providing an opportunity to work out any bugs in the program before broad-scale implementation.[19] He offers six principles as guidelines in conducting a pilot:

1. Don't mix barrier and benefit research with piloting, as this could impact behavior change levels.

2. Use a minimum of two groups to conduct a pilot, with one a control group.

3. Use random assignment to assign participants to groups.

4. Make measurements of behavior change a priority, ideally not relying on self-reports, which can be unreliable.

5. Calculate return on investment, strengthening your opportunity for broad-scale implementation.

6. Revise your pilot until it is effective.[20]

As an example, Doug shared the following pilot effort in Canada: "Turn It Off: An Anti-idling Campaign:"

This pilot project in 2007 sought to decrease both the frequency and duration of motorists' idling their vehicle engines. The project involved staff approaching motorists at Toronto schools and Toronto Transit Commission Kiss and Ride parking lots and speaking with them about the importance of turning off their vehicle engines when parked and sitting in their vehicles. Approached motorists were provided with an information card (see Figure 15.8), and signs reminding motorists to turn off their engines were posted at both the schools and the Kiss and Ride sites (see Figure 15.9). As part of the conversation, each motorist was asked to make a commitment to turn off the vehicle engine when parked. To assist motorists in remembering to turn off their engines, they were asked to place a sticker on their front windshields. The sticker both served as a prompt to turn off their engines and facilitated the development of community norms with respect to engine idling (the sticker, which was static-cling, could be pulled off, was transparent, and was placed on the front windshield of the vehicle with the graphic and

Figure 15.8 These information cards outline the benefits of reduced engine idling and are suitable for distribution at schools and other community locations.

Source: Natural Resources Canada.

text viewable from both inside and outside the vehicle). Over 80% of the motorists who were asked to make a commitment to turn off their engines did so, and 26% placed the sticker on their front window (see Figure 15.10).

This project had three separate conditions. Two Kiss and Ride sites and two schools served as controls and received none of the above materials. In a second condition, two Kiss and Ride sites and two schools received only the signs. Finally, in the third condition, the personal conversations, which involved providing an information card and the sticker described above, were used in conjunction with signs. Note that the signs alone, which is what most municipalities would gravitate toward using, were completely ineffective. Motorists in the sign-only condition were no more likely to turn off their engines than those in the control group. However, the combination of signs, stickers, and information cards (third condition) dramatically affected idling. In this condition, there was a 32% reduction in idling and over a 70% reduction in the duration of idling. These results are based on over 8,000 observations of vehicles in the various parking lots. With the support of NRCan, this pilot project was subsequently implemented across two Canadian cities, Mississauga and Sudbury, with similar results. Most important, NRCan has made the materials from the project freely available to communities so that they can quickly and inexpensively implement their own anti-idling campaigns. As a consequence, municipalities across North America have implemented anti-idling programs based on this case study.

For further information, visit the Government of Canada's Idle Free Zone website (http://www.nrcan.gc.ca/energy/efficiency/communities-infrastructure/transportation/

idling/4397). This site provides further details on delivering effective anti-idling programs as well as downloadable materials that can be used in a local program.

WHEN WILL YOU MEASURE?

Earlier, we distinguished between evaluation and monitoring, referring to final assessments of efforts as *evaluation* and ongoing measurements as *monitoring*. Timing for measurement efforts is likely to happen as follows:

1. *Prior* to campaign launch, sometimes referred to as pre-campaign or baseline measures

2. *During* campaign implementation, thought of as tracking and monitoring surveys; this may occur at one time only or over a period of years (i.e., longitudinal surveys)

3. *Post-campaign* activities, referring to measurements taken when all campaign elements are completed, providing data on short-term outcomes and long-term impact

Baseline measures are critical when campaigns have specific goals for change, and future campaign efforts and funders will rely on these measures for campaign assessment. These are then compared with post-campaign results, providing a pre- and post-evaluation

Figure 15.9   A sign used at schools and Kiss and Ride sites.

Source: D. McKenzie-Mohr and W. Smith, *Fostering Sustainable Behavior: An Introduction to Community-Based Social Marketing*, 2nd ed. (Gabriola Island, BC, Canada: New Society, 1999).

Figure 15.10   Stickers given to motorists for their windows.

Source: D. McKenzie-Mohr and W. Smith, *Fostering Sustainable Behavior: An Introduction to Community-Based Social Marketing*, 2nd ed. (Gabriola Island, BC, Canada: New Society, 1999).

measure. Monitoring efforts during campaigns are often conducted to provide input for changes midstream and to track changes over time. Post-campaign (final) assessments are the most typical evaluations, especially when resources and tight time frames prohibit additional efforts. A few programs will use all points in time for evaluation, most common when significant key constituent groups or funders require solid evidence of campaign outcomes.

HOW MUCH WILL IT COST?

Costs for recommended monitoring and evaluation activities will vary from *minimal* costs for those that simply involve checking records and databases or gathering anecdotal comments, to *moderate* costs for those involving citizen surveys or observation research, to potentially *significant* costs for randomized controlled trials and those needing scientific or technical surveys. Ideally, decisions to fund these activities will be based on the value they will contribute to your program. If such an activity will assist you in getting support and continued funding for your program, it may be a wise investment. If it helps you refine and improve your effort going forward, payback is likely in terms of return on your investment. Once a methodology is determined based on your research purpose, you can assess these potential costs versus potential benefits.

Social marketers François Lagarde, Jay Kassirer, and Lynne Doner Lotenberg suggest four factors that may drive an evaluation budget up or down. In an article for the *Social Marketing Quarterly* in 2012, they first acknowledge the often-referenced "10% rule of thumb." They caution, however, that "10% of $50,000 is very different than 10% of $50,000,000. And why would you want to spend lots of money if you evaluation costs could instead be minimal—as when simply checking records and databases?"[21] They suggest the following considerations in addition to referencing this 10% rule of thumb:[22]

1. *What level of **attribution** is required?* This answers the question "What level of proof will you need to demonstrate that the effort was a success, and can this success be attributed to a specific intervention?" In some cases, a rigorous study of impact (e.g., reduced morbidity) is critical to justifying significant future investments. At other times, these complex designs are not worth the cost.

2. *Is there **existing evidence**?* Can you use findings from similar approaches that have already been rigorously evaluated and shown to be successful? Similarly, if your program has recently been evaluated and is still "on track," your organization and funders may be satisfied with a more limited number of additional outcome measures.

3. *Can you **build in measures** to evaluate and monitor?* This may involve ensuring that existing records or data collection methods are used and, if not, exploring whether new ones can be built into the intervention, providing "automatic" data findings on outcomes.

4. *What **level of precision** is needed?* Costs will vary significantly by primary research methodologies and requirements (e.g., whether you need to have adequate sample sizes of several audience segments for comparative purposes). Costs, versus benefits, will need to be identified.

ETHICAL CONSIDERATIONS IN EVALUATION PLANNING

Ethical considerations for monitoring and evaluation are similar to those discussed regarding research and focus mostly on the respondents surveyed for the evaluation.

One additional issue worthy of mention is the extent to which you should (or can) measure and report on unintended outcomes (consequences) as well, both positive and negative. For example, many program managers are now reporting concerns with their success in encouraging recycling. Although volumes of materials are being recycled that might otherwise have been put in landfills, managers believe the use of recyclable materials has significantly increased. Anecdotal comments such as these confirm their fears: "I don't worry about printing extra copies anymore because I'm using recycled paper and I'll put any copies not used in the recycling bin" and "I don't worry about buying small bottles of water to carry around because I can recycle them." As a result, environmentalists in some communities are now beginning to direct more of their efforts to the other two legs of their "three-legged stool": "Reduce use" and "Reuse."

CHAPTER SUMMARY

Key components of an evaluation and monitoring plan are determined by answers to the following questions:

- Why are you conducting this measurement, and who is the audience for the results?
- What will you measure?
- How will you conduct these measurements?
- When will these measurements be taken?
- How much will it cost?

Reasons *why* you are measuring will guide your research plan, as methodologies will vary according to your reason for measurement. Is it to fulfill a grant requirement? To do better the next time you conduct this same campaign? To (hopefully) get continued or even increased funding? To help you decide how to prioritize and allocate your resources going forward? Or to alert you to midcourse corrections you need to make in order to achieve goals?

What you will measure to achieve your evaluation purpose is likely to fall into one or more of five categories: inputs, outputs, outcomes, impacts, and return on investment.

Input measures report on program resources expended. Output measures report on campaign activities, outcomes on target audience responses, and impacts on improvements in social conditions as a result of adoption of the targeted behavior. The final, ideal metric to report on is return on investment.

Optional techniques for *measurement* include randomized controlled trials and surveys that are quantitative, qualitative, observational, or scientific/technical in nature, as well as ones that use control groups and rely on records and databases.

In this plan you will also determine *timing* for evaluations, considering opportunities to carry out measurements prior to campaign launch, during campaign implementation, and once the campaign has ended.

Finally, you will determine *costs* for your proposed efforts, which should be weighed in light of potential benefits. (See worksheet in Appendix A on potential evaluation measures.)

RESEARCH HIGHLIGHT

Bullying Stops Here

Pledge to Prevent

(2012–2013)

This research case highlights an award-winning effort of a team of five public relations students at Ohio's Kent State University to develop, implement and evaluate a campaign to prevent bullying, the assigned theme for the Public Relations Student Society of America's annual Bateman Case Study Competition in 2013. The setting for their intervention was Rootstown Middle School, about 20 miles from Kent State University's campus, where 72% of students had recently reported experiencing bullying.[23] Their planning process was systematic and inspired by formative research. Their hands-on implementation of their plan provided real-world lessons learned. And their evaluation effort benefited from establishing clear, relevant, and measurable goals, no doubt contributing to their

second-place award among 68 entries as well as increasing the chances that the campaign will be replicated across the school district.

Program Overview

Preliminary research efforts by the team were extensive:

- *Secondary research* identified some of the shared characteristics of programs that had been unsuccessful in the past: they usually lasted only one day; they were expensive and therefore not sustainable; and they focused on telling children not to bully.
- *Demographic research* of the school attendees and the surrounding community helped the team to better

understand what types of bullying were most likely prevalent in the school.

- The team then conducted *formative research*. The first phase involved *one-on-one interviews* with teachers, mental health professionals, parents of bullied children, children who had been bullied, and students currently learning about bullying. A follow-up *online survey* helped quantify their findings. Finally, a *focus group* with students helped to gain a richer understanding of how middle school students defined bullying, and the most common types.

- An online *benchmark survey* of 265 students helped to establish current levels of bullying:[24]

  o Seventy-two percent of students in sixth, seventh and eighth grades said they had been bullied.

  o Forty-seven percent admitted to being a bully.

  o Seventy-two percent said they had seen a bullying situation and not intervened.

This research led the team to a *priority target audience*, students who had witnessed bullying at the school. The desired *behavior* was to sign a pledge to intervene, and the goal was to increase the understanding of bystander techniques by 15% by the end of the 28-day intervention period. *Barriers research* identified major concerns students had to intervening, including fear that they might be taunted by their peers or that they might upset the bully further. Clearly, a norming approach would be key, if not critical, to success.

The team also recognized the need to reach key influencers, the teachers at the school and the parents of middle school students. As the heads of the classroom, teachers witnessed bullying more often than other district employees, and yet formative research identified a lack of understanding in distinguishing bullying from other behaviors (e.g., teasing) and failure to specify appropriate actions to take once witnessed. And formative research with parents revealed similar concerns with spotting signs of bullying, and then knowing what supportive actions to take.

Major strategies for students focused on skill building, first helping students to identify bullying behaviors and then demonstrating what bystanders could do to make a difference:

- "Pledge to Prevent" *cards* listed distinguishing behaviors and actions to then consider.

- A series of short anti-bullying *videos* played during lunch periods, featuring common bullying scenarios, such as bus stop bullying, hallway bullying, and cyberbullying, providing a motivating statistic for each.

- *Printed materials* were provided with actions for bystanders to take, and a norming highlight such as "72 percent of students at the middle school say they have recently been bullied."

- A *poster-drawing contest* was held for students on the first day of Pledge to Prevent week, with team members giving students a sheet of paper and encouraging them to portray how a bystander could stand up and diffuse bullying.

- *Stickers* were passed out in the cafeteria at lunch periods, featuring a list of seven bystander techniques; students were instructed to place the sticker on a folder, notebook, or textbook cover.

- *Face-to-face* communications were carried out, with the team spending an average of three hours a day in the school interacting with students.
- A basic anti-bullying *lesson plan* was provided for teachers, including handouts for students and a take-home sheet for parents.

Additional strategies targeting teachers and parents are noted in Table 15.2, which summarizes campaign inputs, outputs, and outcomes.

Postnotes From the Team

Team members acknowledged that the project was not without challenges, including the short times they had with the students (e.g., at their 30-minute lunch breaks); the inability to use social media platforms, since most middle schoolers were under 13; and the need, they discovered, to tailor face-to-face communication strategies for the three different grade levels.

Commenting on their second-place win, one student felt that "their focus on the bystander role might have been what set them apart from other groups."[25] To help ensure sustainability, program managers left

---

Table 15.2 A Modified Logic Model for Campaign Evaluation

Inputs	Outputs	Outcomes
Kent State Student Team Time: • Program planning • Several hours each weekday spent on site • Meetings with parents • Special events **Funding:** $300 cash for materials $1,000 in-kind donations for prizes	**Students:** • Pledge to Protect cards given to students • Videos played during lunch periods • 85 posters and large sign in school entry • Stickers passed out to students • Face-to-face interactions with students	**Students:** • 70% signed a pledge card • 65% reported knowing more about what to do • 72% reported feeling more comfortable intervening
	Teachers: • Email about the program sent from school administration • Staff meetings • Lesson plans • Facebook and Twitter pages	**Teachers:** • 75% (18) teachers signed a pledge card
	Parents: • Three letters sent home to parents • Information tables at two parent and community events • Facebook and Twitter pages	**Parents:** • 84 parents and community members signed a pledge card to talk with their child about bullying • 16 likes on the Facebook page • 13 followers on Twitter

middle school administrators with posters, lesson plans, information about other campaign tactics for future reference, and copies of their benchmark and post-implementation surveys. They then recommended to administrators that, based on the success of the campaign at the middle school, they should consider adapting and implementing the Pledge to Prevent campaign at the district's high school and elementary school, located on the same campus.

Author Note

A natural question for many after reading this case may be, "Well, did more bystanders take action when witnessing bullying?" This metric is certainly a key *outcome* measure. This team, however, was on a short time frame, and chose the behavior of signing a pledge card, one they could measure and report on during their 28-day intervention period. A longer-term project should certainly have included this behavior as an outcome measure, in addition to an *impact* measure reporting on actual decrease in bullying. Consider as well what a *return on investment* metric might look like. One option would be to calculate the amount of student and teacher time it took to reduce one bullying incident.

DISCUSSION QUESTIONS AND EXERCISES

1. For the opening Marketing Highlight, do you see any advantage, or theoretical argument, for the ParticipACTION effort's first focusing on the problem and then "correcting" audience beliefs? Could these have been important first steps, paving the way to the solution campaign? Or should they have been skipped?

2. Why is establishing the purpose of the evaluation the recommended first step in developing an evaluation plan?

3. Explain the difference between output and outcome measures.

4. Give an example of an actual or hypothetical randomized controlled trial, using the schematic presented in the chapter.

5. Discuss your reaction to the author's note at the end of the research highlight, including what could be another potential ROI measurement.

CHAPTER 15 NOTES

1. P. Kotler, *Kotler on Marketing: How to Create, Win and Dominate Markets* (New York: Free Press, 1999), 185.

2. ParticipACTION, *2013 Annual Report* (n.d.), accessed May 15, 2014, http://www.partici paction.com/AnnualReport2013-en/index.html.

3. Angus Reid Campaign Assessment Study, Spring 2010.

4. 2013 Cassies Awards submission for ParticipACTION's Bring Back Play Campaign. Submitted by J. Walter Thompson, Canada.

5. P. Kotler and N. Lee, *Marketing in the Public Sector: A Roadmap for Improved Performance* (Upper Saddle River, NJ: Wharton School, 2006), 266.

6. Ibid., 268–269.

7. Ohio State University, "National Anti-drug Campaign Succeeds in Lowering Marijuana Use, Study Suggests," *Research News* (n.d.), accessed March 14, 2011, http://research news.osu .edu/archive/aboveinfluence.htm.

8. Ibid.

9. Adapted from an article that first appeared in the *Journal of Social Marketing*, Volume 1, Issue 1, Emerald Group Publishing Limited, February 2011: N. R. Lee, "Where's the Beef? Social Marketing in Tough Times," 73–75.

10. C. Tucker, "National Public Health Week Highlights Return on Investment," *Nation's Health*, accessed May 5, 2014, http://thenationshealth.aphapublications.org/content/43/5/1.3.full.

11. Ibid.

12. J. French, R. Merritt, and L. Reynolds, *Social Marketing Casebook* (Thousand Oaks, CA: SAGE, 2011), 129–139.

13. Ibid., 138.

14. GOV.UK, Cabinet Office "Behavioural Insights Team," accessed May 8, 2014, https:// www.gov.uk/government/organisations/behavioural-insights-team.

15. L. Haynes, O. Service, B. Goldacre, and D. Torgerson, "Test, Learn, Adapt: Developing Public Policy With Randomised Controlled Trials" (Cabinet Office Behavioural Insights Team, June 2012).

16. E. Jaffe, "Watch 'Real-Time' Transit Planning Help North America's Busiest Bus Line" (March 26, 2014), accessed May 5, 2014, http://www.theatlanticcities.com/commute/2014/03/ watch-real-time-transit-planning-helps-north-americas-busiest-bus-line/8725/.

17. Kotler and Lee, *Marketing in the Public Sector*, 266.

18. U.S. Department of Health and Human Services. (n.d.). *What is comparative effectiveness research*. Retrieved March 15, 2011, from http://www.effectivehealthcare.ahrq.gov/index.cfm/ what-is-comparative-effectiveness-research1/

19. D. McKenzie-Mohr, *Fostering Sustainable Behavior: An Introduction to Community-Based Social Marketing*, 3rd ed. (Gabriola Island, BC, Canada: New Society Publishers, 2011), 137.

20. McKenzie-Mohr, *Fostering Sustainable Behavior*, 140–142.

21. F. Lagarde, J. Kassirer, and L. Lotenberg, "Budgeting for Evaluation: Beyond the 10% Rule of Thumb," *Social Marketing Quarterly* 18, no. 3 (2012): 247.

22. Ibid., 247–251.

23. Public Relations Student Society of America, "Kent State PR Students Named National Finalists in PRSSA Bateman Competition" (May 6, 2013), accessed May 5, 2014, http://www .prssa.org/scholarships_competitions/bateman/2013/index.html.

24. Ibid.

25. Kent State University, "Kent State PR Students Named National Finalists in PRSSA Bateman Competition" (May 6, 2013), accessed May 2, 2014, https://www.kent.edu/einside/arti cledisplay.cfm?newsitem=667DBA6C-AC25-DA80-1D9C80B2007C9C2E.

Chapter 16

ESTABLISHING BUDGETS AND FINDING FUNDING

If substantial financial resources are to be raised and sustained over a long period of time, it's essential that supportive partners, especially large corporate partners, get as well as give.

Bill Shore[1]
Founder and CEO of Share Our Strength

In this chapter, not only will you read about how to determine and justify budgets for your proposed plans, but you will also explore options for additional funding. You will read that we encourage you to seriously consider opportunities for corporate support for your initiatives, such as ones mentioned in the opening Marketing Highlight. In the ethical considerations section of the chapter, we will ask you to think back on your reaction to the following examples of corporate initiatives related to decreasing childhood obesity:

Sesame Street. A press release from the Sesame Workshop in September 2005 presented findings from a research study titled "The Effectiveness of Characters on Children's Food Choices" (the "Elmo/Broccoli Study"). It indicated that

> intake of a particular food increased if it carried a sticker of a *Sesame Street* character. For example, in the control group (no characters on either food) 78% of children participating in the study chose a chocolate bar over broccoli, whereas 22% chose the broccoli. However, when an Elmo sticker was placed on the broccoli and an unknown character was placed on the chocolate bar, 50% chose the chocolate bar and 50% chose the broccoli. Such outcomes suggest that the *Sesame Street* characters could play a strong role in increasing the appeal of healthy foods.[2]

Nickelodeon. In October 2005, Nickelodeon held its second annual Worldwide Day of Play, a part of its larger Let's Just Play initiative. The network went dark that Saturday for the first time in its 25-year history, from 12 p.m. to 3 p.m., replacing its usual programming with a broadcast message that encouraged kids to go outside and play. More than 60,000 kids registered online to get a number to wear to Day of Play events, and 40,000 kids attended events organized by Nickelodeon in selected American cities and abroad.[3] The annual campaign continued five years later. On Saturday, September 25, 2010, a special message was shown on the Nick channel screen: "Today is Nickelodeon's Worldwide Day of Play! We're outside playing and you should be too! So, turn off your TV, shut down your computer, put down that cell phone, and go ALL OUT! We'll be back at 3!"[4] The annual event celebrated its 11th season on September 20 in 2014.

MARKETING HIGHLIGHT

Increasing Funding Through Corporate Social Marketing

(2012)

In Kotler, Hessekiel, and Lee's 2012 book *GOOD WORKS!*, six major initiatives under which most corporate social-responsibility-related activities fall are identified. Three are developed and managed primarily by the corporation's marketing function: *cause promotion, cause-related marketing*, and *corporate social marketing*. And three are most often developed and managed by other corporate functions, including community relations, human resources, foundations, and operations: *corporate philanthropy, workforce volunteering*, and *socially responsible business practices.*[5] This research highlight focuses on describing corporate social marketing and making the case that when it comes to gaining a market edge while supporting a social cause, a social marketing effort is the "Best of Breed."[6]

"Corporate Social Marketing uses business resources to develop and/or implement a behavior change campaign intended to improve public health, safety, the environment, or community well-being."[7] It is most distinguished from other corporate social initiatives by this behavior change focus. And, as illustrated in the following six examples, many of the potential benefits for the corporation are connected to marketing goals and objectives.

1. *Supporting brand positioning:* SUBWAY Restaurants

If you were the marketing director at SUBWAY, responsible for securing a brand positioning as the healthy fast-food option, you would be grateful for the long-term partnership the company has had with the American Heart Association, sponsoring many initiatives including Start! Walking at Work, Jump Rope for Heart, and the American Heart Walks. You would also be pleased with the announcement in January 2014 from First Lady Michelle Obama that SUBWAY has committed to promoting healthier choices for kids through a new marketing campaign and additional restaurant offerings. Adding to the applause, a follow-up press release from the American Heart Association also praised the effort:

> For almost 15 years, we have worked with SUBWAY to develop and provide healthier meals to adults and

children. Today is another example of SUBWAY's leadership and its commitment to kids' health. This represents a great step toward marketing only healthy foods and beverages as well as promoting fruits and vegetables to children.[8]

2. *Creating brand preference:* Levi's® Care Tag for the Planet

Levi Strauss & Co. has a corporate commitment to build sustainability into everything they do, exemplified by their Care Tag for Our Planet social marketing initiative. In 2010, they launched an initiative to start a long-term conversation with consumers about what they can do to save water and energy and contribute to communities. A tag on their Levi's® Jeans and Dockers® khakis includes messaging that encourages people to help the planet by washing less, washing in cold water, line drying, and (in the end) donating to Goodwill when the item is no longer needed. A variety of social media channels also support the effort. In the fall of 2011, for example, the company launched a new consumer action campaign, Dirty Is the New Clean, asking consumers to rethink their washing habits by washing their jeans less and to tweet how many times they wear their pants before washing (#Care+OurPlanet).[9]

3. *Building traffic:* Lowe's

In 1999, the Water—Use it Wisely campaign was launched to respond to a sentiment among Arizona residents to "Don't tell us to save water. Show us how." Partners included local city governments, private and public utilities, Arizona Department of Water Resources, and Arizona Municipal Water Users Association, and, in 2005, Lowe's, a partner in the private sector, joined.[10] As part of a radio campaign, the partners scheduled radio broadcasts every Saturday at prominent Lowe's locations to help drive traffic and purchases of water-saving devices. Conservation workshops were presented by Lowe's employees on those Saturdays, using a curriculum created by the water conservation experts from the cities. Promotions included water-saving tips appearing on aisle, register, and door signs. Outcomes for the program as well as Lowe's were impressive, with Lowe's reporting a 50% increase in workshop attendance over prior similar workshops, and sales of water efficient merchandise increasing by an average of 30%.[11]

4. *Increasing sales:* Energizer and "Change Your Clock, Change Your Battery"

According to the U.S. Fire Administration, every year more than 3,400 Americans die in fires and approximately 17,500 are injured, with the majority of these fires occurring in the home, but adding a working smoke alarm can double the chances of survival.[12] Influencing homeowners to ensure the battery in their smoke alarm is functional, and to then replace it, is a natural social marketing campaign for a brand like Energizer to support. And linking this action to another routine behavior, changing your clock in the spring and fall, is an even smarter idea, functioning as a sustainable prompt. For 26 years (as of 2014), Energizer, the International Association of Fire Chiefs, and more than 6,400 fire departments have partnered to remind people of this simple life-saving habit.[13]

5. *Improving profitability:* Allstate and Teen Driver Pledges

Given the statistics put forth by the Centers for Disease Control and Prevention (CDC) indicating that motor vehicle crashes are the leading cause of death for U.S. teens, it might not be surprising that Allstate Insurance is interested in promoting safer teen driving.[14] And given that teens have the highest proportion of distraction-related fatal crashes, it also isn't surprising that reducing texting and driving among teens is a priority for one of Allstate's corporate social marketing efforts, carrying the potential to reduce their claims as well. Their strategic focus is on encouraging teens to pledge not to text and drive. The movement began in 2009, and by 2011, they had received more than 250,000 pledges. Social media are a primary channel for making the pledge, with teens being encouraged on Facebook to add their thumbprint to an oversized pledge banner.

6. *Attracting credible partners:* Clorox and the CDC's "Say Boo to the Flu"

Because of their behavior change focus and potential, corporate social marketing initiatives, perhaps more than the other five initiatives identified, are likely to be welcomed and supported by public sector agencies. A partnership between Clorox and CDC is a great example. The Say Boo to the Flu program was created in 2004 to increase the number of families vaccinated against the flu

and to promote additional simple prevention behaviors. On the campaign's website, for example, a section on "Where is the Flu Virus Hiding in Your House?" identifies five germ "hot spots" and recommends using sprays and wipes that are disinfectant cleaning products, such as Clorox. In the fall of 2013, Clorox sponsored Say Boo! to the Flu events across the country, offering parents opportunities to get their families the flu vaccination and incorporating a fun Halloween theme and a "Boo-mobile" that crisscrossed the country.[15]

7. *Having a real impact on social change:* Pampers' "Back to Sleep" campaign

SIDS is a term used to describe the sudden, unexplained death of an infant

Figure 16.1 A just-in-time reminder on Pampers newborn diapers.

Source: National Institutes of Child Health and Human Development, Back to Sleep Campaign, "Safe Sleep for Your Baby: Ten Ways to Reduce the Risk of Sudden Infant Death Syndrome" (n.d.), accessed October 31, 2006, http://www .nichd.nih.gov/publications/pubs/safe_sleep_gen.cfm#backs.

younger than 1 year of age. In the United States, it is the leading cause of death in infants between 1 month and 1 year old.[16] One behavior to help reduce SIDS is to place infants on their backs to sleep. The Back to Sleep campaign, launched in 1994 by the National Institute of Child Health and Human Development, included an early partner, Pampers, one that helped expand the reach of the campaign message by printing the Back to Sleep logo across the fastening strips of its newborn diapers (see Figure 16.1). This prompt helped ensure that every time caregivers changed a baby's diaper, they would be reminded that back sleeping is best to reduce a baby's risk of dying from SIDS. In 2006, it was announced by the National Institute of Child Health and Human Development that since the campaign had been launched, the percentage of infants placed on their backs to sleep had increased dramatically and the rate of SIDS had declined by more than 50%.[17]

STEP 9: ESTABLISH BUDGETS AND FINDING FUNDING SOURCES

Step 9, the budgeting process, is "where the rubber hits the road." You are now ready to determine price tags for strategies and activities that you have identified in your plan, those you believe are key to reaching quantifiable behavior influence goals. Once this number is totaled, you will evaluate this potential cost by referring to anticipated benefits from targeted levels of behavior change, comparing this with current funding levels, and, if needed, identifying potential additional resources. This chapter section will take you through each of these budgeting phases.

DETERMINING BUDGETS

In the commercial as well as nonprofit and public sectors, several approaches are often cited as possibilities to consider in determining marketing budgets.[18] The following four have the most relevance for social marketing:

The affordable method. Budgets are based on what the organization has available in the yearly budget or on what has been spent in prior years. For example, a county health department's budget for teen pregnancy prevention might be determined by state funds allocated every two years for the issue, and a local blood bank's budget for the annual blood drive might be established each year as a part of the organizational budgeting process.

The competitive-parity method. In this situation, budgets are set or considered on the basis of what others have spent for similar efforts. For example, a litter campaign budget might be established on the basis of a review of media expenses from other states that have been successful at reducing litter using mass media campaigns.

The objective-and-task method. Budgets are established by (a) reviewing specific objectives and quantifiable goals, (b) identifying the tasks that must be performed to achieve these objectives, and (c) estimating the costs associated with performing these tasks. The total is the preliminary budget.[19] For example, the budget for a utility's marketing effort for recycling might be based on estimated costs for staffing a new telephone service center to answer questions on what can be recycled, providing plaques for recognizing homeowner participation, and promotional strategies, including television ads, radio spots, statement stuffers, and flyers. These total costs are then considered in light of any projections of increased revenues or decreased costs for the utility.

Cost per sale. Commercial marketers often set budgets based on sales goals, having (what may seem to social marketers) the luxury of knowing what it has cost in the past to generate leads and then convert to sales. In this case, costs are typically those associated with promotional activities. A company wanting to sell 5,000 more of one of their products may have historic data indicating it takes $10 of advertising to generate one sale, a rate meeting targeted profit margins. This metric would be used to establish the advertising budget for the campaign (e.g., $50,000). For social marketers, the math is similar, with "cost per behavior" substituting for "cost per sale." Consider, for example, a Fish & Wildlife campaign to increase usage of crab gauges to determine whether or not a crab should be retained. Program managers would, ideally through a pilot, divide the total promotional costs for an effort by the number of crabbers they observed, or determined, used a crab gauge as a result of the promotional effort. Future efforts could then use this amount to estimate budgets for desired behavior change goals.

The most logical of these approaches, and one consistent with our planning process, is the objective-and-task method. In this scenario, you will identify costs related to your marketing mix strategy (product, price, place, and promotion) as well as evaluation and monitoring efforts. This becomes a preliminary budget, one based on what you believe you need to do to achieve the goals established in Step 4 of your plan. (In subsequent sections of this chapter, we discuss options to consider when this preliminary budget exceeds currently available funds, including sources to explore for additional funding as well as the potential for revising strategies and/or reducing behavior change goals.)

More-detailed descriptions of typical costs associated with implementing the marketing plan follow. A brief example is included to further illustrate the nature of identifying strategies with budget implications. In this example, assume a hospital has developed a draft marketing plan to decrease the number of employees commuting to work in single-occupant vehicles (SOVs). The campaign *objective* is to influence employees to use public transportation, car pools, or van pools or walk or bike to work, with the *goal* being to decrease the number of SOVs on campus by 10% (100 vehicles) over a 12-month period. The hospital is motivated by a desire to build a new wing, an effort that will require land use permits granted, in part, based on impacts on traffic congestion in the surrounding neighborhoods.

Product-related costs are most often associated with producing or purchasing any accompanying *tangible goods* and developing or enhancing associated *services* needed to support behavior change. Costs may include direct costs for providing these goods and services, or they may be indirect costs, such as staff time. Product-related cost considerations for the hospital will include the need to lease additional vans from the county's transit system, install new bike racks, and construct several additional showers for employee use if marketing goals are in fact met. Incremental service charges as a result of increased efforts might include costs for temporary personnel to provide ride share matching or to build and maintain a special online software program for ride sharing.

Price-related costs include those associated with incentives, recognition programs, and rewards. In some cases, they include net losses from sales of any goods and services associated with the marketing effort. Price-related costs for the hospital may include incentives, such as cash incentives for carpooling, reduced rates for parking spots close to the building, free bus passes, and occasional free taxi rides home promised to staff if they need to stay late. The draft plan also includes providing recognition pins for name tags, a strategy anticipated to make members of the program "feel good" as well as spread the word about the program to other employees during meetings, in the cafeteria, and the like. The hospital might also decide to reward those who have stuck with the program for a year with a free iPod in order to make their ride home on the bus or in the van more pleasant and encourage others to stick with the program.

Place-related costs involve providing new or enhanced access or delivery channels, such as telephone centers, online purchasing, extended hours, and new or improved locations. There may be costs related to distribution of any tangible goods associated with the program. In our example, there may be costs for creating additional parking spots for car pools close to the main entrance of the hospital or for staffing a booth outside the cafeteria for distributing incentives and actual ride share sign-up.

Promotion-related costs are the costs associated with developing, producing, and disseminating communications. Promotion-related costs for the hospital might include developing and producing fact sheets on benefits, posters, special brochures, and transportation fairs.

Evaluation-related costs include any planned measurement and tracking surveys. Evaluation-related costs for the hospital might include conducting a baseline and follow-up survey that measures employee awareness of financial incentives and ride share matching programs, as well as any changes in attitudes and intentions related to alternative transportation.

JUSTIFYING THE BUDGET

First, consider how those in the commercial marketing sector look at marketing budgets—it's all about the return on investment. We begin with a story from *Kotler on Marketing* that illustrates the marketing mindset, as well as a potential budget analysis:

The story is told about a Hong Kong shoe manufacturer who wonders whether a market exists for his shoes on a remote South Pacific island. He sends an *order taker* to the island who, upon cursory examination, wires back: "The people here don't wear shoes. There is no market." Not convinced, the Hong Kong shoe manu- facturer sends a *salesman* to the island. This salesman wires back: "The people here don't wear shoes. There is a tremendous market."

Afraid that this salesman is being carried away by the sight of so many shoeless feet, the Hong Kong manufacturer sends a third person, this time a *marketer.* This marketing professional interviews the tribal chief and several of the natives, and finally wires back: "The people here don't wear shoes. However they have bad feet. I have shown the chief how shoes would help his people avoid foot problems. He is enthusiastic. He estimates that 70 percent of his people will buy the shoes at the price of $10 a pair. We probably can sell 5,000 pairs of shoes in the first year. Our cost of bringing the shoes to the island and setting up distribution would amount to $6 a pair. We will clear $20,000 in the first year, which, given our investment, will give us a rate of return on our investment (ROI) of 20 percent, which exceeds our normal ROI of 15 percent. This is not to mention the high value of our future earn- ings by entering this market. I recommend that we go ahead."[20]

As described in Chapter 15 in the section on ROI, consider the marketing budget as an investment, one that will be judged based on *outcomes* (levels of behavior change) relative to financial *inputs.* Theoretically, you want to calculate your costs for the targeted levels of behavior change and then compare them with the potential economic value of the behaviors influenced. The following examples are the types of simple, but not neces- sarily easy, questions you will want to answer for yourself and others:

- What is it worth in terms of medical and other societal costs for a health department to find 50 HIV-positive men in one city as a result of their testing efforts in gay bath- houses? How does that compare with the proposed marketing budget of $150,000 to support this effort? Is each "find" worth at least $3,000 ($150,000 ÷ 50)?
- What is the economic value of a 2% increase in seatbelt usage in a state? How many injuries and deaths would be avoided, and how do savings in public emergency and health care costs compare with a $250,000 budget for promotional activities pro- posed to achieve this increase?
- How does a budget of $100,000 for a state department of ecology to influence and support remodelers and small contractors to post their materials on an online exchange website compare with the value of 500 tons of materials being diverted from the landfill the first year—the goal in their marketing plan?
- If a county's campaign to increase spaying and neutering of pets is anticipated to persuade 500 more pet owners this year, compared to last year, how does a budget of $50,000 sound? Is it worth $100 for each "litter avoided"?

You may be surprised how grateful (even delighted) colleagues, funders, and management will be when you provide estimates on these returns on investment. This is possible only when you have established specific, measurable, attainable, relevant, and time-sensitive (S.M.A.R.T.) goals for behavior changes, developed calculated strategies to support these goal levels, and then determined a budget based on each marketing-related expense.

FINDING SOURCES FOR ADDITIONAL FUNDING

What if the costs for the marketing activities you propose—ones you believe are needed to reach the agreed-upon goal—are more than is currently available in your agency's budget? Before reducing the goals, you have options for additional funding to explore. Each option will be illustrated with an example, and we use this as an opportunity to recall several of the cases highlighted in this text.

Government Grants and Appropriations

Federal, state, and local government agencies are the most common sources of funds and grants for social marketing efforts. Potential sources, especially for nonprofit organizations, include national, state, and local departments of health, human services, transportation, ecology, traffic safety, natural resources, fish and wildlife, parks and recreation, and public utilities.

Example: The Puget Sound Partnership. Puget Sound, in Washington state, is the second largest estuary in the United States. The Puget Sound Partnership is a Washington state agency serving as the backbone organization for Puget Sound recovery, coordinating the efforts of citizens, government, tribes, scientists, businesses, and nonprofits to set priorities, implement a regional recovery plan, and ensure accountability for results.[21] The agency currently (2014) coordinates more than $650 million to help fund over 800 projects to improve natural resources around Puget Sound; many of those are projects of nonprofit organizations, local governments, and tribes.[22] About $11 million is currently devoted to developing and implementing social marketing efforts that protect water quality and fish and wildlife habitats, and to building regional capacity, such as training, technical assistance, and practitioner networks to implement and evaluate such projects.[23] Examples include increased planting of native plants on shorelines, disposing of farm animal waste properly, using commercial car washes versus washing on driveways, removing invasive plants on streams, properly maintaining septic systems, purchasing safer pesticides, preventing abandonment and assisting in recovery of derelict marine vessels, and testing and fixing vehicle oil leaks (see Figure 16.2).

Counter card for Don't Drip & Drive, a campaign that won a Silver Anvil Award in 2014 from the Public Relations Society of America.

Source: Washington State Department of Ecology.

Nonprofit/Foundations

There are more than 88,000 active independent corporate, community, and grant-making foundations operating in the United States alone (2010) with missions to contribute to many of the same social issues and causes addressed by social marketing efforts.[24] Kotler and Andreasen identify four major relevant groups: *family foundations*, in which funds are derived from members of a single family (e.g., Bill and Melinda Gates Foundation); *general foundations*, usually run by a professional staff awarding grants in many different fields of interest (e.g., Ford Foundation); *corporate foundations*, whose assets are derived primarily from the contributions of a for-profit business (e.g., Bank of America Foundation); and *community foundations*, set up to receive and manage contributions from a variety of sources in a local community, making grants for charitable purposes in a specific community or region.[25]

Example: World Bicycle Relief. To the nonprofit organization World Bicycle Relief, a bike is not a bike; "it's an engine for economic and cultural empowerment."[26] The organization envisions a world where distance is no longer a barrier to education, healthcare, and economic opportunity, and as of 2014, the organization has trained more than 900 field mechanics and provided more than 180,000 specially designed, locally assembled bicycles to disaster survivors, health care workers, students, and entrepreneurs (see Figure 16.3).[27] The bikes are engineered to increase load capacity as well as to withstand rugged terrains. In rural Zambia, for example, where children are at risk for extreme poverty and high HIV/AIDS infection rates, only 60% enrolled in primary school go on to complete high school.[28] It is not uncommon for students to have to walk two or three hours each way to get to school, an effort exposing them further to harassment, sexual abuse, poor nutrition, and inability to provide critical family support. High school students must travel even farther, and often end up having to rent rooms near their school, putting them at risk for transactional sex and other dangers of living away from parental supervision. The Zambian Ministry of Education identified safe, reliable transportation as one way to increase school enrollment, and in partnership with local communities and relief organizations, implemented World Bicycle Relief's Bicycles for

Educational Empowerment Program, providing approximately 50,000 purpose-designed locally assembled bicycles to children, teachers, and community supporters.[29]

Advertising and Media Partners

Advertising agencies often provide pro bono services to support social causes, with contributions ranging from consulting on media buying and creative strategies to actually developing and producing advertising campaigns. Several factors motivate their choices, including opportunities to contribute to issues in the community, give their junior staff more experience, have more freedom to call the shots in developing creative strategies, and make new and important business contacts.[30]

The Ad Council, formed in 1942 as the War Ad Council to support efforts related to World War II, has played a significant role in producing, distributing, promoting, and evaluating public service communication programs. Familiar campaigns include Smokey Bear's "Only You Can Prevent Forest Fires," "Friends Don't Let Friends Drive Drunk," and McGruff the Crime Dog's "Take a Bite Out of Crime." Each year the council supports approximately 40 campaigns to enhance health, safety, and community involvement; strengthen families; and protect the environment, chosen from several hundred requests from nonprofit organizations and public sector agencies. Factors used for selection include criteria that the campaign must be noncommercial, nondenominational, and nonpolitical in nature. It also needs to be perceived as an important issue and national in scope. When a proposal is selected, the council then organizes hundreds of professional volunteers from top advertising agencies, corporations, and the media to contribute to the campaign.[31] Television and radio stations are often approached to provide free or discounted ("two for one") airtime for campaigns with good causes. Even more valuable, they may be interested in having their sales force find corporate sponsors for campaigns,

Figure 16.3 Rugged bicycles are engineered specifically for rural African terrain and load requirements.

Source: World Bicycle Relief. Worldbicyclerelief.org

who then pay for media placement (e.g., for a campaign promoting bicycling, a media partnership between an outdoor equipment retailer, a health care organization, and a local television station). In this win-win-win situation, the social marketing campaign gets increased frequency and guaranteed placement of ads on programs that appeal to their target audience; the local corporations get to "do good" and "look good" in the community; and the television or radio stations get paid, which might not occur with public service advertising.

Coalitions and Other Partnerships

Many social marketing campaigns have been successful, at least in part, because of the resources and assistance gained from participating in coalitions and other similar partnerships. Coalition members may be able to pool resources to implement larger-scale campaigns. Networks of individual coalition members can provide invaluable distribution channels for campaign programs and materials (e.g., the local department of license office airs a traffic safety video in the lobby, where a captive audience waits for their number to be called).

As evidenced by a tally of the cases and examples highlighted in this text, support from coalitions and public/private/nonprofit partnerships appears to be the norm, illustrated by the following examples, to name a few:

- Chapter 1: Funding efforts to end polio, like the one highlighted in India, have included a network of organizations: NGOs like Rotary International and UNICEF, international agencies like the World Health Organization, governmental organizations like the CDC, and foundations like the Bill and Melinda Gates Foundation.
- Chapter 4: Research was key to success in the Democratic Republic of the Congo's Pigs for Peace initiative, and key to this extensive research was the partnership between local community leaders and academic organizations.
- Chapter 10: We doubt that the F'Poon, developed by the Diabetes Association of Sri Lanka, would have the dissemination it needed for impact without its partnership with tea houses and major restaurants, making access convenient and a perceived norm.
- Chapter 13: Influencing fisheries to change their practices involved consumers, nonprofit organizations, restaurants, food suppliers, and retail stores that were organized and influenced by Monterey Bay Aquarium's Seafood Watch program.
- Chapter 13: Persuading 30,000 of the 50,000 unbanked households in San Francisco to open a bank account relied on 75% of the banks and credit unions in the city to offer the branded Bank on San Francisco accounts.
- Chapter 14: No doubt the increase in purchasing of 1% low-fat milk and the decrease in purchasing whole milk, a project of the University of Oklahoma Health Sciences Center's College of Public Health, relied on the contributions of multiple partners, including the participation of the popular NBA spokesperson as well as the cooperation of retail stores for signage and sales data.

Corporations

In the opening quote for this chapter, Bill Shore stressed how critical it is that supportive partners, like corporate partners, get as well as give. He goes on to say, "To find the intersection of public interest and private interest that will work for your partners, begin by sitting down with them to learn about their needs before telling them about yours."[32] As Kotler and Lee describe in their book *Corporate Social Responsibility: Doing the Most Good for Your Company and Your Cause*, three trends in corporate giving are noteworthy, especially for social marketers: First, the good news is that giving is on an upward trend, with a report from Giving USA indicating that giving by for-profit corporations rose from an estimated $9.6 billion in 1999 to $18.9 billion in 2012.[33] Second, there is an increased shift to strategic versus obligatory giving, with a desire, even expectation, for "doing well and doing good." More and more corporations are picking a few strategic areas of focus that fit their corporate values. They are selecting initiatives that support their business goals, choosing issues more closely related to their core products, and expressing more interest in opportunities to meet marketing objectives, such as increased market share, better market penetration, or building a desired brand identity.[34] And this brings us to the third relevant trend. Many corporations are discovering (and deciding) that supporting social marketing initiatives and campaigns can be one of the most beneficial of all corporate social initiatives, especially for supporting their marketing efforts. In an article titled "Best of Breed" in the *Stanford Innovation Review* in the spring of 2004, Kotler and Lee described why corporations find this so attractive:

- It can support brand positioning (e.g., SUBWAY partnering with the American Heart Association to influence healthy eating)
- It can create brand preference (e.g., Pampers' support of the SIDS Foundation to influence parents and caregivers to put infants to sleep on their back)
- It can build traffic in stores (e.g., Best Buy's recycling events at store locations)
- It can increase sales (e.g., Mustang Survival's partnership with Seattle Children's Hospital and Regional Medical Center to help the company capture a share of the toddler market)
- It can have a real impact on social change, and consumers make the connection (e.g., 7-Eleven's participation in the Don't Mess With Texas litter prevention campaign that has helped decrease litter by more than 50% in that state).[35]

Corporations have several ways to support your campaigns, as described in the following sections: cash grants and contributions, cause-related marketing campaigns, in-kind contributions, and use of their distribution channels.

Cash Grants and Contributions

Cash contributions from corporations (as opposed to their foundations) are awarded for a variety of purposes, including sponsorship mentions in communications, potential

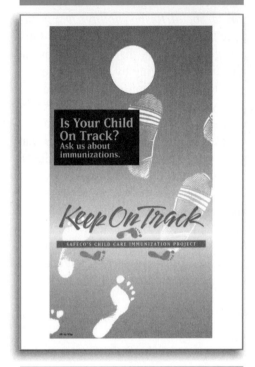

Figure 16.4 Door hanger used at child care centers to remind parents to check immunization status.

Materials developed by Child Care Resources and Safeco Insurance.

for building traffic at retail or Internet sites, and opportunities for visibility with key constituent groups.

Example: Child Care Resources. Child Care Resources is a nonprofit organization in Washington state providing information and referral assistance to families seeking child care, training, and assistance for child care providers and consulting and advocacy for quality child care. In the mid-1990s, Safeco, an insurance company based in Seattle, provided a generous grant to Child Care Resources to strengthen the ability of child care providers to promote and track immunizations of children in their care. Formative research with child care providers provided input for developing training and a kit of materials that included immunization-tracking forms, posters, flyers, stickers, door hangers, and brochures for parents, with refrigerator magnets and immunization schedules (see Figure 16.4). In partnership with numerous local and state health agencies, Child Care Resources developed and disseminated more than 3,000 kits to child care providers in the first year of the grant. An evaluation survey among approximately 300 of the providers indicated that 94% felt the materials helped them encourage parents to keep their children's immunizations up-to-date. The grant was extended for a second year, and trainings and kit distribution were taken statewide under the direction of the Washington state Child Care Resource and Referral Network.

Cause-Related Marketing

Cause-related marketing (CRM) is an increasingly popular strategy with a win-win-win proposition. In the typical scenario, a percentage of sales of a company's product is devoted to a nonprofit organization. The strategy is based on the premise that buyers care about the civic virtue and caring nature of companies. When market offerings are similar, buyers have been shown to patronize the firms with better civic reputations. Carefully chosen and developed programs help a *company* achieve strategic marketing objectives (e.g., sell more product or penetrate new markets) and demonstrate social responsibility, with an aim of moving beyond rational and emotional branding to "spiritual" branding. At the same time, CRM raises funds and increases exposure for a *social issue or cause* and gives *consumers* an opportunity to be involved in improving the quality of life.[36] Well-known partnerships include programs such as American Express and Charge Against Hunger, Yoplait yogurt and breast cancer, Lysol and Keep America Beautiful, and Ethos Water® sold at Starbucks to support water, sanitation, and hygiene education programs. National surveys indicate that the majority of consumers would be influenced to buy, or even switch and pay more for, brands when the product supports a cause, especially when product features and quality are equal. However, if the promotion rings hollow, customers may be cynical; if the charitable contribution doesn't amount to much or the promotion doesn't run long enough, customers may be skeptical; if the company chooses a cause of less interest to their customers, it will gain little; and if the company chooses a cause and other causes feel miffed, it may lose out.

In-Kind Contributions

For some corporations, in-kind donations are even more appealing than cash contributions. Not only do they represent opportunities to off-load excess products or utilize "idle" equipment such as that used for printing, but they also provide opportunities to connect consumers with the company's products and to connect the product with the organization's cause. The following example illustrates this opportunity well.

Example: Mustang Survival. Drowning is the second leading cause of unintentional-injury-related death for children in the United States. In Washington state alone, 90 children under the age of 15 drowned from 1999 to 2003. Sadly, in too many cases, drowning deaths could have been avoided if the child had been wearing a properly fitted life jacket. Although Washington state regulations require that children 12 years and younger wear a properly sized U.S. Coast Guard–approved life jacket on any boat under 19 feet long, not all children are wearing life jackets or ones that are properly fitted. In 1992, Mustang Survival, a life vest manufacturer, made a three-year commitment to a partnership that included Seattle Children's Hospital and Regional Medical Center and other members of a drowning prevention coalition. In addition to contributing free life jackets for special events, they also provided financial support, discount coupons, bulk buy programs, and in-kind printing (see Figure 16.5). Financial support was used to develop a parent's

Figure 16.5   Coupon used to promote life vest use.

Source: Reprinted with permission of Seattle Children's Hospital and Regional Medical Center.

guide, children's activity booklet, and interactive display. Their support of the program continues more than 20 years later.

Use of Distribution Channels

Companies can provide tremendous visibility and support for your efforts by giving you space in their stores for such things as car seat safety checks (at car dealers), flu shots (at grocery stores), energy-saving events like Rock the Bulb (at hardware stores), and pet adoptions (at pet stores). In some cases, this can have a profound impact, as it did in the following example.

Example: Best Buy. "No matter where you bought it, we'll recycle it" is a headline Best Buy uses frequently, and, in recognition for this effort, Best Buy received, in 2013, the first-ever eCycling Leadership Award from the Consumer Electronics Association, recognizing consumer electronics companies that are recycling above and beyond any level mandated by government.[37] As of 2014, 966 million pounds have been recycled at Best Buy stores, representing nearly 50,000 dump truck loads.[38] No doubt this success is due in part to the fact that they make this easy and "cheap" for consumers, offering kiosks just inside the door of their U.S. stores for easy drop-off and taking them at no charge. Although their annual sustainability reports do not comment on the traffic and sales these customer contacts generate, we can imagine it would be substantial, as those bringing their used and unwanted items in are likely looking for replacements.[39]

APPEALING TO FUNDERS

The same principles we have outlined for influencing target audiences are applicable for influencing potential funders as well. They could be viewed simply as another type of target audience, and the same steps and customer orientation are called for:

- Begin by identifying and prioritizing segments (potential funders) who represent the greatest opportunities for funding your program. Several criteria may guide this prioritization, with a special focus on organizations where you have existing contacts and relationships, common areas of focus and concern, and similar target audiences, publics, or constituent groups.
- Formulate clear, specific potential requests.
- Spend time deepening your understanding of the funders' wants, needs, and perspectives. What are potential benefits of and concerns with your proposal? Who is the competition, and what advantages and disadvantages do you have?
- On the basis of this information, refine and finalize your specific request. Your preliminary inquiries, for example, may reveal that a large request (risking the "door in your face") may in fact make it more likely that you will receive funding for a smaller one.

- Develop a strategy using all elements of the marketing mix, a proposal that (a) articulates clear value for the funder (what's in it for them) and benefits to the cause (target audiences), (b) addresses concerns and barriers, (c) ensures a smooth and responsible administrative process, and (d) provides assurance of measurable outcomes.

It is helpful to keep in mind that corporations evaluating an opportunity to support a social marketing effort are likely to consider the following questions:

- Is there a natural bond between the cause and the company?
- Is it an issue that their target audience cares about?
- Is there an opportunity for staff to be involved?
- Can they own or at least dominate the position of corporate partner?
- Can they stick with the program for at least two to three years?
- Is there synergy with their current distribution channels?
- Does it provide enhanced media opportunities?
- Can they develop an optimal donation model that provides sales incentives at an economically feasible per-unit contribution?
- Will they be able to absolutely measure their return on investment?

And, to underscore additional points made in the "Best of Breed" article in the *Stanford Innovation Review*, these partnerships must "pass the smell test"[40] It is crucial that the social issue being addressed avoids any appearance of inauthenticity or hidden agendas. A tobacco company promoting parent–teen dialogue on the dangers of smoking, for an example, is likely to be viewed as inauthentic. Cynical consumers know the tobacco industry counts on early uptake among the youth population for a sustainable customer base. If there is the potential for even the appearance of a conflict of interest, companies should choose a different issue and social marketers should choose a different partner.

REVISING YOUR PLAN

What happens if funding levels are still inadequate to implement the desired plan? In this familiar scenario, you have several options to make ends meet:

Develop campaign phases. Spread costs out over a longer period of time, allowing for more time to raise funds or to use future budget allocations. Options for phasing could include targeting only one or a few target audiences the first year, launching the campaign in fewer geographic markets, focusing on only one or a few communication objectives (e.g., using the first year for awareness building), or implementing some strategies the first year and others in subsequent years (e.g., waiting until the second year to build the demonstration garden using recyclable materials).

Strategically reduce costs. Options might include *eliminating strategies and tactics* with questionable potential impact, *choosing less expensive options* for noncritical executional strategies (e.g., using black and white instead of four colors for brochures or lower-grade paper), and, where feasible, *bringing some of the tasks in-house* (e.g., the development and dissemination of news releases and organization of special events).

Adjust goals. Perhaps the most important consideration is the potential need to return to Step 4 and adjust your goals. Clearly, in situations where you have chosen to spread campaign costs over a longer period of time, goals will need to be changed to reflect new time frames. In other situations where time frames cannot be adjusted and additional funding sources have been explored, and you have decided you need to eliminate one or more key strategies (e.g., television may not be an option, even though it was identified as key to reach and frequency objectives), you will then need to adjust the goal (e.g., reach 50% of the target audience instead of the 75% that television was anticipated to support). You are encouraged to then return to your managers, colleagues, and team members with frank discussions about the need to adjust preliminary goals so that "promises" are honest and realistic.

ETHICAL CONSIDERATIONS WHEN ESTABLISHING FUNDING

Ethical considerations regarding budgets and funding are probably familiar and include issues of responsible fiscal management, reporting, and soliciting of funds. Consider, though, the following additional dilemmas that could face a social marketer: What if a major tobacco company wanted to provide funding for television spots for youth tobacco prevention but didn't require the company's name to be placed in the ad? Is that okay with you? What if a major lumber and paper manufacturer wanted to provide funding for a campaign promoting recyclable materials and wanted the name of the company associated with the campaign? Any concerns? What if a fast-food chain wanted to be listed as a sponsor of magazine ads featuring the food guide pyramid? Is it okay to accept pro bono work from an advertising agency for a counter-alcohol campaign if the parent company has clients in the alcohol industry? In the opening of this chapter, you read about two corporate initiatives to help decrease childhood obesity (the Sesame Street and Nickelodeon projects). What did you think? Did you think they were well intended and a smart move on the corporations' part? Or were you put off in some way?

CHAPTER SUMMARY

Preliminary budgets are best determined by using the *objective-and-task method*, in which budgets are established by (a) reviewing specific objectives, (b) identifying the tasks that must be performed to achieve these objectives, and (c) estimating the costs associated with performing these tasks. These costs will include those related to developing and implementing elements of the marketing mix, as well as funds needed to support the evaluation and monitoring plan. And to justify them, you are encouraged to quantify the intended outcomes you are targeting for these outputs to produce, and ideally the return on investment.

When preliminary budgets exceed current funding, several major sources for additional funds are identified: government grants and appropriations, nonprofit organizations and foundations, advertising and media partners, coalitions and other partnerships, and corporations. You are also encouraged to consider more than cash grants and contributions from corporations, with cause-related marketing initiatives, in-kind contributions, and the use of their distribution channels being excellent opportunities as well.

If proposed budgets exceed funding sources even after exploring additional sources, you can consider creating campaign phases, strategically reducing costs, and/or adjusting the campaign goals you established in Step 4.

RESEARCH HIGHLIGHT

Increasing Participation in Workplace Wellness Programs

A RAND® Health Study

(2013)

Employers interested in increasing participation in workplace wellness programs face decisions regarding what employee behaviors to focus on, what strategies to use to promote desired behaviors, and what support services to offer, all of which will have budget implications. As described in Step 2 (conducting a situation analysis) of this model, existing research on the viability, benefits, and costs of similar programs can help with allocation of funding resources and set expectations for participation levels.

In 2012, the RAND® Corporation, a nonprofit institution in the United States informing policy and decision making through research and analysis, conducted a study intended to inform the development of workplace wellness programs. The work was conducted by RAND Health, a division of the RAND Corporation, and was sponsored by the U.S. Department of Labor and the U.S. Department of Health and Human Services. The following research highlight is a brief summary of the contents of their research report "Workplace Wellness Programs Study," with the full study being an informative resource for those developing workplace wellness programs.[41]

Informational Objectives

The study was designed to answer four major questions related to workplace wellness programs:

- What is the prevalence of these programs, and what are the program characteristics?
- What evidence is there of program impact?
- What is the overall usage level of incentives, what types are used, and who administers them?
- What are the key program success factors?

Method

The project used four data collection methods: (1) a review of scientific and trade literature; (2) a national survey of employers with at least 50 employees in the public and private sectors, including federal and state agencies; (3) statistical analysis of medical claims and wellness program data from a convenience sample of large employers; and (4) analysis of five case studies with existing wellness programs among a diverse set of employers, providing in-depth experiences and insights of individual employers and employees.

Findings

Program Prevalence and Characteristics

Findings from the employer survey indicated that approximately half of U.S. employers offer workplace wellness initiatives. Major program offerings include wellness screening activities to identify health risks as well as interventions to reduce risks and promote healthy behaviors. Data suggest that a vast majority (80%) of employers with a wellness program offer health risk screenings for employees.[42] Prevention interventions include those that focus on primary prevention, targeting employees with risk factors for chronic disease, as well as those considered to be secondary prevention, improving disease control among employees with chronic conditions. In addition to screening and prevention interventions, 86% of employers offer health promotion activities, such as on-site vaccinations and healthy food options.[43] More than half (61%) offer additional health- and well-being-related benefits such as employee assistance plans and on-site clinics.[44] Benefits are offered by employers as well as vendors. Additional findings from the case studies suggest that some employers utilize population-level strategies and use results from employee health screenings for program planning and evaluation and for directing employees to preventive interventions.

Evidence of Program Impact

Three indicators of program impact were summarized in the study:

1. *Program uptake.* The employer survey indicated that among those offering screening, almost half of their employees (46%) undergo clinical screening and/or complete a health risk assessment to identify employees eligible for interventions.[45] On average, among those eligible, 21% participate in fitness programs, 16% in disease management programs, 10% in weight/obesity programs, and 7% in smoking cessation programs.[46]

2. *Program impact on health-related behaviors and health status.* Medical

claims and wellness program data indicated that wellness program participants had statistically significant and clinically meaningful improvements in exercise frequency, smoking behavior, and weight control, but not cholesterol levels.

3. *Impact on health care cost and utilization.* Employers surveyed indicated that workplace wellness programs reduce medical cost, absenteeism, and health-related productivity costs. However, only about half indicated they had evaluated program impacts formally, and only 2% reported actual savings estimates.[47] Conclusions from the case studies were similar, with none of the five case study employers having conducted a formal evaluation of their program in terms of costs.

Incentives: Usage, Types, and Administration

The employer survey suggests that employers do use incentives to increase employee engagement, especially in getting employees to complete the health risk assessment, with incentives over $50 appearing to be the most effective. The use of incentives tied to health standards, however, remains uncommon, with the RAND employer survey indicating that nationally, only 10% of employers with 50 or more employees offering a wellness program use incentives for health standards and only 7% link the incentives to premiums for health coverage.[48]

Key Facilitators

The case study analysis and literature review led to the identification of five factors as key to successful workplace wellness programs:

1. Use effective communication strategies, ones with clear messaging from organizational leaders that uses broad outreach as well as face-to-face interaction.

2. Provide convenient opportunities and locations for employees to engage in wellness activities.

3. Support a corporate culture where wellness is a priority for senior management and is supported by direct supervisors.

4. Leverage existing resources and relationships (e.g., health plans) to expand offerings at little or no cost.

5. Monitor programs for continuous improvement, soliciting feedback from staff to improve future wellness programming.

DISCUSSION QUESTIONS AND EXERCISES

1. Discuss responses to the questions posed in the ethical considerations section.

2. What ideas do you have for a potential corporate partner for a campaign influencing women to know the signs of a heart attack? What about one for literacy?

3. Give an example of a social marketing campaign that has a visible corporate sponsor, one not mentioned in this chapter.

CHAPTER 16 NOTES

1. "Surprising Survivors: Corporate Do-Gooders," *CNN Money*, accessed December 11, 2011, http://money.cnn.com/2009/01/19/magazines/fortune/do_gooder.fortune.

2. Sesame Workshop, "If Elmo Eats Broccoli, Will Kids Eat It Too? Atkins Foundation Grant to Fund Further Research" [Press release] (September 20, 2005), accessed July 26, 2011, http://archive.sesameworkshop.org/aboutus/inside_press.php?contentId=15092302.

3. L. L. Berry, K. Seiders, and A. Hergenroeder, "Regaining the Health of a Nation: What Business Can Do About Obesity," *Organizational Dynamics* 35, no. 4 (2006): 341–356.

4. "Worldwide Day of Play," *Wikipedia* (n.d.), accessed March 16, 2011, http://en.wikipedia.org/wiki/Worldwide_Day_of_Play.

5. P. Kotler, D. Hessekiel, and N. Lee, *GOOD WORKS! Marketing and Corporate Initiatives That Build A Better World . . . and the Bottom Line* (New York: Wiley, 2012).

6. P. Kotler and N. Lee, "Best of Breed," *Stanford Social Innovation Review* (Spring 2004).

7. Kotler et al., *GOOD WORKS!*

8. American Heart Association, "American Heart Association Applauds SUBWAY's Commitment to Marketing Healthy Foods to Kids" (January 23, 2014), accessed May 23, 2014, http://newsroom.heart.org/news/american-heart-association-applauds-subways-commitment-to-marketing-healthy-foods-to-kids.

9. Kotler et al., *GOOD WORKS!*, 118.

10. Water—Use It Wisely, "Campaign History" (n.d.), accessed June 6, 2014, http://wateruseitwisely.com/jump-in/campaign-history/.

11. Kotler et al., *GOOD WORKS!*, 130–132.

12. U.S. Fire Administration, "Home Fire Prevention and Safety Tips" (n.d.), accessed May 23, 2014, http://www.usfa.fema.gov/citizens/home_fire_prev/.

13. Energizer, "Change Your Clock Change Your Battery" (n.d.), accessed May 23, 2014, http://www.energizer.com/learning-center/fire-safety/Pages/default.aspx.

14. Centers for Disease Control and Prevention, "Injury and Prevention & Control: Motor Vehicle Safety" (n.d.), accessed May 23, 2014, http://www.cdc.gov/motorvehiclesafety/Teen_Drivers/index.html.

15. Say Boo to the Flu, "Vaccine Info" (n.d.), accessed May 23, 2014, http://sayboototheflu.com/events/.

16. National Institute of Child Health and Human Development (NICHD), "Safe to Sleep" (n.d.), accessed May 23, 2014, http://www.nichd.nih.gov/sts/Pages/default.aspx.

17. NICHD, Back to Sleep Campaign, "Safe Sleep for Your Baby: Ten Ways to Reduce the Risk of Sudden Infant Death Syndrome" (n.d.), accessed October 31, 2006, http://www.nichd.nih.gov/publications/pubs/safe_sleep_gen.cfm#backs.

18. P. Kotler and G. Armstrong, *Principles of Marketing* (Upper Saddle River, NJ: Prentice Hall, 2001), 528–529.

19. Ibid., 529.

20. Kotler, *Kotler on Marketing*, 31.

21. PugetSound Partnership, "About the Puget Sound Partnership" (n.d.), accessed June 2, 2014, http://www.psp.wa.gov/aboutthepartnership.php.

22. Personal communication from Dave Ward of the Puget Sound Partnership, May 2014.

23. Personal communication May 2014 from Dave Ward, Puget Sound Partnership.

24. Urban Institute, National Center for Charitable Statistics, "Number of Private Foundations in the United States, 2010" (n.d.), accessed March 17, 2011, http://nccsdataweb.urban.org/PubApps/profileDrillDown.php?state=US&rpt=PF.

25. P. Kotler and A. Andreasen, *Strategic Marketing for Nonprofit Organizations* (Englewood Cliffs, NJ: Prentice Hall, 1991), 285.

26. World Bicycle Relief [home page], accessed May 30, 2014, https://www.worldbicyclerelief.org/.

27. Ibid.

28. World Bicycle Relief, "Mobility=Education. Bicycles for Educational Empowerment Program" (2011), accessed May 30, 2014, https://www.worldbicyclerelief.org/storage/documents/wbr_education_field_report.pdf.

29. Ibid.

30. H. Pringle and M. Thompson, *Brand Spirit: How Cause-Related Marketing Builds Brands* (New York: Wiley, 1999); R. Earle, *The Art of Cause Marketing* (Lincolnwood, IL: NTC Business Books, 2000).

31. Ad Council [website], accessed October 10, 2001, www.adcouncil.org, www.adcouncil.org/body_about.html.

32. "Surprising Survivors: Corporate Do-Gooders," *CNN Money*, accessed December 11, 2011, http://money.cnn.com/2009/01/19/magazines/fortune/do_gooder.fortune.

33. Charity Navigator [website], accessed June 4, 2014, http://www.charitynavigator.org/index.cfm?bay=content.view&cpid=42#.U49Hc3l3uUk.

34. P. Kotler and N. Lee, *Corporate Social Responsibility: Doing the Most Good for Your Company and Your Cause* (New York: Wiley, 2006), 9.

35. P. Kotler and N. Lee, "Best of Breed," *Stanford Social Innovation Review* (Spring 2004): 14–23.

36. Pringle and Thompson, *Brand Spirit*; Earle, *Art of Cause Marketing*.

37. Best Buy, "Best Buy Gets Top Recycling Honors" (n.d.), accessed May 23, 2014, http://www.bby.com/best-buy-gets-top-recycling-honors/.

38. Ibid.

39. T. Granger, "Best Buy Targets 1 Billion Pounds of Electronics Recycling" (April 27, 2010), accessed July 26, 2011, http://earth911.com/news/2010/04/27/best-buy-targets-1-billion-pounds-of-electronics-recycling/.

40. P. Kotler and N. Lee, "Best of Breed," *Stanford Social Innovation Review* (Spring 2004), 14–23.

41. S. Mattke, H. Liu, J. P. Caloyeras, C. Y. Huang, K. R. Van Busum, D. Khodyakov, and V. Shier, "Workplace Wellness Programs Study: Final Report" (2013), accessed May 26, 2014, http://www.rand.org/content/dam/rand/pubs/research_reports/RR200/RR254/RAND_RR254 .sum.pdf.

42. Ibid., xv.

43. Ibid., xvi.

44. Ibid., xvi.

45. Ibid., xvi.

46. Ibid., xvii.

47. Ibid., xix.

48. Ibid., xx.

Chapter 17

CREATING AN IMPLEMENTATION PLAN AND SUSTAINING BEHAVIORS

Numerous behaviors that support sustainability are susceptible to the most human of traits: forgetting. Fortunately, prompts can be very effective in reminding us to perform these activities.[1]

—Dr. Doug McKenzie-Mohr
McKenzie-Mohr & Associates Inc.

We envision a world where people are healthy and safe, financially secure, involved in protecting the environment, and contributing to their communities. We have written this book for the thousands of current and future practitioners on the front lines responsible for changing public behaviors to help create this reality.

After reading the prior 16 chapters, we hope you see social marketing as a process with a target audience focus and an intervention toolbox (4Ps) containing more tools than the promotion "P," ones you'll need to get the job done. We hope you appreciate the rigor involved in achieving success and that you picked up on principles that will help ensure your desired outcomes—ones worth repeating and reviewing:

- Take advantage of prior and existing successful campaigns
- Start with target audiences most ready for action
- Promote single, simple, doable behaviors, ones that will have the most impact, greatest target audience willingness, and largest market opportunity
- Identify and remove barriers to behavior change
- Bring real benefits to the present
- Ask your target audience what would motivate them to do the behavior
- Highlight costs of competing behaviors
- Search for and include tangible goods and services in your campaign, ones that will help your target audience perform the behavior

- Consider nonmonetary incentives in the form of recognition and appreciation, commitments, and pledges
- Make access easy
- When appropriate, have a little fun with your messages
- Use communication channels at the point of decision making
- Try for social and entertainment media channels
- Get commitments and pledges
- Use prompts for sustainability
- Create plans for social diffusion
- Track results and make adjustments

You'll read in this final chapter about the importance of creating a detailed implementation plan to ensure accountability, as well as sustainability, discussing:

- Major components of an implementation plan
- Options for campaign phases
- Recommended sustainability strategies
- Anticipating forces against change
- Sharing and selling your plan

MARKETING HIGHLIGHT

Improving Water Quality and Protecting Fish and Wildlife Habitats in Puget Sound and Chesapeake Bay Through Dissemination of a Social Marketing Approach

(2012–Present)

Nearly every problem has been solved by someone somewhere. The challenge of the 21st century is to find out what works and scale it up.

—Bill Clinton,
former U.S. President[2]

We believe that a strategic social marketing approach to behavior change is one of those problem solvers "that works." And that the following two cases illustrate how

two agencies, the Puget Sound Partnership and the Chesapeake Bay Trust, have been scaling up social marketing to support their missions to improve water quality and protect fish and wildlife habitats. By disseminating the practice throughout their respective regions, they are creating a sustainable force for real change.

Puget Sound in Washington State

Puget Sound is the second largest estuary in the United States, the Chesapeake Bay being the largest. The Puget Sound Partnership (PSP) is a state agency serving as the backbone organization for Puget Sound recovery, coordinating the efforts of citizens, scientists, the government, businesses, and nonprofits to set priorities, implement a regional recovery plan, and ensure accountability for results.[3] The Puget Sound Action Agenda identifies three regionwide priorities: (1) Prevent pollution from urban storm water runoff, (2) protect and restore habitat, and (3) restore and reopen shellfish beds.

To support this agenda, as mentioned briefly in Chapter 16, the agency currently (2014) invests about $11 million in developing and implementing social marketing efforts that protect water quality and fish and wildlife habitats. One area of focus is on building regional capacity to implement evidence-based programs, including providing social marketing training and technical assistance to first develop and then implement and evaluate funded projects. Hallmarks of this capacity-building effort include the following:

1. *Social marketing certificate trainings* involve a two-day course offered by adjunct faculty of the University of Washington, leading students through the 10-step planning model presented in this text. Two weeks between the two daylong sessions allow for formative research. Upon successful completion of the course and a draft social marketing plan, attendees receive a certificate documenting contact hours and continuing education units earned for the course through the university.

2. *"Training the Trainers"* involves a half-day training for graduates of the certificate course. Graduates are provided agendas, handouts, and a one-hour presentation for their use in subsequent trainings. Each graduate commits to conducting at least one training with managers and staff engaged in water quality protection initiatives in their region. The objective is to ensure that practitioners in each Puget Sound county have direct access to at least one local social marketing expert.

3. *Executive briefings* are designed for senior leadership from local, state, and federal organizations and emphasize the difference between social marketing and education, outreach, advertising, and social media. They also emphasize principles for success when applying a social marketing approach as well as the potential for high returns on investment.

4. *Social marketing grants* were awarded to some graduates of the certificate course. Experience has shown that social marketing training alone is not enough for students to successfully implement social marketing initiatives on their own. These grants offer recent graduates a chance to apply their learning in a controlled environment, with technical support from recognized experts—a de facto internship in social marketing. In this case, the technical support includes working with PSP staff and consultant contractors to conduct formative research, develop the 10-step social

marketing plan, and complete an actionable evaluation plan.

5. *Technical assistance for Model Stewardship Programs* includes working with PSP staff and consultant contractors to develop a social marketing toolkit that can be disseminated to future grantees working on similar behavior change initiatives. Model Stewardship Programs are locally based behavior change programs that have a track record of filling gaps, systemic change, sustainability, focus on innovation, and Action Agenda implementation. Through this technical assistance, PSP is expanding the scale and geographic scope of these model programs using social marketing techniques.

6. *A Social Marketing Trade Association* for the Puget Sound region provides a community of practice for social marketing practitioners, quarterly forums, and an annual conference.

7. *Additional components* that support partner organizations include online resources with sample social marketing plans and worksheets, project portfolios, formative research, a quick reference guide outlining the 10-step model, and a standard grantee scope of work that follows the 10-step model.

Table 17.1 provides an estimate of the numbers of individuals in the Puget Sound region working on water quality issues who were provided with briefings and/or in-depth trainings in social marketing, most receiving hands-on assistance in developing a strategic marketing plan. Consider the potential impact that these 500-plus individuals can have—all in one geographic region, all focused on the same environmental issue, and all armed with a proven toolkit for changing citizen behaviors that improve water quality and protect fish and wildlife habitats.

Information for this case was provided by Dave Ward and Emily Sanford at the Puget Sound Partnership.

Table 17.1 Puget Sound Partnership's Reach in a Two-Year Period, With Individuals Working on Initiatives to Improve Water Quality and Protect Fish and Wildlife Habitats

Activities	Individuals Trained or Briefed
Social Marketing Certificate trainings	220 (7 trainings)
Training the Trainers	180 (30 trainers)
Executive briefings	80
Technical assistance for social marketing grants	30
Technical assistance for model stewardship programs	20
TOTAL	530 individual in-depth exposures to social marketing in the Puget Sound

Chesapeake Bay

The Chesapeake Bay Trust (CBT) is a nonprofit grant-making organization with the mission of improving the Chesapeake Bay and its rivers. Since its inception in 1985, the Trust has awarded $55 million in grants and engaged hundreds of thousands of citizen stewards in projects designed to have a positive and measurable impact on the Chesapeake Bay and its tributaries.[4] Similar to the Puget Sound Partnership, in 2013 they launched a major effort to disseminate a social marketing approach to behavior change efforts throughout the region. An impressive research study had given them a new direction. In 2011–2012, the Trust worked with a group of graduate students from the University of Michigan to consider the types of outreach programs under way in the Chesapeake Bay Watershed. This study revealed that although the bulk of Trust grantees (97%) seek to motivate individuals to protect the Bay and that a significant percentage of program leaders (62%) seek to measurably change behavior in a given target audience, many organizations were conducting communications campaigns and/or education programs only with the hope of changing behavior. Their recommendations were the basis for the following activities:

1. *Alignment of requests for proposals with the social marketing 10-step planning model* was done in fiscal year 2013. The request for proposals (RFP) now functions as both a call for proposals and an educational tool that encourages projects that follow best practices for behavior change program design.

2. *Social marketing trainings for grantees* have been conducted in two ways. The first major training for grantees was held by Doug McKenzie-Mohr at the annual Chesapeake Bay Watershed Forum in 2012. Additionally, individual and group trainings for grantees have been led by Trust staff since 2010.

3. *Social marketing trainings for technical assistance providers (TAPs)* were led by Nancy Lee in 2013. Nineteen TAPs were trained and received a certificate to better enable them to provide much-needed technical assistance in designing better storm-water outreach programs. An initial indicator of success of this strategy is that 11 of the 13 funded proposals to CBT's outreach grant program sought assistance from one of the trained TAPs. In addition, CBT is working with a funding partner, National Fish and Wildlife Foundation, to integrate qualified social marketing TAPs into their program, which funds technical assistance for local governments and NGOs implementing outreach programs.

4. *Technical assistance for grantees* has been provided directly by Trust staff during the application process and once funding awards are made. The Trust also allows requests by organizations to hire social marketing contractors where appropriate. Moving forward, the Technical Assistance Provider Network will be expanded and TAPs will help to provide technical assistance for grantees in addition to Trust staff.

5. *The Stormwater Outreach Forum* was held in April 2014. Over 40 leaders from nonprofits, local governments, and state and federal agencies currently engaged in storm-water outreach attended a two-day forum, sharing outreach program best practices and generating the following recommendations to assist in the broader application of these practices in local programs:

- Develop a crowdsourced database to promote shared research, results, and materials.
- Support systematic coordination between NGO partners and local governments.
- Document the case for more public investment in storm-water outreach using social marketing best practices.
- Coordinate broad and comprehensive development and implementation of audience research available for application at the local level.

- Increase coordination of "midstream" activities and approaches to avoid duplication, and find economies of scale (e.g., contractor training/certification).
- Develop and promote a tool for a rapid assessment/audit of outreach programs to encourage incorporation of social marketing best practices into program design.
- Expand and promote the stormwater outreach technical assistance provider network.

As indicated in Table 17.2, more than 180 individuals in the Chesapeake Bay region working on water quality issues aligned their RFP with the 10-step model, attended social marketing trainings, received technical assistance in developing a strategic marketing plan, and/or attended the outreach forum.

The Chesapeake Bay Program, a multistate partnership coordinated by the Environmental Protection Agency (EPA), is working toward development and implementation of an indicator of citizen

Table 17.2 The Chesapeake Bay Trust's Reach in the First Two Years With Individuals Working on Initiatives to Improve Water Quality and Protect Fish and Wildlife Habitats

Activities	Individuals Trained
Alignment of RFP with 10-step model	40
Social marketing trainings for grantees	60
Training of technical assistance providers	20
Technical assistance for grantees	20
Stormwater Outreach Forum, April 2014	42
	182 individual in-depth exposures to social marketing in the Chesapeake Bay Region

stewardship, perhaps modeled after the Puget Sound Partnership's Sound Behavior Index, to serve as a baseline and measure of progress toward achieving a recently adopted citizen stewardship goal. The goal calls for an increase in the number and diversity of local citizen stewards and local governments that actively support and carry out the conservation and restoration activities, and the Trust plans to work with the Bay program partners to support social marketing approaches in pursuit of that goal.

Information for this case was provided by Jamie Baxter and Kacey Wetzel at the Chesapeake Bay Trust.

Summary

From these two examples of dissemination of social marketing throughout a region, with a focus on clear issues, we see common components:

- A backbone organization with a mission that lends itself to the support of organizations and citizens in the community with similar interests and commitments
- Social marketing training for grantees, program managers, and staff
- Establishment of a community of practice, with intentional communication and support networks
- Special trainings for trainers and technical assistants
- Piloting and dissemination of program strategies that work
- Web-based resources such as prior research studies and case examples

STEP 10: COMPLETE AN IMPLEMENTATION PLAN

For some, the implementation plan *is* the marketing plan, one that will reflect all prior decisions, and is considered your final major step in the planning process. It functions as a concise working document to share and track planned efforts. It provides a mechanism to ensure that you and your team do what you said you wanted to do, on time, and within budget. It provides the map that charts your course, permitting timely feedback when you have wavered or need to take corrective actions. It is not the evaluation plan, although it incorporates evaluation activities. It is also not the same as a marketing plan for an entire program or organization, as the emphasis in this book has been on developing a marketing plan for a specific social marketing campaign.

Kotler and Armstrong describe *marketing implementation* as "the process that turns marketing strategies and plans into marketing actions in order to accomplish strategic marketing objectives."[5] They further emphasize that many managers think *doing things right* (implementation) is just as important as *doing the right things* (strategy). In this model, both are viewed as critical to success.

Key components to a comprehensive implementation plan include addressing the classic action-planning elements of what will be done, by whom, when, and for how much:

- *What will we do?* Key activities necessary to execute strategies identified in the marketing mix and the evaluation plan are captured in this document. Many were reviewed and then confirmed in the budgeting process activity and will be incorporated in this section.
- *Who will be responsible?* For each of these major efforts, you will identify key individuals and/or organizations responsible for program implementation. In social marketing programs, typical key players include staff (e.g., program coordinators), partners (e.g., coalition members or other agencies), sponsors (e.g., a retail business or the media), suppliers (e.g., manufacturers), vendors (e.g., an advertising agency), consultants (e.g., for evaluation efforts), and other internal and external publics, such as volunteers, citizens, and lawmakers.
- *When will it be done?* Time frames are included for each major activity, typically noting expected start and finish dates. (See Box 17.1 for a bold approach to campaign time frames.)
- *How much will it cost?* Expenses identified in the budgeting process are then paired with associated activities.

Most commonly, these plans represent a minimum of one year of activities and, ideally, two or three years. In terms of format, options range from simple plans included in executive summaries of the marketing plan to complex ones developed using sophisticated software programs. Box 17.2 presents a summary of one section of a social marketing plan developed for the Mental Health Transformation Grant Social Marketing Initiative in Washington state, a section focusing on influencing policymakers. Also see Appendix B for an additional example of a social marketing plan using this 10-step model.

Box 17.1
A "Rapid Results" Implementation Schedule

Rapid Results is a management technique, originally designed to ignite more timely results within large corporations, introduced about 40 years ago by Robert Schaffer, a management consultant. In 2006, the company spun off a nonprofit group to train people all around the world to use the same method for turbo-charging community development as well as public sector performance, setting a short-term goal with a 100-day deadline forcing prioritization, focus, and collaboration. A 2011 article in the *New York Times* described Rapid Results as working like this:

A trained facilitator sits down with people in a business, organization or village to decide what to do. They vote how could we spend it to accomplish that goal in just 100 days? The village chooses its goal and how to get it done . . . At first, the 100 days seems ridiculous . . . Who can accomplish something significant in three months? But this is exactly the point—it takes a project out of the realm of business as usual.[6]

Box 17.2
A Social Marketing Plan for Eliminating the Mental Health Stigma: Special Section for Influencing Policymakers

1.0 Background, Purpose, and Focus

The purpose of this initiative is to reduce the stigma surrounding mental illness and the barriers it creates in the work setting, at home, within the health care system, and in the community. The focus is on increasing the understanding that people with mental illness can and do recover and live fulfilling and productive lives.

2.0 Situation Analysis

2.1 SWOT Analysis

Strengths. Statewide transformation initiative with executive support, multiagency workgroup commitment, and marketing task group with strong consumer participation; recent legislative action on mental health issues, including PACT teams, parity, and increased funding for children's mental health

Weaknesses. Limited budget, unrealistic expectations for a communications solution, and lack of consensus on the use of social marketing

Opportunities. Grant funding, governor endorsement, emerging coalitions, provider interest and support, and political curiosity

Threats. Competing projects/staff time limitations, constituent expectation that "campaign" can be all things to all people, and skepticism that marketing is a legitimate method for social change

This initiative will be built around the framework set forth by Patrick Corrigan, professor of psychiatry at Northwestern University, whose research suggests a target-specific stigma change model, identifying and influencing groups who have the power to change stigma and support adoption of the recovery model. Policymakers, the focus of this section of the plan, were identified as one of three priority audiences and will be addressed in Year 3 of the social marketing initiative. The full marketing plan includes sections targeting consumers and providers.

3.0 Target Audience Profile

- State legislators who are responsible for state-level policies and funding
- State agency officials who set reimbursement rules for the types of services that can be covered
- Local elected officials who are responsible for local policies and allocating funds to regional service providers

(Continued)

(Continued)

4.0 Marketing Objectives and Goals

4.1 We want this plan to influence policymakers to:

- Pass legislation that enables "recovery" and "mental health transformation."
- Reallocate existing funds to put more resources into recovery, resulting in a decreased need for crisis intervention.
- Interpret regulations affecting people with mental illness using a "recovery" lens.
- Ensure adequate funding to support recovery-oriented mental health services, including consumer participation.
- Support the provision of employment opportunities for consumers.
- Eliminate stigmatizing language and views and adopt a language and process that promotes recovery.

4.2 Goals

- Conduct a minimum of four speaking engagements with local elected officials.
- Conduct a minimum of six speaking engagements with state legislators.
- Conduct a minimum of five speaking engagements with state agency officials.

5.0 Target Audience Barriers, Benefits, and Competition

5.1 Barriers

Perceived barriers to desired behaviors include (a) lack of knowledge about mental illness and funding/resource issues, (b) uncertainty that successful recovery is how the consumer defines it, and (c) uncertainty that recovery-oriented treatment systems can be devised where people with mental illness pose no greater violence risk to the community than people without mental illness.

5.2 Benefits/Motivators

Potential motivators include consumer success stories and proof that the recovery model works and is an efficient way to spend tax dollars.

5.3 Competing Behaviors

Responding to public fear and belief in stereotypes; providing funding for crisis intervention before funding recovery-oriented self-help programs.

6.0 Positioning Statement

We plan to develop a speakers' bureau consisting of providers and consumers of mental health services that will educate policymakers about recovery and serve as living examples of success. We want them to view these speaking engagements as an opportunity to hear success stories from consumers and as a good source of information about mental health issues, including recovery and stigma. We will also develop white papers, in partnership with consumers and providers, and want policymakers to see these as a credible source of information about mental illness, recovery and resiliency, and stigma, and as a source of empirical evidence that the recovery model works, can be economical, and is a good investment.

7.0 Marketing Mix Strategies (4Ps)

7.1 Product

Core: Increased knowledge of mental illness and Washington's Mental Health Transformation Project.

Actual: Strategic speaking engagements and presentations throughout the state, highlighting consumer success stories and the recovery model.

Augmented: White papers on the transformation effort in Washington state.

7.2 Price

Speaking engagements and white papers will be free. Media coverage will address public fear and instill hope for recovery. Advocacy awards will honor policy "heroes" who contribute to recovery and the breaking down of myths and stereotypes.

7.3 Place

Speaking engagements will be scheduled at locations and times throughout the state that are convenient for policymakers. White papers will be available on the Internet and downloadable for print. Hard copies will be mailed out individually and made available at speaking engagements.

7.4 Promotion

Speaking engagements will be promoted in association newsletters, on listserves, and at sessions at related conferences. White papers will be promoted via direct mail. A news bureau will be used to publicize awards, conduct editorial board meetings to discuss mental health transformation, and stimulate feature stories. Availability of the speakers' bureau will be promoted through ongoing conversations with elected officials and their staff.

8.0 Evaluation Plan

Purpose and audience for evaluation: Speakers' bureau evaluation will measure change in policymaker knowledge of mental illness and recovery, change in belief

(Continued)

(Continued)

that people with mental illness can live fulfilling lives in the community, disposition toward changing regulations and funding to support recovery-oriented services, and actual changes in policies, regulations, and funding. The marketing team will use evaluation findings to determine continuation, improvement, and expansion of speakers' bureau and policymaker strategies.

Output measures: Numbers of speaking engagements conducted, white papers distributed, news articles and editorials printed, news stories aired, and editorial board meetings conducted.

Outcome measures: Number of policymakers at speaking engagements, number of visits to website, increased knowledge about mental illnesses, increase in knowledge about Washington's Mental Health Transformation Project, and decrease in stigmatizing attitudes and beliefs by policymakers attending speaking engagements.

How and when to measure: Pre- and post-workshop questionnaires by speakers' bureau participants and audience members. Tracking of policy, regulation, and funding changes. Media monitoring for number of letters to the editor, retractions of stereotypical portrayals, feature stories on recovery, and media coverage of award recipients.

9.0 Budget

Budget estimate is for Year 3 for the speakers' bureau and news bureau, aimed at three target audiences—consumers, providers, and policymakers—and does not include all planned activities for Year 3. The project is funded by a Mental Health Transformation State Incentive Grant from the Substance Abuse and Mental Health Services Administration of the U.S. Department of Health and Human Services.

Speakers' bureau	$70,000
Recovery and stigma materials (print and web)	$20,000
News bureau	$15,000
Professional education	$10,000
Management and coordination	$20,000
Total for speakers' and news bureaus	$135,000

10.0 Implementation Plan

Key Activities	Responsibility/Lead	Timing	Budget
Project coordination and oversight	DOH	Ongoing	$30,000
Speakers' bureau coordination and scheduling	Washington Institute for Mental Illness Research and Training; finalize schedule for speaking engagements	1st quarter

Quarterly | $70,000 |
| Continuing availability of recovery and stigma materials in print and on the web | DOH | Ongoing (started in Year 2) | $10,000 |
| Policy white papers | Mental Health Transformation staff with DOH | 1st quarter: Draft for review
2nd quarter: Finalize and print
2nd–4th quarters: Publicity and distribution | (Included in project coordination) |

Source: Heidi Keller and Daisye Orr, Office of Health Promotion, Washington State Department of Health with Washington's Mental Health Transformation Project, Office of the Governor, 2006.

PHASING

As mentioned earlier in our discussion on budgeting in Chapter 16, when funding levels are inadequate to implement the desired plan, one tactic to consider is spreading costs over a longer period of time, allowing more time to raise funds or use future budget allocations. Natural options include creating phases that are organized (driven) by some element of the marketing plan: target audience, geographic areas, campaign objectives, campaign goals, stages of change, products, pricing, distributional channels, promotional messages, or communication channels. The following provide examples of situations in which a particular framework might be most appropriate.

Phases Organized by First Piloting and Refining and Then Broad-Scale Implementation

Conducting a pilot prior to broad-scale implementation is strongly recommended. As Doug McKenzie-Mohr writes, "Think of a pilot as a 'test run,' an opportunity to work out the bugs before committing to carrying out a strategy broadly."[7] And the "bugs" that may be identified can range from discovering that something about the offer (product, price, place) was not sufficient to overcome barriers and provide valued benefits, or that some element or elements of promotional strategies (messages, messengers, creative elements, communication channels) were insufficient to reach and inspire target audiences. The SmartTrip Welcome new mover program in Portland, Oregon, described in Chapter 5, began as a pilot and then, based on results, was transformed to respond to new market opportunities:

Phase 1: Pilot in 2004 appealing to all residents throughout the city to use alternative transportation

Phase 2: Refinements to program strategies based on identification of the most responsive audience segment

Phase 3: Broad-scale implementation in 2011 of a program focusing on new residents

Phases Organized by Target Audience

In a differentiated strategy in which several market segments are targets for the campaign, each phase could concentrate on implementing strategies for a distinct segment. This would provide a strong focus for your efforts as well as increase resources behind them. For the Seafood Watch program highlighted in Chapter 13, deliberate phases included:

Phase 1: Influencing consumers to ask for and purchase "green fish"

Phase 2: Equipping restaurants and grocery stores to favor suppliers of "green fish"

Phase 3: Developing a recognition and certification program that recognizes "green fisheries"

Phases Organized by Geographic Area

Phasing by geographic area has several advantages. It may align with funding availability as well as offer the ability to pilot the campaign, measure outcomes, and then make important refinements prior to implementation. Most important, by using this option, you will also be implementing all of the strategic elements you chose for the marketing mix. You will just be concentrating them in one or a few geographic areas. In the "Bullying Stops Here" case in Chapter 15, the team of five public relations students conducted their intervention in one location and then made recommendations for implementation in additional locations:

Phase 1: Focusing efforts on one middle school in the district

Phase 2: Recommending to administrators that, based on the success of the campaign at the middle school, they should consider adapting and implementing the Pledge to Prevent campaign at the district's high school and elementary school

Phases Organized by Objective

In a situation in which a campaign has identified important objectives related to knowledge and beliefs as well as behavior, campaign phases can be organized and sequenced to support each objective. A litter prevention campaign in Washington state used this strategy, allowing more time to gain the support of partners (e.g., law enforcement), secure sponsors (e.g., fast-food restaurants), and establish important infrastructures (e.g., identifying broad distribution channels for litterbags and incorporating questions on fines for litter in driver education tests). In this example, phases reflect the process of moving target audiences from awareness to action—over time.

> Phase 1: Creating awareness of laws and fines
>
> Phase 2: Altering the belief that "no one's watching and no one cares" by implementing a toll-free hotline for reporting littering
>
> Phase 3: Changing littering behavior

Phases Organized by Goal

Campaigns may have established specific benchmarks for reaching interim goals, in which case, activities and resources would then be organized to support desired outcomes. The advantage of this framework is that funders and administrators "feel good" that the program will achieve targeted goals—eventually. Similar to phasing by geographic area, this approach does not require altering the marketing strategy you developed for the program. For example, a social marketing effort in Japan to increase breast-screening rates from 30% in 2008 set the following milestones:[8]

> Phase 1: To 40% by 2010
>
> Phase 2: To 50% by 2012

Phases Organized by Stage of Change

In keeping with the objective of moving audiences through stages of change, it may make the most sense to phase a campaign effort by first targeting those "most ready for action" and then using this momentum to move on to other markets. In a campaign encouraging food waste composting, for example, efforts might be made to set up demonstration households in neighborhoods with eager volunteers, who can then be influenced and equipped to spread the word to neighbors. In this case, phases might appear as follows:

> Phase 1: Influence households with consistent participation in all curbside recycling (maintenance segment)
>
> Phase 2: Influence households participating in paper and glass curbside recycling, but not yard waste recycling (in action segment)

Phase 3: Influence households that have responded to and inquired about information in the past but are not regular curbside recyclers (contemplator segment)

Phases Organized by Introduction or Enhancement of Services or Tangible Goods

When new or improved services and tangible goods have been identified for a program plan, it may be necessary, even strategic, to introduce these over a period of time. A Supplemental Nutritional Program for Women, Infants, and Children (WIC) clinic, for example, might phase the introduction of service enhancements by starting with those perceived to have the most potential impact on increasing use of farmers' markets and then move on to those providing added value:

Phase 1: Counselor training and support materials

Phase 2: Market tours and transportation vouchers

Phase 3: Clinic classes on freezing and canning

Phases Organized by Pricing Strategies

A program may plan a pricing strategy in which significant price incentives are used early in the campaign as a way to create attention and stimulate action. In subsequent phases, efforts may rely on other elements of the marketing mix, such as improved distribution channels or targeted promotions. In the case of a utility promoting energy-efficient appliances, pricing strategies might change over time as follows:

Phase 1: Rebates for turning in old appliances

Phase 2: Discount coupons for energy-efficient appliances

Phase 3: Pricing similar to competing appliances and increased emphasis on contribution to the environment

Phases Organized by Distribution Channels

A campaign relying heavily on convenience of access might begin with implementing distribution channels that are the quickest, easiest, or least expensive to develop and then move on to more significant endeavors over time. Launching a prescription drug medications return program might progress over time as follows, allowing program managers to develop procedures that ensure secure as well as convenient return locations:

Phase 1: Pilot the program by accepting medications at the county sheriff's office

Phase 2: Expand to major medical centers and hospitals

Phase 3: Expand to pharmacies

Phases Organized by Messages

When multiple campaign messages are needed to support a broad social marketing program (e.g., decreasing obesity), behavior change may be facilitated by introducing messages one at a time. This can help your target adopter spread costs for change over a period of time as well as feel less overwhelmed (self-efficacy). The Ad Council's Small Steps campaign for the U.S. Department of Health and Human Services could phase its 100 recommended actions in the following clustered way:

Phase 1: Steps at Work: Walk during your lunch hour. Get off a stop early and walk. Walk to a coworker's desk instead of emailing or calling.

Phase 2: Steps When Shopping: Eat before grocery shopping. Make a grocery list before you shop. Carry a grocery basket instead of pushing a cart.

Phase 3: Steps When Eating: Eat off smaller plates. Stop eating when you are full. Snack on fruits and vegetables.

Phases Organized by Communication Channels

At the onset of major threats such as the H1N1 flu, mad cow disease, and terrorist attacks, you may need to first reach broad audiences in a very short time. Once this phase is complete, efforts may shift to more targeted audiences through more targeted communication channels. For H1N1 flu, for example, we saw channels progress as follows:

Phase 1: Mass communication channels: news stories on TV, on radio, and in newspapers

Phase 2: Selective channels: posters, flyers, and signage (e.g., hand-washing signs in restrooms)

Phase 3: Personal contact: health care workers making visits to schools to ensure policies were in place regarding attendance for sick children

Phases Organized by a Variety of Factors

In reality, it may be important, even necessary, to use a combination of phasing techniques. For example, campaign target audiences may vary by geographic area (e.g., farmers are more important target audiences for water conservation in rural areas than they are in urban communities). As a result, different communities may have different target audience phasing in their campaigns. As most practitioners will attest, campaigns will need to be meaningful to their specific communities or they will not receive the necessary support for implementation.

Phase 1: Rural communities target farmers and urban communities target large corporations for water conservation

Phase 2: Rural communities target businesses and urban communities target public sector agencies

Phase 3: Rural communities and urban communities target residential users

SUSTAINABILITY

At this point in the planning process, most strategies have been identified and scheduled to support desired behavior change objectives and goals. It is a worthwhile exercise, however, to give last-minute consideration to any additional tactics to include in the plan that will keep your campaign visible and behavior change messages prominent after ads go off the air and news stories die down. Are there other mechanisms you could include in the campaign that will help your target audience sustain their behavior over the long term? In keeping with our stages of change theory and model, you should be specifically interested in ensuring that those in the action stage don't return to contemplation and that those in the maintenance stage don't return to irregular actions. In the following sections, ideas including the use of prompts, commitments, plans for social diffusion, dissemination, and utilizing public infrastructures are presented.

Prompts

In their book *Fostering Sustainable Behavior*, McKenzie-Mohr and Smith offer insights, guidelines, tools, and checklists for the social marketer to consider for supporting continued behavior change. They describe prompts as

> visual or auditory aids which remind us to carry out an activity that we might otherwise forget. The purpose of a prompt is not to change attitudes or increase motivation, but simply to remind us to engage in an action that we are already predisposed to do.[9]

They have four recommendations for effective prompts:

1. Make the prompt noticeable, using eye-catching graphics.
2. Make the prompt self-explanatory, including all information needed to take the appropriate action.
3. Place the prompt as close as possible to where and when the action is to be taken.
4. Use prompts to encourage positive behaviors rather than to avoid harmful ones.

"Anchoring" is similar to prompting, where the desired behavior (e.g., flossing) is "anchored," or closely linked, to a current established behavior (e.g., brushing your teeth). Examples of both are illustrated in Table 17.3, and as a planning note, any new or additional prompts that you identify at this point should be noted in the appropriate 4Ps section of your marketing plan.

Table 17.3 Sustaining Behaviors and Campaign Efforts

Issue	Using Prompts to Sustain Behavior
Tobacco cessation	Electronic alerts during vulnerable times in the day that signal, "Come on, you can do it"
Binge drinking	Small posters in bar restroom stalls showing someone bending over "the porcelain god"
Physical activity	Wearing a pedometer to make sure you get 10,000 steps a day
Unintended pregnancies	Keeping a condom in a small case on a key chain
Fat intake	Detailed data on food labels indicating fat grams and percentage of calories
Fruits and vegetables	Placing fruits and vegetables in glass bowls at eye level in refrigerators
Water intake	Stickers at water coolers saying, "Have you had your 8 glasses today?"
Breastfeeding	Pediatricians encouraging a nursing mom to continue breastfeeding at the six-month checkup
Breast cancer	Shower nozzle hanger reminding about monthly breast self-exams
Folic acid	Keeping vitamin pills by the toothbrush as an established habit
Immunizations	Emails recognizing and reminding parents of when a child's immunizations are due
Diabetes	Using a beeper as a reminder for blood glucose monitoring
Car seats	Keeping a car seat in all cars used frequently by a child
Drinking and driving	Making Breathalyzers available in bars
Booster seats	Air fresheners for cars with reminders about booster seats
Drowning	Providing loaner life vests for toddlers at public beaches
Smoke alarms	Placing reminder stickers in planning calendars for checking batteries in smoke alarms
Waste reduction	Label on a bathroom towel dispenser suggesting, "Take only what you need. Towels are trees."
Food waste composting	Stickers on recycling containers recognizing a homeowner who also composts food waste
Reducing use	Messages at coffee stands suggesting that "the regulars" bring their own cups
Air pollution	Stickers inside car doors reminding car owners when it is time to get their tires inflated
Organ donation	Lawyers asking their clients who are organ donors if they have talked to their families about their wishes

Commitments and Pledges

Gaining commitments, or pledges, from target adopters has also proven surprisingly effective. "Individuals who agreed to a small initial request were far more likely to agree to a subsequent larger request."[10] Examples include a backyard wildlife sanctuary program in which homeowners sign the application promising to follow the natural gardening guidelines, and WIC clinics in which clients who sign a receipt for farmers' market coupons state they are interested in using these in the next three months. Evidently, as McKenzie-Mohr and Smith report, "when individuals agree to a small request, it often alters the way they perceive themselves."[11] Any commitments you decide to add to your plan at this point should be noted in the price strategy section. We consider it a form of a nonmonetary incentive, since making this commitment has been shown to act as an incentive to follow through with the behavior.

In McKenzie-Mohr's 2011 edition of *Fostering Sustainable Behavior*, the following four guidelines for designing effective commitments are among those emphasized:[12]

1. Make commitments as public as possible (e.g., signs on lawns or signatures on a petition).

2. Seek commitments in groups (e.g., members of a church congregation pledging to conserve energy).

3. Engage the audience in performing the activity initially to increase their perception of commitment (e.g., having homeowners check the thermostat on their hot water heater will likely lead them to take the next step, setting it at 120 degrees).

4. Use existing, related contact points to solicit commitments (e.g., when customers purchase paint, ask for a commitment to dispose of unused paint properly).

Framework for Dissemination of Evidence-Based Practices

In the introduction of a 2012 article in *Preventing Chronic Disease*, the authors commented that "although the public health community has developed many evidence-based practices to promote healthy behaviors, adoption of these practices has been haphazard."[13] In response, Jeff Harris, MD, MPH, MBA, and others at the University of Washington Health Promotion Research Center developed a recommended framework for dissemination to serve as a guide for community-based organizations and to help researchers develop and test approaches to dissemination of evidence-based practices.[14] Main elements of the framework are presented in Table 17.4 and illustrated using an example of promoting physical activity among older adults.

Plans for Social Diffusion

Before wrapping up the planning process, also take time to consider additional tactics to facilitate social diffusion—the spread of the adoption of a behavior from a few to many, a concept introduced in Chapter 5. McKenzie-Mohr suggests guidelines for this as well, including:[15]

1. Make support for behavior adoption visible (e.g., affix a decal to a recycling container indicating that "We compost").

Table 17.4   Health Promotion Research Center's Dissemination Case Study Example

Framework Construct	Example From Enhance Fitness (EF)
Evidence-based practice	An older adult exercise program involving aerobic activity and training to increase balance, flexibility, and strength, three times a week
Disseminating organization	Senior Services
User organizations	Senior centers, community centers, and nonprofit and for-profit fitness organizations
Linkages and learnings: working with user organizations to refine practice	Developed and tested a chair-based version of EF for frail older adults
	Developed an online version of EF instructor training to reduce costs associated with training and to reach a wide instructor pool
	Tested EnhanceMobility, an adaptation of EF for people with dementia
Dissemination approach	Senior Services licenses the program for a fee and provides training, materials, and data management and analysis
	A new national licensing agreement with Y-USA is opening up 2,700 YMCA sites across the country
Modifiable context: Policy supports	Acquired CDC Arthritis Program approval of EF
	Acquired approval for EF to be one of five evidence-based disease prevention programs included in the Administration on Aging Choices for Independence grants, 2009.
Modifiable context: funding supports	Selected as a Choices program for AoA funding (26 states)
	Part of a $7.5 million initiative in South Florida
Dissemination results to date	As of 2014, has been offered at 629 community locations in 33 states and has served 42,560 participants, 6,121 in 2014.

2. Use durable versus temporary indicators (e.g., a Mutt Mitt station in a neighborhood vs. yard signs encouraging picking up pet waste).

3. Engage well-known and well-respected people to make their support for a desired behavior visible (e.g., a city mayor speaking frequently about the advantages she sees from taking mass transit to city hall).

4. Make norms visible, especially when "most of us" are engaged in the behavior (e.g., a sign at the entrance to a grocery store stating that 60% of shoppers bring their own bags at least once a month).

Utilizing Public Infrastructures to Increase and Maintain Visibility

If you are working in the public sector, you have numerous opportunities for sustained visibility, as you often have access to public places and signage at public agencies. Those

Figure 17.1 A durable sign at the entrance to a playground provided to recognize cities that support active play.

Source: Author photo.

working on traffic safety can negotiate for signage on roadways; those working on flu prevention have access to public restrooms for signage reminding people to wash their hands; those working on pedestrian safety can negotiate for tougher tests for getting a driver's license; those working on decreasing secondhand tobacco smoke can work with school districts to send home "smoke-free home" pledge cards with the children; and successful programs can benefit from sustained visibility. An example is Playful City USA, a national recognition program honoring cities that champion efforts to make play a priority through establishing policy initiatives, infrastructure investments, and innovative programming (see Figure 17.1).[16] These are resources and opportunities that many in commercial marketing would envy and most would have a hard time paying for.

ANTICIPATING FORCES AGAINST CHANGE

Prior to finalizing the implementation plan, we suggest you consider one last question. "What could happen that would work against our success?" One process to address this question is inspired by Kurt Lewin's *Force Field Analysis*, developed in 1951 to inform decision making, particularly in planning and implementing change management programs.[17] This classic analysis can be best carried out by a small group of people identifying the following, relative to the desired behavior objective and goals for the effort:

1. Forces for change (driving forces)
2. Forces against change (restraining forces)

Once identified, a next best step is to rank-order the forces, for example, by scoring them on a 1-to-5 scale, where 1 is weak and 5 is strong. In the end, you will want to go back to your plan and ensure that there are action items to support the strongest driving forces and address the greatest restraining forces.

SHARING AND SELLING YOUR PLAN

Several techniques will help increase buy-in, approval, and support for your plan. First, include representatives from key internal and external groups on the planning team. Consider those who have a role in approving the plan as well as those key to implementation. For a litter prevention campaign with an emphasis on enforcement, it would be critical that a member of the state patrol have input in the planning process; to increase WIC clients' use of farmers' markets, it would be important to have a representative from the farmers' market association present, especially to hear the results of research with clients on their experiences of shopping at the market; and a city developing a pedestrian safety plan will benefit from having a police officer, an engineer, someone from the communications department, someone from a local business, and a citizen at the planning table.

Second, share a draft plan with decision makers and those key to implementation before finalizing your plan. Identify their concerns and address them. Be prepared to share the background data that led to your recommended strategies, and be prepared to compromise or modify a strategy based on their feedback. And surprise them with the targeted quantifiable goals you are proposing and how you plan to evaluate and report on campaign outcomes.

Finally, once the plan is finalized, consider developing and disseminating a concise summary of the plan. It could be as simple as a one-pager that presents the purpose, focus, target audience, objectives, key strategies, and evaluation plan. Where warranted, it could even be a more portable format, such as a wallet-sized card or a more accessible one, such as one on your agency's website. Your intention is to position your campaign effort as one that is evidence based, strategically developed, and outcome driven.

ETHICAL CONSIDERATIONS WHEN IMPLEMENTING PLANS

In most of the chapters in this book, we have presented ethical considerations related specifically to each phase in the planning process. To highlight final considerations when developing an implementation plan and to summarize ethical considerations in general, we present the American Marketing Association members' code of ethics, published on their website (www.MarketingPower.com), in Box 17.3. Many of the principles apply to social marketing environments, with themes similar to those we have highlighted, including do no harm, be fair, provide full disclosure, be good stewards, own the problem, be responsible, and tell the truth.

Box 17.3
Ethical Norms and Values for Marketers

Preamble

The American Marketing Association commits itself to promoting the highest standard of professional ethical norms and values for its members (practitioners, academics and students). Norms are established standards of conduct that are expected and maintained by society and/or professional organizations. Values represent the collective conception of what communities find desirable, important and morally proper. Values also serve as the criteria for evaluating our own personal actions and the actions of others. As marketers, we recognize that we not only serve our organizations but also act as stewards of society in creating, facilitating and executing the transactions that are part of the greater economy. In this role, marketers are expected to embrace the highest professional ethical norms and the ethical values implied by our responsibility toward multiple stakeholders (e.g., customers, employees, investors, peers, channel members, regulators and the host community).

Ethical Norms

As Marketers, we must:

1. Do no harm. This means consciously avoiding harmful actions or omissions by embodying high ethical standards and adhering to all applicable laws and regulations in the choices we make.

2. Foster trust in the marketing system. This means striving for good faith and fair dealing so as to contribute toward the efficacy of the exchange process as well as avoiding deception in product design, pricing, communication, and delivery of distribution.

3. Embrace ethical values This means building relationships and enhancing consumer confidence in the integrity of marketing by affirming these core values: honesty, responsibility, fairness, respect, transparency and citizenship.

Ethical Values

Honesty – to be forthright in dealings with customers and stakeholders. To this end, we will:

- Strive to be truthful in all situations and at all times.
- Offer products of value that do what we claim in our communications.
- Stand behind our products if they fail to deliver their claimed benefits.
- Honor our explicit and implicit commitments and promises.

Responsibility – to accept the consequences of our marketing decisions and strategies. To this end, we will:

- Strive to serve the needs of customers.
- Avoid using coercion with all stakeholders.
- Acknowledge the social obligations to stakeholders that come with increased marketing and economic power.
- Recognize our special commitments to vulnerable market segments such as children, seniors, the economically impoverished, market illiterates and others who may be substantially disadvantaged.
- Consider environmental stewardship in our decision-making.

Fairness – to balance justly the needs of the buyer with the interests of the seller. To this end, we will:

- Represent products in a clear way in selling, advertising and other forms of communication; this includes the avoidance of false, misleading and deceptive promotion.
- Reject manipulations and sales tactics that harm customer trust.
- Refuse to engage in price fixing, predatory pricing, price gouging or "bait-and-switch" tactics.
- Avoid knowing participation in conflicts of interest.
- Seek to protect the private information of customers, employees and partners.

Respect – to acknowledge the basic human dignity of all stakeholders. To this end, we will:

- Value individual differences and avoid stereotyping customers or depicting demographic groups (e.g., gender, race, sexual orientation) in a negative or dehumanizing way.
- Listen to the needs of customers and make all reasonable efforts to monitor and improve their satisfaction on an ongoing basis.
- Make every effort to understand and respectfully treat buyers, suppliers, intermediaries and distributors from all cultures.
- Acknowledge the contributions of others, such as consultants, employees and coworkers, to marketing endeavors.
- Treat everyone, including our competitors, as we would wish to be treated.

Transparency – to create a spirit of openness in marketing operations. To this end, we will:

- Strive to communicate clearly with all constituencies.
- Accept constructive criticism from customers and other stakeholders.

(Continued)

(Continued)

- Explain and take appropriate action regarding significant product or service risks, component substitutions or other foreseeable eventualities that could affect customers or their perception of the purchase decision.
- Disclose list prices and terms of financing as well as available price deals and adjustments.

Citizenship – to fulfill the economic, legal, philanthropic and societal responsibilities that serve stakeholders. To this end, we will:

- Strive to protect the ecological environment in the execution of marketing campaigns.
- Give back to the community through volunteerism and charitable donations.
- Contribute to the overall betterment of marketing and its reputation.
- Urge supply chain members to ensure that trade is fair for all participants, including producers in developing countries.

IMPLEMENTATION

We expect AMA members to be courageous and proactive in leading and/or aiding their organizations in the fulfillment of the explicit and implicit promises made to those stakeholders. We recognize that every industry sector and marketing sub-discipline (e.g., marketing research, e-commerce, Internet selling, direct marketing, and advertising) has its own specific ethical issues that require policies and commentary. An array of such codes can be accessed through links on the AMA Web site. Consistent with the principle of subsidiarity (solving issues at the level where the expertise resides), we encourage all such groups to develop and/or refine their industry and discipline specific codes of ethics to supplement these guiding ethical norms and values.

Source: American Marketing Association, "Statement of Ethics" (January 1, 2013), accessed June 17, 2014, http://www.dguth.journalism.ku.edu/AMA-Ethics.pdf.

CHAPTER SUMMARY

Developing an implementation plan is Step 10, the final step in the marketing plan model. It turns strategies into actions and is critical to *doing things right*, even if you've planned *the right things*. An implementation plan functions as a concise working document that can be used to share and track planned efforts. It provides a mechanism to ensure that you do what you said you would do, on time, and within budgets. Key components of the plan include the following: What will you do? Who will be responsible? When will it be done? How much will it cost?

Formats for plans vary from simple plans incorporated in the executive summary of the marketing plan to complex plans using software programs. The ideal plan identifies activities over a period of two to three years.

Plans are often presented in phases, usually broken down into months or years. Several frameworks can be used to determine and organize phases, including target audiences, geographic areas, campaign objectives, campaign goals, stages of change, products, pricing, distribution channels, promotional messages, and communication channels. Often it will be a combination of these factors.

Typical strategies to sustain visibility for your campaign, as well as to target audience behaviors, include the use of prompts and commitments, social diffusion, and existing infrastructures. Prompt tactics and mechanisms include signage, stickers, mailings, electronic reminders, labels on packaging, and email alerts. New or additional prompts you identify at this stage in the planning process are most often noted as promotional strategies, and commitments are nonmonetary incentives. Taking advantage of public places and agency partnerships may involve placing signage on government property or messaging in their existing materials (e.g., messages regarding texting and driving in driver's education tests).

Several techniques may be used to increase buy-in, approval, and support for your plan. First, include representatives from key internal and external groups on the planning team. Second, share a draft plan with decision makers and those key to implementation before finalizing your plan. Third, once the plan is finalized, consider developing and disseminating a concise summary of the plan. It could be as simple as a one-pager that presents the purpose, focus, target audience, objectives, key strategies, and evaluation plan.

RESEARCH HIGHLIGHT

The Power of Monitoring and Midcourse Corrections

In June 2014, the authors posted the following message on the Georgetown Social Marketing Listserve and the International Social Marketing Association's website: "We are looking for short cases where a social marketing strategy was implemented; midcourse results were disappointing; a course correction was made; and things turned out better!"

The following four case examples were chosen, as they not only represent the benefits of monitoring and making course corrections, but also illustrate that what went wrong is likely to be related to some "flaw" in principles—in these cases, a flaw related to not following principles of appealing to a unique target audience; selecting a single, simple, doable behavior;

choosing inspiring messages; or utilizing effective communication channels.

The Strategy Wasn't Addressing Barriers for One of the Campaign's Target Audiences

Marian Huhman, professor at the University of Illinois, recalled a mid-course correction for one component of the CDC's VERB™ campaign promoting physical activity to U.S. children ages 9 to 13 (tweens). After the first year of the campaign, a longitudinal survey indicated that although targets of awareness were being met for all ethnic groups, a positive association between increasing levels of VERB awareness and free-time sessions of physical activity was detected for white children, but not for Hispanic children. Garcia 360°, an advertising agency in Texas, recommended a strategic shift. They knew from focus group findings that campaign messages were relevant to Hispanic tweens, but that they needed to reach tweens through more outlets, and they recommended increasing school-based marketing efforts, including distributing a popular bilingual student planner. Garcia 360° also recommended increased promotions to parents, responding to focus group findings that tweens perceived family responsibilities (e.g., babysitting siblings after school while parents worked) as barriers to their participating in structured programs, especially for the girls.

Two years later, the Hispanic tweens' outcome evaluations showed positive associations between increasing levels of reported frequency of exposure to VERB and the number of sessions of free-time physical activity.[18]

They Were Asking for Too Many Behaviors

Stephen Groner at S. Groner Associates in California shared about an EPA campaign in California launched in 2003 with the purpose of reducing the consumption of contaminated fish and a focus on informing anglers of the varying levels of health hazards associated with a variety of fish. Initial interventions primarily included distributing information through flyers. The anglers found the information confusing, resulting in their either ignoring the health warning or not eating any fish at all (see Figure 17.2).

The EPA then hired S. Groner Associates, who recommended a shift in focus from an "information campaign" to a behavior change effort, one aligned to encourage adoption of one specific action: "If you catch white croaker, throw it back." At the time, the white croaker was the most contaminated fish and the third most frequently caught fish along the California coast. Formative research indicated that 53% of anglers said that not knowing white croaker was contaminated was the strongest barrier, and that one of the strongest motivators was protecting the health of their children (see Figure 17.3). Pilot testing confirmed the efficacy of the materials, and an implementation evaluation indicated that during the pre-intervention, 30% of anglers left with white croaker. During the post-intervention period, only 6% left with white croaker.

Words Alone Weren't Enough

Caryn Ginsberg at Priority Ventures Group thinks the Humane Society of the United

Figure 17.2   Initial flyer intended to influence recommended servings of fish.

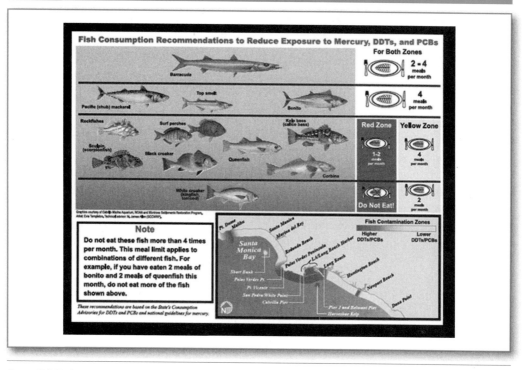

Source: U.S. Environmental Protection Agency, Fish Contamination Education Collaborative.

Figure 17.3   A shift to a focus on one behavior . . . releasing the croaker fish.

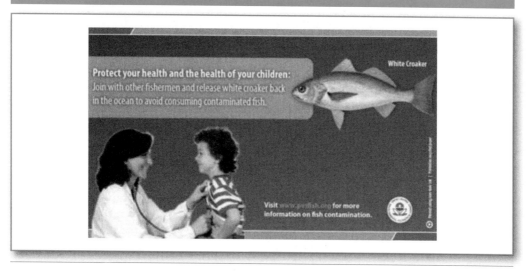

Source: U.S. Environmental Protection Agency, Fish Contamination Education Collaborative.

States is a great example of an organization that practices continuous improvement by regularly collecting data, noting lessons learned, and then making appropriate adjustments and enhancements. One example is their program Pets for Life (PFL), which supports outreach to people and pets in underserved communities, conducting door-to-door outreach and holding community events offering free services such as vaccinations. An important area of focus is the spaying and neutering of pets. Although these community outreach activities are a very useful tool, program managers discovered that more was needed to achieve the desired "end-state" behavior of spaying and neutering pets.

Outreach teams now employ a more specific and detailed process. The PFL approach assumes that once a client says yes to spaying or neutering, the responsibility is on the organization's team from the local shelter or spay/neuter clinic to ensure that the surgery is completed. This requires a shift in attitude and a rigid follow-up process with clients that must be adhered to at all times. Many spay/neuter programs struggle with strategy compliance, yet when the responsibility is shifted away from the client, completion rates increase significantly. "A pet owner's 'yes' to spay/neuter kicks off the PFL spay/neuter process and is bound by the transfer of a voucher that resembles the shape and size of a U.S. dollar."[19] The organization's information and the value of the appointment package of services is listed on the voucher, a concrete representation of what the client is receiving, creating the understanding that the pet will be provided a free veterinarian appointment that includes the surgery as well as rabies and parvo/distemper vaccinations.

Referencing our social marketing model, the program has added several strategies to promotional efforts: augmented products, a prompt, a commitment device, and monetary incentive tools.

The Audience Didn't Get the WIFM: "What's in It for Me?"

Brian Day, director of social marketing at RARE, described a case example illustrating the difference in outcomes we can achieve when the audience understands the benefits they receive in exchange for a desired behavior. In 2012, RARE and a local nongovernmental organization, Ninos y Crias in Merida, Mexico, partnered to implement a social marketing effort with the purpose of reducing the contamination of natural water sources downstream and a focus on influencing best practices among farmers upstream. The 150,000 water users in the city of Merida were the target audience, and the campaign objective was to influence these residents to voluntarily pay an extra fee of 1 peso (0.08 USD) to a Water Fund to provide an incentive for farmers to engage in best practices. Initial strategies included a mass-media campaign utilizing radio and TV spots that highlighted clear benefits to downstream residents, that is, that this fund would provide more and cleaner water. Midcourse monitoring efforts were disappointing, with an assessment indicting that the mass-media buy was inadequate to reach, and therefore influence, a significant portion of the residents, and funds were depleted. As a result, most residents never got the message as to how they could benefit from their contribution.

After negotiations with the Municipality of Merida, the spots were aired "free" in public offices while residents waited in line to pay their water bills. In the end, enough funds were generated to influence farmers to sign an agreement to alter their practices, and incentives also funded skill-building workshops for farmers.

DISCUSSION QUESTIONS AND EXERCISES

1. Share an example you are aware of that has used a dissemination strategy, or one you can think of that would benefit from this approach.

2. Similarly, share an example of a midcourse correction, either one you are aware of or one you can imagine might be needed.

3. What is your impression of the 100-day Rapid Results approach? Can you see any advantages? Disadvantages?

CHAPTER 17 NOTES

1. D. McKenzie-Mohr, N. R. Lee, P. W. Schultz, and P. Kotler, *Social Marketing to Protect the Environment: What Works* (Thousand Oaks, CA: SAGE, 2011), 13.

2. Ashoka Globalizer, "Bill Clinton Quote" (n.d.), accessed June 6, 2014, http://ashokaglobalizer.com/bill-clinton-quote.

3. Puget Sound Partnership, "Leading Puget Sound Recovery" (n.d.), accessed June 6, 2014, http://www.psp.wa.gov/aboutthepartnership.php.

4. Chesapeake Bay Trust [website], accessed June 6, 2014, http://www.cbtrust.org/site/c.miJPKXPCJnH/b.5435807/k.AFFA/About.htm.

5. P. Kotler and G. Armstrong, *Principles of Marketing* (Upper Saddle River, NJ: Prentice Hall, 2001), 71.

6. T. Rosenberg, "Making Change Happen, on a Deadline," *The New York Times* (September 29, 2011), accessed June 26, 2014, http://opinionator.blogs.nytimes.com/2011/09/29/making-change-happen-on-a-deadline/?_php=true&_type=blogs&_r=0.

7. McKenzie-Mohr, *Fostering Sustainable Behavior*, 137.

8. N. Lee and P. Kotler, *Social Marketing: Influencing Behaviors for Good*, 4th ed. (Thousand Oaks, CA: SAGE, 2011), 406–409.

9. McKenzie-Mohr and Smith, *Fostering Sustainable Behavior.*

10. Ibid., 61.

11. Ibid., 48.

12. McKenzie-Mohr, *Fostering Sustainable Behavior.*

13. J. R. Harris, A. Cheadle, P. A. Hannon, M. Forehand, P. Lichiello, E. Mahoney, S. Snyder, and J. Yarrow, "A Framework for Disseminating Evidence-Based Health Promotion Practices," *Preventing Chronic Disease* 9 (2012), accessed June 24, 2014, http://dx.doi.org/10.5888/pcd9.110081.

14. Ibid.

15. McKenzie-Mohr, *Fostering Sustainable Behavior*, 70.

16. KaBOOM!, "Playful City USA Program Details," accessed June 24, 2014, https://kaboom.org/take-action/playful-city-usa/program-details.

17. D. Cartwright, "Foreword to the 1951 Edition," *Field Theory in Social Science and Selected Theoretical Papers—Kurt Lewin* (Washington, DC: American Psychological Association, 1997; originally published by Harper & Row).

18. M. Huhman, J. M. Berkowitz, F. L. Wong, E. Prosper, M. Gray, D. Prince, and J. Yuen, "The VERB™ Campaign's Strategy for Reaching African-American, Hispanic, Asian, and American Indian Children and Parents," *American Journal of Preventive Medicine* 34, no. 6S (2008): S194–S209.

19. Humane Society of the United States, "2014 Pets for Life: An In-Depth Community Understanding," http://www.humanesociety.org/about/departments/pets-for-life/.

EPILOGUE

We see a future world where people are healthy and safe, protecting the environment, contributing to their communities, and enhancing their own financial well-being. We believe that the discipline of social marketing, influencing public behaviors for societal as well as individual good, is a key strategic model to help make this a reality.

For social marketing to be understood, regarded, and adapted around the world, we think there are four urgent needs:

1. Social marketing should be a required course for degrees in public health, public administration, political science, international studies, environmental studies, nursing, and medicine—all degrees whose graduates would benefit from the art and science of influencing patients', citizens', and policymakers' behaviors. Imagine the difference it would make to this field, as well as to the worlds' citizens, if thousands of graduates from these programs each year understood the term, its applications, and its strategic planning model. We think the best place for this to begin is with the master of public health degree.

2. Social marketing professionals need to be united. We need to embrace a common terminology and a strategic planning model, such as the one presented in this text. And all should be encouraged to make it even better and supported in doing so. Accountants have done this. So can we. In 2013, progress toward this was made when the board of the International Social Marketing Association (iSMA) agreed on a definition of social marketing, which was presented in Chapter 1. In 2014, the iSMA Board approved a set of academic competencies for students completing a course or certificate program in social marketing. It appears as Appendix D.

3. Social marketing professionals would benefit from joining the iSMA, which provides information on conferences, jobs, discussion forums, and webinars; discounts on conferences, trainings, and subscriptions; and networking online and in person with social marketing experts. For information, visit http://i-socialmarketing.org.

4. Social marketers need to consistently report on return on investment for programs. For every dollar spent, how many taxpayer dollars were saved? And given this, what is the rate of return on investment? We have presented a detailed discussion on how to accomplish this in Chapter 15.

Thank you to all who are currently helping to complete these action steps, and to those who will be inspired to help in the future.

—Nancy Lee and Philip Kotler

Appendix A

Social Marketing Planning Worksheets

STEP 1: DESCRIBE THE SOCIAL ISSUE, ORGANIZATION(S), BACKGROUND, PURPOSE, AND FOCUS OF YOUR PLAN

1.1 Briefly identify the social issue, sometimes referred to as the "wicked problem," your plan will be addressing (e.g., tobacco use, air pollution, water contamination, homelessness, literacy).

_____

_____

1.2 Identify the organization(s) involved in developing and implementing the plan.

_____

_____

_____

1.3 Summarize key *background* information leading to the development of this plan, ideally using reliable statistics (e.g., percent decrease in salmon populations).

_____

_____

_____

_____

_____

1.4 What is the campaign *purpose*, the intended impact (e.g., reduced teen pregnancies, increased protection of salmon habitats)?

_____

1.5 What is the campaign *focus*, the approach you will be using to contribute to your plan's purpose (e.g., residential gardening practices)? Areas of focus may be solution-oriented (e.g., soft shore buffers), population-based (e.g., homes on streams), or product-related strategies (e.g., native plants).

_____

Refer to Chapter 4 for a detailed description of the process.

STEP 2: CONDUCT A SITUATION ANALYSIS

(Identify Two to Three Bullet Points for Each)

Organizational Factors: Organizational Resources, Service Delivery Capabilities, Expertise, Management Support, Issue Priority, Internal Publics, Current Alliances and Partnerships, Past Performance

2.1 What organizational *strengths* will your plan maximize?

_____

_____

2.2 What organizational *weaknesses* will your plan minimize?

_____

_____

External Forces: Cultural, Technological, Demographic, Natural, Economic, Political/Legal, External Publics

2.3 What environmental *opportunities* will your plan take advantage of?

_____

_____

2.4 What environmental *threats* will your plan prepare for?

_____

_____

Prior and Similar Efforts

2.5 What findings from *prior and similar efforts* are noteworthy, those of yours and others?

_____

_____

Refer to Chapter 4 for a detailed description of the process.

STEP 3: SELECT TARGET AUDIENCES

3.1 Describe the *primary target audiences* for your program/campaign in terms of size, problem incidence and severity, and relevant variables, including demographics, psychographics/values and lifestyles, geographics, related behaviors, and/or readiness to act (e.g., homeowners on shoreline properties engaged in landscaping and interested in protecting the environment.):

_____

_____

_____

_____

_____

_____

_____

3.2 If you have *additional important audiences* that you will need to influence as well, describe them here, to keep them in mind as you develop strategies. They may end up being messengers or distribution channels (e.g., garden centers and nurseries):

_____

_____

_____

_____

_____

_____

_____

_____

Refer to Chapter 5 for a detailed description of the process and Worksheet A on page 518 in this Appendix.

STEP 4: SET BEHAVIOR OBJECTIVES AND TARGET GOALS

Objectives

4.1 Behavior Objective:
What, very specifically, do you want to influence your target audience to *do* as a result of this campaign or project (e.g., plant native plants)?

_____

_____

_____

4.2 Knowledge Objective:
Is there anything you need them to *know* in order to act (e.g., how to identify native plants at the nursery)?

_____

_____

_____

4.3 Belief Objective:
Is there anything you need them to *believe* in order to act (e.g., native plants can be beautiful and easier to maintain)?

_____

_____

_____

Goals

4.4 What quantifiable, measurable goals are you targeting? Ideally, these are stated in terms of *behavior change* (e.g., increase in sales of native plants). Other potential target goals are campaign awareness, recall, and/or response and changes in knowledge, belief, or behavior intent levels.

_____

_____

Refer to Chapter 6 for a detailed description of the process and Worksheet B on page 519 in this Appendix.

STEP 5: IDENTIFY TARGET AUDIENCE BARRIERS, BENEFITS, AND MOTIVATORS; THE COMPETITION; AND INFLUENTIAL OTHERS

Barriers

5.1 Make a list of *barriers* your audience may have to adopting the desired behavior. These may be related to something, physical, psychological, economical, skills, knowledge, awareness, or attitudes. (Try for a list of 5 to 10.)

Benefits

5.2 What are the key *benefits* your target audience wants in exchange for performing the behavior (e.g., a yard that's easier to maintain and increased wildlife on their property)? This answers the question "What's in it for me?" (Try for a list of 2 to 3.)

Motivators

5.3 What does your target audience say will make it more likely that they would do the behavior? Ask them if there is something you can give them, say to them, or show them that would help them (e.g., an easy way to know which nurseries sell native plants and to identify plants at the nursery).

Competition

5.4 What are the major competing *alternative behaviors* (e.g., planting nonnative plants)?

5.5 What *benefits* do your audiences associate with these behaviors (e.g., easier to find)?

5.6 What *costs* do your audiences associate with these behaviors (e.g., requires more fertilizing)?

Influential Others

5.7 Relative to the desired behavior, who does your target audience listen to, watch, and/ or look up to?

5.8 What do you know about what these midstream audiences are currently saying and doing regarding the desired behavior (e.g., staff at nurseries)?

Refer to Chapter 7 for a detailed description of the process and Worksheet C on page 520 of this Appendix.

STEP 6: DEVELOP A POSITIONING STATEMENT

Positioning Statement

6.1 Write a statement similar to the following, filling in the blanks:

"We want [TARGET AUDIENCE] to see [DESIRED BEHAVIOR] as [ADJECTIVES, DESCRIPTIVE PHRASES, SET OF BENEFITS, OR HOW THIS BEHAVIOR IS BETTER THAN THE COMPETITION] (e.g., "We want shoreline property owners engaged in landscaping to see native plants as beautiful, easy to find, less hassle to maintain, and a way to protect water quality and wildlife habitats")."

_____

_____

_____

_____

_____

_____

_____

_____

_____

_____

_____

_____

_____

_____

_____

Refer to Chapter 9 for a detailed description of the process.

STEP 7: DEVELOP MARKETING STRATEGIES

7.1 Product: Creating the Product Platform

7.1.1   Core Product: What is the major perceived benefit your target audience wants from performing the behavior that you will highlight? (Choose one or a few from those identified in 5.2.)

_____

_____

7.1.2   Actual Product: What, if any, tangible goods and services will you be offering and/or promoting (e.g., 100 native plants to choose from, fruits and vegetables, life vests, blood monitoring equipment, low-flow showerheads)?

_____

_____

7.1.3   Augmented Product: Are there any additional tangible goods or services that would assist your target audience in performing the behavior (e.g., workshop on designing a native plant garden)?

Refer to Chapter 10 for a detailed description of the process.

7.2 Price: Fees and Monetary and Nonmonetary Incentives and Disincentives

7.2.1   If you will be including tangible goods and services in your campaign, what, if anything, will the target audience have to *pay* for them (e.g., cost of native plants, life vests)?

_____

_____

_____

7.2.2   Describe any *monetary incentives* for your target audience (e.g., coupons, rebates).

_____

_____

_____

7.2.3   Describe any *monetary disincentives* you will highlight (e.g., fines, increased taxes, higher prices for competing products).

_____

_____

_____

7.2.4   Describe any *nonmonetary incentives* (e.g., recognition, such as yard plaques).

_____

_____

_____

7.2.5   Describe any *nonmonetary disincentives* (e.g., negative visibility, a website with photos of properties where migratory birds have disappeared).

_____

_____

_____

Refer to Chapter 11 for a detailed description of the process.

7.3 Place: Develop the Place Strategy

As you determine each of the following, look for ways to make locations closer and more appealing, to extend hours, and to be there at the point of decision making.

7.3.1   *Where* will you encourage and support your target audience to *perform the desired behavior* and *when*?

_____

_____

_____

7.3.2   *Where* and *when* will the target audience acquire any related tangible goods?

_____

_____

_____

7.3.3   Where and when will the target audience acquire any associated services?

_____

_____

_____

7.3.4   Are there any groups or individuals in the distribution channel that you will target to support efforts (e.g., nursery owners and their staff)?

_____

_____

_____

Refer to Chapter 12 for a detailed description of the process.

7.4 Promotion: Decide on Messages, Messengers, Creative Strategies, and Communication Channels

7.4.1   Messages: What key messages do you want your campaign to communicate to target audiences?

_____

_____

_____

7.4.2   Messengers: Who will deliver the messages and/or be the perceived sponsor?

_____

_____

_____

7.4.3   Creative Strategies: Summarize, describe, or highlight elements such as logos, taglines, copy, visuals, colors, script, actors, scenes, and sounds in broadcast media.

_____

_____

_____

7.4.4   Communication Channels: Where will your messages appear?

_____

_____

_____

Refer to Chapters 13 and 14 for a detailed description of the process.

STEP 8: DEVELOP A PLAN FOR MONITORING AND EVALUATION

8.1   What is the *purpose* of this evaluation? Why are you doing it?

_____

_____

8.2   For *whom* is the evaluation being conducted? To whom will you present it?

_____

_____

8.3   *What inputs, outputs, outcomes, and impact* will be measured?

_____

_____

8.4   *What techniques and methodologies* will be used to conduct each of these measurements?

_____

_____

8.5   *When* will these measurements be taken?

_____

_____

8.6   *How* much will this cost?

_____

_____

Refer to Chapter 15 for a detailed description of the process and Worksheet D on page 521 in this Appendix.

STEP 9: ESTABLISH BUDGETS AND FIND FUNDING SOURCES

9.1 What costs will be associated with *product*-related strategies?

_____

_____

9.2 What costs will be associated with *price*-related strategies?

_____

_____

9.3 What costs will be associated with *place*-related strategies?

_____

_____

9.4 What costs will be associated with *promotion*-related strategies?

_____

_____

9.5 What costs will be associated with *evaluation*-related strategies?

_____

_____

9.6 If costs exceed currently available funds, what potential additional funding sources can be explored?

_____

_____

Refer to Chapter 16 for a detailed description of the process.

STEP 10: COMPLETE AN IMPLEMENTATION PLAN

10.1   Sample Implementation Plan

What	Who	When	How much

10.2   If you are conducting a pilot or plan with several phases, complete a grid for each phase.

Refer to Chapter 17 for a detailed description of the process. For an electronic version of this plan, visit www.socialmarketingservice.com.

Worksheet A

Selecting Target Audiences

1 Potential Target Audiences	2 Size	3 Problem Incidence	4 Readiness to Act	5 Ability to Reach	6 Match for the Organization	7 Average Score (From 2, 3, 4, 5)

1. **POTENTIAL TARGET AUDIENCES:** Relative to a campaign purpose (e.g., improve water quality) and focus (e.g., yard care), brainstorm and then list potential target audiences. A target audience is a segment of a population that has similar characteristics. Potential audiences may be grouped based on one or more variables, including demographics, geographics, values and lifestyles, or current related behaviors (e.g., homeowners with large lawns).

2. **SIZE:** As a segment of a population, what is the actual or relative size of this segment?

3. **PROBLEM INCIDENCE:** How significant is the contribution that this audience makes to the environmental problem (e.g., shoreline properties or frequency of fertilizing)?

4. **READINESS TO ACT**: How concerned is the target audience with the problem issue/behavior?

5. **ABILITY TO REACH:** Can you identify them and do you have efficient ways to reach them?

6. **MATCH FOR THE ORGANIZATION:** Does this audience support your organizational mission, expertise, and positioning?

7. **AVERAGE SCORE:** This can be a "weighted average" to give increased significance to one or more of the items, or it can be an "unweighted average," with each aspect being considered equally important.

A variety of scales have been used to rank these items: (a) high, medium, low; (b) scale of 1 to 10, (c) scale of 1 to 7, (d) scale of 1 to 5. The one used will depend on how much verifiable information is available.

Worksheet B

Prioritizing Behaviors

TARGET AUDIENCE _____

1 Potential Behaviors to Rank	2 Impact on the Social Issue	3 Willingness of Target Audience to do this Behavior	4 Measurability	5 Market Opportunity	6 Market Supply	5 Average Score (From 2, 3, 4, 5, 6)

1. **POTENTIAL BEHAVIORS TO RANK:** Relative to a campaign purpose, focus, and target audience, brainstorm and then list potential single, simple behaviors to promote (e.g., replacing half of lawn with native plants).

2. **IMPACT ON THE ENVIRONMENTAL ISSUE:** What potential impact do scientists, technical staff, and/or engineers determine that this desired behavior will have on the environment relative to other behaviors (e.g., using natural vs. chemical fertilizers vs. reducing lawn in half)?

3. **WILLINGNESS:** How willing is the target audience to do this? In the diffusion model, this would be the percentage or number who are in the *Help Me* group versus the *Show Me* or *Make Me* group.

4. **MEASURABILITY:** Can the behavior be measured through either observation, record keeping, or self-reporting?

5. **MARKET OPPORTUNITY**: Estimate the percentage and/or number of people in the target audience/population who are not already doing the behavior. (Note: The higher the number, the higher the score.)

6. **MARKET SUPPLY;** Does the behavior need more support? If some other organization or organizations are already addressing this behavior, perhaps a different behavior would be more beneficial to the social issue.

7. **AVERAGE SCORE:** This can be a "weighted average," to give increased significance to one or more of the items, or it can be an "unweighted average," with each aspect being considered equally important.

A variety of scales have been used to rank these items: (a) high, medium, low; (b) scale of 1 to 10, (c) scale of 1 to 7, (d) scale of 1 to 5. The one used will depend on how much verifiable information is available.

(Adapted from Doug McKenzie-Mohr, www.cbsm.com.)

Worksheet C

Using the 4Ps to Reduce Barriers and Increase Benefits

Desired Behavior: _____

Target Audience: _____

For each of the target audience's perceived barriers and potential benefits, consider whether one or more of the 4Ps would help reduce the barrier and provide desired benefits.	Potential Strategies using the 4PS To Reduce Barriers and Increase Benefits			
Perceived Barriers to Desired Behaviors	**Product** Goods or services to promote or to provide to help the audience do the behavior	**Price** Incentives and disincentives (includes use of pledges and commitments)	**Place** Where goods and services can be accessed or behavior will be performed	**Promotion** Messages, messengers, creative elements, and communication channels (includes use of prompts)
Desired Benefits				

Worksheet D

Potential Evaluation Measures

Inputs	Outputs	Outcomes	Impact	Return on Investment
Resources allocated to the campaign or program effort: • Dollars • Incremental staff time • Existing materials • Existing distribution channels • Existing partners	*Program activities conducted to promote a desired behavior. These measures do not indicate whether the audience "noticed" or responded to these activities. They represent only what was "put out there," including:* • Number of materials disseminated • Number of calls made • Numbers and types of distribution channels for any products or services • Number of events held • Websites created/ utilized • Social media tactics • Reach and frequency of communications • Free media coverage • Paid media impressions • Implementation of program elements (e.g., whether on time, on budget)	*Audience responses to outputs, including:* • Changes in behavior • Changes in numbers of related products or services "sold" (e.g., native plants) • Changes in behavior intent • Changes in knowledge • Changes in beliefs • Responses to campaign elements (e.g., hits on a website) • Campaign awareness • Customer satisfaction levels • Policy changes • Partnerships and contributions created	*Indicators that show levels of impact on the social issue that constituted the focus of the effort:* • Lives saved • Diseases prevented • Injuries avoided • Water quality improved • Water supply increased • Air quality improved • Landfill reduced • Wildlife and habitats protected • Animal cruelty reduced • Crimes prevented • Financial well-being improved	*Economic value of changes in behavior and calculated rate of return on the spending associated with the effort:* • For every dollar spent, dollars saved or generated • After subtracting expenses, rate of return on investment

APPENDIX B

SAMPLE SOCIAL MARKETING PLANS

1. Reducing Pedestrian Injuries and Deaths by Increasing Use of Pedestrian Flags: Kirkland, Washington

2. Restoring Salmon Habitats: Lake Washington/Cedar/Sammamish Watershed (WRIA 8), King County, Washington

REDUCING PEDESTRIAN INJURIES AND DEATHS BY INCREASING USE OF PEDESTRIAN FLAGS

Kirkland, Washington

(Developed 2007)

STEP 1: BACKGROUND, PURPOSE, AND FOCUS

1.1 Background (as of 2007)

Each year in the City of Kirkland, approximately 20 pedestrian accidents occur, almost two per month. Since 1987, there have been 387 recorded crashes (all types), with 7 fatalities and 371 injuries.

PedFlag, the name of Kirkland's pedestrian flag program, started in 1995 and is installed at 37 locations in the city. At this time (2007), city staff maintain flags at 16 downtown locations and citizen volunteers maintain the other sites, most of which are not in the downtown corridor.

Although pedestrian flags have been used in Kirkland and elsewhere for over 10 years, little is understood about why some pedestrians choose to use the flags and why some do not. Current usage, prior to this study, was assumed to be between 1% and 5% of pedestrians at these crosswalks using the flags. Flags are concentrated at intersections where most pedestrian injuries have occurred.

1.2 Organization Sponsoring

City of Kirkland, Washington

1.3 Purpose

The purpose of this social marketing plan is to decrease pedestrian injuries and deaths.

1.4 Focus

The focus, predetermined by a grant the city received, is on increased use of pedestrian flags versus alternatives such as installation of signals, more in-pavement flashing lights, or increased enforcement.

STEP 2: SITUATION ANALYSIS
AND FINDINGS FROM SIMILAR EFFORTS

2.1 Organizational Strengths to Maximize

- Pedestrian safety is a priority of the council.
- The City of Kirkland has a pedestrian-friendly commitment and image.
- The team working on this plan will provide important vantage points.
- Current locations have been there for years, some managed by volunteers.
- There is the ability to respond to volunteer requests for new locations.
- Staff are available and interested in helping sustain/revive the program.

2.2 Organizational Weaknesses to Minimize

- Lack of (recent) promotions and visibility for the program
- Lack of sustainable promotional vehicles
- Potential for excess demand for flags if they create too much interest
- Ongoing theft and vandalism; some suspicion flags are stolen to be used as flags for water skiing, which may explain why more flags are missing during the summer months
- Because there are only about six flags at each location, often flags all end up on one side of the street

2.3 Opportunities to Leverage

- The Pedestrian Safety initiative, including a recently produced PSA
- The "Step Up to Health" initiative encouraging citizens to be active
- Relationships with several important populations: schools, youth, seniors, neighborhood organizations, businesses
- A senior walk program
- Cultural trends/emphasis on health

2.4 Threats to Prepare For

- A pedestrian who is carrying a flag might be hit.
- Staff attention could be diverted by other projects or unforeseen events.

2.5 Similar Efforts and Findings

A number of cities across the country were found to have similar programs: Portland, Maine; Hudson Falls, New York; St. Paul, Minnesota; Madison, Wisconsin; Cambridge, Massachusetts; Salt Lake City, Utah; and Washington, DC.

Highlights of marketing strategies elsewhere included the following:

2.5.1 Target audiences

- Small children (Alexandria, VA)
- Elderly population (Alexandria, VA)
- Tourist groups (Alexandria, VA)
- Tourists during the Olympics (Salt Lake City, Utah)
- People with disabilities

2.5.2 Product

- Campaign stressing assertive waving and thanking/acknowledging driver (Monroe, Wisconsin)
- Orange/fluorescent colors (Salt Lake City, Utah)
- Emphasized benefit: visibility (Salk Lake City, Utah)
- "LOOK" crosswalk pavement markings (Salt Lake City, Utah)
- Decorative streetlight containers for poles (Salt Lake City, Utah)
- Having flags printed with "Property of Salt Lake City" with a felt marker helped with theft (Salt Lake City, Utah)
- The problem with the bright orange color is that the flags can be used for other purposes, such as construction or skiing, so they get stolen (Salt Lake City, Utah)

2.5.3 Price

- Stepped-up education and enforcement for motorists is needed as well.
- Driver yielding violations in Salt Lake City now require an appearance before the city's Justice Court judge, with a recommended fine of $425.

2.5.4 Place

- Pole holders are most commonly used.
- Trainings are at schools and senior centers.
- Salt Lake City felt that having so many locations (180+) really helped carrying the flags seem like a norm.

2.5.5 Promotion

- Salt Lake City found launching with a lot of publicity helpful (e.g., newspaper, television), including pictures of a clown walking across and using the flags
- "Walk safely. Grab a Flag." billboard (Madison, Wisconsin)
- "Yield to Pedestrians. It's the Law" billboard (Madison, Wisconsin)

- Message to "use the flags even if you don't need them so drivers learn to expect them" (Madison, Wisconsin, press release)
- Signage/slogans on pole holder
- Kids standing at a crosswalk once a month and encouraging others

STEP 3: TARGET AUDIENCE

3.1 Primary (Years 1 and 2)

Pedestrians walking in downtown Kirkland are the primary target and include park users, transit users, seniors, condo residents, teens, workers downtown, those parking in the garage, concertgoers in the park, attendees at the Kirkland Performance Center, restaurant customers, gallery walk participants, shoppers, those going to the library, and bar customers.

Since it is estimated that a significant percentage of nonusers have used the flag at least once (58 of the 94 nonusers interviewed), we will keep in mind that our bull's-eye target market is *infrequent users who we want to persuade to use all of the time, thus helping to create a social norm.*

3.2 Additional (Year 3): All other PedFlag locations

STEP 4: BEHAVIOR OBJECTIVES AND TARGET GOALS

4.1 Behavior Objective

We want pedestrians at crosswalks where there are flags to make it a habit to take a flag with them *every time* they cross and then place it in the holder on the other side. If there is more than one in the group, we want one person to take a flag.

4.2 Goals

Current baseline usage (2007) is 8.6% of all pedestrians in a crosswalk. After the first six months, 14% of pedestrians will take a flag in the downtown locations. (Second measurement March 2008 budgeted.)

STEP 5: TARGET AUDIENCE BARRIERS, MOTIVATORS, AND COMPETITORS

5.1 Barriers (From Research Study March–April 2007)

Theme	Barrier	# = 94	% of 94	Potential Implications
NOT AT RISK	I felt safe	26	27.7%	Data on Injuries
NOT AT RISK	The car saw me	21	22.3%	Data on Injuries

Theme	Barrier	# = 94	% of 94	Potential Implications
NOT A NORM	I'd look silly	17	18.1%	Product Design, Recognition
AWARENESS	It didn't occur to me	13	13.8%	Product Design, Signage
DESIGN	My hands were full	14	14.9%	Product Design
NOT A NORM	Flags are for the young and old	14	14.9%	Product Design, Recognition
DESIGN	It takes too much time	10	10.6%	Product Design
AWARENESS	I didn't notice it	9	9.6%	Signage, Education, Pavement Stencil
AVAILABILITY	There were no flags	8	8.5%	More Flags
DESIGN	It takes too much effort	7	7.5%	Product Design
NOT AT RISK	I used the flashing lights	6	6.4%	None
AWARENESS	I don't know what they're for	6	6.4%	Signage, Education, Product Design

5.2 Motivators (From Research Study March-April 2007)

	All Respondents Interviewed		For Users to Use Flags All the Time		For Nonusers to Use Flags All the Time	
Number of Respondents	*n* = 120	% of 120	*n* = 26	% of 26	*n* = 94	% of 94
More Flags	14	11.7%	6	23.1%	8	8.5%
Better Signs	13	10.8%	2	7.7%	11	11.7%
More Education	13	10.8%	4	15.4%	9	9.6%
Better Flag Design	9	7.5%	2	7.7%	7	7.5%
Enforcement	6	5.0%	1	3.9%	5	5.3%
Media Campaign	5	4.2%	2	7.7%	3	3.2%
More Flags in Kirkland	4	3.3%	0	0	4	4.3%

5.3 Competitors (what they are doing instead)

- "Watching for cars"
- "Making sure cars notice me"
- "Using my hands"
- "Using umbrella to wave"

STEP 6: POSITIONING STATEMENT

We want pedestrians in downtown Kirkland to perceive that carrying a pedestrian flag every time they cross the crosswalk is just like wearing a seatbelt. It is an easy way to be sure they are safe and more effective than just watching for cars or only making eye contact with cars.

We also want pedestrians to see the City of Kirkland and Kirkland businesses as their partners, ones interested in supporting their safety.

STEP 7: MARKETING MIX STRATEGY

7.1 Product

- Redesign flag to look like the official pedestrian crossing sign (color and design) and add a flag to the "icon's" hand, two sided.
- Flag squares should be about 14 inches square.
- Include a City of Kirkland logo on the flag to deter theft.
- Maintain 18 flags at each location, versus 6 flags currently.
- Use a "bucket" for ease of access and to display signage.
- Develop small handkerchief flags for seniors to carry with them—and for others who might like them as well.
- New flags will replace those in all but one managed by the city.

7.3 Price (Incentives and Disincentives)

- The typical fine for not stopping for pedestrians in crosswalks is $101, so for launch, at least, consider increased enforcement periods and ticketing motorists.
- Recognition: Acknowledgment by business partners with coupons or free items.

7.4 Place (Access to Flags)

- Most important is to get the flags closer to the crosswalk. The bucket for the flags will provide easier access and more visibility and should hold more flags. It must, however, be "rainproof" and "spillproof."
- In addition, there will be 18 versus 6 flags maintained at each crosswalk.

7.5 Promotion

Key Messages

- Slogan: "Take It to Make It." This statement gives the behavior as well as the benefit, one that addresses major perceived barriers.

- 62 people have been injured or killed in crosswalks in Kirkland between 1996 and 2006:
  - o Carrying a flag: 0
  - o Not carrying a flag: 62
- Partners: Ben & Jerry's reminds you to "Take It to Make It."

Key Messengers

- City of Kirkland
- City Council (consider pairing to retailers)
- Downtown "Adopt a Crosswalk" partners and other retailers
- Parking enforcement officers
- High school students: Culminating projects

Key Communication Channels to Pursue

- Signage on buckets or pole (three panels)
- Coupon distributed at retail partners and by law enforcement and volunteers
- News articles in *Seattle Times* and local newspapers
- Banners at relaunch: "Take It to Make It"
- Drink coasters
- Plaques in retail partner stores
- Presentations at schools
- School newspapers
- Website
- Cable story
- Emails to neighborhood groups
- Presentations at Kiwanis, Rotary, and Lions clubs
- Presentations at senior centers
- Words on crosswalk reminding pedestrians to take a flag
- Place on police report forms indicating whether pedestrian was carrying a flag to make it part of reports/media coverage

STEP 8: EVALUATION PLAN

Evaluation will be conducted by using the same survey methodology as for the baseline and will be fielded in March 2008.

STEP 9: BUDGET

Total available budget is $20,000 for Implementation.

STEP 10: IMPLEMENTATION PLAN FOR OCTOBER 2007 LAUNCH

What	When
1.0 Flags	
1.1 Finalize design	By 8/17
1.2 Order 2,000 flags (14-in square)	By 8/24
1.3 Delivered	By 10/1
1.4 Reflective tape applied to flag	By 10/1
1.5 Distribute to 15 locations	10/15
2.0 Buckets	
2.1 Finalize design of labels	By 8/30
2.2 Order 30 buckets	By 8/24
2.3 Order labels/signs	By 8/24
2.4 Assemble and mount buckets with divider	By 10/15
2.5 Explore "Thank You" sensor monitor	By 9/15
2.6 Install labels/signs	By 10/15
3.0 Stencil on Sidewalk	
3.1 Finalize design	By 10/15
3.2 Complete stenciling (produce mesh)	By 10/15
3.0 Retail Partners	
3.1 "Agreement sheet" including coupon	By 10/1
3.2 Sign up	By 10/1
3.3 Volunteers for each partner	By 10/15
3.4 In-store signage/displays/materials: Framed sign with logos or poster for windows	By 10/15
4.0 Coupons	
4.1 Finalize concept	By 8/30
4.2 Finalize design	By 10/1
4.3 Print	By 10/15
5.0 Promotion	
5.1 Drink coasters	By 10/15
5.2 Banner (horizontal treatment of banner, two sides. Yellow background and black letters and icon)	By 10/1 3 weeks in October

What		When
5.3	Retail environment materials distributed: Coupons, bar coasters (multiple locations), partner plaque	10/15
5.4	News article: *Seattle Times* and local newspapers	2nd week in October
5.5	Website	By 10/15
5.6	Cable: Consider videos of pedestrians	October
5.7	Emails to neighborhood groups (explain a pilot)	October
5.8	Presentations (2007): Rotary, Kiwanis, schools, Lions Club	Oct.–Dec.
5.9	Work with police to hand out coupons to people using the flag	Sept.–Ongoing
5.10	Work with high school students for culminating project to encourage people to take the flag; link with retail partners	Sept.–Ongoing
5.11	T-shirts with city logo and brand logo for retail partners	October
6.0	**Other**	
6.1	Explore place to notate on accident report	
6.2	Explore getting news to report flag/no flag	

Case information was provided by David Godfrey, City of Kirkland, Washington. See Chapter 15 for the results of the campaign.

RESTORING SALMON HABITATS

Lake Washington/Cedar/Sammamish Watershed (WRIA 8)

STEP 1: BACKGROUND, ORGANIZATION, PURPOSE, FOCUS

The Lake Washington/Cedar/Sammamish Watershed (WRIA 8) is a collaborative effort of 27 local governments, community groups, and businesses. Together they developed and adopted a plan to conserve and restore salmon in the watershed and work together to implement the plan. In 2010–2011, WRIA 8 conducted an analysis of changes in forest cover and riparian buffers in the watershed. The analysis found that many riparian areas lost forest cover and all gained impervious cover between 2005 and 2009, despite regulations designed to protect these areas. WRIA 8 has decided to make riparian areas a higher priority for plan implementation and is developing a strategy to address the many small actions of streamside property owners that reduce forest cover and streamside vegetation.

The *purpose* of this plan is to improve salmon habitats along streams in WRIA 8 watershed.

Its *focus* is on increasing planting of native plants and trees along streams in suburban residential neighborhoods along high-priority (Tier 1) spawning areas.

STEP 2: SITUATION ANALYSIS

Organizational Factors	External Forces
Strengths: • Broad coalition of local governments, NGOs, state agencies, and interested citizens • Data that support the need • Several strong NGOs already working with streamside property owners and doing riparian restoration • Existing marketing materials from prior projects • Existing success stories to highlight/share • Strong expertise in watershed for designing a program	**Opportunities:** • Existing programs would benefit from support • Increase in community volunteerism from students needing community service credit • Families seeking family-friendly activities • Companies wanting team-building events • Riparian planting benefits several water quality issues, which can lead to increased partnerships and funding • New home owners are more willing to change landscaping
Weaknesses: • Limited funding/cuts to programs • Property owner concerns about volunteers on private property • Lack of monitoring of effectiveness of outreach efforts • High maintenance needed for plantings/lack of long-term funding • Lack of infrastructure for ongoing riparian restoration	**Threats:** • Economy • Budget cuts in local governments and NGOs • "Save the Salmon" fatigue • People love their lawns

Similar prior and existing efforts suggest that workshops can be effective, as can contacting property owners and assisting them with physical labor and finding ways to help them cover or discounting costs.

STEP 3: TARGET AUDIENCE

Property owners along the Cedar River, Bear Creek, and Issaquah Creek, especially those with lawn extending to the edge of the stream who are contemplating (or open to) making a change to their landscaping.

Additional important audiences that may warrant separate marketing plans include homeowner associations that may have concerns about replacing lawns and misperceptions regarding native plants, and jurisdictions that own public land along streams that also need restoration. These sites can be good demonstration areas and could be used for kick-off planting events.

STEP 4: SET BEHAVIOR OBJECTIVES AND GOALS

Behavior objective: Streamside property owners will plant and maintain native trees and plants along their streamside property.

Knowledge objectives: How to prepare the site, what nonnative invasive plants need to be removed and how, and where to buy and how to choose, plant, and care for native plants.

Belief objective: Native plants are beautiful and benefit birds, salmon, and other wildlife. They are easy to maintain, save money, conserve water, save time, and are safe for pets and kids, since no pesticides are needed.

Goals: Contact 500-plus streamside property owners, of whom 165 will agree/pledge to remove nonnative plants and plant native trees and plants. Among these 165 willing property owners, 50 will agree to have supervised volunteers assist them with restoring riparian areas. In the end, restore 10 to 15 acres of riparian area, planting 10,000-plus native trees and shrubs.

STEP 5: BARRIERS, BENEFITS, MOTIVATORS, AND COMPETITION

Barriers property owners may have to replacing lawns with native trees and plants along the shorelines include:

- "I want to see/interact with the creek."
- "I don't think my lawn to the creek matters/hurts the stream."
- "I don't want to sign anything."
- "I don't like the government telling me what to do with my property."

- "I don't like the look of native plants—too scraggly, messy."
- "It costs too much."
- "I'm concerned about stream bank eroding, flooding."
- "I don't know how to do it, where to start."
- "I need lawn for my kids' play area."
- "It's too much to do. I'm too busy and overwhelmed."
- "The homeowner association won't let me."
- "The social norm around here is a neat, tidy yard."
- "I think that's critical area by code. I can't touch it."
- "I don't know native plants or where to buy them."
- "I'm not the problem; ___ is the problem."
- "I don't trust government, the messenger."
- "There's no technical assistance available to help."
- "We have a large bulkhead and would need a permit to change anything."
- "I need to have access to my dock/boat."

Benefits desired include increased property value and improved water quality and wildlife and salmon habitats.

Motivators include knowing and believing that native plants are a beautiful, low-maintenance landscaping choice and that property owners will be a part of the community/neighborhood effort to improve their stream.

The *competition* is tidy yards that fit in with their neighborhood and provide space for kids and pets to play.

STEP 6: POSITIONING STATEMENT

We want streamside property owners in WRIA 8 watershed to see planting native plants as easy, beautiful, and beneficial to their property values as well as to bird, fish, and other wildlife.

STEP 7: 4Ps STRATEGIES

7.1 Product Strategies

Core product: A beautiful, low-maintenance yard

Actual product: Native plants and trees

Augmented product:

- Technical assistance to develop planting plan and actual support for planting
- Workshop for streamside property owners in each watershed

7.2 Price Strategies

Monetary incentives:

- Free or discounted plants and compost
- Potentially, compost buckets full of gifts (e.g., Brown Bear car wash coupons, Cedar Grove compost discounts)

Nonmonetary incentives:

- Recognition signage similar to Backyard Wildlife Sanctuary sign

7.3 Place Strategies

Workshops will be held in a convenient location in the neighborhood, where property owners can also sign up for technical assistance/support for planting and receive free plants, compost, and discount coupons.

Technical assistance and planting support will be provided at homes, arranged at a time convenient for the property owner.

7.4 Promotion Strategies

Key messages:

- Planting native plants and trees along streams will create a beautiful, low-maintenance yard.
- In fact, it is the Northwest look.
- It will also improve water quality and habitats for salmon, birds, and other wildlife.

Key messengers:

- NGOs in each target watershed area
- WRIA 8 and local jurisdictions in watersheds will be cosponsors and help to promote events/services

Creative strategies:

- "Easy for Salmon and Me" tagline
- Incorporate into the Puget Sound Starts Here brand and messaging

Communication channels:

- *Special event:* Kick off a volunteer planting event in each watershed on publicly owned property

- *Outreach materials:* Door-hangers for neighborhood canvassing by NGO partners to contact property owners one on one; letters inviting property owners to neighborhood workshops; flyers and electronic invitations to promote volunteer stewardship events; materials for workshops (PowerPoint presentations, planting instructions, plant identification—reuse good existing materials as much as possible); recognition signage; thank-you gifts of donated items for participating landowners

STEP 8: DETERMINE AN EVALUATION PLAN

Inputs	Outputs	Outcomes	Impact	Return on Investment
• Dollars spent • Staff time • Volunteer hours • Partners' contributions (business donations, jurisdictions helping to promote events and workshops, donation of meeting space)	• # of streamside property owners contacted • # of events held • # of partners assisting with program • # of articles/ media messages promoting events/program	• # of streamside property owners attending events • # of streamside property owners pledging • # of streamside property owners removing nonnative plants and planting native trees and plants	• # of square feet/ acres of invasive plants controlled • # of trees/shrubs planted • # of square feet/ acres of riparian area plantings	• For every dollar spent, # of households that removed nonnative plants and planted native trees and plants • For every dollar spent, # of square feet/acres of riparian area plantings

STEP 9: ESTABLISH A CAMPAIGN BUDGET AND FIND FUNDING

Product-Related Costs	Staff time, printing, workshop/stewardship event refreshments
Price-Related Costs	Native plants, compost to give away
Place-Related Costs	Travel costs, room rental for workshops
Promotion-Related Costs	Staff time, postage
Evaluation-Related Costs	Staff time
TOTAL	At least $250,000; program is scalable based on funding available.

STEP 10: OUTLINE AN IMPLEMENTATION PLAN

What	Who	When	How Many
Volunteer stewardship kick-off events to help create buzz around restoring riparian areas along Cedar River, Bear Creek, and Issaquah Creek	NGO in each basin with assistance from WRIA 8 staff, WRIA 8 jurisdictions, King County Noxious Weeds	Beginning of campaign	3+, at least one per basin
Letters to targeted property owners inviting them to workshops and offering technical assistance with restoring their riparian vegetation	NGO in each basin	Before workshops	All property owners along each targeted stream
Workshops for property owners on how to identify and control noxious weeds and plant native plants	NGO in each basin with assistance from WRIA 8 staff, WRIA 8 jurisdictions, King County Noxious Weeds	After kick-off event	3+, at least one per basin
Door-to-door canvassing of property owners in targeted reaches of streams offering technical assistance	NGO in each basin	After workshops	All property owners along each targeted stream
Technical assistance with planning riparian restoration and assistance with actual plantings by volunteers	NGO in each basin	After canvassing	30+ willing property owners

Case information was provided by Jean White, King County WRIA 8.

Appendix C

Social Marketing Resources

Compiled by Mike Newton-Ward, Independent Social Marketing Consultant

BLOGS

Beyond Attitude: Community-Based Social Marketing Tips	www.beyondattitude.com/
Have Fun, Do Good	http://havefundogood.blogspot.com/
Marketing in the Public Sector	http://jimmintz.wordpress.com/
National Social Marketing Centre	http://www.thensmc.com/news-events/blog
Ogilvy PR, Social Marketing Exchange	http://smexchange.ogilvypr.com/
On Social Marketing and Social Change	http://socialmarketing.blogs.com/
OSOCIO: The best non-profit advertising and marketing for social causes	http://osocio.org/
Social Marketing Panorama	www.socialmarketingpanorama.com
Stephan Dahl's Blog	http://stephan.dahl.at/

BOOKS

Andreasen, A. (1995). *Marketing social change: Changing behavior to promote health, social development, and the environment.* San Francisco, CA: Jossey-Bass.

Andreasen, A. (2001). *Marketing research that won't break the bank: A practical guide to getting the information you need* (2nd ed.). San Francisco, CA: Jossey-Bass.

Andreasen, A. (2006). *Social marketing in the 21st century.* Thousand Oaks, CA: SAGE.

Bearden, W. O., Netemeyer, R. G., & Haws, K. L. (2011). *Handbook of marketing scales: Multi-item measures for marketing and consumer behavior research* (3rd ed.). Thousand Oaks, CA: SAGE.

Berger, W. (2010). *Glimmer: How design can transform your world.* Toronto, ON, Canada: Vintage Canada.

Buros Institute. (2013). *The nineteenth mental measurements yearbook.* Lincoln, NE: Author.

Cheng, H., Kotler, P., & Lee, N. (2011). *Social marketing in public health: Global trends and success stories.* Sudbury, MA: Jones & Bartlett.

Deshpande, S., & Lee, N. (2013). *Social marketing in India.* Thousand Oaks, CA: SAGE.

Donovan, R., & Henley, N. (2010). *Principles and practice of social marketing: An international perspective.* Victoria, Australia: Cambridge University Press.

Duhigg, C. (2014). *Marketing social change: The power of habit.* New York, NY: Random House.

French, J., Blair-Stevens, C., McVey, D., & Merritt, R. (2010). *Social marketing and public health: Theory and practice.* Oxford, UK: Oxford University Press.

French, J., Gordon, R. (2015). *Strategic social marketing.* UK: SAGE.

Ginsberg, K. (2011). *Animal impact: Secrets proven to achieve results and move the world.* Arlington, VA: Priority Ventures Group.

Hastings, G., & Domegan, C. (2013). *Social marketing: From tunes to symphonies.* Oxford, UK: Butterworth-Heinemann.

Hastings, G., Angus, K., & Bryant, C. (2011). *SAGE handbook of social marketing.* Thousand Oaks, CA: SAGE.

Heath, C., & Heath, D. (2011). *Switch: How to change things when change is hard.* New York, NY: Broadway Books.

Heath, C., & Heath, D. (2014). *Decisive: How to make better decisions.* New York, NY: Random House Business.

Kotler, P., & Lee, N. (2007). *Marketing in the public sector: A roadmap for improved performance.* Philadelphia, PA: Wharton School.

Kotler, P., & Lee, N. (2009). *Up and out of poverty: The social marketing solution.* Philadelphia, PA: Wharton School.

Kreuger, R. A., & Casey, M. A. (2008). *Focus groups: A practical guide for applied research* (4th ed.). Thousand Oaks, CA: SAGE.

Lee, N., & Kotler, P. (2011). *Social marketing: Influencing behaviors for good* (4th ed.). Thousand Oaks, CA: SAGE.

Lefebvre, C. (2013). *Social marketing and social change: Strategies and tools for improving health, well-being, and the environment.* San Francisco, CA: Jossey-Bass.

McKenzie-Mohr, D. (2011). *Fostering sustainable behavior: An introduction to community-based social marketing* (3rd ed.). Gabriola Island, BC, Canada: New Society.

McKenzie-Mohr, D., Lee, N., Schultz, P. W., & Kotler, P. (2011). *Social marketing to protect the environment: What works.* Thousand Oaks, CA: SAGE.

Resnick, E. A., & Siegel, M. (2012). *Marketing public health: Strategies to promote social change* (3rd ed.). Boston, MA: Jones & Bartlett.

Shea, A. (2012). *Designing for social change: Strategies for community-based graphic design.* New York, NY: Princeton Architectural Press.

Strecher, V. (2013). *On purpose: Lessons in life and health from the frog, dung beetle, and Julia.* Ann Arbor, MI: Dung Beetle Press.

Van Praet, D. (2010). *Unconscious branding: How neuroscience can empower (and inspire) marketing.* Thousand Oaks, CA: SAGE.

Weinreich, N. K. (2010). *Hands-on social marketing: A step-by-step guide to designing change for good.* Thousand Oaks, CA: SAGE.

CONFERENCE OPPORTUNITIES

1. *MARCOM Professional Development Annual Forum* June, Ottawa, Canada
   http://www.marcom.ca/

2. *Social Marketing in Public Health Conference* June, University of South Florida,
   Sand Key, Florida (biennial)

   Continuing Professional Education

   University of South Florida College of Public Health

   813-974-9684

   http://health.usf.edu/publichealth/prc/training.html#conf

3. *World Social Marketing Conference* (Locations and dates rotate)
   http://wsmconference.com/

ELECTRONIC MEDIA

The Basics of Social Marketing	http://socialmarketingcollaborative.org/smc/pdf/Social_Marketing_Basics.pdf
Changing Transportation Behaviours: A Social Marketing Planning Guide	www.tc.gc.ca/media/documents/programs/ctb.pdf
Free-Range Thinking	http://www.thegoodmancenter.com/resources/newsletters/
The Manager's Guide to Social Marketing	http://socialmarketingcollaborative.org/smc/pdf/Managers_guide.pdf
Social Marketing and Public Health: Lessons From the Field	http://socialmarketingcollaborative.org/smc/pdf/Lessons_from_field.pdf
Storytelling as Best Practice	http://www.thegoodmancenter.com/resources/
Why Bad Ads Happen to Good Causes	http://www.thegoodmancenter.com/resources/

JOURNALS AND MAGAZINES

Advertising Age

Crain Communications, Inc.
http://adage.com/

Adweek

VNU, Inc.
http://www.adweek.com/

Health Marketing Quarterly

Haworth Press
http://www.tandfonline.com/loi/whmq20#.VDc32RaTo40

Journal of Consumer Research

University of Chicago Press
http://www.journals.uchicago.edu/JCR

Journal of Health Communication (online)

Taylor & Francis
http://www.tandfonline.com/toc/uhcm20/current#.U8CRDah2fs0

Journal of Marketing

American Marketing Association
https://www.ama.org/publications/JournalOfMarketing/Pages/Current-Issue.aspx

Cases in Public Health Communication and Marketing

Taylor & Francis
http://publichealth.gwu.edu/departments/pch/phcm/casesjournal/

Journal of Nonprofit and Voluntary Sector Marketing

John Wiley & Sons
http://www.wiley.com/WileyCDA/WileyTitle/productCd-NVSM.html

Journal of Public Policy and Marketing

American Marketing Association
https://www.ama.org/publications/JournalOfPublicPolicyAndMarketing/Pages/
current-issue.aspx

Journal of Social Marketing

Emerald Group Publishing Limited
http://www.emeraldgrouppublishing.com/products/journals/journals.htm?id=JSOCM

Social Marketing Quarterly

Taylor & Francis
http://smq.sagepub.com/

LISTSERVES AND EMAIL DIGESTS

Dispatches: Insights on Brand Development From the Marketing Front (email digest)

Brand Development Network International
http://www.competitivepositioning.info/dispatches.php

Fostering Sustainable Behavior Listserv

http://www.cbsm.com/forums/index.lasso

Georgetown Social Marketing Listserve

1. Send an email message (using plain text, not rich text or html) to: listproc@george town.edu
2. In the *body* of the message, type: "sub soc-mktg your name" and type your actual name in place of "your name" (e.g., sub soc-mktg Bob White)

Knowledge at Wharton (email digest)

The Wharton School at the University of Pennsylvania

1. Go to: http://knowledge.wharton.upenn.edu/
2. Enter your email address in the subscription box at the bottom of the page

Social Marketers Global Network of the International Social Marketing Association

http://www.socialmarketers.net/

ONLINE PLANNING TOOLS AND E-LEARNING

CDCynergy-Social Marketing Edition, online

www.orau.gov/cdcynergy/soc2web/default.htm

Cullbridge Marketing and Communications, Tools of Change Webinars	www.webinars.cullbridge.com/
Health Communication Theory Picker	http://www.orau.gov/hsc/theorypicker/index.html
HealthCommWorks, Centers for Disease Control and Prevention	http://www.cdc.gov/healthcommworks/
The Open University, United Kingdom, Social Marketing Course	http://www.open.ac.uk/courses/short-courses/gb017
Social Marketing for Nutrition and Physical Activity Web Course, Centers for Disease Control and Prevention, Division of Nutrition, Physical Activity and Obesity	www.cdc.gov/nccdphp/dnpa/socialmarketing/training/index.htm
Social Marketing Toolbox	http://www.socialmarketing-toolbox.com/

PORTABLE MEDIA

"Starter for 10" teaching and course materials (memory stick)	http://thensmc.com/content/starter-10

SPECIAL EMPHASIS: SELECTED RESOURCES ABOUT SOCIAL MEDIA

e-Marketer	http://www.emarketer.com/
Mashable	http://mashable.com/
Pew Internet and American Life Project	http://www.pewinternet.org/
Social Media at CDC	http://www.cdc.gov/socialmedia/
Social Media Today	http://www.socialmediatoday.com
Social Media Tools, Guidelines & Best Practices (CDC)	http://www.cdc.gov/SocialMedia/Tools/guidelines/
US DHHS Center for New Media	http://www.hhs.gov/web/socialmedia/

TWITTER FEEDS ABOUT SOCIAL MARKETING AND COMMUNICATION

Alexandra Bornkessel, @SocialBttrfly

Australian Association of Social Marketing, @AASM_Aus

Carol Schechter, @Carol_Schechter

CDC e-Health, @CDC_eHealth

Centre of Excellence for Public Sector Marketing, @CEPSM

Craig Lefebvre, @chiefmaven

Jay Bernhardt, @jaybernhardt

Jeff French, @JeffFrenchSSM

Jeffrey W. Jordan, @jeffreywjordan

Jim Mintz, @JimMintz

Luke van der Beeke, @LukevanderBeeke

Marketing for Change, @mktgforchange

Mike Newton-Ward, @sm1guru

National Social Marketing Center (UK), @NSMC

Nedra Kline Weinreich, @nedra

Nicholas Goodwin, @nickgoodwin

Osocio Social Advertising, @osocio

Pew Internet & American Life Project, @Pew_Internet

R. Russell-Bennett, @DrBekMarketing

Rescue SCG, @RescueSCG

Salter Mitchell, @M4Change

Sharyn Rundle-Thiele, @rundlesr

Social Marketers Global Network, @socmarketersnet

Social Marketing at Griffith University, SM@Griffith

Stephan Dahl, @socMKT

Susannah Fox, @SusannahFox

The Social Change Hub, @SocialchangeHub

Worldways Marketing, @worldways

WEBSITES

Ad Council	www.adcouncil.org/
American Marketing Association	www.marketingpower.com
Association of Consumer Research	www.acrwebsite.org
Australia and New Zealand Marketing Academy	www.anzmac.org
CDCynergy Lite	http://www.cdc.gov/healthcommunication/cdcynergylite.html
Center of Excellence for Public Sector Marketing	http://cepsm.ca/home/
Centers for Disease Control and Prevention, Division of Nutrition, Physical Activity, and Obesity, Social Marketing Resources	http://www.cdc.gov/nccdphp/dnpao/socialmarketing/index.html
Centers for Disease Control and Prevention, Gateway to Health Communication & Social Marketing Practice	www.cdc.gov/healthcommunication/index.html
European Social Marketing Association	http://europeansocialmarketing.weebly.com/
FHI360, Social Marketing and Communication Center	http://www.fhi360.org/services/social-marketing
Fostering Sustainable Behavior, Community-Based Social Marketing	www.cbsm.com/
FrameWorks Institute	www.frameworksinstitute.org/
Goodman Center: Where Do-Gooders Learn to Do Better	http://www.thegoodmancenter.com
IDEO	http://www.ideo.org/

Institute for Social Marketing, University of Stirling, Scotland	www.ism.stir.ac.uk/
Knowledge at Wharton	http://knowledge.wharton.upenn.edu/topic/marketing/
LinkedIn Social Marketing Group	http://www.linkedin.com/groups?uk=anct_ug_hm&gid=1846146&home=
Marketing sociale e comunicazione per la salute (Italy)	www.marketingsociale.net/
MRS Market Research	www.marketresearch.org.uk/index.htm
National Cancer Institute, Health Behavior Constructs: Theory, Measurement & Research	http://cancercontrol.cancer.gov/brp/constructs/index.html
National Centre for Health Marketing	www.nsmcentre.org.uk/
Neuromarketing	http://www.neurosciencemarketing.com
Queensland, Australia, Government's Social Marketing Final Report	www.premiers.qld.gov.au/publications/categories/reports/social-marketing.aspx
Social Marketing National Excellence Collaborative (Turning Point)	http://socialmarketingcollaborative.org/smc/
Stanford Social Innovation Review	ssireview.org
Stanford University Persuasive Technology Lab	captology.stanford.edu/
Tools of Change	www.toolsofchange.com/
University of South Florida, Graduate Certificate in Social Marketing and Public Health	https://documents.health.usf.edu/display/COPH/Social+Marketing+and+Public+Health+Certificate

APPENDIX D

COURSES

Table 1 Academic Social Marketing Courses

University	College and/or Department	Course Title	Graduate (G)/ Undergraduate (U)/ Postgraduate Certificate (PGC)
American University, Washington, DC	Kogod School of Business	Marketing for Social Change	U
American University, Washington, DC	School of Education, Teaching and Health	Health Promotion and Social Media	U
Champlain College, Burlington, VT	School of Business	Nonprofit and Social Marketing	U
City University of New York, New York, NY	Baruch College, Department of Communications Studies	Communication Strategy	G
College of Charleston, Charleston, SC	Department of Communication	Addressing Problems in Context: Strategic Communication and Social Marketing	U
Colorado State University, Fort, Collins, CO	College of Business	Integrated Marketing Communications	U
Dartmouth College, Hanover, NH	Tuck School of Business	Social Marketing	U
Edith Cowan University, Perth, Australia	Faculty of Business and Law School of Marketing, Tourism, and Leisure	Social and Not-for-Profit Marketing	G
Emerson College Boston, MA	Communication Sciences and Disorders	Social Marketing	G
Emory University Atlanta, GA	Rollins School of Public Health, Department of Behavioral Sciences and Health Education	Social Marketing in Public Health	G
George Washington University, Washington, DC	School of Public Health and Health Services, Department of Prevention and Community Health	Intro to Social Marketing	G

(Continued)

Table 1 (Continued)

University	College and/or Department	Course Title	Graduate (G)/ Undergraduate (U)/ Postgraduate Certificate (PGC)
Interdisciplinary Center (IDC) Herzliya, Israel	The Sammy Ofer School of Communications	Social Marketing as Communicational Strategy	U
Kazakhstan Institute of Management, Economics and Strategic Research (KIMEP)	Business School	Social Marketing	U
Michigan State University, East Lansing, MI	College of Communication Arts and Sciences	Seminar in Social Marketing	G
National University of Ireland, Galway, Ireland	Marketing Discipline, J. E. Cairnes School of Business and Economics	Social Marketing and Non-profit Marketing	U and G
The Australian National University, Acton, Australia	Research School of Management, ANU College of Business & Economics	MKTG3024 Social Marketing	U
The Chinese University of Hong Kong, Hong Kong, China	JC School of Public Health and Primary Care	Social Marketing Methods	G
The Ohio State University, Columbus, OH	Fisher College of Business	Social Marketing and Public Policy	U
The University of Southern Mississippi, Hattiesburg, MS	Department of Community Health Sciences (College of Health)	Health Marketing	G
The University of the West Indies, Mona, Kingston, Jamaica	The Caribbean Institute of Media & Communications, Faculty of Humanities and Education	Social Marketing Principles and Practice	U
The University of the West Indies, Mona, Kingston, Jamaica	The Caribbean Institute of Media & Communications, Faculty of Humanities and Education	Basic Social Marketing I, 1 of 4 modules	U
The University of the West Indies, Mona, Kingston, Jamaica	The Caribbean Institute of Media & Communications, Faculty of Humanities and Education	Basic Social Marketing II, 2 of 4 modules	U

University	College and/or Department	Course Title	Graduate (G)/ Undergraduate (U)/ Postgraduate Certificate (PGC)
The University of the West Indies, Mona, Kingston, Jamaica	The Caribbean Institute of Media & Communications, Faculty of Humanities and Education	Advanced Social Marketing 1, 3 of 4 modules	U
The University of the West Indies, Mona, Kingston, Jamaica	The Caribbean Institute of Media & Communications, Faculty of Humanities and Education	Advanced Social Marketing II, 4 of 4 modules	U
The University of the West Indies, Mona, Kingston, Jamaica	The Caribbean Institute of Media & Communications, Faculty of Humanities and Education	Social Marketing Laboratory	U
Tulane University, New Orleans, LA	School of Public Health and Tropical Medicine	Introduction to Social Marketing in Health Education	G and U
University of Brighton, Brighton, UK	Brighton Business School	Postgraduate Certificate in Social Marketing	G
University of California, Los Angeles, CA	School of Public Health	Communication in Health Promotion and Education	U and G
University of Illinois, Urbana Champaign	Communications Department	Social Marketing for Health & Behavior Change	U
Universidad Católica Cecilio Acosta Maracaibo, Zulia, Venezuela	Facultad de Ciencias de la Comunicación Social, Àrea Académica de Comunicación y Desarrollo	Comunicación y Desarrollo: Mercadotecnia Social (Development Communication: Social Marketing)	U
Universita della Svizzera Italiana, Lugano, Switzerland	Faculty of Communication Sciences, Institute of Public Communication	Social Marketing I and II	G
University of Greenwich, London, England	Business School	Social Marketing	U
University of Haifa, Haifa, Israel	School of Public Health	Social Marketing for Health Promotion	G
University of Lethbridge, Lethbridge, Alberta, Canada	School of Management, Department of Marketing	Social Marketing	U

(Continued)

Table 1 (Continued)

University	College and/or Department	Course Title	Graduate (G)/ Undergraduate (U)/ Postgraduate Certificate (PGC)
University of Michigan, Ann Arbor, MI	Ross School of Business	Social Marketing	G
University of Montreal, Montreal, Quebec, Canada	Faculty of Medicine	Social Marketing	G
University of North Carolina, Chapel Hill, NC	Gillings School of Global Public Health, Public Health Leadership Program	Public Health and Social Marketing	G
University of Queensland, Brisbane, Queensland, Australia	Business School	Social Marketing and Communication	G
University of South Florida, Tampa, FL	College of Public Health	Advanced Social Marketing	G
University of South Florida, Tampa, FL	College of Public Health	Introduction to Social Marketing for Public Health—Online	G
University of Stirling, Stirling, Scotland	Stirling Management School	Social Marketing, 1 of 4 modules	G
University of Stirling, Stirling, Scotland	Stirling Management School	Research Project Management, 2 of 4 modules	G
University of Stirling, Stirling, Scotland	Stirling Management School	Public Comms, Advocacy & Public Affairs, 3 of 4 modules	G
University of Stirling, Stirling, Scotland	Stirling Management School	Behaviour Change Strategies, 4 of 4 modules	G
University of the West of England, Bristol, England	Bristol Business School (Bristol Social Marketing Centre)	PG(Cert) Social Marketing	G
Utah State University Logan, UT	Emma Eccles Jones College of Education and Human Services, Department of Health, Physical Education, and Recreation	Social Marketing in Health Education	U

University	College and/or Department	Course Title	Graduate (G)/ Undergraduate (U)/ Postgraduate Certificate (PGC)
University of Wellington, Wellington, New Zealand	Victoria Business School	Social Marketing	U
*University of Wollongong, NSW, Australia	**Social Sciences	***Social Marketing Principles & Practices, Certificate, 1 of 4 courses Critical, and Upstream Social Marketing, Certificate, 2 of 4 courses Advanced Studies in Behaviour Change, Certificate, 3 of 4 courses Social Marketing Placement, Certificate, 4 of 4 courses	****PGC
Western Washington University, Bellingham, WA	Physical Education, Health & Recreation Community Health Program	Health Communication & Social Marketing	U
York University, Toronto, Ontario, Canada	School of Administrative Studies Atkins Faculty of Liberal and Professional Studies	Social Marketing	U
Texas State University, San Marcos, TX	Department of Marketing	Social Marketing	U
The University of the West Indies, Mona, Kingston, Jamaica	The Caribbean Institute of Media & Communications, Faculty of Humanities and Education	Social Marketing Laboratory	U

Source: Academic Course Offering were compiled and provided by Kathleen Kelly, Ph.D., Professor of Marketing, Colorado State University. This list was also published in an article in the *Social Marketing Quarterly* 2013 19:390. http://smq.sagepub.com/content/19/4/290

Note: *Repeat University of Wollongong, NSW, Australia for a total of four entries, **Repeat Social Sciences for a total of four entries, ***These are the 4 Course Titles, and ****Repeat PGC for a total of four entries.

Appendix E

International Social Marketing Association's Academic Competencies September 2014

The academic competencies for social marketing outlined in this document are intended as guidance for **instructors of academic courses and designers of academic and nonacademic certificate programs** in social marketing. They provide a set of participant-focused benchmarks for the development of course curricula and certificate completion requirements. These competencies are not meant to prescribe or restrict the content of academic social marketing degree programs. It is anticipated that degree-granting programs in social marketing may have more competencies than are outlined here.

The development of these competencies was formally begun at a collaboratory held at the Social Marketing Conference in Clearwater Beach, Florida, in June 2012. Since then, the full list of competencies generated by that discussion has been reviewed and revised, and was approved in September by the International Social Marketing Association, Australian Association of Social Marketing, and European Social Marketing Association.

It is planned that these competencies will be revisited in 2016 and potentially revised. Comments about these competencies can be sent to Nancy Lee (nancyrlee@msn.com).

ACADEMIC COMPETENCIES IN SOCIAL MARKETING (AUGUST 2014)

Upon completion of a social marketing certificate or academic course, a participant should be able to:

1. Describe social marketing to colleagues and other professionals and differentiate it from other approaches to influencing behaviors and social change.

2. Work with colleagues and stakeholders to identify community, state, province, national, regional, and/or international priorities, and identify those for which a social marketing approach may be appropriate.

3. Identify and segment affected populations and select appropriate, high priority segments.

4. Prioritize and select measurable behaviors (not just awareness or attitudes) of individuals, organizations, and/or policymakers to influence.

5. Design and conduct situational analysis and formative research, employing mixed methodologies needed to understand current audience barriers and benefits, as well as competing behaviors and direct and indirect competition.

6. Select and apply relevant social marketing, behavioral, exchange and social science theories, models, frameworks and research to inform development of a social marketing strategic plan, one that meet the needs and wants of the intended audience.

7. Create an integrated social marketing mix strategy that extends beyond communications only campaigns, with consideration of all appropriate evidence-based tools and theory needed to influence a desired behavior.

8. Critically reflect and test the effectiveness, acceptability, and ethics of potential social marketing strategies with representatives of target audiences and stakeholders and adapt as necessary.

9. Finalize an implementation plan, incorporating opportunities for scaling up and sustainability.

10. Design and implement an evaluation plan, including a monitoring system to assure programs are on track to achieve goals and meet agreed quality and efficiency standards.

11. Apply ethical principles to the conduct of research, developing, implementing, and evaluating a social marketing plan.

12. Document and communicate the results of social marketing initiatives to colleagues, stakeholders, communities, and other relevant organizations and groups.

INDEX

ABOUT THE AUTHORS

 **Nancy R. Lee,** MBA, is president of Social Marketing Services, Inc., in Seattle, Washington, and an adjunct faculty member at the University of Washington as well as at the University of South Florida, where she teaches social marketing and marketing in the public sector. With more than 25 years of practical marketing experience in the public and private sectors, Ms. Lee has held numerous corporate marketing positions, including vice president and director of marketing for Washington State's second-largest bank and director of marketing for the region's Children's Hospital and Medical Center.

Ms. Lee has consulted with more than 100 nonprofit organizations and has participated in the development of more than 200 social marketing campaign strategies for public sector agencies. Clients in the public sector include the Centers for Disease Control and Prevention (CDC), Environmental Protection Agency (EPA), Washington State Department of Health, Office of Crime Victims Advocacy, county Health and Transportation Departments, Department of Ecology, Department of Fisheries and Wildlife, Washington Traffic Safety Commission, City of Seattle, and Office of Superintendent of Public Instruction. Campaigns developed for these clients targeted issues listed below:

- Health: teen pregnancy prevention, HIV/AIDS prevention, nutrition education, sexual assault, diabetes prevention, adult physical activity, tobacco control, arthritis diagnosis and treatment, immunizations, dental hygiene, senior wellness, and eating disorder awareness
- Safety: drowning prevention, senior fall prevention, underage drinking and driving, youth suicide prevention, binge drinking, pedestrian safety, and safe gun storage
- Environment: natural gardening, preservation of fish and wildlife habitats, recycling, trip reduction, water quality, and water and power conservation

She has conducted social marketing workshops around the world (Jordan, South Africa, Ghana, Ireland, Australia, Singapore, Canada) for more than 2,000 public sector employees involved in developing public behavior change campaigns in the areas of health, safety, the environment, and financial well-being. She has been a keynote speaker on social marketing at conferences for improved water quality, energy conservation, family planning, nutrition, recycling, teen pregnancy prevention, influencing financial behaviors, and tobacco control.

Ms. Lee has coauthored seven other books with Philip Kotler: *Social Marketing: Improving the Quality of Life* (2002); *Corporate Social Responsibility: Doing the Most Good for Your Company and Your Cause* (2005); *Marketing in the Public Sector: A Roadmap for Improved Performance* (2006); *Social Marketing*: Influencing Behaviors for Good (2008); Up and Out of Poverty: The Social Marketing Solution (2009); *Social Marketing in Public Health* (2010); and *Social Marketing to Protect the Environment* (2011). She has also contributed articles to the Stanford *Social Innovation Review, Social Marketing Quarterly, Journal of Social Marketing,* and *The Public Manager.* (See more on Nancy Lee at www.socialmarketingservice.com)

 **Philip Kotler** is the S. C. Johnson & Son Distinguished Professor of International Marketing at the J. L. Kellogg School of Management, Northwestern University, Evanston, Illinois. Kellogg was voted Best Business School in *Business Week*'s survey of U.S. business schools. It is also rated Best Business School for the Teaching of Marketing. Professor Kotler has significantly contributed to Kellogg's success through his many years of research and teaching there.

He received his master's degree at the University of Chicago and his Ph.D. degree at MIT, both in economics. He did postdoctoral work in mathematics at Harvard University and in behavioral science at the University of Chicago.

Professor Kotler is the author of *Marketing Management,* the most widely used marketing book in graduate business schools worldwide; *Principles of Marketing; Marketing Models; Strategic Marketing for Non-Profit Organizations; The New Competition; High Visibility; Social Marketing; Marketing Places; Marketing for Congregations; Marketing for Hospitality and Tourism; The Marketing of Nations; Marketing 3.0, Good Works, Market Your Way to Growth, Winning Global Markets,* and *Kotler on Marketing.* He has published over 150 articles in leading journals, several of which have received best-article awards.

Professor Kotler was the first recipient of the Distinguished Marketing Educator Award (1985) given by the American Marketing Association (AMA). The European Association of Marketing Consultants and Sales Trainers awarded him their prize for Marketing Excellence. He was chosen as the Leader in Marketing Thought by the Academic Members of the AMA in a 1975 survey. He also received the 1978 Paul Converse Award of the AMA, honoring his original contribution to marketing. In 1995, Sales and Marketing Executives International (SMEI) named him Marketer of the Year. **In 2012 he received** the William L. Wilkie "Marketing for a Better World: Award of the American Marketing Association Foundation (AMAF). In 2014, he was inducted into the AMA Marketing Hall of Fame.

Professor Kotler has consulted for such companies as IBM, General Electric, AT&T, Honeywell, Bank of America, Merck, and others in the areas of marketing strategy and planning, marketing organization, and international marketing.

He has been chairman of the College of Marketing of the Institute of Management Sciences, director of the American Marketing Association, trustee of the Marketing

Science Institute, director of the MAC Group, former member of the Yankelovich Advisory Board, and a member of the Copernicus Advisory Board. He is a member of the Board of Governors of the School of the Art Institute of Chicago and a member of the advisory board of the Drucker Foundation. He has received honorary doctoral degrees from Stockholm University, University of Zurich, Athens University of Economics and Business, DePaul University, the Cracow School of Business and Economics, Groupe H.E.C. in Paris, the University of Economics and Business Administration in Vienna, the Catholic University of Santo Domingo, and the Budapest School of Economic Science and Public Administration.

He has traveled extensively throughout Europe, Asia, and South America, advising and lecturing to many companies and organizations. This experience expands the scope and depth of his programs, enhancing them with an accurate global perspective.

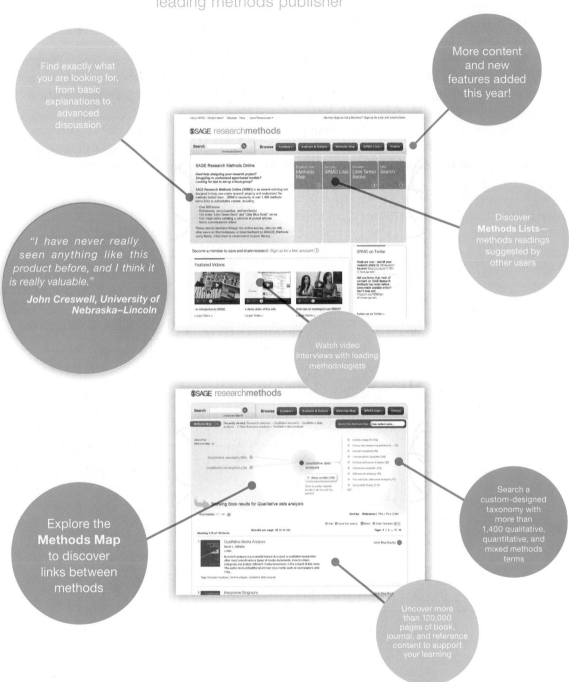